To Phil.

Joe

5/20/97

A CULTURAL HISTORY OF WESTERN EDUCATION

Its Social and Intellectual Foundations

McGraw-Hill Series in Education

HAROLD BENJAMIN, *Consulting Editor*

A CULTURAL HISTORY
OF WESTERN EDUCATION

Its Social and
Intellectual Foundations

R. FREEMAN BUTTS

*Professor of Education, Teachers
College, Columbia University*

Second Edition

McGRAW-HILL BOOK COMPANY, INC.

New York   Toronto   London   1955

THE MAPLE PRESS COMPANY, YORK, PA.

PREFACE

The first edition of this book was published under the title *A Cultural History of Education* in January, 1947. It has been used, therefore, during the period of vast changes that have taken place since the close of World War II. During this time, it has become even more clear that a careful reexamination of our social, intellectual, and educational predicament is an urgent necessity. Attacks upon democracy and democratic ideals of education have widened and intensified in many parts of the world. Attacks upon modern educational beliefs and practices in the United States have also gained in intensity. These make it imperative that we reassess the strengths and weaknesses of our educational traditions. The author believes with increased conviction that the historical study of culture and education is an indispensable means to that end.

As in every critical period, the American people are searching for answers to their persistent problems. When persons holding different points of view come into conflict about the solution of these problems, each person is likely to appeal to the past for support of his own position. This necessitates a study of history, for any present situation is a result of the past. An adequate analysis of the present with a view to the future requires a study of the past. Indeed, any decision in education or elsewhere in the realm of social affairs depends upon an interpretation of history.

History can do at least two things: It can show what historical ingredients have gone into our present beliefs and practices and what problems face us when inherited traditions confront new conditions and new demands; and it can show how other peoples in other times have solved similar (though not identical) problems.

War accelerates social and educational change, and postwar periods usually see disruptions of old patterns. It is the responsibility of educators and the public alike to see that we do not simply seek the past with longing or, on the other hand, clutch at every new fad. Intelligent study of the history of education is an indispensable ingredient in making sound judgments.

This book is designed principally for those who are preparing to enter the educational profession and for those who have had experience and wish to reevaluate it in the light of the perspective to be gained by viewing education in history. The author hopes that the book may also be of value to all who are seriously concerned with the future of American public education.

This book is based on the assumption that education is affected by the dominant institutions and beliefs of a culture and that education in turn affects that culture. The term "culture" is used here to refer to the whole matrix of political, economic, social, and religious institutions as well as to the beliefs, ideas, and ideals that guide a people in their private and public endeavors. The author has therefore utilized some of the major findings and interpretations of the scholarly disciplines of history, the social sciences, philosophy, and psychology. The book has grown out of the author's teaching experience of more than 20 years, principally at Teachers College, Columbia University, where he has had the opportunity to teach courses not only in the history of education but also in the social and philosophical foundations of education.

The author's argument is that, in order to reassess our present educational program, we must understand and evaluate the cultural and educational traditions which make us what we are. We may then be in a better position to use a revitalized conception of democratic education as a guidepost for the future of American education and for a world in desperate need of cooperative action. This book is the author's effort to apply such a "foundational" approach to the history of education as well as to make the discipline of history contribute to the larger foundational task. The author's indebtedness to his colleagues in the Department of Social and Philosophical Foundations at Teachers College is apparent throughout. In great part, the merits of the book may be attributed to the experience of working closely with these and other colleagues; its shortcomings are, of course, the author's own.

Although the book is designed primarily for use in courses in the history of education, it is also designed to be of value in other phases of teacher education. For example, in courses in elementary, secondary, or higher education, students may gain from it the perspective of history upon those specific levels. Similarly, students in courses in the philosophy of education, introduction to education, principles of education, curriculum, administration, guidance, and the subject-matter fields may here find easily available historical materials that are appropriate to their own specialized needs and yet related to the larger developments of education.

The scope of the book has had to be limited to Europe and the United States, and the title of this revised edition reflects this limitation, although it grows out of no narrow provincialism. It has also been necessary to omit discussion of our neighbors on the North American continent. It would have been well, too, if attention could have been given to the problems of colonial peoples and contemporary primitive societies. But this is a task for comparative, international, and anthropological studies beyond the scope of a single book on the history of Western education.

This revised edition has retained the basically chronological organization of the first edition. The commonly accepted "periods" are treated as units, partly because of the familiarity of these periods and partly because of the continuing conviction that the chronological approach is one of the distinctive contributions of history to the achievement of perspective and understanding. In other respects, the materials have been reorganized in order to make more evident the interaction of culture and education.

Each chronological period is treated in four sections, which are occasionally divided into two chapters. The first section deals with the social foundations of education in each period. Emphasis is placed upon the distinctive ways in which the people organized their lives to achieve their purposes. These efforts are principally summed up in the political, economic, social, and religious institutions of the time. An effort has been made not to give a capsule of the whole history of the period but simply to highlight those trends and qualities of institutional life which gave education its distinctive character and which have had the greatest influence upon our time.

The second section for each period turns to the educational institutions that resulted from the organizational efforts described in the first section. Here are indicated the principal ways in which educational institutions were organized, controlled, and supported. Particular stress is put upon those problems of control where conflict of interest appeared or where patterns were set that have influenced our own types of educational organization and control. Attention is also given to the range and extent of educational opportunity made available to youth and adults both within and outside the schools and the changing role of teaching as a profession.

The third section in each period or chapter deals with the intellectual foundations of education, namely, the climates of thought, belief, and values which have had significant influence upon the aims, content, and method of education. Here are described the main currents of thought about the nature of the universe, man's destiny, human nature, and man's capacity for learning and intelligence. Significant developments in the arts and sciences are described, as well as the resultant theories or philosophies of education that were expressive of the intellectual temper of the times and have influenced our own.

Finally, the fourth section in each period or chapter deals with the educational program as it has been shaped by these intellectual and social developments. Particular attention is given to the different levels of elementary, secondary, and higher education. Here again the aim is not to describe the minutiae of curriculum or methods of earlier schools but to gain insight by seeing what happens to the content and processes of education when one point of view is accepted rather than another.

Much is to be gained from seeing education as a whole operating in its cultural setting, but it is recognized that specialized interests should also be served. Therefore, it is likely that a reader with a special concern for some aspect of educational administration will find particular interest in the first and second sections of each period or chapter. Similarly, a reader with a special concern for some aspect of curriculum and teaching or philosophy or psychology may be particularly interested in the third and fourth sections. The intention has been to preserve the values of a chronological perspective and at the same time achieve some of the values of a "problem" approach by fitting the story into a framework of persistent problems.

So that there may be no doubt in the reader's mind, the preferred culture in the author's view is, in short, a culture that asserts the values of democracy, the traditions of liberty, and the methods of free inquiry.

Some chapters of this revised edition have been largely rewritten; the content of others remains substantially the same despite the reorganization. Much of the factual detail appearing in the sections on the cultural setting in the first edition has been deleted in order to tighten the argument, stress the general trends, and shorten the book somewhat. Interrelationships among cultural movements and educational developments have been emphasized. The author recognizes the pedagogical dangers of presenting too much material in a single book and thus giving the impression of encyclopedism, but he also sees the value of viewing education steadfastly as an integral phase of the cultural aspirations and institutions of a people.

The task of writing and of studying is no easy one for author, for teacher, or for student, and the author does not presume to have found the formula that will appeal to all. He hopes, however, that this edition represents a considerable improvement over the first one and that it will set forward the rigorous enterprise of inquiry and education—in the long run the best hope of preserving and promoting the values of a free people.

The author acknowledges with thanks the yeoman service rendered by his secretary, Miss Priscilla Aiken, in preparing the manuscript for the publisher. Special thanks are due to his colleague, Professor Lawrence A. Cremin, who so generously and competently selected the illustrations for this edition.

R. FREEMAN BUTTS

CONTENTS

xi

A CULTURAL HISTORY OF WESTERN EDUCATION

Its Social and Intellectual Foundations

Chapter 1

THE BEGINNINGS OF CULTURE AND EDUCATION
IN THE EASTERN MEDITERRANEAN WORLD

CULTURE AND EDUCATION

One of the most illuminating concepts developed by modern scholarship in the social sciences is summed up in the term "culture." It is a concept and term that educators should find especially useful as they seek to understand and improve the educative process. It is a key to understanding the basic social institutions that affect education and the basic motivations and behavior of the people with whom education deals. It can help us to understand ourselves, to gain some detachment and perspective on our own society, and to appreciate the values and outlooks of other societies. In its broadest sense, culture is the most distinctive characteristic that differentiates human beings from other creatures.

Social scientists, of course, have different ways of defining the term "culture," but it is often referred to as the whole way of life that is created, learned, held in common, and passed on from one generation to another by the members of a particular society. Culture is the sum total of ways of behaving that a group of people builds up and expects its members to acquire, share, and live by. It includes the entire range of social institutions; the organized patterns of behavior; the customs and expectations; the tools and technology; the bodies of knowledge, thought and belief; the cherished ideals, values, and sanctions; the forms of creative expression; and the language and modes of communication.

Different social scientists define the elements of culture differently and emphasize some aspects over others, but the differences are not as important for our purposes as the common agreement that the term is a most convenient shorthand concept for the sum total of ways of living of a human society. Anthropologists like to use the term to apply to simple as well as to complex cultures. Sociologists may prefer to use the term "civilization" and concentrate upon modern societies. Historians may emphasize the term "tradition" to stress the movements of culture through time. All these outlooks are important for the educator. Hence, the basic plan of organization of this book centers upon the conception of culture (see the Preface).

When we consider that culture is *acquired by learning* by the individuals in a society, is *held in common* by many in the society, and is *transmitted* from one generation to the next, we can see how essential *education* is to any culture. Indeed, the very essence of culture is that people "learn" it as they acquire the customs, habits, and ways of behaving of those around them and then in turn "teach" it by the expectations they hold up for others to follow. In this broadest sense, all culture is always "educative," whether by conscious plan or by unintentional imitation. It is most important for educators to understand this broad "educative" function of culture. It is usually more helpful, however, to reserve the term "education" itself for the deliberate, planful, conscious, and directed processes whereby people "learn" their culture and learn to participate in it effectively. Whenever an individual or a group deliberately attempts to guide behavior, education is present. Education thus assumes an enormously important role in the processes whereby a culture is transmitted and changed.

If education is viewed as embracing all the deliberate efforts to "teach" a culture, education is much more inclusive than formal "schooling." Parents, families, churches, governments, and most forms of organized institutions deliberately attempt to educate by influencing the behavior of young and old alike. Schooling, however, usually appears in a culture when particular persons are assigned the specialized task of "teaching." At this point in the history of human culture, the teacher and the school appear on the scene and devote their full attention to deliberate education. Education is thus always an integral part of human culture everywhere, but schooling has not been present in all cultures. As a matter of fact, schooling is a relatively recent occurrence. When it does appear, schooling is deeply affected by the other deliberate educational agencies of the culture, and both schooling and education are molded by the whole culture itself. Because schooling and education are both so much an integral part of the culture in which they operate, it is necessary for educators to study the whole range of educative processes of the culture as well as the more specialized educative function of formalized schooling.

MAN ORGANIZES HIMSELF

Prehistoric Culture

One of the best ways to illuminate the study of modern culture and education is to view our own times in the perspective of the long development of human culture. Paleontologists, archeologists, and anthropologists assure us that man has existed in some form upon this planet for at least a half million years and perhaps for as much as a million years or longer. Archeological discoveries are constantly being made that cause the estimates of the age of man to be changed somewhat, but the general outlines seem fairly clear. Practically all we know about the earliest forms of human culture must be gained by inference from examination of the things that man made long ago. These are principally tools and weapons that have been found in the earth. The problem of reconstructing man's culture in those earliest ages is much more difficult than reconstructing the biological characteristics of man from his skeletal remains. But we do know that from about 500,000 years ago until about 75,000 years ago the tools that man made slowly but gradually became somewhat more refined. Their form and design improved as the skill of shaping tools was presumably passed on from one generation to the next and as one generation was able to learn and profit from some rudimentary forms of learning and teaching. Education in some form must have been present.

Human culture appeared as men were able to pass on what they had learned to the younger generations. During those hundreds of centuries when men improved their tools but slowly, the inference is that their conditions of living and culture were relatively static. When men first found that they could hunt or gather food better by using rough stones to hit or throw at animals rather than by using their bare hands, culture began to change. When they taught each other and their children to use such implements and to make better ones, education began. Some anthropologists even believe that the invention and use of tools may have helped to speed up the processes of biological evolution itself whereby those who had acquired greater skill in toolmaking and tool using tended to be the ones who survived and reproduced themselves.

In any case, from 75,000 to 20,000 years ago much more rapid strides in human culture took place. The stone blades showed much greater skill in design and sharpness, bone tools appeared, fire was used, skins of animals were shaped and sewn, vessels were made to contain food, caves and huts were used for habitation, and art expressions were created in the form of line drawings, painting, and carving of stones. By inference, it seems likely that cooperative effort of an organized sort was achieved to aid in the search for food and for defense and that ceremonies and rites were held for burial, for magical purposes, and perhaps for propitiation of the forces that were believed to rule the life after death. If this is so, the methods of "teaching" and "learning" the culture also became more complicated. Recent evidence indicates, however, that some of these forms of culture deteriorated during a period of several thousand years.

Then, some 10,000 to 8,000 years ago, human culture began to develop more rapidly than ever before. Man greatly improved his stone and bone tools; designed and built more complicated dwellings; domesticated animals and planted crops to provide a more stable food supply; made clothes by sewing, spinning, and weaving; built canoes and boats for travel and trade; developed an organized community life based upon family, clans, and tribes; devised more complicated forms of ceremony, rites, and religious beliefs; and expressed his feelings in more highly developed artistic forms of behavior. We cannot tell very much about prehistoric man's ideas, beliefs, institutions, language, or values, but it seems inescapable that prehistoric man began to use gestures, signs, and symbols that eventually became words for the conveying of ideas. Then he began to write down the words and construct a written language. At that point, we begin to have a record of his thoughts, beliefs, institutions, and ways of behaving. We thus gain more knowledge of his culture than is possible to acquire simply from the material remains. When written language appears, history begins, and prehistoric cultures give way to historic cultures.

In view of these tremendous achievements in human culture, scholars today seldom apply the terms "savage" or "barbarian" or "uncivilized" to prehistoric man. Many anthropologists even avoid the use of the term "primitive" because of its connotation that the people were the slaves of uncivilized and irrational customs, magic, and superstition. It is much more descriptive to use the less colorful but more accurate term "prehistoric" to apply to all peoples who lived before the invention of a written language some 5,000 to 6,000 years ago. Similarly, it is important *not* to identify or to equate prehistoric peoples with present-day "primitive" peoples simply because they do not possess a written language. It may be that the neutral term "nonliterate" is the best term to use to refer to present-day peoples whose cultures are very complex in many respects but who do not use a written language.

The term "primitive" is, however, very difficult to drop entirely. It has been used so extensively by historians and other social scientists that it continues to appear in scholarly literature. Furthermore, we cannot know much about the culture of prehistoric man except as we make informed guesses on the basis of inference from a firsthand study of the customs and cultures of present-day "primitive" peoples. The term "primitive" is therefore used here simply to refer to "early" cultures of prehistoric times and to indicate that the discussion is largely based upon inference from the study of present-day nonliterate societies that do not have a written language. No value judgments may be made, however, that present-day nonliterate societies are retarded, backward, or equivalent to prehistoric societies.

When prehistoric man began to *control* his environment for his own purposes rather than merely submit to it, human culture began to take a form that is somewhat familiar to us. If man had forgotten what he had learned, he would not have been human. In other words, all human beings today stand in debt to the nameless millions of men over thousands of centuries who gradually learned to control their environment and to pass on what they had learned to the younger generations, thus helping to make them human. In prehistoric times, culture and education were of a piece.

Undifferentiated Social Institutions of Prehistoric Cultures (before 4000 B.C.)

In the process of beginning to exert control over their environment, prehistoric men apparently organized themselves into working groups for the more adequate achievement of this purpose. At some time in the long history of man prior to 6,000 years ago, individual men and individual families began to live together, work together, and fight together for common purposes. Family and tribal groupings based upon kinship were probably the first kinds of social institutions. Men found that living together increased the security, protection, and welfare of all the individuals in the group. They found also that some sort of rules had to be made to guide group living and to define the individual's relationship to the group's activities. Thus, customs, habits, and folkways were developed in order to fix the obligations and duties of various individuals in the group. Primitive man apparently sensed that the welfare of the group depended upon the performance by each individual of his obligations, and pressure was therefore put upon the members of a tribe to live up to the folkways of the tribe.

Rule of the Folkways. We are likely to be impressed by the extent to which the fixed folkways of a primitive tribe control the conduct of the tribal members. We are impressed, too, with the great variety of practice that has appeared among different tribes of men in different parts of the world. Despite these differences, however, it remains true that, within a single tribe, folkways were relatively stable and fixed over long periods of time. They changed upon contact with different tribes or when conditions of life reached a crisis which made change necessary, but the apparent intent and effort of most primitive tribes were to see that the tribal folkways were passed on intact.

Quite explicit rules were likely to be formulated concerning the important activities of life, the duties of children toward their parents, the relations between the sexes, attitudes toward property, loyalty to the elders and leaders, division of the spoils of the hunt, the duties of warfare both as to victor and vanquished, taboos against certain kinds of food, the accepted interpretations of natural phenomena, and participation in religious rites and ceremonials. In modern times, such a listing of social activities could be classified into distinct social institutions, such as family and marriage institutions, political institutions, economic institutions, and religious institutions.

Such differentiation, however, was apparently not a large part of prehistoric life. The important thing for educators to note is that, just as these other activities were not differentiated into separate institutions during prehistoric times, so the educational function was not set up as a separate institution but was an integral part of the preservation of tribal culture and folkways.

Growing Complexity of Early Historic Cultures (after 4000 B.C.)

The primitive tribal organization of life reflected the fact that social groups were necessary for protection of men in the nomad state of wandering from place to place in search of food and security. Social organization was even more necessary when men began to settle down in the river valleys of the Tigris and Euphrates in Mesopotamia and of the Nile in Egypt. In these two centers, human culture advanced enormously and became exceedingly complex as man perfected the use of bronze and iron metals and devised elaborate systems of written language.

Life along these rivers required such effective social organization and such long-range guidance that leaders emerged who could plan the ways in which their neighbors could be defeated in war, or canals and ditches could be dug to control the floods of the rivers for agricultural purposes, or the masses of people could be kept at their appointed tasks. These leaders became the kings and priests who gave order to life, organized a government, and commanded obedience because of the belief in their divine guidance. Thus, well-defined political, economic, and religious institutions emerged, which characteristically centered in the fundamental needs of maintaining human life, united people into a cooperative task, and developed bodies of doctrine and special techniques for getting the jobs done.

In the fourth and third millenniums B.C., the centuries were marked by improved skills in manufacture and communication and by continual wars that gradually consolidated the cities into large empires which, for the first time, brought several millions of people under one rule. A close alliance between political and religious leaders gave absolute power and divine authority to the king-priest and his privileged class of office-holders and priests. Class divisions were recognized as normal and morally right, and codes of law and morality were developed to maintain these rights. Commerce and trade achieved material improvements that kept pace with increased skill in art, architecture, sculpture, painting, writing, literature, and science. All these developments increased the complexity of life and made necessary a longer period of training to enable the people to cope with the problems of the culture. Schools and higher institutions of education were thus organized to meet these needs.

As a result of the advances just mentioned, a strong centralized government was achieved by the Babylonians. Government and religion became so intertwined that the king's power was considered to be divine, and he came to exert great control over all phases of life. Inequality was accepted as normal and right in law and in custom which assigned special privileges to the upper classes.

After the Babylonians, a whole series of kingdoms and peoples rose and fell during these early centuries of civilization. The most important in the eastern Mediterranean and Asia Minor were the Assyrian Empire and the Persian Empire. The Assyrians created the first large-scale empire, conscripting an army from the common people and giving them careful training, in addition to developing improved weapons, swift cavalry, and artillery. They are comparable to their modern military and totalitarian counterparts in that they perfected the systematic terrorizing of the enemy through torture and massacre and displaced whole nations by force.

The last great empire of this age was that of the Persians, who conquered most of the then known world west of India. The Persian Empire completed a long political development that started with the tribal organizations of primitive man, progressed through the city and city-state stage to the kingdom stage, in which many cities were united, and finally culminated in a centralized empire covering an enormous amount of territory and ruling millions of people.

The Persians proved themselves much more able empire builders than the Assyrians, not only by treating their subjects more tolerantly and humanely but also by looking upon their empire as an integral whole. They introduced uniform coinage, built military roads, and granted a large measure of local autonomy and freedom to develop local languages, literature, and art. As a result, commerce and trade as well as agriculture prospered. The political and economic forms they developed are extremely important because they set a pattern that was later accepted by Alexander the Great, by the Roman Empire, and eventually by Europe. In this conception, the king's power was considered absolute, unlimited, and divine. There was little tradition of democratic self-government in these Oriental despotisms.

The main outlines of development along the Nile River in Egypt were similar in many respects to those in the Middle East and Asia Minor. Egypt was much more isolated, more self-contained, and less exposed to attacks, and therefore developed a less highly militarized civilization. Politically, Egypt was united under a long series of dynasties of pharaoh-kings. To assist him in his absolute rule, the king relied upon a priestly class, who lived in specially assigned temples, conducted propitiatory rites to the gods, embalmed the dead, and gave instructions concerning the accepted ways for departed souls to receive favorable treatment at the day of judgment. The king also had a large coterie of secular officials to carry out his commands in the army and navy, to collect taxes, to organize public works, and to maintain order. All these officials were accountable to the king, who disposed of their lives and property as he saw fit.

Besides the great empires already mentioned, many other civilizations had their day along the eastern shores of the Mediterranean and among the islands of the Aegean Sea. The Phoenicians were important for their wide-ranging commerce and trade and for their refinements of alphabet and language. The cities on the coast of Asia Minor and the inhabitants of Crete likewise developed a remarkable ability in commerce, architecture, and engineering. The cities on the mainland and islands of Greece were developing a culture and forms of social organization that were much more democratic than those of the Oriental kings. These will be described at greater length in the next chapter.

Important too, because of the impact of their culture upon the whole Western world, was the development of the wandering Jewish tribes who finally settled in Palestine around 1500 B.C. A long period of rule under various patriarchs and judges was followed by a period of rule under such kings as David and Solomon. In 722 B.C. the 10 northern tribes of Israel were conquered and transported to Assyria. The two southern tribes of Judea were conquered in the early sixth century B.C. and taken into exile by the Babylonians under Nebuchadnezzar. After 50 years of Babylonian captivity, the Jews were released by Cyrus, king of the Persians, to return to Palestine. Palestine was later conquered by Alexander and then by the Romans. Although the Jews were dispersed as a nation by the Roman emperors, the Jewish culture lived on to influence Western civilization at innumerable points both religious and scientific.

As one looks back over the long development of human institutions so briefly described in these few pages, an outstanding educational implication becomes clear. Whereas the individuals in a primitive tribe were considered to be more or less equal in importance to the tribe, the practice of inequality and rigid class distinctions grew stronger as social institutions became more clearly differentiated. Whereas in the primitive tribe each individual made his expected contribution to the safety and welfare of the tribe, the Eastern cultures began to place more value upon the persons and rights of the privileged classes and less value upon the mere worker and slave. Consequently, as education also became a differentiated social institution, it was naturally assigned to the privileged classes to be controlled and administered in their interests rather than for the whole people. It was hundreds of years before a kind of culture developed that widened greatly the range of persons deemed fit to be given a formal education. This the Athenians in Greece did.

THE RISE OF THE SCHOOL

Primitive Educational Agencies

Definite and differentiated social institutions for educational purposes were not clearly apparent in primitive societies. This meant that control of the educational process was typically in the hands of the family, who had the responsibility of training the children in the accepted folkways of the tribe. In many tribes, however, some special persons came to be recognized as having peculiar functions in the formulation of tribal customs and ideals. These elders, medicine men, seers, or storytellers began to constitute something of a priestly and therefore teaching class. There is evidence that special training was often given to those who were to be inducted into the priestly class. This consisted of special transmission of the peculiar skills of the class, whether of special knowledge of certain magical formulas or certain songs or of the ability to conduct certain rites and ceremonies. Where secret fraternities existed, they developed their own special initiation processes. In addition, some tribes apparently had certain handicraft or occupational groups that specialized in housebuilding, metalworking, toolmaking, garmentmaking, or tattooing. These groups would then initiate young people into the skills and secrets of the group.

Many tribes also conducted special initiatory or puberty rites for the adolescent or older youth who were to be inducted into full adult membership in the tribe. Although puberty rites were not characteristic of all tribes, they represented a kind of educational agency that was commonly controlled by the elders of the tribe for tribal purposes. It is apparent that education was carried on, not by separate schools or educational institutions, but by the adult members of the tribe in the course of their assigned activities. The teaching function was not delegated to special teaching groups nearly as much as in more complex and more modern cultures. It may be that reliance upon formal schools and specialized teaching in prehistoric cultures was greater than we now believe; the absence of written records makes certainty impossible.

Appearance of the Formal School in Early Historic Cultures

The best evidence seems to indicate that the formal school appeared at that stage of culture when it became important to pass on the written literature and to teach certain people to write. It also seems clear that such schools grew up under the control of the priestly class or of secular scribes to whom the art of writing was essential. It is fruitless to try to state exactly where and when the first school appeared. The main point is that as a culture came more and more to deal with written material it became more and more necessary to develop formal education. In Egypt, it seems apparent that schools developed in connection with the temples and with those aspects of the king's offices that required writing. We have evidence of these schools in the remains of copybooks made by boys who were learning to write. Recent evidence makes it clear that such schools were set up in Sumer and other parts of Babylonia for somewhat similar purposes, to train priests and officials to take part in the affairs of the king.

After the Jews returned to Palestine from Babylonia, they established schools sometime during the fifth century B.C. Lay scribes became the teachers of Hebrew among the Jews, conducting formal instruction in the synagogues. The religious control of education was always uppermost in Jewish culture. During the first century of the Christian Era (about A.D. 65), schools were required to be set up in every Jewish community, and compulsory education for boys was a part of the law.

In the period prior to 1000 B.C., then, it seems clear that schooling was organized and controlled primarily for the privileged classes. It had a high scarcity value for preferment and status in the religious, political, and economic life of the times. One who could write was sought after by king and merchant as well as by priest. For the great masses of people, formal schooling was not part of the prospect; consequently, whatever educative process was available to them was conducted through non-school agencies. Families brought up children to engage in the kind of occupation they knew, whether farming, herding, or artisanship of some kind. Education for the masses of people in Egypt and the Middle East was essentially like that of primitive peoples. They were molded by the culture they found about them, the folkways they accepted, the spoken language and tools they used, the religious ceremonials they observed, the work and fighting imposed on them by their rulers, the stories that were told, the songs that were sung, and the rules of conduct that they obeyed.

THE IDEAS MEN LIVED BY

Relation of Man to Nature and to the Supernatural

The Primitive Mind. Primitive man apparently did a most natural thing when he saw a close relationship between himself and the rest of nature. He was so much at the mercy of the physical and animal world about him it is no wonder that he deified nature, fearing and worshiping it and at the same time describing it in terms of himself. We are likely to look upon the mind of primitive man as excessively credulous and unsophisticated, but in doing so we may not appreciate sufficiently the value of his attempts to orient himself to the world about him in highly

imaginative and colorful ways. The development of magical and religious beliefs was a real attempt to explain the reasons for the natural
and human phenomena that he saw about him. These beliefs were worked
into elaborate networks of folkways and taboos that controlled the conduct of individual men through fear of the consequences of not behaving
in certain ways. When man began to be more successful in controlling
nature, he began to be more sophisticated and logical in his intellectual
approach to it.

Emergence of a Conception of Morality and of God. Sometime during
the fourth and third millenniums B.C., the people of Egypt began to evolve
a more highly developed sense of morality and ethics as a means of controlling human conduct. The gods came to be looked upon not merely as
powerful agents that shaped human destiny out of hand but as moral
beings who ruled wisely and justly. Thus, the conception of human
morality took on a more sophisticated form when men were expected to
behave morally in order to carry out the wish of the gods and thereby
attain greater happiness for themselves. The primitive necessity to wage a
constant struggle against the forces of nature gradually gave way to a
concern to improve the social relationships among men.

In Egypt this attempt took the form of an overwhelming interest in
the future life, for which elaborate preparations were made during this
life. In Babylonia, however, the attempt to devise a moral order tended
to take the form of legal codes and ordered social arrangements on this
earth. The Babylonians and Persians had their rich religious legends, but
they were never as much concerned with the afterlife as they were with
divining the ways in which man should behave here and now in the light
of the influence of the stars and of magic.

The sense of personal responsibility and conscience was most highly
developed of all among the Jews, whose conception of Jehovah came to
influence all Western conceptions of God. The Jews went beyond all
other Eastern civilizations in giving to Jehovah complete control over
the life and destiny of human beings, in the belief that everything in life
flowed from him. In the Mosaic conception, Jehovah was a tribal god
exacting and definitive in his requirements concerning personal behavior
and the acceptance of responsible conduct. The laws laid down precise
prescriptions, not only for moral behavior in general, but for the details
of religious ceremonies and rituals and the activities of personal life. In
the second millennium B.C., Jehovah was conceived somewhat in the
image of man as a stern patriarch who watched over his family, fought for
it, and was jealous of the worship of other gods.

Between the tenth and sixth centuries B.C., the conception of God became more abstract and universal, mainly through the efforts of the
prophets. God was conceived as a single divine being, the creator of the

whole world and the God of all peoples, all-powerful, all-wise, and all-just. The prophets emphasized the ethical and spiritual aspects of God and set Him above time and space as the God not only of power but of righteousness. All knowledge, truth, and wisdom flowed from God to man, who was expected to accept the revealed truth as a divine commandment. This monotheistic conception of one universal God, not confined to one people or one region, has enormously affected all Western civilization since that time, defining as it did the religious and ethical relationships of man to man and of man to the supernatural. Education has felt the impact of this conception for nearly 3,000 years.

Emergence of Written Language and Literature

One of the most far-reaching steps that human culture ever took occurred when men began to write down their ideas for others to read. During the long prehistoric millenniums before writing was devised, the accumulated customs, beliefs, and stories of man had to be remembered and conveyed orally. This resulted in a considerable amount of variation and inexactness in the process of communication. The development of writing made possible the more exact setting down of customs, ideas, laws, stories, and conceptions of nature. Thus, as folkways were crystallized in writing, they gained in accuracy and usefulness, but they also could become more rigid and more stultifying to later generations, who were often brought up to live according to the written materials of the past rather than according to the conditions of life prevailing in their time. The invention of writing must be considered one of the most illuminating steps that was ever taken by human beings, but it must also be recognized that grave educational problems were created in the process. A slavish devotion to the mastery of reading and writing could change education, for example, from an informal and direct induction into a culture to a formal and bookish dealing with written materials of the past that had little meaning for the present. These gains and losses must be properly assessed as one looks at the amazing achievements of human culture.

As primitive man began to scratch on walls rough pictures of the world he saw about him, he was laying the basis for a process that through long centuries in the fourth and third millenniums B.C. culminated in written symbols of communication. In Babylonia and in Egypt this process in general took the form at first of picture writing, or pictograms. These came not merely to refer to the object portrayed but to have a meaning beyond the actual object and eventually to designate a spoken sound, or vocalization. In time the written signs referred to words, syllables, and consonants which, when put into different combinations, enlarged enormously the scope of the meaning conveyed. When single letters were organized into an alphabet, the final stage in the evolution of writing had taken place. The principal western European languages were derived from the Aryan language groups of India and Europe. The principal Semitic languages became Hebrew and Arabic.

As far as we can tell, writing developed not as a sudden inspiration springing from the intellect of man but as a cultural tool by which men exerted greater control over their social affairs. It is probably no accident that written language appeared as culture became more complex and the necessity arose of keeping records of government, commercial, and religious affairs. The earliest written records apparently consisted of accounts, lists of property holdings, legal documents, letters, name lists, itineraries, medical formulas, and magical recipes. Recent discoveries in Iraq have turned up cuneiform textbooks on mathematics used by schoolboys in Sumeria as early as 2000 B.C. Other tablets found in the quarters of professional scribes dealt with myths, epic poems, and hymns. In Babylonia, writing was often used by the kings to commemorate themselves, and in Egypt much use was made of writing for religious purposes. The ease of making paper from the papyrus plant accelerated the process in Egypt. When the process had been developed to a high state of efficiency, the writing included legal codes, religious codes, and stories and songs that had been passed on by generations of oral interpreters, culminating in the Egyptian *Book of the Dead*, the Hebrew Biblical literature, and the Homeric epics.

In general, writing was confined to the privileged few, namely, the upper classes associated with the kings and priests. The ability to write was a means of preferment, both secular and religious, that came to be highly prized. It is no wonder, then, that formal arrangements for teaching grew up in connection with the necessity to acquire the ability to write and the desire to achieve preferred status in the culture. As long as written languages were extremely difficult to learn and to use, the practice of writing was largely confined to small, exclusive, even secret, groups of priests, scribes, and official classes. As written language was simplified and became more available to greater numbers of people, a profound democratizing influence was made possible that has even yet not been fully exploited by the civilizations of the world. When education was made available to wider groups than the kingly or priestly classes, the foundations for a more democratic culture were being laid.

Origin of the Arts and Sciences

Along with written language, the development of more refined tools and more accurate knowledge enabled man to exert greater control over his environment and to emerge from a primitive state of culture to a more advanced kind of civilization. When some modern educators eulogize the universality and permanence of truth and knowledge, it is well to remember that organized knowledge grew up in connection with the social necessities of controlling the physical environment and human conduct. When they speak of the desirability of studying "pure" science apart from its practical applications, it should be remembered that science appeared in the midst of a practical and social situation. When they speak disparagingly of the practical arts in favor of the fine arts, it should be noted that the practical arts and the fine arts were closely related in social origins.

In the third millennium B.C. advances in mathematics and science kept pace with the material and economic improvements in Egyptian and Babylonian culture. Arithmetic was refined as the necessity for counting and the keeping of accounts arose in the commercial process of exchanging goods and building roads and in the political process of levying and collecting taxes. Geometry was advanced in the process of controlling the floods of the Nile, building dams, digging canals and irrigation ditches, and erecting the pyramids, temples, and public works. Astronomy was improved in the process of predicting the annual floods of the river and improving navigation for commercial purposes. The calendar year of 12 months divided into 30 days each, with 5 additional days to make 365, was a result of these computations and also of the desire to determine religious holidays and festivals. The division of the hour into 60 minutes, the day and night into 12 hours each, and the week into 7 days was a mathematical achievement of great practical significance. Medicine was refined as attempts were made to ward off or cure illnesses by the use of magical potions.

The advances in architecture, sculpture, and painting are most impressive when compared with the attempts in such activities made by primitive man before he achieved the necessary technical competence. The pyramids of Egypt remain as almost incredible achievements of planning and mechanical ingenuity. The Babylonians and Assyrians displayed extraordinary skill in portraying massive and realistic warlike scenes. The palace architecture in these societies and especially in the Persian Empire reached a remarkable perfection of technique joined with artistic expression. The skill and knowledge necessary for these achievements had to be acquired through special training and could not be picked up incidentally. Thus, the appearance of the formal teaching process emerged as the culture became so complex that it could not be renewed without special attention. It was at this point in human cultural development that the school as a differentiated institution appeared.

EDUCATION AND THE WRITTEN WORD

In Primitive Cultures

In general, the aim of education in primitive societies was to enable the individual to become an integral part of the cultural life to which he belonged. Primitive education is often cited as a horrible example of a static and fixed molding of the individual by the culture. No doubt this is true to a degree, but some primitive tribes must have achieved considerable flexibility, creativity, and freedom, and probably permitted a good deal of these qualities to be developed among the oncoming generations. Unless this can be assumed, it is difficult to know how the more advanced and complex cultures of the ancient world could have arisen at all.

Insofar as primitive culture sought the perpetuation of the group folkways, education sought to create individuals who would carry on the folkways unchanged and reinforced. Again, it is difficult to generalize about prehistoric education because we know so little about it. We can only infer that each tribe tried to bring up its children in the image of its elders. Some tribes taught respect for property; others did not. Some gave special attention to developing technical and vocational skills; others left these skills to chance and casual imitation. Some gave special instruction in magic; others gave no formal instruction. Some inculcated attitudes of shame and chastity toward sex; others encouraged promiscuity.

In any case, primitive education knew nothing of books and schools. It was motivated by the needs of self-preservation; it was direct and effective; and it was carried on by the active participation of the learner as he imitated adult activities or was shown how to make tools, engage in the hunt, and fight in the wars. The children played at hunting, fishing, and making war, as modern children play at keeping house, running a fire engine, flying an airplane, or driving an automobile. They observed the qualities in action that the culture recognized as good, and they were warned against or punished for actions that the tribe considered inimical to its welfare. They heard the folklore and the songs that made up the approved tradition of the tribe, and they felt the pressures of public approval and disapproval.

In the initiation rites at puberty, the boys and girls often went through elaborate and solemn ceremonies, which served to impress upon them their obligations and duties as accepted members of the tribe in good standing. All sorts of variations were probably found in these rites. Physical suffering was frequently a feature, to test the stamina and endurance of the initiate. Direct moral precepts were preached to the young so that they might learn and emulate the desirable qualities of character.

Many features in various forms symbolized the new status: a change of name, the conferring of magical powers, the imposing of long periods of silence, purification of the body, circumcision, tattooing, drinking each other's blood, and many other kinds of tests and rites.

In Early Historic Cultures

The aim of education in the more complex cultures remained in essentials the same as that in primitive societies, but the means of assimilating the individual to his cultural tradition put much more emphasis upon the acquiring, in schools, of a knowledge of the *written* tradition. The school became the specialized place where the language and written material were learned through memorizing the accumulated knowledge of the past and the accepted modes of conduct.

Egyptian Education. Egyptian boys learned the moral precepts contained in the priestly literature. The most important was the *Book of the Dead*, which described minutely how the departed soul should behave in the afterlife in order to achieve happiness. The copybooks used for teaching the difficult art of writing the Egyptian language also contained didactic stories and precepts that were apparently designed to inculcate the accepted qualities of virtue, obedience, reverence, modesty, and manners. Emphasis was put upon unvarying repetition and exactitude. The more advanced sciences and arts must have been handed down in some more or less formal way, but our knowledge of this is limited. Basic to all kinds of formal education was the insistence upon proficiency in writing.

Jewish Education. In the centuries before the Babylonian Captivity in the sixth century B.C., education among the Jews was much like that among other tribal societies. It was primarily a matter of training within the family in which the father was absolute ruler. The child also learned from watching or taking part in the activities of the tribe as it engaged in harvesting, sheepshearing, wars, religious songs, ceremonies, prayers, and feasts and fasts. Perhaps more than that of any other early people, the education of the Jews centered in religious activities, observances, and commandments. The religious law was handed down orally for centuries and provided a central core of instruction emphasizing the ethical and ritualistic commands of Jehovah. During the eighth century B.C., written language began to be more important, and the prophecies of Isaiah contain passages indicating that children were learning to write as early as that time. In the seventh century B.C., the aims of education as reflected in Deuteronomy apparently centered upon training children to learn the Mosaic Law as the revealed law of God and therefore to be obeyed implicitly.

During the Babylonian Captivity the Jews saw their identity as a people narrowly escape obliteration, and after returning to Palestine, they made strenuous efforts to prize and strengthen their religious customs as a means of preserving themselves as a nation. The synagogue became the central place of instruction as well as of worship. During the fifth century B.C., the books of the Mosaic Law, or Pentateuch (Genesis, Exodus, Leviticus, Numbers, and Deuteronomy), were put in permanent written form and became the basis of instruction and the indispensable core of teaching and learning. In the instruction given by the scribes in the synagogues, the boys memorized large parts of the Pentateuch in the Hebrew language. Thus in the sixth and fifth centuries B.C., as the religion of the Jews became more than ever a religion of the Book, so did education become more than ever instruction in the Book.

In the fourth century B.C. the Jews gave up Hebrew as a spoken language and adopted Aramaic as the common speech of the people. This left Hebrew as the written language of religious law. It became more important than ever that the priestly classes and the lay scribes should be taught Hebrew as a means of preserving the religious and national identity of the Jews. Instruction in Hebrew as a learned language became the major subject of study for those older boys who were to become priests, scholars, and scribes. On the other hand, in the third century B.C. Greek culture began to invade the land of the Jews, as it did throughout the Mediterranean world, and the tendency was strong to develop among the Jews a cosmopolitan culture appropriate to all men everywhere. Presumably, therefore, Jewish education tended to emphasize the moral values and social skills portrayed in the wisdom literature of Job, Proverbs, and Ecclesiastes rather than to concentrate exclusively upon the Mosaic Law and religious views of the prophets.

In the second century B.C., however, the cosmopolitan trend was reversed somewhat, Jewish nationalism was reasserted, and the educational goal of social and moral wisdom was subordinated again to education in the Mosaic Law. In the first century B.C. elementary schools were more widely established outside the synagogues to give instruction in reading and writing to younger children. Significantly, these elementary schools were called "Houses of the Book." The older boys went on to study more of the Biblical literature, oral as well as written. Those who could afford to spend the time would often continue their study of religious literature in order to become scribes, whose status in the community was very high. It is probable that the schools also taught some ciphering and sacred music, and the obligation was put upon parents to teach their sons a trade. In general, the methods of teaching admitted of little deviation, consisting of repetition by teacher and student alike with occasional disputations involving questions and answers. Absolute mastery of the subject matter by thorough memorizing seemed to be the ideal of method. Severe punishments and plentiful application of the rod, along with religious injunctions and precepts, were a large part of the accepted means of motivation to learning.

From this time forward the school as a formal institution was to be one of the major instruments of education in the cultures of the Western world. A major purpose of the following chapters is to assess the role of the school, its potentialities and its limitations, in relation to the other educative functions of the several cultures of the West.

Chapter 2

SOCIAL FOUNDATIONS OF GREEK EDUCATION

THE RISE OF POLITICAL ORGANIZATION

One of the most noteworthy aspects of Greek culture and one that has had a profound effect upon all later history was the gradual shift during the first millennium B.C. from an essentially primitive and tribal organization. When tribes began to settle in contiguous territories and to assign the governing power and sovereignty to the political state, mankind was on the way to creating a social institution that obviously has enormous influence today. The Greek development of *polis* changed the course that education was to take. For the first time, education assumed a broadly political function. We are still struggling to determine what relation education should bear to the state.

Political and Economic Institutions

Aegean and Homeric Times (Prior to Seventh Century B.C.). The origin of the peoples who inhabited the Greek peninsula and the islands of the Aegean Sea is shrouded in considerable mystery. Sometime in the second millennium B.C., however, their culture displayed an extensive seagoing trade and a stock-raising and farming life of advanced proportions as the primitive tribes began to settle down and form themselves into political units. The name given to these units was *polis*, which we have called loosely "city-state."

Between 1200 and 700 B.C. several series of migrations brought various Indo-European tribes down from the Danube region. The number of city-states on the Greek mainland increased rapidly and came to be ruled by kings and aristocratic families. The king was typically a strong leader who achieved power by virtue of prowess, wealth, or fighting skill greater than those of his fellows and who relied for help and advice upon the members of the well-established aristocratic families. The epic poems of Homer, the *Iliad* and the *Odyssey*, describe this period of Greek culture in its various forms. The fact that the political foundation of Greek culture had a somewhat more democratic basis than that of the Middle East is extremely important for the development of education and the political traditions handed down to Western civilization.

In earliest Aegean times economic and social institutions centered in an agrarian way of life. The ownership of land and of livestock largely determined social position and class status, with the large landowners at the top of the social scale, the small landholders next, and the unfree slaves at the bottom. Gradually, however, specialized skills of artisanship grew up in connection with shipbuilding, public defense, and weapon-making. Commerce was increasingly carried on by the seagoing traders from Greek cities with Egypt, Phoenicia, and the Middle East, despite the many wars.

Totalitarianism versus Democracy (Seventh and Sixth Centuries B.C.). From the eighth to the sixth centuries B.C., the city-state pattern of political organization began to take a still more advanced form in which full sovereignty became attached to the state. The city rather than the tribe became the political, economic, and religious center of group life. The inhabitants of the territory were no longer simply members of a family or kinship tribe but became citizens of the state. In general, the political power during this period shifted from the tribal king to the aristocratic families, then to a larger body of property owners, and finally to the citizens in general. Such a process was often chaotic and irregular, and the whole process did not take place in all city-states. Sparta is the most outstanding example of the process that stopped at aristocratic control, whereas Athens is the best representative of the process that continued through to a democracy among the entire citizen class.

In either case, an extraordinary development took place when the conception arose that law was a man-made affair resulting from the efforts of the citizens to draw up regulations for individual and group conduct. This is most important in the history of culture and of education. In the Eastern despotisms the law was the word of the king, who claimed divine revelation, and thus it absolutely controlled all men and could not be changed by the people. In Greece the law, being man-made, could be changed by man if it became too much of a hardship, even though it was considered binding while in force. With this conception of law, men began to exert control over their social institutions in their own interests, just as earlier the Egyptians and Babylonians had begun to exert control over their physical environment.

Sparta. The most powerful state on the Peloponnesus, or lower area of Greece, was ruled by Sparta. The constitution of Sparta has a peculiar and fascinating significance for our own time, which has witnessed the rise of strong totalitarian and militaristic states based upon the conception of a "master race" or elite party. The laws of Sparta provided for three well-defined classes: the Spartan citizens, who ruled the state; the provincials (Perioeci), who had economic but no political rights; and the Helots, who were virtually slaves, had no rights, and made up the great majority of people.

Within the citizen class there was some semblance of democratic forms despite the totalitarian nature of the whole system. Two kings were the heads of the government, ruling with the advice of a Council of Elders and by means of overseers known as "ephors." The council and ephors were elected by the popular assembly, which consisted of all adult citizens, who were, in effect, the army. This system aimed at a completely militarized state run by the military-citizenship class in their own interests. Helots were assigned to work for the citizens, who in turn were not allowed to engage in commerce, artisanship, or any activity but war and training for war. The Helots were kept in a state of subjection, servitude, and surveillance. A particularly active or intelligent Helot was likely to be "liquidated" for his pains. The parallel of the aims and practices of the Spartan state and those of the totalitarian states in the twentieth century is unmistakable.

Athens. One of the most outstanding differences between Sparta and Athens was that the unification of the surrounding territory of Attica by Athens took place more by gradual agreement and cooperation than by harsh military conquest. As a result, the base of citizenship in Athens was much broader than in Sparta. At the beginning of the seventh century B.C. the rulers of the state consisted of a king, or military leader, and the magistrates, or civil officials. Then the king's military and political power began to decline, whereas the civil officials became more important and gradually came to be chosen by the popular assembly, consisting of all citizens of the state. These magistrates were assisted in their decisions by a Council of Elders, made up of aristocrats.

The process of widening the base of Athenian citizenship was one that went on more or less successfully through the seventh and sixth centuries B.C. At first the large property owners constituted the bulk of the army; then, as a stronger army was needed, more and more citizens were admitted on the basis of their wealth. The small landowners, artisans, and workers were still excluded, but throughout this period the underprivileged would often rise up against the entrenched groups in order to achieve more equality under the law.

Solon was the first great lawgiver in Athens who can be verified historically, and to him is credited a substantial improvement in the status of the lower classes. Mortgages and debts were eased; punishment, imprisonment, and slavery for debt were abolished; speculation in land was controlled; and export trade in olive oil was encouraged. Most important of all, the lower classes were admitted to citizenship and thus entitled to a place in the army and the popular assembly. The transition from aristocracy to democracy was thus greatly advanced by Solon and by Pisistratus, who continued the process of weakening the aristocracy by distributing their land to the poor and otherwise limiting the power of the aristocratic institutions.

The way was therefore cleared for the establishment of almost complete democracy among the citizenship class by the great Cleisthenes, whose constitution took effect in 502 B.C. The political basis of suffrage was changed from tribal to geographical groupings, according to which the citizens elected the various military, executive, legislative, and judicial branches of the government. The legislative branch was the popular assembly; the judicial branch was a large elected law court; the executive branch consisted of an elected Council of Five Hundred and the magistrates who carried out the desires of the Council. These were the basic forms of Athenian political democracy. Again, the parallel to modern forms of democratic government is striking. The aristocratic classes continued to hold a high place, however, because public officials were not paid a salary, and therefore it was largely the wealthy who could afford to give full time to politics. It must be remembered, too, that even the Athenian democracy rested upon a large slave class of unfree workers who were not entitled to the privileges of citizenship. The slave class was replenished from prisoners of war from conquered and defeated states.

In the period from the eighth to the sixth centuries B.C. profound economic as well as political changes took place in the Greek world. The Greeks on the Aegean Islands and in Asia Minor found that their olive and wine products were superior to those of the rest of the world; they at last had found products that the Eastern cultures desired. There grew up an active trade of much larger proportions than ever before, as a result of which the Greek countryside began to be converted from farming and stock raising to the cultivation of vineyards and olive trees. This meant that large tracts of land were more profitable than small ones. As a consequence, the class of large landowners grew more powerful, as did the class of merchants engaged in commercial and manufacturing activities, and the plight of the small landowners and free artisans became worse and worse. This, then, is the age when aristocratic control in political affairs reflected the economic supremacy of the upper classes, both landowning and commercial. The lines of future economic and class conflict were being laid in this economic revolution.

Another most important corollary of these economic changes was the need for colonies to produce the foodstuffs and textiles that were no longer being produced in sufficient quantities at home. The struggle for markets led to a most active period of colonization until Greek settlements were found in almost all parts of the Mediterranean world, as far west as Spain and France but more particularly in Sicily and Italy, where they came into contact with the native cultures.

Urban life became much more important than ever before, as dispossessed persons sought a new living in the cities and as others tried to improve their economic status. Each city came into rivalry with other cities, leading to almost constant warfare. Within the cities themselves the conflict grew, on the one hand between aristocratic landowners and a new aristocracy of moneyed wealth, and on the other hand between these aristocracies and the common people. As the common people gained economic power, they also gained political power. When economic opportunity was most widely available, Athenian political democracy was healthiest.

The Golden Age and Decline of Athenian Democracy (Fifth and Fourth Centuries B.C.). The height of the political and military power of Athens was reached in the fifth century B.C., along with the greatest effectiveness of Athenian democracy. Athens was drawn into the scene of international politics and war when the Greek cities of Asia Minor revolted against Persia in the early years of the fifth century and Athens made so bold as to send aid to these Greek cities. This led eventually to the Persian Wars in which the Greek city-states, with Athens at the head, emerged victorious. The Delian Confederacy, formed to ward off further invasions from Persia, was gradually transformed by Athens from a league of independent states to an Athenian Empire, in which the several states were virtually under the control of Athens.

Just as the more flexible commercial and manufacturing development of Athens enabled her in large part to bring about a successful conclusion to the Persian Wars, so the creation of the Delian Confederacy enabled Athens to become the economic center of the Mediterranean world in the fifth century. As the confederacy was converted into the Athenian Empire, wealth poured into Athens. This meant that Athens tried not only to be a political democracy but also to follow a strong imperial foreign policy. Such a policy helped both the commercial and artisan classes of Athens, which joined forces to make up the democratic political party. The popular assembly gained more power at the expense of the Council of Five Hundred, and the most extreme form of democracy yet known took shape. This was achieved by merchants, sailors, artisans, and small farmers against the opposition of the conservative wealthy groups represented by the ancient nobility and large landowners. Pericles was the great leader of the "Liberal Democratic" party between 460 and 430 B.C., a period often known as "the Periclean or golden age of Athens."

Democratic and imperial Athens was bound to come into conflict with the other most powerful military state in Greece, aristocratic and conservative Sparta. Athens, as leader of the "free world" of her day, was trying to unite all Greece into a large political unit under her leadership and control. Sparta, as modern dictatorships have done, upheld the right of self-determination of small states except for those under *her* control. The long rivalry for power and for control of markets led eventually to the disastrous series of military campaigns known as the Peloponnesian

War from 431 to 404 B.C. This was largely a struggle between Athenian sea power and Spartan land power, between a democracy and a military dictatorship. It was not until Athenian sea power was destroyed by a series of mistaken and traitorous actions that Sparta finally was able to impose terms of peace upon Athens. Democracy was discredited in the eyes of many, although it was able to restore itself soon after the war.

For several decades the political situation in Greece was chaotic, not to say anarchic, as each city-state fought against the others. The desire for complete independence was so deeply rooted in Greek political traditions that the cities could not unite voluntarily, and no one city-state could impose its military power long enough to bring about a consolidated state. A strong and selfish isolationism matured by the growth of mercantile and capitalistic interests prevented the building of a social consciousness that might have made for real cooperation and peace.

Excessive individualism proved to be an essential weakness in Greek democracy. It produced an increasingly wide gap between the economic status of the lower classes of citizens and the wealthy upper classes. This led to constant conflicts that weakened the attempts to achieve national unity and international cooperation. When the oligarchs were in power, they would seek to consolidate their own interests. When popular movements gained power, the attempt was to "soak the rich." Citizens began to lose interest in politics and to resist the burdens of military life, so that professional politicians and mercenary soldiers took over the field. Slavery became much more common, and the ground was prepared for the loss of political independence as the number of citizens decreased, the class of noncitizens increased, patriotic zeal weakened, and military preparedness rested with a professional army of hired soldiers.

Hellenistic Age (Third and Second Centuries B.C.). The time was ripe for invasions from the north and east by King Philip of Macedonia, who had been able to solidify all Macedonia under his power. Alexander the Great followed in his father's footsteps, conquering not only Greece, but Asia Minor, Syria, Egypt, and Persia as far east as India. When Alexander died, a series of wars ensued until three large units emerged, Macedonia, Syria, and Egypt, each under its own ruler and each carrying on wars against the others throughout the Hellenistic age, until all were finally brought under the sway of Rome. The ruling classes in the Hellenistic powers were largely Greeks and Macedonians who had brought their Greek culture with them. Alexandria in Egypt, Pergamum in Asia Minor, and the island of Rhodes became great intellectual and artistic centers. Athens maintained the forms of a democratic constitution but lost the vitality of democracy with the loss of political independence. As monarchy was imposed once again in Greece, a long process was consummated, a process starting in kingly rule and shifting to aristocracy, then to democracy, and finally back to monarchy.

Somewhat parallel to these political changes, the nature of education also changed. It seems clear that Greek education was most vital and rewarding when Greek democracy was at its height. It became more sterile and narrowly academic when political democracy was lost.

On the economic side, the excessive individualism of capitalistic-minded Greek city-states that helped to destroy the political supremacy of democracy did not destroy the economic supremacy of Greek commerce. Alexander's empire laid the political groundwork for the spread of Greek traders, who followed the Macedonian armies and became a Hellenistic ruling class, along with the army, among the conquered peoples. In material wealth, the Greek world was more prosperous than ever. This fact doubtless compensated some persons for the loss of political freedom and, indeed, contributed to it. Methods of agriculture, horticulture, stock raising, and manufacturing were improved, and the whole Western world learned the technique from the Greeks. Athens lost her leadership in economic affairs, but Greek became the universal language of business and commerce as well as of intellectual life.

As larger areas of land came under cultivation, the slave class became ever more numerous. Conflicts raged between lower and upper classes, between urban and rural interests, and between agrarian and commercial interests. As the number of free citizens became smaller, the concept of leisure began to be praised by the philosophers of the upper classes. As the number of unfree workers increased, their *manual* labor came to be looked down upon as *menial* labor by the leisure classes whose wealth and status freed them from work with their hands. Thus, the groundwork was laid for a distinction between the *liberal* arts suitable to a *free* man as opposed to the practical arts suitable for an unfree man. Such a distinction arising out of an aristocratic class culture has had enormous influence upon the educational theory and practice of the Western world down to our own times. Another set of forces that has effected the life and education of our times has to do with Greek ideas of the state and of good citizenship.

Contrasting Conceptions of Citizenship

Periclean Ideal of Democracy. One of the most all-inclusive ideas that guided the conduct of generations of Greek citizens was the belief that the *polis* provided the highest means by which the individual could come to the fullest realization of himself. When the conception of the state was limited to warlike concerns, as in Sparta, the individual felt that he could realize himself best by becoming a superb soldier. When the conception of the state was broad and flexible and generous, as in Athens, then the individual felt that he himself must become a well-rounded person in order to be a citizen worthy of his state. Just as today, democracy and dictatorship were leaving their marks upon the personalities of the people, the one generous, free, and devoted to the general welfare, the other narrow, mean, and brutal. The educational aims demanded by these opposing political views are startlingly different in kind and can readily be observed in action in their modern counterparts in the East and the West.

The classic statement of the Athenian ideal of democratic citizenship was made in the funeral oration of Pericles in 431 B.C. during the war with Sparta:

Our constitution does not copy the laws of neighbouring states; we are rather a pattern to others than imitators ourselves. Its administration favours the many instead of the few; this is why it is called a democracy. If we look to the laws, they afford equal justice to all in their private differences; if to social standing, advancement in public life falls to reputation for capacity, class considerations not being allowed to interfere with merit; nor again does poverty bar the way, if a man is able to serve the state, he is not hindered by the obscurity of his condition. The freedom which we enjoy in our government extends also to our ordinary life. There, far from exercising a jealous surveillance over each other, we do not feel called upon to be angry with our neighbour for doing what he likes, or even to indulge in those injurious looks which cannot fail to be offensive, although they inflict no positive penalty. But all this ease in our private relations does not make us lawless as citizens. Against this fear is our chief safeguard, teaching us to obey the magistrates and the laws, particularly such as regard the protection of the injured, whether they are actually on the statute book, or belong to that code which, although unwritten, yet cannot be broken without acknowledged disgrace.

Further, we provide plenty of means for the mind to refresh itself from business. We celebrate games and sacrifices all the year round, and the elegance of our private establishments forms a daily source of pleasure and helps to banish the spleen; while the magnitude of our city draws the produce of the world into our harbour, so that to the Athenian the fruits of other countries are as familiar a luxury as those of his own.

If we turn to our military policy, there also we differ from our antagonists. We throw open our city to the world, and never by alien acts exclude foreigners from any opportunity of learning or observing, although the eyes of an enemy may occasionally profit by our liberality; trusting less in system and policy than to the native spirit of our citizens; while in education, where our rivals from their very cradles by a painful discipline seek after manliness, at Athens we live exactly as we please, and yet are just as ready to encounter every legitimate danger. . . .

Nor are these the only points in which our city is worthy of admiration.

We cultivate refinement without extravagance and knowledge without effeminacy; wealth we employ more for use than for show, and place the real disgrace of poverty not in owning to the fact but in declining the struggle against it. Our public men have, besides politics, their private affairs to attend to, and our ordinary citizens, though occupied with the pursuits of industry, are still fair judges of public matters; for, unlike any other nation, regarding him who takes no part in these duties not as unambitious but as useless, we Athenians are able to judge at all events if we cannot originate, and instead of looking on discussion as a stumbling-block in the way of action, we think it an indispensable preliminary to any wise action at all. . . .

In short, I say that as a city we are the school of Hellas; while I doubt if the world can produce a man, who where he has only himself to depend upon, is equal to so many emergencies, and graced by so happy a versatility as the Athenian. . . .[1]

This was the ideal of the Athenian democracy in the golden age, but it soon lost ground to other conceptions.

Sophists and the Ideal of Expediency. The preceding picture of democratic Athenian citizenship is no doubt somewhat rose-colored. Along with the social conception of citizenship went a strong individualistic strain in Greek life that was unleashed when economic conditions in Athens made material wealth a realizable goal for many citizens and when democracy was put upon the defensive in the Peloponnesian War. The desire to perform the duties of citizenship more adequately by improving the ability to speak and think effectively went along with the desire to gain personal power and advantage in political affairs. Teachers, known as "Sophists," appeared to minister to both these desires. In any case, the cause of individualism was elevated by the practices of the Sophists in fifth-century Athens. When their "practical" teaching concerning citizenship was grounded on ethical common sense, it was beneficial; but when it approached opportunism, it tended to undermine the democratic way of life.

It seems clear that the Sophists not only reflected the growing individualistic temper in Athens but tended to accelerate it. Their arguments went something like this: Since laws and customs are man-made "conventions" and since the individual man is "the measure of all things," the individual need not be bound by conventional laws, for they do not carry universal authority. Individual men should set up their own standards of authority through their own thinking and judgment. Grammar and logic are means by which each individual clarifies his own thinking, and rhetoric is the means by which each individual sets out to change, nay, even to avoid, the conventional laws by making his arguments strong enough to prevail.

[1] Thucydides, *History of the Peloponnesian War*, trans. by Richard Crawley (J. M. Dent & Sons, Ltd., London, 1910), pp. 121–124.

Socrates and the Ideal of Free Inquiry. Against such arguments as these, Socrates arose to do combat in the latter half of the fifth century. He apparently was seeking to define generalized principles of conduct that would be binding upon all men who would be good and just. The measure of all things ethical was to be not any given man, but only the *good* man. What the good man did constituted justice, and the universal principles

Fig. 1. Socrates.

of morality could be discovered if men would only discuss their conceptions and, by mutual agreement, arrive at general concepts of justice. Men needed to criticize their habits and operating conceptions so that they could be refined and reduced to a consistency that would achieve universal consent and validity. In his early life and teachings, Socrates operated from a democratic point of view. His belief that universal ideas emerged from the common social life of man seems to embrace the basic democratic tenet of consent, but it is not so clear that Socrates in his old age remained so staunchly an adherent of democracy.

In any case, the question is still paramount today how far a democracy can go in allowing itself to be criticized and undermined by those who demand the freedom to criticize it. A basic loyalty to democratic institutions and democratic procedures must surely be asked of those who would criticize it, while at the same time the process of criticism must go on. It may ultimately be decided that the greatest failure of Socrates was his failure to stress an education for citizenship that would develop the basic loyalties to the common values of democracy at the same time as it developed the ability to criticize, which was Socrates' chief glory.

Plato and His Aristocratic Ideal. When Plato formulated his conceptions of the state and of citizenship which were to be so enormously influen-

Fig. 2. Plato.

tial for centuries to come, he did it against a thoroughly aristocratic and conservative background at a time when democracy was declining in Athens. Plato, too, was impressed by the excessive individualism of Athenian democracy as well as by the apparent military superiority of the well-disciplined aristocracy of Sparta. He grew up in a chaotic period when the great struggles between Athens and Sparta were dividing the loyalties of men and creating partisan conflicts throughout the Greek world. The temper of the times had an uncanny parallel to the spirit induced by the "cold" wars and "hot" wars of the twentieth-century contests between the forces of Communism and the Western democracies. Note the description by Thucydides of the state of affairs in 427 B.C., the year in which Plato is believed to have been born.

> Later on, one may say, the whole Hellenic world was convulsed; struggles being everywhere made by the popular chiefs to bring in the Athenians, and by the oligarchs to introduce the Lacedaemonians. In peace there would have been neither the pretext nor the wish to make such an invitation; but in war, with an alliance always at the command of either faction for the hurt of their adversaries and their own corresponding advantage, opportunities for bringing in the foreigner were never wanting to the revolutionary parties. . . .
>
> Words had to change their ordinary meaning and to take that which was now given them. Reckless audacity came to be considered the courage of a loyal ally; prudent hesitation, specious cowardice; moderation was held to be a cloak for unmanliness; ability to see all sides of a question inaptness to act on any. Frantic violence became the attribute of manliness; cautious plotting, a justifiable means of self-defence. The advocate of extreme measures was always trustworthy; his opponent a man to be suspected. To succeed in a plot was to have a shrewd head, to divine a plot a still shrewder; but to try to provide against having to do either was to break up your party and to be afraid of your adversaries. . . .
>
> The leaders in the cities, each provided with the fairest professions, on the one side with the cry of political equality of the people, on the other of a moderate aristocracy, sought prizes for themselves in those public interests which they pretended to cherish, and, recoiling from no means in their struggles for ascendancy, engaged in the direct excesses; in their acts of vengeance they went to even greater lengths, not stopping at what justice or the good of the state demanded, but making the party caprice of the moment their only standard, and invoking with equal readiness the condemnation of an unjust verdict or the authority of the strong arm to glut the animosities of the hour. Thus religion was in honour with neither party; but the use of fair phrases to arrive at guilty ends was in high reputation. Meanwhile the moderate part of the citizens perished between the two, either for not joining in the quarrel, or because envy would not suffer them to escape. . . .[2]

[2] *Ibid.*, pp. 223-225.

It was no wonder then that in his _Republic_ Plato dreamed hopefully of an ideal state which would do away with factional conflict, which would give the ruling power to an aristocratic class of the wise and just, and in which all individuals would be strictly subordinated to the state. He felt that all people should be divided into three classes, each person doing the job he was best fitted to do. This would be perfect justice. The masses of people would do the work of the world; the courageous and physically fit would do the fighting and protecting; and the intellectually most able would be the philosopher-kings to do the ruling. Good citizenship, thus, was a matter of doing the state's bidding, whether to work, or to fight, or to rule.

Needless to say, this was a denial of the historic Athenian democracy, which had been built upon the democratic principle that _all_ citizens should be obliged to work, and protect, and rule the state. It is useless, but nonetheless interesting, to speculate what the history of democracy would have been if Plato's genius had been exerted on the side of democracy rather than of aristocracy. The "Great Tradition," which he helped so much to formulate, might thus have given countless generations of men a predilection for democracy rather than a justification for a state in which the intellectual elite was believed to be the only appropriate ruling class. Plato doubtless did a great service in showing that a system of education is integral with the welfare of the state, but he also doubtless did a great disservice to democracy by idealizing an antidemocratic kind of state. The Periclean ideal of democratic citizenship seems more appropriate to the development of democratic education than that handed down in the books of Plato.

Aristotle. Much the same kind of argument can be made concerning the vast influence of Aristotle, whose _Politics_ and _Ethics_ have been textbooks in countless schools and higher institutions down to this day. We certainly are indebted to Aristotle for his insistence that the welfare of the individual is inextricably bound up with the welfare of the state. Man as a "political animal" has been a byword of political economy for over 2,000 years, but it must be remembered that Aristotle felt that a good monarchy or a good aristocracy was just as acceptable as a good commonwealth. He, like Plato, had no particular loyalty to democracy. It must be remembered, too, that Aristotle believed that most men are by nature fit only to be slaves and that only the few are by nature fitted to rule.

Further, Aristotle insisted that the highest form of virtue was sheer speculation, contemplation, and exercise of the intellectual abilities. Man as knower was higher in the scale of worthy citizenship than man as practical citizen. Thus, the educational effect of both Plato's and Aristotle's teachings has been to emphasize the cultivation of the intellect rather than the dealing with the practical problems of politics. Some educators of today would term such intellectualism a dangerous retreat to the ivory tower of academic interests at a critical time when an education devoted to social responsibility is the best hope of an enduring democratic society. Other educators of today would hail Plato and Aristotle as the surest guides through our chaotic world.

Fig. 3. Aristotle.

STATE VERSUS PRIVATE CONTROL OF EDUCATION

As education lost its informal primitive character, it took on institutional forms that set the broad patterns for schools for centuries to follow. The differentiation of political institutions prepared the way for differentiated educational institutions. The Aegean age and the Homeric age exhibited educational agencies that were essentially primitive in character, as described in Chapter 1. In the seventh, sixth, and fifth centuries B.C. the school as a separate educational institution began to appear. In the fourth, third, and second centuries B.C. elementary, secondary, and higher institutions took forms that are roughly analogous to modern levels of education.

As social life lost its tribal character and began to center in the city-state, education dropped its informal tribal nature and became political in form and content. Somewhat the same process took place in Egyptian, Babylonian, and Jewish cultures, but the Greek development differed in important ways. Whereas formal schools did appear in Egypt and Babylonia, they were basically personal in character; that is, they trained people for service to the pharaoh or king or emperor, who literally was the state. Among the Jews, schools were set up for dominantly religious rather than political purposes. Only among the Greeks did education become primarily an instrument for the making of citizens. This meant that the dominant character of the state and the ideal of citizenship shaped the character of education as never before. This close identification of education with politics can reveal to us some of the advantages and dangers that modern education encounters in its relationships with the state.

State Control in Sparta

As Sparta emerged from a primitive tribal society into an aristocratic military dictatorship, the state quite naturally began to control education rigidly for its own purposes, just as it controlled all the other aspects of life in Sparta. The ephors, or ruling magistrates, in Sparta had general supervision over educational agencies along with their other civil and military authority. They exercised this supervision directly until they appointed a special educational officer known as the "paidonomus," who took direct charge to see that regulations were carried out. In this way Sparta set up what was virtually a state system of education under strict state control for state purposes. The Spartan child (that is, the child of a citizen) was considered as belonging to the state from birth to death.

At birth the Spartan boy was brought before the ephors, who decided whether he seemed sufficiently healthy to become a strong warrior and citizen. If the infant seemed sickly or weak, he was likely to be exposed on the mountains to die or to be taken by a foreigner or Helot to be brought up as a tradesman, worker, or slave. The process of elimination of the unfit was thus begun at birth. If the child passed muster, he was taken home to be brought up by the mother and father until he reached the age of seven.

At that age the boy was placed in a boarding-school type of institution that amounted to a public barracks, where he remained until eighteen.

During these years the boys lived a semimilitary existence in which they were organized into bands or packs under the leadership and authority of young adults. The boys ate together, slept together, played and worked together, and in general followed the common life of soldiers. Military organization was always the order of the day, headed by the paidonomus, who had the authority of command, discipline, and punishment.

At the age of eighteen the boys were given 2 years of intensive military training which was operated closely under the supervision of the army. Then for 10 years, from the ages of twenty to thirty, the young men were active members of the army. At the age of thirty they became full-fledged citizens and were compelled to marry for the good of the state, but normally the men continued to live as a standing army while they engaged in the duties of citizenship, which included a large share of training the boys and young men for a like existence.

Young girls were kept at home along with the boys until the age of seven. When the boys left for boarding school, the girls continued to live at home, but they were likewise organized into packs. These packs were the means of giving the girls physical training and of building up their bodies so that they might bear and rear strong sons for the army. They were also given training for household duties connected with the rearing of children and the control of household slaves. In general, they enjoyed a relatively high status in a community that regarded women as essential cogs in the maintenance of a military machine.

The analogy of this type of education to the systems set up by Nazi Germany, Fascist Italy, and Communist Russia in modern times will be apparent to all. The Nazis, Fascists, and Communists saw as clearly as did the Spartans that the development and maintenance of a military dictatorship depended in large measure upon having complete and exclusive control over the life of its children. The various age levels of youth organizations in Germany, Italy, and Russia had many parallels in the Spartan system, along with the dominant military ideal for boys and the childbearing ideal for women as feeders for the military maw. These are supreme examples of the use of education as a political instrument in building a totalitarian society.

Private and State Control in Athens

As might be expected from the more flexible political and economic arrangements in Athens, the Athenian state did not exert the complete control over education that was characteristic of Sparta. The stronger sense of freedom and democracy in Athens seemed to leave the provisions for education more fully in the hands of parents. Nevertheless, there is evidence that the state did concern itself with education. The complete picture of educational control in Athens is, however, far from clear. The broader conception of citizenship that emerged in Athens led to the establishment of a far greater variety of schools than appeared in Sparta. Each of these schools was designed to cultivate a phase of the all-round development deemed necessary to enable a citizen to fulfill suitably all his responsibilities. The more urban character of life, with its attendant commercial class, also gave Athenian education a cosmopolitan and varied scope that was never reached by the rural and agricultural society in Sparta.

Just when the first formal schools appeared in Athens is not certain, but we do know that several educational laws have been attributed to the lawgiver Solon in the early part of the sixth century B.C. The presumption is that schools of some sort existed as early as the seventh century and that schools were rather widespread by the end of the Persian Wars in 480 B.C. It is probably true that before Solon's time some schools already existed concerning which he made the regulations attributed to him. Whether he formulated the laws or not, the state by his time had begun the practice of paying school tuitions for boys whose fathers had been killed in the armies. These were probably among the first educational benefits for families of veterans. Other state regulations concerning education apparently compelled parents to see that their sons learned their letters and acquired the ability to swim. The state also appointed a public supervisor for education, and at some time the law required parents to see that their sons were given an elementary education in gymnastics, letters, and music.

Other general regulations of the state dealt with somewhat obscure requirements concerning the size of schools, the admission of boys to school, the age of admission, the compulsory assignment of a pedagogue to each schoolboy, and the prevention for moral reasons of adult men from becoming too closely associated with the young boys in the schoolrooms or gymnasiums. The state further entered into the support of education by building and maintaining at public expense the principal gymnasiums in Athens, where the boys and men engaged in athletic contests and exercises. It is apparent, therefore, that the state was concerned with the organization and control of educational institutions in Athens, and it is entirely possible that many other regulations were passed and influence exerted by the state in addition to the particular laws of which we now have knowledge.

No matter to what extent the state participated in Athenian education, however, it remains true that, in general, the early elementary schools were run by private teachers who accepted a fee or tuition for the instruction of their students. The state did not establish public schools, in the modern sense, at public expense, nor did it pay teachers' salaries, nor did it require compulsory attendance at specific schools for a specified length

Fig. 4. Greek school scenes.

of time. Three kinds of elementary teachers appeared in Athens during this period: the teacher of letters (grammatist), the teacher of music (citharist), and the teacher of gymnastics (paedotribe). What these teachers taught will be discussed in the second section of Chapter 3. The important thing to note here is that no rigid system of schools existed. It is perhaps more correct to speak of Athenian teachers than of Athenian schools; where the teacher was, there was a school. Parents selected a teacher and sent their boys to him.

Sometimes a teacher of letters and a teacher of music would set up their establishment together so that boys could acquire both kinds of instruction at the same place. The most popular teachers seem to have been those of letters and gymnastics, and the evidence shows that often a boy would spend part of the day with the literary teacher and part of the day with the gymnastics teacher in the palaestra. The school day was long, often lasting from sunrise to sunset. Public opinion was the most potent force impelling parents to have their sons educated.

Advanced education beyond fourteen or sixteen was achieved by attending the public gymnasiums for further physical development and by studying with Sophists for further intellectual development. Three gymnasiums were provided at public expense in Athens. The Academy was the oldest and in a sense catered to the most aristocratic elements in Athens; the Lyceum was founded in the fifth century by Pericles in response to the democratic movements of the day and catered particularly to the newly enfranchised citizens from the commercial and artisan groups of citizens; the Cynosarges catered to the metics, traders, and residents who had not achieved full rights of citizenship. Each gymnasium was under the direction of a public official known as the gymnasiarch.

During the political, economic, and intellectual ferments of the fifth century B.C. the traveling "wise men," or Sophists, gave opportunity for private instruction in a wide range of subjects to be noted later. The Sophists taught for a fee, and young men who could afford to pay the fees sought out the teacher they wished to hear. Modern historians have applied the term "secondary education" to the instruction offered by the gymnasiums and Sophists, but this is something of an anachronism, for the ancient Greeks in this period had no clear-cut formulation of a system of education as we know it in modern Europe or America. It is probably better to speak of these kinds of instruction merely as advanced education beyond the elementary levels. It was all very informal and lacked the kind of prescription, curriculum, degrees, or diplomas that have become customary in modern times.

Military training was a final kind of education that was very common and quite popular for youth of the citizen class who had reached about the age of eighteen. Whether this type of training was compulsory before the fourth century B.C. or not is a matter of debate, but in any case it seems clear that it was common and highly regarded. Growing out of the gymnasial training, a youth would normally engage in 2 years of service as a cadet (*ephebos*) in the army; at the end of this time he would enter into full citizenship at a public ceremony. Even during the Persian and Peloponnesian Wars, the individualistic nature of Athenian democracy apparently had left a great deal to voluntary service in the armed forces of the city. This arrangement seems to have worked very well because of the common expectation that a responsible citizen would engage in military defense of the city-state. As the Peloponnesian War continued, this expectation was weakened somewhat, for the young men grew more interested in the intellectual delights of the Sophists' teachings. As the democracy began to waver under attacks by Sparta from without and individualistic excesses from within, regard for the Sophists naturally diminished. In the fourth century Athens took steps to make military training compulsory—when it was too late to preserve Athenian independence.

During the fourth century B.C. elementary education revealed no such marked changes as did advanced education in Athens, but the foundations were being laid for a more systematic institutionalizing of education and for greater state control, both of which came to considerable fruition in Hellenistic times. The informal teaching of the Sophists gave way to institutionalized schools for advanced education in philosophy and rhetoric as represented by the Academy founded by Plato, the Lyceum founded by Aristotle, the school of the Cynics founded by Antisthenes, and the rhetorical school founded by Isocrates. The first three of these schools were set up near the three public gymnasiums of Athens, from which they derived their names. Each became somewhat monastic in its emphasis upon selected members, or initiates, who made up the inner circle along the lines of modern fraternal orders. Often the members lived together according to regulations accepted by all and sought recruits from the students who were attracted to Athens by the fame of the schools. The foundations for "higher education" were being laid as these philosophical schools incorporated much of the monastic ideal of the earlier Pythagorean and Orphic cults and forecast the monastic ideal of the Christian Era.

State control of education was increased when the Ephebic College was established in 335 B.C. by the Athenian assembly and military training was made compulsory for all citizen youth between the ages of eighteen and twenty. Such training was controlled and supported by the state. At the age of eighteen each youth had to prove his legitimate birth as a citizen, have his hair cut, don a uniform, and be inducted into the Ephebic College. The establishment of compulsory military training grew out of the recommendations of Plato and Xenophon. They had been impressed by the effectiveness of the armies of Sparta, which had long required military training of all citizens. The movement was brought to a head by the Battle of Chaeronea when Philip of Macedonia utterly defeated a combined force of Athenian and Theban armies.

Growing Civil Control in Hellenistic Times

During the third and second centuries B.C. education became more systematized than ever before, and state or civil control exerted itself increasingly in many ways. The three modern levels of education, elementary, secondary, and higher, began to take more definite shape. As less and less attention was given to gymnastics and music for younger boys, the school of the grammatist became the common type of elementary school. With the development of various fields of knowledge to be noted in the first section of Chapter 3, the school of the *grammaticus* came to be recognized as the accepted secondary school for boys from about thirteen or fourteen to sixteen or eighteen years of age. Noteworthy, too, was the disappearance of gymnastic or physical education. Beyond the school of the *grammaticus*, the forms of higher education centered in the various schools of philosophy and rhetoric.

Here, then, was the formation of educational institutions that were carried over into the Roman Empire and passed on to modern Europe by the Christian church. In general, the institutionalizing of education paralleled the rise of distinguishable bodies of organized and systematic knowledge. Even the Ephebic College, which had been set up primarily for military and physical training, took on a more intellectual content around 300 B.C. In following years, not only was the requirement for military training reduced to 1 year and then made voluntary, but also requirements in philosophical and rhetorical studies were made part of the curriculum. The Ephebic College thus lost much of its democratic, civic quality and became more nearly like an aristocratic and fashionable semimilitary academy.

To broaden our view now to include the whole Hellenistic world beyond the walls of Athens, the evidence seems clear that public support and control of education were on the increase. Many cities chose administrators of schools, either appointed or elected, who were somewhat analogous to modern superintendents of schools. Teachers were appointed by the state, their salaries paid out of public funds or from the income of private endowments, and general supervision of the curriculum was exercised.

Higher education also received stimulus during Hellenistic times. Athens remained a great intellectual center. In addition to the Academy, Lyceum, Cynosarges, and the rhetorical schools founded there in the fourth century, two new schools were founded at the beginning of the third century B.C. Epicurus opened his school in a garden, from which the Epicurean school derived its name, the Gardens. Zeno opened his school in the portico of a building, from which his school became known as the Stoa (from the Greek word meaning porch) and his philosophy as Stoicism. Collectively, these schools were quite influential in attracting thousands of young men to Athens over the centuries. Some modern historians have applied the term "University of Athens" to this collection of schools, but this is a misnomer, for few of the institutional forms associated with modern universities were present. The university organization as we know it is essentially medieval in origin, stemming from the thirteenth-century universities.

In Hellenistic times other cities arose to compete with Athens as cosmopolitan intellectual centers. At Alexandria in Egypt the Hellenistic kings established a great library and museum for the carrying on of advanced study and research. Other cities that became famous for their libraries, museums, and schools of philosophy and rhetoric were Pergamum, Antioch, Rhodes, Tarsus, Smyrna, and Halicarnassus. Most of these institutions were founded and supported by the Hellenistic kings, often to glorify themselves, but the effect was to stimulate state interest in higher education as a preparation for the further steps taken in the same direction by the Roman emperors. Often the presiding officials and teachers were appointed, paid, and controlled by the Hellenistic kings. By the end of the Hellenistic period, schools and higher institutions were so widespread that a quite considerable reading and educated public probably existed. Hellenistic education laid the groundwork in content and organization for the Roman educational system, which was patterned upon it and which in turn laid the foundations for the educational institutions of the medieval and modern world.

Educational Opportunity

No simple generalizations can be made concerning the availability of and opportunity for education in Greece. It is too easy, for example, to say that all aspects of Spartan education were aristocratic and all aspects of Athenian education were democratic. In both Sparta and Athens, education was designed for the few, as compared with modern conceptions of democracy; the slave class in both city-states was the largest element in the population, and formal education was not for them. If democratic education is to be measured by the extent to which it serves a whole population, neither Sparta nor Athens set up a democratic education. But, even in this sense, Athens was somewhat more democratic, for some provisions were made for noncitizens. Foreigners in Athens could attend the Cynosarges, foreign Sophists were welcomed as teachers, foreigners were welcomed as students, and in Hellenistic times foreigners were admitted to the Ephebic College. In Sparta, foreigners were never eligible for the educational facilities available to the citizen class.

Within the citizenship class there is a sense in which Sparta treated its students more equally than did Athens, for the public system of education treated all citizens alike, whereas in Athens the ability to achieve an education depended upon the wealth of the student's parents. In Athens the richer the family the more chance there was for the boy to have more and better education. Sparta also gave more attention than Athens to the education of girls. Furthermore, Sparta went further than Athens in providing education free to the citizenship class. However, equality of education and free tuition are not exclusively criteria of democratic education, as is witnessed by modern dictatorship countries, in which education has been provided equally to those deemed worthy of full citizenship and provided free to them at state support.

To reverse the argument, we cannot say that Spartan education was essentially nondemocratic merely because it was compulsory and that Athenian education *was* democratic because it was voluntary. Compulsory education can be combined with the democratic ideal, as our own experience in America has proved. The essential thing about compulsory education is the source of the compulsion. If education is forced upon a people by a dictatorial group of whatever kind, this is doubtless undemocratic compulsion; but if compulsory education arises from the will and consent of the people in order to preserve and improve democracy, then surely compulsory education fits in with a democratic ideal. Similarly, it should be recognized that compulsion is not *necessarily* antidemocratic; the source of the authority is the important thing. No one would say that traffic rules, for example, are undemocratic merely because they limit the freedom of motorists to run down pedestrians. If the duly constituted authorities in a democratically run society decide that laws are necessary for the good of the whole people and if such laws are open to change at the will of the people, then authority and compulsion must be considered democratic.

To sum up, it seems clear that Spartan education (like that of Nazi Germany, Fascist Italy, and Communist Russia) was less democratic than that of Athens because it aimed at training a military elite bent upon preserving an aristocratic dictatorship. It seems clear also that Athenian education was more democratic because it was based on a broader conception of citizenship by which the citizen was expected not only to defend the state by military action but also to become a well-rounded individual worthy of a democratic society. The wider range of interests in Athenian education, reflecting the desire for intellectual, emotional, and aesthetic development as well as physical and military prowess, made it essentially more democratic than the education of Sparta.

From a modern point of view, it seems likely that Athenian education would have been even more democratic had it set out to provide a compulsory, free education with public support for all Athenian youth equally. In this way the individualistic character of Athenian education might have given way to a more socially minded conception of democracy. This was especially true in Hellenistic times, when citizens lost a great measure of their interest in politics, and education became separated by a wide gulf from the common life of the people. A continuing interest and participation in public affairs on the part of the whole population are essential to democracy, and a too narrowly intellectualistic or vocational education can become as undemocratic as an exclusively military and physical education. Democracy requires a proper combination of all these factors.

The Teaching Profession

The status of the teaching profession in Greek society was a mixed affair. In Sparta the teachers of military and physical training were public officials and presumably attained the status of any minor official. The Spartan custom of laying educational responsibility on all adult male citizens was something of a survival from primitive tribal times, and if it had been directed toward democratic goals, the custom would not have been a bad one. It would be an excellent thing if in a democratic society all parents took a greater interest in and responsibility for the education of all youth.

In Athens the status of the teaching profession ranged from extremely low to extremely high and often changed from time to time with the social and political situation. The elementary teacher in Athens was held in relatively low regard, partly because he accepted fees for his instruction and partly because of the prevalent feeling then as now that "he who cannot do, teaches." Satirical statements by some Greek authors bear witness to the feeling that certain persons taught letters when they could not make a success of any other occupation. Furthermore, the practice of assigning slaves as pedagogues to the young boys also indicates the low estate of this group. Some teachers were slaves, but the term "slave" often referred to citizens of another city-state that had been defeated in war, and such slave-teachers may have been ordinary or even extraordinary citizens in their own city. In fifth-century Athens the Sophists, many of whom were foreigners, were held in very high regard by great numbers of Athenians. When democracy was considered safest, these foreigners were welcomed and students flocked to them to study and pay their fees.

Great teachers such as Socrates, Plato, Aristotle, and Epicurus achieved a very high social status at certain times in Athens. But in the end Socrates was condemned to death, and Plato and Aristotle had to leave Athens until their political and social views were considered more acceptable. Social pressure upon teachers and the demand for conformity are not new phenomena. In general, the teachers of advanced studies were held in higher regard, then as now, than teachers of beginning or elementary subjects. The gymnasiarch was a public official and thus entitled to fairly high status, and in many Hellenistic cities teachers as well as administrators were elected by the citizenry. The fact that many wealthy persons gave endowed funds for teaching purposes shows that the teaching profession was not altogether despised. If one considers that the Athenian schools of philosophy and rhetoric lasted for some 800 years and that the great institutions in Alexandria and elsewhere were founded and endowed by a long series of kings, it seems clear that the Greek world had a much higher respect for teaching as a distinct profession than any other culture up to that time.

Out-of-school Education

One of the most remarkable aspects of Greek culture is the way in which nonschool institutions and agencies carried on the educational process of preparing people to live in the culture. The compact nature of the city-state made it possible for a great majority of the citizens to engage personally and actively in the activities of society. Conversely, it made possible a degree of impact by the culture upon the people that is much less characteristic of a large, sparsely settled, and loosely knit society. The people of the city of Athens lived constantly in the presence of the beautiful art objects represented in their public buildings and temples. They participated actively in the political deliberations of the assembly and the economic "deliberations" of the market place. Young people were given special roles to play in the public festivals and holidays, the public theater, and the celebrations attendant upon athletic, musical, and poetry contests. The farmers of the adjoining countryside and the sailors of the nearby port of Piraeus could take part in these activities on many occasions rather than few. The military training of the years spent in the army touched great numbers of the men of Athens and thus contributed to their education, broadly conceived. All these activities carried forward the education begun in the schools, and their effectiveness was a tribute not only to the cultural life of the Athenians but also to the broad range of activities carried on in the schools.

One of the most important cultural agencies of education, however, was not touched by the schools, and that was the preparation for engaging in an occupation or trade. Vocational education was a matter with which the schools of Athens did not concern themselves. It was left to a more or less informal system of apprenticeship. In this respect Athenian education continued along primitive tribal lines. Training for a vocation was cared for in family groups as the father taught his son his own occupational tasks. Apprenticeship also became somewhat specialized and formalized as children were taken into shops and households where they were taught the elements of a trade. As the economic revolution of the sixth and fifth centuries B.C. created a greater demand for skilled labor, small shops were often converted into factories and workmen became more specialized in their tasks. Written agreements were drawn up between master and apprentice, and a workman often cited his teacher as proof of his skill. Sculpture, stonemasonry, carpentry, shoemaking, medicine, law, household affairs, and cooking were arts in which the apprenticeship system was used as a means of training the young for a vocation.

Thus, the arts and crafts necessary for providing consumers' goods were handed down from generation to generation outside of the schools. In Homeric days even the kings and noblemen worked with their hands, and in Solon's time an injunction was laid upon parents to see that children were taught a trade. However, the aristocratic nature of Athenian education, according to which the gentleman of leisure was not expected to work with his hands, was increasingly emphasized from the fourth century on. In Hellenistic times the schools were almost exclusively geared to the interests of the upper classes, despite the fact that for the majority of citizens the job of making a living was still of paramount importance. Increased slave labor further tended to lower the popular estimation of artisanship. As a result, the influence of Hellenistic education has led succeeding centuries to neglect such a vitally important phase of culture and education as the handing down and improving of the practical arts and crafts.

Chapter 3

INTELLECTUAL FOUNDATIONS
OF GREEK EDUCATION

RATIONALITY AS A WAY OF LIFE

The Greeks took giant strides in becoming critically self-conscious as they approached the problems of the world, of human nature, and of society, relying more upon human intelligence than merely upon tradition, superstition, and mysticism. Their conception of well-rounded development of the whole personality of the individual is an ideal for education that still stirs the imagination. The Greek artistic genius created masterpieces of literature, poetry, architecture, and sculpture to which all the world has paid homage. They made tremendous achievements in organizing and systematizing knowledge into the disciplines that we know and cherish. The Greeks created world views, methods of thinking, and bodies of knowledge which have influenced Western culture and education to our own day. Indeed, we think the way we do in large part *because* the Greeks thought the way they did. Thus, to understand our own ways of thinking we need to know how the Greeks thought.

"This-worldliness" versus "Other-worldliness"

The Greek genius perhaps expressed itself no more fully than in the realm of speculation concerning the origin and nature of the universe. The soothsayer and medicine man began to give way to the philosopher and his reliance upon critical reason in the effort to solve the basic riddles of the cosmos. Primitive Greeks had much the same conceptions as other primitive peoples concerning the gods who presumably created the earth and controlled the events that took place upon it. They explained various physical phenomena in terms of the actions of the gods, the most familiar of which are the pictures of Apollo driving his sun chariot across the heavens each day and Zeus hurling thunderbolts during a storm.

In the sixth century B.C. certain men began to seek new explanations for physical phenomena. The important thing for the history of thought and education is that they began to seek natural causes for physical events. In a real sense, an intellectual revolution was taking place along with the political and economic revolutions of this period. These men were no longer content to accept the mythological explanations of tradition but attempted to find consistent natural laws lying behind the observed regularity of physical events. Appearing first in the Greek cities of Asia Minor and later in Athens, such philosophers began to build up rational explanations for the universe, often concentrating upon a single fundamental element underlying all material events.

For example, Thales came to the conclusion that water was the essential characteristic of all matter; he is credited with making geometrical and astronomical observations that led to the prediction of an eclipse. Pythagoras found mathematical consistencies in the movement of the stars as well as in musical tones; he is credited with believing that the stars and earth were spherical in shape and that the essential stuff of the universe was somehow connected with the mysteries of numbers. Anaximander estimated that the universe was infinite in size and that man was a higher form in the long process of evolution. Xenophanes believed that the world was a unity and that reality was guided by a single god or directing force. Anaximenes found the essence of things in air, and Heraclitus found it in fire.

In the fifth century B.C., Heraclitus and Empedocles suggested a theory of evolution based upon their conception that change and flux were the essential characteristics of the universe. Leucippus and Democritus formulated an atomic theory of the construction of the universe that remained substantially as they left it until the scientific developments of the seventeenth century. Hippocrates developed the study of medicine to such an extent that his reputation extends down to the present time in the form of the Hippocratic oath, which young physicians take to express their ideals of service to mankind. Anaxagoras felt strongly the impact of change in the physical world and put much emphasis upon this process in the biological and material world, but he considered that the world must have some fixed point in the midst of all the observable flux. He located permanence in the world of mind (*nous*) that lies behind change and gives order to it.

With the advent of Plato in the fourth century B.C., the forces of materialism, relativity, and change received a tremendous setback from his philosophy of idealism, which stressed the permanent, the absolute, and the eternal. Plato was impressed with the necessity of emphasizing the fixed and unchanging character of reality in the universe as well as in political and economic affairs. Thus he devised an ideal world of spirit in which reside all eternal, fixed, and permanent ideas. This world of ideas contains universal patterns of truth, goodness, justice, and beauty, which give form to the everyday world about us. The everyday world is the realm of matter, a shadowy, fleeting world of change and instability, where individual things exist, are created, grow, decay, and are destroyed.

All individual things or objects are merely imperfect copies subordinate to the eternal forms of things. To take an example from mathematics that so impressed Plato, the idea of a circle is eternal and never changes. Specific, individual circles that men can draw or use are always imperfect and can be destroyed, but the idea of a circle is always there in the spirit world, untouched by human manipulation. The same is true of all physical objects, such as chairs, tables, and houses. Men can make many different kinds of chairs, but it is only because they partake of the eternal idea of "chair-ness" that we can recognize them all as chairs. Finally, then, the same is true of justice, beauty, and goodness; men are just and good only as they partake of the eternal ideas of justice and goodness.

From the foregoing it is possible to gauge how profound an influence Plato's idealism has had upon all Western thought down to our own day. The man in the street is familiar with appeals to forsake the passing fancies and material interests of "this world" for the eternal values and spiritual affairs of the "other world." He does so because his whole outlook has been shaped in a considerable degree by Plato's ideas, especially as they were absorbed by the Christian tradition and channelized into Western thought.

Aristotle followed in large measure in the philosophic footsteps of Plato, despite his much greater concern with physical and biological science. The whole universe, according to Aristotle, is made up of "form" and "matter" integrally bound up together. Form is the active life principle that gives shape and meaning to material things, much as the design or plan of an architect gives form and meaning to the materials that eventually become a house or a bridge. The form exists in the mind of the designer prior to matter, and yet it has no material existence until combined with matter. Aristotle did not set up two worlds of separate existence as did Plato, for he believed that the general, eternal form appears *only* when expressed in the shape of individual things.

This outlook shows Aristotle's greater interest in the everyday world of nature, but his impact upon future thought generally supported the otherworldly views of Plato. Despite his effort to strike a balance between spirit and matter, Aristotle stressed the value of pure contemplation (*theoria*) and meditation upon the spiritual essences of reality.

The Foundations of Intellectualism in Education

Fully as important in their effect upon later times, and perhaps even more obviously related to education, are the conceptions of Plato and Aristotle with regard to human nature, learning, and thinking. In each case their views of human nature correspond closely to the views of the universe just described. Plato formulated a theory of human nature to fit his political and economic arrangements as well as his metaphysical philosophy. Just as the universe is divided into a spiritual and material world, so does human nature consist of spirit (soul) and matter (body). The human soul is eternal, changeless, and nonmaterial, whereas the human body is born, grows, decays, and is destroyed, as do all things of change and imperfection.

Plato's physiology and psychology were worked out into a neat three-fold scheme. Inhering chiefly in man's belly are the appetites, feelings, and desires that seek bodily satisfaction. Residing primarily in the heart or breast are the manly drives of courage, endurance, and will. Centered in the head is the highest aspect of man, his reason, or intellect. The intellect is the only part of human nature that is primarily related to the soul; the other parts are closely related to the body. In Plato's *Republic*, men who act solely in response to their appetites are fit only to be workers, those who possess qualities of courage and hardihood are fit to be the fighters, but only those who act according to the dictates of reason are fit to be the rulers, or philosopher-kings. Thus, human nature is determined entirely by heredity and is fixed from birth. Indeed, the soul is immortal and has existed for all time along with the eternal ideas of the spiritual world. Here again it should be pointed out how this view of human nature has been absorbed by the Christian tradition and has come down to us.

Aristotle's conception of human nature is somewhat similar to that of Plato. Analogous to his view of the world, men were conceived by Aristotle to be made of form (soul) and matter (body). Aristotle's scientific studies led him to make more of the relationship of human life to lower levels of life. For example, human nature is a compound of vegetative, animal, and human characteristics. He uses the word "soul" virtually to mean life. Hence, man has a "vegetative" nature that grows, reproduces, decays, and dies, as plant life does. Man also has an "animal" nature, with desires, sensory impressions, and active movement in common with other animal life. But, in addition, man has a distinctively "human" nature that no lower form of life possesses, namely, the reason. As is so often said in Aristotle's words, "Man is a rational animal." Reason consists of (1) a lower, or practical, reason by which man makes ethical and practical decisions concerning conduct and (2) a higher, or theoretical, reason by which man acquires universal and eternal knowledge and truth. Quite logically, then, Plato and Aristotle assigned to education the task of developing the highest elements in the hierarchy of human nature, namely, the faculty of theoretical reason and contemplation. Rationalists and intellectualists in all ages have found inspiration in these views and justification for intellectual discipline in education.

Plato's theory of the learning process corresponds to the nature of man and of the universe. True knowledge cannot be achieved through the bodily senses, for the body is imperfect, guided by its appetites and representing only the changing, shadowy realm of experience. The body is virtually a prison house that confines and deludes the reason. Therefore, the great majority of people can never acquire knowledge because they are activated merely by the appetites of the body. A slightly higher but still imperfect knowledge may be acquired by those whose hearts dominate their actions. This group can have opinions that are better than sense impressions, but their opinions still are filtered through the body and thus do not rank as true knowledge. Knowledge, properly speaking, is acquired only by those whose intellect, or reason, has been able to cast off the shadows and shackles created by sense experience and opinion.

True knowledge comes only from the spiritual world of eternal and changeless ideas, and this knowledge is innate in the immortal soul, which has dwelt in the spiritual world before being incased in the mortal body. Knowledge is thus acquired, not by sense experience, but by a process of reminiscence by which the intellect remembers what it knew before its association with an imperfect body. To remember perfectly, the intellect must rigorously close the windows of the body to the external world and open only the windows of the intellect so that it may look upon and contemplate eternal truth. Intellectual discipline of the strictest kind, achieved by means of mathematics and philosophy, is the only true road to knowledge. Here, then, is the basis of that intellectualistic conception of the learning process which has dominated educational procedure almost down to the present time and which is still strongly urged by some prominent educators in America today.

Despite Aristotle's emphasis upon sense experience as a road to knowledge, his influence has been largely the same as that of Plato because of the hierarchy of intellectual virtues that he formulated. Aristotle, as did Plato, put much emphasis upon learning good character habits, but he insisted that the intellectual virtues were the highest values of man. Therefore "cultivation of the intellect" has been singled out by his followers as the prime method of learning. It is often forgotten, however, that Aristotle made much of sense experience and scientific induction as proper roads to knowledge, even to universal truths. Educators, like everyone else, are selective in their use of the past. When they found Aristotle saying that the theoretical, or speculative, reason (*theoria*) was the *highest* virtue, they often neglected to notice that Aristotle also emphasized the practical reason by which wise moral decisions are made. The traditional view of Aristotle has thus focused upon contemplation of "first principles" or "final causes" as the source of eternal and absolute truths, to be achieved by the study of mathematics and metaphysics. The weight of Aristotle's authority has been used to emphasize learning as an exclusively intellectual process, with an educational program made to fit it. Intellectualism in education is one of our living traditions. Plato and

Aristotle are by no means dead in American education. Their influence needs to be studied and their value reexamined.

The Distinction between the Practical Arts and the Liberal Arts

The Greeks not only created a great culture; they also put their ideas, techniques, and arts into organized forms and systematic bodies of knowledge. Those intellectual arts appropriate to free men eventually came to be thought of as "liberal" arts and those appropriate to artisans or workmen as "practical" arts. The intellectual side of the tradition became so influential in Western education that it is often forgotten that the Greeks made significant achievements in the practical arts as well.

Technology and the Practical Arts. Beginning in Homeric times and developing more rapidly from the seventh and sixth centuries B.C. onward, great advances were made in the knowledge and practice of shipbuilding, navigation, toolmaking, mining and engineering, architecture, manufacture of goods, and agriculture. The Greeks borrowed technical skills from the East but they improved upon them both technically and artistically, giving them their own character and individuality. Their skill was fully as much a technical ability to work the materials as it was a skill in improving the aesthetic quality of the objects. In the fifth and fourth centuries B.C., the artisan was often not only a skilled master of his craft; he was also an artist, whether potter, sculptor, jeweler, woodworker, leatherworker, or metalworker.

As people flocked to the cities in the Hellenistic age, city planning on an advanced scale was practiced in many places, again combining the arts of the craftsman and of the aesthetically minded. Similarly, agriculture and stock raising took on a new significance as innovations were made in irrigation, rotation of crops, fertilizing methods, vinegrowing, the cultivation of olive trees, and new breeds of animals. But the Greeks for some reason were never stimulated to apply their scientific knowledge fully to the production of goods and to economic affairs in a way to produce the kind of industrial revolution that took place in the eighteenth and nineteenth centuries. Technology among the Greeks never kept pace with pure science.

Informal apprenticeship remained the basic means of handing on technical skills from one generation to the next. These practical skills and crafts were never organized into systematic bodies of knowledge with the conscious aim to improve them in the way in which the liberal arts were systematized and improved. It was largely because the liberal arts *were* so organized that they achieved preeminence over the practical arts in education. The weight of written materials in a field of human activity is undeniably enormous in commanding respect in the academic and educational world. Education more readily utilized those bodies of knowledge which were written down in organized and systematized form and were thus ready for teachers to hand down to students.

Liberal Arts. The Greeks turned rather to the liberal arts appropriate to intellectual pursuits and achieved great heights in the language arts, literature, philosophy, science and mathematics, history, and the fine arts.

By the second century B.C. Greek had become the language of scholarship, education, diplomacy, and trade nearly everywhere in the Mediterranean world. The deliberate efforts to systematize the language as well as the creative efforts to produce a literature speeded up this process.

Grammar as a subject of inquiry and study was stimulated in the fifth century B.C. by the interest of the Sophists in response to the new conditions of life already described. They began to study how the language made use of tense, gender, mood, number, etymology, and syntax and to formulate rules for a correct grammatical usage. The emphasis that Socrates, Plato, and Aristotle put upon the necessity of accurate definitions and classification stimulated further the study of grammar. In the Hellenistic age, scholars at Alexandria and elsewhere worked assiduously at formulating the eight parts of speech and in constructing dictionaries and reference books to help standardize the language.

Rhetoric as a special study was also stimulated by the democratic life of fifth-century Athens. Not only was a strong interest shown in the meanings of words and correct usage, but also a growing interest in the ability to use the language with fluency, ease, grace, and persuasion. Isocrates was a great teacher of rhetoric who added much to the refinement of the study as a body of knowledge, as did Demosthenes and Aeschines whose speeches became models of rhetorical skill and usage. Aristotle contributed enormously to setting the patterns of rhetoric for future centuries in his book entitled *Rhetoric,* which has been used by generations of American as well as European students.

Literary forms created by the Greeks are often used as models to this day. The epic poetry of Homer's *Iliad* and *Odyssey* which had been handed down for centuries by word of mouth was finally refined and written down, probably sometime during the ninth or eighth century B.C., and was worked upon further in Hellenistic times, when the folios were edited and corrected with painstaking care. Lyric poetry also gave expression to the loves, struggles, hopes, and despairs of everyday life and gave glory to the gods and man. The poetry of tragedy took exalted form in the dramas of Aeschylus, Sophocles, and Euripides, who portrayed the fundamental conflicts of man as they arose from the contemporary life of the times. Comedy also played its artistic and political part in the biting and satirical poetry of Aristophanes. Aristotle, in his turn, influenced literature and literary criticism through his work the *Poetics.*

Hellenistic scholars gave an enormous amount of time and effort to editing, commenting upon, and criticizing the creative literary works of others in the scholarly mood of the age—in a way the first Ph.D. approach to literature. Among the editorial and scholarly activities carried on at Alexandria was the long process of translating the Old Testament into Greek, a work known as the Septuagint because it was done by some 70 scholars over a period of many years in the third and second centuries B.C.

Greek philosophy ranged over nearly all the fields of knowledge that have since been subdivided into physical and biological sciences, mathematics, social science, and psychology, as well as the more technical fields of philosophy itself—logic, metaphysics, epistemology, and ethics. The Ionian philosophers in the seventh and sixth centuries B.C. were principally interested in the physical world, whereas the philosophers of the fifth and fourth centuries were interested not only in nature but also in man and his conduct in many fields of activity.

Logic, or dialectics, was created as the Greeks sought to analyze the processes of thinking and devise rules for its conduct. Along with their interest in grammar and rhetoric, the Sophists set in motion earnest effort along this line, and Socrates carried the quest to a high state of perfection in his dialectical method of questioning and answering as a means of arriving at and testing truth. Plato gave a different cast to the meaning of "dialectics" when he used the term to refer to the process of contemplating the eternal ideas of the spiritual world. In his work entitled the *Organon*, Aristotle set the pattern for deductive logic so authoritatively that it is known today as Aristotelian or formal logic.

Metaphysics (the study of the ultimate reality of things) and epistemology (the study of the theory of knowledge) were elaborated especially in the writings of Plato and Aristotle, who put these studies highest in the scale of valuable bodies of knowledge. Centuries of philosophers since then have considered them in the same light. Inextricably bound up in Greek philosophy were descriptions of human nature and human conduct which today we would call ethics, political science, economics, sociology, and psychology. The Sophists and Socrates focused great attention upon these subjects, as did Plato in his *Republic*, and Aristotle in his *Ethics* and *Politics*.

Great strides were made by the Greeks in organizing the study of the physical world and of the living world of plants and animals into a form that modern scientists would classify as astronomy, physics, mineralogy, botany, and zoology. The early philosophers of the seventh and sixth centuries B.C. started the process that was carried on through the fifth century down to Aristotle's epoch-making studies of the fourth century, in which he virtually classified all known knowledge of his day in these areas. The work of this great classifier and encyclopedist was carried on by Hellenistic scholars in astronomy, geography, mechanics, and hydraulics.

As a result of these efforts, enormous advances were made toward a scientific understanding of the world and of natural phenomena. The theory that the world was round and rotated on its axis was enunciated, the earth was measured, the solar system was studied, the heliocentric theory was formulated, and the procession of the stars and their distance and sizes were observed. In addition, considerable work was done in physiology and anatomy in determining the function of the brain as the center of the nervous system and the principles of the circulation of the blood.

Closely related to the work in science went remarkable progress in the field of mathematics. Arithmetic was refined and elaborated by the Pythagoreans and Plato, who were interested in the theory of numbers for the philosophic insight and discipline of the mind that it was supposed to produce. Geometry also received increased attention from the Pythagoreans, Plato, Aristotle, and others. Euclid in the third century B.C. organized and systematized all the known geometrical theorems so carefully that his work remained the authoritative study in the field down to the nineteenth century. Trigonometry was also being put into organized form for the first time.

With Herodotus the real beginnings of history writing were made. Herodotus traveled widely and earnestly collected what historical data he could on the countries he visited. Because of his painstaking history of the Persian Wars, published in 430 B.C., he has been called the "father of history." Thucydides in his history of the Peloponnesian War went much beyond Herodotus in that he not only attempted to put the facts accurately in chronological order but tried to explain their causes as fully as he could. He really introduced critical scholarship into the writing of history and placed it on a high level as a means of interpreting human events and social forces. In the writings of Xenophon in the fourth century history lost much of its objective and painstaking character and became more rhetorical and less scientific in aim. Many other historians became interested in the history of their countries or rulers; outstanding among them was Polybius, who wrote the history of Rome in the third and second centuries B.C.

The Greek creative genius found even greater expression in the fine arts than in the fields just mentioned. Art and music were integrally bound up with the religious, civic, and everyday life of Athens in a way seldom approached in other civilizations. Music, dancing, poetry, and drama were linked together in the religious festivals that emerged from the Dionysian rites and culminated in the tragedies of Aeschylus, Sophocles, and Euripides. Architecture, sculpture, and painting were designed to enhance each other in the temples and public buildings of the city-states, reaching highest perfection in the Acropolis at Athens. Painting attained a high level in the decoration not only of temples and sculptured figures but also of vases and pottery in common use.

The Greeks felt that art and music were closely related to good moral qualities. In fifth-century Athens a good man and good citizen was one who could participate actively in the artistic life of the city, whether in religious celebrations, theater festivals, or everyday affairs. Plato and Aristotle stressed the moral effects of art and music, Plato in the *Republic* and other dialogues and Aristotle in his *Poetics,* an influential treatise on the theory of art and aesthetics.

As was the case with the practical arts and crafts, however, the technical aspects of the "fine" arts were not organized into systematic bodies of knowledge that could be taught in the schools. The *theory* of art was so organized but not its technique or skills. This fact, combined with the growing intellectualistic interests of the educated classes, made easier a diminishing emphasis upon fine arts in the education of Greek citizens. The only exception was music, which came to be justified as a study of intellectual worth because of its mathematical content as emphasized by Plato and Aristotle. Even here the practice or playing of music was disparaged as much less worthy than the theoretical study of its mechanical quality. The fine arts as subjects of instruction lost ground in Hellenistic times just as gymnastics and physical development were minimized as unfit subjects for the liberal education of a leisured upper class in a society that has lost its political freedom and social democracy.

Religious Outlooks

In the early Aegean days of Greek culture the religious beliefs were akin to those of all primitive tribes, that certain physical objects and animals had mysterious and divine powers and that gods inhabited the heavens and earth, directing the destinies of man. These beliefs were shaped into the classic religious tradition of Greece by the Homeric epics, the *Iliad* and the *Odyssey,* which gave a clear picture of the family of Greek gods who helped to bring about a common feeling of nationality among the various Greek cities and tribes.

Besides the open worship of the civic gods, many secret and selective cults limited to chosen initiates grew up in Greece. The worship of Demeter took on such a character, and the worship of Dionysus became perhaps the most widespread after the seventh century B.C. The ecstatic revels and dances of the Dionysians especially attracted women to the mysteries of the god of suffering and regeneration. When the worship of this cult took the form of extreme orgies, a group of religious reformers appeared who tried to spiritualize and moralize the ceremonies. These reformers, known as "Orphics," emphasized in their teachings the purification of the soul through a regimen of strict morality and asceticism as a means of everlasting happiness in the next world. The Orphics banded together as a sort of missionary society, traveling throughout the Greek world. Pythagoras was one of the best-known teachers to become associated with them. The Eleusinian mysteries constituted another well-known cult, somewhat similar to that of the Orphics but related to the worship of Demeter.

Thus, religious institutions among the Greeks included two aspects: the "daylight" aspect connected with the worship of gods of the cities, and a mystical aspect associated with the secret cults open only to the initiates. The civic religion was celebrated in public ceremonies, song, dance, drama, athletic games, and public shrines by means of which the individual citizen found his social identification with his group. The secret societies emphasized the selective character of their membership and special interests related to specific gods or rites. The functional character of the civic religion can easily be indicated by the fact that the temples or homes of the gods were public buildings upon which was lavished the artistic skill of architects, sculptors, and painters. The great works of poetry and drama were often written for competitions held to honor the gods, and such famous athletic contests as the Olympic games were at once civic and religious celebrations. The Acropolis at Athens remains the oustanding architectural triumph of a city-state that was honoring itself in the process of honoring the gods.

Religion thus consisted largely in the performance of accepted and stated ceremonies. When, in the fifth century, the traveling teachers, the Sophists, began to question the authority of the gods and the validity of the public rites, the Athenians felt not only that their cherished religious traditions were being threatened but also that attacks were being made upon their city itself. Socrates was condemned as a corrupter of youth not only because he preached doctrines considered subversive of the traditional religion but also of the security of the state.

In the third and second centuries B.C. religion began to lose its civic function and to become more attached to spiritual and otherworldly affairs. The concern of religion shifted from public celebrations invoking the aid of the gods in present endeavors to a concern for what was to happen in the next life. Religious writings began to give a picture of what to expect after death and instructions on how to behave. The conception of divinity was gradually separated from specific gods and associated with a general and spiritual idea of the divine. Plato's philosophy surely helped to form this pattern, along with the growing awareness of Eastern and

Jewish ideas of religion. In general, the new mood of "otherworldliness" provided a receptive attitude congenial to the growth of Christianity when it was introduced to the Western world.

Generalizations are difficult, but it seems possible that the shift from a "daylight" religion of interest in this world to a spiritual interest in the future life reflected the political change from a free and vigorous social life to the restricted political life that occurred when the Greek cities lost their independence under Macedonian and Roman rule. When the civic ideal of the city-state no longer had a vital meaning for the Greek mind, many of the intellectuals sought refuge and the meaning of life in religious contemplation and mysticism. This change in religious outlook was another influence that tended to diminish the civic, practical, and moral character of education and to emphasize its more narrowly intellectual and academic character.

Theories of Education Appear

The purpose of this final part of the discussion of Greek intellectual life is to emphasize the fact that Greek writers for the first time in history began to give special thought and attention to the role of education in their culture. A reader who is interested especially in the theory of education should, however, give close attention to the foregoing sections of this chapter, for much educational theory is present in the discussions of the ideas that men lived by. This section simply indicates that certain Greek writers were charting the course that they felt schools should follow. In most cases, such discussions of education were incorporated in larger treatises on politics or philosophy.

Plato's "Republic." Perhaps the most important and influential discussion of educational theory is contained in Plato's *Republic*, which is, in a larger sense, a thoroughgoing treatment of the ideal state that Plato was proposing to the people of Athens. His conception that education is to be viewed as an integral part of the larger social questions of politics and philosophy is a most provocative and rewarding one for modern times. Judgments concerning the validity of Plato's educational proposals thus must be closely related with judgments concerning Plato's political proposals. If we agree with Plato that an aristocracy is the best kind of society, we might agree that Plato's educational theory is the best for us to follow. However, if aristocracy does not appeal to us, then we must be skeptical of Plato's educational proposals.

Plato paid little attention to education for the great masses of people who did the work of the world; he was interested only in the education of the warrior and ruling classes. Education is designed not only to form the character appropriate to the ideal society but also to act as a selective agency by means of which the most able are brought to light. Children should be reared in state nurseries before the age of six, and during this time they should be taught fairy tales, nursery rhymes, and stories of the gods, with emphasis upon the virtuous gods and omission of immoral stories. From the ages of six to eighteen the main ingredients of education should be music and gymnastics. Music should include not only training in music and dancing that would create the proper moral spirit but also training in letters that would enable the youth to read, write, and count. Gymnastics is to develop the spirited element in human nature just as music develops the reason. The object of all education is to blend these two elements into harmonious proportions. From eighteen to twenty, further physical training and especially military training should occupy the time of the men.

At the age of twenty those who are to become warriors should begin their assigned tasks, whereas those destined to become philosopher-kings should continue a course of higer study for 10 years, this course to consist primarily of mathematics (arithmetic, geometry, astronomy, and music). It should be noted here that these studies are those of the quadrivium, which made up the higher studies of the Middle Ages (see pages 151 to 152). This testifies to the influence of Plato's theories upon all higher education after his time.

At the age of thirty the less brilliant of the ruling class should go into the lower civil offices of the state, and the most brilliant should continue their studies for 5 years more. After a regimen of philosophy (dialectics and metaphysics), which makes up the highest study of all, dealing as it does with pure reality and pure knowledge, the true philosopher-kings will have finished their preparation for ruling at the age of thirty-five. They then are to go out for 15 years into the actual world of practical experience and take part in the military and political affairs of the state. At the age of fifty they are ready to become "elder statesmen," spending most of their time in philosophical pursuits but taking their unavoidable turns in office as a matter of public duty. Their main task, however, is to contemplate and think about the essence of the good life by which the state should be regulated.

Plato's predilection for mathematics and philosophy is clearly revealed in this plan. He believed that such mental training is the best discipline for the conduct of public affairs. Once the philosopher-kings are trained in the pursuit of knowledge, they are ready to solve problems of all kinds. Thus Plato not only affected the content of the higher education of the Western world to come but also set the pattern of mental discipline that has been so much a part of English, French, German, and American higher education almost to the present time.

Any estimate of the validity of Plato's proposals for us must include not only what Plato said but also what his followers over the centuries have interpreted him to mean, for the influence of Plato upon us has included both. Some of Plato's followers in higher institutions have overemphasized his intellectualism, and his followers in lower institutions have often forgotten his insistence that the well-rounded development of the individual through a balanced attention to the role of music and gymnastics (in the Greek sense of these terms) is a means of developing personality and character.

Aristotle. The distinct educational proposals that Aristotle made are more difficult to describe, for they are incomplete and are scattered through his writings, especially in his *Politics* and *Ethics*. It seems clear, however, that Aristotle looked upon education as a branch of politics in the sense that education is necessary for the building of a cohesive community life and public morale. Therefore, education should be under state control and should be approximately the same for rich and poor alike so that disparities and class inequalities will not grow up among the free citizens. That Aristotle did not envisage equality among *all* people is clear from his distrust of democracy and from his conception that some human beings are fitted by nature to be free and others to be slaves, or unfree. For example, Aristotle believed firmly that education should be liberal (that is, for free men) rather than practical or vocational. The proper occupation for free men, according to Aristotle, is citizenship, whereas the lower occupations of trade, artisanship, or farming are illiberal because they distort the body, destroy harmonious development, destroy leisure time, and do not allow for the pursuits of citizenship and intellectual investigation. Our inherited tradition that a liberal education is something opposed to preparation for earning a living grew out of an aristocratic conception of society and of human nature and was firmly entrenched in Western education through the efforts of the followers of Plato and Aristotle.

Aristotle further believed that the organization and curriculum of education for free citizens should follow the growth patterns of children. Infants, who are virtually animals, should be given opportunities for play, physical activity, and proper stories. For children before adolescence the main emphasis should be upon moral and physical education, for the preadolescent period is primarily one of irrational or nonrational development. Little or no intellectual training should be attempted before the age of fourteen; rather, the emphasis should be upon inculcating correct moral habits through practice and through turning to good account children's natural imitativeness, sense of shame, and desire to be successful. This means, in respect to curriculum, an emphasis upon gymnastics for bodily control, music for its ethical value as a control over the emotions, and enough reading and writing to make thoroughly familiar the fundamental operations. Aristotle firmly believed that moral education and development of character are attained, not through the study of theory or the preaching of precepts, but only through establishing stable habits of conduct.

For adolescent youth up to the age of twenty-one in whom the rational faculties are developing, Aristotle would turn to such intellectual studies as mathematics (arithmetic, geometry, astronomy, and music), probably grammar, literature, poetry, and rhetoric, and perhaps ethics and politics. Aristotle is not very definite on these matters, but it is likely from his own teaching in the Lyceum and from his other writings that the highest study of all, for those beyond twenty-one years of age, would include the sciences (physics, cosmology, biology, and psychology) and philosophy (logic and metaphysics). This assumption is made in the light of Aristotle's insistence that the theoretical reason is a higher function than the practical reason. Science and philosophy are the subjects appropriate to theoretical reason or knowledge for its own sake, whereas ethics and politics are appropriate to the practical reason or the making of moral decisions.

It is clear that Aristotle proposes different educational aims and procedures for different levels of instruction, and it is this fact that leads to different estimates of his influence on later times. His suggestions are not highly original but agree in their main outlines with those of Plato. Perhaps the most important difference is the neglect by Plato and the inclusion by Aristotle of the study of physical and biological science. Plato finds little place for such science inasmuch as it deals with the changing natural world rather than with eternal ideas. Aristotle feels that such science can reveal first principles and true knowledge just as well as philosophy can. In fact, Aristotle emphasizes the role of experience and the inductive method in arriving at first principles or real knowledge. Aristotle's conception of educational method and learning probably included much more emphasis upon direct experience. Indeed, this difference in outlook led to violent intellectual controversies in the Middle Ages, when the realists looked to Plato for support and the nominalists sided with Aristotle (see pages 142 to 144).

Xenophon is interesting principally as one of the most reactionary Athenians who wrote on educational theory. He had no love for Athenian democracy and therefore quite naturally turned to Sparta for his social and educational ideals. He lived for long in Sparta as an exile from Athens; and when he set forth his educational proposals in his *Cyropaedia*, he idealized the military state and a military education that would support such a state. In turn, the state should rigidly control education for its own purposes. The boys should begin military training as early as seventeen or eighteen years of age and then should continue active duty for some 10 years. His scheme was much narrower than that of Plato, and in effect he stood as an apologist for the Spartan system as it actually existed, with little or no attention to literary, musical, or philosophical pursuits. Xenophon also wrote about the education of women in his *Oeconomicus*, in which women are consigned exclusively to the household, and about his military exploits with the Greek armies in Persia in his *Anabasis*, which has been an elementary textbook for countless generations of students in their study of the Greek language. To anyone interested in democracy, Xenophon's theory of education is interesting principally for its warning as to what might happen if the disgruntled conservatives should have their way in education.

Isocrates stands out in contrast to Xenophon as one of the most forward-looking of Greek educational theorists. Through his long life, Isocrates was a most effective teacher of rhetoric. His ideals had a great influence not only upon the Greek world but upon Rome and Roman education. Isocrates saw clearly that the genuine orator must be primarily a man of good character, devoted to the public good. Rhetoric is not merely a means of persuading people to action; it lays upon the rhetorician the obligation to work for the welfare of the state. Thus an orator must be a good statesman if he is to be a good orator. The preparation for such an ideal, therefore, not only must include a study of rhetorical principles and techniques but also must emphasize a broad background of the liberal arts, including literature, logic, history, political science, ethics, art, and music, as a basis for forming good judgments of public policy.

Of immense interest, also, is the emphasis Isocrates put upon the practicality of knowledge. Philosophy is the means by which knowledge is used for the practical business of making judgments and decisions concerning proposed courses of action. Knowledge for its own sake and without relation to action is not properly to be called philosophy. Here, then, is a most important educational ideal for democracy. Isocrates realized the necessity of education as a process of building up a sense of community responsibility. He worked long and arduously for Panhellenic unity, but his efforts were never crowned with genuine success before Greece fell to the Macedonian conquerors.

In general, it may be said that, despite the influence of Isocrates upon Cicero and Quintilian in Roman times, his ideals were never as fully accepted by the Western world as were those of Plato and Aristotle. One of the reasons may be that Isocrates' conception of the relation of knowledge to action was appropriate only to a flexible democratic society, whereas the democratic ideal was to go into an eclipse from which it did not emerge for some 2,000 years.

EDUCATION FOR CITIZENSHIP AND INTELLECTUAL DISCIPLINE

Spartan Education: the Military-dictatorship Ideal

The aim of education in ancient Sparta can be simply stated: to train the warrior-citizen to take his place in the military state. In the communal life of the public barracks, boys aged seven to eighteen were drilled constantly in habits of obedience and respect for authority. They were subjected to rigorous discipline designed to develop their physical stamina and endurance and to instill qualities of loyalty and courage, all leading to the skills that would produce success in war.

Beds were purposely hard, food was simple, and clothes were light in order to accustom the boys to the conditions they would find in the field. Fighting and physical contest were emphasized as training for combat. Strong and agile bodies were developed by gymnastic activities such as wrestling, archery, javelin and discus throwing, running, jumping, riding, and swimming—all essential in the kind of warfare they engaged in. Flogging and other severe corporal punishments were employed to promote obedience and also to toughen the body. Hunting and tracking down animals and human opponents helped to instill habits of effective field work and concentration.

Martial music, singing, patriotic and military dancing in the form of close-order drills were used to develop agility, morale, and teamwork, as well as to give physical training. Moral qualities were instilled by causing the boys to memorize the laws and the Homeric poems. Literary education apparently played only a small part in Spartan training, for there is little evidence of attention to reading, writing, or arithmetic. The formal pursuit of such intellectual studies as grammar and logic seems to have been wholly absent, and the negative reaction to rhetoric is typified in the glorifying of brief, clipped, "laconic" speech. Girls were given as much of this training, both physical and moral, as would fit them to become strong, healthy mothers.

When the youth went into regular military drill at eighteen, they began to apply all they had learned to the art of warfare. War games became a feature of the training. The youth continued their physical and military training, and studied the geography of their land and the strategy of defense and attack. Organized military bands roamed the countryside, learning how to care for themselves, sleeping in the woods, foraging for food, and, for practice, attacking farmers and Helots in the Spartan version of *blitzkrieg*. In this way, the youth not only learned the methods of Spartan warfare but helped to police the subject populations in the interests of the Spartan rulers. Qualities of stealthiness, cunning, and resourcefulness and skill in spying were thus built up in a manner that would do justice to a modern *gestapo*. With such an educational ideal designed to fit the military-dictatorship ideal of the state, it is no wonder that Sparta produced no lasting literature, art, science, or philosophy. Again, the parallel with modern dictatorships is all too obvious.

Athenian Education: the Democratic Ideal (700 to 400 B.C.)

Aims. In contrast to the Spartan education just described, the aims and content of Athenian education revealed a great advance toward the democratic ideal. Reflecting the broader Athenian conception of citizenship, Athenian education set out to provide youth with an intellectual and aesthetic as well as a physical and military foundation for citizenship. In the Athenian educational ideal, these four aspects were brought into a well-rounded whole in which none of the four was emphasized to the exclusion of any other and in which all reached a perfect balance. The Athenians called this final result harmony; we often call it integration of the whole personality. The ultimate goal was the achievement of emotional stability and qualities of character that would enable the individual to become a properly functioning member of the democratic community. This is an ideal worthy of emulation, but it should be noted that the Athenian ideal gave no place to occupational or vocational training.

Elementary Education. Although the earlier Athenian ideal of education called for harmonious development of the intellectual, aesthetic, physical, and military powers of the individual, a certain specialization developed in the means of achieving this ideal. Different teachers were assigned the task of developing the several aspects of the citizen's character. The teacher of letters (grammatist) began to concentrate on what might be called the intellectual development. He taught the boys to read, to write, and to count. They learned to read by memorizing the alphabet, learning rhymes and songs about the various letters, and eventually reading from such books as the *Iliad, Odyssey,* Hesiod's *Works and Days,* and Aesop's *Fables.* They practiced oral speaking freely in order to learn correct pronunciation. They learned to write on wax tablets or papyrus as the teacher dictated materials for them to copy. Counting was usually done on the fingers or with stones.

The teacher of music (citharist) gradually came to have the somewhat specialized function of developing a sense of rhythm and melody. The boys learned to play the seven-stringed lyre, to sing, to chant, and to dance. These abilities not only developed the individual's aesthetic senses but also prepared him to take part in the civic and religious festivals and celebrations of his city. He could thus participate in the instrumental, poetic, and singing contests, in the war dances, in the rites to the gods, and in family celebrations connected with birth, marriage, and death.

Most of the direct training for dancing was accomplished, not in the schools, but in connection with the Greek chorus that was so important a feature of the dramatic and religious festivals. A choregos (chorus master) was appointed to choose and train the members of the chorus for the various public occasions.

In the earlier stages of Greek education the teaching of letters and of music went hand in hand, instruction in both being sometimes given by the same teacher or by two teachers in the same school, which then often came to be known as the music school. It is important to note, however, that eventually the teaching of letters was separated from the teaching of music.

The development of physical ability was in the hands of the gymnastic teacher (paedotribe), whose task was to develop physical stamina, grace, and health through exercises in the palaestra. The boys were taught how to run, jump, swim, throw the javelin, and wrestle and how to stand and walk gracefully. As far as we can tell, considerable emphasis was put upon the ability to control one's body easily and gracefully as well as skillfully. The boys exercised individually or in pairs, and careful supervision was exerted to see that the boys were matched evenly and played the game fairly and in a sportsmanlike fashion. Individual instruction seems to have been characteristic of all elementary education, and the class, or graded, method of teaching does not seem to have played a large part.

When all aspects of elementary education were properly related, the literary, musical, and gymnastic training was integrated into an organic whole, each aspect supplementing and complementing the other. The ultimate aim was then found in the moral ideal of an individual fitted to participate in the activities of the state and to promote its welfare. Literature and poetry, music and song, dancing and physical prowess all had their proper place, not as separate subject matters to be learned separately but as integral parts of a larger purpose.

Advanced Education. Beyond the kind of elementary education just described, the Athenians prior to the fifth century B.C. laid their principal emphasis upon physical and military training. The state gymnasiums provided physical education of an advanced type, where the youth from fifteen or sixteen to eighteen years of age gained further athletic training. They now concentrated more fully upon achieving excellence in the sports of the pentathlon, which constituted the high light of such great sports contests as the Olympic games. The pentathlon consisted of running races, jumping contests, discus throwing, javelin throwing, and wrestling. Modern outdoor track meets are still based upon these basic contests, with the exception of wrestling, which has become an indoor sport in America. The training in the gymnasiums was built upon the elementary exercises of the palaestra and was designed to give the physical skills necessary for Greek warfare.

Military training was emphasized for Athenian youth from the age of eighteen to twenty during a 2-year period of cadet training. At this time the boys learned military drill and methods of defensive and offensive tactics, studied the topographical features of the country, and began to specialize in cavalry, infantry, or naval maneuvers. At the age of twenty the young man was ready to take his place as a full citizen and as a full-fledged member of the armed forces. Physical education and military training thus comprised nearly the whole of advanced education in Athens during the early Athenian period (prior to the fifth century B.C.).

Sophists. During the fifth century, however, a new type of advanced education began to grow in favor. This was an intellectual type of education conducted by the Sophists and stimulated by the political, economic, and philosophical changes that took place in Athens between 500 and 400 B.C. The Sophists were mainly itinerant teachers who came from Asia Minor and the Aegean Islands, attracted by the active life of Athens. Their teaching was highly informal; they came and went, talked on street corners, frequented the groves and gymnasiums, and sometimes rented rooms, gathering student followers as they could. Some specialized in certain subjects, but as a group they were often opportunists catering to the dominant intellectual interests of the times. They were the "practical educators" who tried to adjust their teaching to the interests and desires of the potential students.

Gradually, the Athenian Fathers began to be prejudiced against the Sophists, to think of them as superficial, shallow, and overdialectical, and as sellers of tricks of the trade instead of as seekers after the truth. So long as Athens rode the crest of prosperity and power prior to the Peloponnesian War, the Sophists were not only tolerated but greeted with enthusiasm, especially by the young men; but when Athens began to shake and crumble under the impact of war, the conservative Fathers began to be suspicious of these newfangled teachers who, in their view, were doubtless corrupting the youth of the city.

They were professionals who charged a fee, a practice not congenial to the Athenian love of the amateur. Some were actually quacks and boldly professed to teach anyone anything, even to the point of guaranteeing to teach a young man how to win either side of an argument. Worst of all, they seemed to be questioning the old customs, political traditions, the state gods, and religious beliefs. In time of war such skepticism could not be tolerated. The urge to reaffirm the ancient loyalties led to attacks upon the Sophists. Many of them had to leave Athens because it was too "unhealthy" for them, and the most famous of all,

Socrates, was tried and condemned to death for his allegedly impious teachings.

Despite the attacks upon them, the Sophists gave an enormous impetus to education. They were creatures of their day, reflecting the rampant individualism, the enthusiasms, and the skepticisms that swept Athens in the later fifth century B.C. Their contribution in widening the scope of advanced education and in helping to organize large, nebulous bodies of knowledge into teachable form was no mean one. Theirs was a transition task that was eventually overshadowed by the towering educational structures erected by Plato and Aristotle.

Socrates. Socrates is the only fifth-century educator who has continued to rank in fame and importance with such figures as Plato and Aristotle. Some who would glorify Socrates as one of the great teachers of all time resent attempts to classify him as a Sophist; but if the term is used to refer to all the informal teachers of the fifth century and not just to the quacks, then Socrates was a Sophist, and the greatest of them all. He left no record of himself or his ideas in writings of his own, and thus his story must be pieced together from what others wrote about him. He has been a most difficult figure to estimate because of the different pictures of him painted by Plato, Aristophanes, and Xenophon. Most historians and philosophers have seen Socrates principally through the eyes of Plato, in whose dialogues Socrates is the central character. The problem that has troubled philosophers ever since has been to determine how much of Plato's description of Socrates stems from Socrates himself and how much from Plato's own conceptions. In any case, the reputation of Socrates as one of the most famous teachers of all time has remained strong.

Socrates differed from other Sophists in that he was a native-born Athenian and spent all his life in Athens. He did not charge fees, but he did accept gifts from his students. He professed great humility and ignorance, and yet he was disliked by many for the way he disconcerted those who were cocksure of their knowledge. He quickly gained great popularity among the young men of Athens because of his keen analytical powers, his ability to puncture the pompous and boastful, and his constant interest in a broad range of subjects. He asked the profound questions concerning the future of Athens and concerning the general nature of justice, truth, good, and beauty. He was at once a typical Athenian citizen and yet, through the magic of his tongue, the force of his personality, and the weight of his ideas, he was the outstanding intellectual figure and teacher of his time.

Of all that might be said about Socrates, perhaps his most important educational contributions were his methods of teaching and of seeking knowledge and his conception of the role of knowledge in conduct. The

"Socratic method," as it has been known ever since, is essentially the method of discussion, conversation, and question and answer. Socrates always insisted upon rigid and strict definition of the terms and subject under discussion. He aimed at making clear the conceptions of justice, truth, and beauty that people used and always tried to see what they would mean in action. In his conferences, he assumed the role of a simple and humble seeker after truth. He would challenge someone's statement, refute and confute it with adroit questioning, bring his opponent from "unconscious ignorance" to "conscious ignorance," lead him to a blank wall, and then begin to build up his own account of the problem. His questions could usually be answered by "yes" or "no" and were intended to serve as a guide to a general proposition to which the group would agree.

Socrates spent his days and nights in such discussions, talking with all sorts of men on all sorts of topics. He recognized that his method was not popular with those who had been discomfited, but he persisted in it because he said that he felt himself divinely commissioned to criticize and to be the "gadfly of the state." His method was thus one of criticism, to convince men of their ignorance when knowledge was uncriticized, to test moral standards and the goals of effort by criticism, to break down overconfidence, and to seek the truth. He relied upon the ability of human reason to achieve through this method true knowledge and proper guides to action.

Socrates' interest in the role of knowledge in conduct led him to be primarily concerned with the ethical and moral problems of individuals and society. Knowledge, true knowledge, is the highroad to good conduct. He heard many of the Sophists preaching that the individual man is the measure of all things and that therefore each man can decide for himself what is right or wrong. Socrates set himself against such excessive individualism and insisted that true knowledge determines what is right or wrong. If a man knows, *really* knows, the truth, then he will act rightly. Knowledge is virtue, and virtue is knowledge, and never the twain shall be separated. Acceptance of this insight into the aims of education means that the ultimate goal of education is moral and ethical, to produce good people. This is one of the most important features of the heritage that Socrates has bequeathed to posterity.

Hellenistic Education: the Intellectual Ideal

After the fifth century the ideal of a well-rounded development of the whole personality as the best road to good citizenship began to give way to a greater emphasis upon the intellectual training of the mind and a corresponding de-emphasis upon aesthetic and physical development. In general, this was a reflection of the decline of the democratic ideal of culture. The fifth-century conception of education as primarily the shaping of character for moral and social purposes faded before the newer conception that the best educated person is the one who has developed his intellectual capacities to the highest point. The conception of a "free" man became identified with the man of intellect rather than with the man of action.

Elementary and Secondary Education. By the end of the Hellenistic period the dominant elementary school teacher was the grammatist, or teacher of letters, who concentrated on the teaching of reading, writing, and counting. The teacher of music (citharist) and the teacher of gymnastics (paedotribe) began to play a smaller and smaller part in the elementary education of Greek boys. This meant that a literary education became the basis of elementary education, and aesthetic and physical education virtually dropped out of the picture. An education for literacy replaced an education for well-rounded development. This was a most important change in emphasis, for it was the school of the grammatist that set the educational pattern for the Romans and thus was carried to western Europe and eventually to America.

Much the same sort of thing happened to the new, advanced schools that came to be known as secondary schools. Here again the physical education of the gymnasiums declined in public esteem, and a new secondary teacher, the *grammaticus*, began to dominate the field. The *grammaticus*, as the name implies, was most interested in the study of grammar and rhetoric. Grammar included the rules of syntax and the study of literature, poetry, and meter. Rhetoric included composition, declamation, and the rules of oratory. The *grammaticus* sometimes taught some arithmetic and geometry also, but his prime purpose and effort were devoted to linguistic and literary ends. Even the Ephebic College, which had been established originally for military training in Athens, after 335 B.C. began to require its members to study literary and linguistic subjects.

In the case of both elementary and secondary education, music suffered because of a change in public taste. In the fourth century the character of the music changed from the religious, civic, and martial type to a softer, more romantic, and sensuous kind. The flute became more popular than the lyre, and words became incidental to the melody. Almost the same sort of thing happened in the United States in the twentieth century, when jazz and "popular" music became the rage as against religious and "classical," or "good," music. The Greek Fathers objected to the enervating new music and ruled it out of the schools. As a result, music in practice lost much of its honorable place in Greek education.

The same sort of thing happened to physical education. With the loss of political freedom, the need for a citizen army disappeared. Having no longer a direct relation to general military service, physical education became the plaything of the upper classes or the prerogative of professional athletes, who engaged in sports for money and popular acclaim. When spectator sports became more popular than participation in sports, bribery and gambling increased. Again, the Greek Fathers condemned such practices, and physical education lost its role in the schools, both elementary and secondary. When music, physical education, and military training were gone from Hellenistic schools, the intellectual studies remained.

Higher Schools. With the institutionalizing of higher education in the fourth century B.C., a great tradition was launched that has affected Western civilization ever since. Plato's Academy and Aristotle's Lyceum became virtually world-famous and lasted for several centuries. In this way the works of these philosophers were handed down from generation to generation, and their teachings became imprinted on the mind of the Western world. The very names of these schools have been preserved down to the present day in the academies of France, England, and the United States and the *lycées* of France, the *Lyzeum* of Germany, and the lyceums of the United States. As the informal teaching of the Sophists gave way to the institutions of the Academy and Lyceum, so the "practical" intent of the Sophists gave way to the "philosophical" purposes of Plato and Aristotle.

Plato's Academy gave itself largely to the study of philosophy (dialectics, physics, metaphysics, ethics, politics, law, and literature) and of mathematics (arithmetic, geometry, music, and astronomy). The Lyceum carried on the tradition of Aristotle's interest in the sciences, and thus its philosophy included not only attention to metaphysics, logic, aesthetics, ethics, politics, and rhetoric but also a great emphasis upon the natural sciences (physics, mechanics, meteorology, botany, zoology, anatomy, geography, geology, and medicine). Aristotle's vast range of writings was largely in the form of lecture notes that he used in his teaching. In the fifth century the various bodies of knowledge available today were not highly systematized or organized. It was largely Aristotle's work in the Lyceum that led to the classifying and organizing of the great fields of knowledge. Alexander the Great subsidized Aristotle's researches with large amounts of money, and many men were commissioned to gather scientific data for Aristotle as they marched with Alexander's armies on their extensive campaigns in all parts of his enormous empire.

A much more "practical" type of education was given in the rhetorical schools that were established in the fourth century, again as an outgrowth of the interest aroused by the Sophists. The most famous of these rhetorical schools was founded by Isocrates, who opposed the verbal tricks and subtleties of the Sophists. As noted earlier, Isocrates insisted that the power of speech should be used only for democratic purposes.

He urged that, if rhetoric were to be an instrument for promoting democracy, the orator must be a genuinely virtuous person devoted to the common good. Only in this way could rhetorical training be training for good citizenship. In a 2-, 3-, or 4-year period of training, he tried to furnish not only the principles and practice of good oratorical style but also a broad background in the liberal arts as a basis for the use of rhetoric. Isocrates apparently understood the importance of proper loyalties and ideals as the groundwork upon which to build specialized skills.

These philosophical and rhetorical schools continued into the Hellenistic period of the third and second centuries B.C., but their emphasis shifted somewhat as Athens became a conquered state. The rhetorical schools found less and less practical outlet for their teachings, for young men could no longer find genuine use for their talents in the absence of a vital democratic society. They therefore began to emphasize the delights of rhetorical style for its own sake. The turning of a nice phrase or a witty saying became more important than achievement in the assembly or courts. The philosophical schools likewise turned to knowledge for its own sake and became more like semireligious groups. Religion had long been identified with the city-state; but as Hellenistic control reduced the independence of the city-states, the state religions became less important, and new philosophical religions arose to satisfy men's desire to explore their fate and to describe the nature of things.

Some of these philosophical religions developed around new schools at Athens during the third century. The most important of these were conducted by the Stoics and the Epicureans. When Zeno set up his school, the Stoa, he followed generally the tradition of Socrates and Plato. The Stoics preached that, since nature is inherently reasonable, conformity to the natural order of things is living according to the dictates of reason. Nature is rational because it is directed by a single, omnipotent, and rational God. They taught that tranquil acceptance of what life brings and calm indifference to painful circumstances are the highest goods in life. The moral life is to find reason in nature and to live resolutely in the light of these findings. Hence, Stoicism came to imply an imperturbable acceptance of the difficulties of life. Through its doctrines and its semireligious nature, Stoicism was a forerunner of Christianity and, indeed, helped to shape the characteristics of Christian thought and practice.

The Epicurean school operated from a quite different philosophical orientation. Epicurus, who set up a school known as the Gardens in Athens, had been influenced by Democritus, a traveling Thracian philosopher. Democritus had taught that matter was eternal, indestructible, and uncreated, and that the universe was merely infinite space filled with material atoms, operated by chance rather than by a creative intelligence or reason. Thus, Epicurus believed, not in a divinely inspired natural world, but in a mechanistic universe. Happiness-consists in avoiding pain of the body and anguish of soul and in seeking pleasure. The good life is found in achieving freedom from the evils of pain, useless desires, and obstructing fears; the highest good is the pleasure of intellectual pursuits. Epicurus specifically stated that sensual pleasures did not constitute happiness, but nevertheless successive generations came to believe that Epicureanism meant "Eat, drink, and be merry, for tomorrow we die."

Both the Stoics and Epicureans resembled evangelical orders in some respects. They went about preaching and seeking converts to their ideas, and they held fraternal festivals, took care of their sick, and provided burials for their dead. But they did not become churches; they remained primarily "schools of thought." They had no creeds or dogma, no priests, no public worship, and no ecclesiastical organization.

The higher education that grew up in other parts of the Hellenistic world did not partake so much of this religious character but rather resembled research institutes of various kinds. The most famous of these was at Alexandria, where scholars came together to pursue their own studies and where young men came to work with the older ones. As described earlier in this chapter, considerable work was done in advancing the knowledge of the physical world through the study of mathematics (astronomy, geometry, trigonometry), physics, geography, medicine, language, literature, and philosophy.

The accumulation of knowledge at Alexandria and at other Hellenistic centers was important in its own right but also because it provided a link between the Greek world and the Roman Empire and western Europe. The Athenian schools were favorite places to send Roman youth during the height of the Roman Empire. They even outlasted the fall of the Western Roman Empire, finally being closed by Justinian in A.D. 529 because they were pagan. The other Hellenistic centers of learning continued more or less active under the Roman Empire and then received another stimulus from Arab and Jewish scholars between the eighth and the thirteenth centuries.

It is difficult to assess the contributions of Hellenistic higher education. It might be put this way: In respect to the accumulation of knowledge and information through research and investigation, the Hellenistic period took enormous strides forward. It made knowledge more easily available to scholars who wished to continue research work for the joy of it. But in respect to the *aim* of education, the influence of Hellenistic higher education was less desirable. The intellectual ideal of knowledge for its own sake was exalted to the extent that the welfare of the student and of society was largely overlooked. Hellenistic education lost the earlier Greek fervor for creating good citizens in a free and democratic state, and it lost concern for the development of the physical, aesthetic, and moral qualities of the well-rounded individual. In modern terminology, Hellenistic education exalted the "graduate school ideal" of research and neglected the "college ideal" of teaching for social and individual values. Its dominant concern was the pursuit of organized knowledge.

Chapter 4

THE ROMAN WORLD

LARGE-SCALE SOCIAL ORGANIZATION

In the third and second centuries B.C. the center of political and economic gravity shifted from the eastern Mediterranean to Rome. The chronological sequence of our story, therefore, must be interrupted briefly in order to describe the cultural developments that had taken place on the Italian peninsula before Rome became a world power.

Political and Economic Institutions

Early Times in Italy (Prior to Fifth Century B.C.). The history of the Italian peninsula in primitive times is clouded with uncertainties. The evidence seems to show that, for many centuries, Italy was the scene of several migrations from eastern Europe, Asia Minor, and northern Europe. By the eighth century B.C. the Etruscans dominated the west coast of Italy above the Tiber River, the Latins dominated the central portion of the west coast, and other Italian tribes elsewhere. Their culture was presumably much like that of other primitive tribes. The city of Rome, whose legendary founding is usually put at 753 B.C., became the center of the Latin tribes.

Between the eighth and sixth centuries B.C. primitive tribal life gave way to a political organization similar to that of the early Greek city-states. The rulers of Rome as well as of the other tribes were kings and noble families. At Rome the Senate, which functioned as an advisory council to the kings, was made up of the noble families whose descendants were known as "patricians." These patricians, who were the highest class of landowners, fought in the army as mounted cavalry, providing their own armor and horses, and came to be a hereditary aristocratic class. The Etruscans conquered Rome and ruled it during the sixth century B.C., until they were finally overthrown at the end of the century by the Latin tribes. Rome emerged from this period as a leading military and political center with the landed aristocracy more powerful in military, political, and economic affairs than ever before.

The Roman Republic (Fifth to First Century B.C.). The legendary founding of the Republic is usually given as 509 B.C., the time when the Romans threw off the rule of the Etruscans and at the same time did away with their kings. The aristocratic class of patricians continued to be the dominant political power in Rome during the fifth and fourth centuries, expressing its power through the Senate, which, instead of choosing a new king, set up a constitution by which the Senate chose two consuls to be joint executives for a period of 1 year. These consuls were given complete power over military, civil, and religious affairs during their term of office; since they were elected by the Senate, Rome has been called a republic. However, it was much less democratic than Athens at the same period under the reforms of Cleisthenes, for the control was virtually in the hands of the aristocratic patrician or senatorial class.

The plebeian class of citizens (or common people) now began to increase in numbers and in political importance. They were citizens who did not have the standing of the patrician families but who were free inhabitants of the city of Rome—the artisans, foreigners attracted to Rome, and small landowners. As a result of wars with the Gauls who fought their way into Rome, the Latins sought to make the army stronger than ever. In this process the plebeians were called upon to serve in the army to help out the depleted aristocratic class. The plebeians thus became more important because of their military power and were often rewarded with grants of land in the conquered territories. As the number of free landowners among the plebs increased, they became more important economically and eventually became full citizens and members of the army. Thus, a citizen army was created, made up of all landowners divided into classes depending on the amount of their wealth.

The plebeians henceforth had a sense of common interests and demanded some sort of organization for the furtherance of these. As a consequence, they began to choose representatives known as tribunes, who probably were originally the leaders of the plebeian armies. Several tribunes came to be elected annually, and gains were made for plebeian rights in the code of civil law published as the Twelve Tables about 450 B.C.

In the fourth and third centuries the popular Assembly was organized and gained political power at the expense of the Senate. The Assembly was made up of all citizens who served in the army; thus it consisted of all free landowners. The Assembly came to have the power to pass laws, elect consuls, and decide matters of war and peace. Plebeians achieved the right to be elected to the consulship, and the tribunes acquired the power to defend plebeians against discriminatory laws and to exercise a veto on the rulings of the consuls. The steady democratizing process that was under way in the fourth and third centuries brought the great bulk of the population into the exercise of responsibilities, rights, and duties as citizens of the state.

Despite these gains, however, the political control of Rome was never as democratic as in Athens. The public officials still came largely from the aristocratic classes, who had time and money to spend in politics, and the weight of tradition caused the people to lean upon the aristocratic families as persons who had greater experience and better judgment in political affairs. Although the Assembly had achieved the supreme power in the state, the citizens did not vote as individuals as in Athens but by five classes divided according to wealth. The first class, made up of patrician families, had 98 divisions with 1 vote each, whereas all the other four classes had a combined vote of only 95 votes. Thus, the minority of patricians could outvote the majority of plebeians.

The political fortune of the plebeian classes under the Republic paralleled the waxing and waning of their economic and social status. By the fifth century B.C. class distinctions in Rome were fairly well established. At the top were the patricians who were principally the large landowners, traders, and stock raisers. Then came the plebs, or plebeian classes, composed of the free persons who owned their own small plots of land. Finally, there were the slaves, who had no political or economic rights. The most significant development in the fifth and fourth centuries B.C. was the growth of the *free* plebs; this represented a great widening of the base of economic and social life.

As already noted, this expansion of the free plebeians came about as the common people were granted conquered land as a reward for their services in the army. The number of free plebs increased also as men drifted to Rome and to other cities in order to take advantage of the commercial and manufacturing activities that were becoming increasingly important. These plebs became shopkeepers, tradesmen, and skilled workers. Guilds, or associations of workmen (*collegia*), were formed to establish standards of workmanship and to give certain privileges to the guild members. Here is an early framework of economic organization that later became most important in the guilds of the Middle Ages.

The fourth and third centuries B.C. were the economic heyday of the small landowner, or yeoman, in Rome. Most of the land was held in relatively small plots, the yeoman-owner tilled his soil with his own hands, and large estates were relatively less common than in later centuries. Here was a broad basis of economic democracy that helped to make Rome a strong and powerful state and seemed to augur well for the extension of political democracy commensurate with the economic democracy that the land policy had fostered.

However, this trend toward economic democracy was abruptly terminated during the second century B.C. The class of free plebs declined rapidly as men were killed in the Punic and Eastern Wars and as the returning veterans could not keep their lands in cultivation. They fell into debt and often lost their lands to those who had money to lend and to buy land. Thus the proportion of large estates increased, and the class of free plebs and small landowners began to decline. As the yeomen went into debt, they moved to the cities or stayed on the land as tenants or hired hands, and similarly the city classes of more or less idle plebeians grew in numbers. This meant that the economic base was narrowed and the chances for lasting political democracy grew much less.

The converse of the decline of the small-landowner class was the growth not only of large estates but also of the business and merchant classes. Businessmen grew rich by obtaining government contracts for providing war supplies and for making ships, roads, and the weapons of war. The capitalists bought up the small lands of the debtor yeomen and imported plentiful supplies of slaves from the East for labor.

Meanwhile, the military power of Rome was rapidly being extended abroad. A series of Latin Wars in the fourth and third centuries enabled Rome successfully to defeat the other major Italian cities on the peninsula until by 275 B.C. Rome had united all Italy under its control. Then, through the Punic Wars with Carthage, Rome gained control of Sicily, Corsica, Sardinia, and Spain by 201 B.C. Turning their attention to the East, the Roman legions carried on a series of wars against the Hellenistic kingdoms until Macedonia, Greece, Asia Minor, Syria, Egypt, and the entire Mediterranean world came under their sway. The Greek city-states at first welcomed the Romans as liberators in their struggle against Macedonia, but the Roman legions that came to free them remained eventually to rule.

At home, the second and first centuries B.C. saw a long-continuing struggle between factions which professed to represent the common people as against those which represented the Senate. Intrigue and counter-intrigue often erased any clear lines of demarcation, and sometimes the struggle became merely a contest for power among rival groups or individuals. On the whole, the Senate emerged victorious over the Assembly in the series of civil wars that lasted intermittently for a century. First the wars between Marius, representing the people, and Sulla, representing the Senate, resulted in a further strengthening of the Senate and a further weakening of the tribunes and the Assembly. Then came the struggle between Pompey and Julius Caesar, the Senate at first supporting Pompey against the democratic proclivities of Caesar and ultimately opposing both under the leadership of Cicero. Caesar was victor and made himself virtually a complete dictator, concentrating all important offices in his own person; but he reckoned too lightly with the continuing power of the Senate, which contrived to assassinate him and thus set loose another series of wars, culminating in the struggles between Antony and Octavian.

When Octavian emerged victorious, all the Mediterranean world and most of western Europe were under his rule and the old city-state conception had given way to the conception of a world-wide empire.

The Roman Empire (27 B.C. *to Sixth Century* A.D.). Octavian became princeps, or first citizen of Rome, and took the name Augustus and the title imperator. Augustus apparently had good intentions about restoring the old forms of constitutional government, which he felt had been usurped by Caesar. In fact, all that he did was according to the scrupulously correct forms; he laid down all his extraordinary powers and thus afforded the Senate the opportunity of giving them back to him. Despite his good will and integrity, however, Augustus was the source of ultimate authority in all political as well as military affairs because of his complete control of the army. The army was more important politically than ever, for it became a standing professional army rather than a citizen militia. All its officers were members of the aristocracy, and the legions were made up of citizens who began to consider themselves as special recipients of privilege.

The Senate continued to command considerable respect from Augustus and from the people. It was a sort of training ground for the great number of public administrators and officials who were needed to rule the vast empire. Its activities still provided a route to promotion, an outlet for the energies of the aristocratic class, and a focus for their interests and loyalties. It remained true, however, that the real authority rested with Augustus despite his respect for and attentiveness to the Senate. Its tradition was a great one despite its actual lack of final power. Senators favored Augustus because he favored them. In fact, the power of Augustus was widespread among a population that was weary of constant wars and welcomed the 40 years of peace and prosperity that accompanied his reign.

During the first and second centuries A.D. the power and grandeur of the Roman Empire were at their peak. Commerce and trade prospered under relatively peaceful conditions, and the magnificent systems of roads vied with the seas as arteries of trade. Town life became common as provincial cities were founded and developed in imitation of the glory of Rome itself. The provincial cities came to have a large measure of local autonomy and legal rights, and the people continued to display a keen interest in their local political affairs. Above the local governments, of course, was the authority of the central government at Rome, which kept control of the armies, finances, and taxes through the central agents and secret police. The immediate successors of Augustus ruled merely because they were related to Augustus, but every now and then strong and capable emperors appeared who ruled with a sense of their obligation to the people. Such were Vespasian, Trajan, Hadrian, Antoninus Pius, and

Marcus Aurelius. It is probably no accident that these were the emperors who were interested in fostering education in various ways.

The economic and social life of Imperial Rome in the first and second centuries A.D. presented striking contrasts. On one hand were the wealth, beauty, comfort, and conveniences that combined to produce the "grandeur that was Rome." On the other hand were the undercurrents and signs that the economic situation was unhealthy and would lead to decay and decline.

The grandeur rested on uneasy foundations that were eventually to topple the whole edifice. In agriculture the large estates remained large and even increased in size, but methods of farming declined in technique and efficiency. The owners moved to the cities and leased the land on long- or short-term leases to small tenants, who began to drop the scientific and specialized methods of farming. Ever more primitive methods were universally resorted to, for estates came to be managed by freedmen or slaves, who did not see the advantage of better methods. Finally, the use of slave labor made it impossible for farmers or laborers to organize for protection against the owners in order to improve their status.

Likewise, in commerce and manufacturing deterioration in methods and products began to be evident. The large factories at Rome were broken up into smaller shops, and their products declined in quality and beauty. In the mines as well as factories the methods of mass production gave way to smaller workings, and the techniques declined in the hands of workers who worked alone or in small groups. It was apparently not recognized that the dissemination of technical information among the individual workers by a widespread education might have enabled the small farmer and worker to keep his standards high; widespread education for the ordinary people was not part of the Roman conception.

In the third and in following centuries the Empire fell upon evil days, and its weaknesses became more evident. After Marcus Aurelius, the army began to play an ever greater part in raising and overthrowing emperors. For example, in the 50 years between A.D. 235 and 285 there were 26 emperors, only one of whom died a natural death. Intrigue and counter-intrigue on the part of the army and of the Senate produced a chaotic situation. The autonomy of local governments virtually disappeared as the emperors took more and more direct power into their own hands. The emperor became less and less a "first citizen" and more and more an Oriental despot. The Senate had no political outlet for its energies, and the aristocracy became a pampered leisure class depending for preferment upon the fancy of the emperor. This development had enormous implications for education.

In the fourth century the authority of the Empire was divided between the eastern and the western parts. Diocletian began this process, which became even more pronounced under Constantine, who founded Constantinople on the site of ancient Byzantium as the seat of the Empire. By the fourth century, then, virtually two empires existed, one with a capital and Senate at Rome and another with a capital and Senate at Constantinople, although for years many emperors tried to keep alive the legal fiction of one unified empire. This theory became even more fictional as the many Germanic tribes began to press against the boundaries of the Empire.

During the fourth, fifth, and sixth centuries the Germans swept along the whole front of the Empire. In the fourth century they invaded Macedonia, Greece, and Asia Minor. In succession they conquered Italy, Spain, France, and England. The bishops of the Christian Church in Rome maintained authority over a greater or lesser part of Italy, and the nominal rule of the Eastern Empire was acknowledged more or less sincerely by the various Germanic kings, but they nevertheless held the real power.

In the sixth century, Justinian, as emperor of the Eastern Empire, made vigorous attempts to reassert his rule over the West by conquering Italy and much of the western areas of the Empire in northern Africa and southern Spain. He was a strong administrator and exerted great authority. Although Justinian made great gains in reestablishing the authority of the Empire, his successors were unable to maintain these gains, and the Eastern Empire was confined to the eastern Mediterranean and became identified more than ever with Greek and Byzantine culture. Its powers of resistance were strong, and it tenaciously held on to some sort of order and continuity down to the fifteenth century. In order to explain more fully why the Western Empire disintegrated and made way for the appearance of a medieval civilization, we must look more specifically at the economic and social developments that took place in the course of the decline of the Empire.

The most striking generalization concerning the economic and social development of the Roman world is that expansion and general prosperity were greatest under the Republic, when the base of economic ownership was broad, whereas contraction and depression set in when ownership of land became exclusive and confined to the upper classes in the days of the Empire. This development paralleled in major elements the course of economic events in Greece. Economic democracy was accompanied by a measure of political democracy under the Republic; but when the aristocracy gained economic and social superiority under the Empire, political power and freedom passed out of the hands of the great masses of people. Finally, when the emperors turned on the aristocracy and destroyed it, all groups lost political as well as economic power, and the emperor became supreme dictator.

As the emperors became complete despots, civil freedom and self-government disappeared, and a prevading spirit of servility replaced the independence of thought and attitude that was prevalent when individuals had a sense of participation in the government and a sense of self-realization through the opportunities that freedom provided. The plebs and peasants were gradually bound completely to the soil by the emperors, and all semblance of economic freedom was lost. Such persons became serfs of the emperor, working and producing for his benefit. In some degree the same thing happened to workers in the cities and even to the merchants and manufacturers. They had to keep at work for the benefit of the emperor. They could not move or quit their jobs. Here was an ancient groundwork for the later development of medieval feudalism.

To all these factors were added the constant wars against the Germanic tribes that kept beating against the borders and invading the Empire. Population declined rapidly as a lowering of the birth rate was added to an increase in the death rate caused by the wars, plagues, and famines. The old aristocratic families no longer maintained themselves for generations but now died out rapidly and were replaced by other and newer aristocratic families from the provinces. The status of marriage declined, and vice increased. Taxes became overpowering; the richer classes could no longer maintain themselves, while the lower classes had no means of income beyond subsistence on the land as serfs or by doles in the cities.

As a result of all these forces, society took the form of a great pyramid, with the emperor, his family, followers, army officers, and high ecclesiastics at the top, catered to by the wealthy merchants and speculators, and all resting upon the work of the masses in the city, the serfs on the land, and the slaves who rendered personal services in the houses of the rich. When the Germanic tribes invaded the Empire, the emperors could not summon up enough enthusiasm or stamina to stave off conquest and disaster. A heavy attitude of psychological weariness and loss of nerve had so weakened the mental and moral fiber of the people that they could not respond with the courage, devotion, and loyalty that were needed to face the invader. The weaker turned to whatever immediate pleasures they could find in such a life, and the stronger turned to faith and hope in a better life to come in the next world. The ideal of a good life on this earth was apparently impossible of realization, and thus more and more people began to seek salvation in the other world after death. Such an intellectual climate was fertile soil for the spread of religious faith and devotion. It was apparent that the failure to establish and maintain a genuine social, economic, and political democracy was largely responsible for the decline of Roman civilization, as had been true in Greece.

All these developments had enormous significance for education, which became increasingly exclusive and aristocratic as the process just described ran its course. It is possible that a more generous conception of the importance of widespread education would have played a part in bringing about and maintaining a more healthy political and economic condition, and would have provided a bulwark against the aristocratic exclusiveness that was at the root of cultural decay.

Religious Institutions

Family and State Religions. Throughout the period of the Roman Republic and Empire the religious institutions of family and state played a large part in the private and public life of the people. The earliest religious beliefs of the Romans were similar to those of other primitive peoples, but the Romans emphasized family ties and the religion of the family. Drawing upon primitive beliefs that the heavens and earth were peopled by gods like human beings who helped or hindered the projects of man, the Romans developed a set of deities who were thought to rule the destinies of the family, each deity representing an important phase of the family's activities. On stated and proper occasions, as well as in their informal daily life, the members of the family looked to these gods to bless their work and to protect the family from evil spirits and evil days.

The civic religion of the Romans was in large part a projection on a national scale of the family religion, but it became much more formalized and definitely prescribed as to ritual and ceremony. The state eventually took complete control of the worship of the gods, and special guardians of the religious functions were set up by the state in the form of priestly guilds, or colleges (*collegia*). The Pontifical College was the highest of these groups; it fixed the religious holidays and the kind of rituals to be observed and, in general, acted as the state's official custodian of all things religious. All important state ceremonials and undertakings were begun and closed with religious rites in order to discover whether the time and conditions were auspicious in the view of the gods and to ask their help. A citizen was thus obligated to know his place in the religious life of the state and to be able to fulfill his obligations. It is no wonder, then, that early educational practices of family and state included much of a religious character.

With the advent of Augustus as emperor in the first century B.C. the character of the Roman state religion took another important turn, this time in the direction of a personal worship of the emperor himself. The belief in some sort of divine human being who would act as messiah and savior of the world had long been common among the people. When Augustus brought peace after the horrors and destruction of the civil wars, the people began to attribute divine powers to Augustus himself. He was not averse to this idolatry and encouraged it to such a degree that he became the personification not only of the majesty of the state but also of divine will. He united in his own person the ultimate religious as well as the ultimate civil power. The emperors after Augustus saw the desirability of keeping alive this union of civic and religious authority, but the ceremonies gradually became less meaningful and more formal until finally, by the time of Constantine, the emperors were obliged to give up the conception.

Eastern Religions. In Greece and in the eastern part of the Empire the intellectual classes of the second and first centuries B.C. found little satisfaction in the ancient gods, in worship of the emperor, or in the strictly rationalistic philosophy and science of earlier Greek culture. They began to be pessimistic about the conditions of everyday life as they had seen it disrupted by the Roman conquests. They thus turned to such philosophies as Stoicism, Epicureanism, and Cynicism, which dropped their earlier emphasis upon rational inquiry and built up systems of belief that were organized into bodies of doctrine to be accepted with little or no question. Stoicism was the most popular among intellectuals of the time of Augustus and reached its heyday in the first and second centuries A.D., finding expression in the writings of Epictetus, Seneca, and Marcus Aurelius, respectively a slave, a senator, and an emperor.

Those with less sturdy intellectual interests turned to Epicureanism, which had lost almost entirely the character that Epicurus had given it and had become a justification for simply enjoying life to the full. Still others who were enticed by the mysteries of life and death turned to the Eleusinian mysteries of the Orphics or to Neo-Pythagoreanism and Neoplatonism, which gained a considerable following in the third century A.D. under the leadership of Plotinus and his disciples. All these philosophic religions represented attempts to combine a philosophic interest with religious emotionalism.

For the common people who had no capacity for philosophic interpretations, the ancient local religions of the various parts of the Empire provided an outlet for their emotional and religious desires in the face of the political and economic disasters of the times. These ancient cults took on the character of evangelical religions and developed a body of doctrine, a definite theology, prescribed rites, ceremonies, costumes, and priestly hierarchies. The Empire was swept from one end to the other by religious beliefs that mingled or established themselves side by side with the family and civic religions of the Romans.

The Triumph of Christianity. In the first two centuries of the Empire,

Christianity, in the eyes of most people, was simply another Eastern religion among many. Beginning as a local Jewish sect in Palestine, the Christian groups and beliefs gradually gained adherents in all parts of the Empire, especially among the lower classes of the towns and cities. St. Paul was especially instrumental in universalizing Christianity and in promoting the faith among many of the peoples of the Eastern Empire. He had studied Greek philosophy, particularly Stoicism, and after his conversion wrote extensive letters and preached in person through most of the Greek world of Asia Minor, the Aegean Islands, Thrace, and Greece itself.

As the Christian sects and congregations gained followers, they came into conflict with the other religions and eventually with the emperors. It is not altogether clear why the Christians were persecuted by the emperors. Perhaps it was their insistence upon the worship of one God and their refusal to worship the emperor, which could be construed as an illegal or traitorous act; perhaps it was their refusal to engage in the usual civic ceremonies and games, which exalted the emperor and pagan gods; perhaps it was their refusal to serve in the army because they believed it involved useless killing; perhaps it was their growing reputation for living strictly moral lives, which led them to be looked upon as "queer" and therefore as dangerous. Whatever the reasons, they increasingly became a concern to the public officials of the state. Nero found them a useful scapegoat upon whom to blame the burning of Rome. Under other emperors in the first and second centuries A.D. there were intermittent and irregular persecutions, which arose from distrust or fear of these groups who could not be swayed by punishment but even thrived on martyrdom, supremely confident in the righteousness of their cause and their faith.

With the increasing trials of the Empire in the third century and the ever-increasing strength of the Christians, the emperors apparently felt that the time had come to call a halt. Under Decius and Diocletian systematic attempts were made to reassert the absolute power of the emperors and to wipe out the Christian congregations as a means to this end, but the Christians could not be stopped. As the Empire emerged from the third century weakened and shaken, the church emerged stronger than ever. The church had won the first of its many centuries of battles with the state.

Finally, in the fourth century, the attitude of the emperors changed; they found apparently that it was the better part of wisdom to be tolerant and eventually to gain the support of such a powerful institution. An edict of Galerius in A.D. 311 granted to Christians the legal right to worship their God, in 313 Constantine gave the Christians full legal rights, and in 325 he recognized Christianity as the official state religion. From this time on, church leaders began to argue that the state and the church should cooperate. Ambrose and Bishop Gelasius I claimed that the state should protect and support the church, and in points of conflict the church should be supreme. Here are foundations of the idea of "an establishment of religion."

Despite a temporary setback under Julian in the fourth century, when the pagan gods were again brought into prominence, the triumph of Christianity was achieved when Theodosius set out to suppress the worship of the old Roman gods as a crime against the state and to give legal protection *only* to Christians. Theodosius was the last emperor to rule over the full extent of the Empire; after the beginning of the fifth century, the separation into a Greek Empire of the East and a Latin Empire of the West was complete. The greatest power in the Western Empire was the Roman Church. In the sixth century the Eastern emperor, Justinian, made the last great attempt to unify the Empire once more into a single world state. A strong believer in Christianity as a means to this end, he showed his desire to stamp out paganism in A.D. 529 by closing the doors of the philosophic schools at Athens, which had existed since the time of Plato and Aristotle. This was another sign that the classic culture was giving way to medieval culture.

In its rise to power the Christian Church was favored not only by the force of its doctrine and faith but also by the gradual perfecting of its organization as an institution. Over the centuries the church patterned its organization after that of the Empire and thus became increasingly hierarchical in form. At first the Christian sects were relatively independent communities of believers, but gradually a more centralized organization was built up. A new and effective organizational discipline was achieved when the priesthood was distinguished from laymen and a clerical hierarchy developed. In the local communities and small districts within cities, the church appointed parish priests; in the cities, the church established bishops to be in charge of all church affairs in their jurisdiction; in the imperial provinces, the church established metropolitans, or archbishops, who governed the bishops in their territory; and in the diocese (a group of provinces), the church appointed patriarchs. This type of centralized control was fairly well established by the fourth century.

Eventually, the bishops of Rome were able to claim jurisdiction over the entire Western Church and to exert their power as popes. This process seems to have been well on its way by the time of Pope Leo the Great in the fifth century. The supremacy of the bishop of Rome was aided by the fact that Rome was still looked to by the West as the physical, spiritual, and economic center of the Empire. In addition, the claim was increasingly made and established by the bishops of Rome that since the church at Rome had been founded by St. Peter, who had been designated the chief apostle by Christ himself, therefore the bishops of Rome were the legitimate apostolic successors of Christ through Peter. The conception of a united Christendom played an enormous role in political and religious affairs as well as in the intellectual and educational enterprises of the Empire and the Middle Ages.

DIVERSITY IN EDUCATIONAL CONTROL

Early Education by the Family. Before 300 B.C., Roman education, like that of primitive and tribal societies, was directed by the family and guided by the aim to induct the children into the customs and life of the group in order to preserve its folkways. We may presume that ideals of

Fig. 5. Roman school scene.

piety, integrity, courage, and prudence were inculcated as the children imitated and watched their parents going about the ordinary business of living. The general aim of family education was to help the boy become healthy and strong, to instill in him reverence for the gods, his parents, and the laws, and to help him become effective in war and in peacetime occupations.

The boy of a privileged family was taught to ride, box, swim, and use the spear. Girls were taught by their mothers the details of managing a home and were trained in the conduct becoming to a Roman woman who held a relatively high position in Roman homes and society. At the age of sixteen or eighteen the Roman youth put on the dress of a citizen and accompanied his father to the Forum and to the public religious cere-

monies. He thus learned the ideals and duties of a citizen, set forth not as
theoretical abstractions but as matters of everyday practice and action.
This type of education applied only to the upper-class families associated
with the senatorial class. Children of the plebs and slaves received only
enough instruction to enable them to fulfill whatever economic, religious,
and military duties might be expected of them.

Private Control of Schools in the Republic. It is possible that formal
schools may have existed in Rome as early as 500 B.C., but if so they did
not play a very large part in comparison with the family type of education just described. In general, schools as formal institutions appeared in
an important way on the Roman scene sometime following 300 B.C. and

Fig. 6. An educated slave calculating before his Roman master.

had become fairly common by the end of the third century B.C. The institutionalizing of Roman schools was in large measure a part of the spread
of Greek culture to the western Mediterranean world during the Hellenistic period. The elementary school in Rome came to be known as the
ludus and was presided over by the *ludi magister,* or *litterator,* who was
the Latin equivalent of the Greek grammatist in Hellenistic schools of
the East.

Children from the ages of seven to ten or twelve, often girls as well
as boys, were taught to read and write Latin and to count on their fingers,
with pebbles, or with an abacus. In comparison with the Greek schools
of the time, instruction in music and gymnastics seems to have been
lacking in Roman schools; the first step in the intellectualizing of Roman

education had taken place. These schools were private and voluntary, with little supervision by the state. The pedagogue who took the boys to school and acted as guardian was prominent in Roman education as well as in Greek countries. He sometimes even acted as tutor or teacher, for in an upper-class household he was often a Greek slave who was quite equal to such a role. Inasmuch as elementary education was a private affair, it is clear that Roman education was designed principally for the upper classes, who could afford to buy their children an education.

The secondary school was imported into Rome sometime in the third century B.C. As might be expected, it was thoroughly Greek in character, taking its pattern from the Greek secondary school of Hellenistic times. It was basically a grammar school and was taught, as in Greece, by a teacher known as a *grammaticus*. In the school of the *grammaticus* boys from the age of ten or twelve to sixteen were taught Greek grammar and literature, again with little or no attention to music or gymnastics, for Rome copied the intellectualistic pattern of education that was developing in the Hellenistic East. Interestingly enough, the first secondary schools in Rome were foreign-language schools, representing the interest of Republican Rome in all things Greek. This was likewise a part of the general Hellenizing of the West brought about by the Roman economic, military, and intellectual contacts with Greece. The *grammaticus* was also a private teacher or tutor, supported by fees, and for the most part during Republican times he was not controlled or supervised by the state.

Parallel with the growing awareness of Latin as the national language of Republican Rome in the first century B.C., a new type of secondary school appeared, this time a grammar school for teaching Latin. By the end of the Republican period the growth of a Latin literature had made it possible for the Latin grammar school to exist alongside of the Greek grammar school. For many generations Rome had the two kinds of grammar schools, one Greek and one Latin, the favored boy perhaps attending both in order to achieve the best all-round education. These schools became the means by which the upper-class boy was prepared for a life of activity suitable to his class in Republican Rome. They were the roads to attainment and preferment in the realm of public office, whether in the Senate or in the army.

For the very best education during Republican times it was considered desirable to supplement secondary education with study at the rhetorical or philosophical schools in Athens or at other Hellenistic centers of the East. Rhetorical schools had not made great headway in the West prior to the time of the Empire. Thus, in all its foundation elements, the education to be obtained in Roman schools was basically borrowed from Greek education. But the earlier type of family education continued to play a large part in Rome during the Republic, and, for most children, school education was no part of their lives whatsoever.

Growing Civil Control of Schools in the Empire. During the Roman Empire the basic pattern of schools did not change radically from that of the Republic. The most outstanding changes were in matters of emphasis and support. Throughout the Empire the school of the *litterator* was the most common elementary school, designed principally to teach reading. The school of the *grammaticus* was the common secondary school, increasingly emphasizing the study of Latin grammar in the West and Greek grammar in the East. Eventually the Greek grammar school virtually disappeared in the West (although, interestingly enough, the study of Greek seems to have continued to some extent in the schools of Gaul and Ireland). The school of the rhetor, or rhetorical school, became the most popular higher school in the Imperial period, again emphasizing Latin rhetoric in the West and Greek rhetoric in the East. The philosophical schools were maintained in the Eastern cities throughout most of the Imperial period, but they were never established in Rome or in the West to any like degree. Other higher institutions, maintained and established in the East and to a lesser degree in the West, included technical institutes, libraries, museums, and centers of research in scientific fields.

The most important change in Imperial schools was the increasing patronage and support given to teachers by several of the emperors and by the municipal authorities. In this way, the civil government came to play a larger and larger role in the control of Roman schools so that in some sense it may be said that Rome established "public" schools on a wide scale. In general, however, such schools were designed principally for the senatorial or knightly classes, in other words, for the wealthy landowning and commercial classes of Roman society. Imperial patronage was more or less haphazard, depending upon the personal interest of individual emperors in promoting learning or upon their desire to gain personal support for certain sections of the population. Even before Imperial days, Julius Caesar had given the franchise and rights of citizenship to certain foreign teachers and physicians who had come to Rome. Augustus also gave such favors when he allowed foreign teachers and physicians to remain in Rome when all other foreigners were being banished because of widespread famine.

In the first century A.D., the Emperor Vespasian is notable for his patronage and support of educational institutions. He established considerable library facilities in Rome and endowed chairs of rhetoric in Greek and Latin, paying the rhetoricians' salaries out of the public treasury. He also granted extensive exemptions from certain civic obligations to grammarians, rhetoricians, physicians, and philosophers, removing the burdens of taxes, service in the army, and the obligation to quarter soldiers. Nerva provided allowances for certain boys and girls to continue their education up to the ages of eighteen and fourteen, respectively, and Trajan provided for the care and education of several thousand poor children in Rome. How effective or how widespread were these attempts to broaden the base of educational opportunity is not known, but the surface could only have been scratched under the best of conditions. Nevertheless, the eagerness for education seems to have been very widespread in this period, and thousands of schools in the East and the West taught children to read Greek or Latin.

In the second century A.D. even greater advances were made in extending schools at all levels throughout the Empire. Most of this activity was undertaken by the towns and municipal authorities, especially in the East, with occasional help and stimulation by the emperors when financial depressions affected the towns. In the East, but not in the West, all towns had their palaestrae and gymnasiums; the public games and athletic competitions served to keep up the interest in music, dancing, and athletics. Schools, however, were confined to the towns and restricted to children of the upper social classes. The Emperor Hadrian helped to rejuvenate Athens as a center of learning and established in Rome the Athenaeum as an institute for Greek and Latin scholars interested in science, literature, and philosophy along with engineering, architecture, and the more practical arts.

Antoninus Pius laid upon the towns the obligation of paying the salaries of teachers and of giving them exemptions; this had the effect of stimulating the already established custom of municipal control and support of education. Capital cities had to support up to 10 physicians, five rhetoricians, and five grammarians; small cities, five physicians, three rhetoricians, and three grammarians; and others in proportion to their size. In general, the cities were to pay these salaries at public expense, and the emperor to pay the salaries from the imperial treasury if the cities could not do so. Marcus Aurelius was primarily interested in the schools at Athens; he endowed a chair for a rhetorician and authorized the payment of salaries for eight philosophers, two each for the philosophic schools originally founded by Plato, Aristotle, the Epicureans, and the Stoics.

In the third century A.D. Alexander Severus established a new center of higher learning in Rome, with public professors of grammar, engineering, architecture, medicine, and astronomy, and offered scholarships for the children of the poor. Constantine encouraged education by Christian teachers, especially in Constantinople, and reaffirmed the principle of immunities and honors for higher teachers. Gratian extended imperial patronage in the schools of Gaul. During the reaction against Christianity under Julian, the effort was made to cancel the privileges for Christian teachers. Julian's edict of A.D. 362 prohibited Christian teachers from offering instruction in the publicly supported schools, bringing all appointments under the emperor's thumb for confirmation or rejection.

Theodosius further sponsored public payment of salaries for teachers in the higher schools of Constantinople, authorizing 10 grammarians and three rhetoricians to teach in Latin and 10 grammarians and five rhetoricians to teach in Greek and appointing as well a philosopher and a jurist. An interesting development was his ruling that public teachers could not have private pupils and that private teachers could not teach publicly. The rule of Justinian marked a decline in the practice of imperial patronage of education; he ordered the schools of Athens to be closed because they were pagan. There is evidence, however, that Roman imperial schools continued to exist in the East and also in Italy well into the Middle Ages. Some of the Italian towns managed to maintain their secular schools for centuries despite the difficulties of the times and the growing importance of religious schools conducted by the Christian Church.

Church Control of Christian Schools. The Imperial period of Rome was marked by the entry of the Christian Church into the educational field alongside of the secular schools controlled privately or by the civil governments. In point of numbers of schools and pupils, the Christian schools probably did not equal the secular schools during the greater part of the Imperial period, though in the absence of statistics such a generalization is perhaps open to question. However, it seems likely that at some time between the fifth and seventh or eighth centuries the preponderance of educational effort was definitely the church's.

Whatever the merits of a generalization concerning the relative proportion of secular versus religious control of schools, the church made beginning efforts to set up its own schools in the first three centuries of the Empire. At first the church hesitated to establish schools, but it soon became clear to an increasing number of church leaders that some kind of special instruction should be given to those who were about to become members of the church. In the early days of Christianity, baptism and joining the church were adult affairs. In order to be sure that the candidate for baptism (catechumen) was well grounded in the faith, it was necessary to give him 2 or 3 years of probationary instruction. At first, this was usually done informally by the elders of the Christian community; but as this instruction became more formal, the term "catechumental school" was applied to the process by which the candidate for baptism was made familiar with the services, moral precepts, and doctrines of the faith. These schools probably reached their height in the fifth century A.D. and then gradually declined until they had all but disappeared by the eighth or ninth centuries, and other types of church schools took their place.

Another and much more important kind of school sought to give the advanced type of education available in the Greek philosophical schools. Outstanding schools were conducted by Clement at Alexandria, Origen at Caesarea, Chrysostom at Antioch, and Justin Martyr at Rome. In general, these schools came to include in the curriculum the whole round of studies deemed proper for an educated man of the second and third centuries A.D., and were eventually found in all the principal intellectual centers of the Empire. Schools of this sort were not always highly institutionalized in form; they were most commonly conducted by a bishop or other church leader. They may have been the forerunners of the cathedral schools, which were so important and influential in the Middle Ages.

That the church became interested in expanding its educational efforts as early as the fourth century A.D. is attested by the decree of the General Church Council in Constantinople, which in A.D. 381 required the establishment of schools in all towns and villages for the free instruction of children. This doubtless was a response to a demand that the church try to replace the secular control of emperor and town in the establishment of schools. In the sixth century a church council decreed that priests throughout Christendom should follow the example of the priests in Italy and give attention to the training of their successors. In these ways the idea of education for prospective members of the priesthood became a growing concern of the church before the end of the Roman Empire.

One other aspect of church organization and development had a profound effect upon the organization and control of education. That was the growth of monasticism. As early as the second and third centuries A.D. the practice of retiring from the world in order to follow the religious life attracted an increasing number of Christians. In the earliest days this practice was represented by the solitary hermit who dedicated himself to a strictly ascetic and rigorous life of denial of all things of the body and of glorification of the spirit. Self-abnegation, self-discipline, and even extreme physical mortification became the ideals of the hermit's ascetic life.

In the fourth and fifth centuries a change took place in the form of ascetic practices when individual hermits began to live near one another and eventually to live together and develop a communal life. In this process the original forms of religious monasticism were created, paving the way for the Benedictine movement, which began in the sixth century and eventually spread throughout most of Europe. Although the place of formal education in these early monastic groups is uncertain, it is clear that rules were developed for the conduct of the members, including definite expectations concerning mental and moral discipline. Eventually, the monasteries became important centers of the educational and intellectual life of the Early Middle Ages.

Status of the Teaching Profession. Much has already been implied concerning the role and status of teachers in the Roman period, but a few generalizations may be made here. The teacher of the elementary school, as always, was held in fairly low repute and paid haphazardly through fees or gifts. Little can be said with assurance concerning his position, but it is probably significant that so little comment upon him appears in the records of the Roman period. This is presumably a rough measure of the estimation put upon his services. As often as not, the elementary school teacher in Rome was a slave or a captured national of some country conquered by Rome.

The story is much different, however, with respect to teachers in the higher schools. In Republican days the most notable teachers were Greeks who came to Rome first as political equals, later as slaves, and then as enfranchised Roman citizens. In any case, the Greek scholars were often lionized in the intellectual circles of Rome, receiving patronage and special privileges of different kinds. The status of grammarians, rhetoricians, physicians, philosophers, and scientists rose and fell at different times in Imperial days, but in general the fact that some of the emperors and many of the towns were willing to pay their salaries means that they had a rather high position in the life of the period. Quintilian, a foremost rhetorician and teacher, held high public office under Vespasian in the early days of the Empire, and other examples could be noted.

When Christians were a minority and therefore a "dangerous" group, Christian teachers suffered the same fate as other Christian believers. When Christianity became the dominant religion, the pagan teachers in turn were often in trouble, notably when they were obliged to leave Athens under Justinian's edict closing the philosophical schools. Within the church itself many of the notable Fathers were at the same time teachers, philosophers, and scholars. During the Imperial period the teaching process was a part of the function of the priest, bishop, and church leaders; in general, a special teaching class within the church did not emerge until the Middle Ages. The mark of a teacher was not a degree or the passing of examinations after a formal course of study so much as it was the fact that a person had studied under some recognized teacher and was then able to establish his own claim to be a teacher, to attract students, or to be appointed to a teaching position by the emperor, by municipal authorities, or by a bishop.

Although familiarity with the liberal arts came to be more and more accepted as the minimum requirements for one who would be known as a teacher, it was left to the Middle Ages to outline specific courses of study to be required as the avenue to a teaching license and a teaching degree. Until that time teachers had little cohesiveness as a professional group except as they belonged to a rhetorical or philosophical school, and admission to the profession was much less formal and more individualized than in the centuries to come. In the later days of the Empire the secular teachers, reflecting the general intellectual life, became less creative and more sterile in their approach, and the religious teachers were hemmed in by the restrictions of religious doctrine as well as by the desiccation of the intellectual life. It is likely that many of the teachers of the Later Imperial period knew little more than was contained in the digested textbooks that were written in the fourth and fifth centuries.

Aristocratic Character of Roman Education. Just as Roman civilization itself was largely aristocratic in character, so was Roman education confined in large measure to the privileged and wealthy classes. In the days of the Republic, when the basis of economic and political life was rather broad, education in schools was a common expectation for relatively large numbers of people; but as the economic and political life became more restricted in the later days of the Empire, education became virtually limited to the aristocratic senatorial and knightly classes. Even though some remarkable advances were made in respect to the public support of teachers and a few gestures were made toward scholarships for the poor, there was little chance that the children of the lower classes could take advantage of such schooling. In general, the opportunity to rise from the lower classes was a fairly small one and became smaller and smaller as serfdom and despotism increased after the third century A.D.

When the church began to take over control of much of Roman education, it did little to change the essentially aristocratic character of education; its purpose was primarily to train leaders for the church, and these leaders increasingly came from the more privileged classes. The church did not develop a conception of education for all—a religion and a church for all, but not an education for all. The reservoir of religious doctrine was conceived to be, not the people at large, but the priesthood; hence education and intellectual opportunities were by and large reserved for priests and prospective priests.

Out-of-school Agencies of Education

The most pervasive educational agency outside of the school in Roman times was, as in most cultures, the family. Much has already been said concerning the role of the family in educating children for their place in society. Only two more points need be mentioned. (1) The ability of a family to provide an adequate introduction of the child to the culture was determined in large measure by the social and economic status of the family. Therefore, the increasingly exclusive character of Roman society meant that fewer and fewer families could do much in this direction, and consequently the family as an educational agency could do little to check the deterioration of Roman life. (2) The early Roman family directed youth toward the whole life he was to live in the Roman Republic in all its religious, political, economic, and social aspects. However, as the church became all-inclusive, the obligations upon any Christian family that tried to live up to the expectations of Christianity led the family to concentrate more and more upon the religious, moral, and spiritual aspects of family instruction and to shy away from the political and economic aspects. Thus, family education, along with other types of education, became otherworldly in its influence and less concerned with the introduction of the child to the matters of everyday living in this world.

Other nonschool agencies of education have also been touched upon. In Republican days the educational effects of the activities of the Forum, the Senate, the popular Assembly, and the civic religious observances were enormous. Under the Empire the Roman citizen lived in the presence of great architectural, sculptural, and artistic monuments that served as a constant reminder of the greatness of Rome and of the emperor. Likewise, the games, circuses, theaters, public baths, festivals, and holidays had a largely public character, influencing the public mind; and for the intellectual classes the libraries, museums, and institutes provided a further means of education, in addition to the schools. Above all, the Christian Church in its whole early development took on an educational aspect as it went about the process of spreading the gospel and converting a whole civilization to its beliefs. In order to win a position of supremacy, the church engaged in an all-inclusive teaching and educative process.

Two other agencies remain to be mentioned. (1) The army was extremely important as a means to success and achievement in Roman public life. Under Augustus particularly, the education of the youth of the privileged classes was directed toward leadership in the army, emphasizing physical education as well as military training. The youths practiced their horsemanship in the reviews and games held on the Campus Martius in Rome and on similar fields in the provincial cities. Whereas in the East physical education had remained a function of the palaestra and public gymnasium, in Rome physical education became either an adjunct of military training or was directed toward participation by the professional athlete in the games and circuses.

(2) The system of apprenticeship provided vocational education for the lower classes of tradesmen and craftsmen. As in Greece, vocational education in Rome was not a part of the schools but was left to a period of apprenticeship in which the boy worked with a practicing craftsman.

As these tradesmen and workers formed into guilds, or associations, certain requirements for entrance to the guild were set up to ensure the adequate preparation for the aspiring young person. For the rest, the plebs on the farms and in the cities learned what they could of semi-skilled and unskilled labor from their families or landlords or employers.

THE CORPUS OF KNOWLEDGE

The Cycle of the Roman Mind

Prior to the third century B.C. the Romans developed their own peculiar qualities of character and intellect largely untouched by Greek culture. Quite naturally, they idealized the characteristics and qualities of mind that were appropriate to rugged, agricultural, and warlike primitive tribes. Apparently the ideal Roman was one who undertook seriously, almost overzealously, his family obligations, his civic duties, and his business or farming activities with sincerity, dignity, and forethought.

In the third, second, and first centuries B.C. Roman intellectual life received a tremendous stimulus from the introduction of Greek thought, literature, philosophy, science, and religion. Beginning as a result of the very practical need to meet Greek traders on even terms, the desire to learn the Greek language grew apace, until at length Greek scholars began to pour into Rome and Roman intellectuals began to study and be influenced by Greek thought. Of course, there was opposition to the Greek influence by such men as Cato the Elder, who saw nothing but evil for Rome in Greek culture; but even he capitulated finally. In general, most Roman intellectuals of the later Republic period were nourished on Greek thought.

A new period began in the time of Augustus and lasted into the second century A.D. This was the period when a unique Latin literature expressing the national spirit of Rome ushered in what is usually called the "golden age" of Latin thought. In these days of Cicero, Lucretius, Vergil, Horace, and Ovid, Latin literature for the first time rivaled the creative literature of Greece, and the purely imitative phase of Latin literature had passed. With regard to intellectual patterns, however, most of Latin thought was at its basis Greek in origin and content, and it produced no creative genius that towers in intellectual history along with Plato or Aristotle.

The last creative stage of Roman thought began in the second and third centuries, when Christian thought produced a new optimism in the form of faith through religion and hope in the next world. The church Fathers of the Greek and Latin worlds formulated the teachings of Jesus into a body of doctrine that would appeal to the despairing intellectual classes, who had lost their faith in Greek philosophy as a solution to their intellectual and moral problems. The center of gravity shifted from an interest in political and social improvement to an enchantment with salvation of the spirit, which had become more important than physical freedom and happiness.

On the positive side, Christian thought gave new hope and new vitality to Greek thought by injecting into the old Greek forms of philosophy the new impetus of salvation and theology. On the negative side, the wellsprings of creative thought that had caused Greek classical philosophy to flower had apparently dried up, and creative conceptions in physical science and political philosophy had to await the passing of the centuries before they received new form and new substance. As the third, fourth, and fifth centuries progressed, Roman intellectual life, with the exception of Christian thought, passed into its decadent and antiquarian phase, from which it did not emerge until the Later Middle Ages.

Man and Nature and God

The principal formulations concerning the nature of the world and the relation of man to nature revealed a continuing opposition between otherworldly and this-worldly outlooks. The dominant "otherworldly" trends in Roman thought were shot through with Stoicism and the idealism of Plato. They stressed the permanent and absolute character of spiritual affairs as against the transitory quality of everyday life.

According to the Stoicism of Epictetus, Seneca, and Marcus Aurelius, the individual should guide his own life with rigid discipline and unconcern for the vagaries and passing fortunes of the material world. In the first century A.D. Philo the Jew attempted to achieve a synthesis between Judaism, Stoicism, and Platonism. He argued that the personal God of Judaism was the same as the abstract and transcendent spirit described by Plato. He glorified the contemplative life and mystical union with God and deplored the life of the bodily senses and passions. Philo was a most important bridge between Judaism, Greek philosophy, and Christian theology. In the third century A.D., Plotinus developed a school of Neoplatonism which stressed a mystical process by which the individual could be drawn into complete union with the divine by means of faith, restraint of bodily desires, and exaltation of the spiritual qualities.

At the opposite extreme, Lucretius used his poetry as a philosophical vehicle for Epicureanism. Lucretius preached the materialistic doctrine that the world is made up of atoms falling in space, there being no spiritual or divine control over human destiny and no life after death. Blasting the Platonic and Stoic conception that man is essentially spiritual, Lucretius insisted that man's soul is mortal, as well as his body, and that therefore there is no need to spend one's days in preparing for death nor to fear divine punishment afterward. Lucretius preached atheism with the passionate zeal of an evangelist and used all his poetic artistry to attack religious superstitions and extol what he believed to be the rational life.

Whereas the Greeks had looked upon the dualism of the body and the soul as an opportunity to develop both harmoniously, the tendency of Roman times was to exalt one or the other to the extreme. Stoicism and Neoplatonism glorified the soul, whereas most Epicureans glorified the body even to the extent of denying the existence of the soul. The problem thus posed was settled for centuries by the victory of Christianity.

By the force of his teaching and the power of his message, Jesus gave to the world a belief having for its main doctrines that man should obey God's laws and love Him and that each man should love his fellow men and treat them as he would have them treat him. Jesus made a personal appeal to the heart and emotions of men, assuring eternal salvation if one's relationship to God is right. Each person must be guided by a righteous heart and soul and not merely by correct forms and ceremonies if he is to achieve lasting happiness and blessedness in the kingdom of heaven. Jesus also taught that every human being is the child of a loving, heavenly Father. This personal care of God for His children was a new element in the tired world of the Empire. This ethical and spiritual message of the fatherhood of God and the brotherhood of man began the conquest of the Roman world.

It was soon discovered, however, that the size and complexities of the Empire, the varieties of peoples that made it up, and the strength of Greek philosophic traditions were problems to be overcome if Christianity were to become the universal religion. Thus it was that the church had to be organized on a large scale to meet the demands of the size of the Empire. It therefore appealed to practically minded persons who found a new outlet for their organizational energies. Because the common people were so accustomed to ceremony and ritual, the Christian Church soon set up its own ceremonies and customs, which had much in common with those of the other religions of the day, such as the reverencing of minor saints, martyrs, and relics, baptism, and religious holidays. Not only did Christian belief absorb much from the various religions of the time; it appealed to the depressed and underprivileged, who gained hope for the future. It also appealed to the intellectual classes who became weary of the purely contemplative philosophies.

Finally, Jesus' teachings were institutionalized over the centuries into bodies of doctrine that incorporated much of the form and content of Greek, and especially Platonic, philosophy. The first step in this process was the writing down of the oral stories about Jesus in the books of the New Testament. This took place during the Apostolic Age in a period of 100 years beginning about A.D. 50. As a result, the conception of Jesus began to change from the simple teacher to the divine Christ, Son of

God, who was the incarnation of God in human form and who atoned for man's sins through the Crucifixion and made possible man's salvation through the Resurrection. St. Paul and the authors of the Fourth Gospel were influential in bringing about this change and identifying Platonic idealism with Jesus.

Then during the Patristic Age from the second to the sixth century A.D. the church Fathers developed, organized, systematized, and elaborated Christian doctrine, using the teachings of Jesus, Biblical writings and commentaries, the decrees and writings of the bishops, the decisions of the church councils, and Greek philosophical writings. The church Fathers thus brought a great flood of Greek philosophical content into Christian theology from which it has never completely departed. Above all others, St. Augustine helped to fix the pattern of Christian theology into the Middle Ages.

In general, the Christian theology of the Fathers sided with the idealism and dualism of Platonism as against the materialism of Epicureanism. In this view, the world is ruled by an all-wise, all-good, all-powerful God, whose essence is spirit and who wages perpetual war against the world of matter, of evil, and of the devil. Man consists of a soul and a body and is thus an admixture of potential good and evil. The evil of the body triumphed in the fall of Adam, but spiritual grace and salvation may be achieved through the immortal soul. The means by which man may be saved through faith in the intervention of Christ are revealed and fixed by the church. Cyprian established as early as the third century A.D. that communion with Christ was impossible without adherence to the church.

The church found it necessary to reconcile all sorts of differences that arose concerning the true doctrine. One of the most important of these controversies was settled at the Nicene Council called in A.D. 325 by Emperor Constantine. Arius had maintained that God and Jesus are *similar* in substance but that Jesus was essentially a human teacher rather than completely divine, whereas Athanasius insisted that the Father and the Son are identical in substance and that the Divinity is manifested in the Trinity, God the Father, God the Son (Christ), and God the Holy Ghost. The council decided in favor of Athanasius, whose doctrine of the divinity of Christ became the orthodox one. From that time on, all deviations from the orthodox were increasingly persecuted as a danger to the church, to the state, and to morality.

Despite its reliance upon Greek philosophy, Christian theology departed from the Greek emphasis on reason by insisting upon the moral, ethical, and emotional role of faith as against the ability of human intelligence alone to achieve happiness. It further established the realm of true happiness to be in the future life of the "other" world of spirit rather than in the present life of this world of matter and things. The primary motive for good conduct was now not in human reason or in the welfare of human society but lay in the strength and authority that comes from reliance upon God and belief in the justice and peace of the next world. As moral authority thus was changing its center of gravity, the classical tradition of ancient Greece and Rome was giving way to the Christian tradition of the Middle Ages.

The Uses of Intelligence

During the Republic the most outstanding formulation of the role of intelligence in human affairs was made by Cicero. In general, Cicero argued that knowledge should be viewed as a practical guide to action in the affairs of public and private life. Following the lead of Isocrates, Cicero centered his interest in the orator as the best type of public figure, maintaining that the good orator must have a broad general education, a knowledge of the whole range of liberal arts, and a philosophical background in order to make sound decisions and to guide others in arriving at wise practical judgments. Knowledge was not to be sought simply for its own sake. The "more humane letters" were viewed not as a frosting of "culture" but as a means of putting intelligence to work at the job of solving the problems of this world.

Quintilian in the Early Empire followed in Cicero's footsteps in his interest in human reason as the supreme guide to conduct. He insisted that the principles of moral conduct should rest not with the philosophers but with the orators, who ought to be recognized as the leaders of public policy. Quintilian's antagonism toward the philosophers of his day revealed that he felt that philosophy was forsaking important everyday concerns for flights into the nonpractical world of spiritual affairs. The sweep of political, economic, and religious events in the Empire, however, was against Quintilian. His voice was less and less heeded until rediscovered in the time of the Renaissance thirteen centuries later.

The trend was in favor of the philosophers, Stoics, Epicureans, and Neoplatonists, all of whom became less and less interested in the public and practical affairs of the community and the Empire. Stoicism lost its early interest in the affairs of the state, became indifferent to the ordinary business of life, and held that the principal use of reason was to attain a perfect equilibrium of the soul. Epicureanism played down rationalism as a guide to the improvement of conduct and gave itself up to enjoyment of the incidentals of life. Neoplatonism, especially in the hands of Plotinus, glorified the mystical and spiritual powers of the soul as the guide to conduct. Thus the Roman philosophies took a religious turn and dropped the original rationalistic emphasis of Greek and Republican times.

Christianity completed the process by making human reason and intelligence an instrument for the explanation and justification of religious doctrine rather than the ultimate resource for human beings as a guide to their conduct. For example, St. Augustine insisted that reason is given to man by God in order that man may comprehend all things, including God Himself. Reason is the eye of the soul, by which man is enabled to see truth directly without reliance upon the senses. Wisdom is the highest truth, and wisdom is God. True philosophy is therefore true religion, and both strive for the same eternal truth. St. Augustine followed Plato's idealism in believing that truth, knowledge, goodness, and beauty are eternal, permanent, and unchanging. They constitute the will of God and thus are given to man as innate ideas. Although faith is possible only to a person endowed with reason, yet faith is superior to reason. Chronologically, faith precedes reason; in order to understand a thing we must first believe in it.

With these arguments, human intelligence and human reason were made to serve the cause of religious faith and belief. When St. Augustine made reason subservient to theology, he set the pattern for Christian thought until the Scholastic battles of the Middle Ages. Likewise, the long struggle between rationalism and empiricism that had arisen in Plato's time turned in favor of a religious rationalism. The empirical point of view with its reliance upon sense experience as the source of knowledge and upon human intelligence as the guide to human conduct was kept in abeyance, save for exceptions to be noted later, until the time of the Renaissance.

The Role of the Arts and Sciences

The Rise and Decline of Scholarship. The cycle of intellectual life in Roman times, as just described, can be further illustrated in the development of the various bodies of organized knowledge. Three fairly well-defined periods of development seem to stand out. The first period, which consisted of the third, second, and first centuries B.C., may be called the Hellenistic-Republican period. During this time much creative work was done in Greek science and mathematics, especially in the eastern part of the Mediterranean world, with centers at Alexandria, Rhodes, Pergamum, and Antioch. In the field of language arts, literature, and philosophy the Greek scholars of the East were beginning to codify and systematize the bodies of knowledge that have come down to us as grammar, rhetoric, and logic. Meanwhile, the Latin authors of the West were beginning to assimilate for their own uses the great creative products of Greek literature and philosophy.

The second period, which covered the first century B.C. and the first and second centuries A.D., may be called the Early Imperial period. During this time the creativeness of Greek thought in the East lost its force in philosophy and literature as well as in science and mathematics, and the emphasis on systematizing and reworking older materials remained strong. Meanwhile, creativeness in literature and the language arts shifted to the Latin writers of the West, and in turn the Western world began to assimilate the results of Greek science and mathematics of the Hellenistic period.

The third period, which lasted roughly during the third, fourth, and fifth centuries A.D., may be called the Later Imperial period. During this time scholarship in both the Greek and the Latin worlds lost its creativeness in nearly all fields and turned almost wholly to editing and digesting the knowledge that had been codified and systematized in the earlier periods. It was almost as though the Later Imperial authors saw hard times ahead and eagerly sought to reduce scholarship to the compact form of small compendiums, so that it might weather the rigors of the intellectual depressions to come. Only in the field of religious thought and theology was the creative spirit alive in the Eastern and Western world as the church Fathers sought to reconcile Greek philosophy with the doctrines of Christianity. Much systematizing and editing were inherent in this process.

Rome Formulated the Seven Liberal Arts. One of the best illustrations of the course of intellectual thought in the three periods just mentioned is the development of the liberal arts as they were drawn from Greek sources, modified by the Latin authors, and made ready to be passed on to the Middle Ages. As we have seen, the liberal arts appropriate to the "free man" of Greece were more or less commonly regarded as including, on the elementary level, grammar, gymnastics, music, and sometimes drawing, and on the advanced level, logic, rhetoric, philosophy, arithmetic, geometry, astronomy, and musical harmony.

Meanwhile, in the West, the Latin scholars had begun to draw upon the Greek studies and to proclaim the values of the liberal arts. The work of Varro in the first century B.C. was outstanding. He sought to establish nine of the Greek studies as the necessary equipment of the liberally educated man. He wrote treatises on the following: grammar, rhetoric, logic, arithmetic, geometry, astronomy, music, architecture, and medicine. Interestingly enough, he dropped gymnastics and drawing from the usual Greek curriculum and added architecture and medicine. Varro's selections have been explained on the theory that he was attempting to carry over into Latin education only those phases of Greek knowledge in which Greece was superior to Rome.

Inasmuch as he did not include all the fields of knowledge developed systematically by the Greeks, Varro apparently had concluded that Greece was not superior to Rome in agriculture, mechanics, and engineering. Furthermore, he apparently could find no *science* in the fine arts of painting, drawing, and sculpture, but he could justify architecture and medicine, as well as the other seven, on the basis that they had been developed systematically to such a degree that they could be handed down from teacher to student and taught to others. Thus, in Varro's compendium of the liberal arts, two principles of selection were at work, namely: (1) Liberal arts were confined to Greek studies; (2) liberal arts were confined to what Varro believed were Greek scientific studies, that is, bodies of organized and systematic knowledge.

In the Later Imperial period the number of liberal arts was fixed at seven. This was done by Martianus Capella. It is interesting to note, as revealing the intellectual temper of the times, why it was that Capella in the late fourth century A.D. turned to Varro's list of nine liberal arts and then cut them down to seven. In his influential allegorical compendium called the *Marriage of Philology and Mercury*, Capella described a heavenly wedding in which the seven liberal arts acted as bridesmaids. He named grammar, rhetoric, logic, arithmetic, geometry, astronomy, and music. His justification for reducing the number to seven was that he wanted to keep only those arts that would interest a group of celestial and spiritual beings. He left out medicine, because celestial beings had no earthly ills, and he left out architecture, because spiritual beings needed no physical habitation. In other words, he did not include the physical or mechanical sciences, because they were so closely related to material and mundane interests that they were not suitable for spiritual, intellectual, and therefore liberal beings. Music could stay in the list because it was primarily a "pure science" and therefore fit for "supermundane" interests. Thus, a third principle of selection was at work, namely, Capella's interest in spiritual and intellectual rather than in practical or physical things.

Here, then, by the end of the fourth century was a compendium of knowledge that did not comprise the entire range of subjects known to Greece or Rome but that did eventually fix the bounds of the medieval curriculum of the liberal arts. The liberal arts had been formalized and condensed from the Greek heritage into small literary packets of knowledge. They had come to be identified with those systematic studies of Greece which had been translated into Latin and which were thought to be suitable to spiritual and intellectual affairs rather than to material affairs. These are some of the historical reasons why a "liberal education" in its traditional form has so often been exclusively linguistic, literary, and mathematical in content and has so often been opposed to a "useful" or "practical" education.

It should be noted further that Capella was not a Christian but represented the Later Imperial interest in otherworldly affairs, a spirit highly appropriate to the intellectual climate in which Christian theology and doctrine were being formulated. Many of the church Fathers in the East had favored Greek philosophy and literature as suitable for study by Christian scholars. In the West, however, the story was different; most of the Latin Fathers turned against the pagan studies. Among these were Tertullian, St. Jerome, St. Augustine, and St. Gregory the Great. In general, however, it was difficult even for these men to divorce themselves completely from the cultural and intellectual heritage of the times in which they lived. In the fourth century, before his conversion, St. Augustine himself had written treatises on the values of six of the seven liberal arts. His influence was so strong that despite his later antipathy for pagan studies he really helped to prepare the way for assimilation by the church of the secular liberal arts, a process completed by Cassiodorus in the sixth century. By that time the pagan schools had so declined and the church had become so victorious that church leaders had no longer any cause to fear the pagan liberal arts. In any case, they had been so transformed in spirit and content that they had become appropriate to the medieval outlook of religious otherworldliness.

The Trivium: Grammar, Rhetoric, and Logic. In the Hellenistic-Republican period the term "grammar" had a far wider meaning than in modern times. It meant not only the study of syntax, syllables, parts of speech, declensions, and conjugations but also the study of poetry and literature in general. Countless Greek grammarians in the third and second centuries B.C. made of Greek grammar a logical and systematic body of knowledge through their work in compiling word lists, dictionaries, and reference books. Latin grammarians then began to assimilate and copy into Latin the work of the Greek grammarians in order to build up an organized study of Latin grammar.

Perhaps the most influential grammar of all time was the *Ars grammatica minor* written by Aelius Donatus in the fourth century A.D. It is a short description of the eight parts of speech, elaborating the definition and characteristics of each in question-and-answer form. Another most influential grammar, that of Priscian, is a much longer and more advanced work containing more than 250 quotations from many different Greek and Latin authors, as well as material on syntax, conjugations, and declensions. The grammars of these men and scores of others went through many editions. They were copied, edited, and commented upon in turn by generations of other grammarians. As the Middle Ages approached, the content of grammar came to be more and more condensed into small digests for use as textbooks in the schools rather than as tools for scholarly research.

Much the same cycle of events took place in the field of literature. In the Hellenistic-Republican period the peak of creative production in Greek literature had passed, but the creation of a native Latin literature was beginning. In giving creative form to Latin prose, Cicero was greatly influenced by Greek philosophy, rhetoric, and literature. His development of a refined style, formal diction, and literary allusions made his letters and orations the most popular prose examples of Latin style for centuries.

In the Early Imperial period Latin poetry reached its creative peak in the works of Vergil and Horace. Vergil's *Aeneid* stands as the greatest epic poem of Roman national life and became the textbook for countless generations of students of Latin as well as a model of the sweep and power of Latin verse. A master of Latin lyric form, Horace criticized from the viewpoint of the sophisticated artist the life and times of Augustan Rome. Soon, however, Latin literature became more romantic in form and content; it turned to escape, imagination, overcultivated refinement, mysticism, or bombast in place of the classic emphasis upon simplicity, restraint, and austerity.

The outstanding literary achievement of the Later Imperial period was the Latin Vulgate of Jerome who translated the Old Testament directly from the Hebrew into the everyday Latin of the fourth century.

Most of the Later Imperial writers compiled textbooks, digests, and collections of quotations, many of which were used as readers to aid in the learning of Latin. Perhaps the most famous and influential of these readers was the book of rhymed couplets written by the fourth-century Stoic, Cato; his *Distichs* was studied for centuries down to the time of Benjamin Franklin. Such textbooks became the provender on which the Middle Ages were nourished. They contained much of the heritage of Greek and Latin literature in a predigested form, but although they sustained life they provided scant nourishment.

Rhetoric, as one of the language arts dealing principally with the study of the art of expressive speech, both oral and written, went through an interesting course of development. In Hellenistic-Republican times it was looked upon as the highest of the studies that the aspiring Roman youth could follow. This is revealed in the rhetorical writings of Cicero, who leaned upon Aristotle and Isocrates for his inspiration and reached the height of Latin rhetoric in style and content. In the Early Empire Quintilian followed in his footsteps and called for a return to the classic ideals of rhetoric as exemplified by Cicero. As the Imperial period progressed, however, there was less and less practical outlet for the arts of rhetoric and oratory, for public discussion no longer had the determining effect upon public policy that it had in the Senate and Assembly of Republican Rome. Rhetoric came to be increasingly a dilettante exercise in formal language for the benefit of a wealthy, leisured, and sophisticated class. The study of rhetoric changed from a broad preparation for public service to a narrow study of the details and techniques of delivering formal speeches and orations.

What had been the art of persuasion to the Greeks and to Cicero and Quintilian became an artificial elegance of language without conviction or strong feeling. The oration, which had been an important instrument for deliberation and decision, became an elaborate discourse to be delivered on some special occasion such as a funeral, anniversary, or ceremony when "celebration" was important but not decision. Whereas hundreds of textbook editions were being prepared in grammar, there were relatively few such books on rhetoric written in the Later Imperial period. The best known were those of Capella and St. Augustine. Cicero and Quintilian were always the models, but their original works were seldom used in full. These small handbooks and manuals illustrate the way in which the creative literary heritage of Rome was wrapped up in small packages for the use of scholars and students in the Middle Ages.

One of the most important phases of the transition in Roman intellectual history was the change that took place in the meaning of and regard for philosophy. To Plato and Aristotle philosophy had been the highest form of study dealing with the ultimate reality and nature of things. Philosophy fell into disrepute in the Early Empire, but by the end of Roman times it had emerged again, not as one of the liberal arts and not as the highest study of all, but as the handmaiden of theology.

Logic, meanwhile, became firmly established as one of the seven liberal arts, gradually losing its identification with philosophy as a whole. Among those who helped to pass on Aristotle's logic, which was the basis of all medieval logic, was Porphyry, a Neoplatonist of the third century A.D., who wrote a textbook in which he edited Aristotle's logical works and added an introduction of his own. This book was handed down through many commentaries and editions for centuries. Although Porphyry was interested in the whole range of metaphysical and philosophical thought, he specifically ruled out such problems as beyond the scope of logic. This distinction apparently suited Capella and St. Augustine, who wrote the other two notable texts on logic, both of which became important handbooks during the Middle Ages. These books treated of the definitions of words and propositions and the use of the syllogism. Logic came to take its place along with grammar and rhetoric as one of the three elementary liberal arts, the so-called "trivium" of the medieval liberal arts.

The Quadrivium. The quadrivium, or four higher liberal arts, came to include arithmetic, geometry, astronomy, and music, all conceived as basically mathematical studies. Despite the advances made in the field of arithmetic by Hellenistic scholars at Alexandria, little use was made of these developments in the liberal arts and thus little was known of them in medieval times. Capella's very brief chapter on arithmetic made much of the mystical significance and properties of numbers but gave virtually no attention to the problems of computation. Arithmetic thus became, not a practical means for solving useful problems as it had been among Egyptians and earlier Greek scholars, but an intellectualized and theoretical exercise in mysticism.

Geometry followed a similar decline. The great advances made in geometry in Hellenistic-Republican times in the hands of Euclid and others were largely discarded in the Later Imperial period. In this way geometry lost much of its mathematical character, reverted more or less to the literal meaning of the word, measurement of the earth, and thus became principally geographic in character. As a result, the great achievements of Hellenistic geometry were scarcely known to western Europe until the tenth and eleventh centuries.

The story of astronomy was again similar. The Hellenistic scholars of the East had made enormous advances, as we have noted earlier. Much of this knowledge seems to have escaped the attention of the Early Imperial astronomers, who turned to Aristotle's work *On the Heavens* with its geocentric theories that the earth was the center of the universe. Ptolemy in the second century A.D. brought together much of the ancient information on astronomy and wrote a book that was enormously influential in all western Europe, for its principles were passed on to the Middle Ages through the medium of Capella. These Ptolemaic doctrines prevailed until the reassertion of the heliocentric theory by Copernicus in the sixteenth century.

In Greek life music had been joined with poetry and dancing as a part of the moral, civic, and religious expression of the times. In Hellenistic-Republican times, however, music as a medium of instruction became separated from playing, singing, and dancing and became identified with theoretical and mathematical exercises. Pythagoras and Plato had emphasized the mathematical properties of music, and Plato had disparaged the practical musician as a mere practitioner. It was this latter conception of music that was selected by Roman writers and exalted as early as the time of Cicero. Hence it is no wonder that Capella followed their mathematical and theoretical interests when he came to define music as one of the liberal arts. The Roman world dropped the Greeks' functional use of music in actual life but retained the Greek theory of music with its tetrachordal scale and lack of harmony. On the practical side, church music became more creative than the theoretical study of music based on Greek theory. It was not until the Middle Ages broke away from the "liberal arts" conception of music as mathematics that the modern developments of music were possible.

Other Sciences and Arts. Mention has already been made of the creativeness of the Hellenistic scholars in the fields of physical and natural science. In the Later Imperial period investigations in science fell off in originality and relied principally upon borrowing from former works, reminiscent and credulous and much concerned with miracles and revelations. Because science dealt with the natural and physical phenomena of the changing world men live in, it was not considered as one of the liberal arts, which were to be devoted to the unchanging and spiritual realm of the intellect. Plato's idealism had won its point over Aristotle's emphasis on science and was to maintain this superiority until the thirteenth century.

The science of medicine was advanced considerably during the Hellenistic-Republican period both in the East and in the West. At Alexandria and other Hellenistic centers, Greek physicians continued their investigations in anatomy, physiology, and dissection to the extent that some fundamental conceptions were established concerning the brain's relationship to the nervous system, the character of veins and arteries, and the processes of digestion and reproduction. The fact that Varro included medicine as one of the liberal arts indicates that he believed that the Greek science of medicine had been greatly developed and was worthy of a high place in Roman estimation. The most famous physician of all was Galen, whose books written in the second century A.D. were used extensively throughout the Middle Ages until the development of modern medicine in the sixteenth and seventeenth centuries.

In the fields of engineering and architecture Rome made great strides in respect to both technical perfection and artistic quality. Public buildings, aqueducts, roads, bridges, and city planning were developed on a grander scale than the world had known up to that time. In the Hellenistic-Republican period, the engineering and architectural forms of Greece were brought to Rome, and Rome became the architectural center of the world during the Early Imperial period. In the Later Imperial period a decline may be noted in Roman architecture, little originality being displayed except in the building of Christian churches. The technical skills of the stonemason had apparently deteriorated to the extent that the achievements of the Augustan Era were no longer possible.

In general, the development of sculpture, painting, and the crafts followed along with that of architecture. Borrowing from the Greek models, Roman sculpture became highly realistic in style and was characterized by massiveness and grandeur. Creativeness and originality seem to have lasted longer in painting, portraiture, and sculpture than in architecture or in the intellectual fields, but by the Later Empire sculpture and painting were losing detail and individuality and were substituting size, weight, and garish color. The arts of sculpture and painting remained "nonliberal" arts largely because of their close connection with craftsmanship and artisanship.

Law. Among the contributions to western Europe made by Rome the influence of Roman law stands very high. The judicial system, the codi-

fying of the civil law, and the imperial system of governmental administration proved to be working models for other times and places. The
conception of one unified state ruling the world captured men's minds for
centuries and found a counterpart in the ideals of the Christian Church
and the Holy Roman Empire of later periods.

The notion that law should be based upon reason rather than simply
upon precedent began to be accepted during the Republican period, and
much attention was given to creating new legal arrangements to keep
pace with the expansion of Rome. During the Early Imperial period the
legal theory that the Empire was a vast federation of self-governing towns
and provinces overlaid by the central government at Rome gave a large
share of self-government to the cities and municipalities. This was most
important in the Middle Ages, when the Italian cities began to assert their
rights of independence against the feudal nobility and invoked the Roman
law for justification (see pages 162 to 163). The theory stated that the
self-governing communities should direct their own affairs, with merely
a superstructure of central government to defend the frontiers and police
the seas, but it was apparent that the emperor, through his control of
finances, taxes, jurists, and secret police, was in a position to interfere
more and more with local governments.

The codifying of the law in the Later Imperial period became an important concern to many jurists and to some of the emperors. In their
hands the Roman law received its formulation as the law of the whole
civilized world. Perhaps the most important codification was undertaken
during Justinian's rule in the East in the sixth century, when the *Corpus
Juris Civilis* was published in four parts: The "Code" comprised the cur-
rently accepted edicts and laws of the emperors that were still in force;
the "Digest" was a compilation and digest of the jurists' opinions; the
"Institutes" was a textbook for students of the law; and the "Novels"
included the new laws issued after the publishing of the "Code" up to
the time of the death of Justinian.

THE SECULAR AND THE RELIGIOUS IN EDUCATION

Conflicting Theories of Education

The Liberal Arts in Action. Cicero had the greatest influence upon
Roman educational theory during Hellenistic-Republican times. In his
book entitled *De Oratore* Cicero outlined his conception of the art of
rhetoric and oratory and indicated the kind of education he felt appropriate for the development of the orator or public leader. He insisted
that the orator must have a broad general education as a background for
the attainment of true success in his professional and public life. Only in
this way could he become a wise and judicious leader; anything short of a

broad liberal education in the studies appropriate to man would leave the
orator narrow, mean, and warped in his judgments. The conception of
the "humanities," the studies proper to humanity, is the outstanding idea
in Cicero's theory of education.

Although his enumeration of the humanities was not too specific, it
seems clear that Cicero would include grammar (which was primarily
literature), rhetoric, logic, geometry, astronomy, music, physics, history, civil law, and philosophy as the important branches of knowledge
necessary for the well-educated orator. It should be noted that these are
studies broader in scope than the seven liberal arts, which later came to
be recognized as constituting the whole of a liberal education. Even more
important, Cicero constantly stressed that the aim of such study was not
simply intellectual or spiritual exercise but usefulness in public and
private life. All the humanities were to be focused upon the art of leadership in public affairs.

Another example of the Roman ideal of maintaining a vital connection
between theory and practice is afforded by a contemporary of Cicero
in quite a different field. In his works on architecture, Vitruvius Pollio
maintained that theory and knowledge must go hand in hand with practice and craftsmanship. For example, not only must an architect be a
good craftsman, know how to use his tools, and be proficient in his
practice, but he must also have a broad and deep acquaintance with the
basic fields of knowledge—mathematics, science (especially physics),
literature, and philosophy—and be familiar with art, music, law, and
medicine. Only in this way can an architect or engineer become a true
leader in his field. If the educators of following centuries had paid more
attention to the proposals of Vitruvius and if the movement of society
and culture had not been so much in the other direction, it is possible that
there would not have been so wide a gap between knowledge and action,
between theory and practice. Many engineering schools and other professional schools today have not yet learned the lesson that the liberal and
the technical must go together.

In Early Imperial times the most important and influential treatise
on education was written by Quintilian. In the preface to his *Institutes
of Oratory* Quintilian gave a general picture of the character of the orator
as the well-rounded man of affairs or statesman who must not be merely
an accomplished speaker. The orator's role of leadership in the formulation of public policy should be based upon a broad intellectual background, knowledge, and sound character. In Book I of the *Institutes*
Quintilian described the kind of education that should be given to
children prior to the study of rhetoric itself; in this respect his treatise
put considerable emphasis for the first time upon educational method and
procedures.

Quintilian stressed the fact that boys differ in their individual capacities and that teachers should take account of these individual differences. Recognizing that the vast majority of boys are capable of improvement, Quintilian emphasized not only individual differences but also the desirability of allowing a choice of studies in order to give the greatest opportunity for the development of special talent. The good teacher will ascertain the disposition and abilities of his pupils so as to adapt his methods to each individual. Play, games, and amusements should be used for relaxation and increased efficiency as well as to stimulate interest through competition and rewards, rather than through corporal punishment. Instruction in reading and writing can be given to very young children. Despite his emphasis on amusements and rewards, Quintilian also stressed memorizing and the use of moral admonition. Nurses, parents, and teachers of small children should be very careful of the language they use and the morals they display. In learning to read, the child should start with Greek first, on the theory that he would learn his native Latin anyway; since Greek came before and acted as a foundation for Latin, it was only natural to learn Greek first. Quintilian set a pattern in this respect that generations of educators in the Renaissance and in following centuries used to support their argument for study of a foreign language as the best way to learn one's own language.

Quintilian apparently had a well-developed conception of the social aspects of education, for he insisted that public education in the school was much to be preferred to private education with a tutor. He stressed the values of the group education that comes when boys learn together in classes; the emulation, friendships, and incitements to success thus experienced are superior to the advantages of private teaching at home. He refuted the arguments that schools hurt the morals of boys and that a teacher is likely to give unfair attention to certain individuals. Quintilian pointed out that morals are corrupted at home too and that if classes are not too large the teacher in school can give adequate attention to all pupils. In general, his arguments pointed to the modern idea that school is a society in which children learn from each other as well as from the teacher.

In the final 11 books of the *Institutes* Quintilian gave detailed descriptions of the advanced education suitable to the training of the orator. Beyond the elementary instruction just described, the boys should have a grammar school training, which should lay great emphasis upon grammar, composition, and extensive reading of all kinds of authors, including the tragic, comic, and lyric poets. In Book X, Quintilian set forth perhaps the first list of "great books" that should be included in a liberal education. In addition to the study of grammar and composition, word usages, and the art of style, and memory training, Quintilian mentioned music to help train the voice, mathematics for the methods of proof, training in elocution, and a certain amount of physical education to promote the graceful use of the body and effective use of gestures. For the most advanced training of the orator, he prescribed a thorough study of composition and declamation, reading of the prose authors, and the formal theory and practice of rhetoric, including the various types of oratory, style, delivery, figures of speech, allusions, and analogies. Reading in law, jurisprudence, and philosophy was also deemed desirable; but since Quintilian was distrustful of the philosophers, he did not stress philosophy very much. Quintilian's views on education are important not only for what they reveal concerning the highest ideal of Roman education but also because the *Institutes* was rediscovered during the Renaissance, when it became virtually the educational bible for generations of Humanist educators.

No other writer in the Imperial period approached Quintilian in the scope or detail of his proposals for education. The trend after his time was away from the close relation between education and society that Quintilian had proposed. An occasional voice arose in protest against educational isolationism, notably that of Seneca, who complained, "We learn our lessons, not for life, but for the schools." Similarly, Tacitus wrote with approval and nostalgia of the education that Cicero had gained by studying a wide range of liberal arts, mathematics, philosophy, and science, topped off by practical apprenticeship to a jurist. Likewise, Galen, the last of the great Greek scientists, urged that the writings of the classic authors should be constantly tested and verified by observations of nature. But most writers in the first and second centuries A.D. were beginning to glorify, as did Plutarch, the training of the memory, strict mental discipline, and inculcation of good moral habits through precept and practice. The way was being paved for the medieval Christian outlook in educational theory.

The Ascetic Ideal of the Church Fathers. Although many of the Greek Fathers of the East (such as Clement and Origen) had approved the study of secular authors and philosophers for Christian youth, the trend in the third and fouth centuries was in the other direction. The Latin Fathers of the West, as mentioned earlier, had always been less favorably inclined toward Greek learning. Tertullian was one of the most outspoken in his condemnation of the Greek philosophers; his attitude doubtless stemmed from his conception that human nature is essentially sinful and human reason as expressed in Greek philosophy not to be trusted. St. Augustine and St. Jerome also renounced in their later years their earlier enthusiasm for secular learning, and Gregory the Great despised Greek grammar and rhetoric. In general, the effect of the Western Christian Fathers upon educational theory was to deny the

values of the material and practical affairs of life and to discount the values
of the Greek intellectual life. This left only the values of a strictly moral
and disciplined mental life as contributory to spiritual salvation.

Something of an exception to this generalization is to be found in the
educational writings of St. Chrysostom in the fourth century A.D. He
urged parents and teachers to use the stars, the flowers, and the fields
as objects of instruction, but he tempered this with the injunction that
although the senses are the gates of the soul they must be carefully
guarded by constant moral precepts and memorizing of religious poetry.
Clement of Alexandria went much further in advocating physical exercise
for the attainment of health and music for relaxation, but Clement and
St. Chrysostom were both Greeks and thus reflected the secular Greek
ideal of well-rounded personality even though they were good Christians.
By and large, the educational theories of the Western church Fathers
showed no such breadth of view.

St. Ambrose, St. Augustine, and St. Jerome were much more influential
than the Eastern Fathers in setting the pattern and tone for Christian education in western Europe for centuries to come. In their view, the ascetic
ideal became most important as a means of subjugating the desires of the
body and elevating the soul. The life of sense experience came to be
considered evil; thus physical education and gymnastics were worse than
useless, for the more they helped to develop the body, the more they
interfered with progress toward salvation. Secular music was likewise
viewed as harmful because it diverted the emotions from religious affairs,
whereas church music as represented by the Ambrosian chant was desirable because it directed the emotions into the proper religious channels.

Secular learning was to be shunned in that it elevated human reason
improperly above religious faith. The child's nature was evil and not
to be trusted. The child must be subjected to constant supervision and, if
necessary, to severe discipline in order to achieve the proper measure of
obedience and submissiveness. Particularly with reference to the education of girls, retirement, seclusion, and careful supervision were universally favored, the discipline of the nunnery admired, and the life of
perpetual virginity glorified. Thus, when the Western Christian Fathers
rejected gymnastics, music, rhetoric, and secular philosophy and when
they denied the value of education as preparation for an active life in
practical affairs, they narrowed the Greco-Roman educational ideal to
the religious studies and liberal arts deemed suitable to Christian doctrine.

The Program of the Schools

Secular Elementary Schools. When Rome began to import Greek educational ideas during the Republican era, it was the Greek literary school
of the grammatist that was copied, not the school of music or of gym-

nastics. Roman elementary schools made paramount the aim of literacy and paid little or no attention to the Greek ideal of a well-rounded individual, versed in music and physically well developed. Roman elementary schooling simply stressed the ability to read and to write and to count. Just why the accent should have been put upon the three R's to the exclusion of music and gymnastics is not clear, but some reasons may be advanced. The fact that the Latin language was just taking literary form during the Early Republican period made it only natural that the new language should be stressed in the elementary schools. Another factor may be that when Rome began to be interested in Greek education in the third and second centuries B.C. the Hellenistic schools of Greece and of the East had already begun to drop their attention to music and gymnastics and to glorify the intellectual ideals even at the earliest levels of education. It has further been claimed that the early Roman people were cold to the values of music and physical development in much the same way as the American pioneers found little time for such accomplishments when a wilderness continent was to be won by so much hard physical work that interest in more than the rudiments of literacy was lacking.

In any case, the lot of the elementary pupil in Rome was apparently a hard one. Most of the literary and pictorial references to elementary schools attest to strenuous discipline and corporal punishment as integral parts of the learning process. Learning to read was a matter of memorizing the letters of the alphabet, constructing syllables, learning the meanings of individual words, and studying sentence structure. Writing was a matter of copying down the dictated statements of the teacher into copybooks or on wax tablets. The materials used were, at first, such books as the Latin translation of the *Odyssey* and Vergil's *Aeneid*, but in the Imperial period grammar textbooks such as that of Donatus began to replace actual literary works. Pupils then simply copied down definitions and grammar rules and memorized them. Likewise, they copied reading materials taken from such readers as Cato's *Distichs*, learning the prudential maxims concerning morality, caution, self-control, courage, moderation, and shrewd adaptation to the fortunes of life. Counting, whether on fingers, or the abacus, or with bags of stones or pebbles, was an important part of the three R's; arithmetic was probably emphasized because of the necessity of keeping business and household accounts in the growing complexities of a commercial and mercantile society. Memorizing, drill, and discipline seem to have been the major features of the Roman educational method.

Secular Secondary Schools. The Latin grammar school held a large place in the education of the well-to-do Roman youth and has left its mark upon generations of European and American youth down to the present day. Like elementary education, and for much the same reasons,

Roman secondary education was more narrowly conceived than that of the Greeks, lacking the Greek interest in gymnastics. It is interesting, too, that the first secondary schools in Rome were foreign-language schools; the native Latin had a long struggle before it could pretend to be as valuable an educational experience for Latin youth as was claimed for the Greek language. From Roman times to the present nearly every European country has gone through the same experience, and the parallel in America is striking. The first secondary school among English-speaking peoples in the American colonies was a foreign-language school in the form of the Latin grammar school. The belief that someone else's language is better than one's own for educative purposes has had a long tradition. Only the Greeks did not believe it; they felt at home with their own language.

In its best days, the school of the *grammaticus* in Rome was a liberating and effective instrument of education, conceiving of grammar so broadly that it included the great literature of Greece and Rome. Under farseeing teachers the study of grammar could include much of what we today would call history, ethics, and the social studies as well as poetry, grammar, composition, and literary criticism. More often, however, it became a routine study of words, phonetics, conjugations and declensions, paraphrasing, memorizing, repetition, dictation of sentences, and explanation of allusions. The best grammar schools in the Early Empire began to include in their curriculum the whole round of liberal arts as defined by Cicero and Quintilian. But in the declining days of the Later Empire the grammar schools repeated the rules of the professional grammarians, emphasized quotations and selections from the great authors instead of the literary works themselves, and handed down such allegorical and intellectualized pabulum as Capella's digest of the liberal arts.

Secular Higher Schools. The most outstanding of the higher schools in Rome were the rhetorical schools established for the wellborn Roman youth who was destined for a career of politics and public service. Interestingly enough, the rhetorical schools were not very common until after the Republic had died and the real professional outlet for the schools had largely vanished. They were patterned in their best days on the ideals of Cicero as promulgated by Quintilian in the first century A.D. In the conception of such leaders, the rhetorical school was the culmination of training for the all-round development of the public orator and statesman. But by the time the rhetorical schools were well established the opportunity for guiding the destinies of the state through public oratory and statesmanship had practically disappeared with the passing of the Republic. The rhetorical school's usefulness had virtually been outlived before it began to function.

In the hands of a Quintilian the rhetorical school was much more than simply the study and practice of rhetoric. Its course of study was designed to include all the major fields of knowledge as a means of developing a person of broad understanding and good practical judgment. Under the rhetoricians of the Later Empire the study of rhetoric became an end in itself, living in the dead past and out of touch with the contemporary currents of life. The study of oratory, when there was no longer an outlet for it in practical life, turned its attention from subject matter to correct and elegant expression.

Other institutions of advanced education maintained a more or less effective life throughout the Empire. In Rome the Athenaeum as well as other institutes and libraries became centers for research and study in medicine, architecture, engineering, law, rhetoric, and literature. In the East the Athenian schools of philosophy and rhetoric maintained themselves over the centuries, and the museums, libraries, and schools at Alexandria, Pergamum, Antioch, Rhodes, and elsewhere provided centers where scholars and students could gather together and explore a wide range of fields, including law, medicine, architecture, engineering, mathematics, language, literature, philosophy, and ultimately religion. In these institutions, however, the creative character of education diminished in ways that have already been described.

Christian Schools. The basic outlines of the catechumenal and philosophical schools set up by the Christian Church in the Imperial period have already been suggested. The great question facing Christian educators was what attitude to take concerning secular schools and their "pagan" learning. We have noted that the answer to this question varied from time to time and from place to place. Some Christian leaders stood out strongly against secular schools and secular learning, urging Christian parents to have nothing to do with such sources of evil and paganism. Others preached moderation and told parents that children could be sent to secular schools if care were taken that they were not corrupted by the religious mythology and pagan morality contained in secular literature. Still others were not at all fearful of secular learning but included in their philosophical schools the whole round of liberal arts and philosophy as preparatory to the highest study of Christian doctrine and theology.

In general the church accepted and assimilated most of the noncontroversial elements of the secular liberal arts stripped of their pagan influences. After all, grammar, rhetoric, and logic could be taught in such a way as not to corrupt the morals of youth but even to contribute to the intellectual discipline necessary for the Christian scholar. The study of the mathematical elements of arithmetic, geometry, astronomy, and music would not be morally harmful if employed as purely intellectual exercises or as instruments for the delineation of human reason as subservient to faith. In like manner the idealistic philosophy of Plato was absorbed by church doctrine.

Two large areas of human knowledge, however, were considered to be not germane, or even harmful, to the dominantly religious concern of Christian schools. One was the field of the practical sciences of architecture, engineering, mechanics, medicine, and law. These subjects dealt with the means of controlling the physical or human environment for the betterment of life on this earth; therefore, they were, in religious terms, of much less significance than the liberal arts as defined in the foregoing pages. They consequently declined from neglect at the hands of the church during the Empire, despite the occasional books on these subjects found in church libraries and schools. The other field was that of the natural sciences and materialistic philosophies, which were deemed definitely harmful to the spiritual and idealistic philosophy accepted by the church. Thus the science of Aristotle and of the Alexandrians was not assimilated into Christian learning at this time and was therefore not passed on to western Europe through the church and its schools. Rather, it was driven into exile in Syria and Egypt, where it was later reworked and finally introduced into western Europe by the Islamic and Jewish scholars of the twelfth and thirteenth centuries. The point is that the church schools selected, reconciled, and assimilated much of the secular learning but also rejected much, which was therefore virtually sentencing it to exile from the West for centuries.

Chapter 5

THE MIDDLE AGES:
SOCIAL FOUNDATIONS OF EDUCATION

THE STRUGGLE FOR STABILITY AND ORDER

The emphasis that many historians have put upon the "decline and fall" of the Roman Empire engenders the feeling that everything went to pieces in the fourth, fifth, and sixth centuries and that there was nothing but anarchy, confusion, and hopelessness for several centuries thereafter. Although the Middle Ages had its share of cultural dislocation, it is also true that political, economic, and religious institutions were gradually shaped in such a way that life not only continued but eventually prepared the groundwork for many of the institutions and ideas that we call "modern." In general, the most difficult days were encountered in the Early Middle Ages, designated in this book as roughly from the sixth to the eleventh centuries, whereas life took on an increasingly fertile and flourishing character in the Later Middle Ages, namely, from the eleventh to the thirteenth centuries. These divisions are fairly arbitrary, but they do represent in some sense the fact that order and stability were gaining headway in the Later Middle Ages over the confusions of the Early Middle Ages.

Conflicts between Empire, Nations, and Church

Early Middle Ages (Sixth to Eleventh Centuries). As recounted in Chapter 4, the seat of the Roman Empire had been shifted from Rome to Constantinople from the fourth century on. This meant that Greece and the eastern Mediterranean became more than ever distinctly separated from western Europe in political affairs. In the West, Italy was the scene of a series of political upsets marked by the Germanic tribal invasions of Ostrogoths, Lombards, and Franks.

Meanwhile, the center of political authority began to move from Italy northward to the Frankish kingdoms located roughly in what are modern France and Germany. The many small Frankish kingdoms were gradually consolidated under the leadership of the Merovingian kings. In the eighth century Charles Martel united, organized, and cemented the Frankish kingdom and strengthened the Roman Church in Frankland with the aid of the great churchman St. Boniface. Charles Martel's son, Pepin the Short, went to the aid of the Pope against the Greek Empire and the Lombard kings. In return, the Pope made Pepin king of the Franks, and Pepin granted to the Pope a strip of land across central Italy, which later became the Papal States of Italy.

Later in the eighth century Charlemagne, son of Pepin, became king of the Franks and set out to extend the boundaries of his kingdom east to the Elbe River, north to the North Sea, and south to the Mediterranean. On Christmas Day in the year 800 Charlemagne was crowned Roman emperor by the Pope and in theory became the legitimate successor to the emperors of the ancient Roman Empire. As such, Charlemagne was the towering political figure of the Early Middle Ages and made great strides in reestablishing the authority of a strong central government over most of western Europe. In general, under the rule of Charlemagne political authority was made more effective, economic and agricultural life was improved, and religious and educational reforms were instituted. It was a period of considerable intellectual achievement.

In the ninth century the successors of Charlemagne in state, church, and family began to quarrel among themselves for control of the Empire. As a result of a long series of civil wars, the Empire was gradually split up into three large parts; the western Frankish kingdom ultimately became France, the eastern Frankish kingdom became Germany, and the rest became Italy. The central administration could not be maintained in the face of the growing strength of local aristocracies, the nobility, the churchmen, and the landowning rulers.

The Empire was further weakened by a series of invasions in the ninth and tenth centuries. The Northmen, or Vikings, swept in from the Scandinavian lands from the north; the Slavs and Magyars attacked the Empire from the east; and the Arabs, or Saracens, came over the sea from the south to harass Greece, Italy, Spain, and France. As a result, lawlessness, terror, and warfare became ever more common. Safety and political authority were to be found increasingly in the hands of a local strong man who had land, a well-fortified castle, and subordinates who would fight for him. Political authority thus became extremely decentralized, for these feudal lords were the only ones who could promise some protection against marauders, although the kings continued to exercise a nominal control.

Much of the political history of the Frankish kingdoms following the breakup of Charlemagne's empire in the ninth century was written in terms of the struggles between the kings and the nobility. The kings, who claimed power either by election or by hereditary right, constantly sought to make their powers more than nominal, whereas the nobility were eager to keep one ruler from becoming too strong. By 962 Otto I (the Great) was strong enough to conquer Italy and establish himself as head of the Holy Roman Empire, reviving the theory that he was the successor of Charlemagne and thus the legitimate heir of the Roman Empire. The name, Holy Roman Empire, shows that the church had become vastly important in the political affairs of western Europe and that the emperor was considered the guardian of the secular branch of a universal Christendom. By the end of the Early Middle Ages the Holy Roman Empire was a power to be reckoned with in European political life.

Meanwhile, a development had taken place in Arabia that eventually had great influence upon Europe. In the early seventh century Mohammed appeared as the great political and religious leader of the Arab people. Building up a strong following and a strong army, he was able to conquer most of Arabia by the time of his death in 632. When he died, strong men known as "caliphs" arose to take his place and continue the policy of conquest. Because of the weakness of the Eastern Roman Empire and the strength and fanatic fighting quality of the Arab horsemen, the caliphs were able to conquer most of the Middle East and spread their empire beyond the borders of Arabia to the Turks in the north, to India in the east, and across northern Africa to Spain and Italy in the west.

Mohammed's religion is known as Islam, and his followers, of whatever nationality, are called "Moslems." The term "Saracen" had earlier been given to the Arabs by the Greeks and Romans, but it was gradually expanded and eventually came to include all those who adopted the religious tenets of Islam, not only Arabs, but also Persians, Turks, and others who were affected by the religion and culture built up in the southern and eastern Mediterranean world from the eighth century onward.

Later Middle Ages (Eleventh to Thirteenth Centuries). From the middle of the eleventh century to the end of the thirteenth century the process of centralizing political authority in the hands of the kings continued in France and England, but less headway was made in Germany and Italy because of the complicated struggles between the emperors and the nobility on the one hand and the emperors and the Papacy on the other. In the eleventh and twelfth centuries, the Papacy gradually won more and more power in its contest with the Empire (the investiture struggle). This struggle was carried on into the thirteenth century, particularly between Pope Innocent III and Emperor Frederick II. Innocent III was perhaps the greatest medieval Pope, exerting more secular power than any other Pope before or after his time. He believed that Christendom should be a great unified commonwealth with the Pope at the head, inspiring governments everywhere to righteousness. In his view, the Pope was clearly superior to secular authorities; he was successor of Peter and feudal overlord of the kings. Innocent III joined with the Lombard cities of northern Italy against Frederick II, after whose death the Empire was so weakened that the Papacy remained the greatest single political power in Europe in the thirteenth century. The struggle had kept Germany and Italy so divided within themselves that strong centralized governments could not be established. Until the nineteenth and twentieth centuries these countries were never unified as were France and England.

In contrast to the essentially decentralized state of affairs in Germany and Italy, the monarchies in France and England became ever more centralized and powerful. Outstanding among the French kings who made such gains were Philip II (Augustus), who conquered many of the lands in France still claimed by the Norman kings of England; Louis IX (St. Louis), who gave France a long period of peace and improved the courts of law throughout the land; and Philip IV (the Fair), under whose rule the States-General began to take shape, giving the nobility and merchant classes more voice in the government.

The kings of England likewise made headway in unifying their country. Beginning with William the Conqueror, the Norman rule established a highly centralized and effective central government; yet when King John was forced to sign the Magna Charta in 1215, the English nobility gave notice that they did not intend to be brought under the king's rule without a struggle. Under Henry III the great council was expanded to include representatives from the principal towns as well as members of the nobility. Although the great council was intended simply to approve the acts of the king, the constitutional forms were being established out of which grew the English parliamentary government. At the end of the thirteenth century, under Edward I, representatives of the middle classes were admitted, and shape was being given to the House of Commons.

Social Institutions Based upon Class Distinctions

Feudalism. The foregoing section on medieval political institutions may give a one-sided conception of medieval political life unless it is understood that a complicated framework of personal and landowning relationships supported all political arrangements. This whole complex of relationships, which came to be known as "feudalism," gained increasing strength with the breakup of Charlemagne's empire. The roots of feudalism went back to at least two ancient sources, which gave form to two types of personal relationships known as feudal tenure and servile tenure. Technically speaking, feudal tenure, the relationship between two persons of noble birth, the overlord and his vassal, probably had its basis in the customs of the Germanic tribes in which a free man would bind himself to obey a leader or king; servile tenure, the relationship between a noble and an unfree peasant or serf, had its roots in the latter days of the

Roman Empire, when agricultural workers were forced by the Roman emperors to remain on the land and work for the owner.

In theory, the king was the chief overlord, and all nobles owed allegiance to him; but, as has been noted, the nobles did not often pay this respect unless they were forced to do so by strong methods. In France and England the kings were able to command this loyalty earlier than in Germany, where many strong nobles were able to prevent for a long time the emperor and kings from becoming too strong. The church was involved in these feudal relationships, for monasteries and churches owned much land and gradually acquired more until the church is said to have owned as much as one-third of the land of Europe in the Later Middle Ages.

A person of lower class who owned no land and was not able to fight on horseback received servile tenure. In return for protection, he worked in the fields or on the roads or fought as a foot soldier in the wars. The serf, or villein, was an unfree tenant, bound to the land assigned to him, the produce of which he had to divide with the lord. The serf also usually worked a share of his time on the lord's demesne land, all the produce from which went to the lord. Once freedom was lost, by the hereditary nature of feudalism, the serf's descendants were born serfs, bound to the soil.

Thus, rigid class distinctions grew up in Europe as a result of feudal arrangements. It became very difficult to rise out of the class one was born into. The church and the nobility made up the aristocratic upper classes, the first and second estates, and the lower classes made up all the rest of the people, most of whom were unfree serfs. In the Later Middle Ages the growth of commerce and the rise of towns made possible the appearance of a middle class with rights above those of the unfree serfs and below those of the aristocracy. The middle classes of merchants, traders, and craftsmen became the nucleus of the third estate.

On its positive side, feudalism bequeathed to modern Europe an emphasis upon political contract and reciprocity of obligations. The king could command obedience only so long as he fulfilled the terms of the contract. This was the focal point of the struggles between the nobles and the kings. On the negative side, Europe was saddled with an entrenched and hereditary aristocratic class cut off from the common people by distinctions that marked all aspects of life, including educational opportunity. In this respect, America has had less class stratification than most of Europe, for it has had no entrenched feudal nobility.

The Revival of Economic Life

Growth of Commerce and Towns. In its earliest days, medieval economic life was almost entirely agricultural and rural. The economic unit was basically the lord's manor, which was also for a long time the political, social, religious, and educational unit. The manor was largely a self-sufficient economic unit consisting of the noble's family, the serfs' families, and artisans. In general, trade and commerce were a local affair in the Early Middle Ages.

However, trade with the East had apparently never died out completely, although it had declined greatly during the days of the Germanic invasions of the Roman Empire. As early as the tenth century a revival in East-West trade took place in which the Italian cities of Venice, Genoa, and Pisa took the lead. The Crusades gave further stimulus to trade, for the Crusaders relied upon the fleets, sea routes, and knowledge of the traders. In the twelfth and thirteenth centuries a great upswing in commerce occurred as the wares from the East were brought to the Italian cities and then carried by caravan or river routes into the rest of Europe and distributed at the fairs and market places. Traders wandered in bands along the rivers, selling their goods and sometimes settling on the outskirts of a castle or monastery. Being free men, foreigners, or strangers, they were not bound to the local lord or bishop.

As traders began to gather at advantageous spots, town life became ever more important. The centers were likely to be on the sites of old Roman cities, near monasteries or castles, or near a river crossing or bridge, wherever people could gather conveniently for the markets. At first, of course, the local noble or bishop laid claim to the towns, but soon the traders and townspeople organized themselves into town governments to break the control of the feudal lords and win their freedom.

In the twelfth and thirteenth centuries towns grew rapidly in number and in size in all parts of western Europe. The growth of towns created greater demands for agricultural products, and these demands resulted in an increase in the amount of land under cultivation; forests were cut down, swamps drained, and agricultural techniques improved through the use of fertilizer and crop rotation. As a result, the population of Europe increased so rapidly that it is estimated that by 1350 it was greater than under the Roman Empire. Freedom was increased, for if a serf could get to a town and stay for a year and a day he became free. All in all, an astonishing energy, versatility, and vitality went into the constitutions of towns in the thirteenth century. In the main, the cities were a source of increasing secularization and interest in the everyday affairs of this world.

Merchant and Craft Guilds. One of the most characteristic features of medieval life was the forming of associations among persons with common interests for their mutual protection and welfare. This grouping together for certain purposes characterized nearly all aspects of medieval life from church choirs, churchmen, scholars, knights, and soldiers to merchants and artisans of all types. In the eleventh century the growth of cities and commerce was closely connected with the formation of guilds of merchants and of craftsmen. The merchant guilds were organized as traders banded together for their travels from market to market. These bands selected their own leaders, devised regulations, formed common funds for the purchase of goods, and otherwise helped each member. The guilds soon garnered a monopoly on foreign trade and then obtained the legal right to such monopoly from the feudal lords and in turn began to exert great influence upon the development of municipal governments. From these beginnings the merchants rapidly grew in wealth and power until, as the "middle class," they made their way into the privileged company of the nobles and clergy. The winning of power by the middle class was a notable step in the march of democracy.

The craft guilds arose somewhat later for the purpose of regulating the making of goods. By the thirteenth century craft guilds had been organized in almost every city of northern Europe. The artisans organized themselves into distinctive groups according to their craft in order to protect themselves from shoddy work, low prices, and inferior workmen and to gain a monopoly of production. Working hours and conditions, quality of goods, wages and prices, and the number of tools and employees in each shop were rigidly regulated by the craft guilds and by the town authorities.

Membership in the craft guilds was strictly regulated, and workers were excluded unless they met the requirements of the guild. The master usually owned his own shop and his own tools. The attempt was ultimately made to restrict membership ever more closely, even to the point of making membership hereditary. Within the circle, however, the effort was made to provide equality for all members and to achieve stability to such an extent that advertising, cutting prices, and instituting technical improvements were considered disloyal and were thus prohibited. The guilds also had a religious and fraternal aspect. They often maintained altars in the churches or supported priests of their own. They helped the poor members, the sick, and the aged; they built roads and schools, and they even organized military defenses.

By the beginning of the sixteenth century the guild economy of restriction and protectionism began to decline in the face of the capitalistic enterprisers, who fought against the restrictions that had been laid upon prices and profits by the guilds. Even before the sixteenth century, conditions for apprentices and journeymen had become more difficult under the excessive limitations put upon entry into the guild.

The Role of the Religious Orders

Perhaps the most characteristic aspect of medieval life was the large part played by the Christian Church in nearly all fields of endeavor.

Growing rapidly during the later centuries of the Roman Empire, the church provided a large measure of security and stability in the difficult days of the Early Middle Ages, when political authorities were changing so rapidly. The church continued to grow in political and economic power throughout the Middle Ages until it reached its peak in the thirteenth century.

Monasticism. During the Early Middle Ages much of the strength of the church was to be found in the monastic institutions. The distinction between the "regular" clergy (monks who lived in monasteries according to strict rules, or *regulae*) and the "secular" clergy (priests who ministered directly to the people) became more marked. The most influential of the monastic groups was organized by St. Benedict, an Italian monk of the sixth century, who developed at Monte Cassino an elaborate scheme of regulations for the conduct of his followers. Benedictine monasticism spread over all of Italy by the seventh century and over most of Europe by the ninth century. At its peak the Benedictines maintained several thousand monasteries, from which came a great number of bishops, popes, and scholars. The rules of St. Benedict emphasized three main principles, obedience to God and the abbot, simplicity of life, and constant industry.

The manual and agricultural arts were often highly developed, for monasteries had to be completely self-supporting in the chaotic economic conditions of the early days. At a time when the secular authorities and the secular branch of the church were not yet highly organized, the

Fig. 7. Mathematician monks.

monasteries kept the religious spirit alive and did much to convert western Europe by spreading the gospel through their missionaries. They were also often the literary, artistic, intellectual, and educational centers of Europe in the Early Middle Ages. The preservation and copying of ancient manuscripts became one of their important functions, promoted under the rule of constant industry. From the twelfth century on, however, the relative importance of the monastic orders began to decline in the face of the newer emphasis upon the secular branches of the church, which resulted from the influence of the rise of towns, cathedral leadership, the universities, and the mendicant orders.

Mendicant Orders. Although the church was a great power economically and politically in the thirteenth century, many of the people were seeking a religion of the heart as well as one of authority and obedience. The retreat of the Benedictine monks to their monasteries had left the way open for a new kind of ministering to the needs of the people. This need was met by the mendicant friars, especially the Franciscans and Dominicans. St. Francis of Assisi, responding to the demands of his time, determined to go abroad among the people as Jesus had done, helping the poor, healing the sick, and preaching the gospel of love. Soon after the year 1200, St. Francis gathered about him a few apostolic followers, and in a few years he had organized several thousand members into the Friars Minor, or Minorites.

The ruling ideas of St. Francis included an ardent love for Jesus and the determination to imitate His life as closely as possible; a belief in the latent goodness of all men to be developed through the power of love; an emphasis upon poverty as the best way to serve God; an acknowledgment of the duty of joyfulness; and love of all the things of nature as creatures of God. In general, the Franciscans did great service to the church by reconciling the masses of the people through the example they set of returning to the humble and simple spirit of ancient Christianity. St. Francis has been given credit for synthesizing the best of the religious spirit of his age with the best of the secular spirit. Many believe that his influence caused artists and writers to portray Jesus in a more human aspect and thus stimulated appreciation of nature, music, poetry, and the arts.

St. Dominic, on the other hand, was a severe ascetic, noted for the rigorousness of his life and for his activities in organizing the Dominican friars. St. Dominic tried to convert heretics not by the sword but by preaching to them and showing them that clerics could live the good life in poverty. Like the Franciscans, the Dominicans abandoned the idea of monastic seclusion and went among the people, especially in the cities. Profiting from St. Dominic's genius for organization, the Dominicans soon became a powerful and centralized agency of the church. They were most eager for education and began to flood into the universities in the belief that an educated clergy was one of the best ways of combating heresy.

CIVIL AND RELIGIOUS CONTROL OF EDUCATION

Just as some of the earlier misestimates of the culture of the Middle Ages have been corrected by newer historical investigations, so must some of the earlier judgments on medieval education be revised. It has often been thought, for example, that education virtually disappeared in the Early Middle Ages, but now we know that there was an essential continuity of education following the decline of the Roman Empire and that despite a decrease in educational facilities there were many schools that continued almost without interruption. It is true that the evidence is rather meager, but it seems clear that schools not only continued to exist but became much more widespread in the Later Middle Ages than has often been recognized. Another misestimate is that all schools in the Middle Ages were conducted by the church. It now is evident that secular schools and lay teachers continued to function throughout the period.

Secular Control of Schools

Continuity of Secular Education. In Italy the currents of Roman life continued without complete interruption despite the long period of invasions and disasters that beset the Roman Empire from the fifth to the seventh or eighth century. Especially important for education was the fact that town life remained stronger in Italy than in any other part of western Europe. The process of Latinizing the new peoples who swept into Italy continued apace, slower in some periods and swifter in others. One of the principal means of assimilation of the Germanic tribes was the existence of the secular schools that had been sponsored by the later Roman emperors and the Roman towns. The Ostrogothic king, Theodoric, took steps to reestablish the town schools during his reign, and the Lombard kings and nobles did likewise as soon as conditions were a little more settled after the disruptions caused by their coming.

In the sixth century the secular schools were still at work. Although the level of instruction in Italian schools was doubtless very low in the seventh and eighth centuries, the desire for knowledge of grammar, medicine, and law was always present. The uninterrupted existence of secular schools was apparent in most of the principal towns of Italy from the eighth century to the Later Middle Ages. These secular schools, conducted both by private teachers and by public teachers supported by the towns, did not give religious instruction but emphasized grammar (including classical literature), rhetoric, law, and medicine.

Despite the intellectually low level of much of this instruction, the desire for these schools and the instruction given originated not in religious feelings but in a wish for whatever intellectual and practical advantage such studies could afford. The fact that such scholars as Paul the Deacon and Peter of Pisa could be called from Italy to the court of Charlemagne in the ninth century shows that instruction in the classics continued in Italy. Salerno was mentioned as a center of medical study as early as the ninth century, and the Emperor Lothaire I in 825 published a decree naming eight or nine Italian cities as places eligible for the establishment of higher schools to which scholars from their surrounding districts could go.

Although the evidence is sparse, there is reason for believing that some schools also continued to exist during the Early Middle Ages in northern Europe. Certainly the secular and druid schools of Ireland were for long maintained alongside the religious schools. In France the schools at Chartres probably had their origins in druid schools established by the Celts and persisted until refounded and stimulated by Charlemagne in the late eighth and early ninth centuries. Although there is not much direct evidence, the inference is that there was much more continuity of education in the Early Middle Ages than was formerly supposed. By the tenth century and following, the evidence is much clearer that fairly widespread secular education existed in many of the Italian towns. Gerbert sent to Italy for ancient manuscripts that he knew could be obtained there; in 1028 a chaplain for Emperor Conrad II contrasted the ignorance of Germans with Italy where "the entire youth is sent to sweat in the schools"; and Bishop Otto of Freising made a similar contrast between the Germans and Italians of his day in the middle of the twelfth century.

Town Control. In Italian towns, the presumption is that schools were maintained throughout the Middle Ages by municipal authorities. The study of grammar, rhetoric, law, and medicine had not died out in the Italian cities, and the continuous existence of these cities as centers of trade and commerce and intellectual activity makes it probable that these subjects, constantly useful to the merchants and scholars of Italy, were widely taught. The reconquest of parts of Italy by the Byzantine Empire meant that the continuity of Greek learning in the schools of Italy was probable. When the early struggles of the Italian cities to achieve independence from the feudal nobles began, the towns turned to their schools for the study of law as well as for the groundwork of instruction in grammar and rhetoric that was necessary for such study.

With the acceleration of trade in the tenth and eleventh centuries, attention to secular learning increased. Villani's *Chronicle* estimates that by the middle of the thirteenth century there were between 8,000 and 10,000 children learning to read in the schools of Florence; there were also six schools in which 1,000 to 1,200 children were learning arithmetic; and there were four advanced schools where 550 or 600 children were learning grammar and rhetoric. This surely must mean that schools had existed for a long time in Florence. Likewise, before 1250 in Siena several masters were employed by the republic to give instruction in grammar, medicine, and law in an effort to rival the schools at Bologna and Padua. The estimate has also been made that in this period there were some 70 teachers of reading in Milan, along with eight teachers of grammar. The inference is thus that many of the Italian cities were rivaling each other in providing schools under the control of the city authorities.

The movement for town control of schools took place somewhat later in northern Europe, just as the growth of the cities themselves occurred later. In Germany, for example, in the thirteenth century, many towns were taking steps to establish schools under the control of town authorities. Similar steps were being taken in the Netherlands and to a lesser degree in France. In general, these schools were religious in aim and Latin in content and represented not so much an effort to establish secular instruction as simply to exert civil control over religious schools. The continuity of secular schools was not nearly so clear in northern Europe as it was in Italy, but nevertheless the growth of interest in town control of education reflected the growing economic and political power of the middle classes in medieval life.

Royal Control. The most notable of the efforts by kings and emperors to establish and control schools under their jurisdiction was that of Charlemagne, whose political attempts to establish a strong centralized government were paralleled by his interest in extending education. In addition to his capitularies on political matters, Charlemagne issued many decrees on religious and educational affairs. He required the clergy to improve their ability to read and write and to raise the level of their scholarship in general so that they could write good letters, be able to calculate the date of Easter, and know the grounds of their faith. He thus required schools for teaching reading to be established where they were lacking. Abbots and priests were to be examined in respect to their educational attainments by their bishops, and corrupt manuscripts were to be corrected in monastery scriptoria. In response to this stimulus, Bishop Theodolphus of Orléans ordered his priests to see that schools were provided in every town or on every feudal manor where children might learn to read and write without payment of a fee.

In addition to this general stimulation of education, Charlemagne revived the palace school at his court, which had apparently been in existence from the time of Charles Martel, and called Alcuin from York in England to be its head. The school apparently was attended by the family of Charlemagne and other nobility of the court, adults as well as children, including Charlemagne himself on occasion. He also summoned from Ireland, Spain, and Italy as well as from England other scholars to aid in preparing a learned clergy and officialdom for church and state. In general, the efforts of Charlemagne loom large when compared with those of earlier and later times; and although he was not interested in education for all, he recognized it as a potent force for maintaining the Empire. Despite weak successors, civil war, and invasion, learning and schools never sank as low after the time of Charlemagne as they had before his time.

Under Louis the Pious the Irish scholar Clement was called to head the palace school. Under Charles the Bald, who ruled the western part of the Empire, the greatest scholar of his time, Johannes Scotus Erigena, conducted the palace school. Under this stimulus a provincial church council meeting in Paris in 824 decreed that bishops should become more attentive to fostering schools in their dioceses so that church scholars might know better the grounds of their faith. At the same time Lothaire I, who ruled the central and Italian part of the Empire, issued his decree, already mentioned, for the establishment of higher schools in several Italian cities. Imperial stimulus again had effect, for Pope Eugenius II saw to it that a church council translated Lothaire's decree into practice by directing the bishops to establish schools in their parishes and dioceses for the teaching of grammar, the liberal arts, and religious doctrine.

Meanwhile, in the German part of the Empire, the scholar Rabanus Maurus was establishing monasteries and schools so extensively that he has been called the "preceptor of Germany" in the Middle Ages. When Otto the Great revived the concept of a unified Holy Roman Empire in the late tenth century, he installed his younger brother Bruno as virtual head of all the schools in the Empire. Bruno made the palace the intellectual center, much as Alcuin had done; he stimulated learning in the monasteries and gathered together the best scholars and collected the finest manuscripts he could find. The interest of emperors in education was certainly not directed at the ordinary people, but it existed intermittently throughout the Middle Ages.

In England, royal interest in education was spasmodic, but considerable progress was made by Alfred the Great in the latter part of the ninth century. In addition to his interest in learning and scholarship, Alfred established a palace school at his court for the sons of the nobility, decreed that sons of the wealthy should attend school until they were fifteen years of age, and brought to England many scholars from the Continent.

Under the leadership of St. Dunstan, schools were established in the churches, as well as in monasteries, in order to foster and improve learning among the priesthood, for St. Dunstan did not feel that the monasteries alone could attain the goal of learning set by Alfred. In the eleventh century William the Conqueror appointed Lanfranc Archbishop of Canterbury, and St. Anselm became his successor. Both were patrons of learning in the monasteries and cathedral schools and helped to consolidate Norman institutions and ideals in England.

Among other rulers who sponsored education and scholarship the most outstanding in the Later Middle Ages was Frederick II. At his court in Sicily, the streams of Arabic, Greek, and Norman cultures joined with the Italian. Sicily thus became an important center for the translation of manuscripts and the gathering of scholars eminent in medicine as well as in the liberal arts.

In general, secular authorities were active in sponsoring education, especially in the Early Middle Ages. To be sure, they operated through the clergy. When kings gathered scholars about them, the scholars were always clerics; and when kings ordered schools to be established, the schools were established in monasteries or churches or cathedrals (with the exception of the palace schools themselves). The fact remains that the kings and emperors did occasionally prod the clergy and did stimulate educational activity in the church. However, the direct control of most schools was in the hands of the clergy; and as the political power of the Carolingian emperors declined in the ninth and tenth centuries, the Pope and the church councils began to take more and more independent action toward the encouragement of schools and education.

Church Control of Schools

The interest of the church in education, especially for the prospective clergy, continued to increase throughout the Middle Ages. For example, the council of Toledo in Spain in 531 prescribed that boys destined for the clergy should be instructed in the cathedral schools under the supervision of the bishop. A hundred years later another council at Toledo elaborated similar arrangements. However, the most important steps taken by the church in the establishment of schools during the Early Middle Ages were represented by the monastic schools. The Benedictine and the Irish monasteries, which between them covered most of western Europe and the British Isles, soon came to have schools as a regular part of their establishments. From the ninth century on, the monastic schools seem to have included instruction for boys going into the secular priesthood and for nonclerics (*externi*) as well as for those who were to become monks (*oblati*). The monastic schools dominated the educational scene of Europe from the sixth to the eleventh century.

The obligation of parish churches and cathedral churches to maintain schools was set forth time after time by church councils and by the Popes. Some of these statements that were prompted by kings and emperors have already been mentioned in the foregoing section. Then, as the church itself became more powerful, it began to take independent action. A council held in Rome in 853 decreed that elementary instruc-

Fig. 8. A cathedral school.

tion should be given in all parishes and that schools for instruction in the liberal arts should be established in all cathedrals. In 855 a council at Valens supported this view. In 908 the Bishop of Modena in appointing a new priest put as his first duty the task of maintaining a school and educating the boys under his jurisdiction. The Third Lateran Council in 1179 decreed that every cathedral church should have a master assigned not only to teach boys who wished to become clerics but also to teach without fee poor children whose parents could not afford to pay for the instruction. These and other ordinances show that the church took some steps to provide free instruction for the needy.

Thus, a wide range of schools was maintained by the various agencies of the church in the Middle Ages. The parish churches in the towns or on the manors provided elementary instruction in reading, writing, and music through their parish or song schools. The monasteries, collegiate churches, and cathedrals provided not only song schools for elementary instruction but also secondary and higher instruction in the seven liberal arts, medicine, law, and theology. To be sure, not all monasteries, parish churches, or cathedrals gave all this instruction all the time. The fact that so many church councils, popes, and bishops on so many different occasions issued orders for increased attention to schools doubtless meant that the earlier injunctions had been neglected and that new pressure had to be exerted upon a reluctant clergy. Nevertheless, the evidence of the *intent* of the church is clear.

Private Control of Schools

In the Later Middle Ages there is evidence that individuals and groups began to establish schools that were not directly responsible either to public authorities or to the church. The most important of these were the chantry schools and the guild schools. A chantry school was most likely to be established by a wealthy person who wished to endow a foundation where a priest might chant masses for the salvation of his soul after his death. At first, the teaching function of the chantry foundation may have been more or less incidental to the work of the priest, who usually gathered some boys together to form a choir for the Latin services. Later, the school often became an integral or even principal part of the original foundation. Likewise, as the guilds became important factors in town life, they often appointed a priest to teach the children of the guild members in a guild Latin school. The guild schools should not be confused with the vocational preparation provided in the apprenticeship system to be described later. Although these chantry and guild schools were not yet very common, nevertheless a pattern of private control of education was started in the Later Middle Ages that was to become most important, especially in England, during the Renaissance and Reformation periods.

The Control of Higher Education

As has already been mentioned, the principal agencies of higher education in the Early Middle Ages were the monastic schools and the cathedral schools. In general, the monastic schools were predominant until about the eleventh century, when the cathedral schools began to surpass them in importance. As the numbers of students in the cathedral schools began to increase, the actual teaching function and direct control of the school were often delegated by the bishop to a church official known as the "chancellor." The chain of authority was from Pope to bishop to chancellor. Gradually, the most important power delegated to the chancellor was the right to issue a teaching license (*licentia docendi*) to qualified students within the diocese. As certain of the cathedral schools grew to still greater prominence, the Pope often gave to the chancellor through the bishop the right to issue a license to teach anywhere (*licentia docendi ubique*). This meant that some cathedral schools gained authority beyond their diocese.

Certain of these cathedral schools acquired the name *studium generale,* a place of general study, so called because it attracted students from a wide area and its license to teach was recognized beyond its own jurisdiction. By 1100 the most flourishing of such schools were those at Chartres, which was particularly famous for the study of grammar and literature, Paris, for logic and theology, Bologna, for law, and Salerno, for medicine.

Origin of the University Type of Organization. In the twelfth century, as the number of teachers and students increased at some of these schools, the teachers began to follow a typical medieval pattern of group action and organize themselves into a guild, or *universitas.* The university was designed particularly to protect the teachers against the chancellor, the bishop, the king, or anyone else who tried to bring them under control. Likewise, the students often organized themselves into guilds for protection against the teachers, the townspeople, and each other. These early student "universities" usually followed nationality lines according to the region or country from which the students came.

The term *universitas* was originally applied simply to any group of people who were organized in a guild for common purposes, but gradually it began to be applied specifically more and more to universities of faculties and students. As the masters and students organized themselves into guilds and corporate organizations, the cathedral school became a university. The process of transformation was gradual, and no exact date can be given for this transition in the case of the universities that appeared in the later twelfth and thirteenth centuries. The typical guilds of teachers were the faculties of liberal arts, law, medicine, and theology. Not all medieval universities had all these faculties, and some universities were more famous for one faculty than for another, for example, Paris for theology and Bologna for law.

University of Paris. Since the greatest of the universities in the Middle Ages was the university of Paris, a short description of its rise to power may reveal some of the factors at work in the general university movement. By the eleventh century the number of students in Paris had increased enormously, for they were attracted to the schools of Notre Dame Cathedral, the collegiate church of St. Geneviève, and the abbey of St. Victor. Guillaume de Champeaux had attracted many students to Notre Dame, and then Abélard far overshadowed his former teacher and colleagues in his drawing power, which he displayed at various times at St. Victor and St. Geneviève as well as at Notre Dame. There is evidence that before the end of the twelfth century the masters of these schools

Fig. 9. A university lecture.

had organized themselves into guilds of arts, law, medicine, and theology because they felt themselves fettered by the control of the chancellors of Notre Dame and St. Geneviève.

The masters wanted to control their own affairs, appoint new members to their group as other guilds did, and issue the licenses to teach. They turned to anyone who would give them help in their struggles to achieve greater autonomy. Thus, on occasion, they turned to the king for help against the townspeople, and Louis VII gave them the right to strike whenever they were molested by the town. In the frequent riots that broke out between town and gown, the university came to be recognized as exempt from the civil courts, and students and faculty gained the right to be tried by ecclesiastical or university courts. If the king issued orders to the university, as Philip Augustus did, the faculty turned to the Pope for help. If the chancellor required obedience of them, as the chancellor of Notre Dame did, they again turned to the Pope or struck. Whenever the faculty felt that restraints were intolerable, they would strike and leave the city or threaten to strike; and as the students often joined the faculty, the university could often bring the king, the town, or the church to their terms.

In their disputes with the chancellor, the faculty won from Pope Innocent III in 1212 recognition of their association, and Innocent ordered the chancellor to wait for recommendations from the faculty before appointing new professors. Again in 1229 the faculty appealed to the Pope over the chancellor's head, and in 1231 the papal bull of Pope Gregory IX became the main fortification of the autonomy of the university. Thus, the Papacy showed itself willing to overrule its own appointed officials and to protect the university in order to gain more direct control over it. In general, the faculty was willing to accept this help; for the Pope was far away, whereas the chancellor was on the ground and was therefore thought to be more immediately dangerous to them.

Soon, however, the faculty began to have its troubles with the Pope. When the Dominican friars began to teach in the University of Paris, they often sided with the Pope rather than with the other professors. In the years 1252 to 1257 there was a series of struggles with the mendicant friars. When the rest of the professors went on strike, the Dominicans kept on teaching and attracting students. The Pope supported the Dominicans, insisted that they remain at work, and the strike was broken, but the university had shown that it was hard to control.

Gradually, the arts faculty became the largest and strongest of the faculties, and by the end of the thirteenth century the rector, who was the executive and disciplinary head of the arts faculty, came to be recognized as the head of the whole University of Paris. Increasingly Paris was regarded as *the* great medieval university, and the saying was "Italy has the Papacy; Germany has the Empire; and France has the University of Paris; all is well."

One of the significant results of the struggle for autonomy at the University of Paris was the growing recognition of the faculty as the full legal body of the university. The faculty had corporate existence, could set the curriculum, issue a license to teach, confer degrees, and appoint its own members. In fact, the very idea of a university in its origins was this corporate existence of the faculty empowered with the right to run its own affairs without responsibility to administrative officers or a board of control outside its membership.

Other Medieval Universities. In Italy the most famous university of the thirteenth century was at Bologna, where the university type of organization developed out of a cathedral school of arts, a monastic school of law, and a municipal school of rhetoric. An interesting but not very influential characteristic of Bologna was the power of the student guilds to exert control over the affairs of the university. The rector of the student guilds was recognized as the head of the university, and the professors were obliged to take an oath of obedience to the student rector and abide by the regulations of the student guilds concerning the length and content of lectures and the length of the academic term. Other universities that achieved some status in Italy during the thirteenth century were at Siena, Padua, Naples (founded by Frederick II), and Rome (founded by the Pope).

In England the universities at Oxford and Cambridge took form during the Middle Ages and remained the only English universities for several centuries thereafter. Having achieved a university type of faculty organization by 1167 or 1168, Oxford was modeled in large part upon the faculties of Paris but was not so closely supervised by the Papacy or by the local bishop. Cambridge was established later, when a group of masters became dissatisfied and moved from Oxford in 1209. This practice of secession from one university to another accounts for the establishment of many universities throughout Europe.

By the end of the thirteenth century the only other universities in France outside of Paris were those at Montpellier and Toulouse. Montpellier was especially noted for its work in medicine; and Toulouse was founded by the Papacy in the 1230's as a means of combating heresy in southern France. Universities appeared in Spain at Salamanca and Seville and in Portugal at Lisbon before the end of the thirteenth century. In the fourteenth and fifteenth centuries the university movement spread to north and central Europe. More than 75 universities were known by the end of the fifteenth century.

Aristocratic Nature of Medieval Education

Viewed from the perspective of modern times, with our stress upon widespread public education, the opportunity for education among the ordinary people of the Middle Ages seems limited indeed. In general, the modern estimate is that medieval education was highly aristocratic as compared with education in our own day. Yet, viewed from the standpoint of the medieval period itself, the opportunity should probably not be discounted too heavily. Even though the church was not widely concerned with giving every child a chance for education, it is apparent that some steps were taken to provide free education for poor children. To be sure, this was a charity conception of education, for if parents had the wherewithal they were expected to pay for the education of their children. Yet the fact that free education existed at all is not to be taken too lightly.

Furthermore, recent investigations seem to point to the conclusion that great numbers of children were attending school in the larger towns of Italy, France, Germany, and England before the end of the thirteenth century. There is even reason to believe that educational opportunity was more widespread in the thirteenth century than in the fourteenth or fifteenth century. There seems to be some evidence, too, that at least a few opportunities for schooling for girls outside of the convents and courts began to appear late in the thirteenth century.

When all these exceptions have been noted, however, the generalization still seems to hold that compared with Roman Imperial times before the Middle Ages and compared with Reformation times of the sixteenth and seventeenth centuries the opportunity for education in Europe was relatively limited.

Status of the Teaching Profession

Since most of the teachers in the elementary schools of the Middle Ages were clerics, minor church officials, or priests, their status was similar to that of the lower levels of the clergy. There were also lay teachers, especially in the towns of Italy, who made their living instructing children by private contract with parents. But the great weight of instruction was carried by monks in the monasteries or priests in their parishes, who taught school as a part of their regular duties. At the lower levels of instruction, the church had not yet organized a special corps of teachers or separate profession of teaching whose principal task was education. The clergy did the teaching primarily because it was the only group in society with sufficient education to carry out the teaching function. Education was not an end in itself as much as a means of fulfilling the religious duties of the church. Teaching in general was truly a handmaiden of the church as far as elementary instruction was concerned.

At the higher levels of instruction, however, the situation changed during the Later Middle Ages. Advanced instruction in the liberal arts, law, medicine, and theology soon became the principal business of certain monks in the monasteries and of the chancellor or *scholasticus* in the cathedral schools. Here the change from instruction as incidental to the other duties of the clergy to instruction as a principal duty was a gradual one. By the eleventh and twelfth centuries the job of the *scholasticus* and his staff in the cathedral schools began to be a full-time one. Many such persons became noted as scholars and teachers rather than as clergymen. Such, for example, were Bernard of Chartres, John of Salisbury, Guillaume de Champeaux, and Abélard. However, the real transition to an independent profession of teaching took place in the process of university organization.

In the thirteenth century a career in university life became so important that it began to challenge a career in church or state as an outlet for the energies of able young men. It is noteworthy that virtually all the important thinkers, writers, and intellectual leaders in the thirteenth century were university-trained men or professors. The universities were the molders of the intellectual life of the times to a greater degree than at any time since, for there were few scholars outside the universities. The status of the teaching profession in the universities was very high, surrounded with privileges, exemptions, and immunities. University professors never gained the great wealth of the noble or great churchman, but they enjoyed much better than average living and held a high place in public respect and social esteem. At Oxford and Cambridge they gained special representation in Parliament, and as a group they were often sought out to decide important questions of heresy or theology or political disputes.

Chapter 6

THE MIDDLE AGES:
INTELLECTUAL FOUNDATIONS OF EDUCATION

CONFLICTING CLAIMS UPON THE MEDIEVAL MIND

The medieval period has often been described as a time of intellectual uniformity when the scholars were satisfied that they had settled the fundamental problems of man and the universe, but closer inspection reveals many of the conflicts, uncertainties, and differences of point of view that mark most periods in history. At almost every stage of the Middle Ages there were those who stood out as "reconcilers," those who attempted to keep the course of thought to what they believed were the main highways of orthodoxy; but there were also the "recalcitrants," those who kept tugging at the leashes and trying to pull off in one direction or another. The capacity of the church to assimilate and control these different elements was enormous. What was condemned as near heresy in one period was likely to be incorporated into orthodoxy in another.

The central intellectual problem of the Middle Ages was the attempt to reconcile the main religious values of the church with the widely varying secular interests of all kinds. For example, the ideal of a universal Christian commonwealth was a strong intellectual factor throughout the Middle Ages, but it had to win its way by force, by threat, by argument, and by compromise over the secular interests of feudalism, the ideal of national sovereignty, and the ideal of independence as expressed by emperors, kings, towns, and universities.

The religious ideal of hope for eternal security in the other world through salvation was in conflict with the secular interests of this world. The church itself entertained a mixture of otherworldly and this-worldly interests, for many of the popes were great political organizers and economic administrators as well as spiritual leaders. It is too easy a generalization to say that the Middle Ages were completely otherworldly in outlook. It is probably better to say that the strength of the religious outlook was such that it tried to include and harness the secular drives of people as well as their spiritual energies. In this respect the church was not altogether successful, but it is also true that the church perhaps came closer to achieving this ideal than at any time before or after the Middle Ages. Perhaps this is the essence of medievalism.

Within the realm of religious thought itself there were the same tuggings at the leash and recalcitrance. The established doctrines of orthodoxy were often challenged by the heresies and near heresies, and church officials were constantly on the alert to keep the recalcitrants from stepping too far over the bounds of orthodoxy. Very often the conflict centered in the problem of reconciling the religious literature of the Bible and church Fathers with the secular literature of the classical authors of Greece and Rome. This was a terribly difficult problem and often resulted in attributing Christian characteristics to some aspects of the thought of Plato, Aristotle, Cicero, and Vergil and then ruling out of consideration other aspects.

The intellectual efforts to reconcile the claims of human reason as against the claims of faith led to the gigantic quarrels of the Later Middle Ages that took the form of Scholasticism. Here we find such men as St. Anselm and St. Bernard of Clairvaux swinging far in one direction in their emphasis on faith, emotion, and mysticism, whereas Roscellinus, Abélard, and Roger Bacon were tugging at the leash in exalting the claims of reason, intellect, and dialectics. The balance was then struck between faith and reason in the thirteenth century in the synthesis of St. Thomas Aquinas, the greatest of all the "reconcilers."

In general, it is fruitful to think of medieval intellectual efforts as though a young and immature people were attempting to gain maturity through a long and arduous process of learning their lessons in order to be able to solve their own problems in their own way. In this process there were two great lessons to learn, namely, the whole thought of the pagan world of Greece and Rome, found in the writings of the ancient Greek and Latin writers, and, second, the religious thought of the Patristic Age, contained in the writings of the church Fathers. To these two great lessons the young peoples of western Europe brought their own energies, capacities, and qualities. The Italians, the Spaniards, the Gauls, the Germans, and the Northmen all had to learn their hard lessons from the beginning before they could make the classical and Christian traditions their own. It took some four centuries simply to absorb these lessons and to become Latinized. In this process of interaction from the sixth to the tenth centuries medievalism was taking form. By the eleventh and twelfth centuries the assimilation had become easier, and by the thirteenth century the whole intellectual fabric could be restated in distinctive, but not entirely new, terms.

Christian World View and Human Nature

During the Early Middle Ages the main body of medieval belief about the structure of the universe, the nature of God, and the nature of man and his relation to God was taken from the theology of St. Augustine. It was thus largely Platonic in its philosophical foundations and was framed of the Judaic monotheism of the Old Testament, the ethical teachings of Jesus as contained in the New Testament, and the elaborations of the church Fathers of the Patristic Age. To these were added rational, emotional, and mystical elements of Neoplatonism, Stoicism, and the Eastern religions. Out of this variety of influences came an outline of belief that formed the basic traditions of Christianity.

Central in the picture of the universe was belief in one God whose essence is infinite and spiritual, an all-good, all-wise, and all-powerful being who created the universe and all the forms of inanimate and animate existence. The universe revolving about the earth was created for a purpose—to provide a home for man, the highest form of creation. The world operates according to natural processes created by God; but if occasion requires, God can intervene directly in the processes of nature, for moral purposes, to reward the good and punish the wicked by means of miracles and special acts of providence. A heaven above the earth and a hell below the earth were constituted as a reward for goodness and punishment for evil in the life after death.

Man was placed on the earth for the ultimate object of achieving salvation and grace in the sight of God. He was created with an immortal soul, which links him with the spiritual nature of God, and he has an intellect, a conscience, and a free will as means of choosing the good life and shunning evil. Man also has a material body, which links him with the natural world, often tempting him to corruption, weakness, and sin. The original sin of Adam and Eve made it necessary for all men thereafter to seek help in living the good life, but God provided for man the means of escape from evil through the life and death of Christ. If man believes in Christ and seeks to follow His way of life, he may be saved from eternal punishment in the hereafter and his immortal soul will unite him with God in salvation and grace. If man does not choose to believe in Christ and in God, he will suffer the torments of hell forever. The means of salvation were instituted on earth by God in the form of the universal church, which provides the holy sacraments by which man may begin his journey to salvation.

With these fundamental tenets of the Christian world view there was relatively little dissent among the scholars of the medieval world. The oneness of God, His power in creating the world and all things, the essential spirituality behind the outward material forms of things, and the inherent moral and rational nature of the universe were generally not questioned. The world of material things was definitely considered to be in a subordinate position to the realm of spiritual affairs and man's own nature to reflect this distinction between spirit and matter. If man elevates his soul and subdues his body, he will be following the moral order of the universe as planned by God. If he elevates the things of the body and his sense experiences, he will be flying in the face of the universe and thus be sinful. Since the things of this world are inclined to evil, man must prove his desire to rise above the distractions and temptations of this world and keep his eyes upon the salvation to be achieved in the other world. In this respect, the dominant theology of medieval Christianity was otherworldly.

Heresies. In the Later Middle Ages the principal heresies centered upon criticisms of the worldliness and authority of the clergy. The Albigenses originated in the eleventh century and gained their name from the town of Albi in southern France. They conceived of themselves as Cathari (pure ones) in their protest against the corruption of the church and the priesthood. They emphasized that desire for material things is sinful, because matter is evil, and they thus classified as mortal sins the gaining of material wealth, the telling of falsehoods, and waging war. In these ways they attacked the worldliness of the clergy and the authority of the church. Another group that criticized the church was headed by Arnold of Brescia, whose followers were known as Arnoldists. They also attacked the corruption of the priesthood, the greed of the Pope, and the assumption by the clergy of authority in secular affairs, and preached the values of poverty and the simple life.

A much more influential sect was known as the Waldenses, followers of Peter Waldo, who were numerous in southern France and northern Italy. The Waldenses preached against the worldliness of the clergy, insisting that obedience was owed to Pope and priest only if they were good men and that God rather than man was to be obeyed. They argued that *all* men and women can be preachers if they are good, that prayers, masses, and almsgiving are of no avail to the dead, that prayer is just as efficacious outside of a church as inside, and that the reading of the Bible is an important means to salvation. In attacking the problem of the authority of the priesthood and feeling the necessity of living according to the spirit of the sacraments, these "heretics" were incipient Protestants in their point of view.

Intelligence and Learning

Within the general framework of the Christian world view, the most vital and widely varied points of view were expressed with regard to the role of human reason or intelligence as a means of arriving at truth. The debates and argumentative writings of the "schoolmen" of the medieval period are usually referred to as Scholasticism.

The term "Scholasticism" has been used in a number of widely varying ways. Sometimes it is used to refer to the whole body of thought and writings of the schoolmen of the Middle Ages, originating with the term *scholasticus*, the person who became a teacher or scholar in the cathedral schools and universities. As a method of thought, Scholasticism is often identified with the deductive and syllogistic logic of Aristotle, as interpreted by the medieval scholars of the Later Middle Ages. In general, Scholasticism was a method of selecting and classifying general principles or statements taken from religious and classical authorities, comparing these authorities, commenting upon these statements in systematic order, examining the arguments on both sides, drawing conclusions, and refuting the arguments of the other side in detail by marshaling evidence in support of the conclusions accepted. Argumentation, disputation, and dialectical analysis played a large part in this process.

The reasoning and the content of Scholasticism were often stated in terms of the problem of "universals." Is the universal proposition the most real, or is the individual thing the most real? Does reality lie in the universal proposition, or does it lie in the individual statement of fact? Despite the widely varying interpretations, there seem to have been two principal points of view with regard to these questions.

One position, known as "realism," stated that the most universal concept, the most general class of things, is the most real and therefore the most important. Universal ideas exist independently of and prior to individual things. Since God is the most universal substance, God is the most real; the universal concepts of man, goodness, justice, truth, and beauty give form to individual men, individual acts of goodness and justice, and individual examples of truth and beauty.

Platonic idealism, at work here in medieval realism, generally sided with the religious emphasis upon the world of spiritual ideas and spiritual values as the revealed sources of faith and of the authority of the universal church. The universal propositions laid down by the Scriptures, the Fathers, and the Papacy were considered to be the most real and most binding propositions. The religious temper, faith in the unseen, and the authority of tradition and revelation favored realism. Faith should be reasonable; but if reason does not agree with revelation, then faith is uppermost and must prevail.

In the Early Middle Ages realism was the dominant outlook, stemming from St. Augustine and elaborated in effective terms by St. Anselm, St. Bernard of Clairvaux, and St. Guillaume de Champeaux in the eleventh and twelfth centuries. St. Anselm stated with St. Augustine that all reasoning and discussion about religious affairs must be preceded by faith in revealed and authoritative truth. In order to arrive at knowledge we must first believe the doctrines of the church. Guillaume de Champeaux asserted that individual things are mere names; only the universal is real. For example, the universal genus Man is the only reality in human nature; all men are fundamentally the same because they partake of the universal characteristics of Man; individual differences among men are merely accidental variations that have no importance.

The opposing position, known as "nominalism," drew for support upon the scientific outlook of Aristotle rather than upon the idealism of Plato. Nominalism stated that the most real thing is the individual object and that the universal is simply a name or a term given for convenience to a collection of individual things that have similar characteristics. Universals exist only as propositions or generalizations *after* individual things have been examined and found to be like each other. Universals have no independent power or force but simply are convenient ways of handling a group of similar individual objects. To arrive at truth we must start with the individual objects, see how they operate and what their characteristics are, and then arrive inductively at generalizations useful in classifying new objects or new knowledge as it is discovered. Thus, the test for reality is not in faith or authority but in the efforts of the human reason to find the reality of things as individuals and describe them in terms of general concepts, or universals. The secular temper of nominalism was tugging at the leash of religious orthodoxy. In its dependence upon logic and dialectics as the supreme agencies in arriving at knowledge, nominalism elevated human reason above faith.

The nominalist position came into clear prominence in the eleventh century, when Roscellinus began to criticize the realist position and to insist that the universal is merely a word, a name, a breath of the voice. The cause of nominalism and the claims of reason against faith received their greatest justification in the hands of Peter Abélard in the twelfth century. Abélard was a nominalist of a sort, but more important than his specific doctrine of universals was his attitude of questioning, criticism, and doubt concerning the tenets of faith and authority. Finding himself successful in confounding the realist doctrines of his teacher Guillaume de Champeaux in the field of dialectics and logic, Abélard turned to theological questions with the same critical attitude.

Abélard's willingness to treat the three persons of the Trinity and other sacred topics not as objects of worship but as subjects for analytical and logical dissection caused two church councils under the leadership of St. Bernard of Clairvaux to condemn him. Whereas St. Anselm had said that we must believe in order to understand, Abélard was saying that we must understand in order to believe. Abélard's book entitled *Sic et non* (*Yes and No*) illustrated his critical method. He listed some 150 specific religious theses and then quoted authorities from the Scriptures and Fathers to support both sides of the questions. Thus he showed dramatically how the authorities contradicted one another and that it was the business of the Christian scholar to arrive at the truth by the use of human reason. His attitude of protest was probably more significant than his thought or his systematic theology, but it was so effective that the great theologians of the thirteenth century were prompted to effect a reconciliation. Abélard was the greatest of the recalcitrants; he gave stimulus to the work of St. Thomas Aquinas, the greatest of the reconcilers.

During the twelfth and thirteenth centuries the whole range of Aristotelian science was introduced into western Europe through the activities of Arab and Jewish scholars who had translated the materials from Greek into Arabic and then into Latin. By the middle of the thirteenth century Christianity was once more in possession of careful literal translations of Aristotle's scientific works on biology, physics, astronomy, metaphysics, ethics, politics, and poetics. With this enormous mass of "new" material to digest, absorb, and argue over, the dialectical arguments were ever more divergent. The church became alarmed at the degree to which Christian faith seemed to be contradicted by the scientific investigations of reason as represented by Aristotle.

To the problem of reconciling Aristotelian thought with Christian faith St. Thomas Aquinas addressed himself, arriving at a synthesis in his *Summa theologica*. This eventually was accepted as embodying the official doctrine of the Catholic Church, and it remains so, in effect, today. St. Thomas Aquinas achieved reconciliation by sharply distinguishing between natural philosophy and supernatural theology. Philosophy deals with the natural world, where things are created, change, and decay; it includes everything that is open to argument or that can be demonstrated by human reason. Theology, on the other hand, deals with revealed truth, which involves the supernatural world of changeless, uncreated, eternal, and ultimate reality. These truths are the universals that make up the content of faith and are not open to question by human reason.

There can be no contradiction between theology and philosophy, no contradiction between revealed truth and human reason, for God is the author of all truth. Faith may be reasoned about as far as reason can go, but some articles of faith are beyond finite human reason. They are not "unreasonable"; they are simply not open to rational demonstration. By his elevation of faith above reason St. Thomas Aquinas aided the realist outlook; at the same time, his position gave greater autonomy to the workings of human reason within the bounds of the natural world of science. Science and religion may handle the same facts or ideas, but they look at them from different sides. Science and human reason start from the individual and particular thing and work up, whereas religion starts with God, the most universal of all, and works down to the individual.

Augustinian theology had not separated philosophy and theology in this way but had asserted the identity of the two, whereas St. Thomas

Aquinas gave science free rein over natural phenomena within its own restricted province. This illustrated the adaptability of the church but also showed that Aristotle could be used to regulate Scholastic philosophy and circumscribe the ranges within which human reason could work. If left to itself, reason would tug at the leash and threaten to cause trouble, but when codified and formalized by the authority of Aristotle it could be disciplined and made to serve the higher ends of theology. St. Thomas Aquinas's method was basically that of Abélard, but he went one step beyond Abélard; he not only stated the problem and gave authorities on both sides, but he then added the "correct" solution.

The dominant medieval conceptions of the thinking process and learning process were set by these basic assumptions of St. Thomas Aquinas. Truth is anchored in eternal reality; it is fixed, universal, objective, and permanent. Truth is not created by man; it is created by God; it is simply *discovered* by the human reason and intelligence. Truth is static and unchanging in the supernatural world, for God made knowledge perfect to begin with; but man is imperfect and change is necessary if human beings are to proceed from ignorance to knowledge through learning. Therefore, man has been given intellect as an active agent that enables him to achieve truth and bring his knowledge into actuality.

The primary aim of human intellect is to reach out and grasp truth, but intellect cannot achieve truth unaided; it must rely upon faith, revelation, and grace to arrive at the truths of theology and religion. The highest objective of knowledge is God Himself as the source of all truth. All men are endowed with the faculty of intellect as a part of human nature in order to give them a start on the road to truth. In summary, then, human reason is viewed as made up of the higher, or theoretical, intellect, having to do with science, mathematics, and philosophy, and the lower, or practical, intellect, having to do with decisions about political, economic, and everyday affairs of action, conduct, and experience.

In this respect, St. Thomas Aquinas followed in the tradition of Aristotle in elevating the virtues of the theoretical intellect and theoretical knowledge above the claims of practical intellect and the knowledge to be obtained from experience. This distinction has been a characteristic of the traditional intellectual outlook from the Middle Ages to the present time and provides the hard core around which much educational and philosophic controversy has revolved. But the attack upon Thomism was not long in appearing; it was delivered in the thirteenth century by such opponents as Roger Bacon.

Bacon, not satisfied with the complete system as set forth by St. Thomas Aquinas, attacked its assumptions of universal authoritativeness. He raised his voice, often querulous and rasping, in criticism of the growing reliance upon Aristotle for authority in scientific as well as in theological matters. He went far in arguing that conclusions concerning the operation of the natural world should be verified by actual and active experiences. He was perhaps the first to urge the use of experimentation as a check on the abstract results of theorizing and as a means of reconstructing the past and estimating the future. Bacon's recalcitrance caused him to be attacked and imprisoned as a disturber of the peace and a causer of disharmony.

In the fourteenth century the argument was kept alive by the acute nominalism and skepticism of William of Ockham and by the extreme realism of Duns Scotus. Scholasticism became involved in the subtleties, the intricate and complex arguments, and the abstract terminologies that finally led to its decline and the reaction of Humanism against it in the fourteenth and fifteenth centuries. On the positive side, however, five centuries of hard intellectual labor by Scholastic thinkers had prepared the way for the emergence of scientific thinking in the sixteenth century.

Role of the Arts and Sciences

General Development of Scholarship. The sixth and seventh centuries were periods of transition in the handing down of the scholarly materials from the Later Imperial period of the Roman Empire. Some of the writers of the early medieval period who transmitted the work of earlier authors were competent and careful; others were dry and lifeless. The most outstanding was Boethius, who was the only scholar of his period with a real flair for the classical spirit; he translated much of the best Greek science and philosophy into Latin and made good commentaries upon this material. His *Consolation of Philosophy* provided most of what western Europe knew of Greek thought for several centuries.

Another of the intermediaries between classical and medieval scholarship was Cassiodorus, a Christian scholar and monk, who made a great contribution to the preservation of classical and Patristic scholarship by his inauguration of manuscript copying in the monasteries in special rooms known as *scriptoria.* In his own work, Cassiodorus wrote extensively on religious topics, on history, and on the various liberal arts. He was not the scholar that Boethius was, but he had great influence in that he put much material, both secular and religious, into a form that was usable by the church. A third transmitter of materials to the medieval world was Pope Gregory the Great, whose writings and letters were a principal means by which the theology of the church Fathers was made available to medieval scholars. A fourth of these early intermediaries was Isidore of Seville, Spanish bishop, who compiled an encyclopedia called the *Etymologies*. According to modern standards, this is lifeless and dull, containing hundreds of excerpts, terms, and definitions arranged according to no particular order or system. To the naïve and uninstructed the *Etymologies* must have been welcome; but as far as creative reworking of classical thought is concerned, it is barren indeed and reflects the decline in scholarship that had taken place by the seventh century.

In the eighth and ninth centuries the level of medieval scholarship rose considerably, culminating in the so-called "Carolingian revival" of the ninth century. The most outstanding scholarly performances in England were those of St. Bede, Alcuin, and Alfred the Great. St. Bede, often called the "father of English learning," knew Greek and Hebrew as well as Latin and wrote on music, history, biography, science, theology, pedagogy, and the liberal arts. Alcuin, called from the cathedral of York by Charlemagne to conduct the palace school at his court, established a curriculum of wide range. Alfred the Great stimulated scholarly learning in England after the destruction caused by the wars with the Danes not only by his encouragement and promotion of the arts and sciences but also by his own achievements in vernacular Anglo-Saxon prose. He translated into English or Anglo-Saxon the works of St. Bede, St. Augustine, Boethius, and Gregory the Great. The revival on the Continent continued under the leadership of Rabanus Maurus and Johannes Scotus Erigena.

In the tenth and eleventh centuries the level and pace of intellectual activity accelerated considerably, much as was the case in economic life when commerce began to increase and the towns to grow. Bruno, Archbishop of Cologne, brought together the best scholars and collected the best manuscripts he could find; and Gerbert (later Pope Sylvester II), *scholasticus* at the cathedral school of Reims, was the most learned man of the era around the year 1000.

Meanwhile, an enormously important development was taking place on the fringes of European scholarship. This was the Arab scholarship, which had absorbed a great deal of Greek philosophy and science, especially that of Aristotle. The Arabs had carried much of this material to Sicily and Spain as their empire expanded. In the process of translating Greek materials into Arabic, the Arabs assimilated Greek ideas along with Hindu, Islamic, and Christian thought. Thus, as the Christian scholars of the eleventh and twelfth centuries came into contact with Arabic civilization in Spain, Sicily, and Syria, a great interest arose in translating these materials from the Arabic into Latin. The Jewish scholar Maimonides reconciled Aristotle with the Jewish religion, and Avicenna and Averroes reconciled Aristotle with Islamism. As these writings flooded into Europe, Aristotle now had to be reconciled with Christianity, and to this task St. Thomas Aquinas and others addressed themselves in the thirteenth century.

Meanwhile, also, another intellectual movement had gained headway in the twelfth century, often known as the "twelfth-century Renaissance." This took the form of an enthusiasm for classical literature as opposed to the philosophy and logic of Aristotle. The greatest centers of this movement were the cathedral schools of Chartres and Orléans in France, and the greatest exponent of "Humanism" was John of Salisbury, who had come to be head of the school at Chartres. John of Salisbury battled against the inroads made by logic and philosophy upon the literary studies of grammar and style, but his was a losing battle, for Aristotelian science soon captured the intellectual energies of most of the scholars of the thirteenth century. Classical Humanism thus had to wait until the Renaissance of the fourteenth and fifteenth centuries before it could win its way over the dialectical interests of Scholasticism.

General Development of the Liberal Arts. Before the end of the Roman Imperial period the number and framework of the seven liberal arts had been stated by Capella (see pages 101 to 102). Although Boethius and Isidore wrote treatises on the subject, there was in general a good deal of skepticism among Christian scholars concerning the use of the pagan liberal arts. However, in the sixth century, Cassiodorus found sufficient scriptural sanction for the seven liberal arts to fix them securely as the necessary preparation for the study of theology throughout the Middle Ages. The Christian Cassiodorus hated the pagan Capella and wrote his own book in the hope that it would supersede Capella's compendium, which had survived the destruction of the Roman Empire. If Cassiodorus had held his peace, Capella might have been forgotten, and his list of liberal arts might never have been known beyond the Early Middle Ages.

Medieval ecclesiastics in general looked with considerable suspicion upon the pagan character of Capella's small compendium, but the notion grew that the spiritual, literary, and philosophical character of the seven studies was suitable for higher education in the church (particularly in view of the fact that so little other material was available). When to this growing feeling was added the emphatic assertion of Cassiodorus that the seven liberal arts were specifically justified by the Scriptures, his testimony could not be ignored. He quoted to such good effect the text "Wisdom hath builded her house, she hath hewn out her seven pillars" (Prov. 9:1) that the church eventually accepted all seven liberal arts for use in the monastic and cathedral schools. The medieval limitation of the liberal arts was thereupon established in fixed form as early as the beginning of the seventh century.

It must be remembered, however, that many changes and adaptations were made in each of the seven arts as knowledge expanded in the various stages of the Middle Ages. In accordance with the varying needs of the times, certain subjects were emphasized more than others. Prior to the eleventh century, Latin grammar was emphasized because the scholars needed a thorough grounding in Latin as a preparation for religious study. During the eleventh and twelfth centuries, the study of classical literature was promoted by such Humanistic schools as Chartres and Orléans. During the twelfth century, logic became the predominant study when Abélard made questions of metaphysics and theology the most interesting topics of the time. Still later, with the rise of Aristotelian philosophy and science, interest turned to the mathematical subjects, astronomy, arithmetic, and geometry. It is thus apparent that the church was by no means entirely hostile to secular literature, for there was continuous interest in the classics all through the Middle Ages.

The Trivium: Grammar, Rhetoric, and Logic. One of the most striking phenomena of the Middle Ages was the Latinizing of western Europe. Latin gradually became the universal medium of discourse among educated persons. However, its character changed enormously over the centuries as "classical" Latin gradually become "medieval" Latin. Medieval Latin had a closer connection with the spoken Latin of the people than with written Latin of classical literature. It was affected by the spoken tongues of the various European peoples.

Grammar was consequently the most important of the liberal arts during the Early Middle Ages, for the non-Latin peoples had to be taught the rudiments of Latin in order to be able to take part in the religious and intellectual life of the times. The works of Donatus and Priscian and Cato's *Distichs* remained the most influential grammar texts and readers.

With respect to the literary side of the study of grammar, the Middle Ages knew much more of the secular classical literature than has often been supposed. There was no century during which classical learning was unknown; it may have been known by fewer scholars or in more condensed form in certain periods, but the continuity is clear. The so-called "Carolingian revival" was not a revival or rediscovery so much as it was a bringing together in western Europe of what had been preserved and known despite long years of civil war and invasion during the sixth and seventh centuries. From the eighth century onward appreciation of classical literature steadily increased until it came to its height in the Humanism of the twelfth century, the most outstanding exponent of which was John of Salisbury at Chartres.

Rhetoric, on the other hand, was largely in eclipse during the Early Middle Ages, although it maintained its place as one of the recognized seven liberal arts. In the hands of the early church scholars rhetoric lost the predominantly oratorical and practical character it had achieved as the highest of the liberal arts under the Roman Empire. In the popular manuals the material was condensed from Cicero and Quintilian, but their emphasis upon the public uses of rhetoric was reduced. One phase of rhetoric did become very important, however, and that was the study of letter writing and the drawing up of such legal and feudal documents as contracts, wills, immunities, and appointments to office. The *ars dictandi*, or dictamen, had a most practical value at a time when the economic, political, and legal affairs of the church were expanding at such a rate that record keeping was of the utmost importance. The investiture struggles and the consequent delving into legal and historical documents also stimulated attention to dictamen in the towns and schools of northern Italy.

Many handbooks and textbooks to aid in the study and practice of dictamen were compiled as early as the ninth and tenth centuries, but the height of interest was achieved in the eleventh and twelfth centuries. It became so popular that John of Salisbury lashed out in bitter attack against the "shyster" professors of dictamen, who were exalting "practical" education and tricks of the trade at the expense of the development of taste, judgment, and character, which could be achieved only by the study of classical literature. In the twelfth century most of the arguments of Humanism as against "practical" education were the same kind of issues that the humanists and intellectualists of today are raising against practical education in the United States.

Aside from the scholarly development of language and literature in Latin, the Middle Ages saw the appearance of a vital and original literature in the vernaculars of Italian, Spanish, French, German, and English. Taking form as early as the tenth and eleventh centuries, vernacular literature achieved a great development in the twelfth and thirteenth centuries. It included love lyrics, songs of war, romances, fables, animal stories, sermon stories, and mystery plays, all of which became enormously popular among the unschooled people of the upper as well as the lower classes.

The development of this vernacular literature was of enormous importance for education, because it foreshadowed the eventual demand that schools should teach the vernacular as well as Latin. It was a long struggle, however; it took eight or nine centuries for the vernacular languages and literatures to be recognized as of equal educational value with the classical. In some countries and in some educational circles in the United States this equality has not yet been achieved.

In the Middle Ages the study of logic as one of the seven liberal arts was sharply distinguished by most scholars from "philosophy" in general. Logic was looked upon simply as the rules of deductive thinking designed as a preparatory study to be undertaken before advancing to the higher studies of the quadrivium and philosophy. Philosophy, on the other hand, was considered to be a study of the metaphysical problems dealing with the origin and nature of the universe as well as the epistemological problems dealing with the origin and nature of knowledge. However, the method of Scholasticism enhanced the importance of the study of logic until it overshadowed the other subjects of the liberal arts from the time of Abélard onward. The most important textbooks on logic reflected the influence of Aristotle's logic.

The Quadrivium. Important developments were made in mathematics during the Middle Ages that helped to lay the groundwork for scientific and mathematical investigations of later centuries. In the Early Middle Ages the primary consideration of arithmetic continued to be the computation of the date of Easter with some attention to the theory of numbers. During the eleventh and twelfth centuries considerable achievement was made, notably in the work of Gerbert, who developed a better method of columnar computation and reconstructed the abacus so that it could be used more easily for the four fundamental processes of addition, subtraction, multiplication, and division. The most important change in arithmetic came in the thirteenth century, when the use of Arabic numerals including the zero made possible the use of the decimal system, which enormously simplified computation and began to replace the cumbersome Latin numerals, the duodecimal system, and the Roman abacus. These developments were indispensable to the development of modern science.

Much of the same sort of development took place in geometry and astronomy. Gerbert was able to bring together virtually all that the Western world knew of Euclid's definitions and of geometry in general. Then, in the twelfth and thirteenth centuries, the whole of Euclid's geometry, along with other mathematical works of the Greeks, Arabs, and Hindus, was translated into Latin. Astronomy was for long a peculiarly fascinating study for the Middle Ages because of its mystical and astrological possibilities, its relation to the calculation of Easter, and the whole notion of the earth as the center of the universe. Gerbert devised ingenious models of terrestrial and celestial spheres to illustrate the motions of the earth and heavens as he understood them. In the twelfth century the astronomy of Ptolemy along with great amounts of Greek astronomy was translated from the Arabic into Latin, and in the thirteenth century Aristotle's work *On the Heavens* was also made available.

As one of the seven liberal arts, music continued to be almost exclusively theoretical, speculative, and mathematical in nature. Indeed, the applied side, playing and singing songs, was not considered properly a liberal art; it was thought appropriate only to the wandering minstrel or jester. This intellectualizing of music remains a strong tradition in the colleges and universities of the United States, where performance is often not considered as important as the historical and theoretical study of music. In the Early Middle Ages the all-inclusive work was that of Boethius, which was influential nearly everywhere that music was taught as a liberal art and which passed on to western Europe the Greek tradition in music. Meanwhile, the performance of music became more important in the church and in secular life. Hymns, chanting, part singing, and pipe organs became features of church services, and the troubadours and minnesingers sang their folksongs for the secular entertainment of the nobles and the common people.

THE INTELLECTUAL AND THE SPIRITUAL IN EDUCATION

General Bookish Character of Schooling

In general, medieval education was highly bookish in character. In an age when books were so scarce, it was only natural that they should be regarded with great respect and even reverence. The written word was virtually the essence of authority, and medieval education was based upon it. Submissiveness and obedience were qualities which the schools set out to instill in the pupils. Although many advanced scholars showed critical abilities, initiative, and originality, these were not qualities to be encouraged in students.

Many of the most popular textbooks of the Middle Ages were written during the period of decadent scholarship in the later Roman Empire. The digest, the compendium, and the manual in which the lore of the past was condensed, simplified, and made easy were typical. The Middle Ages represent the heyday of reliance upon the textbook. If a teacher had a textbook, he was lucky, and perhaps he knew little more than was in the textbook. Indeed, it might almost be said that a person could be identified as a teacher by the fact that he had a textbook or had memorized one. The principal practical aim of education was the ability to read Latin, and the principal method was to memorize the required books. The whole educational process was largely a passing on of the content of textbooks from teacher to student.

The outlook on education of the Middle Ages must be deduced from the materials put into textbooks rather than from special treatises devoted to the theory of the aims, content, and methods of education. We can gain these insights from the compendiums of Cassiodorus, Isidore, and others on the liberal arts. We know what they expected of students, namely, the mastery of the textbooks. We can tell what different scholars considered important for students to learn and the methods they considered desirable: for example, the Humanistic study of grammar required by John of Salisbury, the dialectical study of logic by Abélard, the practical competence in dictamen by the Bolognese rhetoricians, and similarly for law, medicine, and theology as developed by Irnerius, Gratian, and St. Thomas Aquinas.

We know something also of the attacks upon Aristotelian dominance of education from the statements of Roger Bacon. According to Friar Bacon, the education of his day had four great defects: its utter dependence upon the authority of Aristotle; the reliance upon established custom; its undue reliance upon popular opinion; and the concealment of real ignorance by the pretensions of knowledge. His remedies were a more thorough study of languages and literature, science and mathematics, and the methods and spirit of experimental inquiry.

An interesting exception to these generalizations about the Middle Ages is an anonymous work discovered recently in the archives of the Vatican.[1] In this manuscript the author proposed that the boy begin his study of grammar at the age of seven years and continue grammar as the principal study along with some arithmetic and music until he is fourteen. For the next 7 years he should study rhetoric, logic, and astronomy, until the age of twenty-one; then for another 7 years he should study geometry, metaphysics, and natural philosophy until he reaches twenty-eight; he may then go on to the professional study of theology or law. As will be noted, the seven liberal arts, with the addition of Aristotelian science and philosophy, were conceived to be the staples of higher education in the liberal arts by the end of the thirteenth century.

Interesting, too, is the author's concern for the physical health and intellectual abilities of the younger boys from seven to fourteen. The health of the boys should be maintained by protection from the cold; those with physical defects and contagious diseases should be barred from school; and all should have a recess for play, sports, and games as a means of recreation in preparation for further study. The personality, or *complexio*, of different students should be carefully considered, as well as their capacity for learning. Different adaptations in instruction should be made for the sprightly and the subdued, for the bright, normal, and dull.

Despite the modern tone to this document, it is questionable just how much these admonitions were put into actual practice. Doubtless some good teachers always considered such factors in their day-to-day teaching, but it is also significant that so few such statements have come down to us from the Middle Ages. Acquisition of subject matter was the overpowering concern of medieval educators, along with the desire to instill proper religious attitudes among the younger students. These two concerns were the greatest legacies of the medieval heritage to education.

The concern for the development of the individual and for his preparation to engage in the society in which he would live outside of the church

[1] See Lynn Thorndike, "Elementary and Secondary Education in the Middle Ages," *Speculum*, 15:405–406 (October, 1940).

was notable by its absence. Notable too was the fact that, although such concerns were paramount in the educational theory of the Greeks and of Cicero and Quintilian in Roman times, they were overshadowed by the religious concerns of the church in the Middle Ages. When the dominant influence of the church was lessened in the Renaissance, we find again an upswing of interest in the individual and in the secular aspects of society.

Elementary and Secondary Instruction in the Schools

Education as conducted in the monastic schools, parish or song schools, and elementary branches of cathedral schools revolved around the ability to read Latin and take part in the church services. The minimum amount of learning needed to become a priest was the ability to read Latin and conduct the prayers, chants, hymns, and religious ceremonies of the church services. Latin syllables, Latin words, and the rules of Latin grammar were taught from the elementary textbooks such as that of Donatus or Cato or from the Latin psalter or prayer book. Often, no doubt, the material was committed to memory by the boys without understanding of the meaning of the words. Writing may sometimes have been learned too, but it was not universally taught. Music took the form of instruction in the accents of words and training in singing or chanting the phrases. The finger elements of arithmetic and some simple fundamental operations may also have been taught. Since there were few books, the boys had to learn mainly by memorizing and drill, accompanied by considerable corporal punishment and severe discipline.

In general, the most common method of teaching was probably as follows: The teacher read from his book and dictated the words to the pupil, who repeated the words aloud or perhaps copied them on a wax tablet. The pupil then memorized the words by repetition; if he had a wax tablet or slate, he memorized the words before he wiped it clean for the next day's lesson. Apparently, little attempt was made to explain the meaning of the words, or the attempt was made without using objects or pictures. However, a good teacher perhaps used vernacular words to explain the Latin words as soon as the phrase, hymn, or chant was memorized.

It seems clear that this elementary instruction in letters and secondary instruction in grammar were more or less carefully distinguished from the more advanced study of the liberal arts during the Later Middle Ages, for by that time elementary and secondary instruction were given by teachers different from those who taught the liberal arts. In the Early Middle Ages in the monasteries there was probably little differentiation, except of course that the boys needed to learn the elements of reading Latin before they could go on to the study of the liberal arts. Schools for the most part were not institutionalized in the modern sense and indeed perhaps should not be called "schools"; rather, a monk or a priest would teach a few boys informally at more or less regular hours. In the days when there was no literature or fund of knowledge recorded in the vernacular and when all knowledge handed down by the church was in Latin, learning to read and write Latin had a most practical value. Without it one could not broaden his horizon beyond his own little niche. Nevertheless, the Latin of the church was a foreign language to the Germanic and Celtic peoples of western Europe. It was therefore an astonishing achievement to whip into shape countless generations of youth who must have found the learning of Latin in the schools a difficult and sometimes distasteful task.

Fortunately for the church and unfortunately for the youth, the religious doctrine of original sin made it seem natural for youth to be stubborn and rebellious. Bodily punishment as a means of discipline was deemed good for the mind and for the soul. It is likely that western Europe would not have been Latinized if these doctrines had not been insisted upon by the church, but it was hard on the pupils. Such methods could doubtless be justified when they had practical values; but when in later centuries the vernaculars became scholarly carriers of knowledge, there was no longer the same educational justification for such mental and physical discipline. Resistance to the doctrine of corporal punishment and mental discipline for their own sake appeared as early as the fifteenth century, but little headway was made in changing educational practices until the eighteenth and nineteenth centuries.

Education through Apprenticeship

Chivalrous Education of the Knight. As the complicated system of personal relationships associated with feudalism grew up among the nobility in the Early Middle Ages, methods of preparing the young noble for assuming these obligations were devised. The ideals of chivalry became the guide for the education and conduct of the noble class. Chivalry was based on the usages appropriate to warfare, religion, and courtesy. Warfare demanded training for strength, courage, endurance, and skill in fighting on horseback. The church contributed ideals of mercy, honor, generosity to the fallen foe, protection for the weak, and loyalty to the Christian religion. The social graces and manners developed at the courts of the nobles added the notion of *courtoisie*, or courtesy. The ideal knight was thus a man of action, a soldier, courtier, and Christian gentleman, who had reverence for the church as well as loyalty to his overlord and his feudal obligations.

Although there were no special schools for training knights, chivalric education became somewhat standardized and systematized. It was usually conducted at the court of the overlord and included three fairly well defined stages of training. The first stage was designed for the younger boy from the ages of seven or eight to fourteen or fifteen; during this time he acted as page or valet at the court of his father's overlord. As a page, he was attached particularly to the ladies of the court, whom he served and from whom in general he learned about the life of the court. If he were lucky, he might learn how to practice the courtly graces and courtesies, how to sing and play a musical instrument, how to take part in religious ceremonies, and perhaps how to read and write in the vernacular.

From the ages of fourteen or fifteen to about twenty-one years the boy acted as a squire, or attendant, for the overlord or one of the knights of the court, helping with the armor and arms, caring for the horses, and ready to assist in war, tournament, or chase. He learned to ride, hunt, and fight. He perhaps improved his social accomplishments by singing, playing, reciting and composing verses, dancing, and entering into the games and storytelling activities of the times. He also learned about the coats of arms and devices of heraldry.

At the age of twenty-one or so the young man was ceremonially inducted into knighthood by the overlord and church officials upon proof of his worth on the field of battle or tournament. As he was dubbed knight, he dedicated himself to service to his overlord and to the church and took the oaths of allegiance to both. The ritual might include a symbolic bath, prayer, or vigorous exercise as a ceremonial means of purifying himself of sins.

The young knight was now ready to enter upon his duties at the court and undertake his obligations as a vassal, in return for which he might receive some land or other means of subsistence as a fief. His training perhaps had included some instruction concerning feudal laws and how to manage a manor and estate, or perhaps he had simply gained experience by watching others deal with the workmen and serfs. In any case he was sure to acquire the accepted attitudes of superiority toward the common people and the art of commanding others of lower position. The whole training was a class education for entrance into the aristocracy.

Girls of the noble class were also inducted into adult life by learning the religious faith and ceremonies, the social accomplishments of dancing, singing, and instrumental music, and the accepted practices of courtesy. A young girl might also receive instruction in sewing, weaving, and handcraft and might learn how to manage household servants. She perhaps also learned to read and write in order to be able to conduct her correspondence and to keep books if occasion required. She was trained in these duties either at home or in a convent, and then in her teens she was likely to be assigned to the overlord's court to learn the social graces of the chivalrous life and to act as a lady in waiting or attendant upon the mistress of the court until marriage. In contrast to the bookish character of the church schools, the education of youth of the noble classes was a direct and practical induction through experience.

Vocational Education of the Craftsman. In the Early Middle Ages, as in most preindustrial societies, the most common methods of occupational education were simply direct imitation and handing down of skills from father to son. With the rise of towns and the acceleration of trade in the eleventh and twelfth centuries the skills of artisans improved noticeably, and by the time of the emergence of the medieval guilds in the twelfth and thirteenth centuries the methods of vocational education were also refined. Since the primary purpose of the guilds was to protect the quality of products and to keep down overproduction, many rules developed concerning entrance into the craft. One of the most important nonschool agencies of education was the system of apprenticeship that developed as a means of preparing youth for their occupation.

Like the education for knighthood and roughly equivalent in purpose to the training of page, squire, and knight, the education of the artisan also had three stages, apprentice, journeyman, and master. As an apprentice the boy was assigned to a master craftsman, often on the basis of a written contract, or indenture, which bound both parties to keep certain obligations. The master promised to teach the boy the skills of the trade, look after his morals and religion, give him his keep and perhaps a small stipend, and teach him whatever reading and writing might be needed to carry on the trade. In most cases the reading and writing were probably negligible. In return, the boy promised to work hard and faithfully, keep the secrets of the trade, and not cause the master too much trouble. The period of apprenticeship varied greatly and might last anywhere from 3 to 10 or 11 years. The boys might start any time after seven or eight years of age.

The next stage was that of training as a journeyman, during which the young man might travel about, working as a day laborer for different masters in their shops, or might work in a larger shop for a longer period of time for a wage to be set by the guild. Then, if he proved his worth and could present a masterpiece showing that he had mastered the skills of the trade, he would be admitted to the guild as a full-fledged member, with appropriate ceremony. As a master craftsman, he could set up his own shop, hire journeymen, take on apprentices, and become an instructor in the art of the craft.

Higher Education: The Seven Liberal Arts

Prior to the rise of the universities in the twelfth and thirteenth centuries, the principal content of higher education was the seven liberal arts, as described earlier. In general, the trivium (grammar, rhetoric, and logic) came prior to the more advanced studies of the quadrivium (arithmetic, geometry, astronomy, and music). Beyond these liberal arts came the professional studies of law, medicine, and theology.

Grammar at Chartres. The highest point in the medieval teaching of grammar was reached at the cathedral school of Chartres during the twelfth century. The textbooks of Donatus and Priscian were still the basis for the study of grammar, but it was by no means confined to these authors. Students and masters alike studied many of the classical authors and wrote compositions for development of style. The methods, ideas, and attitudes of Chartres can best be illustrated by a consideration of two of the noted teachers.

Bernard of Chartres was an eminent teacher who reflected the reverent dependence on the classics that was a main feature of Chartres. Learning, for Bernard, was the fruit of long and patient thought, careful study of worthy models, and a tranquil life free from distractions. He considered grammar to be the basis of all culture and protested against the hurried and unintelligent drill based on textbooks. He assigned portions of the works of classical authors to be memorized; he had his students write daily compositions with particular attention to content, style, and quality; and he corrected carefully his students' prose and verse, criticizing their knowledge and taste. Bernard was mindful of Christian piety, but he loved the classics so much that he believed that grammar in its broadest sense should be studied for itself.

John of Salisbury, Bishop of Chartres when he died in 1180, wrote a pure, gracious Latin. Cicero especially influenced his style, philosophy, attitude toward life, and writings, which ranged from letters, history, and politics to poetry, education, and philosophy. John also knew the Bible and the Fathers, but he believed the classics were worthy of study for their own sake. He saw no essential antagonism between the secular Romans and Christians, but he fused them into a rounded Christian Humanism. He bitterly attacked those whom he termed "Cornificians," who would offer students a "get-learning-quick" method of study so that they could cut their academic course short and proceed to the practical business of living.

John advanced nearly all the arguments that have ever been made in favor of Humanistic training as opposed to practical or synthetic education. True education, he considered, required a thorough grounding in the classics in order to obtain knowledge, develop critical judgment and discriminating taste, and acquire the mature understanding necessary to the contemplative mind. Rhetoric or logic he thought to be of little value and even harmful unless based on wisdom gained through patient study of the humanities. John of Salisbury's own writings give evidence of an amazingly wide knowledge of classical authors. There is considerable evidence that John was not an exception at Chartres, for the Latin that was written in the twelfth century seems to have been of higher literary quality than that of the thirteenth.

Abélard at Paris. As Chartres was famous for its teaching of grammar in the twelfth century, so was Paris famous for its teaching of logic; and preeminent among the teachers at Paris was Abélard. So famous did he become that he was instrumental in turning the attention of students from the humanities to the delights of dialectics. A brilliant lecturer, a skillful dialectician, a witty classroom entertainer, Abélard was bold, lucid, original, and sharply controversial. He was always fresh and stimulating, and therefore he was just the sort of teacher to attract youthful attention at a time when the usual method of teaching was dry lecturing, eternal glossing of materials, reciting of propositions and counterpropositions, citing of authorities, and abstruse disputation. His remarkable range of reading permitted him to illustrate his lectures and enliven them with concrete examples. By his brilliance, criticism, and pugnacity Abélard fired interest and enthusiasm until students flocked to his schools in Paris by the hundreds and even thousands.

When he was forced to leave Paris, his hold upon his students was so great that they followed him wherever he went, seeking him out in the woods and repeatedly forcing him to return to teaching throughout his life. It was characteristic of Abélard that he aroused either violent dislike or equally devoted loyalty. Great teacher as he was, as well as shrewd and fearless critic, nevertheless, for profound insight, constructive power, and mastery of synthesis, he could not be compared with St. Anselm or St. Thomas Aquinas. His poetry and love songs, however, exhibited emotional qualities of versatility and genius that the works of these others did not.

Origin of the Prescribed Curriculum. With the rise of the university system, an expansion of the liberal arts curriculum followed. To the seven liberal arts were gradually added the newly discovered works of Aristotle on the physical sciences ("natural philosophy"), ethics and politics ("moral philosophy"), and metaphysics ("mental philosophy"). For example, the faculty of theology at the University of Paris was slow to accept the scientific works of Aristotle; and, because they did not seem to fit in with church doctrines, the Papacy made many efforts to keep them out of the university faculties.

The arts faculty, however, was much more receptive to Aristotle's philosophy and set out to digest and assimilate it. In this way, the arts faculty made itself more vital and attractive to students. As Aristotle gradually became "respectable" and as his works were reconciled with church doctrine, particularly through the efforts of Albertus Magnus and St. Thomas Aquinas, the philosophical and scientific studies of Aristotle came to be prescribed along with the traditional seven liberal arts in the arts curriculum.

Whence came the power to require these and only these studies for a liberal education? The origin of prescription seems to be in the church's practice of licensing its teachers. Since all teachers in the Middle Ages were clerics and since it was felt that all clerics should be trained properly in religious orthodoxy as well as in the tools of scholarship, the church found it expedient to control entrance into the teaching profession. This was done by granting a license to teach (*licentia docendi*), the condition for receiving which was the successful completion of the course in the liberal arts. Before the rise of the university system, the *licentia* was granted by the bishop or chancellor of the cathedral schools, but, with the spread of university organization, the license, or degree, came to be granted by the faculty of arts. The first complete prescribed curriculum in arts seems to have been laid down at the University of Paris in 1215.

In general, when the student had finished the study of the elementary liberal arts, he was granted the baccalaureate degree (bachelor of arts, or B.A.), which indicated that he was ready to be an assistant teacher. He then studied the higher liberal arts and Aristotelian philosophy for some 3 years more, at the conclusion of which he was granted the final license to teach and was entitled to become a master teacher (master of arts, or M.A.). To win the master's degree, the student usually was required to prepare a thesis and defend it against disputants in much the same manner that a journeyman presented his masterpiece to the guild members as proof of his qualification to become a master workman.

The specific requirements in the English universities, which were directly the progenitors of the American college, were somewhat as follows: At Oxford, the student followed a 4-year course of study under a tutor for his B.A. degree; a first examination included grammar and arithmetic, and a second included rhetoric, logic, and probably music. Three years more of study beyond the B.A. were required for the M.A. degree, during which the student read prescribed books on geometry, astronomy, and Aristotelian "philosophy" (physical science, ethics, and metaphysics). The arts course at Cambridge as well as at Oxford included the prescription of the old seven liberal arts and the new philosophical studies of Aristotle. Remnants of all these studies were found in the early American colleges.

It might be noted here that we are peculiarly the inheritors of the medieval tendency to organize and institutionalize. For example, the grouping of studies into separate faculties, the requiring of students to confine themselves largely to one faculty, the allotment of a definite period of years to the student's course, the giving of examinations, and the granting of degrees or titles with formality and ceremony are all distinctly medieval in origin. The most important educational characteristic of the medieval university institution, however, was its tendency to mark out a definite course of study or curriculum, and to prescribe certain books to be read by the students.

Colleges and University Life. When a boy or young man went to the university in the Middle Ages, he simply sought out the master under whom he wished to study, signed his name on that master's roll, and paid him his fees directly. The student then lodged where he could and acquired the clerical gown as a sign that he was a student and thus a minor cleric. Since many of the students apparently began as mere boys in their teens, the question of lodging often became a problem, especially for the poorer students. Gradually, philanthropy came to their rescue, and rich benefactors provided buildings where they could live, or the friars opened their houses to take them in.

A college in its origin was thus simply a rooming and boarding house for young and indigent scholars. As would be natural, the matter of discipline soon became a problem, and some universities began to assign masters to these colleges to keep order. Then, in the centuries following the Middle Ages, these masters, or tutors, in the colleges began to take on teaching functions, until at length the colleges became the most important teaching agencies of the English universities at Oxford and Cambridge. Most of the early American colleges were modeled upon the college ideal of the English universities.

The methods of instruction at the medieval universities were principally in the form of lectures, repetitions, and disputations. The lecture consisted primarily of reading aloud from the textbook by the master and then his commenting upon the material line by line. These commentaries when written out were called "glosses." The lecturing might be very complicated as one master elaborated upon certain passages by referring to the glosses of a whole series of scholars who had commented upon each other. The repetition was basically a review of the materials of the lectures and textbooks, and the disputation was a formal elaboration by students who argued, defended, and attacked certain theses according to established rules for argumentation.

The life of the student was doubtless an exhilarating one when it came to the "extracurricular" side. As antidotes for complicated lectures and texts, students engaged in all sorts of activities that were frowned upon by the university authorities, who made little or no effort to provide acceptable physical or social activities for students. The regulations listing prohibited pastimes reveal what the students enjoyed doing. Fighting and brawling were perhaps the most popular. Regulations were also issued against cock fights, tennis, gambling, singing and playing musical instruments, and the keeping of such pets as parrots, hawks, monkeys, bears, wolves, and dogs. The singing of student songs, storytelling, and drinking apparently took much time. These were natural activities in institutions where organized sports and physical education, scientific investigations of nature, and social intercourse were not admitted to standing along with intellectual training, mental discipline, and the study of books.

Professional Instruction: Law, Medicine, and Theology

In the Early Middle Ages some of the monastic schools and cathedral schools often taught elements of law, medicine, and theology along with the liberal arts, without much differentiation. For example, at Chartres before the twelfth century, law and theology were taught incidentally whenever material on these subjects was found in the writings of the various church Fathers or in the various compilations of knowledge. However, from the twelfth century on, the study of law, medicine, and theology gradually became recognized as separate, advanced professional studies; and the liberal arts came to be looked upon as preparatory to these more advanced studies. With the development of university organization, separate faculties of law, medicine, and theology were created in many of the universities.

Law at Bologna and Elsewhere. The revival of interest in legal studies at Bologna in Italy paralleled somewhat the acceleration of intellectual interest that marked the growth of grammar at Chartres and logic at Paris, but in Italy this revival took a somewhat different turn. Whereas education was largely a function of monasteries and cathedrals in the north, the revival had great effect among the secular teachers in Italy. Scholars and masters were often laymen interested in civil careers and were thus not automatically clerics or priests, nor were they subject to any greater ecclesiastical supervision than were other laymen. In Italy the subject matter of the schools emphasized the seven liberal arts; but grammar was not taught as a literary and Humanistic study as at Chartres, nor was logic taught as a dialectical exercise as at Paris. Rather, grammar and rhetoric were looked upon as a preparatory, practical preparation for the study of law, medicine, and dictamen. The reasons for this doubtless lay in the different cultural conditions that obtained in Italy; municipal life instead of feudalism, political rather than theological and religious interests, the struggles of the cities for independence, and the investiture struggles between pope and emperor.

The Roman law had remained strong in the use and tradition of the Lombard towns of northern Italy from the later days of the Roman Empire. Justinian's *Corpus Juris Civilis* had been handed down by the lawyer class, and elementary law had often been taught wherever instruction was given in the schools of liberal arts. Law was often thought of as a branch of rhetoric; and schools at Rome, Pavia, and Ravenna were known for the study of law in the eleventh century long before Bologna gained preeminence. The study of law permeated much of the instruction in Italian schools; Bologna simply became the outstanding example among many cities where the tradition was strong.

Bologna became well known as a *studium generale* for the arts in the eleventh century, but its reputation for legal studies came to overshadow all else at the time of the investiture struggle in the twelfth century. The legal revival was accelerated in the early twelfth century by Irnerius, whose fame attracted students to Bologna much as Abélard's attracted them to Paris. Under the leadership of Irnerius, a greater attention was given to the close technical and professional study of the *Corpus Juris Civilis* for its practical usefulness rather than as a literary or philosophical treatment. An organized and systematic study of the whole *Corpus Juris Civilis* became the required curriculum of an ordinary legal education. The differentiation of the law from a general education in the liberal arts accompanied the growth of a new class of students who were older and more independent than elsewhere.

Those who favored the emperor's side in the investiture struggle found support in the Roman civil law. So the supporters of the Papacy had to look for better justification of the Pope's claims. This they found in 1142 in the great work of Gratian, who did for canon law almost what Justinian's code did for the civil law. He codified and systematized authorities from the Bible, writings of the church Fathers, canons of the church councils, letters and decrees of the popes, edicts of the Roman emperors, Justinian's laws, capitularies of the Frankish and Lombard kings, and the customs of the church. Gratian arrived at the position that ecclesiastical law was superior to secular law and that therefore the authority of the church was paramount. Gratian's *Decretum* had a very wide vogue as a textbook in law schools until it became the fundamental authority for the study of the canon law, and it has never been entirely superseded. From this time on, Bologna became famous for its canon law as well as for its civil law, and the way was paved for the rise of the University of Bologna.

Medicine at Salerno. The revival in medicine during the eleventh and twelfth centuries was fully as marked as that in grammar, logic, and law. For more than two centuries Salerno, as a school of medicine in southern Italy, rivaled in academic fame the schools at Chartres, Paris, and Bologna. The origins of the school at Salerno are obscure, but there are traces of the study and practice of medicine at Salerno as far back as the ninth century. By the tenth century it was famous for the skill of its physicians, and by the middle of the eleventh century its celebrity in Europe was established. Since Salerno was purely a medical school, it never developed other faculties and did not arrive at the completed university type of organization. It was, nevertheless, important, for it revealed how the medical traditions of Greece and Rome had continued in southern Italy much as the legal tradition had persisted in northern Italy.

In the eleventh century the courts of Salerno acknowledged the authority of the Eastern emperors and were in constant communication with Constantinople. The concentration of medical science and its revival at Salerno were thus a counterpart of the survival of the Greek language in southern Italy. Medical study was further stimulated by the fact that Salerno had long been noted as a health resort with a mild climate and mineral springs. In addition to the Greek and Roman medical science of Hippocrates, Galen, and others, Arabic science began to influence Salerno through the efforts of such scholars as Constantinus Africanus, who translated many Greek, Arabic, and Hebrew medical books into Latin. Arabic medical science was thus disseminated among the medical faculties of the universities of Europe.

Theology at Paris. The twelfth and thirteenth centuries saw a great upswing in the study of theology that paralleled and then came to surpass the other studies of higher and professional learning in the Middle Ages. We have already noted that the introduction of Aristotelian science in the thirteenth century greatly influenced the faculties of arts and theology. The arts faculty of Paris, for example, eagerly welcomed this new scientific material, and it was now the turn of the quadrivium to enjoy huge popularity, for all else was subordinated to Aristotle's scientific and mathematical philosophy. Many arts professors were attracted by the interpretations of Aristotle made by the Islamic scholar Averroes. These Averroists, who were strict Aristotelians, began to dominate the arts faculty, but the church became alarmed at their doctrines of the eternity of the world and the indestructibility of matter. If the world were eternal, God could not have created it; and if matter were indestructible, it would rank with the soul as immortal.

Therefore, the first move of the church was to condemn Aristotle's *Physics* in 1209 and his *Metaphysics* in 1215, outlawing them from instruction in the university. Its second move was to assimilate Aristotle and correct his errors. Outstanding in their efforts to accomplish this task were Alexander of Hales, Albertus Magnus, and St. Thomas Aquinas, all of whom taught at one time or another at the University of Paris. By the time St. Thomas Aquinas had completed his work and the Dominicans had taken up the cudgels for Thomism, Aristotle was installed permanently within Catholic doctrine. Theology had become the keystone of all university study, the highest of the high, with all other studies subordinate to it. The faculty of theology at Paris and elsewhere ultimately became virtually an arbiter in matters theological, deciding disputes, defining heresy, and on occasion even correcting the theology of the Pope himself.

Chapter 7

THE RENAISSANCE

The term "Renaissance," in historical usage, has been applied principally to the period of the fourteenth, fifteenth, and early sixteenth centuries. Some historians have heretofore looked upon the Renaissance as a time of sudden rebirth of the classical spirit and have attributed most of its cultural changes to the revival of interest in classical learning. More recently, however, it is generally agreed that there was much more to the Renaissance, and that many of its institutional and intellectual trends had their origins deep in the Middle Ages. The Renaissance, however, did reveal a general efflorescence of life and a speeding up of institutional as well as intellectual and artistic change. If there is a single key to the explanation of the Renaissance, it is probably in the growing secularism of the times. This can be seen in the complicated interweaving of nearly all aspects of Renaissance life. Secular forces had already become strong in the Middle Ages, but the clue to the Renaissance is that secularism began to permeate Renaissance culture to a greater degree.

EMERGENCE OF THE MODERN STATE

Centralization and Decentralization in Political Institutions

In general, the striking thing about political development in the Renaissance was the continued and rapid growth of the centralized political authority of the monarchies in France and England. In this process the medieval political traditions of feudalism were giving way to the modern institutions of the national state. In contrast, however, political developments in Germany and Italy reflected a much more decentralized and confused situation. The earlier rise of France and England to national sovereignty gave them a head start in the world scene and enabled them to acquire great colonial empires, whereas Germany and Italy were not strong enough to achieve such power until much later.

At the beginning of the Renaissance in France, King Philip IV (the Fair) began to assert his rights to full sovereign power rather than merely as overlord to the nobles. He gathered about him professional lawyers trained at his court and loyal to him. With their help he struck severe blows at the nobles and at the Pope, two of the powers that stood in the way of his effort to become supreme ruler of France. Philip IV also enlisted the middle classes on his side by giving them a voice in the States-General, and thus gained further support to consolidate his power. By the end of the Hundred Years' War with England, the French nobles and the States-General had lost power, and the king emerged as the absolute ruler. The king was now able to levy his taxes directly upon the nobles and the middle classes without the intermediaries that had been set up under feudalism. Finally, with the reign of Francis I (1515 to 1547), France became one of the great powers in Europe.

A similar process of centralization of political power was occurring in England and at an even more rapid rate. Edward I was more quickly successful than Philip the Fair in establishing his royal machinery at the expense of the nobles and in setting up courts of law responsible directly to himself. The decisions of the king's judges began to give to the English common law the form that it was to maintain for centuries. The feudal laws and local customs were gradually replaced by the common law as expressed by the king's courts. Likewise, Parliament gained during the fourteenth century the power of introducing legislation in return for granting money to the kings.

The House of Commons, made up of middle-class representatives from the cities and the landowning gentry from the rural sections, became more representative of the whole country at an earlier date than did the States-General in France. Furthermore, a spirit of national consciousness was heightened as the common man felt himself more a part of the nation because he had fought in the wars as a foot soldier. Henry VIII, who personified the Renaissance life of England at its height, much as Francis I did in France, made rapid gains in further weakening the nobles and gaining the adherence of the merchant classes by aiding English commerce and industry.

In contrast to the growing centralization of political authority in France and England, the German, Slavic, and Magyar states of central and eastern Europe were marked by confusion, rivalries, and constant changes of boundaries and peoples. Much of this region of Europe was nominally a part of the Holy Roman Empire, but there existed little of the authority usually associated with the word "empire." Dozens of states, large and small, were ruled by family dynasties and joined together only by more or less loosely held loyalties and responsibilities, all supposedly owing allegiance to the emperor. The crown was bandied from family to family and contended for by the princes who could get the necessary political or military support. The emperor was chosen by a College of Electors, which consisted for a long time of seven members, three church and four secular rulers. Although the emperors usually tried to maintain and extend their powers, the College of Electors and the many coalitions formed among the other states were able to keep alive during most of the

Renaissance period the forces of particularism against the dynastic ambitions of the Hohenstaufen and the Hapsburg emperors.

Politically, Italy was made up of a number of independent city-states. There was no central political authority to weld the various cities into a nation as was being done in France, England, and Spain. The Italian cities had begun to win their independence from the feudal nobles during a long process of legal and military conflicts in the Later Middle Ages. This process was accelerated in the fourteenth century when it was found that common foot soldiers with guns and gunpowder were more than a match for armored knights.

In those cities where the merchant guilds were strongest republican forms of government were set up, as in Venice, Florence, and elsewhere. In other cities the nobles were able to maintain power, as in the duchies of Milan and Mantua and the kingdoms of Naples and Sicily. For nearly the whole of the Renaissance the Italian cities exerted great leadership in economic and cultural affairs, but their eventual decline was forecast by the invasion by France in 1494, after which Italy became a battleground for the French, Spanish, and Germans. Italy, of course, had great political influence in Europe through the Papacy, but the political power of the Pope was declining as a result of the attacks from many secular sources, to be described shortly.

Economic Expansion

The upswing in European commerce and trade that had begun in the twelfth and thirteenth centuries was accelerated during the Renaissance. In general, the free cities of Italy and of northern Germany were the leaders in the early Renaissance, but by the sixteenth century the center was beginning to shift to the Atlantic trade routes as the discoveries of Vasco da Gama, Columbus, and Magellan opened up new horizons for commerce across the ocean rather than simply across the Mediterranean, the Baltic, and the North Sea.

Of great importance was the growing political power of the middle classes in the English Parliament and French States-General, as well as their dominance of the Italian cities. This trend reflected the increasing wealth and economic power of the merchant groups, known as "burghers" or *bourgeoisie*, congregated in the cities. The same process was taking place in Germany, where rich trading families were appearing.

In nearly every country of Europe, the Renaissance period was marked by the outbreak of violent and bloody revolts of the peasants. In the middle of the fourteenth century the overcrowded and unsanitary conditions of town life, the famines, and the Black Death killed off vast numbers of persons. As a result of this depopulation, there was a greater demand than ever for workers to till the fields and work in the cities. This helped to hasten the freedom of the serfs and the commutation of their feudal ties. Stirred to action by their conditions and the possibility of improvement, the peasants revolted in England in the fourteenth century. By the end of the fifteenth century most English serfs had obtained their freedom and had become tenant farmers, hired laborers, independent yeomen, or city workingmen.

Although the economic status of the peasants was actually better in the late fifteenth century than it had been, the discontent was greater because of the obvious inequalities in the distribution of wealth as revealed by the extravagant display of the wealthy merchant classes and because of the injustices of the system of land ownership. Discontent was heightened by bad harvests and rising prices, but the nobles were not disposed to be generous, nor was the church. Even Luther, who was preaching the equality of men in the sight of God, exhorted the nobility to put down the peasants' revolts with all the means at their disposal. The age of the common man was not yet.

Protests and Revolts against the Church

Decline of the Papacy and the Conciliar Movement. Attacks upon the Papacy by the kings grew in intensity during the Renaissance; the most outstanding of these involved Pope Boniface VIII and King Philip IV of France. Boniface issued a series of papal bulls in which he exhorted his clergy not to pay taxes to the kings, denied the right of secular courts to try the clergy, issued a proclamation (*Unam Sanctam*) of his complete sovereignty over all secular rulers, and specifically declared Philip IV deposed. Philip IV in turn sent his agents to Italy, who raised a small army, captured Boniface, and demanded that he quit the Papacy. The result of the whole episode was a terrible fall in the prestige of the Papacy.

For some 70 years afterward the popes were Frenchmen. They were controlled by France, and the seat of the Papacy was located at Avignon in France. During this so-called "Babylonian captivity" of the Papacy (1309 to 1377), rival Italian popes at Rome made claims to legitimacy, and the church was further torn by the Great Schism as these contestants carried on their claims and counterclaims. Finally some of the cardinals called the Council of Pisa in 1409 to heal the schism. This heralded the so-called "conciliar movement" in the church.

At the Council of Constance in 1414 the principle was specifically asserted that the council rather than the Pope was supreme in church matters. Many more church councils were held, all of which revealed an attempt to establish authority over the Pope and make him a sort of spokesman for a constitutional body rather than the supreme authority in the church. As these nationalistic movements increased, the councils became in effect a league of strong national churches rather than representatives of one international church. Finally, in the sixteenth-century Reformation, the national churches became strong enough to break away entirely under the leadership of Luther, Calvin, and others.

By 1500 attacks upon the church were increasing and were being delivered from many directions. Not only were many of the secular rulers, kings, and emperors trying to extend their authority at the expense of the church, but the peasants were seething with discontent and the middle classes were restless under the taxes and tithes that were expected by the church. The cry was that the clergy were so incredibly worldly and rich that they neglected their religious duties.

Forerunners of Protestantism. John Wycliffe, a teacher of theology and philosophy at Oxford in the fourteenth century, was one of the most effective of those who protested against the worldliness and abuses of the church and urged reforms in theology and practice. The most important of his ideas on religious reform were as follows: (1) Since each person is a direct vassal of God and holds his possessions by His grace, he should enjoy them only on condition that he render due service and loyalty to God. (2) The terms by which men enjoy these possessions are set forth in the Bible, and therefore everyone should have access to the Scriptures in order to know these terms. (3) It is the duty of the clergy to be pious, to live modest lives, and to give up worldly concerns; if the clergy fail in these respects, it is the duty of the state to reform the church.

Acting upon these principles, Wycliffe attacked papal authority, urged the direct responsibility of the individual to God, and sponsored the translation of the Bible into English so that all could read it. His followers, known as the Lollards, followed his ideas with a petition to Parliament in 1395 to enact a series of church reforms, but Parliament not only paid no attention to the petition but was induced to pass a law in 1401 for the burning of heretics. In 1408 the Archbishop of Canterbury issued a series of decrees prohibiting the publication of Lollard books and the English translation of the Bible without the license of the bishop concerned. Wycliffe was apparently one of the first learned men to claim the discrepancy between the Bible and the practices of the church and thus paved the way in idea for the Protestant reformers who were able to break away from the church 150 years later.

Wycliffe's ideas were directly transferred to Bohemia where the University of Prague became the center of a reform movement in that country. Religious reforms were linked with a nationalist Bohemian movement under the leadership of John Huss, who launched a special protest against the sale of indulgences. He was summoned to the Council of Constance on charges of heresy and was given the promise of safe conduct by the emperor; but the promise was retracted, and he was tried, condemned, and burned at the stake.

The stirrings of religious unrest were found also in Italy as revealed in the preaching of Savonarola, famous Dominican friar in Florence. Savonarola was a zealous reformer who brooded over the low state of morality and religion in Italy and forecast that Italy was doomed if a reformation did not occur. He became a powerful preacher against sin, lashing the practice of simony, the wealth of the church, and lax popes. He gained a strong grip on the lower classes by his inflammatory preaching and his prophecies of doom and destruction, but his friendliness toward France and his accusations against Pope Alexander VI led the city government to try, torture, and hang him. Too much revolt against the church could not succeed in Italy any more than it could elsewhere in the fifteenth century.

Attacks upon Established Authorities

The increasing emphasis upon the secular aspect of life can be seen in the development of Renaissance social thought much as it can be seen in Renaissance political, economic, and religious institutions.

Rights of the State against the Church. Just as political institutions became more secular in practice, so did Renaissance thought begin to give more attention to man as a political, economic, and social being. One of the outstanding exponents of this viewpoint in the fourteenth century was Pierre Dubois, royal advocate to Philip IV of France, whose chief work is entitled *The Recovery of the Holy Land.* The main point of his argument was that the church should give up its secular ambitions and leave all matters of secular authority to the state. He did not criticize the religious functions of the church but insisted that it drop its activities in respect to business, landed property, and war, so that the clergy might concentrate on religious interests. Establishment of perpetual peace was a major concern of Dubois, who envisaged, not a world government, but rather a world religion headed by the Pope, who should call a world council in which the states would swear to maintain peace, substitute arbitration for war, and ship all warlike people to the Holy Land.

Another plea for world peace in the fourteenth century was made by Marsiglio of Padua, an Italian who became professor of arts and rector of the University of Paris. Marsiglio's *Defender of the Peace* took a quite different position from that of Dubois. Marsiglio insisted that the state was the true defender of the peace and that the church and especially the Pope were the enemies of peace. In his treatise, Marsiglio expressed the fundamentally democratic doctrine that the source of all coercive power is the sovereign people, who are the true legislators but who may delegate this power to a committee or to one individual. In thus stating the elective rather than the monarchical principle, Marsiglio insisted that the obligations of government apply to the ruler as well as to the ruled and that the ruler may be removed when he does not fulfill his obligations to the people.

Moreover, Marsiglio claimed that the clergy should have no coercive power whatever. The Scriptures state all that is necessary for salvation, the clergy may interpret the Bible and define heresy, but all penalties and punishment are the province of the state, and heretics should not be punished unless guilty of overt acts of treason or attempt to overthrow the state. In these ways Marsiglio elaborated the doctrine of the supremacy of the state in a widely defined area of secular affairs.

The principle of the political authority of the state was carried much further by Machiavelli in the late fifteenth century. Machiavelli's basic assumptions were that men are by nature evil, selfish, greedy, and self-seeking and that a good state is one which is conducive to the common welfare of its members. All states will decay because of the inherent nature of man, but the best way to hold back the process is to set up a state that has a basis of liberty, a religion to keep people within reasonable control, a native army, and an efficient excutive. Machiavelli extolled the *real politik* of a ruler who will refrain from nothing that will benefit the state. It is at this point in his book called *The Prince* that he defended an executive who will not hesitate to go back on his word, to shed blood, or to use all manner of ruthlessness if such acts benefit the state, as judged by the results. Despite his belief in a limited monarchy or republic as the best forms of the state, Machiavelli had lost his faith in the sovereignty of the people, and thus his very name became the symbol of ruthless and totalitarian dictatorship.

Rights of the People against the Ruler. However, several other, albeit less influential, voices were raised to assert the principle that government should be based upon the consent of the people. In the fourteenth century Nicolas Oresme, writing on the theory of money, held that the king cannot alter the coinage without the consent of the governed. In his commentaries on Aristotle, Oresme argued that the community of citizens is free by nature and should never consent to tyranny. Nicolas of Cusa argued for constitutional government in which the strength of law depends upon consent, and freedom of election is the proper basis of orderly government. In England the parliamentarian cause was upheld by Sir John Fortescue, who preferred the English constitutional arrangements to the principles of the French monarchy or the Roman law.

Rights of the Individual against Authority. While the church and the state quarreled about whose authority should be supreme in the lives of men, there were some who began to assert the right of the individual to throw off the restraints of all authority and to develop his own individuality as he sees fit. The spirit of individualism began to claim that the individual man should be loyal principally to himself and should develop his own personality in all its aspects, creative, artistic, emotional, and physical as well as intellectual. On its best side this spirit approached the ancient Greek doctrine of the development of the well-rounded personality; on its worst side, it laid claim to such freedom as amounted to license. In the lives of the nobility and newly rich merchant classes the spirit of individualism could and did easily lead to the throwing off of all restraint and to the indulgence of all tastes no matter where they might lead. An opportunity had arisen to swing to the opposite extreme from the medieval ideal of self-abnegation, asceticism, and discipline.

On its more positive side the ideal of individualism was expressed in such books as the *Courtier* by Castiglione, in which he described the courtly gentleman of affairs who can fight, love, paint, compose poetry, and discuss the affairs of state with equal ease and effectiveness. Perhaps the best representative of the many-sided interests of the Renaissance was Leonardo da Vinci, who combined the achievements of the scientist, practical inventor, and artist. He seems to have been interested in virtually the whole range of human experience.

STRUGGLES OVER THE CONTROL OF EDUCATION

Many of the political quarrels between the kings and the church and between the people and the nobles were reenacted in struggles over the control of schools. Just as modern nations have realized anew that political power rests, in the last analysis, not only upon military and legal power but also upon the control of education, so the Renaissance began to realize dimly this important relationship. Although the church maintained its strong position in the face of attacks, nevertheless definite gains were made by kings and other rulers in establishing, maintaining, or interfering with the schools and universities. This was not a time when complete national or state school systems were set up, but the groundwork was being laid for national systems of schools in later centuries.

Likewise, the rise of commercial and business interests, personified in the increased power and status of the middle class, was reflected in at least two changes in the schools. One was an impetus given to vernacular schools that would give to the children of the middle classes the rudiments of reading and writing as a means of preparing them to engage in the everyday affairs of business, legal, and commercial transactions. The other change was the growing interest of the middle classes in the Latin schools as a means by which their children could gain social and intellectual access to the company of the upper classes. By putting their new sources of wealth at the disposal of schools, the middle classes began to make available to their children a "gentlemanly" education that could not otherwise be attained.

The faint outlines of the modern organization of schools began to appear in the distinction between vernacular, or "elementary," education for the ordinary people and classical, or "secondary," education for the upper classes. This distinction was not solidified or standardized during the Renaissance, but, as in so many other fields of endeavor, the roots of such distinction were gaining strength in the soil of Renaissance life and were being made ready to sprout during later centuries.

Claims for Civil Control of Schools

The medieval pattern of school control had been centered in the church, with the Pope in supreme authority but with local administration in the hands of the bishop for his diocese or delegated by him to his *scholasticus*. The licensing of teachers came from these officials, who exerted general supervision over the schools in their jurisdiction. This pattern was naturally carried over into the Renaissance, for the church continued to maintain its parish schools, monastic schools, and cathedral schools and to play an important role in the universities of Europe. As the cities grew, however, it became necessary for the larger cities to locate schools in outlying parishes and in different parts of the town, because it had become difficult for children to travel from the outskirts of town to the central church. Conflicts over the control of new schools arose between church officials, who felt that the control of education was properly theirs, and other agencies, who began to lay claim to the right to establish and maintain schools. Among these agencies were the town governments, the secular rulers, private teachers, and voluntary associations of persons who wished to endow schools.

Town Schools. The Italian towns had continued to maintain their schools throughout the Middle Ages, some of them doubtless exhibiting more or less continuity with their original foundations in the days of the Roman Empire. A decree in Ferrara in 1443 stated that new grammar schools could not be established unless the town council approved such a school. In Germany severe struggles arose between the church officials and the town authorities concerning whether or not the towns could set up schools under their own jurisdiction. Gradually, the towns won the right to establish schools by appealing for support either to the local ruler or to the Pope over the head of the local bishop. In general, the foundations of Germany's modern public-parochial system were being laid as the town and church often reached agreements for joint operation of the schools. Often the priest would do the teaching, but the town would pay his salary and looked upon him as a public official. As many of the Netherlands towns won freedom from the control of the feudal nobility, they also began to assert their rights to build schools and to choose and pay teachers.

Authority of the Ruler. As a part of the general assertion of the rights of the state against the church, rulers began to lay greater claim to the control of education. The dukes and rulers of Italian cities often set up schools at their courts for the education of noble children and for the greater glorification of the court. Such were the schools of Vittorino da Feltre at Mantua and Guarino at Ferrara. In Brussels the Duke of Brabant established several elementary schools for both boys and girls in the early fourteenth century. In Scotland King James I in the early fifteenth century decreed that public schools should be maintained as one means of reforming the clergy and promoting the ability to read and write.

In England the authority of the kings was increasingly being asserted in educational control. In 1391 Richard II denied a petition from the House of Commons that children of villeins should be prevented from attending school. Some time later it was decided through legislation and court decisions that all parents could freely send their children to any school in England, provided, of course, that they could afford to do so. In the fifteenth century Henry VI and, later, Henry VIII were instrumental in founding many new grammar schools.

Private Teachers. As the clientele available for school instruction grew larger and as the lucrative possibilities in school teaching were realized, the private teacher began to appear on the scene with a view to making his living from the fees and tuition he could obtain. In general, the private and unauthorized teacher met with resistance both from the church and from the civil authorities. It has already been noted how the city of Ferrara tried to prevent unauthorized teachers from operating. In Ypres the town ruled that the three established schools should be the only ones to give instruction outside of individual homes; private tutors could be employed in the home if they gave instruction only to the children of the family and admitted no others. The Duke of Brabant established his own schools in Brussels to settle a quarrel that arose when certain private teachers kept on teaching without the approval of the *scholasticus.* In Gloucester, England, the masters of the established grammar school brought court action to restrain an unauthorized teacher from operating in the locality, but the court decided that there could be no private monopoly in the right to conduct grammar schools.

As time went on, private teachers began to organize themselves into guilds in order to protect themselves and to gain the right to teach. For example, in Germany the teachers of writing, commercial arithmetic, and bookkeeping organized themselves into the guild of *rechenmeisters.* They took an apprentice for several years, at the end of which he became a journeyman, known as a *schreiber*, until he became a full-fledged master in the guild.

Voluntary Foundations. During the Renaissance the endowment principle in England went beyond the medieval chantry foundation, which had as its basis a religious motive, and was extended to include foundations designed specifically for the establishment of schools. When wealthy individuals or groups contributed money for the founding of schools, secular control was being exerted where church control had been present before. These foundations were the origins of the English "public schools," the first of which was founded by William of Wykeham in 1382 at Winchester and the second at Eton in 1440 under Henry VI. The teachers were thus not directly responsible to church authorities, for the schools had a corporate existence independent of church control, although they remained highly religious in content and character. Boards of trustees were set up for the general supervision of the schools, and, in some cases at least, these included representatives of the merchant or craft guilds. Whereas the schools of the medieval guilds were regularly taught by the clergy, the trend in the later Renaissance was to appoint and even to require the appointment of secular teachers in these public schools and guild schools.

Universities. In general, the older universities of the Renaissance remained freer from civil controls than did the lower schools. This was doubtless a result of the long struggles carried on by the universities during the Middle Ages to achieve autonomy from church and state, but the rulers were gaining strength. In France the universities were centers of conservatism as far as Humanist learning was concerned; hence Francis I set up the Collège de France to be hospitable to Humanism, and the city of Bordeaux established the Collège de Guyenne under civil control. In the fifteenth century Louis XI decreed that the University of Paris was giving too much attention to the philosophy of nominalism and insisted that only realism should be taught in the arts and theological faculties; professors were required to take an oath to comply with this, and degrees were denied to students who did not conform. Although the decree was rescinded a few years later, it showed the increasing tendency of rulers to try to interfere in the affairs of the universities. Likewise, Henry VIII was trying to build up Humanist learning at the universities of Oxford and Cambridge by establishing new colleges that would be favorable to this interest.

Aristocratic Nature of Renaissance Education

In general, the education of the Renaissance was intended mainly for the youth of the upper and wealthy classes. The church was primarily interested in developing scholars and clergy for future leadership in the church; the rulers were interested in surrounding themselves with trained and loyal adherents who would be gentlemen as well as scholars; and the middle classes were interested in breaking into these two charmed circles. There were, however, certain tendencies toward a more democratic approach. The demands for vernacular schools for the common people were gaining in force, although such schools had to take a definitely inferior place in comparison with the classical and Latin grammar schools. Also, the provision of schools for girls at the lowest levels began to increase in some of the towns in Germany, the Low Countries, and France. Despite these gains, however, Renaissance education, which had an enormous effect upon both Europe and America, was definitely in favor of an aristocratic education of the elite centering in the ideals of classical Humanism and the cultivation of the gentlemanly graces.

Improving Status of the Teaching Profession

Teachers doubtless gained in respect, social standing, and income during the Renaissance, especially those who were teaching in secondary schools. The patronage of teachers in the courtly schools gave them a high standing as the tutors of the youth of royal and noble birth. The wealth that flowed into town schools and private foundations gave impetus to the financial backing of education on a larger and larger scale. The fact that church officials held so tenaciously to their educational and teaching prerogatives and that others were so eager to obtain a share of teaching revenues indicates that teaching as a means of livelihood was increasing in public esteem. The increase in the number of secular teachers shows that teaching could be a full-time job and not merely incidental to the other tasks of the priest.

This improvement in status was not so true of the vernacular school teachers, who constantly had to fight for their rights to be teachers at all and who were always considered to be in an inferior position. This class distinction between secondary school teachers and elementary school teachers was a basic quality of European education that has lasted for centuries and that continues in considerable force in the United States to the present time. However, the fact that there were any vernacular teachers whatever in the Renaissance was a matter of some achievement.

Other Agencies of Education

Among the various nonschool agencies of education, the systems of apprenticeship set up by the guilds continued to be the most important methods of preparing youth of the lower and middle classes to enter upon their responsibilities as workers and citizens. The guilds continued to be strong and powerful in the political and economic life of the times throughout most of the Renaissance. For upper-class youth the training for knighthood and chivalry was losing its power as the nobility lost its former monopoly in the arts of war and politics. These youth turned to the courtly schools and the Latin grammar schools for whatever formal training they might gain. The vernacular literature began to provide wider sources of enjoyment for greater numbers of people, as did the public display of the art forms that were so profusely created, especially in the Italian Renaissance. The church, of course, continued to exert a powerful influence upon the people despite the attacks being made upon it. Finally, the first dim realizations of the possibilities of popular enlightenment through the printing press were beginning to appear, although not much headway was made in this respect until the Reformation and after.

THE GROWTH OF SECULAR THOUGHT

Appeals to Man and to Nature

In the realm of intellectual affairs, the center of gravity began to shift from the religious to human experience and from the spiritual interests of the other world to the natural interests of this world. The beginnings of modern science were taking the form of such beliefs and assumptions as the following: a certainty that the secrets of nature could be revealed and that the progress of such knowledge was inevitable; a belief that "science" should mean what we can learn by looking at nature rather than a body of knowledge inherited from the past; and, finally, the development of a scientific technique for obtaining such knowledge through the observation of nature, collection of facts, objective verification of facts, use of mathematical formulas in the process, and the application of the results to nature.

The Renaissance did not produce developments in science that can be compared with those of the seventeenth or eighteenth century, but the groundwork was being laid, the methods formulated, and the restraints of religious dogmatism gradually weakened. The discovery of the Americas led to intellectual questioning of the established social forms and the opening of new horizons through which the study of nature might reveal the fundamental nature of man as well as of things. Exploration and acquaintance with the primitive societies to be found in the Americas prompted interest in the "natural man" and the unspoiled "noble savage." Montaigne was struck with the fact that untutored savages with no ancient religion or "civilized" heritage could show such qualities as courage, honor, and integrity. The feeling grew that nature could produce a purer and better form of moral conduct than an oversophisticated civilization could.

Despite all the inroads made by secularism upon the medieval conceptions of the nature of the universe and man's relation to it, the dominant outlook concerning human destiny continued to be Christian theism. The challenge of the Renaissance thundered against the abuses of the church as an institution rather than against the basic foundations of Christian theology. The voice of criticism was rising, but science did not lay claim to the intellectual allegiance of men in any such degree as was achieved in later centuries. The movement, however, was under way in such writings as those of Copernicus, who formulated the heliocentric theory of the universe, though the implications of this revolutionary doctrine were not to be realized and championed for a long time. In general, the philosophical spokesmen of the Renaissance couched their writings in a way that kept within the general framework of Christianity.

With regard to the conceptions of human nature, there was considerable restiveness. The doctrine of original sin and the emphasis upon the inherent evil of human nature were beginning to be called into question. The spirit of naturalism began to say that human nature had qualities for potential goodness within itself. The example of aboriginal native Americans led some to stress the fact that primitive peoples could be good without the benefits of civilization and religion. The Renaissance murmurings against a pessimistic view of human nature formed the background for the clarion call of naturalism that was to be sounded by Rousseau and others in the eighteenth century. In general, however, Renaissance writers were content with urging the claims of human individuality and human creativeness to be achieved within the accepted religious framework. The accent upon the "human" in human nature led to indifference to or unconcern with the religious preoccupations of the Middle Ages but not to open revolt against the underlying conceptions.

With regard to the role of human intelligence in solving human problems and the methods to be followed in achieving knowledge, however, the revolt of the Renaissance thinkers was much more pronounced. In determining what knowledge was of most worth, the intellectual of the Renaissance was besieged by the authoritative claims of three major forces. These were (1) the Scholastic methods of theology, which looked to religious doctrine and Aristotelian philosophy for authority, (2) the inductive methods of science, which looked to nature for authority, and (3) the literary and linguistic methods of Humanism, which looked to the ancient classics for authority.

Scholasticism was the target for considerable criticism at the hands of the naturalists and the Humanists and, as a result, began to decline in importance as an intellectual method during the fourteenth and fifteenth centuries. This decline was a corollary of the attacks upon the institutional authority of the church during the same period. Scholastic method became much more complicated, elaborate, and difficult. One professor at Vienna took 13 years to expound and comment upon five chapters of Genesis. As the arguments became more abstruse, the Schoolmen seemed to delight more and more in arguments for their own sake and exhibited less freedom and originality of thought. Their achievements became less valuable in solving the vital problems that confronted human society.

The scientists and naturalists turned away from religious tradition and toward investigation of nature. They stressed observation of natural phenomena, the collection of facts, and the inductive methods of generalizing from the observed facts. They spent less time on the deductive methods of argumentation and commentary upon the works of Aristotle. Whereas the Scholastics had elevated the study of logic to a preeminent position among the liberal arts, the scientists concentrated upon the mathematical arts of arithmetic, geometry, and astronomy as well as the subject matter of natural history and natural philosophy.

The Humanists took up the hue and cry against Scholasticism and put emphasis upon grammar and rhetoric as the prime methods of human intelligence. They considered the literary accomplishments of reading, writing, and rhetorical exposition as the best achievements of the human mind and as the means by which the intellect might be cultivated in its highest forms. In this process the standards of value and of appreciation as well as of literary excellence were found in the great masterpieces of Greek and Latin literature. The best subject matter was considered to be, not religious doctrine or the secrets of nature, but the style and content of the ancient classics.

This shift of intellectual interests can be illustrated in many of the fields of knowledge of the Renaissance and represents one of the most important intellectual trends in the history of education. From the time of the Renaissance to the present, classical Humanism has played an enormous part in the ideals and methods of education in Europe and America, especially at the secondary and higher levels. By and large, because of the educational consequences of Humanism, the revival of ancient classical learning was the most influential intellectual factor of the Renaissance, just as the reassertion of religious interests was paramount in the Reformation, and as science had its turn in the Enlightenment.

Flowering of the Arts and Sciences

Humanism and the Revival of Classical Learning. Beginning in the fourteenth century in Italy and continuing through the fifteenth and sixteenth centuries in most of western Europe, men began to be more and more interested in ancient classical literature. The Humanists did not break violently with medievalism or with religion, but intense love for the classical languages and literature led them to scorn all other authority. In a narrow sense, the Humanists were no more interested in the investigation of nature itself than were the Scholastics.

In its broadest sense, Humanism found a new interest in human nature and in freeing human individuality from the restricting demands of church, guild, manor, and monastery. The Humanists claimed that the best portrayal of the perfection and development of *human* nature was to be found in classical literature. It was in this sense that those interested in the revival of classical learning liked to call themselves Humanists. The widespread interest in classical literature and civilization was expressed first in the cities of Italy, where a general efflorescence of political and economic life was taking place in the fourteenth century.

Francis Petrarch is usually considered the initiator of the revival of a specialized interest in the Latin classics. Petrarch despised the principal medieval instruments of knowledge and tried to emulate the Latin style of the ancient writers, especially Vergil and Cicero. In his desire to re-establish the glory of the Roman Empire, he was indefatigable in his search for classical manuscripts; he edited many of them, using only pagan sources as his authority; and he became acquainted with nearly all the accessible Latin authors.

Stimulated by Petrarch, a growing number of Humanists became interested in asserting the values and superiority of classical Latin over medieval Latin as the best expression of the human spirit. Despite all other claims that were made in praise of the classics, the one above all others was the claim for the superiority of the classical *style*. This meant that every effort was made to substitute classical Latin for medieval Latin as the medium of discourse among educated men everywhere.

By the fifteenth century the interest in reviving classical Greek was also apparent. Greek scholars, headed by Chrysoloras, began to come to Italy and lecture on Greek literature and to bring Greek manuscripts from the East for editing and translation. Reuchlin was outstanding in his promotion of Hebrew as a scholarly classical language. In his defense of Hebrew writings against those who would burn the books of Jews as heretical, he was able to strike an early blow against the book burners and in favor of tolerance and intellectual freedom in the field of scholarship.

Above all others in asserting the claims of Humanist learning was Erasmus of Rotterdam, the outstanding scholar of his age. He taught at universities in England and France and traveled widely in Europe preaching the Humanist gospel. He edited some 25 Greek and Latin authors and many of the works of the church Fathers, including St. Augustine, St. Gregory, and St. Jerome's Vulgate; he translated the New Testament into a scholarly Greek edition, which was later used as the basis for the King James translation into English.

Meanwhile, despite the concerted efforts of the Humanists to raise the classics to a place of undisputed authority in nearly all the countries of Europe, the vernacular literature continued to exert a wide popular appeal and to enlist the efforts of first-rate writers, including some of the Humanists themselves. In Italy Dante produced the great poetry of his *Divine Comedy*, Petrarch himself wrote many Italian lyrics, and Boccaccio wrote much Italian poetry and prose, the most famous of which is his collection of mirthful and carnal tales known as the *Decameron*. The essentially medieval and religious temper of Dante's *Divine Comedy* in contrast with Boccaccio's earthy *Decameron* reveals the wide range of human interests existing in Italy in the fourteenth century.

In England the *Canterbury Tales* of Chaucer and Sir Thomas More's *Utopia* found an increasing audience. In France the tales of *Gargantua* and *Pantagruel* by Rabelais appealed to a public that appreciated his caricatures of the institutions of his day, and the essays of Montaigne pictured the cultivated ideal of scholarly letters for the pleasure of the intellectual classes. Even though the Humanists were likely to belittle literary expression in the vernacular tongues, these were being developed and refined until at length the English, French, German, and Spanish masterpieces of the following centuries were produced.

No contributions to philosophy were made during the Renaissance that could compare with the contributions in other fields. This was perhaps the result of the Humanists' overpowering interest in literature and style. The principal organized effort to probe the fundamental problems of philosophy was the formation of the Platonic Academy in Italy in the fourteenth century. In general, the Humanists were interested in reconciling and showing the essential unity of all religions and philosophy. They gloried in the methods of the contemplative life and they relied upon allegories and mysticism. They "proved" the identity of religions by simply asserting in complicated ways that all religions are identical and by working up an emotional ecstasy over the assertions. They virtually lost sight of distinctions among philosophies, religions, and sciences in their attempts to achieve harmony.

The prominent Humanist historians in Italy of the fourteenth and fifteenth centuries discarded the straightforward chronicling of events and tried to emulate the style and rhetoric of Livy. In their hands, all events became great events, as they sought for the epic dignity of Livy and described battles and couched speeches in the resonant phrases of Cicero. The best Italian historians, however, were Machiavelli and Guicciardini, neither of whom was a Humanist. They wrote in Italian but their style rivaled that of the Humanist historians. They used good sources, checked with documents and archives, and they grouped their facts in such a way as to show causes and results. On the other hand, much of our long tradition of respect and reverence for the achievements of the Renaissance is the result of the self-glorifying and self-admiration of the Humanist historians, who saw greatness in their own day but little of value in the preceding "Dark Ages."

Other Sciences and Arts. A general skepticism concerning Scholastic notions of natural philosophy was on the increase in the fourteenth century. Duns Scotus was more interested in natural science than most Scholastics, but Scholasticism was losing favor and Humanism was largely indifferent to natural science. When Humanists *were* interested in the subject, they were likely to go back to the oldest texts, and even then they were more interested in philological accuracy than in scientific content.

However, notable gains were made by a growing number of scientists. As a result of his studies in mathematics, astronomy, and physics, Copernicus decided that Ptolemy was wrong about the earth being the center of the universe and arrived at the conclusion that the sun is the center. The groundwork was thus laid for Galileo later to complete the heliocentric theory. Likewise, Vesalius laid the foundations of the modern study of anatomy and Agricola promoted the scientific study of mining and metallurgy in addition to his Humanist interests. Although progress was not very rapid, a solid basis was being laid upon which modern science rests.

Whereas medieval art had been largely didactic, aiming at the teaching of religious lessons, as in the great Gothic cathedrals, Renaissance art began to depict the human body and landscapes with greater realism. Early Renaissance painting displayed a detailed realism that later became more dignified, restrained, and expressive of emotional content rather than being confined simply to depicting nature as it is. Much of the glory of the Renaissance was, of course, embodied in the masterpieces of fine art. It scarcely influenced formal education, however, because the Humanist interest in literature preempted the field.

The development of certain practical arts and techniques had attained such a state of refinement by the Renaissance period that enormous social and intellectual effects were the result. For one thing, the rise of the national state rested upon new arts of warmaking, which resulted from the development of gunpowder, gun barrels, cannon, fortifications, and military engineering. Scientific measurement was made more accurate by the development of mechanical clocks and watches. Improvements in the size and shape of sailing vessels, rigging, and rudders accompanied the demands of exploration and expanding commerce.

Above all, the invention of movable type and refinements in papermaking and inkmaking led to the development of the printing press in the fifteenth century through the efforts of Gutenberg and others. The implications of the printing press were, of course, enormous. The sheer fact that knowledge could now be more easily disseminated made popular education a possibility and eventually a necessity. Without the presence at hand of the technical means of cheap printing, no amount of argument could have achieved widespread popular education. Indeed, it might never have been thought of.

HUMANISM IN EDUCATION

Of the rival claims on the intellectual loyalties of men during the Renaissance, namely, religion, science, and Humanism, the one that educators championed most actively was Humanism. Many educators echoed the cry of the Humanists that classical Latin should be substituted for medieval Latin in the schools and universities of the day. This movement for educational reform, which started in Italy in the fifteenth century and soon spread to Germany, England, and France, met with a good deal of resistance from the established church schools. By dint of much writing, speaking, and traveling, the Humanists made good their claims, either by winning over the church schools, by refounding them, or by setting up new schools.

Educational Theory of the Humanists

Italy. In Italy written statements on educational theory were made by such Humanists as Vergerius, Guarino, Vittorino, Aeneas Sylvius, Alberti, and, most famous of all, Castiglione. Although they had many differences in their points of view, the composite of their outlook was somewhat as follows:

The aims of Humanistic education were to produce a broadly educated person possessing a well-rounded personality and capable of assuming leadership in church or state. He should be at home in the field of classical knowledge and yet be an effective man of action and citizen. He should possess a wide range of accomplishments; be able to express himself in poetry, song, and dance; exhibit good health and physical dexterity; and withal be a Christian gentleman with all the social graces. The Humanists drew heavily upon the ideals of Quintilian and Cicero, to which they added their own interpretations of the versatile accomplishments appropriate to a scholar and gentleman in Renaissance times. The education of girls should be such that the ideal woman would be a versatile and charming companion for the ideal courtier. The aims were broad and generous but they far outstripped the ability to devise a curriculum or methods entirely appropriate to the ideal.

The curriculum designed to produce the "courtier" leaned heavily, as already suggested, upon the classical literature of Greece and Rome. In their enthusiasm for the classics, the Humanists attributed all-inclusive values to them. They believed that they would develop a well-rounded personality, would give practical aids to a life of action, would instill the qualities of artistic enjoyment and moral worth, and would afford the wide learning which they desired. In comparison with the classics, only slight attention was given to mathematics, natural history, music, and dancing, and none to the vernacular. History and ethics could be studied from the classical historians and writers. Physical education was important in a few schools and in the written treatises, but the *sine qua non* was an emphasis on grammar, composition, versifying, and rhetoric.

As to methods of teaching, the common assent of the Humanists was that memorizing was the most important, although they agreed that it would be well if the student could understand the rules as he learned them. Considerable importance was conceded to recognizing individual differences among pupils, but the Humanists were always a little vague as to how this could be achieved in the study of Cicero or Vergil. Also, it was urged that the rigors of corporal punishment be lightened in favor of appeals to the pride and ambition of pupils in rivalry with one another for social approval. There is no doubt that Humanist theory went far beyond the practices of the day, far beyond the actual achievements of the Humanist grammar school as well as those of the traditional church schools. It is interesting, however, that the Humanist theory gave little attention to the way in which education could contribute to those great arts of painting, sculpture, and architecture in which the Italian Renaissance was leading the world of the time. The explanation seems to be that these arts were not considered "liberal" arts despite the magnificent heights they reached. They were still technical crafts in the eyes of the literary Humanist.

England. The viewpoints of the English writers on education had much in common with those of the Italian Humanists. Vives, a Spaniard who taught Catherine of Aragon and went to England with her, advocated that the school should reduce its lag behind society, adapt instruction to the individual differences and interests of pupils, and use the classics as the foundation for wisdom rather than merely as examples of good literary style. He was one of the few who declared that the vernacular could be of value in education, and he emphasized the importance of the education of girls. His aim for girls was the development through letters and moral teaching of the high-principled lady of the court, wife, and mother who would become the intelligent companion and mistress of the household.

Another and even more influential writer was Sir Thomas Elyot, a nonchurchman, statesman, and scholar who promoted Greek learning and translated Plutarch and Isocrates into English. In his *Boke Named the Governour*, written in English, he set forth the curriculum desirable for educating the statesman, namely, Greek, Latin, rhetoric, logic, geometry, astronomy, music, history, geography, drawing, sculpture, and physical education. His book is notable for its inclusion of the social sciences, the arts, and physical education, in which respect he went beyond many of the Humanists of his time. He urged that a university education in these fields was as essential for a successful career in the secular world as in religious offices, but, as always, the Humanist came out in his insistence upon Plato and Cicero as the prime studies.

A third writer was Roger Ascham, tutor to Queen Elizabeth and professor at Cambridge. His *Scholemaster* is full of learning and common sense, revealing the methods of his time and recommending reforms. For example, the custom was apparently to learn Latin by memorizing the rules of grammar and then repeating the Latin sentences directly until learned. Ascham recommended the startling notion that the student learn his English first, then translate the English into Latin and back into English. Ascham also wrote extensively on physical training and outdoor activity, which he felt were important for scholars and students as well as for the nobility and leisure classes.

France. One of the outstanding Humanist scholars in France was Budé (or Budaeus), who wrote an outline for the liberal education of a prince, hoping that Francis I would take the hint. The crux of his proposal was that a prince should love letters, Greek above all, and cultivate his interest in style and in history. The most popular author in France was doubtless Rabelais, who set the people laughing at the schools in his *Gargantua* and *Pantagruel*. Writing in French and reaching a popular audience, Rabelais ridiculed the dry formalism of the Humanist schools as well as other social excesses of his time. He depicted his own ideas of educational reform in exaggerated form, caricaturing the older methods as compared with newer and more realistic methods. He advocated the classics, to be sure, but he insisted that they should give real and useful guidance to conduct rather than simply represent bookish, linguistic, and literary values. His proposed curriculum apparently included all the subjects he could think of, not only Latin and Greek but also Hebrew, Arabic, Chaldee, grammar, arithmetic, geometry, astronomy, music, history, geography, civil law, philosophy, natural science, and physical education. Rabelais revealed his naturalistic bent in his own study and teaching of science, medicine, and anatomy; in this respect he was more than a literary Humanist.

Another scholar who perhaps had more direct influence upon educational content was Petrus Ramus, who went even further than Rabelais in his adherence to the naturalistic interest in science and mathematics. Ramus lashed both the Aristotelian Scholastics and the Ciceronian Humanists, and the word "Ramism" was coined to represent his attack upon these twin scourges of education. He set out to reform each of the liberal arts by improving the material studied and by making the methods of acquisition simpler and easier. His efforts were directed toward a careful systematizing and simplifying of the knowledge of the ancient authors and the eliminating of the superfluities and intricacies of medieval commentaries. In this way he helped to make knowledge more applicable to actual social situations, to free it from ecclesiastical control, and ultimately to clear the way for a new mathematics and science. He wrote new textbooks on all the subjects of the seven liberal arts, as well as on physics, ethics, metaphysics, and theology. They gained relatively wide vogue in Germany, Switzerland, at Cambridge in England, and later in colonial America.

Finally, the man who perhaps represented as well as anyone the living ideal of Castiglione and Elyot was Montaigne, not a churchman, not a teacher, not a scientist, but a scholarly gentleman and man of affairs and letters. In his urbane and sophisticated essays Montaigne combined the streams of Humanism and naturalism in his attacks upon formalism, verbalism, and blind reliance upon authority. He urged that the proper education of a gentleman should include the classics as sources of wisdom in action and not merely as models of literary style; modern languages as well as the classics; history, travel, and wide social contacts; and physical education.

Erasmus. Whereas Montaigne may have personified the ideal of the courtly gentleman and scholar, to the Humanists Erasmus was the scholar's scholar. His thoroughgoing research and editing of classical and religious manuscripts commanded the respect of the whole scholarly world, and his Latin schoolbooks became the texts for countless numbers of students in Humanist schools. In his *Liberal Education for Boys,* Erasmus joined in denouncing Ciceronian formalism and in praising the broad study of the classics to achieve knowledge, taste, and judgment. He urged that the interest of boys should be awakened in the work at hand rather than destroyed by disciplined drudgery. Gentleness should be substituted for flogging as an invitation to learning. He mildly recommended physical exercise and bitterly opposed the dialectical methods of Scholastic philosophy and theology.

He believed that man is naturally good; nature is beneficent and benevolent; and human nature is perfectible if only it be allowed to develop through the classics. To him religion was a matter, not of mystical or emotional faith, but simply of human intelligence; man can arrive at correct religious doctrines if proper scholarly texts are made available. The violence of the Reformation with its theological quarrels, devastating wars, and appeals to the doctrines of original sin and the pervading supernatural world left him cold. His belief in reasonableness led him to

Fig. 10. Erasmus.

exalt the classical humanities as the prime means whereby education could distill the best from the classical and religious writings of the past and pass it on to students. His great influence gave enormous support to the belief that all persons who would be considered cultured and educated must know Latin and Greek. This, above all, has been the educational legacy of the Renaissance to the modern world.

Schools for Scholars and Gentlemen

Italy. The most outstanding of the many Humanist schools in Italy was that of Vittorino da Feltre, who was called in by the Duke of Mantua to establish a school for his children. Vittorino set out to create a school according to the ideas of Cicero and Quintilian as he interpreted them. He accepted in his school not only the children of the nobility but apparently a few lower-class boys as well. The aims of the school were couched in terms of the Roman ideal, of a wellborn youth with a broad and rounded background of knowledge, the manners and social graces suitable to the ruling classes, and loyalty to basic Christian principles. The principal means to this end were the study of the classics and mathematics.

Vittorino's course of study is interesting in that all the seven liberal arts were present in it except logic. This represented the Humanist's distaste for medieval Scholasticism and his glorification of grammar and rhetoric. Much attention was given to the study of Latin and Greek grammar at an early age and to declamation, composition, and the elegances of style to be achieved through rhetoric. Much use was made of

Fig. 11. Lecture in a fifteenth-century Italian academy.

imitating and memorizing long passages from Cicero, Vergil, Ovid, Horace, Homer, and Demosthenes as well as other standard Latin and Greek authors. Arithmetic, geometry, astronomy, and a little music were also studied.

The significant thing is that the basic medieval liberal arts were taught, with the reinterpretation given to them by the Humanist emphasis upon classical literature. This might mean a revitalizing and stimulating experience for those fifteenth-century youth who could catch the enthusiasms of the early Humanist educators. Vittorino went beyond the liberal arts to try to recapture the classical ideal of well-rounded development and made much of physical training, games, sports, athletic contests, and exercise. Whether this was considered a good in itself or simply a means to provide recreation so that intellectual studies could be pursued even more profitably is hard to determine. Certainly the ideal of physical development as a prerequisite for military training was also part of the picture.

This whole experience was doubtless refreshing and exhilarating to many students in comparison with what was to be found in the church schools of the day, and the study of the great authors might have become a liberalizing education. The fact is, however, that in other Humanist schools throughout Europe the Humanists' supreme interest in style and composition overshadowed the classical ideal of well-rounded development. It was not long before slavish attention to grammar and rhetoric led to the charges of "Ciceronianism," from which Humanist schools never completely recovered.

Northern Europe. Much the same story could be told of Germany, the Netherlands, and France. Scholars went to Italy, studied in the Humanist schools, and returned home fired with the zeal to reform the schools along classical lines. In the north there seemed to be a much stronger alliance between religion and Humanism than in Italy, and consequently the interest in the classical languages was stimulated by the desire to study and investigate the original sources of the Scriptures in Greek, Latin, and Hebrew. The classics were thus studied as sacred languages as well as secular languages.

One example of this tendency is furnished by the clerical and lay society known as the Brethren of the Common Life, founded in the Low Countries in the fourteenth century by Gerhard Groot. The members of this society spent much of their time and earned their livelihood by copying manuscripts. Gradually they began to give instruction in the town schools and eventually established their own schools in such cities as Deventer, Brussels, and Antwerp. Under the influence of Erasmus and other Humanists who had been students in these schools, the classics were introduced into their curriculums in the late fifteenth century; with the onset of the Reformation the importance of the Brethren's schools began to decline.

England. The Humanist enthusiasm struck England in the late fifteenth century and gradually found its way into the cathedral grammar schools of the church, into new church schools set up for the purpose, and into the "public schools" as they were founded. The public school ideal was greatly influenced by the Renaissance ideal of gentlemanly education, and Eton soon had a large playing field designed to give physical exercise and training for the "battles of life," as Vittorino had proposed. In this respect the English public schools differed from the grammar schools of France and Germany, which had insisted upon the intellectual rigors of classical discipline almost to the exclusion of all else. Classical Latin and Greek had entered Eton by the sixteenth century.

Among the church grammar schools of England that at St. Paul's Cathedral was notable in introducing classical learning, under the leadership of John Colet, who had been in Italy and had caught the Humanist enthusiasm. He spent a considerable amount of money to convert the medieval cathedral school at St. Paul's into a Humanistic grammar school. Although it was not the first Humanistic school, its eminence and the influence of Colet helped to introduce classical Humanism into the dozens of other grammar schools of this time. The stress was usually upon learning the rules of Latin and Greek grammar, declensions of nouns and conjugations of verbs, and the reading of such authors as Cicero, Horace, Vergil, Cato, Aesop, and Erasmus.

The actual practices in Renaissance schools were, as is often the case, at wide variance with the theory propounded by the writers on education. Indeed, it was the imputed evils of practice that led to much of the theorizing. The accounts of actual practice seem to show that memorizing and whipping were the chief tools of learning in most Renaissance schools. For example, an account of how grammar was taught in an Italian town in the fourteenth century shows that the master read aloud from selected authors for the first 5 days of the week; during this time the students memorized selections from Cicero and Vergil, and on Saturday they reviewed all that they had learned during the week. Meanwhile the submaster taught Donatus and Cato to the younger pupils. In a school in Aberdeen in the early sixteenth century the regimen seems to have been something like this: Before 7:00 A.M. the pupils knelt and saluted the Virgin Mary; at 7:00 A.M. the master arrived and flogged them for the faults of the day before; then they had breakfast; during the morning and afternoon, selected authors were read aloud by the master and submaster, and the selections were memorized by the pupils; at 7:00 P.M. they had prayers and went to bed; all were forbidden to speak in the vernacular, and the beginners were forbidden to speak at all.

In summary, the Humanist influence established the classics as the heart of European secondary education. It helped to make secondary schools in essence preparatory institutions for further study in the universities. Above all, Humanism established the tradition that no person might be counted as truly educated who had not had training in the classics. This was, to the Humanist, the mark of the scholar and the gentleman. The aim of education had been broadened to include preparation for service in the secular life of the times, in the state as well as in the church, in the social life of the nobleman, and in the work of the great merchant. But, for any of these purposes, the Humanist insisted that the common background of the truly educated and cultured person must be knowledge and training in the classics.

Schools for the Common Man

In comparison with the influence and achievements of Humanist education, the progress of the vernacular schools during the Renaissance seems to have been slight indeed. Part of the reason for this was doubt-less the general feeling that one's mother tongue was learned sufficiently well in the family circle and that therefore there was no particular need to offer special instruction in what everyone learned in any case. So long as the vernaculars were simply *spoken* tongues, there was undoubtedly much justification for their not being taught in schools. When, however, law courts began to use the vernacular in their records, when contracts, wills and deeds, business and commercial transactions, and the whole record of an increasingly complex society began to be kept in the vernacular, the merely incidental acquisition of the mother tongue was no longer as satisfactory as it had been.

Thus, here and there, schools to teach reading and writing in the ver-nacular and the elements of arithmetic and computation began to appear during the Renaissance. They suffered in comparison with the Humanist schools because they had no "intellectual content" or mental discipline, but they persisted in response to the demands of the people and began to make real headway in the Reformation period. In later centuries they were recognized as part of the national systems of education, but they were nearly always considered to be inferior schools for lower classes of people—at least they were so considered by the "truly educated" persons as defined by the Humanists.

Humanism in Higher Education

In Italy, classical learning was promoted largely by court and mu-nicipality rather than by church or university. It made little impression upon the older universities whose conservatism and medieval learning resisted its entrance, and it was accepted only in a very subsidiary position where it was accepted at all.

In France, the story was much the same. The courts led the way in the acceptance of Humanism, whereas the church and the universities gave little but opposition. The University of Paris kept aloof from the movement, which it rightly considered as a reform that would threaten the vested interests of theology, Aristotelian philosophy, and canon law. It kept to its Scholastic ways of thinking and remained engrossed with the subtleties of discussion concerning universal principles instead of ad-mitting the new Humanist spirit, with its enthusiasms for style and beauty. Humanism did gain entrance into some of the higher schools, however. Francis I with the aid of the scholar Budé founded the Collège de France in which chairs were established for professors of Greek, Hebrew, Latin, French, law, philosophy, mathematics, and medicine. Classical learning was also promoted by such institutions as those set up by municipal governments at Bordeaux, Lyons, Orléans, Reims, and Montpellier.

Again, in Germany, the courts and schools accepted the new learning before the universities did. Lectures on classical antiquity were attempted as early as the latter part of the fifteenth century but met with little response by the universities until after 1500. Then, as the religious reformers adopted the new learning, it gradually was accepted by the universities under the leadership of a reform group at Erfurt and Tübingen and especially under the impetus of Melanchthon at Wittenberg and Nuremberg.

In England, a somewhat different situation obtained. The Oxford Reformers, a group of orthodox Catholics, aiming at the general reform of church and society as well as of school and university and aided by Henry VIII, were able to make substantial gains for the new learning in actual educational practice. Lectures on Greek were read at Oxford in the late fifteenth century; but neither Oxford nor Cambridge made official provision for Humanistic studies until the early sixteenth century, when Erasmus began to present the new learning at Jesus College at Cambridge.

Soon the first avowedly Humanistic colleges recognizing Greek and Hebrew were founded. Erasmus taught at Cambridge for four years from 1511, and Vives taught at Oxford in 1522. Even greater advances toward Humanistic studies were made at Cambridge when Aristotle began to be studied from the commentaries of the Humanists, Agricola and Ramus, rather than from the glosses of the medieval Schoolmen. Thus, Humanism steadily gained ground in the subjects of both the trivium and the quadrivium, until finally the founding of Trinity College, Cambridge, in 1546 with its several fellows in Greek along with the regius professorships in Greek, Hebrew, and civil law, appointed earlier by Henry VIII, set the seal upon the transition from the medieval to the Humanistic tradition.

Actual modifications in the prescribed curriculum of the English universities meant a decline in the importance of logic and a reemphasis upon grammar and rhetoric. In the hands of the Humanists, grammar lost its purely medieval aspect and was expanded to include the grammar and literature of classical Latin, Greek, Hebrew, and other Oriental languages. Rhetoric also began to receive a greater attention characteristic of the Humanists' interest in the style and form of written and oral speech. Under the influence of Ramus, logic was simplified and freed of the complexities of Scholastic treatment. The most obvious effect of the Renaissance upon the arts curriculum was the substitution of ancient classical language and literature for medieval and religious language and literature. As the classics became "polite letters" particularly suitable for the education of a "gentleman," the Renaissance tended to reaffirm the aristocratic conception of a liberal education, which the Greeks and Romans had praised so highly.

It may be interesting to note how the passage of time has reversed the position of educational "progressives" and "conservatives." During the Renaissance, the Humanists were the progressives, urging that the new and vital Humanistic studies should be substituted for the outworn and obsolete studies of the Middle Ages. The Humanists justified their position with such arguments as the following: The development of the individual is of prime importance; the interests and nature of the individual should be considered in education; the student should be given freedom from the obscurantism of medievalism; the student should pursue more "realistic" studies. The Humanists insisted that the classical studies of literature, poetry, and oratory were admirably suited for attaining these ends.

The curious thing is that in the eighteenth and nineteenth centuries these were the very same arguments that were used by the new progressives, who were then favoring the scientific and social studies as a means of breaking down the very classical curriculum that the Humanists had been at such pains to set up during the Renaissance. The Humanists who had been progressives in the Renaissance became the conservatives of a later date. They insistently harked back to the Renaissance ideal of culture and the Renaissance conception of a liberal education to bulwark the prescribed classical curriculum against the "barbarians" who advocated newer subjects. The explanation of this rather common educational phenomenon may be that when the Renaissance was at its height the classical curriculum, in comparison with the medieval curriculum, probably did stimulate the imagination and tend to develop the individuality of students. But as new social, intellectual, and technological conditions arrived on the scene, the older conception of a liberal education was no longer appropriate to the changed situation. The once flexible and liberal curriculum of the Humanists became the rigid and conservative curriculum remote from the realities of a later time.

Chapter 8

RELIGIOUS REFORMATION
AND SCIENTIFIC REVOLUTION

In the sixteenth and seventeenth centuries four principal cultural forces were striving for the loyalties of men and competing for control of educational institutions, curriculum, and methods. They were (1) the social institutions of government and economics, (2) the religious institutions and beliefs of Catholic and Protestant Churches, (3) the new outlooks described by science and the scientific method, and (4) the continuing influence of Humanism. All these forces had their roots deep in medieval and Renaissance times, but they became so interrelated in such significant ways that they gave rise to the culture now known as the "Reformation."

THE CENTRALIZING OF ORGANIZED LIFE

Consolidation of the National States

Centralization of Royal Power. The trend of the late medieval and Renaissance periods to put more political power in the hands of the kings progressed during the Reformation to such an extent that the seventeenth century has often been called the "age of absolutism." The medieval conception of a universal Christendom with the Pope as head received mortal blows, and constant difficulties beset the long-lived Holy Roman Empire. Kings were able to raise money for their armies by cultivating the friendship of merchants and bankers, who saw economic gain in thus allying themselves against the nobility and the Catholic Church. Kings also found a source of ready money in taking over the property and funds of the Roman Catholic Church, which was enormously wealthy in many countries of Europe. The time seemed ripe for a coalition of kings, merchants, and Protestant reformers within the various national states to break the military, political, economic, and religious control of the Catholic Church in Europe.

The states most successful in their efforts to centralize royal power were Spain, France, and England. Because of the strength of local rulers and the fortunes of war, Germany and Italy were delayed for generations in achieving a similar national unity. Spain emerged as one of the strongest national states and colonial empires in the sixteenth century. Then gradually in the seventeenth century Spain began to lose her place as an international power, but at home the principle of absolute authority in the hands of the king remained paramount, and the close relationship between king and Catholic Church continued.

In France the trend toward royal supremacy proceeded apace, especially in the hands of the supreme absolutist of all, Louis XIV. During this process France became a great European power as a result of a series of wars against England, Spain, Germany, and the Italian states. The ideal of state sovereignty received effective statement by the scientist Jean Bodin, who argued that the sovereign state was completely free in its movements and could not be challenged legally by any other authority. This, of course, gave sanction to secular rather than religious authority over men's conduct.

In England Henry VIII hastened the process of consolidating royal authority as he strove to build up the navy, took over the Catholic monasteries, disestablished the Catholic Church in favor of the Church of England, and won over many nobles as well as the merchant class to his side. The long reign of Queen Elizabeth further strengthened the power of the monarchy; the tremendous multiplication of statutes issued by the crown concerning nearly all aspects of life revealed its increasing importance and power.

When the Stuart kings, James I and Charles I, came to the throne, they forcefully asserted the doctrine of the divine right of kings, only to be set back by the revolution in which Parliament, under the control of the Puritans, established the Commonwealth for a decade or two during the middle of the seventeenth century. With the restoration of the Stuarts in 1660, Charles II and James II again claimed rule by divine right. Thomas Hobbes supported absolutism, but argued that it rested upon an original contract among men. In his *Leviathan* he asserted that laws are the commands of the political sovereign, who is subject to no legal limits; the people obey the laws of the absolute state because they realize that such obedience is the only sure means of preventing anarchy. The English people, however, found that absolutism was less to their liking than constitutionalism; therefore, William III was brought from the Netherlands to rule with Mary in a limited monarchy.

Constitutionalism and Civil Liberties. The revolt of the Netherlands against Spain, the setting up of the Dutch Republic and the English Commonwealth, and the limitations that Parliament put upon the power of William and Mary heralded the growth of constitutional government, in which the civil rights of the merchant class and gentry were protected against autocratic usurpation by an absolute monarch. In the Netherlands and England the merchant classes grew strong enough to prevent the kind of absolutism that was achieved in France and Spain. In both cases the economic motive and the religious motives of Calvinism were joined in a drive that asserted the right of the merchant class and gentry to share with the nobility and king in the control of public affairs. It is interesting to note that several of the important documents on civil and economic freedom were written by John Milton, the great Puritan poet and philosopher. In England, too, the Petition of Right in 1628 and the Bill of Rights and Act of Toleration in 1689 laid the foundations for the civil liberties that have been written into most democratic constitutions since that time.

The Spirit of Nationalism and Education. One of the most far-reaching corollaries of the consolidation of the national states in Reformation times was the growth of a spirit of nationalism and the accentuation of national differences. The constant wars, the growing use of vernacular languages, and a mounting sense that each nationality was different from (and better than) all other nationalities gave rise to a feeling of national importance and patriotism. In the process of building up a spirit of nationalism, schools and education have played an enormous share. The inculcation of national loyalties through the schools and the teaching of the vernacular language became eventually a primary task of the national school systems. That is why the story of the national state in the Reformation is so important for the present day. The groundwork for state control of educational organization, aims, and curriculum was being laid in this period. The control of education was being taken out of the hands of the Catholic Church and put into the hands of national churches with the authority of the state to back them up.

The Commercial Revolution

Geographic Discoveries. Stimulated by the desire for economic gain among the merchant classes and among the state rulers, the great period of exploration and discovery began in the late fifteenth and continued into the sixteenth and seventeenth centuries. Because they were strong and consolidated national states, Spain, Portugal, France, and England were the first to take over the trade routes of the world. As the Netherlands became a strong merchant state, it took the place of Spain and Portugal and in the seventeenth century competed with England and France for commercial supremacy. Men's imaginations and economic desires were stimulated by the visions of conquest and wealth thus opened up by the New World. Religious, nationalistic, and capitalistic motives were closely interlocked, and the scientific and technological advances in navigation, shipbuilding, and warfare made the explorations and conquests possible.

Growth of the Middle Class and Capitalism. The progress made by the merchant class in earlier centuries increased rapidly in the Reformation period, and corresponding changes took place in the economy of Europe. Its agricultural and feudal economy began to shake. Prices went up; money became even more important than land as a source of wealth; and merchants and bankers began to take the place of the feudal nobility as economic powers. Cities became ever more important and replaced the medieval manors as centers of economic life. The characteristic institutions of commercial capitalism were being developed in the form of stock companies on a large scale, money exchanges, credit, interest charges, insurance, and banks.

The guild economy of the Middle Ages had been bulwarked by the Catholic Church, with its insistence upon a fair price and its outlawing of usury, and was based upon a doctrine of subsistence and subordination of worldly goods to the demands of the hereafter. However, the secular temper (always present but now sharply emphasized) of the merchant classes led to a growing respect for productive work, a greater regard for the acquisition of worldly goods, and a decline in respect for the monastic ideal of retirement from the affairs of this world. The "get-rich-quick" spirit was born and proved a lusty infant.

Naturally, the merchant wanted the source of raw materials to be easily available to him, and he wanted his finished goods to arrive safely at their destination. Thus, he wanted the king to suppress robbers and highwaymen both at home and abroad. He gave his support and money to the ruler who would establish stringent civil laws at home for the protection of property, who would build an army and navy to protect trade routes on land and sea, and who would conquer new lands as potential sources of raw materials and potential markets for finished goods.

This earliest phase of modern capitalism was known as "mercantile capitalism," or mercantilism. According to this doctrine, wealth is measured not so much by land or labor as by the abundance of gold and silver money in a country. Consequently, the state must see to it that it has colonies or other available sources of the precious metals. The state must not only win and preserve the colonies, but it must ensure that internal order is maintained so that business may proceed efficiently and safely. The state must do all in its power to regulate, protect, and promote business interests through protective tariffs, subsidies, taxation, and new colonies. In effect, then, mercantilism meant strict state control of business, but always, the businessmen hoped, in the interests of business.

It is plain why such a doctrine appealed to both merchants and kings. The merchants gained protection at home and new colonies and trade abroad; the kings gained the money and support necessary to consolidate their own power at home and wage successful wars abroad; both were able more easily to break the hold of the universal church upon the political, economic, and religious loyalties of their people. Medieval restraints upon the political power of the king were broken, the flow of money in tithes and taxes to Rome was slowed down, religious injunctions against the building up of material wealth were denied, and Reformation religious reformers were, for the first time, able to break the yoke of Catholic doctrine and authority in a way that earlier reformers had not been able to do.

The New Class Structure of Society. One of the most important results of Reformation economic developments was the shifting of power among the classes of society and the greater power achieved by the middle classes. In general, it may be said that the class structure of society in seventeenth-century Europe was somewhat as follows:

1. Rural classes:
    a. Nobility, who were large landowners and were recognized by the crown as a privileged noble class
    b. Gentry, who were also large landowners but not entitled to the social respect and prerogatives of the nobility
    c. Free farmers, or yeomen, who owned and worked their own small plots of land
    d. Renters, farm laborers, servants, and serfs, who worked for someone else
2. City classes:
    a. Merchants, bankers, and employers, who owned the greatest wealth and hired the most employees
    b. Small merchants and professional men, who had considerable independence and social respect
    c. Skilled artisans, who could command a certain amount of respect because of their skill
    d. Servants and menial laborers, who were often not free in their movements
3. Clerical classes:
    a. Higher clergy, who were virtually as important as the nobility and wealthy merchants
    b. Lower clergy, who traditionally had a position of respect and influence

There was, of course, some fluidity among the classes, but in general they were rather rigidly defined. The important point is that the rural gentry and the city merchant classes became much more powerful during the Reformation than ever before. In the process of change from a rural and agricultural economy to a commercial and city economy, the lower classes were often so severely affected that the national state sometimes had to come to their aid by passing, as in England, a series of poor laws.

The Commercial Revolution and Education. Just as the political changes of the Reformation profoundly affected education, so did the economic changes influence educational organization and curriculum. The primary effect of the economic developments was to create for the schools a new group of students from the gentry and merchant classes. Giving their children the advantages of an education was one of the ways that the newly rich could achieve respectability. Therefore the merchant classes poured their money into schools of all kinds. One of the easiest ways was to give money to schools already established or to help found classical and Humanistic schools. Another way was to demand new types of schools of greater practical and vocational use for a life of business. In some countries this end was achieved through voluntary gifts and subscriptions to the private schools. In other countries the merchant class used its newly won political power to pass laws creating state and city schools supported at public expense for the benefit of all children. The extremes at each end of the social scale were also not overlooked. The nobility were interested in setting up special academies to train their children in the proper courtly ways. Religious and philanthropic agencies set about giving free or charity education to those whose parents could not afford to have them educated. In any case, the religious motive was nearly always combined with the political and economic in the efforts to provide education, especially among the Protestant Churches of northern Europe.

The Religious Reformations

In 1500 the Catholic Church was still the universal European church in fact as well as in name, but during the sixteenth and seventeenth centuries a series of religious revolts took place, backed by the military power of the national states and by the economic power of the middle classes. These revolts gave rise to a number of different national churches that were destined to play an important role in the European and American scene of future generations. The fact that political and economic factors were involved does not mean that the religious reformations did not represent genuine changes in men's beliefs and attitudes. It means primarily that *successful* revolts were made possible by the political and economic changes already noted. In many ways the religious reforms represented a truly religious reaction against the growing secularism of the Catholic Church, and in other respects they represented a reaction of the more conservative rural attitude against the more secularized interests of city life.

Lutheranism in Northern Europe. Martin Luther, who became the spearhead of attack upon the Catholic Church in Germany, tried for several years to achieve reform from within the church in his capacity as monk and university professor. When in 1520 Luther was threatened with excommunication by the Pope, he broke with the Catholic Church and began his attempts to set up a new church. He wrote many pamphlets in both German and Latin, calling upon the nobility, clergy, and common people of Germany to throw off the shackles of Catholicism. At the famous Diet of Worms in 1521, called by Emperor Charles V, Luther again refused to recant and was outlawed by the Emperor as well as by the Pope. Interestingly enough, the nationalist phase of this event is illustrated by the fact that the Spaniards and Italians hissed his speech and the Germans cheered. The papal legate reported to the Pope that during Luther's processional nine-tenths of the people shouted "Long live Luther" and one-tenth yelled "Down with the Pope." Luther was committed to the custody of the Elector of Saxony, and during his stay at the castle of Wartburg he translated the New Testament into idiomatic German for the use of German-speaking peoples—another sign of the importance of the new national spirit as shown through the use of the vernacular language.

During the following decades Lutheranism became ever more closely reliant upon the civil authority of those German rulers who embraced that doctrine. This principle of close alliance between church and state was formally recognized at the Diet of Spires in 1526, when the rival Catholic and Lutheran rulers met to prevent further revolts of the peasants. In the face of the common enemy the rulers decided to declare an armistice on religious warfare and announced that each ruler should decide for himself and for his subjects which should be the established religion of his state. The famous doctrine of *cuius regio eius religio* (whose rule, his religion) was enunciated. Three years later, at another Diet of Spires, the Catholic majority decided that Lutheran rulers must tolerate Catholics but Catholic rulers were not obliged to tolerate Lutherans. Against this decision the Lutheran minority protested so vigorously that henceforth they were dubbed "Protestants." Finally, at the Peace of Augsburg in 1555, the right of the state to determine the religion of its subjects was again accepted; but although the right of the state to secede from the Catholic Church was won, the right of the individual person to choose his own religion was not won. The individual could legally be only a Catholic or a Lutheran, this decision resting in the hands of his ruler.

In the next hundred years the Lutheran religion alternately waxed and waned, until finally the Thirty Years' War (1618 to 1648) left Germany exhausted, though Protestantism was still triumphant in the states of northern Germany. As a result of these bloody religious wars, the efforts of Protestant rulers to break with the Roman Church and the Holy Roman Empire were crowned with success. At the Peace of Westphalia (1648) the foundations of the present national states of Europe were laid, and each state was recognized as completely sovereign and no longer as subject to the Empire. In the eyes of some historians the Peace of Westphalia is one of the most important treaties ever signed in view of the nationalistic wars waged since then, culminating in the World Wars of the twentieth century. Hitler's "new order" was in a real sense the effort to destroy the fruits of Westphalia in 1648 fully as much as it was aimed at the Treaty of Versailles in 1918. Since each ruler was considered as a sovereign power, Calvinist rulers were admitted to equality along with Catholics and Lutherans and given the right to choose the religion for their peoples.

Calvinism in Western Europe. The Protestant revolt in Switzerland was led by Huldreich Zwingli and John Calvin. Zwingli gained control of the city of Zurich and led an open revolt that resulted in his death, after which Calvin became the leader of anti-Catholic forces in Switzerland. First at Basel and then more fully at Geneva, Calvin wielded almost complete power over the lives of the people of Geneva.

The political import of Calvinism was subordination of the state to the church. Whereas Luther's reliance upon the state had resulted in the church becoming an arm of the state, Calvin felt rather that the state should be considered the political and civil arm of the church to do its bidding and carry out its injunctions. The political term for this doctrine is "theocracy," literally "the rule of God." Since God is not present in person on this earth, the true church (Calvinism) must rule according to God's unchangeable, authoritarian laws. Theocratic rule meant that the Calvinist church leaders must exert strict control over all the affairs of men, economic, political, and social as well as religious. Education, of course, was one of the facets of institutional life included in this range of control. Discipline was a primary necessity of life, for the church could not afford to let affairs fall into the hands of sinners who were outside the pale. Thus, a church consistory, or court, was set up to enforce the commands of the church, to investigate the personal lives of everyone, to punish those who were not leading godly lives, and to censure harsh creditors, usurers, monopolists, and tricky or light-fingered merchants. The influence of Calvinist theocracy can be seen clearly in the New England colonies (see pages 240 to 249) and in many of the puritanical aspects of American life.

Calvinism spread from Geneva through Switzerland into Germany, where it was known as the German Reformed Church, into France, where its followers were known as Huguenots, into the Netherlands, where it was known as the Dutch Reformed Church, to England among the Puritans, and to Scotland among the Presbyterians. Calvinist immigrants of all these nationalities came in great numbers to America.

The Calvinist often looked upon himself as the aristocrat of the Protestants. He was typically an effective, energetic, and aggressive fighter, supremely confident that God was on his side, and more often than not an earnest, hard-working artisan, merchant, or professional man. The Calvinist's success can be seen in the part he played in the Bohemian revolt, the Huguenot wars, the Netherlands' revolt against Philip of Spain, the Presbyterian revolt against monarchy in Scotland, and the Puritan revolts in England and later in the American Revolution. Integral to all the Calvinist's success was his great belief in the value of education and his insistence that education be made available to all.

Anglicanism and Puritanism in England. The Reformation in England produced no single great religious and evangelical reformer such as Luther or Calvin. Two hundred years earlier Wycliffe and the Lollards had made a stand, but the time had not been ripe for revolt. The Reformation in England rather took place from the top down as successive kings and queens took the initiative in overthrowing or restoring the power of the Catholic Church. In these efforts Parliament sometimes supported the king and sometimes opposed him. In 1534 Henry VIII caused Parliament to pass the Act of Supremacy, which recognized the king as the sole head of the church in England. From a religious point of view, the newly formed Church of England was a change more in name than in fact, for doctrinal changes were not marked. Priests were allowed to marry; church services were in English instead of Latin; the Bible was translated into English by Tyndale; and the English Book of Common Prayer (containing the Creeds, Ten Commandments, Lord's Prayer, and much liturgical material) was published as a beginner's church book or primer and subsequently became an important schoolbook. Henry VIII took over the land and wealth of the monasteries that remained as outposts of loyalty to the Pope and used the money primarily to build up his own power as king.

After Henry VIII, Protestantism had varying fortunes in England. It continued to grow strong under Henry's son, Edward VI, whose affairs were run largely by Cranmer, Archbishop of Canterbury, but it received a setback under Mary. Mary restored Catholicism and Roman control of the church, expressed allegiance to the Pope, caused Parliament to repeal the Act of Supremacy, dismissed Protestant clergymen and priests who had married, abolished the English Book of Common Prayer and restored Latin as the language of the church, executed such leaders as Cranmer, and forced many Protestant churchmen to flee from England. These exiles were welcomed by the Calvinists of the Netherlands and Switzerland, and when they returned under Elizabeth they brought Calvinism back to England with them, laying the foundation for Puritanism.

Under Elizabeth's long reign from 1558 to 1603 the so-called "Elizabethan settlement" was achieved, whereby the Church of England became the established church and enough reforms were made to satisfy large numbers of Englishmen. Richard Hooker in his *The Laws of Ecclesiastical Polity* argued that the state and the church were simply two aspects of a single commonwealth whose head was the royal sovereign, that church and state should be close allies, and that subjects owed allegiance and obedience to both.

In effect, the Church of England departed less in doctrine, organization, and form from the Catholic Church than did any other Protestant church. The main point of interest here is that the religious settlement was enforced by the authority of the state. The Calvinist Puritans, however, felt that the Church of England had not gone far enough in reform and wished to "purify" it further of its remnants of Catholicism.

When the Stuart kings, James I and Charles I, came to the throne, they persecuted the Puritans and other noncomformists. Outraged by the attacks of Archbishop Laud, the Puritans increased their demands for religious liberty, and many fled from England to America. Turning the tables under the Commonwealth, the Puritans were not sorry to see many Anglicans emigrate to America. With the coming of William and Mary to the throne in 1688, the Church of England was firmly implanted in England as the established church but with toleration of dissident Puritans. The successes of Calvinist Presbyterianism in Scotland left only Ireland as a stronghold of Catholicism in the British Isles.

The Catholic Counterreformation. Despite all the space devoted here to the Protestant reformations, it should constantly be borne in mind that the Catholic Church remained by far the strongest single church in Europe. Southern Europe, France, and southern Germany continued basically loyal to Catholic doctrines, for the Roman Church had many great advantages in addition to the custom and tradition that kept people in the centuries-old fold of their fathers. The Catholic organization, with a single head in the person of the Pope and a well-organized hierarchy of officials who looked to the head for authority, aided the church immensely when it faced the often scattered efforts of several struggling Protestant groups. Furthermore, the church made many effective doctrinal as well as military efforts to stem the tide of Protestantism. In 1537 an important report (the *Consilium delectorum cardinalium*) on necessary reforms in the church was made by a group of cardinals. This report deplored the fact that men of worldly interests were admitted to the clergy, criticized the laxity of the monastic orders, the easy dispensations, the selling of indulgences, and urged that better educational facilities be provided throughout the church.

In 1542 the Court of the Inquisition in Rome began to decide questions of doctrine, to try suspected heretics, to punish those convicted of heresy, and to keep a watchful eye upon spoken and published statements of doctrine. The Pope wanted the Inquisition to work in all countries, but its effectiveness was often blocked by the kings or powerful bishops of northern Europe. However, Spain conducted it under state control with peculiar pitilessness, secrecy, and terror. Schools and universities in Spain and Italy were kept under close watch, and Humanism and liberal ideas in religion, science, and scholarship were set back for generations in comparison with intellectual progress in other countries. It should be said, however, that the procedures and attitudes of the Inquisition were not confined to the Catholic side; Calvin, for example, was fully as terroristic and authoritarian in his efforts to stamp out opposition to his ideas. His persecution and torture of Servetus were as bloodthirsty as any of the acts of the Inquisition. Authoritarianism and intolerance were characteristics of the times.

Another effective counterattack by the Catholic Church was the Council of Trent, which met for 25 different sessions in the middle years of the sixteenth century. The council met at Trent in the effort to prevent the Germans from breaking away as the English had done. Despite the presence of a liberal party who wished to reconcile the Lutherans by making radical doctrinal changes, the Pope's party won, and' the decrees on doctrine and matters of belief were restated without breaking from traditional Catholic positions. In the end, full authority in matters of doctrine was given to the Pope; this reversed the conclusion of the Council of Constance, which had said that the church council was supreme. Many decrees were also passed, aimed at reforming the abuses listed in the report of 1537 and including plans for the reform of education. The Index was set up to publish a list of books harmful and prohibited to faithful Catholics, to approve acceptable books, and to censor parts of books that verged on heresy. The Index continues in existence today.

Perhaps the most effective counterreformation agency of all, from the point of view of education, was the organization of the Society of Jesus under the leadership of Ignatius Loyola. The Jesuits rejected the monastic type of church order and became a militant order to war against heresy and win back ground, both geographical and doctrinal, lost to the Protestants. Loyola knit his organization into a highly centralized and effective agency, with strict eligibility tests enforced for new members. As preachers, as missionaries, and as teachers, the Jesuits ranged over the whole world, setting up their missions and schools. They became eloquent preachers and untiring missionaries for converting the heathen in the Far East and in the Americas as well as in Europe. They established an extremely efficient system of schools for training future leaders to carry on the work of the church. From the beginning, Loyola was convinced of the necessity of superior educational training as an effective religious weapon against Protestantism.

The Jesuits became so successful, so subtle, and so facile that they gained the reputation of upholding the doctrine that "the end justifies the means." For this they met the opposition of other church movements, notable among which was that of the Jansenists, who were imbued with a desire for stern moral discipline. They represented something akin to Puritanlike reform within the Catholic Church. In their contests with the Jesuits the Jansenists came off second best and were themselves declared heretics, but they exerted an educational influence far beyond their numbers and length of life.

As a result of the various agencies of the Catholic Counterreformation in the later sixteenth and seventeenth centuries, the Protestants gained no new victories and captured no new territory. In fact the Catholics won back Bohemia in the seventeenth century. The church was successful in reorganizing without surrender and without compromise. A new interest in education was expressed through several newer teaching orders, such as the Fathers of the Oratory and the Institute of the Brothers of the Christian Schools, in addition to the older Franciscan and Dominican orders. Such orders were extremely influential in carrying the religious doctrines of Catholicism and the ideals of Catholic education to the Americas, where they have continued to the present time.

ROOTS OF NATIONAL SYSTEMS OF EDUCATION

The organized educational efforts of the Reformation reflected these developments in political, economic, and religious institutions. The first effects of the Reformation wars were doubtless harmful to the educational institutions already in existence. The ravages of war and persecution meant great destruction of the physical plants and endowments. The middle of the sixteenth century saw a great depression in education, and the first half of the seventeenth century, especially in Germany during the Thirty Years' War, witnessed even worse conditions. However, as longer periods of peace were achieved in the various states of Europe, the outlines of educational order and organization began to appear. The Catholic schools and universities that had been destroyed by war or seized by Protestant sects were reestablished and reformed along somewhat new lines, and in Catholic countries the educational institutions themselves went through considerable change at the hands of the Catholic Church. The outlines of the modern European systems of education were being drawn along national lines.

Foundations of Modern Organization

The Two-track System of Universal Education Emerges. Much of the effort of Protestant reformers was directed toward providing wider opportunities for education among the common people. The class structure of society was deeply ingrained in all the countries of Europe. The principal change contemplated was that some opportunity for education should be given to the lower classes as well as to the upper classes, but the two classes were to receive different kinds of education. In general, the effect of the Reformation was to crystallize the distinction between a vernacular elementary education for the lower classes and a classical secondary education for the upper classes.

The demand for common schools for the masses of the people met with little response among the upper classes and even from some of the Protestant reformers. Luther and Calvin were both much more interested in the classical type of secondary education than they were in vernacular education, despite their appeals for the latter type of school. Anglican leaders in England and Catholic leaders in France were in general more willing to expand and reform secondary education than they were to provide common education for the lower classes. The traditional aristocratic conception of medieval and Renaissance education still held a predominating position in Reformation ideas of education.

Suggestions for a More Democratic Organization. However, the roots of a more democratic conception of education were being nourished. In Luther's earlier statements he vigorously urged that all children, rich and poor, boys and girls, should be educated. Calvin and his followers in the Netherlands, Scotland, England, and America envisaged universal education for all. John Knox in Scotland, Puritan educational reformers in England, and Dutch Reformed leaders in the Netherlands all proposed, and in some respects were able to achieve, a measure of universal education during the Reformation period. Perhaps the most democratic proposals of all were stated by the Moravian leader, Comenius, who urged the establishment of a complete "ladder" system of schools reaching from the lowest levels to the university. Despite the strength of the aristocratic conception in practice, the democratic conception was being stated in theory here and there in preparation, as it were, for the realization of the democratic ideal that was achieved in the late eighteenth and nineteenth centuries.

It should be pointed out that *universal* education for all is not necessarily identical with *democratic* education, in which equal opportunity is afforded to all. The Reformation made great strides toward providing a universal education in which everyone was given some schooling, but the lower classes had one type of education and the upper classes another. Achievement of a democratic education in which everyone is looked upon as equally entitled to the kind of education from which he can profit most was only occasionally contemplated, even on paper. State control of schools to provide universal education became a typical European product, but state control of schools to provide not only universal education but also democratic education was achieved first in the United States in the nineteenth century and to a lesser degree in some of the European countries in the early decades of the twentieth century.

Education for Girls. In several quarters proposals that girls should be educated as well as boys were heard during the Reformation. As a part of their general conception of universal education for religious and political purposes, Luther, Bugenhagen, and, to a lesser degree, Calvin urged that girls be educated. Dutch schools apparently were far in advance of any others in actually providing opportunity for girls to attend the town schools in the Netherlands. The organization of Catholic teaching orders of nuns, notably the Ursuline Sisters, gave evidence that the Catholic Church was also concerned to provide greater educational facilities for girls. In France the second wife of Louis XIV, Mme. de Maintenon, established a school for upper-class girls at St. Cyr, and Archbishop Fénélon made notable written proposals for the education of girls to equip them appropriately for the duties of household, society, and church. Insofar as the education of girls actually widened the range of educational opportunity, it helped to contribute to the spread of universal education.

Civil Control by State and City

One of the most far-reaching and profoundly important results of the Reformation was the growth of civil control of education as opposed to private and religious control. In the sense that "public" education means civil control, the movement toward public education was begun during the Reformation. However, as noted above, public education is not necessarily democratic education. Public education through civil control can be universal, compulsory, free, and supported by taxation without being democratic. Public education can be instituted by monarchies, by state churches, and by dictators for their own purposes, just as it can be instituted by democracies for the welfare of the whole people. The autocratic states of Europe moved toward public education during the Reformation, but this must not be confused with democratic education, which did not emerge until the states themselves became democratic. It is true, nonetheless, that universal public education helped in some respects to provide the seeds for democratic political arrangements when the time was ripe.

Civil Control in Germany. The stimulus to civil control of education in the Reformation often stemmed from a religious interest. Under the impact of political, economic, and religious events in Germany, for example, the church became closely allied with the state and became in effect a part of civil administration, for religious leaders were often appointed by the head of the state. Thus, under the stimulus of Luther and his followers, Bugenhagen and Melanchthon, the Protestant rulers were urged to study their schools and to reform them by civil authority. Reorganization of schools often accompanied the transformation of the Catholic churches into Lutheran churches. As a result of surveys conducted by Melanchthon and others, several of the German states and free cities issued civil codes for the conduct of schools. Only one or two of these can be mentioned.

The school code of Württemberg in 1559 was one of the most far-reaching, providing for the establishment of vernacular elementary schools to teach boys and girls reading, writing, arithmetic, music, and religion. These schools were to be established in every village and to be taught by the church sexton. Latin secondary schools were also to be set up to train boys for leadership in the church and state through preparation for higher religious schools and eventually the university. Other states followed the Württemberg code, notably Saxony in 1580. Another important code was issued by the state of Saxe-Gotha in 1642, providing for compulsory attendance, higher salaries for teachers, free textbooks, supervision of instruction, a graded class system, and more realistic studies. Among the important cities that also reorganized their schools by civil authority were Brunswick, Weimar, Nuremberg, Hamburg, Wittenberg, and Strasbourg. In the seventeenth century several states enacted compulsory-attendance laws, including Württemberg and Saxony.

Civil Control in Calvinist Lands. Calvin's theocratic theory, according to which the state is essentially an arm of the church, stimulated the growth of civil control in Calvinist countries. In Geneva, Switzerland, the state set up religious schools and enforced attendance for the benefit of the Calvinist Church. In the Netherlands, when the Dutch Reformed Church came into power, it proceeded to adapt the town schools already in existence to its religious purposes and to provide for extension of schools. The Synod of the Hague in 1586 provided for the establishment of schools in the cities, and the Synod of Dort in 1618 provided for the establishment in all villages of schools under the control of civil magistrates, to give free instruction to poor children. In Scotland the General Assembly of the Presbyterian Church recommended to the Scottish Parliament as early as 1560 that schools should be set up in every parish. After the Presbyterian Church was made the state church in 1592, Parliament passed in 1646 a law providing for schools in every parish, but the strength of the upper classes prevented the realization of this aim for many years.

Civil Control in France. In the seventeeth century the French States-General clearly called upon the church to establish schools in all towns and villages and to institute compulsory education. France, however, had followed the line of allowing the church to conduct schools without much civil control. In the wars between Catholics and Huguenots it was, among other things, the zeal of the Huguenots to establish schools and colleges along Calvinist models that aroused the ire of the Catholics. After the Edict of Nantes one of the civil liberties that the Huguenots gained was the right to conduct their own schools and universities in their free cities and towns. After Louis XIV came into power, education was left largely to the Catholic Church but civil control was exerted primarily over universities in a series of edicts about what university professors could and could not teach. Louis XIV required universities to teach the French civil law as well as canon law, and several edicts were issued to prevent instruction on the works of Descartes and others.

Civil Control in England. The Church of England retained control over education in England much as the Catholic Church had in France, but all Protestant rulers in England issued edicts of one kind or another about schools and universities inasmuch as they asserted that the king was the supreme head of the church. The Chantry Acts under Henry VIII and Edward VI dispossessed the Catholic foundations for chantry schools, and Henry VIII took over the monastic schools. Universities were inspected and supervised by agents of Henry VIII and Elizabeth. Henry VIII made the church primers required reading in schools. Thus the beginning church book became the beginning schoolbook. He also required Lily's *Grammar* to be studied in grammar schools. The Oath of Supremacy under Elizabeth in 1562 required all teachers to take the oath of loyalty to the monarchy and subscribe to the Thirty-nine Articles of Anglican faith and gave supervision of grammar schools to bishops.

In other areas affecting a different kind of education, the Statute of Artificers issued in 1563 set up national standards of skill in the trades, took control of apprentices away from the guilds, and put it into the hands of the civil magistrates. A series of poor laws culminating in the Poor Law of 1601 required the parishes to take care of their poor by taxation and required the compulsory apprenticeship of poor boys and girls, the parish overseers being empowered to carry out the orders. The poor laws helped to provide the seeds of civil control and public support for education in England and America.

When the Puritans came to power in England, their Calvinistic doctrines led many of their leaders to recommend the establishment of a state system of schools. Especially prominent in this respect was Samuel Hartlib, but the Puritan regime was so troubled and ended so soon that these ideas were not realized, and education reverted to the Church of England under the Restoration. The Act of Uniformity of 1662 required all teachers to take an oath subscribing to the established religion and to acquire a license from church officials. A few years later the Five-Mile Act levied fines upon any nonconformist who taught in defiance of these regulations. The state in England was coercing education in the interests of religion. The Puritans defied these laws by setting up schools in secret for their congregations, the so-called "Dissenters' Academies," but with the Act of Toleration of 1689 under William and Mary the Puritans were free to teach openly once more.

Private and Religious Control of Education

In general, civil control of education progressed further during the Reformation in Lutheran and Calvinistic countries than it did in England, France, Italy, or Spain. The latter countries, despite the many instances of civil control, adhered primarily to the traditional conception that education is a function of the church and of private philanthropy. Civil requirements that schools be established played little part in the provision of educational facilities in comparison with religious and private sources.

In England. When the Catholic Church was largely eliminated from the religious scene in England and the foundations of the monastic and chantry schools were confiscated, the state made little or no provision to fill the educational gap. Elementary education was provided in a rather haphazard and unsystematic way. Parents taught their children whatever they could, hired a tutor if they could afford one, or sent their children to the parish priest if he could and would teach them their letters. In some instances more or less formal instruction was given to neighbors' children by a housewife, while she did her housework, for which a fee was paid. Such arrangements have been called "dame schools." The most fortunate children were often sent to the preparatory department of a grammar school, sometimes called a "petty school." By and large, then, education was available principally to those whose parents could afford to provide it. Of course, as the merchant class grew in wealth and numbers, more parents could afford education, and proposals were made for charity schools for the poor; but, by and large, formal education did not affect the lower classes to any considerable extent.

Much more interest was expressed in a classical secondary education. Many new grammar schools were established, some estimates stating that as many as 500 such schools were newly founded or refounded during the Reformation. The financial stimulus for this interest came substantially from the new middle classes, whose desire to improve their social status often kept pace with their improving economic status. As funds were poured into the endowments for these Latin grammar schools, the bases were being laid for the English "public schools." The desire to give free instruction to poor children was doubtless a motive in this movement, as witness the plea of Archbishop Cranmer that poor boys be admitted to Canterbury School; but, on the whole, the clientele for these schools came from the more well-to-do classes.

They were "public" in the limited sense that the funds and income were used for the benefit of the schools rather than for the private profit of those who conducted them. They were also "public" in the sense that all children were "free" to attend them if they could pay the tuition or gain a free scholarship. They were not "public" in the American sense that they were open to all free of charge and supported by public funds or taxation. The most notable of these "public" schools were Winchester, Eton, Westminster, St. Paul's, Shrewsbury, Rugby, Harrow, Charterhouse, and Merchant Taylors' (the name of the last reflecting the influence of the merchant class).

In France, Spain, and Italy. In the predominantly Latin countries the Catholic Church maintained a firm hold upon the control of education. The stimulus of the decrees of the Council of Trent bore fruit in the establishment of many schools by church teaching orders in these countries. Among the most energetic bishoprics was the diocese of Paris, where schools were organized for the poor and laboring classes and where by 1675 some 5,000 pupils were taught by 300 teachers. The Jesuit schools were doubtless the most numerous and outstanding of those established by the church orders. Their efficient system resulted in several hundred institutions, attended by some 200,000 students, by the end of the Reformation. The estimate is made that several thousand students were in attendance in the Paris region alone in the middle of the seventeenth century. The Fathers of the Oratory became another very influential teaching order in Italy and France, concentrating primarily on secondary education.

Before the end of the Reformation period some 10 or 12 church orders were at work in elementary education, the most important of which were the Ursulines, Sisters of Notre Dame, Piarists, Port-Royalists, and Institute of the Brothers of the Christian Schools. The purpose in founding many of these was to provide free schools for poor children of the working classes. The number and success of the schools of these orders should caution against the belief that the Protestants alone were interested in elementary education for the masses. The Protestants turned to the civil authority, but the Catholic Church continued largely under its own widespread authority. The Piarists, for example, established schools not only in Italy and France but also in Bohemia, Poland, Austria, and Hungary, and the Jesuits covered the whole of Europe with their schools. The widespread activities of the teaching orders brought them into conflict with the state provisions of other countries. The long fight between public control of education as against religious or private control was entering a new phase.

Beginnings of Special Preparation for Teachers

In general, the Reformation began to emphasize the importance of teaching and of better prepared teachers. Although the improvement was necessarily slow, the combined interest of state and church in religious orthodoxy led to the setting up of standards for the teaching profession and marked the beginnings of certification and examination of teachers by the state churches. Luther visualized a teaching profession that would be well trained, achieve a greater amount of dignity, and be licensed by the government. In Germany the remuneration of teachers came primarily from student fees and tuition, often supplemented by funds from the government or church treasury. Teachers were required to abide by the state laws and by the ordinances that laid down prescriptions for curriculum, discipline, and religion. Some state laws even provided a measure of social security through old-age pensions and sickness aid. In England, teachers were subjected to similar oaths and prescriptions laid upon them by king and church.

Supervision of instruction grew out of the desire of the religious groups to see that teachers remained orthodox in their religious teachings. It represented a kind of fear of what harm unsatisfactory teachers might do, as well as a growing respect for the potentialities and efficacy of education. Perhaps the most careful of all in supervising teachers through civil and religious authorities were the Calvinists in the Netherlands and Scotland and the Puritans in England and America.

The Catholic teaching orders were likewise careful in their supervision and made progress toward the better training of teachers. The Jesuits, Fathers of the Oratory, Port-Royalists, and Institute of the Brothers of the Christian Schools set up teacher-training programs to ensure the better preparation of teachers. Of particular significance was the work of St. Jean Baptiste de La Salle in transforming teaching in the lower schools from a haphazard occupation to a vocation worthy to be called a profession. Through his leadership in establishing the Institute of the Brothers of the Christian Schools, La Salle demonstrated the value of an organized effort to prepare teachers and improve instruction. Edward A. Fitzpatrick has given an excellent summary of La Salle's educational contributions in his recent study.[1]

The Institute made it possible to create a continuing corps of teachers specially selected and trained for the task. Whereas elementary teachers had usually received little or no specialized preparation, La Salle saw the necessity of elevating the professional status of those who taught in the elementary schools. Free education of poor children was thus visualized to be of value to society and to religion on a level of equality with secondary school teaching. To this end, the Institute's normal schools gave theoretical, religious, and practical training to lay persons who were not destined for the priesthood but who were to make a profession of

[1] Edward A. Fitzpatrick, La Salle, Patron of All Teachers (The Bruce Publishing Company, Milwaukee, 1951), Chap. XIII.

teaching itself. The ideal, of course, centered upon religion at the heart of the educative process and of the preparation of teachers. In addition to religion, however, prospective teachers gave attention to the three R's and practical and vocational training as basic ingredients for the teaching of young children and juvenile delinquents.

Other contributions of the Institute included the use of the vernacular language rather than Latin as the medium of instruction, the application of more humane methods of teaching, concern for the individual child, and the creation of an orderly and effective school atmosphere. Children were taught in graded classes rather than exclusively by individualized instruction. Special attention was given to a secondary school program of modern subjects without Latin, to meet the needs of the new middle classes, and to continuation of education on Sundays for those who worked throughout the other days of the week. In these and many other ways La Salle demonstrated the importance of institutionalized and organized effort in the improvement of education. The existence of the Institute for more than 250 years and its spread to many countries of the world testify to his vision and leadership.

Another trend of great importance in improving the preparation of teachers was the effort to apply the principles of the new science to educational methods. This tendency received a good deal of attention in the educational literature of the Reformation. Mulcaster urged the establishment of teacher-training institutions, and Comenius elaborated a thoroughgoing system of method that laid the foundations for later improvements in the preparation of teachers (see pages 236 to 239).

Other Agencies of Education

As already noted, not only the schools but the whole of a culture educates the people through the institutions that they live by and through the guiding beliefs that they come to accept. During the Reformation, ideas and actions were affected by the growing respect for the state and for the benefits of material wealth. The authoritative leadership of the clergy in the various churches also affected the motives and actions of all classes.

The family as an educative institution was emphasized by most of the Protestant reformers. Luther stressed the importance of the family in stimulating moral and religious discussion through Bible reading and teaching the child his catechism as well as in training the child to a trade. The Calvinists likewise emphasized the importance of the family in the early education of youth, calling for extensive Bible reading and prayer in the family circle and often dwelling on the possibility of eternal punishment for the lost souls of children. Comenius urged that there should be a school at the mother's knee in every family.

The spread of printed books and growing literacy had an enormous educative effect. The possession of books and the creation of private libraries began to increase among wealthy families. The extensive pamphleteering on religious subjects, spurred by the conflicts between sects, attracted the attention of the intellectual classes. But, even more, they became interested in things scientific as reflected in activities of the newly organized scientific societies in most of the countries of Europe. Such nonschool agencies of education stimulated organized educational effort and in turn were aided by the spread of elementary and secondary education.

RELIGIOUS CREEDS AND HUMAN REASON

One cannot but be impressed with the tremendous importance of religious creeds during the Reformation. They acted as rallying centers for the loyalties of men. They gave people prime motives for living, fighting, and dying. So much of Reformation culture depended upon religion that it cannot be minimized; its effects lie deep within the loyalties and heart of American life. Yet, during the course of the Reformation, the political loyalties of nationalism also began to play an ever larger part, until finally the patriotic sentiment became so inclusive that persons of different religious faiths could join together in a common national cause to fight against nations made up of their own religious beliefs.

From the modern viewpoint, one of the most important aspects of Reformation culture is the authoritative character of the Reformation religious faiths. They were held so confidently by the people because it was widely believed that the religious leaders of each sect had special insight into the supernatural, beyond which there was no appeal; consequently, the word of the religious leaders was taken to be the word of God. From ancient times to the present day the ruler who wishes his word to be law has proclaimed that he rules by divine right. Another factor was the belief that moral conduct depended upon religion; a man could not be morally good unless he held orthodox religious beliefs. A third reason was the belief that civilization would fall if dissidents were allowed to argue as they pleased. Most religious sects were reluctant to tolerate what they considered to be heresy.

Characteristics of the Protestant Position. In general, Protestants put more direct emphasis than did Catholics upon the Bible as the rule of faith and as the basis of religious and moral authority. Protestantism denied the claims of the Pope and Catholic clergy to be the authoritative interpreters of Christian doctrine. In theory, the Protestant point of view stressed the right of the individual to gain salvation directly through faith rather than through mediation of an authoritative clergy. The ultimate conclusion of Protestantism would have been to allow individuals or small sects to interpret the Bible and believe as they pleased. However, this represents the more liberal and tolerant aspects of the Protestant revolt. In practice, all but the most radical of the Protestant sects became as intolerant in their persecutions of dissidents as the Catholic Church had ever been and used the civil power to enforce their convictions. In this respect the Protestant groups reflected the age of absolutism in which they lived; indeed, they contributed in large part to the authoritarian quality of Reformation life.

The Protestants most often objected to sacraments, indulgences, pilgrimages, devotion to relics, and ritualism that the Catholic Church had insisted were the "good works" necessary for salvation. The Protestants tended to insist that the essential road to salvation is "justification by faith" alone, whereby the individual soul comes into direct communion with God. Along with this insistence upon faith alone, the Protestants emphasized the necessity for each person to establish the grounds of his belief by reading the Bible for himself. This meant that all true believers must know how to read the Bible. The demand for a widespread education thus arose from religious as well as from political and economic motives. The conjunction of these motives in the national states of northern Europe and America gave rise to the conditions out of which a popular education appeared. Popular education was, indeed, something new under the sun, and its achievement has had far-reaching effects upon the history of modern culture.

In 1536, when only twenty-six years of age, Calvin wrote his *Institutes of the Christian Religion* in an attempt to justify Protestantism to Francis I of France. Even more than Luther, Calvin tried to base all his writings on the positive authority of the Bible. Whereas Luther had said that some changes were necessary but that he would retain in his doctrine everything that was not expressly forbidden by the Bible, Calvin kept only those doctrines and rituals that were expressly authorized by the Bible. Therefore, Calvinists did not use pipe organs or stained-glass windows in their churches because the Bible made no mention of them.

In many other respects, Calvinism, of all the Protestant churches, represented the most extreme break with Catholicism. Calvin was made of stern stuff, rigid, intolerant, authoritarian, and an implacable foe of Catholicism. He put great emphasis upon the doctrine of predestination, a doctrine more or less present in all Reformation creeds, but he made of it a big stick with which to force reluctant worshipers into line. According to Calvin, all men are divided into two unchangeable classes: the saints whom God has chosen from the beginning of time to be saved, and the sinners whom God has irrevocably chosen for eternal damnation. Since no one can tell before death whether or not he has been elected to be saved, it is incumbent upon all to live an absolutely moral and upright life. Modern men are likely to think that so rigid a conception of the human lot would lead to fatalism, but those under the influence of Calvin were led to the strictest modes of life in the hope that by complete adherence to the faith, a supremely correct life, and a minute fulfillment of religious duties they could prove to themselves and to others that they were among the elect. Failure to comply meant, of course, that there was no hope either here or in the hereafter, and no thoughtful man could overlook the awful possibilities of eternal punishment.

Despite the power of the Calvinist position, the logic of Protestantism was, however, carried in two directions by certain rebellious groups of sectarians who rejected Calvin's doctrines of predestination. One reaction led to an extreme emphasis upon the role of faith and piety in achieving salvation. The only really important thing was a right relation between the individual and God. Prominent among these groups were the Anabaptists who gained strength in the sixteenth century in Germany, Switzerland, and the Low Countries, and the Quakers who gained adherents in seventeenth-century England. The term often given to these rebellious groups was "antinomian" (*anti* = against and *nomos* = the law), meaning that they saw salvation through faith and the "inner light" rather than through obedience to the moral or civil law. They therefore rejected on principle the idea of a state church and a religion established by law. They fought bitterly and were persecuted mercilessly for their adherence to the radical idea that the church and state ought to be separated.

A second kind of reaction against the rigid predestination of Calvin was a heavy emphasis upon "good works" and living a good life as the road to salvation. In the seventeenth century a dissident group of Calvinists followed the Dutch clergyman, Jacobus Arminius, in believing that man's efforts were a great factor in salvation and that all men who were regenerated by faith could be saved by the exercise of free will and a good life. These Arminian views were rejected by the orthodox Calvinists at the Synod of Dort in 1619 and thenceforth Arminianism was looked upon as a heresy, but its views flowed into the Methodist movement of the eighteenth century and rapidly thereafter gained strength in Europe and America.

Christian Theism

The dominating conceptions of the world, of man's place in the universe, and of man's destiny remained throughout the Reformation period closely identified with Christianity. Despite the quarrels between Protestants and Catholics, neither departed substantially from the medieval conception of God and the universe. Although this may not be entirely accepted by adherents of either group, it does seem clear that there was a basic agreement among Christian Catholics and Christian Protestants that linked them closely together, as against the world view of empirical science. Both accepted a universe created by God in which man played a role assigned to him by God. Both accepted the distinction between a supernatural world and a natural world, of which the supernatural, or spiritual, world was by far the more important.

Both Catholics and Protestants believed that man's nature is essentially dualistic, that is, made of spiritual elements and material elements, a spiritual soul and a material body, of which the soul is, of course, the more important. Calvinists and Jansenists tended to place more emphasis upon original sin, but this was largely a matter of emphasis, for most Christians of the day would have denied a suggestion that man is inherently good or that he is born neither good nor bad. Both Catholics and Protestants agreed that the ultimate judgment of man's success upon this earth does not come until the next world; being good here and now is necessary for the glory of God and to escape eternal punishment. Both would have joined against a doctrine that preached that man's ultimate justification comes from the social good that he is able to accomplish.

Both Catholics and Protestants believed that knowledge and truth are fixed and revealed to man from supernatural sources. Both agreed that man's primary aim in education is to arrive at a true knowledge of God's laws and commandments. If the Protestants objected to the educational system of the Catholics, their remedy was primarily to set up a system of language study whereby they could read the word of God for themselves, unfettered by the commentaries and interpretations of Catholic scholars. Knowledge of the physical world was considered by both as far less important than knowledge of the spiritual and moral world. The learning process was conceived by both Catholics and Protestants as primarily a matter of bringing to light the innate ideas with which God has endowed each person. This was to be done most effectively by a kind of mental and moral discipline and achieved principally through the study of language and literature in which reading and memorizing were paramount. Both Catholics and Protestants were in large part opposed to the implications of much of the new scientific investigation. The burning of Giordano Bruno by the Catholic Church in 1600 and the forced abjuration of Galileo can be matched by Luther's condemnation of science as "That silly Little fool, that Devil's bride, Dame Reason, God's worst enemy."

Science and the New Rationalism

In spite of these convictions of the authority religious beliefs, however, the Reformation saw the rise of doubt, skepticism, and inquiry concerning the ideas that men lived by. The mere fact that the leaders of each religious sect battled so vigorously against unorthodox beliefs showed that doubters and unbelievers were present. By the end of the Reformation the sheer physical destruction of the religious wars had led many to wonder whether perhaps all religious doctrines were wrong in some respect and whether a new way to truth could be found. The impact of new geographic horizons and the knowledge concerning how other peoples lived and thought led many to reexamine their own cultures.

Most powerful of all, in the long run, was the growing respect for science and the scientific spirit. Despite the authoritarianism that was dominant in the Reformation, the growth of rationalism and intellectual liberalism was being nurtured in a few fertile areas. Although no complete victory was won, the skeptic, the scientist, the rationalist, and the heretic were freer and safer in 1700 than they had been a hundred years earlier. A growing reliance upon human reason and science had, of course, tremendous implications for education from the lowest to the highest levels.

Modern man does not need to be told about the importance of science in the world of today. He sees its importance on every side, but he sometimes does not realize that the foundations of modern science were being laid in the sixteenth and seventeenth centuries, often against great odds of intolerance, antagonism, and persecution. Some historians are inclined to believe that the scientific developments of the Reformation were the most thoroughgoing revolutions that occurred in that age of many revolutions. However that may be, the faith in science was growing despite opposition.

Philosophy of Science. One of the most outstanding proponents of science in Reformation times was Francis Bacon, not a scientist himself but a master of popularizing the value of science through his many writings and his influential political position as lord chancellor in England. Bacon's real influence lay largely in his ability to set forth the claims of the scientific method in an eloquent, persuasive, and effective style. Bacon felt that men were too enslaved by superstitions and tradition, relied too exclusively on Aristotle and Scholastic philosophy, and were too engrossed in the niceties of words and language. His remedy for these defects of thought and education was a thoroughgoing reliance upon the study of nature by the scientific method. In his *Dignity and Advancement of Learning* Bacon surveyed and defended the scientific aspects of learning. In his *New Atlantis* he let his imagination revel in describing a Utopia on an imaginary South Sea island where scientific research had developed unbelievable machines that flew in the sky, skimmed under the water, kept perpetual time, and conveyed music afar.

In his *Novum Organum* (*New Method*) Bacon described in detail the inductive, or scientific, method whereby authentic knowledge could be obtained. The scientist should observe nature, collect a wide range of facts, generalize from these individual facts to their common qualities, and express these likenesses in general formulas. Today Bacon would be criticized for recording masses of useless data just because he observed them and for a neglect of the supreme importance of mathematics in modern science. Nevertheless, his insistence that knowledge arises out of experience rather than through traditional authority and his perception of the use of a controlled method of investigation were of supreme importance. He was not the first to urge these procedures, but he helped enormously to make them respectable, despite jibes and sneers for trying to extract sunshine from cucumbers and build houses from the roof down when any sensible person knew this was impossible.

As profound as any revolution that has occurred in human history was the change in world view that gradually emerged from the scientific investigations of the Reformation. It took a long time for the implications to be felt; but when they were realized, the whole fabric of human thought was altered by the conception of a heliocentric universe. The Christian tradition had conceived of the universe as centering in the earth, with the stars and sun surrounding it, all originally created by God for His own purposes. However, when Copernicus, Kepler, Galileo, Brahe, Bruno, and Huygens had completed their scientific investigations, the outlines of a limitless universe with the sun at the center and with the earth as merely one of many satellites burst upon the consciousness of men with terrific force.

All the churches, Catholic and Protestant, viewed such a conception with alarm and took active steps to combat it, for they saw the world made especially for man paling into insignificance before the immensity of the universe. Copernicus died before his views were published; Kepler was denied hospitality by Lutheran theologians; Galileo was forced by the Catholic Church to abjure his writings; and Bruno was burned at the stake for his.

Nevertheless, the scientific revolution proceeded against all odds. Gilbert studied magnetism and coined the word "electricity," Boyle formulated his famous law of gases, and many others made great strides in the study of optics and mechanical principles. Most important, too, were the possibilities opened up by the tremendous advances made in mathematics, so essential for scientific measurement and computation. The sixteenth and seventeenth centuries saw the development of decimals and logarithms and improvements in algebra, the calculus, the theory of probabilities, trigonometry, and analytical geometry.

The most radical result of the application of the findings of science to new conceptions of a world view was the philosophy of materialism. Thomas Hobbes in England and Pierre Gassendi in France began to develop the philosophy of materialism to the point where they claimed that the universe was nothing but a huge machine operating according to purely mechanical laws. They saw nothing in nature but matter in motion; everything could be explained in material terms. Materialism thus represented the most extreme reaction against the Christian idealistic view that looked upon spiritual ideas as the basis of the universe. As might be expected, both Catholic and Protestant Christians were violently opposed to materialism, which gained only a few adherents among the intellectual classes until the eighteenth century, when it became somewhat more popular.

Descartes and Dualism. Much more effective in the Reformation and in later centuries was a kind of compromise called "dualism," worked out in considerable detail by René Descartes, the great French philosopher and mathematician. Just as modern science continued along the lines laid down by seventeenth-century scientists until the epoch-making discoveries of relativity in the twentieth century, so did philosophy continue to struggle with the problems defined by Descartes until the development of pragmatism in the later nineteenth and early twentieth centuries. Descartes was able to incorporate into the traditional world view of his time much of the results and methods of the new science, but he was also concerned not to antagonize the prevailing theology too much.

In his attempt to harmonize theology and science, Descartes reasoned that the universe is made up of two absolutely separate and distinct substances, namely, mind and matter. Mind is the spiritual substance by virtue of which thinking is possible; mind is completely independent of matter, free from mechanical laws, and free to make choices. Matter, on the other hand, is the material substance consisting of the physical world and made up entirely of material objects in time and space and moving according to fixed mechanical laws. Mind is a free agent, but matter is a machine. Both mind and matter are created by and controlled ultimately by God, but they cannot act upon each other. Thus, Descartes left mind to theology but made way for science by assigning matter to it. Western education has virtually been built upon the assumptions of dualism, many educators believing that education properly should devote itself to mental and spiritual activities rather than to material and practical activities.

Human Nature. Conceptions of human nature likewise underwent a change in the Reformation. In anatomy and medicine William Harvey was making enormous strides in discovering what the structure of the human body is like and how it functions. Others like Hobbes and Gassendi were applying their doctrines of materialism to human nature, saying that the body, being matter, works exactly like a machine according to mechanical laws and that the so-called "mind" is not a different sort of thing but merely another, more refined, case of matter in motion. The mind or consciousness is merely the body in motion. Such materialists were attacked as atheistic and in league with the devil, for they obviously denied the existence of an immortal soul.

In this dispute, again, Descartes came to the rescue with the doctrine of dualism. He asserted that, like the universe, human nature is made up of both mind (or soul) and matter (or body). Man's mind partakes of the mental substance and thus can think, exert free will, and control the body, whereas the body partakes of the material substance and thus is a machine obeying scientific and mechanical laws. The dualistic conception of human nature conceded that the human body is a proper object of scientific study but again reserved the human mind or soul for spiritual and higher scrutiny. Education has often been viewed since then as being properly devoted to the higher cultivation of the mind and soul rather than to the lower cultivation of the body.

Learning and Knowledge. With regard to the learning process somewhat the same kind of development took place. Materialists like Hobbes were inclined to say that man learns about the external world through the senses of seeing, tasting, touching, hearing, and smelling. Knowledge is built up through experience coming to the body through the senses. This doctrine, often called "empiricism," stemmed from the scientific methods of observing and testing the natural phenomena of the external world.

Idealists were inclined to say that man learns best through his mind or reason, because sense experience is limited to knowledge of physical objects, whereas reason can achieve permanent and absolute knowledge and truth. This conception is usually called "rationalism" because it assigned to human reason a more important place than that of the senses in getting at the real knowledge that lies behind everyday experience. Because of his great reliance upon mathematics as one of the best examples of achieving permanent truth, Descartes tended to support rationalism, as did such philosophers as Spinoza and Leibnitz, who felt that reason alone can give universal and certain knowledge. Religious thinkers were likewise inclined toward rationalism, although they also tended to say that human reason is subordinate to religious faith; in any case, reason to them provided a more acceptable way to learn than did sense experience.

Education, especially at the higher levels, has long been considered to be rationalistic in aim and content. Rationalists in education tend to stress the importance of mathematics, language, and literature because these studies, they say, develop the reason more effectively than does science, which, after all, depends upon sense experience. Up to the latter part of the seventeenth century, rationalism was often closely allied with religion, but Hobbes and Bacon had fired the opening guns for empiricism, soon to be supported by Locke and by Hume and other eighteenth-century thinkers. In any case, the claims of human reason as against the claims of religious faith, revelation, mysticism, authority, and tradition were once more being staked out in the Reformation. They were developed with great enthusiasm during the eighteenth-century Enlightenment.

Role of the Arts and Sciences

Scientific Knowledge and Instruments. Scientific investigation depended upon the development of such new technical tools and instruments as the telescope, microscope, thermometer, barometer, pump, and clock. These all made scientific discoveries easier and more accurate, but other technological instruments also had far-reaching social effects. Navigation instruments and the science of shipbuilding aided the geographic discoveries, and the opening up of new lands and the availability of new products stimulated in turn the desire to improve shipping and manufacturing. New methods of mining, farming, stock raising, cloth-making, and manufacture of finished goods were under way, laying the groundwork for the far greater developments of the eighteenth and nineteenth centuries.

The invention of movable type in the fifteenth century was improved upon until cheaper printed matter brought closer the possibility of a wider literacy and dissemination of knowledge. The growth of a middle class and a larger reading public stimulated in turn the demand for the publication of books on an ever-widening range of topics. Inasmuch as the universities seemed reluctant to take up the new science, the growing interest in scientific knowledge and its dissemination took place in scientific societies outside of the universities. These societies, such as the Royal Society in England and the Academy of Sciences in France, provided the principal means of applying science to social affairs until the universities of the late eighteenth and nineteenth centuries awoke to the tremendous social possibilities of scientific knowledge.

Languages and Literature. Despite the tremendous strides made in Reformation science, Humanism remained the dominating factor in scholarship and education. Humanism was so strong that throughout the Reformation period Latin remained the language of many of the great scientific as well as religious writings. The preoccupation of the schools and universities with the Latin and Greek classics not only shows the sustaining force of Humanism but explains in large part why science, the vernacular languages and literature, and the arts and music played so little part in the organized secondary and higher education of the Reformation.

A narrow study of the curriculum of Reformation schools and universities would not reveal the tremendous strides being made in the various countries of Europe toward developing national languages and literature of supreme importance. The history of education, however, must note the developments in these fields occurring outside of formal educational institutions in order that the later battles between the Ancients and the Moderns do not come as a surprise. Here is a singularly effective example of how the traditional schools lagged behind the culture of the day. By the end of the Reformation period the vernacular languages were regularly used in courts, business, and the market places of Europe. Stimulated by the growing consciousness of nationality and sponsored by the wealth of a new middle class, the vernacular literatures of England, France, and Spain gained tremendous impetus in the Reformation period.

Vernacular "classics" were being created to challenge the Greek and Latin. One need only mention the English literature of Shakespeare, Milton, and the King James Version of the Bible, and the French of Racine and Molière. French began to replace Latin as the international language of court and society, and the founding of the French Academy in 1629 stimulated the purifying of French as a standard language. When the political states realized the importance of a ready knowledge of a common language among the great masses of people and when the economic advantages of a knowledge of vernacular language for business purposes were realized, the study of vernacular languages and literature came into its own in the eighteenth and nineteenth centuries.

Art and Music. Remarkable advances in art and music paralleled the advances in science and vernacular literature. The trend in painting toward more realistic representations of persons and landscapes showed the increasingly secular tone of Reformation society. Drawing heavily upon the Italian Renaissance and yet each developing unique qualities of his own, the outstanding masters of the Reformation were Rubens and Van Dyck in Flanders, Hals and Rembrandt in the Netherlands, El Greco and Velásquez in Spain, and Dürer and Holbein in Germany.

In like manner the music of the Reformation made tremendous strides in technique and in the development of new instruments and new musical forms. New forms of group singing, the opera, the oratorio, the violin, and keyboard instruments laid the foundations for the great musical developments of the eighteenth and nineteenth centuries. In these artistic manifestations, the formal schools and universities took little interest. Indeed the Protestant groups, especially Lutheranism and Calvinism, felt that the secular music of the times, like the secular literature and science, was not properly part of an education whose prime aim was the saving of souls and the discipline of the mind.

Here, again, the religious factor was closely connected with the doctrines of rationalism, which saw the educative process confined to those "intellectual" studies of mathematics and language which would be not only good discipline for the mind but also safe for the spiritual development of the young. It should be said, however, that secular art and music and even science were of great interest to the aristocratic classes, whose social and leisure activities were enhanced by them. In general, Reformation education reflected Reformation culture but only a part of it. The hand of Humanism, now supported by the hand of religion, continued to direct the basic educational program as it has come down to us.

THE RELIGIOUS AND THE SECULAR IN EDUCATION

The usual description of sixteenth- and seventeenth-century education as dominated by religious aims is true, but it is only a half truth that needs considerable modification. Although much of the impetus for education came from religious leadership, the effects of political and economic, scientific, and Humanistic influences were apparent even in the days of the most energetic religious reform.

The aims of the Catholic teaching orders in Italy, Spain, and France continued to be principally religious. The ideal of preparing youth to become good Christians and devout Catholics dominated all that they did. Although this same aim was essential in the educational proposals of the Protestant reformers, many of them began to widen the conception to include education for the state as well. Luther, always vigorous in his pronouncements, insisted that all children should be educated for the good of the state as well as of the church, even though his earlier zeal that all should read the Bible was relaxed in later life, when he lost some of his faith in the common people and believed that the study of his catechism was probably enough. The close alliance between church and state always meant to Calvinists that education for the glory of God would also improve all aspects of the commonwealth, both political and economic. Even Milton, who, good Puritan that he was, believed thoroughly that the end of all learning was to know God and to love and imitate him for the purposes of salvation, nevertheless formulated an all-inclusive definition of education in which religion is not mentioned specifically: "I call, therefore, a complete and generous education, that which fits a man to perform justly, skillfully, and magnanimously all the offices, both private and public, of peace and war."

Likewise, Comenius, an ardent Moravian bishop who was deeply pious and felt that all knowledge was revealed ultimately in the Scriptures, insisted that children were not born human but became human through education as they grew up in a culture. He was impressed by reports of wild children who had lived apart from human society and thus were less than human. In some respects he was in agreement with modern cultural anthropologists, who make exactly the same point. He viewed the school as the manufactory of society, shaping children into human beings and playing a large part in the improvement of society. In any case, to him the aims of education were wider than merely religious, for children must be taught to live not merely for the church but for all of life. Here is definitely a widening of the aim of education, even to the point of a democratic aim, for he opposed a separate Latin school for the aristocracy, believing that everyone was equal in the Christian republic.

In other respects, too, the aim of education was widened in the Reformation. Economic and political influences can be seen in the new provisions for vocational education and the interest in teaching a trade to poor children. Economic factors were at work in the attempts of the middle classes to widen the scope of vernacular education so that it would meet more adequately their commercial needs. When the Humanist tradition was incorporated into the Reformation schools, it tended to widen narrowly religious outlooks by acquainting students with the secular cultures of Greece and Rome. The aristocratic character of Reformation culture impelled the courtly classes to establish new academies that would meet their needs in military and social accomplishments. Finally, the scientific influence produced a wider curriculum that included the sciences and a scientific method of teaching.

Vernacular Education for the Common People

In Lutheran Lands. The effort to spread vernacular education among the people in Lutheran lands met with considerable success. The older Catholic parish schools and town schools were reorganized wherever possible, and new schools were established. The growing use of printed books made possible the wider dissemination of Luther's German translation of the Bible, his catechism and hymnbook, and schoolbooks written by Luther and his followers. Bugenhagen was especially instrumental in organizing vernacular schools in the various German states, even to the extent of attempting to legislate against the private schools already in existence. Denmark and Sweden also took steps to reform their schools along Lutheran lines. It should be noted, also, that the Moravian denomination developed good vernacular schools before the Thirty Years' War virtually wiped them out.

The vernacular curriculum came to include reading of the Bible, learning of Luther's catechism, reading of Aesop's *Fables* translated by Luther, singing the Lutheran hymns, and possibly some history, physical activity, and arithmetic (although the earlier reckoning schools maintained their superiority in arithmetic). The basic four R's (reading, writing, arithmetic, and religion), along with music and some history and physical education, became the principal curriculum of the common vernacular schools in Lutheran lands.

In Calvinist Lands. Like Luther, Calvin strongly advocated vernacular schools in which children could learn the Calvinist catechism, the three R's in the vernacular, and the singing of Calvinist hymns. The Huguenots carried this type of school wherever possible into France, and the German Reformed Church (teaching in German, of course) attempted to do so in the territories of western Germany, where they made some gains. In the Netherlands the Dutch Reformed Church set up what may have been the best vernacular schools of any country of Europe. Here again, stimulated by the practical needs of the commercial cities of the Netherlands, the Dutch schools taught the three R's and religion for boys and girls and doubtless had an influence upon the Puritans of England and America as well as the Dutch settlers in America. The Scottish schools followed somewhat the same pattern when they were established in the seventeenth and eighteenth centuries.

In Catholic Lands. The teaching orders of the Catholic Church also developed vernacular schools during the Reformation, perhaps in response to the Protestant gains in this area. The Port-Royalists and Institute of the Brothers of the Christian Schools taught in French, as did several of the women's teaching orders. Even the Fathers of the Oratory, who were interested primarily in secondary education, developed a good deal of teaching for the early school years in the vernacular. These schools corresponded in large part to the Protestant schools, with the emphasis, of course, upon Catholic religion rather than Protestant. Parish schools taught by the local priest also multiplied in response to the admonitions of the Council of Trent, and these gradually turned their attention to teaching in the vernacular of the country in which they were located.

In England. An essential phase of the Reformation in England was the change of the language of the Church of England from Latin to English. This meant that the language of the parish schools taught by Anglican priests came to be English. Mention has already been made of the use of church primers, the Prayer Book, and hymnals in such teaching. The destruction of the Catholic monastic and chantry schools destroyed the bulwarks of Latin teaching in elementary schools. Family tutors, private teachers, and dame schools supplemented the English instruction of the priests, all giving their attention more or less to reading, writing, the catechism, hymns, and perhaps some arithmetic, along with attention to the manners and proper behavior of children. The alphabet and Lord's Prayer were learned from a hornbook, a small board covered with parchment on which the words were printed and protected by a thin covering of transparent horn.

Among the Puritans in England the use of vernacular English became extremely important. In elementary schools conducted by the ministers, English was the language through which the Calvinist religion was taught.

When the Act of Uniformity drove the Puritans underground, these schools continued to operate. As toleration was won late in the seventeenth century, it was decided by the courts in several legal cases that elementary school teachers were not required to be licensed by the bishop as was the case with grammar school teachers. Thus, the dissenters' schools began to flourish in the eighteenth century.

Even at the secondary level the teaching of the vernacular became common in the so-called "Dissenters' Academies" taught by Puritan ministers. Although these academies began by emphasizing the classics, they gradually widened their program under economic and scientific pressures until they furnished the widest curriculum of any secondary schools in the seventeenth century. In addition to the standard classical studies they offered English instruction in six of the seven liberal arts (grammar, rhetoric, logic, arithmetic, astronomy, and geometry), trigonometry, algebra, geography, surveying, navigation, ethics, history, economics, politics, natural science, anatomy, metaphysics, and some of the modern languages. Although any one school did not give instruction in all these subjects, nevertheless the type of school as a whole (of which there were 50 or 60) included this range of studies. In the eighteenth century they came to exert a great influence upon the private schools and academies of America. The influence of science and of the practical business of making a living was evident in the study of natural science, practical arts, and social science.

Vocational Education. In addition to the vernacular schools provided for the children of the ordinary person, some strides were made toward providing a modicum of vocational training, especially for the children of poverty-stricken families. In Germany Luther had stressed the importance of teaching all children a trade, but he felt that this should be done in the home. Other provisions for a kind of vocational education for commercial purposes have already been described in connection with the development of the writing and reckoning schools that grew up in German towns in the fifteenth century (see pages 174 and 191). These schools continued through the Reformation period to teach writing, commercial arithmetic, and bookkeeping. In the Netherlands considerable attention was given to commercial and trade education, as might be expected in a country with widespread commercial interests. As early as 1531 a law required that children either be compelled to go to school or be apprenticed to a trade, and municipal governments were directed to establish schools to give vocational training. Here was a tradition of vocational education that was to influence the Dutch and English settlers in America. It was no accident that vocational education received its most effective start in those countries most advanced commercially, namely, Germany, the Netherlands, and England.

In Elizabethan England early steps had been taken to provide by law compulsory apprenticeship and workhouses for poor children. The Statute of Artificers in 1562 and the Poor Law of 1601 were designed to take care of the economic shift from agriculture to commerce and manufacturing. This shift had thrown many lower-class people off the land and out of work. In the seventeenth century several of the Puritan reformers advocated the extension of vocational education into the schools. Petty proposed that technical schools be set up for tradesmen; Dury urged greater attention to the practical subjects of agriculture, navigation, and commerce; and Hartlib advocated the study of how to apply science to commerce, industry, agriculture, and education. These men represented the commercial and practical interests of the Puritans, but they could not break the hold of the religious and classical tradition in education, although the Dissenters' Academies did begin to pay some attention to these recommended subjects.

The important thing to note is that economic conditions were ripe for still greater attention to vocational subjects during the eighteenth and nineteenth centuries, when they actually began to be taught in the schools as well as through apprenticeship. The incorporation of vocational studies into the schools is one of the most important events of modern education, though it raised one of the most violent of all educational controversies, namely, the role of liberal versus vocational studies. The Reformation at least *expressed* the doctrine that education should fit children directly for the active pursuits of life by means of practical and vocational studies.

Education for the Upper Classes

One of the most extraordinary aspects of Reformation education is the way in which all the warring religious groups agreed on one thing, namely, that the classical curriculum provided the best secondary education for training leaders for church and state. This did not seem extraordinary at the time, for the historic documents of the Christian Church were written in the classical languages and Renaissance Humanism had established the classics so firmly as the basis of secondary education that few people even considered questioning their validity. The wholehearted way in which both Protestants and Catholics continued to rely upon the classics served to maintain their influence in secondary and higher education much longer than would otherwise have been the case. The educational marriage of religion with classical Humanism has brought forth untold progeny even to the present generation.

The upper track of the two-track system consisted of the classical secondary school, used in the Reformation for religious, political, and social purposes. The classical humanities became the mark of religious scholarship, political superiority, and good breeding and manners. Gentility could be won indeed by financial success but even more so by the accomplishments bestowed by a classical education. The classical ideal prevailed in secondary education, despite the dreams of certain educational reformers who saw possibilities in the vernacular languages and in science. The Reformation built the framework for the classical secondary school that was to dominate secondary education in Europe for the next two centuries in the form of the *Gymnasium* in Germany, the *lycée* in France, and the grammar school in England.

Lutheran Classical Schools. Despite his interest in vernacular education for the common people, Luther always felt that the Latin school was the prime educational agency for promoting the Reformation in Germany. It was the Latin school that was to train leaders for the church and state and prepare for the universities. In those days of intense religious controversy it was the classical school that would prepare Lutheran leaders to defend and propagate the Lutheran faith on an equality with the Catholic leaders. Luther wanted even the elementary schools to teach Latin; but when he despaired of the abilities of the common people, he put more emphasis than ever upon the secondary schools.

Luther's faithful lieutenant, Melanchthon, who had charge of reorganizing secondary education in Lutheran Germany, was a thoroughgoing Humanist; he loved Greek as well as Latin and had a contempt for the vernacular. Melanchthon was extraordinarily active in establishing classical schools, wrote numerous textbooks on all the seven liberal arts, and was a constant adviser to the Lutheran rulers in setting up their school codes and secondary schools. Also influential was Johann Sturm, whose organization of secondary schools into regular classes laid the foundations of the German *Gymnasium*. In his school at Strasbourg Sturm divided the curriculum into 10 graded classes, each to be taught by a different teacher and each to follow a prescribed curriculum. In this curriculum were found a selection of the ancient secular classics, ancient religious writers, the medieval liberal arts, and the Humanist and reform writers, so patterned as to conform to the Reformation conception of a liberal education.

Calvinist Classical Schools. Little essentially different can be seen in the secondary school set up by Calvin in Geneva. He, too, put great emphasis upon the study of the classics in order that "true" religious scholars might read the Scriptures in their original languages and not be obliged to depend upon Catholic interpretations. He once said that only those boys who could not study the classics profitably should, as second best, study the vernacular. Calvin had taught at Strasbourg and modeled his schools upon Sturm's. He shortened the curriculum to 7 years and introduced some vernacular French, but the prime object was still to train leaders in classical scholarship and rhetoric in order to defend and propagate the Calvinist faith.

Catholic Classical Schools. The most effective of the secondary schools under Catholic auspices during the Reformation were the schools of the Jesuits, called *collèges*. These schools were often physically well equipped, and characteristic Jesuit thoroughness led to the systematizing and standardizing of the curriculum into what has been called the *Ratio Studiorum* since 1599. The Jesuit *collège* consisted of six rigidly prescribed grades in each of which were taught Latin, Greek, religion, and religious history. The Latin authors most commonly read were Cicero, Ovid, Vergil, Catullus, and Horace; Greek authors were Chrysostom, Aesop, Isocrates, Basil, Plato, Aristotle, Plutarch, Demosthenes, Thucydides, Homer, Hesiod, and Pindar. The religious writings of the church Fathers were mingled with secular prose, poetry, rhetoric, and philosophy (the latter carefully selected for moral and religious purposes so as not to conflict with Catholic doctrine).

Beyond this standard course the Jesuits instituted a 3-year philosophy course in which more classical grammar and literature were studied as well as rhetoric, logic, mathematics, ethics, metaphysics, and natural science. During the last year of the philosophy course, instruction was given in the theory and practice of teaching. The Fathers of the Oratory also developed successful secondary schools, deviating from the Jesuit schools somewhat in the attempt to incorporate Descartes' philosophy, science, and mathematics and utilizing the vernacular to a greater extent.

Anglican Classical Schools. The Latin grammar schools of England came to be the English equivalent of the German *Gymnasium* and French *collège*. The very title describes eloquently what the main business of the schools was. In curriculum the grammar school was pronouncedly classical in content, but very often the art and practice of letter writing was included, as a concession to the practical interests of the commercial classes. Even more characteristically, the "public schools" of England came to put much emphasis upon sports and physical activity on the playing field. To a much greater degree than in the German *Gymnasium* or French *collège* the English relied upon games and the spirit of fair play in athletic contests to develop not only physical prowess but also moral habits of sportsmanship and the ability to "take it."

Standardization and Discipline. In general, then, the secondary school of the Reformation came to be carefully graded and divided into classes, with regularly prescribed books to be read in each year. This process of standardizing the curriculum has provided educational reformers ever since with ammunition with which to criticize traditional methods. The age-old struggle of rigidity versus flexibility in the curriculum was being won during the Reformation in favor of rigidity as far as the secondary schools were concerned.

During the Reformation the flexibility characteristic of the wandering students of the Middle Ages and Renaissance began to give way to order, discipline, regular attendance, a prescribed curriculum, and regular classification and promotion from one grade to the next. Constant attempts were made to make students "toe the mark." Innumerable rules were passed to prevent fighting, carrying weapons, lying, cheating, drinking, gambling, swearing, card playing, dicing, and even swimming, skating, fishing, and birdcatching. Severe punishments were meted out in the attempt to enforce discipline. Part of the necessity for discipline was doubtless the fact that the Reformation secondary schools, especially in Germany and France, began to take over many of the subjects of the traditional liberal arts that had formerly been taught in the medieval university. The effort to teach difficult classical studies to young boys, who began the course anywhere from the age of seven to fourteen and finished at from fourteen to seventeen years of age, must certainly have taxed the ingenuity of the masters in matters of discipline.

Courtly Academies for the Nobility. The political, economic, and social changes affecting the highest social classes during the Reformation caused them to be dissatisfied with the classical curriculum just described. The older medieval training for knighthood was no longer suitable for a life that centered more and more in the royal courts of Germany and France, where social graces, and dueling, horsemanship, and other "gentlemanly" means of fighting became the aim of life. The children of the nobility needed a more practical kind of education to prepare them for a military, courtly, and social life. The ideal type of education for "gentlemen" had been described in Renaissance terms by Castiglione, Elyot, and Ascham. Now in the Reformation a good many academies began to fulfill the needs of this group. By 1649 there were over 40 princely academies near Paris alone. They rapidly were copied in the *Ritterakademien* of Germany. In such schools, children who were destined or hoped to live their lives at court were taught dueling with sword and pistol, riding, gunnery and fortification, music, heraldry, geography, history, mathematics and science, and the vernacular languages, especially French.

One of the most complete proposals for such a school, although never put into practice as such, was *Queen Elizabeth's Academy* written by Sir Humphrey Gilbert, himself almost an English prototype of the kind of courtly gentleman whose education he was proposing. His ideal was to provide an education that would include training for a life of action appropriate for the practice of peace and war. In this book Gilbert proposed the teaching of the classical languages, the social sciences, the intellectual weapons of logic and rhetoric, military theory and practice, and the social accomplishments of the modern languages, music, and dancing. The influence of such an ideal eventually affected student life in universities. Students dropped the drab clerical garb, took to wearing swords and jaunty clothes, and measured their social, if not intellectual, success by the number of dueling scars they could exhibit.

University Instruction

In general, the universities of Europe overlooked the new science and philosophy in favor of the study of theology and religious disputation. The earlier battles of the Renaissance to make the universities Humanistic were given further impetus by the Reformation desire to use the classics to prepare the clergy for theological controversy. The universities were not yet becoming centers of free inquiry and investigation. In fact, they were lagging considerably behind other cultural developments and holding so vigorously to their religious-classical emphasis that they gave little attention to new scientific developments.

Italian and Spanish Universities. During the Renaissance the freest universities had been in Italy. The University of Padua, under the protection of the free city of Venice, had become the great scientific university, particularly in mathematics, medicine, and anatomy. Copernicus, Vesalius, and others did outstanding work there as students and professors. However, the growing vigor of censorship instituted by the Catholic Counterreformation in the later sixteenth and seventeenth centuries served to reduce the Italian universities to impotence for centuries to come. Much the same sort of thing happened in Spain, where the universities had prospered under Charles V and Philip II. The University of Salamanca, for example, in 1561 provided for the books of Copernicus to be taught in astronomy and those of Vesalius in anatomy, the first such provision in any European university. But, again, the decline of Spain as a first-rate power and the force of the Spanish Inquisition brought about a corresponding decline in the Spanish universities.

German Universities. The Reformation wars, dogmatic religion, and state control made the German universities dominantly centers of theology-mindedness. Lutheran rulers molded their universities to serve Lutheran purposes, and Catholic rulers did likewise for Catholic purposes. The universities at Wittenberg, Leipzig, Frankfurt, Tübingen, and Rostock became Lutheran, and new Lutheran universities were founded at Marburg, Jena, Strasbourg, and Königsberg. Although the union of theology with Humanism had preserved some of the vitality of the Humanistic interests, most German universities reached a low level under the weight of theological interests by the end of the seventeenth century. The revival in the eighteenth-century Enlightenment was to see the German universities emerge into the first rank among the universities of the world, a position they maintained until the Hitler regime of the twentieth century.

French Universities. The French universities also declined into impotency under the oppression of religious fanaticism and national despotism. The Huguenots had established eight or nine higher institutions during the period of toleration, but they were wiped out as the Huguenots were driven to cover or into exile in the seventeenth century. Francis I tried to reform the University of Paris along Humanistic lines, but failing in this he set up the Collège de France. Henry IV put the University of Paris under civil rule in 1600 and regulated minutely the order of studies and exercises in the faculty of arts; but the classical study was largely dry and formal, and the science and mathematics depended upon Aristotle, whereas the new science of Copernicus and Descartes was rejected or overlooked. A new and even less fruitful scholasticism was being handed down, having little life, vitality, or connection with the new cultural trends of the day.

Calvinist Universities. Calvin's higher institution of learning at Geneva was the capstone of his educational system. The academy at Geneva was apparently very successful at the outset, enrolling several hundred students the first year. Emphasizing constant religious devotions, the curriculum included the classics, the usual liberal arts, ethics, poetry, physics, and theology. Obviously designed to prepare preachers, theologians, and teachers for the Calvinist world, Geneva was used as the model for the University of Leiden in the Netherlands, University of Edinburgh in Scotland, and Emmanuel College of the University of Cambridge in England, all of which were to have an influence upon colleges in America. Of the several universities established in the Netherlands in the sixteenth and seventeenth centuries, the Universities of Leiden, Amsterdam, and Utrecht became outstanding centers of scholarship and Calvinist religion. Several of the Scottish universities were founded in this period under Presbyterian auspices, among which Edinburgh and Aberdeen soon achieved preeminence, especially during the eighteenth century.

English Universities. In England the Humanistic interest was associated with religious sectarianism as the various colleges at Oxford and Cambridge supported different creeds. Humanistic and classical studies were used as new weapons with which to fight old theological battles. Some colleges became Anglican, and others remained Catholic. When Catholics were excluded by Queen Elizabeth in 1575, battles were then fought between Anglican Protestants and Puritan Protestants. The Puritans went mainly to Cambridge, where endowments had been made favorable to them, especially St. John's College, Emmanuel College, and Sidney Sussex

College. These colleges became the avowed centers of a militant Puritanism, which trained many of the Puritans who came to America. Theology remained the predominant study at the higher levels, and the new science was almost entirely ignored. The theological instruction at Oxford and Cambridge was largely suited for training clergymen who would be well versed in Latin, Greek, Hebrew, and the art of disputation so that they could go forth and defend their religious doctrines against all assailants.

The system of college instruction as opposed to university instruction was more firmly embedded than ever by the Reformation emphasis upon discipline, mental, moral, and religious. The college retained its communal aspects, marked by the hall and quadrangle, in which masters and students lived and studied together. The continued enforcement of celibacy upon masters and tutors also helped to preserve the communal life of the English college long after the Reformation had seen its disappearance in German universities. The English conception of a college with its discipline and prescribed curriculum was most influential in the development of higher education in America. Harvard, the first American college, was virtually a copy of one of the colleges at Cambridge.

Ingredients of a Liberal Education. In England, at the time of the colonizing of America, the liberal-arts course consisted of (1) the medieval liberal arts (grammar, rhetoric, logic, arithmetic, geometry, astronomy, but no music); (2) the philosophy of Aristotle (ethics, politics, physics, and metaphysics); and (3) the Renaissance studies of classical Humanism (Latin, Greek, Hebrew, and rhetoric). The Reformation made all these studies more or less subservient to religious and sectarian interests as well as to the demands of a political state closely allied with the church.

Each of these historic ideals was based upon a liberal education essentially of linguistic and literary studies. Therefore, the Reformation educators assumed that the best way to develop a man of action was through the study of books. (The courtly academies were a denial of this principle, but they did not receive much acceptance in England.) Moreover, only a few men were considered capable of higher education in language and literature and only a few were considered capable of leadership in society. In these respects, the liberal education of the Reformation was founded upon an aristocratic conception of society and upon the scarcity theory of higher education, whereby academic degrees and a liberal education were valued even more highly because they were attainable by only a few.

A liberal education meant principally that the student was more or less conversant with Latin, Greek, mathematics, and philosophy. This conception, as embodied in the prescribed curriculum and disciplinary methods, was tenacious.

New Conceptions of Educational Method

Common Practices. The most common methods of teaching grew out of the bookish, linguistic, and mathematical studies that dominated the classrooms of the Reformation period. This meant that success at school was determined largely by the ability to memorize quantities of material and to recite to the teacher what was in the book. Ever since the wide-spread use of written language as a cultural tool the most obvious method of school learning had been memorizing. When grammar was organized into a body of rules, then the study of grammar included the memorizing of grammatical rules. When English grammars were written, they followed the precedents found in Latin grammars. As rules for other studies such as logic, rhetoric, and mathematics were developed, the learning of those subjects likewise included memorizing of rules.

Practice in the rules of rhetoric and logic led to the use of the "disputation," whereby students argued according to the rules of formal logic. Likewise, the "declamation" gave students the opportunity to declaim, or recite, excerpts from the classic writers or pieces of their own composition according to the rules of rhetoric and oratory. Some of the more advanced secondary schools gave a good deal of opportunity for the reciting of lines from ancient plays in order to develop a sense of the style and usage of the classic authors. These methods of bookish learning grew out of the general adherence to a rationalistic conception of mind. When the imitation of classic authors was so pronounced as to be slavish, the method became known as "Ciceronianism."

Formerly, pupils of a wide range of age and ability were grouped together. One schoolmaster attempted to teach all the pupils together even though they ranged in age from six or seven years to fifteen or sixteen years. Classifying the pupils according to age and grade was an outgrowth of the Reformation period. Discipline was often severe, even brutal, including whipping and the ridicule attendant upon the use of the dunce's cap and dullard's stool.

Newer Methods of Sense Realism. The growing influence of an empirical point of view in science and philosophy had its educational effects in the doctrines of sense realism. Several educators began to react against the rationalistic formalism of Ciceronianism and the irrational excesses of discipline. In general, the sense realists urged that learning through the senses by means of actual things is far more effective than merely learning words and rules from books. The inductive method of science whereby the learner begins with actual and simple observations of what he knows best and proceeds to more complex and unfamiliar things was stressed as the basis of educational method. Efforts to arouse the interest of students in what they were learning and to adapt the materials to their abilities were praised as an improvement over traditional formalism and mere bookishness. In such ways as these the sense realists showed that they were becoming aware that Reformation schools lagged behind Reformation culture. They insisted that school methods and curriculums should be widened to meet appropriately the changes that were occurring in the culture.

Many of the doctrines of sense realism stemmed from the empirical philosophy as it was being stated by Francis Bacon, who insisted that education should cultivate the scientific spirit and method. Bacon attacked the "contentious" learning of traditional dialectics and theology, the "delicate" learning of Ciceronian Humanism, and the "fantastic" learning of superstition and witchcraft on the basis that all these neglected the study of nature and depended upon mere speculation or authority. Instead, education should encourage original investigation, should cultivate the habit of suspending judgment until the facts were in, and should foster a critical attitude that would free the individual from the shackles of preconceived prejudices and fixed ideas.

Luther and Ratke. In his various writings on education Luther expressed some ideas consonant with sense realism, but apparently they were the result not so much of an awareness of sense realism as of an effort simply to make the teaching of young children more effective. His conception of a classical secondary education seems not to coincide with some of his recommendations that elementary instruction should be adapted to the capacities of the learners and should be made more pleasant by appealing to the interest of pupils, by studying things as well as words, and by softening discipline.

Nearly a century after Luther, a strange man who embraced Lutheranism made several efforts to apply the Baconian doctrines to the teaching of languages. Wolfgang Ratke had read Bacon in England and came back to Germany, promising mysteriously effective methods of teaching. He captured the fancy of the Prince of Anhalt, who set up a school for him that several hundred boys and girls attended. Ratke urged that the order of nature should be followed in teaching, but his suggestions were somewhat confused. He recommended learning one thing at a time until it was thoroughly mastered through repetition, based upon questioning and understanding rather than upon mere memory. Direct knowledge of things should precede the learning of words about things. In the study of the classics, arithmetic, singing, and religion, the use of the German vernacular should predominate. Ratke's influence was limited because of the criticism evoked by his narrow spirit and secretive methods.

Comenius. The eminent Moravian bishop, Johann Amos Comenius, was perhaps the outstanding writer upon educational theory during the Reformation and paved the way for the wider application of sense realism in the eighteenth and nineteenth centuries. Comenius tried to apply

Ex sump M: S.   G. Glouer fc.

. Loe, here an Exile! who to serue his God.
Hath sharply tasted of proud Pasturs Rod.
(Whose learning. Piety, & true worth, being knowne
To all the world, makes all the world his owne.
                                                    F. Q.

Fig. 12. Johann Amos Comenius.

the methods of science, as he understood them, to educational theory, curriculum, and method. All instruction should be carefully graded and arranged to follow the order of nature as revealed in the child's development. This meant proceeding from the simple to the complex, from the known to the unknown. Throughout all teaching, the understanding of the child should be approached through appeals to his sense experience. Comenius urged that the child learn by acquaintance with actual objects wherever possible and in any case through pictures and representations of things. His many textbooks were profusely illustrated and thus introduced the idea of picture books for school children. His *Orbis pictus* is

Cornix cornicatur, The *Crow* crieth.	à à	A a
Agnus balat, The *Lamb* blaiteth.	b è è è	B b
Cicàda stridet, The *Grasshopper* chirpeth.	cì cì	C c
Upupa dicit, The *Whooppoo* saith.	du du	D d
Infans ejulåt, The *Infant* crieth.	è è è	E e
Ventus flat, The *Wind* bloweth.	fi fi	F f
Anser gingrit, The *Goose* gagleth.	ga ga	G g
Os halat, The *Mouth* breatheth out.	hà'h hà'h	H h
Mus mintrit, The *Mouse* chirpeth.	ì ì ì	I i
Anas tetrinnit, The *Duck* quaketh.	kha, kha	K k
Lupus ùlulat, The *Wolf* howleth.	lu ulu	L
Ursus murmurat, The *Bear* grumbleth.	[mum mum-	M

Fig. 13. Page from *The Orbis Pictus* by Comenius.

perhaps the best known. He improved language teaching by giving simple descriptions of the pictures, with the vernacular and the Latin sentences written along together.

In *Didactica magna* Comenius set forth his educational theory and his plans for reforming the curriculum and organization of schools. In general, he was impressed with the possibilities of social reform through pansophism, that is, teaching all knowledge to all children. In the school for infants up to the age of six (School of the Mother's Knee) Comenius would train the senses and bring about moral, religious, and physical development through play and games, fairy tales, rhymes, music, and manual activity. In his vernacular school for ages six to twelve, he would teach the three R's, singing, religion, morals, economics and politics, history, and the mechanical arts. In the classical school for ages twelve to eighteen would be taught German, Latin, Greek, Hebrew, grammar, rhetoric, logic, mathematics, science, and art. The university would be the top rung of this ladder system. At all levels, the subject matter should be carefully organized into classes and graded to the pupil's ability. The school year must be carefully determined, as well as hours for specific activities during the school day. Classes should be taught as groups for the social advantages thus to be gained, and the various subject matters should be correlated as far as possible. In all activities the school should be made practical for life and pertinent to an upright religious life.

Comenius was far in advance of his day and probably had little effect upon his own time, but the modern tone of much that he proposed is proof of his insight into some of the cultural stirrings of modern times. Although his advice was sought in Poland, Sweden, Hungary, and England (and even some mention was made of inviting him to be president of Harvard), Comenius suffered successive defeats and failures in his homeland because of the ravages of the Thirty Years' War. His religious sect was so generally persecuted that his influence was doubtless much less than it would have been if he had belonged to a majority group.

English Theorists on Method. The effects of sense realism upon several English writers of the seventeenth century are worthy of mention. Richard Mulcaster urged that instruction should be adapted to the pupil's interests and capacities and that great use should be made of physical activity, music, drawing, and games in the development of sense experience. Edmund Coote, John Brinsley, John Dury, Charles Hoole, and Sir William Petty from various approaches put emphasis upon actual perception of things rather than the mere study of words, the use of English in the study of all school subjects, the grading of subject matter and division of pupils into classes so that their abilities might be more appropriately considered, and the lightening of discipline so that learning might become more pleasant and thus more effective. Actual practice in the school seldom, if ever, came up to the proposals of the educational reformers, but their importance is none the less real. Their ideas took root among later educators, who could achieve greater success because the new cultural situation was more favorable. Herein lies, perhaps, one of the great values of educational theory.

Chapter 9

THE REFORMATION IN AMERICA

Currents of life and thought in America in the seventeenth century were so closely related to those in Europe that the founding of America should be considered a part of the broader aspects of the Reformation as discussed in the preceding chapter. In this process, political, economic, and religious factors were closely interrelated. The motives that sent English, Scottish, Dutch, Swedish, German, French, and other colonists to America were a result of the complicated events of the Reformation in Europe. Some came because of political or religious persecutions at home; others came in the hope of greater economic gain than was possible at home; and still others came in a spirit of adventure or desperation or compulsion. Happily, the soldier of fortune and the military adventurer were so rare that the North American colonies were spared the economic exploitation and military control that characterized Mexico and South America. Some were sent out to gain colonies for the political and economic purposes of the homeland. But, fortunately, again, the economic patterns of feudalism and rigid class stratification never gained a firm foothold in the colonies.

Still others chose to come in order to establish the kind of constitutional political institutions that had been expressed in theory at home but had not operated in practice for their particular group. A desire for religious freedom motivated many to come to America to practice the kind of worship that was forbidden at home. Some of these revealed a typical Reformation sectarianism when they refused to allow religious dissent from *their* way of belief once they had been able to establish in the New World the kind of religion they wanted.

Colonization and Government

New England. The political institutions set up in New England in the seventeenth century were a curious mixture of authority, stemming from Calvin's theocratic conception of the state, and the constitutional liberties being won by Englishmen in Parliament at home. The Puritans who settled in New England were imbued with Calvin's doctrine of theocracy. In this conception, the state was viewed as the protector and supporter of the church, to do its bidding and enforce its pronouncements.

In the "True Blue Laws of Connecticut" (1672), for example, the state imposed the death penalty, on authority of the Bible, for such crimes as blasphemy, worship of false gods, witchcraft, and insubordination to parents. This theocratic conception of the state made it appropriate for the civil authority to require and support religious education as the Puritans conceived it.

The structure of the theocratic state is revealed further in the political institutions organized in New England, the best example of which is the system set up in Massachusetts. The charter granted by the king to the Massachusetts Bay Company vested the government in a governor, a deputy governor, and the freemen (stockholders) of the company organized into the General Court, which was the legislative branch of the government. The aristocratic and religious basis in this arrangement is shown by the laws that gave voting privileges only to those male persons who were landowners *and* church members. The estimate has been made that even in 1674 only about one-fifth of the men in the colony fulfilled these requirements for the suffrage. Thus, there was no popular government in the modern democratic sense; government favored the church members and the landowning group. At various times, settlers had to win the right to vote by petitioning and arguing for it. When the original charter was revoked and a new royal charter was issued in 1691, the government was vested in a governor appointed by the king to act as his agent and in the General Court to be elected by the property owners. The religious qualification for voting was abolished, and only the property qualification remained. This change, made by William and Mary, transformed Massachusetts into a royal province and attempted to force the Puritans to grant more religious freedom under the principles of the Act of Toleration of 1689.

Even before 1691 resistance to the absolutistic doctrines of the theocratic state was being expressed in America by various individuals and groups. Constitutionalism and civil liberties were more fully expressed by the spirit of separatism than by the autocratic spirit of the theocrats. The separatists believed that the state should deal only with public or common affairs and that the individual should have a greater amount of personal freedom in his beliefs. They denied the right of the Puritan churches, as well as the Catholic Church or Church of England, to determine authoritatively the religious beliefs of individuals. Therefore, they argued, the church and the state should be separate in order to maintain the largest measure of toleration and civil liberty. It was this separatist, or independent, strain in American culture that laid the foundations for religious freedom.

The Pilgrims who settled in Plymouth were Calvinist in general religious outlook, but they were more separatist in practice and believed in a more individualistic democracy than the Puritans. Roger Williams and Anne Hutchinson in Rhode Island and the Quakers were all exponents of the individualistic freedom of religious conscience as represented by the separatist movement.

Middle Colonies. The political institutions of New York were established first by the Dutch West India Company, which sent over its first permanent settlement in 1630 and directed in large part the affairs of New Netherlands from Holland. A Swedish trading company formed in 1624 sent settlers up and down the Delaware River from 1638 on. In 1655 the Dutch governor of New Netherlands wrested control of the Delaware from the Swedes, but in 1664 the English took over all of New Netherlands and made it an English royal colony under the name of New York. After 1664 New Jersey also became an English royal colony, with its mixture of Quakers, New England Puritans, French Huguenots, Swedes, Finns, Germans, Scots-Irish, and English.

Pennsylvania received its name and a great impetus to settlement from William Penn who, despite being a Quaker, received a large grant of land from Charles II. Penn's advertisements extolling the advantages of free government, economic opportunity, and religious freedom in his land induced many to flock to Pennsylvania, beginning in 1681. Pennsylvania attracted 7,000 to 8,000 settlers by 1685 and rapidly became one of the most populous colonies, made up as it was of many different nationalities and religious sects. Before 1700 not only Quakers but English, Welsh, German, French, and Dutch with their own distinctive religious beliefs poured into eastern Pennsylvania.

Southern Colonies. The London Company took the lead in settling Virginia for commercial purposes at a time when England very much needed raw materials. A governor and a council of wealthy families were set up soon after the London Company was formed in 1606–1607, and by 1619 a representative assembly called the House of Burgesses was established as well. The aristocratic council became the upper house and the representative assembly the lower house of the legislative branch of the government. The lower house was made up of two representatives from each county elected by the free (property-owning) citizens. Late in the century the Carolinas were established on a similar pattern, and in the eighteenth century Georgia was founded. Maryland was founded by a grant of land to Lord Baltimore in 1634 as a haven for Catholics, but other colonists poured in so rapidly that by 1700 the Catholics were outnumbered by Puritan and Anglican settlers.

Although, in general, commercial motives were strong in sending persons to the southern colonies, the political-religious events in England had much to do with stimulating emigration to the Anglican colonies of the South. Just as the Puritan exodus to New England was accelerated by the persecution of Puritans by Archbishop Laud in the 1630's, so the establishment of the Puritan Commonwealth in 1649 tended to drive Anglicans and royalists to the southern and middle colonies during the 1650's. Likewise, the revocation of the Edict of Nantes by Louis XIV in France enriched America by sending many French Huguenots to the middle colonies, and the Thirty Years' War in Germany (1618 to 1648) eventually sent many Germans to America hoping for a greater measure of religious tolerance.

Economic and Social Institutions

The fact that so much of the early settling of America was conducted under the sponsorship of trading companies formed in England, Holland, and Sweden reveals the part that the New World was playing in the commercial revolution of Europe. Trading companies sold shares to stockholders and merchants whose interests back home were primarily to make money. The quest for colonies in the New World and the granting of charters by rulers to the Massachusetts Bay Company, to the London Company, and to the Dutch West India Company emphasize the close tie-up between governments and the middle class in the characteristic form that mercantile capitalism took in the seventeenth century.

In New England people centered their economic life in towns and in more or less compact social units. Land was granted by the king to the Massachusetts Bay Company, and the land in turn was granted to groups of people who held much of the land in common for joint use as pasturage and for other purposes. The "common," or green, remains a prominent feature of many present-day New England towns. The farmers often lived together near the meetinghouse, church, and school and went out to work their farms, which radiated from the populated center. This provided a degree of community spirit not found in the same degree in the southern colonies. Similarly, such a community became much more self-sufficient in providing its own food, clothing, and shelter. A variety of skilled workmen became an integral part of the town life, providing useful articles for other members of the community and giving a diversified character to New England economic life. It could thus support merchants, farmers, sailors, fishermen, shipbuilders, and the like. This need for skilled labor rather than unskilled labor meant that slaves never became the economic asset in New England that they did in the South.

Two things, then, should be noted concerning the population of seventeenth-century New England. One is that the class structure of society in England was transferred to New England as well as to the South. The other is that the beginnings of a more democratic society were evident in the policy of town making and land granting. Three rather distinct classes appeared in New England, somewhat parallel to the classes of old

England. These were the aristocratic upper classes (clergy, magistrates, landed gentry, and merchants), the free classes (skilled artisans, tradesmen, and freehold farmers, or yeomen), and the unfree classes (unskilled laborers, indentured servants, and a few slaves). In general, members of the lowest class had no vote because they owned no property, but the artisans and yeomen gradually fought for and gained the vote as they acquired property or land. They represented an independent individualism never entirely controlled by the theocratic leaders of the upper classes. The policy of granting free land to small holders so bolstered the free classes that a large share of economic democracy eventually provided a firm basis upon which later political and social democracy could be built.

These democratic tendencies, however, had to struggle hard against the privileges imported from England by the upper classes, who had preferential status in the matters of voting, less severe punishments for minor and major offenses, and certain distinctions in matters of title, dress, and seating in church. These distinctions eventually led to a conflict between the agricultural interests of the backwoods farmers and the commercial interests of the towns, and between the skilled artisans and the merchants within the towns. Education reflected these economic conflicts in the eighteenth century.

The middle colonies paralleled somewhat the economic and social patterns of New England, but in the South a different pattern emerged by the beginning of the eighteenth century. In Virginia, for example, the original population was similar in class structure to that of England. Contrary to the usual conceptions, the social stratification of life in seventeenth-century Virginia was not much different from that of New England. Not many more of the aristocratic classes appeared in the South than appeared in New England. The great majority of people were free landholders. The economic systems of Virginia and Maryland in the seventeenth century were based almost entirely upon free labor. It was not until after 1680 and 1690 that wide disparities grew up between unfree labor and the owner classes. This process took place when the profits of trade with England from tobacco cultivation stimulated the plantation system. Large holdings became desirable because tobacco wore out the land rapidly and it therefore had to lie fallow after a few crops in order to restore its fertility.

Establishment of Religion

Following the pattern of church-state relations developed in European countries in the sixteenth and seventeenth centuries, several of the American colonies instituted their respective establishments of religion. In the seventeenth century in America an establishment of religion always meant two things. First, it meant that the legal power of the state was enforced to give financial support to a single preferred church. This was done by levying taxes upon all and granting public lands to the church for the support of established ministers and for the erection of church buildings and maintenance of church services.

An establishment of religion meant, secondly, that the state used the force of law to support the preferred church by requiring its doctrines to be accepted, by requiring people to attend its public worship, and by preventing public worship according to any other religion. This included trial in civil courts and punishment by fine, jail, or torture of those who persisted in holding or expressing dissenting views. Civil rights were denied to dissenters, including their right to vote or hold public office.

In New England (outside of Rhode Island) Puritanism was the guiding genius of the Congregational churches and other social institutions that were set up according to Calvinist doctrines. The dominance of the Puritan theocracy is testified to by the "blue laws" of the General Courts in Massachusetts and Connecticut, by the witch hunts, by the punishments and fines levied for religious offenses, and by the general puritanic quality of the life.

Although many settlers in New England were separatists, a strict rule of orthodoxy was established by John Cotton, John Winthrop, and others who had determined to impose an established religion. Laws required all to attend church, whether they were members or not, and provided public financial support for the ministry. Clergymen exerted great social pressure upon the whole public and personal life of the population. They were the great shapers of public opinion in all matters, including education. Tolerance was definitely not a part of the religious picture in New England outside of Rhode Island. Dissidents were persecuted on the grounds that a person could not be considered to be morally trustworthy or to be a good citizen of the state unless he embraced the established religion.

The Congregational-Puritan form of church organization was established by law by the Massachusetts and Connecticut legislatures, and in fact if not by specific law in New Hampshire. In contrast, no church was established in Rhode Island, where religious freedom was sturdily maintained by Roger Williams and his followers in line with the principles of separation of church and state earlier expressed by the Anabaptist sects of Europe. Rhode Island thus became the principal haven for religious dissenters and freedom of conscience in New England.

The Congregational form of church organization itself contained the seeds of difficulty for Puritan theocracy, for it vested administrative authority for church affairs in the hands of the local congregation. This more democratic type of church organization was opposed to the Anglican, Lutheran, and Roman conception of an authoritative clerical hierarchy, and even opposed to the Presbyterian organization, which gave full authority to the presbyters, or elders, of the church. Eventually, the Congregational type of organization began to undermine the authority of the old theocrats.

In the middle colonies a wide variety of national stocks and religious sects prevented the effective establishment of state churches, although the Church of England was claimed to be established in the four southern counties of New York. The Dutch and the Presbyterians never admitted this Anglican claim. The barriers of language, custom, and denomination between the Dutch Reformed, the Anglicans, the Puritans, the Quakers, the French Huguenots, the German Lutherans, the Scots-Irish Presbyterians, the Swedish Lutherans, and the many other groups that arrived later prevented the dominance of one state church. This religious heterogeneity played a large part in the educational development of the middle colonies.

In the South the Church of England was early the established church, although it is estimated that Virginia was the only colony in which the majority of people were actually members of the church. In North and South Carolina and later in Georgia the Church of England was established but was never so enthusiastically supported by taxation as was the church in Virginia. Even there it was difficult for the church to flourish in the seventeenth century because the lack of towns, the sparse population, the poor salaries paid to the clergy, and the primitive conditions of life made it hard to persuade priests to leave their parishes in England. Nevertheless, the Church of England gradually grew more powerful in the South and exerted considerable control over the political, economic, and educational institutions of the day. Although Maryland had been settled by Catholics, a law of toleration was passed in 1647 permitting all Christians to worship as they pleased, but after the turn of the century the Church of England was established by law.

Despite the emphasis here upon the establishment of state churches (which was a strong characteristic of Reformation culture), America did provide a haven for all sorts of religious sects that could not exist peaceably side by side in the Europe of that day. This fact eventually led to the enormously important doctrine of civil liberties and religious freedom, which has saved America from the worst excesses of the religious wars of Europe. Our achievement in this regard has been great, though our record has been marred with religious antagonisms, persecutions, and bigotry that began with the witch hunts of colonial times and have plagued minority religious groups down to the present.

In this connection mention should be made here of the influence of Spanish Catholic institutions and culture upon seventeenth-century America. Too often histories of America and of American education have neglected the Spanish influence upon American life. Admittedly, the Spanish did not set the major patterns for American culture and education, but in these times of world interdependence it is important to recognize this authentic strain in American history. One cannot live or travel in the American Southwest, for example, without being conscious of its existence, its contribution to American culture, and the problems that it has bequeathed us. As early as 1565 the Spanish had founded St. Augustine in Florida, but the effectiveness of the Spanish settlement was destroyed by 1650 as a result of Indian wars and the influence of the English colonies to the north.

More permanent and more extensive in its influence was the Spanish activity in the American Southwest. The Spanish governors that ruled Mexico began to push their authority up into New Mexico and Texas before the end of the seventeenth century. Coronado's expedition in 1540 was the culmination of a series of expeditions that established the claims of the Spanish government to much of the western territory of the American continent. Franciscan friars followed hard on the heels of the conquistadors in New Mexico and Santa Fé and soon came into conflict with the governors over the right to control the Indians. The Indians, however, were determined to have some say in their own disposition, as shown in the revolts led by Popé from Taos against the control of the Spanish settlers. Although there was much destruction and the Spanish suffered defeat, their influence continued and was later reestablished even more firmly. By 1689 the Spanish had made gains in Texas, and San Antonio was emerging as another center of influence. In the eighteenth century the Spanish and Catholic control was extended over the southwestern territory and much of California, leaving a permanent tradition of great importance in those areas.

Authoritarian Collectivism versus Libertarian Individualism

The ideas and beliefs that motivated men's actions in seventeenth-century America clustered about two opposite poles that pulled them now one way and now another. At one extreme was the authoritarian collectivism of the Puritan theocracy; at the other extreme was the libertarian individualism of the separatists and dissidents of various kinds. These extremes of thought and action revealed themselves throughout the whole range of religious, political, and economic activities of the colonists and laid the foundations for two authentic strands of the American tradition, both of which have come down to us in modern forms.

The religious and political aspects of authoritarian collectivism were revealed best in the absolutist and aristocratic conceptions of the Puritan theocracy. Drawing upon the doctrines of Calvin, such early Puritan leaders as John Cotton, John Winthrop, and Increase Mather set out to exert absolute control over the lives of the Massachusetts Bay colony (authoritarianism) and to weld the diverse social groups into an interdependent community in which each part of the community played its proper role in the whole (collectivism). As a clergyman, John Cotton believed that the clergy should be the absolute interpreters of the divine will to the people and that the "sinner" should be completely subordinate to the "saint." Religious conformity was thus of greater import than political rights; the whole community should be ruled by the "best"—the best to be interpreted by the small group of church members, headed by the clergy and magistrates.

As a magistrate, John Winthrop supported these aristocratic beliefs and insisted that the magistrates had special talents and insights that qualified them to make decisions unhampered by the will of the common people. If democracy were the best form of government, why had God not ordained it? Instead, God had ordained theocracy to be the best form of government, as witness Calvin's picture of God as a sovereign, arbitrary, and absolute ruler whose will must be carried out on earth through his appointed agents, the state and the church, the former being the servant of the latter. It was God's will that had made the masses of people sinners and the aristocratic few wise enough to direct their destinies. Increase Mather carried on this conception in the later days of the seventeenth century and redoubled his efforts to use the state's authority to stamp out any divergent views. With such ideas as these for weapons the Puritan theocrats were able to maintain a fairly closed system of authority over the Massachusetts community until late in the seventeenth century, when the Puritan edifice began to weaken.

In contrast to the authoritarianism of the Puritan theocracy the opposite extreme of libertarian individualism found expression among many of the colonists. It was quite natural that the separatists objected both to the authoritarianism and to the collectivism of the Puritan aristocracy. They wanted to be free from religious control by the state, and their way out seemed to them to lie in emphasizing not only freedom but also individualism. In the religious realm, the separatists insisted upon freedom of religious conscience, and in the political realm they insisted upon a greater democracy than the Puritan leaders would admit.

Thomas Hooker and Roger Williams insisted that the structure of the state should rest not upon the will of the aristocratic few but upon the sovereignty of the people at large. They rejected the conception of the divine right of state authority as expressed by the English kings, by the Church of England, and by Puritanism. Their compact theory of the state was based upon the assumption that political authority comes from the consent of the people as contained in a written contract or constitution which can be changed when necessary, and that the state should be responsible to the will of the majority.

Roger Williams, especially, reflected the logical extension of the original Protestant position of individualism. Believing in a Christian fellowship in which the individual reaches an intimate personal relationship with God, he saw no reason why the state should establish an official church through its civil power. Rather, he felt that the spiritual and intellectual life should not be subject to the state or to any church. Each small group and indeed each individual should be allowed to think and believe as they pleased. These doctrines of civil liberties and religious freedom easily translated themselves into political and economic terms, and the seeds of American individualism were being sown in ground that was most fertile for its eventual flowering.

From the perspective of the twentieth century, we can see clearly why the reaction of the separatists should have taken the direction it did. The separatists automatically linked authoritarianism and collectivism, for all their experience had shown them that where one was, the other was also. Their quite reasonable response was to throw both overboard and to identify freedom with individualism. It did not occur fully to them that it might be possible for social control to exist without authoritarianism on a large scale. Hooker and Williams did sense this distinction when they proposed a public-service state to deal with *common* affairs but not with religious conscience. But in their desire to defeat authoritarianism, they only faintly perceived that perhaps a state and a society that seek the welfare of the whole people might somehow be libertarian and free. They faced but did not solve the great social issue of our time, the way to achieve both liberty and security.

THE STANDING ORDER IN EDUCATION

The pattern of institutions described in the foregoing section was dominated by groups of people and sets of social relationships which were often known collectively as the "standing order." This was a complex arrangement serving the interests of the ruling groups who held political power and the aristocratic classes who exerted religious power. Control of education in seventeenth-century America was largely shaped by the institutions and outlooks of the standing order.

Naturally enough, the main examples of state control of education were found in the authoritarian collectivism of Calvinist America, rather than in the doctrines of libertarian individualism as reflected in Rhode Island, where no steps were taken at this time toward state control of education. It was not until the eighteenth and nineteenth centuries when the collective ideal was joined with humanitarian liberalism that the idea of a democratic system of schools supported by the state appeared. Likewise, the two-track system of different schools for different classes of people appeared in America as a result of the class structure of the colonies.

Civil Control of Schools in New England

The greatest attention to education on the part of civil authorities appeared in New England, where the Calvinist ideals of religion and education prevailed. At first the initiative in establishing schools was taken by the various towns, and then the colonial legislatures added their influence and authority to the process. As early as 1635 the town of Boston voted to establish a school to be supported by private subscription and income of a parcel of land set aside for this purpose by the town. Before the end of the century some 30 New England towns had made similar provisions for the establishment of schools; the earliest of these were Charlestown, Salem, Dorchester, New Haven, Hartford, Cambridge, and Roxbury. The authority exerted by the town meeting was often administered by the selectmen or an interim school committee. The principle was soon fairly well established in New England that the towns should not only take the initiative in seeing that schools were established but also take at least partial responsibility for supporting them. Financial support came from several sources, tuition from those parents who could afford it, rate bills levied in proportion to the number of children in the school and the amount of time spent there, income from town lands or fisheries or tolls, fines and licenses, and property taxes.

The next step in civil control of schools came when the colonial legislatures stepped in to give an impetus to those towns which had failed to establish schools on their own initiative. The Massachusetts Bay colony took the lead in this process in two famous school laws that had considerable influence upon other colonies. The Massachusetts law of 1642 was the first general law requiring elementary instruction for children. In the law, the state assumed the authority to tell town officials that they had the power to require parents to educate their children. The law did not establish schools, nor did it require the towns to establish schools. It did call for compulsory instruction of children by parents or masters. It set up minimum essentials to be taught (reading of English, knowledge of the capital laws, the catechism, and apprenticeship in a trade). It gave the selectmen authority to enforce the ruling by fines and compulsory apprenticeship.

The principle that education is necessary for the welfare of society was thus stated very early on American shores. Apparently, however, the towns did not respond with enough alacrity to suit the General Court, for 5 years later another law was passed that went still further in establishing the authority of the state over education. In the law of 1647, the legislature required each town of 50 families to provide an elementary school teacher, and the establishment of a Latin grammar school in every town of 100 families. The law made it legally permissible for towns to levy taxes for the support of teachers and tried to give teeth to enforcement by providing for the payment of fines by towns that failed to live •up to the provisions of the law.

When this law is considered in conjunction with the law of 1642, it can be seen that the state now asserted its right to require towns to establish schools and that civil authorities had the right to manage, supervise, and control schools. As yet the principle of *compulsory attendance at schools* was not enunciated. Parents were still free to educate their own children, to hire tutors to teach them, or to send them to school, as they wished. The state was trying to make it more likely that children would actually receive instruction by making public instruction more easily available.

In 1650 the colonial legislature of Connecticut passed a law like that of the Massachusetts law of 1647; and New Haven followed suit in 1655, Plymouth in 1677, and New Hampshire, when it was separated from Massachusetts, in 1680. Considerable debate has since arisen as to how important these laws were in laying the foundations of the American public school system. Some believe that they set the legal precedent for the nineteenth-century establishment of state systems of schools; others believe that they were merely tools by which the Calvinist Church made sure that its doctrines would be inculcated in all children. In any case, the important thing is that the state did establish its authority over education. When the established churches were separated from the state in the late eighteenth and early nineteenth centuries, the state reasserted and was able to maintain its earlier legal right to control and support schools. In the light of later developments, the steps that the New England colonies took in the Reformation period were exceedingly important for American education as a whole, even though many towns did not at the time live up to the spirit or letter of the law.

What the New England colonies did was to combine (1) their Calvinist conceptions of education required by a state-church and (2) the English tradition of state control over the apprenticeship of poor children, as expressed in the English Poor Law of 1601. The state in New England was establishing its right to require vocational education through compulsory apprenticeship at the same time as it required education in language and reading. Similar developments took place in Dutch New Netherlands, where at least 12 towns had established their Calvinist schools by 1650. In Pennsylvania the colonial charter stated that the government should establish schools; a law of 1682 required parents and guardians to teach their children reading, writing, religion, and a trade. The middle colonies, however, were not able to maintain for very long the principle of state control, for large groups of different religious and national stocks insisted upon schools taught in their own languages and according to their own religion. This meant that the private and religious control of education became more common in the eighteenth century.

Varied Control of Schools in Other Colonies

Just as the New England colonies were the best representatives of civil control of education, so were the southern colonies the best representatives of the policy of private control. The middle colonies not only were middle colonies geographically but in a sense reflected a combination of the other conceptions. After the English took over New York in 1664, the civil policy of the Dutch gave way to the more typical English approach under the Stuart kings. Pennsylvania followed suit as German Lutherans, Moravians, Mennonites, and Scots-Irish Presbyterians upset the original plans for state education in that colony.

In the South, however, from the beginning, education was normally looked upon as a private affair for those parents who were capable of providing it. In this respect the South reflected the fact that the Church of England dominated educational policies. Instruction was provided by private tutors when parents could afford to pay them, by any parish priests who had the ability or inclination to do so, and by endowed schools. Several such endowed schools were established by interested persons in order to provide free education for those who could not afford it. Usually the endowment took the form of gifts, bequests of land, produce, or livestock to be used for the sustenance of the teachers. In general, however, "free education" in the South meant charity education for the poor, and upper-class parents naturally did not want free education for their children.

Here was a considerable difference, even in the seventeenth century, between New England and the South that was to have lasting importance. New England soon built up a tradition of free education as perfectly proper for self-respecting members of the community, whereas a stigma was long connected with free education in the South because of its connection with charity. The principal educational concern of the state in the South was for orphans or children of poor and indigent parents who could not take the responsibility of educating their children. In Virginia, for example, an act of the legislature in 1642 required guardians and masters to give their apprentices proper training, and a law in 1656 stated that an orphan child should be educated at the social level of his parents. If his parents had not been free, the child was to be apprenticed to a trade and given proper moral and religious training. The aristocratic class structure of society was also revealed in several acts that made apprenticeship and religious instruction compulsory for poor children in order to protect the rest of society from a possible vagabond and "dangerous" class. In these respects the South followed the tradition of the English poor laws but did not show the zeal for popular education through public schools that is reflected in the New England laws of the same period.

In some of the colonies, but more particularly in other parts of continental America, the Catholic Church was carrying on its educational and missionary activities. In Maryland, for example, some Jesuit schools were established on an endowed and free basis; but by the end of the seventeenth century the Catholics were a small minority, and their schools had virtually disappeared. In New York two Jesuit priests conducted a Latin school until toleration of Catholics declined in the latter part of the century. In Spanish Florida the Franciscans were soon at work establishing their missions, and by 1606 a classical school was operating in connection with a seminary at St. Augustine. By 1634 several mission schools were flourishing, but they declined by 1650 as a result of the wars with Indians and the English colonies. In New Mexico, likewise, the Franciscans had arrived as early as 1598 and by 1630 had established some 50 missions that carried on active educational work among the Indians until the Indian uprising of 1680 virtually wiped them out. Although the Catholics were not able to maintain their hold in America in the seventeenth century, they set a precedent for the efforts of the eighteenth and nineteenth centuries and bequeathed much of the heritage of Spanish culture that remains in the American Southwest.

Status of the Teaching Profession

The social status of teachers in Reformation America varied widely from place to place and with the type of school. In general, teachers in New England and New Netherlands were probably more respected than in the South. Everywhere the range of qualifications was very wide, from the poorly prepared women who conducted dame schools to college graduates and ministers who taught the Latin grammar schools. Teachers scarcely ever had enough property or wealth to be listed in tax books or records of wills. In general, their financial status would class them below ministers and the gentry, above unskilled labor, and probably about on a level with such skilled laborers as carpenters, wheelwrights, and masons. Their salaries came from tuitions, voluntary gifts of money, or income from the rental of town lands; or perhaps they were paid in kind with livestock or foodstuffs.

In general, teachers complained a good deal about their income. Although grammar school teachers usually received more than elementary teachers, the form and time of payment for all were likely to be highly irregular. Consequently, a large turnover resulted; many teachers became virtually itinerants, while many more merely waited for a better job to appear, particularly in the case of young clergymen waiting for a pastorate. The difficulty of making a living entirely out of teaching meant that teachers often had a great many additional duties. A survey of the data reveals that teachers also preached; kept records; rang the church bell and dug graves; cared for the sick; served as jurymen, janitors, appraisers, translators, and letter writers; and engaged in tavern keeping, farming, herding, and skilled labor.

Teachers of town schools were usually appointed at town meetings or by the selectmen with the approval of ministers. Teachers of church schools were usually appointed by church officials or clergymen. This meant that the qualifications of teachers were passed upon by towns, by churches, by royal companies, by royal governors, and often by the bishop of London in the case of Church of England teachers. It meant, too, that the most important qualification for teaching was religious orthodoxy.

Licenses for teachers were regularly issued by civil authorities in all the colonies—another evidence of civil control of education. Teachers were supervised and inspected by clergymen, selectmen, and committees that visited the schools to see if students were actually learning correctly the grounds of religion and the rudiments of reading, writing, and arithmetic. Tenure thus depended mainly upon religious orthodoxy, civic loyalty, and good moral character. In general, teachers revealed about as good moral character as the rest of the population as far as drunkenness, profanity, legal and financial troubles, or crimes of violence or sex were concerned. Most teachers were men, but women also found some place as keepers of dame schools in New England and as substitutes in the summer when the men were in the fields; similarly, the wives of planters in the South sometimes carried on instruction for their children.

Out-of-school Education

As in all frontier societies, colonial Americans learned relatively little from their schools in comparison with the education that came from the everyday struggle for a living in a new and strange land. The early settlers eventually learned much from the Indians of ways to trap, hunt, fight, and grow the new crops of corn and tobacco. In such pioneer circumstances, the younger generations were educated largely in their own local groups and through the traditions that their elders brought with them from Europe. Quite naturally, one of the most important of such groups was the family, which had to be virtually self-supporting within itself or in cooperation with other families. In New England the Calvinist conception of the role of the clergy gave great authority to the ministers in all kinds of matters having to do with the upbringing of children. Thus, rules of conduct, recreations, and punishment were set largely by the family under the leadership of the church.

The town-meeting process also furnished rudimentary political education to those who were entitled to take part. In general, books and written materials were relatively scarce, except, of course, for the Bible, which in Calvinist hands became an important source of reading material as well as being an inspiration and a guide for conduct. Books were not entirely absent, for some of the well-to-do gentry such as John Winthrop built up considerable personal libraries. But the communication of news and ideas was largely through word of mouth, in which process again the clergy took the lead in and out of meeting. In the South, where the population was scattered and sparse, the process of communication was even more difficult.

THE RULE OF ORTHODOXY

Christian Theism

The dominating world outlook among the colonists was, of course, Christian in its origin despite the divisions and sectarian quarrels that often raged among the various groups. Whether Catholic or Protestant, Calvinist or Lutheran, English or Dutch, church member or not, the whole atmosphere of belief and attitude was that of Christianity. Puritan and Quaker, separatist and Anglican could quarrel about the proper way to reach salvation, but they all agreed that salvation was important. They could disagree concerning the role of the clergyman in bringing the individual into proper relationship with God, but they all agreed that making one's peace with God was the prime purpose of life. The Calvinist may have emphasized total depravity a little more, and the Quaker may have stressed the "inner light" of conscience, but they both operated from a point of view that was at odds with the new philosophy of science that was developing in Europe.[1]

The whole structure of the Christian tradition as developed for centuries in Europe was reenforced anew in American culture with every shipload of colonists. For these colonists took for granted that the universe is made up of a material and natural world ruled by a spiritual and supernatural world. They assumed and were constantly reminded by their preachers that human nature is also divided into material and spiritual elements, the body partaking of nature and the soul linking man's spirit to the highest spirit of all. Calvinism was perhaps more gloomy and pessimistic than any other sect about the inherent depravity

[1] For a picture of Christian theism that applies to the American colonies as well as to Reformation Europe, see pp. 216–217.

of human nature, but all Christian faiths put *some* stock in the Fall of Adam and hence the sinfulness of all mankind. Finally, it was assumed that all knowledge emanates from God and is implanted in man for His purposes. This meant that the highest type of knowledge is revealed to man through the Scriptures. Learning is a matter of disciplining the mind in such a way that the reason will be prepared to understand the highest reaches of truth. Knowledge of nature or material things was deemed important only as it reveals the higher nature of God and His handiwork. It was this inherited outlook on the world, on human nature, and on knowledge and learning that dominated the education of seventeenth-century America.

We can learn much about the prevailing climate of opinion concerning human nature from the writings of some of the Puritan spokesmen who wrote for and about children. They took pains to emphasize that children, born in sin, must be taught to fear God, obey His commandments, and submit to their parents' authority. One of the earliest catechisms designed especially for children was written by the eminent Puritan divine, John Cotton, and was entitled *Spiritual Milk for American Babes Drawn out of the Breasts of Both Testaments for their Souls Nourishment*. Cotton emphasized that, since children were infected with the original sin and naturally inclined toward evil, they must be especially obedient to parents, teachers, ministers, magistrates, and all others in authority. They should pray constantly, repent their sins, attend church, learn their catechisms, and observe strict discipline in all that they did. Cotton even proposed that rebellious children, if sufficiently incorrigible, should be put to death.

Another very gloomy view of child nature was expressed by Michael Wigglesworth, minister and a teacher at Harvard, in his lengthy poem entitled *The Day of Doom*. He gave especial attention to the poor children who had died in infancy without the benefit of baptism and who faced eternal damnation because of the original sin of Adam. When they pleaded piteously that they did not deserve such punishment, they were told that they must pay for Adam's sin even though they themselves had had no opportunity to sin. The most that could be done for them was to offer them the "easiest room in Hell."

Perhaps the most elaborate statement of attitude toward children in the seventeenth century was a booklet written by Cotton Mather in 1699, entitled *A Family Well-ordered*. The first part of the book told parents how they should bring up their children to be pious, to fear God, to pray, and to obey their elders. Parents must constantly be on the alert to keep their children under control, to rule them with an iron hand of authority, justice, and fear. If "charging them" to be good did not work, the rod should be vigorously applied. The second part was addressed to the children themselves, painting a most vivid picture of the torments and punishments in store for the undutiful child in the endless darkness of eternal Hell. The dutiful child, on the other hand, could expect reasonable well-being if he behaved himself, gave proper reverence to God, and gave obedience and recompense to his parents.

It is no wonder that educational method should have relied so heavily upon instilling fear in children, demanding obedience, and resorting to strict discipline, physical as well as mental. An authoritarian age produced an authoritarian education.

Social Role of the Arts and Sciences

The status of the arts and sciences in seventeenth-century America was about what it was among the equivalent classes in England at the same time. Owing to the Protestant emphasis upon learning to read, the general literacy was probably fairly high in comparison with the average of the countries of Europe. There is some evidence that about 50 per cent of the men and about 25 per cent of the women in certain counties in Virginia could sign their names to public documents, and the percentage in New England was probably higher. The percentage of college-trained men in New England was probably higher than anywhere else in the world.

Science and Superstition. In view of the supernaturalism of the religious outlooks, the sciences did not receive much attention in seventeenth-century America. It is true that several ministers wrote treatises about the interesting flora and fauna that they had observed in the New World, but these could hardly be classed as scientific investigations. The center of greatest interest in science was Harvard College, but even there the classical tradition overshadowed the scientific trend, just as in European universities.

Despite the acquisition of scientific knowledge among a few well-educated persons, the great majority of people were constantly plagued by superstition. They were sure that secret events went on behind the world of everyday occurrences. Belief in astrology and the mysterious effects of the stars upon human life was widespread. Ghosts, devils, witches, and demons peopled a terrible unseen world, waiting to wreak their vengeance upon the unsuspecting or the careless. When these superstitious fears were linked with the repressions and inhibitions laid upon the people by an authoritarian Puritan clergy, persecutions for witchcraft followed. In the middle of the century several hangings of persons accused of practicing witchcraft took place, eight in Connecticut and six in Massachusetts. At the end of the century these feelings were again touched off in the Salem witch hunts.

To say the least, tolerance was not a part of the seventeenth-century

American scene. Quakers and other dissident groups were often among those accused of witchcraft. The superstitious motive frequently was linked with religious intolerance. In general, however, it should be said that a spirit of rationalism and human sympathy ultimately softened fanaticism. After the Salem outbursts a more liberal, rational, and humanitarian outlook began to replace superstitions and intolerances.

Classics and Vernacular. The respect for the classical languages as basic to scholarship and to religion was carried from England and Europe to

N   *Noah* did view
     The old world & new.

O   Young *Obadias,*
     David, Josias,
     All were pious.

P   *Peter* deny'd
     His Lord and cry'd.

Q   Queen *Esther* sues,
     And saves the *Jews.*

R   Young pious *Ruth,*
     Left all for Truth.

S   Young *Samuel* dear,
     The Lord did fear.

Fig. 14. Pages from *The New-England Primer.*

America. The Protestant zeal for getting at the sources of faith in the original languages of the Scriptures supported the Humanistic outlook. It is interesting, in this connection, to note that a Boston bookseller in 1684 ordered among other books 100 copies of Latin readers, 50 copies of Cato, 20 Latin rhetorics, 18 Greek grammars, and 50 Latin grammars. The grammar schools and Harvard College became the repositories of a religious Humanism. The spoken language of the colonial peoples was, of course, the language of the country from which they came, English, Dutch, French, German, Swedish, and so on. From its very beginnings the polyglot character of the American language was being formed. However, the English tongue gradually won out as the common language, modified by all the variations that have since come into the "king's English" from the various elements in our population.

There seems to have been relatively little reading of the new vernacular literature that was being created in Reformation Europe. Part of this neglect may have been due to a general lack of time for reading in the face of the hard frontier life; part was doubtless due to the superior claims of religious literature upon the time of the reading public. A printing press was established in Massachusetts in 1639, and for some 30 or 40 years approximately half the books were religious in nature. In many families, of course, the Bible was virtually the only reading matter available. When books were expensive and most of them had to come from abroad,

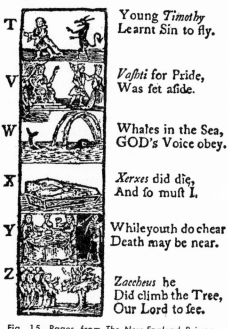

T Young *Timothy* Learnt Sin to fly.

V *Vashti* for Pride, Was fet afide.

W Whales in the Sea, GOD's Voice obey.

X *Xerxes* did die, And fo muft I.

Y Whileyouth do chear Death may be near.

Z *Zaccheus* he Did climb the Tree, Our Lord to fee.

Fig. 15. Pages from *The New-England Primer.*

the careful person was likely to be sure he got his money's worth from the tried and true "classics" of the past rather than risking his time, his money, and his morals on such newfangled authors as Spenser, Marlowe, Shakespeare, Jonson, and Dryden.

The artistic products created by the American colonists themselves were mostly inspired by Old World outlooks rather than by the New World. Most of the "literature" was religious in tone and content. What poetry there was, in the hands of an Anne Bradstreet or a Michael Wigglesworth, was likely to be stolid and gloomy. History took the form of letters, biographies, and sermons. Music in New England was dominated by the hymns of the church, but the usual interpretation that New Englanders had no other music has been recast somewhat by recent investigations. In the South, dance music came to play a part in the social life of the plantations and scattered towns. In general, the relatively barren status of the arts in colonial society was reflected in the neglect of the arts in colonial education.

RELIGION AND HUMANISM IN EDUCATION

Typical Reformation Aims

As might be expected, the schools in seventeenth-century America from the lowest to the highest were dominated by the religious aims of the churches that sponsored them. Whether the schools were Puritan, Dutch, Anglican, Lutheran, Huguenot, or Quaker, the primary aim was to teach the respective grounds of faith to the children. However, the aim to teach children to read was also grounded in the belief that society and the state were served better by a literate citizenry than by an illiterate one.

Typical of the Reformation, too, was the economic aim, which appeared in the form of requirements that children be taught a useful trade and that they be apprenticed if parents failed to give the proper vocational training. Such requirements stemmed from a middle-class interest in seeing that children could support themselves through the practice of useful skills. That such training was acquired by apprenticeship rather than inside the schools does not mean that it was considered unimportant by the settlers. In 1685 a Quaker writer, Thomas Budd, proposed that children should learn a useful trade in public schools along with their academic studies, but his ideas did not catch on. The Humanistic and sectarian religious traditions were too strong.

Humanism was entrenched in the Latin grammar schools and in Harvard College from the beginning. It gave a sanction to the study of Latin as a preparation for college and for the professions that would not otherwise have existed in a frontier society. It explains why the colonists kept out of their schools the vocational training so badly needed, for "education," especially liberal education, had long been conceived as the study of language and literature, especially in Latin. Thus, in the midst of a wilderness, Latin schools were set up and accepted as the proper type of school for upper-class boys to attend, leaving to apprenticeship the job of training for the skilled vocations. This would have been less likely to happen if the Humanistic tradition had been missing. That it was present was due in large part to the leadership of the churches and to the desire of the middle classes to achieve and maintain an enviable social position.

Vernacular Elementary Schools

All the colonies in the seventeenth century made some provision for teaching children to read a vernacular tongue. In New England the town schoolmaster and the women in charge of private dame schools taught reading and sometimes writing in English, along with the Puritan catechism. Writing was often too difficult for the ordinary teacher to cope with, in view of quill pens, poor ink, and very coarse paper, or none at all. The law of 1642 said nothing about writing as a general requirement. It was customary in the late seventeenth century for writing

Fig. 16. A hornbook.

schools to exist alongside of reading schools. Boston, for example, established two such writing schools in 1683, both of which also taught arithmetic.

Whereas elementary education included reading, writing, arithmetic, and religion, the only subjects that were fairly common to all instruction were reading and religion. If a child obtained more than that, he was rather lucky. The basic reading materials for children were the Bible, the catechism, and the psalmbook, whenever these were available. As a guide in learning to read, the hornbook became quite popular in New England.

With minor variations, the same story applied to the Dutch schoolmasters in New Amsterdam, who taught in Dutch, the Anglican school-masters and tutors of the South, who taught in English, the Huguenots, who taught in French, the Lutherans, who taught in German or Swedish, and similarly for others. There was little uniformity in the number of hours a day during which schools were open or the number of days a year for which they operated. Much depended upon the zeal and sense of responsibility of the teacher and his community. In general, the Calvinist communities were likely to be most zealous in keeping schools open the year round. In the hands of a conscientious teacher, hours were likely to be long and arduous, marked with prayers, hymn singing, memorizing, severe discipline, and corporal punishment. "Spare the rod and spoil the child" was the universal maxim. The newer theories of sense realism and educational method being formulated in Europe had not yet touched these shores. Pupils of all ages went to the same teacher, who may have taught two or three or several dozen in the same room. The room was usually at the teacher's home, at the church, at the town meetinghouse, or in some specially constructed shelter, which was likely to be very rough and inhospitable in winter or summer.

Classical Secondary Schools

American secondary schools of the Reformation, following the English model, were called "grammar schools" or, more correctly, "Latin grammar schools." Their major and almost only task was the teaching of Latin grammar. Sometimes such schools had preparatory departments for teaching the younger boys the four R's in English. In general, when they appeared in America, the grammar schools had lost the vital spirit of Humanism that had characterized the better European classical schools of the Renaissance. Their main job was preparation for college work, although the ideal was also to prepare boys for public service and for any occupation into which they might go. As it happened, in the state of American society at the time, the ministry, the magistracy, and teaching Latin in a school or college were virtually the only occupations in which Latin was very helpful.

These schools, therefore, were not particularly adapted to the social situation of the times. It is no wonder that they were not too popular among the great majority of people. As a result, the fines for failure to set up such schools were several times raised by the colonial legislatures of New England in an effort to compel reluctant towns to establish them. Even where they were maintained as town schools, they tended to be class schools frequented by the more wealthy families. They existed not only in New England, where they were most prevalent, but also in New Amsterdam as early as 1659, in Philadelphia, and occasionally in the South, especially in Virginia.

Some grammar schools became well-known institutions, especially the Boston Latin School founded in 1635. Other towns such as New Haven, Hartford, Charlestown, Ipswich, Salem, Dorchester, Newbury, Dedham, and Roxbury had important schools.

Perhaps the most famous grammar school teacher of the early period was Ezekiel Cheever. What went on in his school has had to be reconstructed from the books he wrote and from the testimony of some of his famous students, among whom was Cotton Mather. From these sources it is clear that students probably studied Cheever's own grammar, Lily's *Grammar*, the Bible, Aesop's *Fables*, Vergil's *Aeneid*, Cicero's *Orations*, Ovid's *Metamorphoses*, St. Paul's *Epistles*, and selections from Corderius, Erasmus, Ovid, Horace, and Cato (the fourth-century Latin author of the *Distichs*). The combination of religious books and secular classical authors is clearly evident here. Hours were long, discipline was strict, and punishment severe and frequent. Other grammar schools probably approached this curriculum in essentials if not in breadth.

Some grammar schools also taught the rudiments of Greek if they prepared students to meet the entrance requirements of Harvard College, which included in 1642 the following: ability to read Cicero at sight, ability to speak Latin prose and poetry, and ability to decline Greek nouns and conjugate Greek verbs. Here is the origin in America of the tradition of requiring Latin for entrance to college, a requirement that was maintained in all colleges throughout the eighteenth century and in most colleges throughout the nineteenth and into the twentieth century. Here also is a clear example of the way in which colleges dominated the curriculum of the secondary schools of America, another tradition that persisted into the twentieth century.

College Education at Harvard

Three colonial colleges were founded under the impetus of the Reformation. Harvard College, founded in Massachusetts in 1636, was the only institution of higher education in the colonies until William and Mary was founded in Virginia in 1693 and Yale in Connecticut in 1701 (the latter two will be discussed in a later chapter). Motivated by the Calvinist zeal to provide for an educated ministry and stimulated by the high percentage of university-trained men who had come to Massachusetts (well over 100 by the 1640's), the General Court founded Harvard by law and gave land, income from ferry tolls, and the proceeds from a tax for support. An endowment in the form of John Harvard's estate and library represented the private interests. Thus, the typical Reformation combination of religious and civil motives was involved in the founding of Harvard. In its origin it reveals all three of the typical forms of college control in America, denominational, state, and private.

To say that the religious motive in founding Harvard was strong is true enough, but to say that therefore Harvard was merely a training school for ministers is less than true and misses the point of Reformation higher education. It *was* intended that Harvard should provide an education for future ministers, but it also was intended that Harvard should be a general liberal arts college for all who would achieve a liberal education as then conceived. Direct religious instruction was only a small part of the curriculum of Harvard; only five of the first nine graduates became ministers, and in the later years of the seventeenth century the proportion who became ministers decreased. Although the interests of future ministers were not overlooked, it was assumed that a minister should have the liberal arts education appropriate for any other liberally educated man.

The conception of a liberal education is revealed in the curriculum that was instituted in 1642 on the model of an English college. Henry Dunster, the president who formulated the curriculum, was a graduate of Magdalene College at Cambridge. The first college in America combined in its curriculum three major influences from the past: the medieval seven liberal arts, long considered necessary for a liberal education; the Renaissance and Humanistic study of the classics as a means of producing an educated gentleman; and the Reformation ideal of religious education valued for sectarian purposes and for the preparation of ministers.

The medieval seven liberal arts were present in the form of grammar, rhetoric, logic, arithmetic, geometry, and astronomy (only music was absent). Latin grammar was expected to be mastered in the grammar school, for Latin was the language of instruction at the college, but the college curriculum also included the study of Greek and Hebrew grammar. Rhetoric and oratory had a large place; declamations were considered good training for preaching and the art of persuasion. By the end of the seventeenth century logic was present in the study of Aristotle, Ramus, and Descartes; practice in disputations was regularly held. Arithmetic and geometry were taught but sometimes rather neglected because they were looked upon as practical subjects. Astronomy at first was virtually that of Aristotle, Ptolemy, and Dante, but by the middle of the century Copernican astronomy was filtering in. With the use of a telescope acquired in 1672, one of the tutors, Thomas Brattle, made observations of the Great Comet of 1680; these proved useful to Newton in his work.

In addition to the seven liberal arts, the philosophy of Aristotle, rediscovered in the thirteenth-century universities, was present in the form of physics, politics, ethics, and metaphysics. Ancient history and Aristotelian botany were given some attention on Saturday afternoons. Harvard reflected little of the great scientific discoveries and theories that were so much a part of Reformation developments in Europe. In this regard, however, Harvard was not different from most European universities, which were also neglecting science in favor of the classical languages and philosophy.

Greek and Hebrew, representing the Renaissance interest in the classics, were considered to be of general cultural value for a scholar as well as of practical value for ministers who would be well grounded in the original languages of the Scriptures. The study of specific Calvinist religious doctrines, however, was confined largely to Saturdays, when all undergraduates studied the catechism. The only other religious study was the reading of selections from the Old and New Testaments in Hebrew and Greek. Genuine theological study for ministers was not present in the curriculum but was usually pursued after graduation through apprenticeship to a minister or in residence as a graduate at the college.

At first Harvard had only three classes, but when the fourth class was added by 1655, the college followed the European model of 4 years of undergraduate work leading to the B.A. degree. After a 3-year interval, the M.A. was granted upon payment of a fee, defense of a thesis, and evidence of good moral character. Often the first item was the most important requirement.

The undergraduate curriculum was completely prescribed, all students in a class studying the same subjects at the same time, and all taught, in Dunster's day, by the president himself. The college was small in the seventeenth century, varying from 20 to 50 in number. The students were considerably younger than now, probably varying from thirteen or fourteen to seventeen or eighteen years of age. Discipline was severe, and riots were frequent; much of the restlessness doubtless resulted from the fact that the methods of teaching were almost entirely bookish. The students listened to the instructor read the assigned books, they read the books themselves, they recited from the books, drew up outlines from the books, disputed on questions drawn from the books, and gave declamations.

Much has been made of the fact that students were classified at Harvard according to the social status of their parents. Some evidence has been compiled to show that students were assigned places in class, seated in the dining hall, allotted bedrooms, and assessed fines on the basis of their fathers' rank, wealth, and occupation. The sons of clergymen, magistrates, and gentry headed the list. Insofar as this was true, it reveals the aristocratic nature of colonial society, but the best historian of Harvard, Samuel Eliot Morison, has pointed out that the classification of students in the seventeenth century was as likely to be according to intellectual qualifications as social distinction and that the social rank of parents did not play a great part until the middle of the eighteenth century.

Harvard has been described in such detail because its ideal of a liberal education has affected American colleges and universities down to the present time. This tradition had great value in bringing to America the fundamentals of the Western intellectual outlook, but it was accepted so wholeheartedly and defended so vigorously against criticism that higher education was slow to respond to great new influences that appeared in the life and culture of eighteenth- and nineteenth-century America. The close connection between religion and Humanism kept the colleges from adapting themselves readily to new economic, scientific, and philo-sophical currents. Prospective lawyers and physicians found no specific training at Harvard but had to rely upon apprenticeship to practicing lawyers and physicians, and prospective surveyors, navigators, shipbuild-ers, farmers, and businessmen, to say nothing of skilled workers, found no help in preparing for work that was so important to America. Their needs were not to be met by higher education until later centuries.

Chapter 10

THE AGE OF REASON AND ENLIGHTENMENT

The term "Enlightenment" has come to refer to a whole range of ideas that captured the imagination of men during the eighteenth century. The Enlightenment was a reaction against the abolutist and authoritarian regimes of the Reformation—against absolute monarchy, closed economic systems, rigid social stratification, religious authoritarianism, an unscientific world view, the doctrine of original sin in human nature, and the domination of intellectual life by ancient and medieval conceptions of truth and knowledge. Underlying this protest was a growing faith in the common man, in science, and in human reason. This period has often been called the "age of reason" to indicate the humanitarian faith that man, by taking thought, could reform his institutions as a means of promoting the general welfare. These currents of thought flowed into the great liberal and democratic traditions of Europe and America.

As the reformers sought a justification of their revolt against absolutism, they formulated the conception of "natural law" as an instrument with which to attack all forms of entrenched interests. They appealed to "nature" and the "natural rights" of man as superior to the inherited rights of groups that had retained privileges for themselves to the exclusion of the great masses of people. The conception of natural law was borrowed from the new scientific conceptions of the world and was applied to nearly all areas of human activity. Although the middle classes used these conceptions to further their own interests, their efforts resulted at the same time in enormous strides toward freedom and democracy.

LIBERALISM AND REVOLUTION IN INSTITUTIONS

The Enlightenment in Social Ideas

Political Liberalism. By the opening of the eighteenth century the doctrines of political liberalism had been set forth clearly and forcibly in England by John Locke in his *Treatise on Civil Government.* Locke used the "contract theory" to justify taking away the king's absolute powers by a middle-class Parliament. The social contract is an agreement by which the citizens delegate authority to the government, in return for which the government agrees to protect the natural rights of all citizens. These are the rights to life, liberty, and property.

According to this constitutional view of the state, the government must rest upon the consent of the citizens and should exercise its authority through their representatives. The liberal aspects of Locke's ideas are revealed in his insistence upon civil liberties as a natural right of all citizens. His fear of absolutism is revealed in his view of the state as a "policeman," according to which its powers are restricted merely to the *protection* of rights. The government may not invade the rights of individuals except to protect the rights of nature. Locke's middle-class orientation is reflected in his claim that property is a natural right and in his definition of a citizen as one who owns property.

Three agencies of government are necessary. The legislature (representing property owners) must define the crimes against the natural rights of life, liberty, and property. The judiciary must mete out punishment for these crimes impartially. The executive must give force to the laws of the legislature and decisions of the judiciary. In case of a conflict among these agencies of government, the legislature must be supreme, for it rests upon the sovereignty of the citizens. If these representatives ever betray the interests of the people, revolution is justified. It is not difficult to see how greatly the framers of the American Constitution relied upon Locke's doctrines of liberalism, constitutionalism, and property ownership.

Among French political reformers Montesquieu wrote his *Spirit of the Laws* to show how laws rest upon the sovereign will of the people and thus should be adapted to the people for whom they are made. He elaborated the theory of "checks and balances" among the legislative, judicial, and executive branches of government. Several shades more radical than Montesquieu or Locke was Rousseau. According to his "social contract" the will of *all* the people is the ultimate sovereignty for the state. Natural rights include not only life, liberty, and property but the general pursuit of happiness and welfare of all the people. Since the purpose of government is to promote the general welfare, representation in government must be based upon the will of all the people and not just upon that of property owners.

This radical democratic conception gave great comfort to the oppressed peoples of France and Europe and greatly affected the American Revolution as well as the French Revolution. The middle-class constitutionalism of Locke and Montesquieu was taken up by such men as Hamilton in America and the democratic humanitarianism of Rousseau by such men as Jefferson. In general, the cause of free, public, democratic education owed much more to the social humanitarianism of French liberalism than it did to the individualistic constitutionalism of English liberalism.

Liberalism and Laissez-faire Capitalism. Whereas French liberalism was motivated by a belief that if men work together they can improve their common lot, English liberalism rested upon a much more individualistic outlook. Thus rugged individualism of English liberalism grew out of its greater attention to the economic aspects of life. Stemming from Locke and reaching its culmination in Adam Smith, the protest against

Fig. 17. Jean Jacques Rousseau. (From Gabriel Compayre, Jean Jacques Rousseau and Education from Nature, Crowell, New York, 1907. Courtesy of Thomas Y. Crowell Company.)

the mercantile capitalism of the Reformation resulted in the doctrines of laissez-faire capitalism. Smith's *Wealth of Nations* makes it clear that individual effort will result in appropriate productivity if it is unrestrained by the government. The individual knows best what is good for himself and for society. Natural laws must therefore not be interfered with, for they will work automatically for the good of all.

Here again is the appeal to "natural law." Human nature is such that man is basically motivated by the economic desire for profit. It is the urge to acquire wealth that makes the world go around; for if man did not have this inherent profit motive, goods would never be produced. The conception of the "economic man" was also basic to other "natural laws" of economics, most important of which was the law of supply and demand. According to this law of laissez-faire economics, prices will always reach their natural level when goods are bought and sold in an unrestricted market kept open for free competition. A seller tries to get the highest price possible, and the buyer tries to get the lowest price. Competition among sellers tends to force prices down, and competition among buyers tends to force prices up: the greater the demand for goods, the higher the price. In order to allow this natural process to operate, the government must let business alone—hence laissez-faire capitalism. In France much the same kind of doctrine was preached by Quesnay and Turgot, who gave it the name "physiocracy," which means literally "rule of nature." These doctrines helped to pave the way for the American and French Revolutions.

European liberalism revealed two major strands, individualistic, laissez-faire liberalism and social, humanitarian liberalism. The interplay of these two strands has characterized the development of America as well as European political and economic life down to the present time. American businessmen of the nineteenth and twentieth centuries have tended to exalt the individualistic and laissez-faire ideals to the exclusion of the humanitarian ideals, insisting that the public interest rests upon unrestricted private enterprise. Social reformers and humanitarians in politics, economics, and education have tended for two centuries to exalt the social ideals of liberalism.

Ebb and Flow of Political and Economic Power

The eighteenth century witnessed great political and economic rivalries on a world-wide scale. The great powers were England, France, Prussia, Russia, and Austria. Most of the wars were fought by these countries in different combinations, but underlying all of them was a steady and growing duel between England and France for colonial supremacy. The religious rivalries that marked the Reformation largely gave way to imperialistic and nationalistic rivalries. As a result of almost constant warfare, Britain acquired vast colonial possessions ranging from Canada and America in the West to India and Australia in the East. The Treaty of Paris in 1763 made England the world's leading commercial and colonial power, a position that was maintained despite the loss of the 13 American colonies a few years later. Meanwhile, at home, Parliament was increasing its political power in relation to the crown, and the commercially minded middle class was increasing its power in Parliament.

Absolutism and Revolution in France. At the opening of the eighteenth century France was the great nation of Europe and of the world. However, the series of wars with England and other countries during the long reign of Louis XV (1715 to 1774) lost for France not only her colonial supremacy but her commanding place in Europe—until the day of Napoleon.

Domestically, France was being torn by several factions that eventually came to a showdown in the French Revolution. The *bourgeoisie*, or middle class, sensing its growing power, began to clamor for free trade and release from governmental restrictions. In addition, the peasant classes were growing stronger than in most other countries of Europe. When these groups encountered the resistance of the kings, the nobility, and the clergy, they were ready to take more drastic steps in order to achieve greater freedom.

When the economic disasters of the colonial wars abroad were added to increased governmental extravagance, heavier taxation, and continuing social injustice at home, the situation was ripe for revolution. Louis XVI became so bankrupt in 1789 that he called the States-General together for the first time in 175 years. Thereupon the Third Estate proclaimed itself the National Assembly (1789 to 1791), proceeded to abolish feudal obligations and privileges, and drew up the Constitution of 1791. This established a constitutional monarchy, abolished primogeniture, freed the remaining serfs, confiscated the lands of the church, transformed the clergy into state officials subject to election by the people, and suppressed the teaching orders of the church.

The Declaration of the Rights of Man and of the Citizen, drafted by the Marquis de Lafayette, who had returned to France impressed by the principles of the American Declaration of Independence, was adopted by the Assembly in 1789. It enunciated the liberal principles that were the basis of most of the democratic constitutions of the nineteenth century: Men are born and remain free and equal in their rights. The principle of sovereignty rests with the people. Since liberty consists in the freedom to do anything that does not injure others, there should be freedom of religion, the press, and assembly. Laws are the expression of the general will, and therefore the people should participate in drawing up the laws. The rights of the people, especially the rights of property, shall not be infringed except by due process of law.

The middle classes would have been content to stop with these political and economic reforms, but the laborers and peasants wanted to go further; and go further they did in the second and more radical phase of the French Revolution, represented by the Legislative Assembly (1791–1792). Louis XVI had professed to accept the Constitution of 1791 but he soon tried to flee with Marie Antoinette in an effort to gain support from foreign powers friendly to royalty. Austria and Prussia went to war with France.

Thereupon the First Republic (1792 to 1804) was declared by the National Convention, which executed Louis XVI and Marie Antoinette, issued the Constitution of 1792, and carried on a war against a coalition of Austria, Prussia, England, Spain, and Holland. Meanwhile, the radical Jacobins won their civil war against the more conservative Girondists. The Jacobins carried on the foreign war and ruled France with an iron hand. Their Reign of Terror, under Robespierre, lasted from June, 1793, to July, 1794, until he himself was guillotined. Then middle-class reaction set in, and power was seized by the moderate forces, with the help of Napoleon.

Still under the guise of the First Republic, the Directory (1795 to 1799) was established by the middle class in order to prevent both the royalists and the popular democrats from regaining power. When Napoleon emerged as a great military leader he acquired virtually dictatorial powers under the Constitution of 1799 and then ended the life of the First Republic by making himself emperor in 1804. The middle classes had won more than they had bargained for when they backed Napoleon. However, the French Revolution had loosed upon Europe the ideals of democracy. *Liberté, égalité, fraternité* were to prove powerful companions despite the setbacks they received at the hands of kings, would-be emperors, reactionaries, and dictators in many lands.

Rise of Prussia. Situated strategically in central Europe and at the same time a crossroads for the warring armies of eastern and western powers, Prussia emerged from the eighteenth-century wars not only intact but strengthened and expanded. Under Frederick William I (1713 to 1740), the Prussian kingdom was highly centralized, a civil-service bureaucracy was established, and a strong army was developed. Then, under Frederick II (the Great) (1740 to 1786), Prussia became a first-rate political and military power to be reckoned with therafter in the destinies of Europe.

In addition to expanding Prussian territory and attempting to bring other German and non-German states under his control, Frederick tried to make Prussia self-sufficient by making internal improvements, levying protective tariffs, distributing free grain, and lowering taxes. His strong paternalistic monarchy in Prussia not only strengthened his own power but served to mollify the discontented merchants and lower classes to such an extent that no revolutionary movement was able to achieve the strength it had in France. Frederick the Great thus became known as one of the "enlightened despots" of eighteenth-century Europe.

Rise of Russia and Decline of the Holy Roman Empire. In the latter part of the seventeenth century and increasingly in the eighteenth century, Russia under Peter the Great (1682 to 1725) began to expand westward into Europe, taking land from Poland and Sweden. Peter tried to introduce Western customs and culture into Russia by sending students abroad, inviting Europeans to Russia, making trade agreements, changing the Russian calendar and number system to fit Western arrangements, and establishing schools, hospitals, and printing presses. Symbolizing his attitude, Peter established St. Petersburg (Leningrad) on the western frontier as the center of Russian life in place of the traditional Moscow. Catherine the Great (1762 to 1796) continued the Westernizing process whenever possible and hoped to reform the laws and establish schools throughout the land. Along with Frederick the Great and Joseph II of Austria, she too has sometimes been called one of the enlightened despots of the eighteenth century.

The Holy Roman Empire had become little more than a name for the geographical territory of central and southern Europe. As France had gained in power, the Hapsburgs had lost it. Spain had declined by the end of the seventeenth century and continued gradually to be stripped of her colonial empire by the rising Western powers in the eighteenth century. The Italian states continued to decline, for the frequent invasions by French, Austrian, and Spanish armies kept Italy divided.

The Great Awakening

In most countries of Europe legally established churches continued to maintain their power. In Italy, Spain, France, and the countries of the Holy Roman Empire the Catholic Church was the state church; in England, the Church of England; in German states, either the Lutheran, Calvinist, or the Catholic Church, as arranged at the Peace of Westphalia in 1648 at the conclusion of the Thirty Years' War. The Catholic Church in France, however, was subject to bitter attack throughout the Enlightenment and was disestablished during the French Revolution. It was restored by Napoleon in 1801.

A noteworthy development in religion in the eighteenth century was the emergence of many new religious organizations and churches, many of them beginning as reform movements to improve the established churches. In German Lutheran lands the Pietistic movement grew up under the leadership of such men as Spener, Francke, and Zinzendorf to revitalize and reform Lutheranism. In England, the Wesleyan movement appeared as a similar revivalistic effort to reform the Church of England. Led by John and Charles Wesley, Methodism attempted to replace the formalism and ritualism of the church by more faith, emotion, and feeling. The Baptists and Quakers represented radical protests against the authoritative practices of most established churches.

Many other religious groups, large and small, began to gain strength and confidence as a result of the more liberal attitudes of the eighteenth-century Enlightenment. These groups contributed their share to the revivalistic feeling that affected great areas of Europe and America. The movement became so widespread that historians have named it the "Great Awakening." Hundreds of thousands of people were swept into various religious institutions on the wave of a religious emotionalism sometimes reaching the proportions of hysteria. This movement affected education in all countries, especially in England, Germany, and America. A missionary spirit stimulated all sorts of educational philanthropic efforts in informal as well as in organized ways. The Great Awakening was a popular movement often at odds with the rationalism of the Enlightenment.

LARGE-SCALE EDUCATIONAL ACTIVITIES

The organization and control of education in the Enlightenment reflected the changes taking place in political, economic, and religious institutions. As national governments became stronger, the idea of national control of education came to the fore, and preliminary steps were taken, especially in Germany and France, to make it a reality. As democratic and liberal forces gained strength, they turned to education as a necessary agency of democracy. As the middle classes gained ascendency, the aims and content of education were reshaped to meet their interests. As new religious ideas swept across the land, education received fresh religious impetus. On the whole, the Enlightenment gave a new humanitarian impulse and vitality to education.

Control by State and Church in Germany

Beginnings of National Control. Building upon the efforts of Luther and his followers in the Reformation to create a public-religious system of schools in the various German states, the united Prussia of the Enlightenment period carried national control further than any other European country. In this process much of the stimulus came from the religious enthusiasms of Pietism, led by August Hermann Francke who had caught the humanitarian desire to aid the unfortunate as well as the religious desire to spread the gospel. At Halle, Francke established a series of "institutions" that virtually ran the gamut of a whole educational system.

Francke's institutions included: a free school for poor and orphan children; a vernacular German school at the elementary level; a Latin *Gymnasium* for paying students at the secondary level; a higher school (*Pädagogium*) originally intended for noble students but eventually something of a scientific academy; and, finally, a teacher-training institution that prepared university students to teach in the elementary and Latin schools. Francke gained the support and interest of King Frederick William I, who established several hundred schools in Prussia on the model of Francke's schools and issued school laws in 1713 and 1717 making it compulsory for all parents to send their children to school. Tuition fees were

Fig. 18. Johannn Bernhard Basedow.

to be paid for poor children by the communities. In 1737 a general school code authorized government aid to build schoolhouses and pay schoolmasters.

National control in Prussia was pushed another step forward when Johann Hecker, a Pietist clergyman and educator, joined forces with Frederick II, who had a philanthropic concern for the poor and downtrodden but no democratic urge to give them a voice in their own affairs. He called Hecker, who had worked with Francke, to draw up the famous Prussian School Code of 1763, which laid the basis for a national Prussian system of elementary education.

In these regulations religion and literacy were the predominant interests, the state setting standards for the church teachers to meet. Attendance was made compulsory from five to thirteen years of age, and definite school hours were prescribed. Children were required to pass state examinations prepared by the church. New state inspectors were entrusted with the regular inspection and supervision of schools. Teachers had to obtain a license and be approved by the state inspectors as well as by the church consistory before they could be employed. Curriculums, textbooks, and the qualifications of teachers were prescribed in detail. In 1765 Frederick issued a similar school code for the Catholic country of Silesia, which he had conquered from Austria. These were important transition steps toward national control of education, but they met great opposition and were never fully realized in practice despite the important principles they laid down.

Full State Control. The final step in establishing state authority over Prussian schools came some years later in 1787 under Frederick William II, when a school code took the supervision of schools out of the hands of the clergy and put it in the hands of a state ministry of education. Johann Bernhard Basedow, who had become well known for his educational writings and his school, the Philanthropinum, was influential in creating a demand for secular control of schools. He insisted that children of all religious faiths should have fair access to public schools; in this respect, he reflected the new ideas from France. The law of 1787 established a central agency of education in control of all elementary and secondary schools. It also instituted the "leaving examination," which all graduates of a secondary school had to pass for admittance to the university. The principles of public education under state control for authoritarian purposes were thus established in Germany.

The French Conception of National Education

At the opening of the eighteenth century the control and support of schools in France were largely in the hands of the various teaching orders of the Catholic Church. At the elementary level, for example, the Institute of the Brothers of the Christian Schools had made strides in providing charity education for the poor and unfortunate, and several orders of sisters gave elementary instruction to girls. The Jesuits and Fathers of the Oratory dominated the field of secondary education. The Jesuits, however, had become so powerful in political affairs that they became a symbol of the old regime with its abuses and injustices. Their schools were therefore closed in 1764, and the order was suppressed by the Pope from 1773 to 1814. In the middle of the century the Encyclopedists and others began to agitate for a national system of education exclusively under state control. Appealing to the new humanitarian democratic ideology, they usually argued that education should be universal, free, compulsory, and secular. The idea soon became an integral part of the French Revolution.

As the revolutionists set out to create a new and more democratic society, they realized the importance of education as a means of achieving and maintaining the new society. Among the proposals drawn up by the States-General of 1789 were demands for public education that would be less classical and would put more stress upon modern and practical studies. During the National Assembly Mirabeau and Talleyrand drew up plans for secular education in order to produce persons with a patriotic rather than a religious outlook. Under the Constitution of 1791 the Legislative Assembly made proposals for a free, public system of education. The most elaborate plan of all was drawn up by Condorcet at the request of the Legislative Assembly.

Condorcet set forth detailed plans for a complete state system of secular schools to provide equal opportunity for all children, free, compulsory, and universal. The aim was to develop citizens devoted to civic, national, and democratic purposes. He proposed that elementary schools should be established throughout the country within walking distance for all pupils, one school for approximately every few hundred children. Next, intermediate schools should be located in all medium-sized towns to provide more advanced education for the common people. Third, there should be secondary schools, or institutes, located in the largest towns to provide not only classical education but a wide variety of subjects adapted to the needs of the people. Finally, there should be nine *lycées* to provide higher and professional education, to take the place of the traditional universities. Capping all would be a National Society of Arts and Sciences through which scholars could exert influence over the whole educational system. Condorcet's plan was not put into practice, but it provided germinal ideas that were embodied later in other plans and laws.

After the Republic was established, the National Convention made several attempts to set up a state system of schools and to destroy the church schools by confiscating their properties and by suppressing the teaching orders. The Lakanal law of 1794 provided for an elementary school for every 1,000 people, to teach the three R's in French, along with geography and nature study. They were also to instill republican ideals by teaching patriotic songs and stories and inculcating the doctrines of the Declaration of the Rights of Man, much as American youth are taught the Declaration of Independence and the Constitution. A law of 1795 provided that each of the several thousand communes should establish an elementary school for the three R's and that also a secondary, or intermediate, school should be established for every 300,000 people to give instruction in classical and modern subjects for children from twelve to eighteen years.

Many of these schools, designed to replace the classical *collège*, were actually established, but they lost ground when Napoleon set up his own system of secondary education in 1802. The National Convention also tried to establish several higher institutions in the arts, music, medicine, engineering, and science, but their fortunes proved to be precarious in the hectic days of the French Revolution's later phases. If the First Republic had been able to maintain itself on a genuinely democratic basis, it is possible that France would have achieved the first democratic system of education in Europe. But the reaction, typified by Napoleon and the restoration of the Bourbons in the nineteenth century, reestablished an aristocratic type of education.

Private Control in England

In England the control and support of education remained predominantly in religious and private hands. Schools were supported by Anglican parishes, dissenting churches, private endowment, and subscription societies. The most influential of these societies were conducted under Anglican auspices. The Society for the Promotion of Christian Knowledge, founded in 1699 for missionary work in England, soon set up dozens of charity schools as a part of its activity. The Society for the Propagation of the Gospel in Foreign Parts was established in 1701 to work among British colonies. It was energetic in conducting schools in connection with its missions and was particularly active in the middle and southern colonies of America. The Methodists gave considerable attention to the founding of schools as a part of their enthusiastic philanthropy.

Many endowed schools, apart from direct religious control, were a result of the increasing wealth of the middle class. A court decision in 1670 that a teacher in an elementary school did not require a bishop's license in order to teach stimulated the founding of private schools by endowment. Bishops did, however, have the right to license secondary school teachers. These philanthropic efforts to provide free education were England's way of responding to the educational needs of the eighteenth century.

This "voluntary" conception of education typified England's individualistic humanitarian approach to society in contrast to the social humanitarianism of the French Revolution. Whereas the French would have set up state systems of schools for all children in order to improve the welfare of all, the English solution was to give free education by philanthropic means to the poor and needy. In addition to the societies already mentioned, several other movements were taking shape just at the end of the eighteenth century, but inasmuch as their principal impact was in the nineteenth century they are described elsewhere (see pages 364–366 and 407–408).

Along with the voluntary and philanthropic agencies for providing free education, a few voices were raised late in the century in favor of state support of education. Adam Smith argued for state education, but not for the reasons advanced by the French reformers. Smith was interested in the protection of the "better" classes in society from the delinquencies and dangers to property that might rise from an uneducated and illiterate mass of people who might derive "wrong" ideas from the French Revolution. Therefore, he urged public education for the poor as a means of giving the lower classes a useful occupation and a realization of their "proper" place (of inferiority) in society. Much the same notion was expressed by Malthus, the proponent of the survival of the fittest in population trends. These early expressions for public education in England had uppermost in them a desire to protect the economic interests of the propertied classes, a far cry from the French Enlightenment and the American doctrines of democratic education.

Educational Control in Other Countries

In most Catholic countries the Catholic Church remained in virtual control of education. Interest by the state in education, however, was increasing. Charles III in Spain, affected by the Enlightenment, drove out the Jesuits and hoped to set up secular schools and require state examinations of prospective teachers, but his plans never were realized. Some gains were made in Spanish Florida and California under the tutelage of the Franciscans. In Austria Maria Theresa tried to adopt Frederick the Great's plans for state education and reform of schools; and Joseph II planned to set up a centralized system of all educational institutions in the Empire. Though the hopes of these "enlightened despots" may have been in the right direction, the difficulties of issuing edicts from the top down were too great to achieve much success in a short time with peoples not accustomed to the privileges of education.

In Protestant countries the educational systems of the Reformation continued to function in the hands of the state churches. The Scandinavian countries continued their Lutheran schools and the Netherlands and Scotland their Calvinist schools. In Switzerland the effects of the Enlightenment began to appear in the formation of the Helvetic Society in 1762, which began to work for union of the several loosely federated cantons into a stronger national state, with a national system of education as an integral part of the plan. This union was not achieved until the French Revolution was well on its way, but the groundwork was laid and the setting made ready for the work of the Swiss educational reformer, Pestalozzi.

Aristocratic and Democratic Elements in Education

During the Enlightenment more people had the opportunity to go to school than at any previous time in history. The philanthropic and charitable motives fanned by the Enlightenment led churches, rulers, and private individuals to give more money than ever before to educational institutions. The advantages of an increased literacy and popular enlightenment cannot be denied, but they must not be confused with democratic education. Charitable societies and state schools can be established with little or no thought of democracy. Indeed, aside from the French reformers, few writers or educational leaders were concerned with educating the common people to rule themselves. Saving their souls, making them better workers, and making them better subjects were the prime motives of most "enlightened" rulers of the eighteenth century. The importance of this kind of education cannot be overlooked. It should be remembered, however, that most of the advances of the Enlightenment were but a transition to the more truly democratic education of the nineteenth and twentieth centuries.

Status of the Teaching Profession

In general, the status of the teacher remained at a low level during the Enlightenment. More often than not the teacher of the elementary school was a person who had some other job or jobs and taught school as a side issue. The church sexton who rang the bell and dug the graves might also teach the school; the woman who needed extra funds would keep a dame school; war veterans who could no longer fight might be assigned to schools (as was the case in Prussia). Sometimes the process was reversed. Teachers who could not make a living at teaching would take up tailoring, carpentry, weaving, or other trades in order to make both ends meet.

The teachers in grammar schools and secondary schools were likely to be somewhat better off because of the higher fees paid in the secondary schools. There were even some straws in the wind indicating a better future for the teaching profession. Some of the church teaching orders were maintaining high standards; state regulations in Germany were calling attention to the need of certification for teachers; and such reforms as those of Francke and Hecker were leading the way in giving special preparation for prospective teachers. With universal education around the corner, the necessity of better trained teachers was soon to be much more fully recognized.

Out-of-school Agencies of Education

One of the great achievements of the Enlightenment was the progress made toward expanding the agencies of public opinion and literacy. The increase in newspapers, magazines, pamphlets, and written materials in the vernaculars created a wider audience than ever before. Libraries and museums became much more popular and easier of access, if not to the masses of people, at least to the growing middle class, who had the ability and money to take advantage of them. Scientific academies became extremely popular and even international in scope. Indeed, most of the great scientific discoveries and writings were made by men who worked within the scientific societies rather than in the universities. The reluctance of the universities of eighteenth-century Europe to abandon their traditional interests in literary and religious subjects prevented them from becoming centers of scientific and social research until the nineteenth and twentieth centuries.

INTELLECTUAL FOUNDATIONS OF MODERN EDUCATION

New World Views

Much of the intellectual life of the Enlightenment grew out of interpretations of the universe based upon the new science. Typifying the scientific world view was Sir Isaac Newton, whose epoch-making *Mathematical Principles of Natural Philosophy* was published in 1687. Building upon the immense advances made by science in the Reformation period, Newton's "laws of nature" remained scientific gospel until the late nineteenth century. As a result of the elaboration of the "law" of gravitation and the "law" of cause and effect, the universe came to be described as an orderly system of atoms moving in absolute space and time, essentially simple in structure, obeying fixed laws, and operating in a causal and uniform way. The universe was looked upon as a great machine, not subject to caprice, novelty, or divine intervention, but operating naturally and according to mathematical laws. Scientific "natural laws" became the model for scientific and "natural" explanations in most other fields of thought.

The most radical of the new world views was materialism. The materialists (such as La Mettrie, Holbach, and Helvetius) quickly jumped to the conclusion that nothing exists but matter in the form of atoms operating according to mechanical natural laws. They eliminated all conceptions of a spiritual world, of a soul or a mental substance.

At the opposite extreme were such idealists as Bishop George Berkeley of the Church of England. Berkeley bitterly attacked science and materialism, insisting that the essence of the world is spiritual and mental. In justifying religious principles and proving the existence of God, he elaborated the idealistic view that all apparently material objects are really only perceptions in the mind of God. They seem to exist in space and time, because God's mind exists continuously through space and time. Material substances are merely figments of the imagination; they change their qualities as perceptions change.

The middle-of-the-road conception of the universe that became popular with Enlightenment intellectuals was Deism. The deists, typified by Voltaire, tried to embrace the scientific interpretations of Newtonian science; they broke with traditional Christian theism but still did not go as far as materialism. According to Deism, the world is a great machine operating according to natural laws, but God is its first cause and initiator. God is conceived, not as a personal being who created the world in 6 days and can interfere with it at will, but as the great spirit that lies behind the physical universe. Even God cannot interfere with natural laws once they are in operation. Indeed, it would be a reflection upon the wisdom and power of God to imply that He needed to interfere with His handiwork. The deists attacked the traditional religions for their reliance upon miracles, supernatural revelations, and providential interference with nature. They accepted only what scientific investigation, mathematical description, and human reason could accept and describe.

Natural Law in Human Nature

Many Enlightenment thinkers tried to conceive of human nature in a way that would be appropriate to the kind of universe that Newton had described. Preeminent in this attempt was John Locke. Reinforced by Newtonian conceptions, Locke set out to elaborate the laws of human nature in a scientific manner. His basic assumption was that human nature is not preformed at birth but is a result of the impact of environment upon the unformed and pliable raw material of the human organism. At the same time, Locke did not become an extreme materialist. He believed in a soul and a mind having certain independent qualities. In this sense he was to the eighteenth century what Descartes was to the seventeenth century. He moved a considerable distance from traditional religious conceptions, but he tried to fit the older moral values into new categories.

Extremists followed Locke just as they followed Descartes. On the subject of the existence of the soul or mind as an independent element in human nature, the materialists went to one extreme. Some materialists like Toland, La Mettrie, Helvetius, and Holbach said that human nature is entirely materialistic. No such thing as a soul or mind exists apart from the movements of the body. Other materialists like Hartley, who admitted some distinction between soul and body, said that the difference is merely one of degree and not of kind.

At the other extreme, idealists like Berkeley said that the essence of human nature is the soul or perceiving mind. The body is dependent for its existence upon the spiritual functioning of the soul. Hume carried Berkeley's conception several steps further and arrived at skepticism. He felt it is not necessary to assume the existence of a unitary substance of soul, for all that exists is a flow of perceptions and experiences. Not only is the material world imaginary, but the soul and mind are imaginary. Thus, the range of opinions concerning human nature began with the dualistic belief that human nature is both mind and matter; the materialists insisted that human nature is only matter; the idealists believed that human nature is really mind; the skeptics considered it neither.

One of the most important eighteenth-century conceptions concerning human nature avoided these questions somewhat and directed itself at the question of good and evil. Here Rousseau's ideas were immensely important, for he reacted violently against the age-old belief that human nature is inherently evil and born in original sin. Rousseau went to the opposite extreme and insisted that human nature is essentially good. The child is born with inherent impulses that are right; social institutions make the individual evil, grasping, and bad. Here is a "natural law" of human nature that has had enormous influence upon the social and educational practices of the past two centuries. Out of it grew the doctrine that human nature is perfectible and can be made constantly better. When joined with the doctrines of social humanitarianism, this belief in human perfectibility became one of the great traditions that leavened the life of Europe and especially of America. It fitted in with the growing belief in the essential equality and dignity of all men. New impetus was given to respect for each individuality as a part of the democratic heritage of Western civilization.

Natural Law in Learning and Intelligence

Among the important thinkers concerning the operation of human reason and the way people learn, Locke stands out for his formulations of the doctrines of empiricism. In briefest terms, he stressed experience and environment as the sources of knowledge and learning. He attacked the religious and Platonic notions that ideas are innate in all men at birth. Applying Baconian and Newtonian conceptions of science to the study of the mind, he tried to find the natural laws of learning. He maintained that the child is not born with a preexistent mind or soul or with innate ideas concerning God, justice, morality, or other values. Rather, in Locke's view, the newborn child merely possesses a blank tablet (*tabula rasa*) upon which perceptions from the outside world are imprinted. Ideas, values, and knowledge have their origin in experience received from the external world and from other people.

Simple ideas come from two sources, sensation and reflection. Sensations come through the five senses and give rise to simple ideas concerning the shape, size, number, color, and qualities of things in the external world. The power of reflection is the capacity to gain ideas about the inner workings of memory, judgment, and volition in one's own mind. Complex ideas concerning moral conduct and social and physical relationships are then built up as the mind works over the raw sensations and puts simple ideas into more complex combinations. Locke's famous books, *Of the Conduct of the Understanding* and *Essay Concerning Human Understanding,* had great influence upon educational thought in Europe and America.

More extreme in their empirical views were such men as Hume, Hartley, and Condillac, whose position came to be known as sensationalism. They put almost exclusive emphasis upon the five outer senses as the source of ideas and ruled out Locke's inner faculty of reflection. They were thus often bitterly attacked by traditionalists for eliminating the role of the mind and stressing only the body as the instrument of knowledge.

A most important aspect of sensationalism was the doctrine of association of sensations and ideas. Developed by Hume and expanded greatly by Hartley, associationism was the forerunner of much of the experimental and scientific psychology of the nineteenth and twentieth centuries. To Hartley the basic natural law of learning was the fact that sensations, repeated often enough, leave traces in the nervous system. When different sensations are often enough associated, the occurrence of one sensation will call up a memory of the others. Simple ideas are thus built up into complex ideas merely by association. The principles of associationism sound a good deal like modern doctrines of "synaptic connections," "conditioning," and "frequency and recency."

However, empiricism and sensationalism had not won the day among eighteenth-century thinkers. They were new and startling and were gaining adherents, but the forces of rationalism were still predominant, especially in schools, universities, and churches. Rationalism had its great defenders in such men as the German philosopher, Leibnitz. Leibnitz attacked Locke for saying that ideas are not innate. He insisted that, although experience may bring out ideas, experience does not create them. Since the universe is a rational, intelligible order created by God, only reason (and not sense experience) can arrive at universal and assured ideas, as, for example, in mathematics. The doctrines of rationalism also have a ring familiar to us from the theories of modern educators who speak of "cultivation of the intellect" and "intellectual virtues."

Above all others, rationalism had its most notable defender in the great German philosopher, Immanuel Kant. Disturbed by the extremes of

Hume's skeptical empiricism and yet unwilling to give up the validity of sense experience, Kant set out to reconcile the empiricism of Hume with the rationalism of Leibnitz. His own critical philosophy is thus something of a middle-of-the-road philosophy aimed at reconciling science and religion.

Knowledge in Kant's view is made up of two elements, (1) the *content* of knowledge, which in turn is made up of impressions coming from the external world through experience, and (2) the *form* of knowledge, which is made up of the categories of the mind that give organization and order to experience. A crude illustration might be a stamping machine, which can "predict" what *form* a coin will take but cannot predict whether the raw material submitted to it will be silver, gold, copper, or what not. In the same way, the mind will necessarily give certain forms to knowledge no matter what the raw material of experience may be. The mind will count things, will classify things by kinds, and will see causal relationships among occurrences, no matter whether it is dealing with apples, dogs, or people.

These categories of the mind Kant called "transcendental categories." They exist in the minds of all rational beings prior to and above the external world of experience. Kant believed that there is an external world that causes our experience, but he insisted that we cannot *prove* it and therefore cannot *know* it. We know only our impressions and perceptions as ordered by the mind. Also, we cannot know what lies beyond or above experience, but we can believe that such a realm exists. He argued that we cannot prove the existence of God, or the immortality of the soul, or the freedom of the will. But he accepted their existence on faith, because he believed that morally they *should* exist; therefore, he was morally certain that they do exist. Kant thus believed in a supernatural world that cannot be invaded by reason or science but remains the province of religion. His enormous influence upon the philosophy of Europe and America helped idealism and rationalism to maintain themselves against the onslaughts of materialism and empiricism, especially in higher education.

Rationalism, however, held a more precarious position in lower schools, because it was soon challenged by the doctrine of naturalism, most powerfully stated by Rousseau in his famous book *Émile*. Stemming from the doctrine of the inherent goodness of human nature, Rousseau's theory stated that learning takes place best when the child is free to develop and grow according to his natural impulses. Restrictions and discipline should be discarded and a setting provided in which the child can engage in those activities which interest him. Revealing its affinity with empiricism, naturalism held that the best learning comes from dealing with natural objects, with the manual arts, and with persons in a natural way. Learning is hampered by too great insistence upon memorizing the heralded tools of rationalism, namely, mathematics, language, and books. The keywords of naturalism (freedom, growth, interest, and activity) sound familiar to a generation acquainted with the exponents of modern "progressive" education. This aspect of the lineage of American progressive educators of the 1920's is clear.

The Power of Knowledge

Never has a generation been so confident that knowledge could improve society as were the scholars and intellectuals of the late seventeenth and eighteenth centuries. Taking their cue from the physical sciences, they felt it most important to study and carry on investigations in all the arts and sciences. Consequently, the eighteenth century made great advances in nearly all organized bodies of knowledge.

Science and Mathematics. Preeminent in expanding the horizons of knowledge were the scientists and mathematicians. Setting the stage in the field of astronomy and physics was Newton, whose formulation of the law of gravitation began a new era in science and whose scientific and experimental method provided a tool for other workers in many scientific fields. Important gains were made in the study of light, heat, magnetism, hydraulics, mechanics, electricity, and chemistry. All these developments, when finally harnessed to steam engines in the late eighteenth century, made possible the new industrial society of the nineteenth and twentieth centuries, one of the most important events in all history. Fundamental to science were the spectacular advances in mathematics, signalized by Newton's work and by the formulation of differential calculus by Leibnitz.

In the biological sciences an enormous mass of facts was gathered. The objects of earth and nature were classified by such able scientists as Linnaeus, but few laws or theories were developed to bind the facts together into fruitful generalizations. Chemistry, geology, biology, physiology, and medicine had to await the next century for a Darwin, a Pasteur and all the others. However, new subject matters for schools and higher institutions were being made ready, eventually to challenge the supremacy of the classical and traditional subjects.

Language Arts. In general, the classical languages maintained their hold on the schools and universities of all lands, but unmistakable evidence of their decline was seen in many directions. Whereas Newton had written his *Principia* in 1687 in Latin, by the end of the eighteenth century most scientific and philosophical treatises were being written in the vernacular languages. Even more important was the creation of a new vernacular prose style in newspapers, journals, essays, novels, and dramas. The vernacular languages were coming into their own. French became virtually the universal language of fashion, diplomacy, and international discourse, and English and German were becoming refined, clear-cut, and "respectable."

Social Sciences. The social sciences began to improve their status in the eighteenth century as scholars and philosophers looked for the natural laws of society and political economy. Historical documents began to be treated as though they were scientific data to be gathered, classified, checked, criticized, and combed for evidences of careless acceptance of hearsay or authority. Considerably more attention was paid to social and cultural history than theretofore and less to political, military, and religious history. Voltaire was particularly interested in broadening the scope of history, in order to gain historical justification for many of the reforms he wanted in a broad range of fields. Underlying much of the historical writing of the period was the same optimism that prompted scientific investigation, belief that history is essentially orderly, simple, and subject to natural law. "Progress" came to be stated as a fundamental law of history. The world was constantly getting better, and the philosophers were confident that the future held more of goodness for the race than did the past.

One of the most characteristic elements of the Enlightenment was the pervading missionary zeal for reform. Whereas Reformation zeal had gone into religious fervor, the enthusiasm of the Enlightenment was directed toward reform of all kinds of institutions. Campaigns were organized for the aid of the weak, the poor, the persecuted, and the unfortunate. Fed by the liberalism that came from England in the late seventeenth and early eighteenth centuries, the propaganda for popular enlightenment found its climax in France in the middle and late eighteenth century. It became the ideological forerunner of the French Revolution. Appealing not only to the growing intellectual and middle classes, the reformers also worked hard for the alleviation of the conditions of the masses of people.

A great increase in the agencies of public information took the form of books, pamphlets, newspapers, journals, encyclopedias, debates, scientific academies, libraries, and museums. Perhaps most outstanding of all such activities was the *Encyclopédie,* published in France from 1751 to 1772 under the editorship of Diderot and D'Alembert. Lashing at superstition, persecution, and intolerance of all kinds, the Encyclopedists worked for freedom of thought, reform of harsh and unjust laws, and elimination of poverty, disease, slavery, and war. Here again the fight for civil liberties, for religious and political freedom, for popular education, and for the natural rights of man laid the basis for our Western heritage of humanitarian democracy. In this struggle public education as we know it had its birth.

THE ENLIGHTMENT IN EDUCATION

Realism and Naturalism in Educational Theory

In general, it may be said that the Enlightenment period was more productive of germinal theories concerning education than it was prone to apply such theories in actual practice. The common methods employed in vernacular schools and secondary schools reflected traditional disciplinary assumptions closely related to an uncritical rationalist outlook. In most schools the primary attention was given to the acquisition of verbal symbols through unrelieved memory work, reading, lectures, and recitations. The mental discipline took the form of rigid assignments, drills, and recitations; the physical discipline took the form of severe whippings and cruel punishments of all kinds. Learning to read was a matter of practicing the alphabet, building up syllables, and writing down dictated words and phrases. Advanced language work centered in learning the formal rules of grammar, conjugating verbs, declining nouns, and drilling in style and composition. On the whole, these methods were based upon the conception that the aim of educational method is to discipline the mind.

Empiricism and Sense Realism. One of the most noteworthy attempts to break this pattern grew out of the empirical philosophy of Locke, who went beyond the sense realism earlier expressed by Comenius. Locke's empirical conception of the role of experience in learning gave theoretical justification for sense realism in education. Insisting that ideas and knowledge come from the impingement of the external world upon the human mind in the form of sensations and perceptions, Locke opened the way for more attention in educational methods to the development of all the senses of the child, not merely through reading, but through the senses of sight, taste, smell, touch, and hearing. In line with this point of view, Locke quite logically put great stress upon the importance of the physical development of the body. He gave wide popularity to the famous conception of education as the achievement of "a sound mind in a sound body."

In his *Some Thoughts Concerning Education* Locke paid considerable attention to early care for the child's health through proper diet, sleep, clothing, hygienic habits, sports, and games. He blasted disciplinary compulsion in teaching methods by insisting that children learn best when they are interested in what they are learning. The best way to gain their interest is through play, which provides pleasurable incentives and prevents the building up of aversions to education.

In contrast to the disciplinary conception that the faculties of the mind can be trained by a few linguistic studies, Locke set forth the theory that the curriculum should be based upon studies that will be useful in adult life. He attacked narrow classical training and urged the study of English, drawing, arithmetic, writing, shorthand, geography, history, science, and mathematics. Even though he had aristocratic youth in mind, he advocated the values that can be achieved through manual activity in carpentry, gardening, and the like, as well as through ability in active sports of all kinds.

Above all, he protested against a training that relies upon the learning of moral precepts, verbal injunctions, and memorized religious doctrines. Throughout, he made it clear that moral discipline is the supreme aim of education but that it can be achieved only through diligent practice in good conduct and the building up of desirable moral habits through appropriate activities.

Much discussion has been expended on the question of whether or not Locke was the author of the doctrine of formal discipline. It seems clear in his writings on educational method, particularly in *Some Thoughts Concerning Education*, that his intention was to break down the traditional disciplinary methods in favor of an empirical approach that stressed the role of learning through experience. However, Locke's philosophical outlook, as stated in his works on the human understanding, embraced the necessity of exercising the faculty of reflection much as one exercises his muscles to bring about maximum development.

Therefore, the answer to the question depends on which of Locke's writings is taken as authority. If the *Thoughts* is taken as a guide to the education of young children, then mental discipline was foreign to Locke. If his essays on human understandiung are taken as guides to the development of the more mature mind, Locke does somewhat justify the theories of formal discipline and transfer of training. Inasmuch as the latter works of Locke had the greatest influence in American colleges in the eighteenth and nineteenth centuries, it was quite natural that they should have been cited in support of mental discipline as the ideal of college education.

The most outstanding example of the actual application of the empirical outlook to educational practice in the eighteenth century was the development of sense realism in some of the German schools of the day. The very name of Hecker's *Realschule* gives a clue to the interest in sense realism. In his school, actual objects (*Realien*) were used to illustrate the lessons from books. These were small-scale models of ships, buildings, and machines, life-size examples of everyday articles, and collections of plants, rocks, and small animals.

Basedow went even further to see that all teaching made extensive use of objects, models, and pictures. He wrote a very popular and influential textbook, the *Elementarwerk*, profusely illustrated with pictures to explain the text. Excursions gave students a firsthand acquaintance with farms, shops, markets, mines, and museums. Physical exercise and games also played a large part in the whole conception of education through experience. Through the efforts of Francke, Hecker, Basedow, and others, the first real taste of sense realism was given to education in Germany. But their efforts were opposed by the classical Humanists, and the realistic movement had to await the nineteenth century to gain wider approval and incorporation into the regular school system of Germany.

Rousseau's Naturalism. The most radical of all the theories of educational method that came out of the Enlightenment was the doctrine of naturalism as defined in Rousseau's *Émile.* In many ways it eventually proved to be the most influential in prying teaching methods loose from traditional practices. Although Rousseau's ideas were never fully put into practice in any single school, they did shape in large degree the thinking of many educational reformers of the nineteenth and twentieth centuries.

Rousseau's main point was that educational methods should follow the natural stages of development through which children grow to maturity. He listed four such stages: infancy, childhood, early adolescence, and late adolescence. Each stage has its physical, intellectual, and social characteristics upon which appropriate educational methods should be based.

During infancy, from birth to five years of age, the child is virtually an animal in its physical need for activity, its reliance upon feelings, and its nonmoral social development. Education at this stage should consist primarily in giving free play to motor activities, allowing free and healthy growth of the body, and providing for the development of the senses through contact with a wide variety of objects. The child should be free to do things for himself and should not be subjected to external compulsions or authority, for he can understand, not precepts, only the necessities that follow from dealing with natural objects and things.

During childhood, from age five to twelve, much the same kind of negative education is appropriate, for the child is still fundamentally an animal interested primarily in activity and should not be subjected to social or moral controls from without. Therefore, Rousseau swept aside study of books and language as harmful to the child's nature and substituted play, sports, games, and the manual arts as the means of developing sense experience.

The first great change in child development comes during the stage of early adolescence, from age twelve to fifteen, when reason and self-consciousness appear. Since it is curiosity that leads to the development of reason, the curriculum should be built around curiosity and useful activities, which are the only real motives to learning. Rousseau cited Robinson Crusoe as the great model in this stage of development, for the child is still largely nonsocial in his development; but he can and should begin to investigate the nature of things and see their relationships. Therefore, the child should be introduced to studies that reveal nature, astronomy, science, and the arts and crafts, and he should deal with these problems, as Crusoe did, on his own resources independent of the authority or precepts of other people. He should learn by his own efforts through the observation of nature. Here in its extreme form is the theory of learning by doing, not by words.

It is not until later adolescence, age fifteen to twenty, that the youth should deal with social problems. At this stage the greatest change of all occurs as the sex impulse appears. It is most important for the reason to develop rapidly so that it may serve as a check upon the desires of sex and direct them into socially approved activities. The study of society, politics, economics, history, and religion are appropriate for the youth as an aid to understanding complex social relationships. The development of a moral view, spiritual aspirations, and aesthetic tastes is now important. Youth can understand these things for the first time through the study of language, philosophy, psychology, religion, and the arts. The culmination of such a natural education is achieved in marriage.

Much controversy has been aroused by Rousseau's ideas. Some believe that he saw a great vision of the possibilities of human nature released from the shackles of tradition and obscurantism. Others believe that he set education upon a wrong track from which it has not yet been diverted. In general, Rousseau did a great service in directing attention to the desirability of studying the child so that education can be adapted to the child's characteristic needs. His conceptions of freedom, growth, interest, and activity were greatly needed at the time as leverages against an overweening authority and absolutism in education. However, Rousseau overstressed the individualized character of human development and understressed the role that education and culture play in the formation of the human personality. He neglected the importance of the culture in human development and turned the eyes of teachers away from the necessity of realizing that society has great influence upon the development of individual personality. A more adequate educational theory for the present day requires a new synthesis of education's role in developing wholesome individuals in a wholesome society. Education must work on both fronts, on the individual *and* on society.

New Educational Aims

One of the most far-reaching results of Enlightenment theories of education was the development of education for citizenship. The political aim of education in the Reformation had been to produce a citizen who would be ready to take his place in a state that was closely allied with a ruling church. Thus, the political aim had also a religious meaning. The Enlightenment reformers, on the other hand, believed in the separation of church and state and therefore sought the values of good citizenship in secular terms. This conception of secular education for citizenship came largely from French sources.

Some of the French reformers who emphasized the political aim for education were De la Chalotais, Turgot, Diderot, and Condorcet. They advocated that the schools be taken out of the hands of the church and placed in the hands of lay teachers responsible to the state. Only as education became a civil affair could the schools educate people to serve the state properly in their capacity as citizens. A state system of education should be set up to achieve these aims through secular instruction free to all, universal for poor and rich alike, and compulsory. Despite the fact that the secular point of view reached effective expression, it was not widely put into practice during the Enlightenment.

Other aims, religious and Humanistic, continued to dominate educational practices. Much of Enlightenment education followed the Reformation pattern. The Pietistic schools in Germany, the Catholic schools in France, and the Anglican schools in England adhered to their religious aims at the elementary level; and secondary schools in all countries maintained both the religious and Humanistic aims. The intellectual struggle known as the "battle of the Ancients and the Moderns" in the late seventeenth and early eighteenth centuries had its repercussions in educational theory. Such new Humanists as Lessing and Herder argued that the ancient classics, especially those of Greece, were the fountainheads of good taste and reason and that therefore the classics should be revivified in the secondary school curriculum. On the other hand, such men as Fontenelle insisted that modern science and the study of nature would produce all the values claimed for the classics, and more. Modern men were extolled as equal to if not superior to the ancients.

Besides the political, religious, and Humanistic aims, the Enlightenment also emphasized education for social status. Perhaps the most famous suggestions for the education of a gentleman's son were made by Locke in his *Some Thoughts Concerning Education*. The aims of education as stated by Locke were, in order of importance, virtue, wisdom, breeding, and learning. Virtue is conceived as good character achieved through practice in sound moral habits; wisdom is acting with foresight and prudence in the management of one's personal and social affairs; breeding is the achievement of correct behavior, bearing, and manners; and learning is the achievement of intellectual power through mental training, rather than through the acquisition of mere facts or knowledge. These ideals not only reflected the attitude of the English upper classes but played a great part in shaping the liberal education of American colleges. The aristocratic conception of education found expression in the knightly academies in France and Germany, Francke's *Pädagogium*, Basedow's *Philanthropinum*, and, in large part, the secondary schools of most countries.

Middle-class aims also came into considerable prominence during the Enlightenment. More and more educators began to stress the importance of practical subjects to prepare youth for the various trades and occupations. They began to urge that education give the greater attention to the useful arts needed by youth who would enter business, manufacturing, building trades, agriculture, and mining.

An interesting point is the degree to which the economic aim was bound up with the religious. Such Pietists as Francke, Semler, and Hecker stressed not only religious studies but realistic and useful subjects. In England the religiously inspired Dissenters' Academies went far in providing a practical education. The reason for this is undoubtedly the fact that the religious-reform groups were also middle-class groups, to whom it seemed not at all strange that a person could best serve God by becoming a self-reliant and capable merchant or artisan.

Vernacular Elementary Schools

Despite the formulation of new educational aims and effective statements of them, the elementary schools of Europe remained essentially reading schools. When all else is said and all the major exceptions are noted, the fundamental task of the elementary schools was the task of literacy. However, attention to writing and arithmetic was growing in response to the middle-class interest in such studies for their usefulness in business. Singing and music also gained a larger place as religious revivalism stimulated hymn singing and as a nationalistic spirit began to stress patriotic songs. Wherever the elementary school curriculum contained more than these studies, it was the exception rather than the rule.

In addition to the previously mentioned studies, Francke's elementary school in his institutes taught some history, geography, and nature study. These were also characteristic of other schools as ordered by the Prussian School Code of 1763. In France the schools of the Institute of the Brothers of the Christian Schools concentrated largely upon the standard studies but made special efforts to suit the work to the different age levels of the pupils. In England the schools of the Society for the Propagation of Christian Knowledge and of the Society for the Propagation of the Gospel in Foreign Parts often reflected the missionary aspect of their task by teaching not only the four R's but also on occasion farming, navigation, and such household arts as spinning and sewing. Workhouses, set up for the poor children of the various parishes, also provided a kind of vocational education in addition to the system of apprenticeship.

The most common means of teaching reading and religion were the catechisms, hornbook, the Psalter, the Bible, and especially the primer, which was a first religious book containing the Creed, Lord's Prayer, Ten Commandments, and Psalms. A whole series of books, modeled on the primer, became eventually first schoolbooks as well as first religious books. The Church of England authorized many of them. The dissenting churches authorized their own, the most famous one in America being the *New England Primer*. In the middle of the eighteenth century new aids to reading took the form of spelling books. One of the most famous of these was Dilworth's *New Guide to the English Tongue*, which included lists of words, with their proper pronunciation, rules of grammar, prayers, and some fables and moral precepts. Arithmetic books also appeared at this time, giving further recognition and stimulus to this increasingly popular subject of the elementary school curriculum.

Secondary Education

Interestingly enough, secondary education in the eighteenth century was more responsive to the new trends in educational thought than was elementary education. This has seldom happened in the history of education. Considerable headway was made in introducing the realistic studies and practical studies into secondary schools. Nevertheless, the classical tradition remained so strong in the older grammar schools that new types of schools had to be established to care for the realistic and practical studies. The fact that the new studies were not welcomed in the regular secondary schools shows the grip of Humanism upon these schools.

Germany. The secondary schools of Germany were doubly stimulated during the eighteenth century by sense realism and by a new Humanism. The Pietistic influence promoted sense realism largely through the efforts of Francke, Semler, and Hecker. In Francke's Latin school the curriculum was much broader than in the usual classical school, including not only religion and the ancient languages but also mathematics, physics, botany, anatomy, history, geography, painting, and music. In his *Pädagogium* the realistic studies found an even larger place; considerable provision was made for the study of mechanics and work with glass, copper, and wood, along with laboratory work in natural history and the physical sciences. Semler's mathematical and mechanical school followed somewhat the same lines, even omitting the classics, and Hecker's school in Berlin went still further in offering practical work in mathematics and science.

These were the origins of a new type of secondary school called the *Realschule*. It eventually took its place alongside the classical *Gymnasium*, though it was not until the onset of the Industrial Revolution in the nineteenth century that it came into its own. Sense realism also entered German schools through the *Philanthropinum* of Basedow, in which the useful sciences and mathematics were prominent, as well as many of the manual arts connected with carpentry, woodwork, and the practical arts.

The other enlivening factor in German secondary education, the new Humanism, had its effect directly upon the *Gymnasium*, the most important curricular change being a new emphasis upon Greek language and literature. As the French influence was cast off in the middle of the century, the new crop of German literary men turned to Greece for their inspiration. The old Latin schools became *Gymnasiums*, the very name harking back to the ancient Greek secondary school of that name.

France. In general, the secondary schools of France remained fixed in the traditional classical mold, especially under the influence of the Jesuits, who concentrated upon Latin, Greek, philosophy, and ancient history. The Fathers of the Oratory had achieved a somewhat more modern curriculum in their secondary schools; in addition to Latin, Greek, and Hebrew, they taught the vernacular French, and Cartesian mathematics, science, history, and geography in the vernacular French. Nevertheless, the French reformers began to call more vigorously for greater attention to French history, language, and literature as well as mathematics, science, the practical and fine arts, and physical education.

England. English secondary education was ruled by the Latin grammar schools in the eighteenth century. Within the grammar schools, the grammarians held the fort against mounting criticism. They insisted that Latin grammar was the only means of achieving the truly disciplined mind of the liberally educated person. Among their critics even those who agreed as to the importance of the classics tried to soften this approach by urging more attention to the direct *use* of Latin through speaking it and reading the great literary masterpieces. The Church of England often sided with the grammarians, and legal support was invoked to prevent an expansion of the curriculum. It was pointed out that the foundation grants for the grammar schools had stipulated that Latin and Greek should be taught free to worthy students. The grammarians insisted that these terms meant that nothing else besides Latin and Greek could be taught.

Gradually, however the grammar schools became so pedantic, so brutal and violent in their discipline, and so marked by unrest and rioting among the students that their clientele fell off decidedly. It was then that these schools began to be reformed in the late eighteenth century. They kept their classical emphasis but began to yield to Locke's conception of the education proper for a gentleman. The point of view of the pedantic scholar or grammarian had never appealed very much to the aristocratic or to the middle class; but when the schools began to emphasize the importance of virtue, wisdom, and breeding, as defined by Locke, and play down learning, the upper classes became more interested. By the end of the century these classes began to patronize the secondary schools more freely, and the great "public" schools began to take their modern form.

The real response to new educational trends, however, took place in the early and middle part of the Enlightenment in the Dissenters' Academies conducted by nonconformist clergymen for their congregations. Starting as Latin schools they soon began to pay more attention to "realistic" studies that would appeal to the middle classes. By the beginning of the eighteenth century the academies were teaching, in addition to the classics, the English language and literature, modern foreign languages, mathematics (geometry, astronomy, trigonometry), natural science and anatomy, history, geography, politics, and philosophy (ethics, logic, and metaphysics).

By the middle of the eighteenth century science and mathematics played a larger role than ever, and commercial subjects became more important. Texts in spelling, grammar, and arithmetic appeared in English. Toward the end of the century the Dissenters' Academies began to decline as the Church of England became stronger, the nonconformist groups lost ground, and the "public" schools began to reform and draw off the clientele. Nevertheless, they had served a most useful purpose in awakening secondary education in England at a time when the traditional schools were especially hidebound; they also influenced the rise of American academies in the later eighteenth century.

Higher Education

Libralism in German Universities. A vital intellectual life was allowed to develop in Germany in the eighteenth century by the despotic rulers who professed an "enlightened" care for the interests of the people, though this activity was largely confined to science, philosophy, and literature. Under Frederick II, for example, the new science and literature gained favor not only at court but also at the universities, which began to lose their original ecclesiastical character and to take on the character of public institutions intended to train the good citizen and the able civil servant.

In the seventeenth century the German universities had declined under ecclesiastical control; but, in the latter part of that century, a revival took place. The University of Halle was founded (1694), and there Christian Thomasius, the rationalist, and August Hermann Francke, the Pietist, led a revolt against Lutheran orthodoxy. After 1706, Christian Wolff infused the new science and rationalism into Halle and insisted upon the right and duty of free investigation. Philosophy was separated from authoritative theology and began to absorb the modern sciences of mathematics and physics. Wolffian philosophy eventually permeated nearly all Protestant German universities during the eighteenth century.

Another step forward occurred when a university was founded at Göttingen in 1734. Here the ideas were even more liberal than at Halle, and almost complete freedom was given to a professor once he had been appointed. Other universities followed the lead of Halle and Göttingen somewhat slowly, but gradually both Protestant and Catholic institutions adopted the new learning.

Some of the essential changes that occurred in the German universities as a result of the eighteenth-century Enlightenment were as follows: The Scholastic philosophy of Aristotle was superseded by a more modern philosophy founded upon the principles of the physical sciences and

Fig. 19. Ceremonial at the establishment of Erlangen University.

mathematics. The hard-and-fast curriculum was replaced by one embodying the principle of freedom of research and instruction. Mere exposition of a canonical text was replaced by the systematic lecture. The disputation was replaced by the seminar. A vital classical scholarship replaced the formal imitation of the classics. Finally, the German language ousted the Latin as the medium of instruction. The vast development of science within the German universities made some choice of studies by students virtually a necessity and directly affected the rise of the elective system in American colleges in the nineteenth century.

French Universities. Although the "enlightened" despotism of Germany aided the introduction of the new science and philosophy and encouraged academic freedom in the German universities, the despotism of France wrought exactly the opposite effect. The universities remained dominated by conservative religious groups backed by the monarchy, which kept a watchful eye on their political and social teachings as well as their religious teachings. The faculty of theology of the University of Paris set the pace for the whole institution when it prohibited the study of such books as Montesquieu's *Spirit of the Laws* and Rousseau's *Émile*. Some attempts to heed the cry of the reformers were made, notably by the rector, Charles Rollin, who tried to modernize the system of studies by introducing Cartesian science and philosophy and French history, language, and literature. But his Jansenist leanings brought him afoul of the powerful Jesuit groups, and he was driven into retirement.

English and Scottish Universities. With all the intellectual activity and scientific progress in England during this period, it might be expected that the universities would have been radically changed. However, tradition and the religious hold of Archbishop Laud and of the Restoration kings kept the English universities behind the times throughout most of the eighteenth century. Despite a few brilliant names, such as Newton, Gray, and Blackstone, the favorite studies at Oxford and Cambridge remained the classics, logic, and Scholastic philosophy. Some gains were made in introducing Newtonian science and mathematics, especially at Cambridge. Chairs in chemistry were established at both Oxford and Cambridge as early as 1685; modern history was established at Oxford in 1724; and a tripos, or honors, examination in mathematics was established at Cambridge in 1747. But these were relatively small ripples in the great sea of classicism.

However, the Scottish universities were able to make major reforms by the middle of the eighteenth century. At Edinburgh, the professors of Latin, Greek, logic, and natural philosophy were joined by professors of mathematics and of moral philosophy, who gave lectures open to voluntary attendance. By 1741, the course of study in the arts at Edinburgh was far in advance of that in the English universities. The utilitarian spirit of the reform at Aberdeen involved recognition of such activities as dancing, writing, bookkeeping, and French. Here, then, are early evidences of Enlightenment trends: the impact of the new science upon the arts curriculum; the notion of "useful," or "practical," subjects as equivalent to the older studies in a liberal education; and the actual practice of the "voluntary," or elective, principle.

Teacher Education. Some strides were made in the professional preparation of teachers, especially in Germany. At Francke's institutes in Halle special attention was given to the problems of prospective teachers, and Hecker established regular seminars for training teachers at his *Realschule* in Berlin. Frederick the Great was so impressed by Hecker's work that he urged teachers to attend his *Realschule*. Other teacher-training institutions were established in Austria, Saxony, and Silesia. The new Humanists in Germany also influenced teacher education, not so much through special pedagogical training as through the efforts of Gesner, Heyne, and Wolf to give a thorough grounding in classical scholarship to teachers who were to go into the *Gymnasiums*. This scholarly conception of teacher education became very popular. It was assumed that all a good teacher needed was mastery of subject matter. American teacher education adopted this conception and perpetuated it until well into the nineteenth century when a running battle began between the "professional" and the "academic" elements in the preparation of teachers. Other evidences of special attention to teacher education were present in the Jesuit, Port-Royalist, and Oratorian orders and in the school societies of England.

It seems noteworthy that special education of teachers was undertaken principally under two conditions, when an organization or institution, such as the state or church, gave it impetus, and when such organized groups found it desirable to reform school practice or curriculum along new lines. So long as schools were in purely private hands dominated by traditional universities, no pressure for teacher education arose. But when a teaching order, or an evangelical movement, or a sense-realistic movement became so organized that it wished to change the kind of schools in existence or to set up new schools, then special forms of teacher education appeared. The crusading character of many teacher-education movements has long shown that the training of teachers has often been considered a strategic point in the reform of education.

Chapter 11

THE AMERICAN RESPONSE TO THE ENLIGHTENMENT

FROM COLONIES TO NATION

The period between 1690 and 1715 was perhaps the low point in American intellectual life. Puritan theocratic ideals were being attacked, and the new impetus from Europe had not yet affected American thought. But as America was caught up in the European imperialist wars and as new blood from many national stocks started to flow into America, political and intellectual life began to take on a new color and vitality. English ideas of middle-class liberalism were accepted by many American merchants and traders, and French ideas of democratic humanitarianism were accepted by the ordinary man in city and country. As John Adams put it, the revolution was effected before the Revolutionary War began. The revolution was first of all in the minds and hearts of the people.

Political and Economic Ideas of Good Citizenship

The most remarkable shift in political and economic ideas during the eighteenth century was the change from an absolutist conception of the state to the republican and democratic ideals of representative government. At the beginning of the century sovereignty had been in the hands of a few; when the century was over, it rested on a much wider popular base. In the process, the theocratic and the English aristocratic and royal conceptions were overthrown, and the battle was on as to whether sovereignty should rest with the relatively few propertied persons or with the whole adult male population. In the course of the century, three general positions became quite well defined in America: aristocratic Toryism, middle-class Whiggery and Federalism, and democratic Republicanism.

Toryism. In England the Tory party had been the supporters of the Stuart kings in the seventeenth century against the rights of Parliament. The name lived on and was applied to the English royal officials and their loyal friends in America, who envisioned an America ruled by the wealthy upper classes. Perhaps the outstanding exponent of the Tory view was Thomas Hutchinson, the last royal governor in Massachusetts. He felt it only right and just that gentlemen of property should rule the state and that the welfare of the colonies should be determined by English control from abroad. He hated the "mob," and he hated the town-meeting

300

idea of popular control. The ignorant and stupid people should be ruled by the intelligent few. In general, the Tory insisted that the primary duty of the ordinary person was to obey the king and be loyal to the constituted authorities, for the worst evil was disorder and rebellion. This was the ideology against which most Americans united to wage the Revolution.

Whiggery and Federalism. In their opposition to the Tories the American middle classes were attracted to the English Whig position. The Whigs had been the proponents of parliamentary rights against the king in the seventeenth century, and they continued to be the spokesmen for middle-class and laissez-faire liberalism in the eighteenth century. William Pitt was the leader of the Whigs in England who saw justification in the claims of the colonists for freedom from the colonial restrictions imposed by Lord North and the Tories.

The American Whigs fought royal and Tory control on the basis of their rights as Englishmen. They wanted to be treated without discrimination as other merchants and traders were treated in England, but, when that argument failed, they appealed to their "natural rights" as defined by Locke, the rights to life, liberty, and property.

One of the outstanding American Whigs was John Dickinson, who insisted that the primary aim of government is to protect property. When he felt that the English government was usurping American property rights by levying taxes from England without American representation, he was ready to take part in the Revolution. He was not a democrat or a Republican, for he believed that a legislature should represent the property owners. At the Constitutional Convention he favored property qualifications for voting and a strong stable government in which the Senate should act as a check on the House of Representatives.

Thus, when the debate was being waged over the kind of government that should be set up in the new nation after the war was won, the Federalists carried on the tradition of the English Whig position. The preeminent spokesman for the Federalists was Alexander Hamilton, who assumed that the difficulties of the "critical period" following the war grew out of the lack of a strong centralized government that would protect property.

In general, the Federalists were opposed to a wide extension of democracy. They felt that a written constitution was necessary as a safeguard against the uninformed will of the common people. They were the spokesmen for the wealthy merchants and professional men, who leaned toward the principles of merchant capitalism. Hamilton recognized the necessity of a government that would fit the capitalistic conception of a sound financial system and economic structure. He had no faith in the "turbulence" of the common man and urged that the rich and wellborn should have a permanent share in government to check the unsteadiness of the masses.

Democracy and Republicanism. Although joining with the Whigs and Federalists to win the war, the more democratic elements subscribed to different conceptions of man and society. They found leaders in Franklin, Samuel Adams, Paine, and, above all, Jefferson. These men and others found their ideological base not in English capitalism but in French humanitarianism. They appealed not so much to constitutional rights as to the natural rights of all men, to the inherent equality of all men, and to the possibility of social improvement through a government that rested upon the sovereignty of the whole people, not the propertied classes only. Theirs was the faith in the common man.

Franklin advocated universal manhood suffrage as well as federal union. At the Constitutional Convention as well as in London and Paris he was a democrat in aristocratic surroundings. Samuel Adams was an ardent believer in the local rule of town-meeting democracy. He took it upon himself to organize the rank and file of people to play their part in control of the political state. He expounded the right and competence of the people at large to manage their own affairs, in contrast to the attitude of Hamilton. He fought the Tories and Federalists alike, worked hard for the Bill of Rights, and supported Jefferson for President as a return to democracy after the Federalist administrations of Washington and John Adams.

Thomas Paine was an outstanding representative of French ideals of equality and democracy in America and Europe. As Parrington so well says, he was "a delegate at large in the cause of human freedom." In his *Common Sense* Paine blasted the aristocracy and privileged interests, expressed implicit belief that the majority will is the supreme law, and urged that the people can and should remake the law at any necessary time. He extolled natural rights above property rights in his famous *Rights of Man.*

Representing the French humanitarian ideals above all others and shaping them to fit America as he knew it, Jefferson gave an enormous impetus to the cause of democracy through his writings and his Republican party. He combined a faith in the common man and in human nature with his faith in the agrarian freeholder. He felt that political freedom arises from economic freedom, political democracy from economic democracy. He mistrusted capitalism, mercantilism, and city life and glorified an agrarian society of freeholders as the root of liberty, equality, and fraternity.

Jefferson took to himself the equalitarian doctrines of Rousseau and the French physiocrats and applied them to the American frontier scene. He saw in America the opportunity to work out in practice the ideals of the

French reformers. He favored a government resting upon popular sovereignty, but he hated and feared a strong centralized government operated by the few, whether English aristocrats or American merchants and landowners. His bills introduced into the Virginia legislature reflected his deep concern for freedom of religious conscience and freedom

Fig. 20. Thomas Jefferson.

from vested interests of all kinds. His formulation of the basic ideals of democracy in the Declaration of Independence gave America its best statement of the "American dream."

The motives for men's actions in Enlightenment America were, as always, not of one piece. Not only were men swept up by the political and social idealism of the Revolution; they were also beginning to glorify another and, eventually, a most powerful motive, the making of money. Until the eighteenth century most men had been almost wholly occupied in the struggle to survive, but now the ideal of money-making and profit, as well as of equality and freedom, came to be incorporated in the American dream. Benjamin Franklin was an outstanding spokesman for both these ideals. When he glorified the virtues of industriousness and frugality, Franklin reflected the economic ideals of merchant capitalism as well as the political ideals of equality and freedom.

During the Enlightenment in America the currents of European influence continued to sweep over the colonies; but before the period was over, something new had appeared in the form of political, economic, and religious institutions. As a result, the beginnings of a new species of educational institution had emerged.

The Winning of Representative Government

Changes in Colonial Government. Several of the earliest colonies had been founded and controlled by commercial stock companies to which the European governments had granted considerable political and economic power. Among these were Virginia, Massachusetts, New Netherlands, and New Sweden. Others had been founded and controlled by proprietors to whom the king of England had granted land along with political, judicial, and military authority. Among these were Maryland, the Carolinas, New Jersey, Pennsylvania, Georgia, and New York.

Then in the late seventeenth and early eighteenth centuries the new mercantilist and commercial interests in England began to force a change in governmental policies. Several of the colonies were transformed into royal colonies, with governors appointed by the king and vested with the major share of political authority. By the time of the Revolution nine colonies had been so constituted. Along with the royal government, the colonies were allowed to maintain legislatures consisting of upper houses appointed by the governor or king and lower houses elected by property owners. Virtually all colonies had some sort of self-government through which grievances could be expressed and through which eventually the colonists gained more local self-rule.

In the course of the eighteenth century England began to exert greater direct control over colonial affairs from London by the creation of many councils, special commissions, and legislation. The colonists gradually became restive under British restrictions. Some began to suggest a greater measure of self-rule. When the governors of seven colonies met in Albany to negotiate a treaty with the Iroquois in 1754, Benjamin Franklin proposed a colonial union that would set up a federal congress to maintain an army, deal with the Indians, control lands, and levy taxes, but neither the colonists nor England was ready for it.

Finally, the conflicts grew more bitter over such actions as the quartering of British troops in colonial homes, the closing of the port of

Boston, the prohibition of town meetings, and the establishment of the Catholic Church in Quebec. As a result of many more such grievances as these, the colonists called convention in Philadelphia in 1774 to draw up the list of grievances for petition to the king. The battles of Lexington and Concord set off the explosion in 1775, and the Declaration of Independence was issued in 1776, after a year of fighting.

The Emergence of the New Nation. The first stage of the political organization of the new nation took place under the Continental Congress, consisting of delegates from the 13 sovereign states, which conducted the war until its conclusion in 1781. The Articles of Confederation had been drawn up by those who feared a strong central government and who preferred a more loosely constituted confederation of virtually sovereign states. Their experience with strong nationalistic governments in Europe had made them fearful of an overweening centralized government. Therefore, the central government was first designed merely to deal with such necessary tasks as war, commerce, coinage, and the disposition of the public lands that had been created when the states gave up their claims to the west.

The weakness of the Confederation soon precipitated a struggle over the creation of a Constitution to take the place of the Articles. This struggle was fought between the Federalists, who urged a stronger central government, and the Anti-Federalists, who desired a less powerful government but a more democratic one. At the Constitutional Convention, many of the Anti-Federalist leaders who had so well conducted the Revolution were absent. Thomas Jefferson, Samuel Adams, Thomas Paine, and Patrick Henry, for example, were not there. The new government was given greater power to levy taxes directly on the people, regulate commerce, control the currency, and prevent the impairment of contracts.

Ratification by the states was finally won after considerable opposition. In general, the propertied classes favored adoption, but the debtor groups and back-country people were fearful of the degree to which their rights would be protected under a constitution that did not contain a bill of rights consonant with the Declaration of Independence. Finally, the requisite number of states ratified the Constitution. At the first session of Congress in 1789 the first 10 amendments were drawn up under the leadership of James Madison as a bill of rights and were finally ratified by 1791.

In general, the struggle for power was won at the Constitutional Convention by the merchant and propertied interests, but the Bill of Rights and the new constitutions of the states reflected the demands for more democratic control and wider suffrage. The more radical agrarian and populist groups captured many of the new state governments, but the propertied group continued to favor a stronger government that would protect property, provide checks on the supremacy of the legislative branch, and give more power to the executive and judiciary.

When the new government was launched by the Federalists with Washington as president in 1789, much effort was devoted to establishing a solvent financial structure as favored by the propertied classes. To these measures the debtor classes, of course, objected, and they found a leader in Jefferson, who sponsored Republican ideals in opposition to those held by the Federalists. Washington, however, was reelected in 1792, and John Adams followed in his footsteps in 1796. By the end of the century, the Americans had won the right of home rule, but also central in the political affairs of the day was, as Professor Carl Becker has put it, the struggle to see who would rule at home. In this struggle the Federalists and propertied interests were winning up to 1800, but the Republicans came to power in that year, when Jefferson was elected as third president. The Federalist party as such soon disintegrated after that defeat.

The Clash of Economic and Social Interests

Rise of Merchant Capitalism. Throughout the eighteenth century, agriculture continued to be basic to the economic institutions of the American colonies, but one of the most important developments of the period was the rise of commercial interests. A great upswing in trade and commerce was achieved as the European wars created a huge demand for American agricultural, forest, and fur products. This meant an increase in power for the merchant classes, who began to carry American trade to and from Europe.

The great increase in trade and commerce in the New England and middle colonies led to the rapid expansion of cities along the eastern coast near the good harbors like those at Boston, New York, Philadelphia, Baltimore, and Charleston. Commerce became a quicker way to get rich than through land, although land speculation was popular too. With the increase of wealth from trade, the Yankee merchants began to challenge the political and social authority of the landed gentry and the clergy. City life and the new spirit of profit-making gave a character to American life that became increasingly prominent decade after decade. In the cities, a working class of clerks in the business houses and mechanics in the manufacturing shops also gained in numbers and importance.

Social Classes. The population of the colonies was fairly homogeneous up to 1690, but by 1750 great numbers of non-English people had come to America. The total population by the Revolution reached about 2,500,000 or 3,000,000. The newcomers were principally German, Scots-Irish, and French, who tended to push beyond the settled regions of the eastern seaboard to the back country bordering on the Appalachian range.

In New England and the middle colonies a strong class of small farmers who owned their land or rented it became ever more important in the social structure. The colonial land policy of granting land free to those who would take it produced a powerful class of freeholders, or yeomen, in the back country, who developed a strong democratic and individualistic temper. Together with similar groups in the back country of the South, they began to accept the French conceptions of liberalism based upon "natural rights" rather than upon the rights of king, church, or merchant.

In the South the unfree labor group was made up of indentured white servants and Negro slaves. Very often the indentured servant could gain his freedom after 5 years of service and would then take up land in the West or become a wage earner. The possibility of freedom for white workers increased, but the social status of those who remained in the South declined as the wealth of the planters grew and as wave after wave of Negro slaves were brought in. In 1670 the Negroes represented only about 5 per cent of the population in Virginia but by 1756 they represented nearly 75 per cent. By 1760 there were about 400,000 Negroes in America. They accounted for more than one-third of the population in the South. With the invention of the cotton gin, the South turned more than ever to cotton and established Negro slavery securely until the time of the Civil War.

The conflict between classes intensified during the eighteenth century as the result of increased concentration of wealth in the hands of the merchant and planter classes. The debtor classes resented a policy by which legislatures had granted land to speculators who held it for profit, who did not live on it or work it, but who nevertheless could control a town by virtue of being a large landowner. In many respects, such policies of legislatures, speculators, and absentee landlords were more outrageous to the farmers than were the trade acts of England. Therefore, they became loud in their protests against absentee ownership, high taxes, and heavy interest rates on loans and mortgages. Similarly, in the South the small landowners resisted the power of the planter, who was trying to build up a social life on the model of the English gentry and aristocratic classes.

In general, the working and clerical groups in the larger towns and cities began to feel somewhat akin to the small farmers in that they too had their grievances, namely, low wages. They joined the farmers in supporting Jefferson's democratic Republican party. These groups began to adopt more and more of the French humanitarian devotion to political, economic, and educational progress. They were the backbone of resistance during the American Revolution, and they became the spearhead of the campaign to spread political and social democracy during the nineteenth century.

The Winning of Religious Freedom

Decline of Puritan Theocracy. With new currents of thought sweeping into America from England and France, the Puritan clergy found it ever more difficult to maintain its control in New England. The high hand of John Cotton and John Winthrop began to be replaced by the querulous complaints of Cotton Mather and the sharp jibes of John Wise. Theocracy could no longer hold out against the rising tide of democratic faith, commercial interests, and the influx of new national and religious groups.

Bitter arguments arose concerning the kind of organization the churches should have and what their relation to the state should be. Cotton Mather thundered against lay control of the church and demanded more complete control by the clergy. Wanting to preserve the old theocratic church-state, which he saw slipping away, he told the people that they should be willing to be ruled by the godly. He resented any interference by the merchant classes, and he ranted against the popular unrest of the common people. He had no shred of liberalism in his outlook; yet he was more widely read than most others of his time. In Parrington's words, he was a twilight figure.

John Wise was the outstanding spokesman for a more liberal conception of a democratic church in a democratic state. He wrote effectively in favor of the separation of church and state and in favor of democratic control within the church. To him the best form of church organization was congregationalism, according to which the people themselves are the ultimate authority. By analogy with political theory, the church could be monarchical in rule (episcopal), aristocratic (presbyterian), or democratic (congregational). He subscribed to French humanitarian beliefs in natural rights, equality, and general welfare through good government. He reflected the free and independent spirit of the New England back country in contrast to the aristocratic spirit of Boston Toryism and merchant groups.

The Separation of Church and State. At the opening of the eighteenth century the colonies revealed three kinds of practice with respect to the relation between church and state. In some colonies a strong and long-standing establishment of religion had given preference to a single church. Massachusetts, Connecticut, and New Hampshire had singled out the Congregational Church, and Virginia and the Carolinas had given special privileges to the Church of England.

In a second group of colonies the place of established religion was uncertain, precarious, or changeable. These included Maryland, Georgia, New York, and New Jersey, where claims for the establishment of the Church of England were only more or less successful at different times. In a third group of colonies a relatively large measure of religious freedom over a long period of time had prevented the establishment of religion. These were Rhode Island, Pennsylvania, and Delaware.

In the course of the eighteenth century the trend toward separation of church and state accelerated in all colonies until by the end of the century only four states had the remnants of an establishment of religion. These were Massachusetts, Connecticut, New Hampshire, and Maryland, all of which adopted the majority practice early in the nineteenth century.

The transition from a single establishment of religion to full separation of church and state was a most difficult and painful process. In several colonies an intermediate step was taken. It permitted several religious groups or churches to use the power of the state to help support their ministers and church services. This has been called a "multiple establishment of religion." For example, in Massachusetts, Connecticut, and New Hampshire the Anglicans were given the privilege of using the religious taxes they paid for the purpose of supporting their own Church of England ministers. Later *all* Protestant societies were given this privilege in the organic laws that governed these states after the Revolution. Similarly, South Carolina and Maryland continued for long to require everyone to pay a general assessment for religious purposes but each person could have his assessment paid to the church of his choice. He was, however, not free from religious taxation. A similar proposal created bitter battles in Virginia during the Revolutionary period and nearly succeeded, but it was defeated under the leadership of Jefferson and James Madison. The Virginia statute for religious freedom drawn up by Jefferson became a model for other states throughout the nineteenth century.

Fresh from these battles, Madison saw the necessity of guaranteeing religious freedom and separation of church and state in the federal constitution. As a result, he led the fight for a bill of rights in which the First Amendment proclaimed, "Congress shall make no law respecting an establishment of religion, or prohibiting the free exercise thereof."

Reflecting the unmistakable trend toward religious freedom, eight states had already disestablished their state churches before the First Amendment determined national policy. They did this in their early state constitutions (by charter in Rhode Island). Significantly, the states where the more liberal and democratic forces had influence in framing the state constitutions were the ones that decreed separation of church and state. The more conservative institutions held on to the principle of establishment of religion, in every case, however, embodying the principle of multiple establishment and not preference for a single church. Even these states eventually followed suit: South Carolina in 1790, Maryland in 1810, New Hampshire in 1817, Connecticut in 1818, and Massachusetts in 1833.

This struggle for separation of church and state was another phase of the struggle to see "who would rule at home" which, as we have seen, had its political and economic counterparts. The democratic and republican forces eventually won their way against the "standing order" of the colonial period. This was one of the most important triumphs of the Enlightenment over the Reformation in American life, heralding significant changes for the control and program of education in the nineteenth century.

The influx of a wide variety of religious groups during the eighteenth century created the conditions wherein the ideals of religious freedom could become a reality. Great numbers of German Lutherans, Moravians, Mennonites, and Scots-Irish Presbyterians settled in Pennsylvania, and the Methodists and Baptists gained followers in all colonies. After the Revolution, the churches broke their ties with Europe, and American versions of the Church of England, Methodist, Presbyterian, and other churches were organized. The established churches could not survive the rising political power of these large sectarian groups.

The Great Awakening. An American version of the Pietistic and Methodist movements in Europe affected most of the large denominations in America. Outstanding among the many religious leaders who stimulated the revivals of the "Great Awakening" were Jonathan Edwards in New England and George Whitefield, who traveled the length and breadth of the land preaching literally thousands of sermons over a 30-year period.

As a result of the efforts of the various revivalists, thousands of new members were swept into the churches, and many new congregations were added to each denomination. Religious leadership gained greatly in power and importance as a result of the nationwide movement, but the fact that many churches grew more powerful made it more certain than ever that established churches were doomed. The revival doubtless increased genuine religious feeling, but it also resulted in hysterical emotionalism or "enthusiasm" among many people. It increased philanthropy and altruism either through a broadened sympathy for the unfortunate or through fear of the everlasting torments of punishment in the next world. It prompted the merchant classes to devote some of their money to churches, to philanthropic societies, and to schools and colleges.

Jonathan Edwards reached the peak of revival technique with his threats of eternal damnation and the horrors of burning brimstone for sinners. Much of the evangelism, of course, was more restrained. In either case, the purpose was the same, to persuade people to repent their sins, regenerate their souls, and join the churches. As a result, many American schools and colleges of the Enlightenment stressed religious beliefs more than the new political ideals of the impending revolution. The hold of the churches upon American education was made much more firm, and that hold was maintained much longer than would have been the case without the Great Awakening. New colleges and new secondary schools were hammered out in the crucible of religious revivalism.

DENOMINATIONAL, PRIVATE, AND CIVIL CONTROL OF EDUCATION

The over-all picture of educational control in eighteenth-century America is complicated and confused, but certain general patterns can be detected. For the most part, denominational control of schools continued to be predominant. However, the new commercial interests produced new types of private schools taught in English and emphasizing appropriate practical subjects. Later in the century the political motive came to the fore, and proposals were made that the new states should sponsor public education. Some writers even proposed that the new federal government should support and control education for democratic purposes.

Denominational Control of Schools

As would be natural, the inherited traditions of Reformation times remained strong in the American colonies of the early eighteenth century, and consequently it was generally considered proper that education was a function of the churches. With the exception of Rhode Island, the established Congregational Church provided stimulus for education in the New England colonies through colonial and town laws. In New York and the southern colonies the Church of England made some efforts at expanding education through legal means. Outside of New England the most important means of providing education came to be the Society for the Propagation of the Gospel in Foreign Parts, which established many free schools under Anglican auspices in virtually all the 13 colonies. These beginnings of philanthropic, charity education for poor and underprivileged children were greatly accelerated by the religious enthusiasms of the Great Awakening.

As thousands of people flooded into the several denominational churches, the strength and material wealth of the churches were greatly increased. With the emotions of altruism, philanthropy, and religious zeal for spreading the gospel thus awakened, the people were more than ever ready to pour money into establishing religious schools and colleges. Extensive campaigns to establish schools were carried on by the various Protestant denominations, Presbyterian, Dutch Reformed, Anglican, Congregational, Lutheran, Moravian, Mennonite, Quaker, Baptist, and Methodist. The philanthropic motive combined with religious fervor produced the denominational form of school control.

As an outgrowth of the Enlightenment ideal of religious liberty, America accepted the idea that churches could put this liberty into effect by providing their own schools. In this sense denominational control of education was a great victory for religious tolerance. It is also true, however, that in time to come the religious control of schools was to stand in the way of the idea that education should be under public control for all children, regardless of creed. America is still struggling with the problem of reconciling secular education under civil control with the demands of the churches for religious instruction.

Private Control of Schools

In addition to the increased trend toward denominational control of education in the middle of the eighteenth century, there appeared a new type of private-venture school which provided a secular education in subjects that would be useful and practical for the expanding occupations of a commercial society. These private schools were established principally in the coast towns of the eastern seaboard, where commerce and trade were becoming so important, in Boston, New Haven, New York, Philadelphia, Baltimore, and elsewhere. The private schoolmasters were responsible, not to the churches or to the towns, but only to their clientele, consisting of prospective merchants, clerks, bookkeepers, accountants, mechanics, engineers, and seamen. Such schools had largely disappeared by Revolutionary times, but their influence was strong, for their ideals of practical usefulness were absorbed by a still newer type of school, the academy, which was to make a much greater mark upon American education.

With the appearance of the academy a new form of school control appeared on the scene. The private-venture schoolmaster just referred to was an individual enterpriser seeking students where he could and adapting himself to various interests of the people. There was, however, no continuity or formal organization to carry on his work when he passed from the scene. Therefore, in the middle of the eighteenth century, the incorporated type of private school took form. Typically, a group of men were organized into a board of trustees along the model of English commercial corporations. The state would then grant a charter to this board of trustees, constituting it a corporation and authorizing it to own property, receive money, endowments, and bequests, and conduct the affairs and control the policy of a school. Many such corporate boards were granted the right by the state to be self-perpetuating.

Such schools were thus able to maintain continuity, achieve permanence, and build distinctive traditions. Typical ones were the William Penn Charter School and Franklin's Academy in Pennsylvania, the Newark Academy in Delaware, the Washington Academy in New Jersey, the Dummer Academy and Phillips Academy in Massachusetts, and the

Union School at New London, Conn. Henceforth, the private corporate school was to become an important aspect of American education. The state had formally delegated part of its authority over education to private institutions. How much *control* the state should exercise over these private schools proved a matter of much controversy.

Civil Control of Education

Town and District Control. Just as the states delegated some of their authority in education to denominational and private groups, so they began to delegate some of the management of their public schools to smaller units. The pattern of town control of schools in New England had been established in Massachusetts by the school laws of 1642 and 1647 and by similar laws in Connecticut and New Hampshire. Now, in the eighteenth century, a trend toward greater decentralization of state control took form. The district school system became a new educational pattern for generations to come.

During the eighteenth century people pushed back from the seacoast to settle in the rural frontier regions of Massachusetts, Connecticut, New Hampshire, and Vermont. As settlements were made on isolated farms or on the outskirts of the central towns, the town schools become less convenient for the children of the backwoodsmen; furthermore, the back-country farmers saw little value in the town Latin schools. To be sure, they wanted elementary education for their children, but they did not want to pay for Latin schools that their children would probably not attend.

The outlying districts therefore proceeded to supply their own elementary schools through their local committees and selectmen, just as they provided churches and built roads and bridges. Inasmuch as the New England town included the surrounding rural area as well as the inhabited central town, these districts, or parishes, were still a part of the larger town authority, but they began to agitate for greater control over their own local or district schools.

At first the town teacher would travel from one district to another and spend a part of his time each year in the outlying districts. This arrangement has sometimes been called the "moving school." The teacher was hired and paid by the town authorities. Later, the districts sometimes obtained an arrangement whereby the town appointed and paid several teachers, one of whom was to spend all his time in one district. This was sometimes called the "divided school." Finally, the districts achieved full legal autonomy and authority over their own schools in the Massachusetts law of 1789. Thus, decentralized control was achieved in New England. The districts thereafter were free to build their own schoolhouses, appoint the teachers, set the length of school terms, and control the curriculum. By 1800 the local districts were empowered to levy taxes to support their schools.

The growth of the district system was distinctly a frontier and make-shift arrangement, suitable for an agrarian society where other governmental agencies could not function, population was scattered, and communication was difficult. As people moved from New England westward in the nineteenth century, they carried the district system of schools with them, but it soon showed its limitations. Its aspirations were low, its funds restricted by the resources of the neighborhood, and its ability to provide equal educational opportunity for all American youth exceedingly limited. Yet it elicited great loyalty and enthusiasm, and the "little red schoolhouse" has become a part of American folklore. This spirit fought the idea of state control of education in the nineteenth century and has fought federal support of education in the twentieth century.

State Interest in Education. Whereas the actual control of education was increasingly in local hands, the *idea* of state control of education began to gain greater headway as the political struggles of the Revolutionary period progressed. To be sure, nearly every colonial legislature before the Revolution had passed some laws concerning education, but outside of New England they had amounted to little. For example, the attempts of the colonial legislatures in New York and Pennsylvania to establish public schools broke down in the face of the influx of varied religious sects, each stimulated by the Great Awakening to run its own denominational schools. This pattern prevailed in the middle and southern colonies, just as the district system prevailed in New England, but the growing interest of the states in public education before the end of the eighteenth century was a force later to be reckoned with.

The outstanding spokesman for state control of education in America before 1800 was Thomas Jefferson. Accepting the French ideals of humanitarianism, natural rights, equality, and liberty, Jefferson introduced into the Virginia legislature in 1779 a comprehensive document for the reform of the state's institutions. His bills called for the repeal of the laws of primogeniture and entail and abolished taxation for the established Church of England. Jefferson also advocated a state system of free universal education as a corollary to these political, economic, and religious reforms. His bill proposed that free elementary schools be established throughout the state to provide secular education for all children. Secondary schools for the more intelligent youth should be maintained at state expense. The most promising should then be sent free to a reorganized and enlarged College of William and Mary, which would become in effect a state university to cap the state system. Jefferson's plan for education was not adopted by the Virginia legislature largely through the opposition of religious groups and the College of William and Mary. But the ideal of free universal education had been stated, and it was later to achieve success in most American states in the nineteenth century.

When the colonies were reorganizing themselves as states during the Revolution, several of them expressed interest in education. Approximately half of the first state constitutions mentioned education, stating that schools were needed and should be established or in some cases simply that schools should be cheap. Likewise, the early laws of some of the states made provision for establishing schools, in a range from secular schools to pauper and parochial schools; but some states had taken no action whatever by 1800.

Outside of New England the most comprehensive attempt to establish a state-wide system of education was made by New York when the University of the State of New York was established in 1784 as an administrative agency to exert control over the academies and Columbia College. New York also appropriated state money for aid to schools in 1795, and more than a thousand schools were established; but the time was not yet ripe for state support of education, for the money was withdrawn in 1800. Headway was being made but slowly. The ideal of public education under state control had to wait for nearly half a century before it could be fully realized with the help of Horace Mann, Henry Barnard, and other school reformers.

Federal Interest in Education. Scarcely had independence been assured when a flood of pamphlets, articles, and essays began to set forth new theories of educational control for the new republic. The public discussion of education was stimulated by the American Philosophical Society, which offered a prize for the best description of a liberal education suitable to the new United States. Most of the writers who engaged in this contest were imbued with the French humanitarian doctrines of the perfectibility of man and the possibility of social progress by reforming social institutions, of which education was deemed one of the most important. The currents of thought represented by liberalism, democracy, and nationalism were caught up in these theories and focused upon American education.

Samuel Knox, Samuel Harrison Smith, Benjamin Rush, and Robert Coram argued that education should be practical, flexible, and adaptable to new conditions. It should be democratic and universally free to all in order to provide equal opportunity and prepare citizens for their responsibilities in a democracy. It should embrace a complete system of elementary, secondary, and higher institutions under national control and federal support in order to contribute to secular rather than religious outcomes and to ensure the greatest progress toward social welfare. President

Washington was much interested in a national university as a means of unifying the new country and proposed to Congress that it be established. He even set aside some 50 shares in the Potomac Canal Company to help subsidize the university, but nothing ever came of the idea, despite subsequent proposals by other presidents and leaders.

It is interesting to note that these theories of national education were not put into practice. The tradition of religious and decentralized control of education was too strong to allow the federal government to set up a national system of schools; yet some steps were taken that were to have great influence upon American education. While the American states were operating under the Articles of Confederation, two ordinances were passed concerning the disposition of the vast public lands in the West, the claims to which the various states had given up to the federal government.

The Ordinance of 1785 established a policy for the sale of this public land. It provided that the land should be surveyed into square plots 6 miles on a side, to be known as townships. Each township was to be further divided into 36 sections, or squares, 1 mile on a side. The income from the sale of the sixteenth section, located in the center of each township, was to be used for common schools when the land was sold.

Two years later the Ordinance of 1787 confirmed this land policy and set forth the governmental principles to be followed when the Northwest Territory was settled (an area represented by the present states of Ohio, Indiana, Illinois, Michigan, Wisconsin, and part of Minnesota). The ordinance provided that the states carved out of this territory should assure free religious conscience, trial by jury, prohibition of slavery or involuntary servitude, good faith with the Indians, and common schools.

What might be called the charter of public concern for education was contained in the following famous sentence: "Religion, morality, and knowledge being necessary to good government and the happiness of mankind, schools and the means of education shall forever be encouraged." This meant that the income from the sixteenth sections would be dispensed by civil authorities and therefore some of the support of common schools would come from public sources. Important policies on education were thus being formulated by the federal government even though a national system of education was not established.

When the Constitution was drawn up and ratified in 1789, no mention of education was made in it. Apparently most of the members of the Constitutional Convention felt that other matters were of more pressing concern. Many considered education properly to be a function of the churches and of local or state government rather than of the national government. The Federalists were interested in a strong federal government but not in education for the common people; therefore they did not desire national education. The Anti-Federalists were interested in education for the common people but opposed a strong national government; therefore they did not want national control of education.

Even the Bill of Rights did not mention education directly. But the First Amendment guaranteed religious liberty, which the churches took to include the right to conduct schools, and the Tenth Amendment reserved to the states or to the people all powers not delegated by the Constitution to the federal government or prohibited by it. This was later interpreted to mean that the states could assert their rights to establish and maintain schools. By ignoring the opportunity for federal support of education, the framers of the Constitution made it difficult for the states to put into practice their legal right to control education and for the federal government to win the right to support general education.

Types of School Support

The sources of revenue for American schools in the eighteenth century were varied and often complicated. In general, schools were supported in two principal ways: (1) direct payment by parents for the education of their own children, primarily by tuition fees and rate bills, and (2) direct or indirect means that helped to educate other children as well as one's own. Fees were paid to teachers of dame schools, to parish priests in the South, to private tutors, to teachers of private Latin grammar schools, to teachers of the private-venture schools, to the academies, and to the colleges. Rate bills were of the same general nature except that they were the fees paid by parents whose children went to town schools set up by civil authorities. Rate bills were usually fixed *pro rata* according to the length of time the child attended in relation to the total expenses of the school.

The second type of support involved a good many methods of indirect help. Individuals gave money, land, or income-producing property of various kinds to private schools, to specific charity schools, to churches for the support of their schools, or to such school societies as the Society for the Propagation of the Gospel in Foreign Parts. These gifts, bequests, and endowments were put into the operation of the schools to help defray expenses; poor children were often given free or charity education, whereas parents who could afford to pay were charged tuition.

The civil authorities used a variety of means to support schools, including local taxes, income from land grants, appropriations from general funds, the proceeds of licenses, and taxes on liquor, peddling, and lotteries. These funds were often given by civil authorities to private and religious schools as well as to town and public schools. For example, the state of Massachusetts in 1797 gave land grants to certain private academies, and other states did likewise. Colleges as well as lower schools were often the recipients of governmental aid. Near the end of the century some states began to set aside "common school funds" into which they would put a variety of revenues to be used for the benefit of the public schools.

Control of Higher Education

The principal stimulus to higher education during most of the eighteenth century came from the churches. The Great Awakening prompted denominations to set up colleges that would provide a setting favorable to their faiths and would aid the training of ministers in their particular beliefs. Princeton was founded by the Presbyterians of New Jersey in 1746, King's College (Columbia) by the Anglicans of New York in 1754, Brown by the Baptists of Rhode Island in 1764, Rutgers by the Dutch Reformed of New Jersey in 1766; and Dartmouth by the Congregationalists of New Hampshire in 1769. The College of Philadelphia, built upon Franklin's Academy, was given a charter in 1755. Together with Harvard, William and Mary, and Yale, these colleges comprised the institutions of higher education founded in the colonies before the Revolution.

Two trends of great importance to American higher education took place in the control of colleges before 1800. The first was the increase in power of the corporate board of trustees, which became the full legal authority for the colleges. When Harvard was founded, the corporation consisting of the president, treasurer, and five resident tutors was intended to be a full legal governing body, having all the powers of a corporation at law. This followed the British models in which the faculty was the autonomous, self-governing university. Gradually, however, the Harvard Corporation came to be made up of nonresident members, and control began to shift from the faculty to this nonresident board. Much the same sort of development took place at William and Mary during the eighteenth century. When Yale was founded, the nonresident governing board was made up of 10 ministers and did not even include the president until 1745. Most of the other colleges followed this pattern, doubtless reflecting the desire of the churches to keep a fairly close watch over the affairs of the colleges. Despite considerable actual autonomy often given to the resident faculty, the legal authority remained with the nonresident board.

The second noteworthy trend in college control came with the upswing of republican and democratic ideals following the Revolution. Impressed by the humanitarian arguments for a complete system of education under state control from the lowest schools to a university at the top, the democratic forces took what seemed to them a logical step, namely, to transform the private, religious colleges into state institutions. Spectacular but little known battles raged over this issue from the middle of the eighteenth century on. Harvard, William and Mary, and Yale resisted successfully several attempts by the states to increase their control. A bitter struggle took place in Connecticut as an outgrowth of the religious revivals and the antagonisms between the "Old Lights" and "New Lights." Yale College had remained staunchly Calvinistic and conservative, whereas the New Light forces of revivalism felt that Yale should be more responsive to the religious needs of the revivalistic groups, inasmuch as it received public moneys paid by all groups alike. But President Thomas Clap won the battle, insisting that Yale was a private autonomous college and not a public institution and therefore had the right to require strict religious discipline of its students, no matter what religious views their parents might hold.

If Virginia had followed Jefferson's lead in 1779, the College of William and Mary might have become one of the earliest state universities. Indeed, the very first state university might have been achieved in New York in the 1750's had the battle over the founding of King's College turned out differently. Two factions were in conflict. One, representing the Church of England and the Tory classes loyal to the crown, wanted the college to be founded by royal charter. The other, representing Presbyterian, dissenting, and democratic forces under the leadership of William Livingston, wanted the college to be founded by enactment of the colonial legislature. The plans of the latter group could have made King's College virtually a nonsectarian state university, but the "church party" won the fight for a royal charter, as the original name of Columbia University so clearly reveals.

New York State did move toward greater state control of higher education, however, when the legislature created the Regents of the University of the State of New York in 1784. Under this law, the Regents were essentially a private corporation which could found colleges, give them the right to grant degrees, and inspect the conduct of their affairs. Columbia was included in the "University" and was given special privileges. By 1787, however, New York made the Regents a full-fledged state agency for the visitation, inspection, and regulation of higher education. Columbia's special status was removed by this act. From this time forward, the Regents took special cognizance of academies as well as colleges in their jurisdiction over higher education. Again this control amounted principally to visitation, inspection, and report to the legislature, rather than the actual management of higher institutions. Genuine state control of elementary education awaited the nineteenth century, and a genuine system of higher education under state control in New York awaited the twentieth century.

When the college in Philadelphia, which had originally been nonsectarian, came under Anglican and Tory control, the democratic forces in Pennsylvania in 1779 set out to convert it into the University of the State of Pennsylvania. The old college, however, refused to give up its charter and continued to exist for 10 years alongside the state university. In 1789, when the religious and political interests in the state were realigned, the original college was given back its charter. After 2 years of struggle the Presbyterians became so powerful that the two institutions were merged in 1791 into the University of Pennsylvania, a private and independent institution, which it has since remained.

Meanwhile, the democratic forces began to establish new institutions created from the beginning as state universities. Four were established before 1800, in Georgia, North Carolina, Vermont, and Tennessee, notably in states where no colonial religious college had been established. The real impetus for state universities, however, arose in the nineteenth century.

Status of the Teaching Profession

It was only natural that the strong religious character of American schools in the eighteenth century should mean that the most common qualification for teaching was religious orthodoxy. Academic qualifications ranged from the ability to read and write to a college education. The qualifications of secondary school teachers were usually higher than those of elementary teachers. In many instances, loyalty to the existing government was expected, and other qualifications were usually good moral character, "sober conversation," and, in general, an exemplary personal life as a guide for the pupils.

In colonies and states where religious control of schools was uppermost the local clergy and higher church officials were usually charged with the appointment and supervision of teachers. In New England, where civil control was dominant, the local town meeting, selectmen, or school committee took the responsibility for appointment and supervision, although the local minister often had the power of approval as well. It was common for citizens to visit the schools, observe their conduct, and judge the achievements of pupils as displayed in public ceremonies or on special occasions. The interest of the citizens and parents of a community in what went on in their schools was early present in American education and helped to set the pattern of public concern for schools. This had the advantage of keeping the schools close to the people but also raised the knotty problem of how to achieve a balance between the public's interest in education and the teaching profession's responsibility for the conduct of schools.

During the eighteenth century, pay for teachers, still quite low, took varied forms. Teachers were paid in money (often at irregular intervals), in services such as "boarding around," in gifts or produce, or in exemptions from taxes. The social respect accorded to teachers was doubtless higher than their salaries, even as now. Schoolteaching was often considered a part-time job to be performed along with other religious or civic duties or while a young man was waiting to go into law, the ministry, or some other more lucrative profession.

Out-of-school Education

The agencies of public enlightenment and the dissemination of knowledge gained great headway during the eighteenth century. The reading public expanded rapidly. More than 30 newspapers were being published by the time of the Revolution, books were published in several centers, and a mass of pamphlets was being issued. Franklin's efforts in the newspaper field and in the publishing of his *Poor Richard's Almanac* were representative of many others. Paine's stirring pamphlets had wide circulation; these, along with the propaganda efforts of Sam Adams, helped mold public opinion in the Revolutionary cause. Several noteworthy private libraries and many public libraries were founded. Of the societies established for the wider dissemination of knowledge, the most important was the American Philosophical Society founded in 1769. The New England town meeting became an influential center where people could express their opinions, debate public issues, carry on public discussion, and make decisions of common concern. Vocational education was commonly acquired, as it had been for centuries, in the process of apprenticeship, which was extended by state and local laws.

ORTHODOXY AND RATIONALISM IN AMERICAN THOUGHT

Christian Orthodoxy

By and large, the dominant conceptions of the world and of man's place in it continued to be shaped largely by the tradition of Christian theism, especially by Calvinist orthodoxy. The doctrine of innate depravity, promulgated by Cotton Mather early in the century, was reaffirmed by Jonathan Edwards, the most outstanding spokesman for the conservative theological position in the middle of the century. Edwards pictured a universe completely controlled by an angry God who manipulates the world for purposes of granting salvation to the elect and meting out eternal punishment to sinners. He rejected the idea of free will and insisted that God exerts complete control over man's will and destiny. He rejected the Arminian notions that man can be saved by a life of good works and argued that man can be saved only by conversion. He took up the cudgels against the conception of man as a part of nature and viewed "natural man" as sinful and evil.

Edwards applied his doctrines of original sin directly to children. He defended the revivalistic preachers who deliberately used the terrors of hell and damnation to make children conscious of their sins and to seek salvation by repentance and conversion. He told approvingly of a little girl, Phebe Bartlett, who was so affected by his own preaching that she spent her days and nights closeted in her room praying, reciting her catechism, talking incessantly with other children about death and salvation, or being seized with fits of hysterical crying.

Not all religious thought was so extreme by any means. The reactions against a rather harsh Calvinism began to grow by leaps and bounds. The Baptists, Quakers, and German Pietists gained strength with their emphasis upon individual faith and piety. On the other hand, the Wesleyan movement advanced rapidly in the latter parts of the eighteenth century as people responded to Methodism and its emphasis upon good works and human effort as the road to salvation. Within Congregationalism itself were found more liberal spokesmen in favor of a greater role for human reason, and greater reliance upon God's mercy and benevolence, along with revelation, as a means of salvation. Such were John Wise, Jonathan Mayhew, and Charles Chauncey. These views were likely to take a more humane and sympathetic view toward child nature. Gentleness and tenderness toward children found expression in the writings of the Quaker John Woolman, the Anglican Samuel Johnson, and the Mennonite Christopher Dock.

Rationalism

The still more liberal doctrines of rationalism in religion pictured the universe as a safer and better place for man than Edwards would allow. By the end of the century these doctrines began to take the shape of Unitarianism, which rejected the doctrines of special election and original sin and began to preach the inherent goodness of human nature and the indefinite perfectibility of man along the lines of French humanitarianism. The Unitarians rejected the theology of Trinitarianism and spoke of Christ not as divine but as a great human teacher. They stressed God's beneficence and sympathy rather than fear of His wrath and punishment. They emphasized the humanitarian, rational, and ethical qualities of religion rather than the divine, the dogmatic, and the theological. As these liberal views began to win recognition, more room was made for individual responsibility in religion and less room for the witch hunts, the persecutions, and the intolerances of the early period. In this respect the Enlightenment was living up to its name.

Still more radical than Unitarianism was the scientific religion known as Deism which gained some sympathetic reception in America late in the eighteenth century. Deists could not give up the conception of God but neither could they adhere to the belief in a jealous or angry God who visited punishments upon His wretched creatures. Indeed, they could not think of man as wretched or conceived in sin. They had faith in man's essential dignity and decency. Deists were impatient, too, with the theo-

tury progressed the medical profession began to avail itself of some of the mounting interest in science and to achieve a higher position in public estimation. Much of the medical world remained, however, at the level of quackery and nostrums. Special instruction in medicine was established at the College of Philadelphia in 1765, at King's College in 1767, and at Harvard in 1782. As early as the 1720's, smallpox inoculations were introduced in Massachusetts, but a great battle was aroused between science and religion. Medical science had to win its way gradually against great odds.

Early in the eighteenth century there was a strong prejudice against lawyers, who were looked upon as tricksters and sycophants. However, as legal arguments based upon natural law and natural rights began to gain a hearing, the lawyer began to find a larger place in American life. By 1730 there were some 30 lawyers in New York City, some of whom joined together to form a small bar association. The real emergence of the legal profession occurred as business and commerce created a greater demand for lawyers. By the middle of the century, legal advice became virtually necessary for the businessmen, merchants, and landowners as more complicated forms of corporation and partnership were developed, as land titles came up for dispute, and as business agreements needed adjudication. The Albany convention in 1754 signalized the fact that lawyers would thereafter take a leading role in shaping public opinion. The clergy began to lose its preeminent place to men like Patrick Henry, Thomas Jefferson, John Adams, William Livingston, and many others.

THE LIBERALIZING OF EDUCATION

New Aims Added to Old

The religious, Humanistic, and rationalistic aims that had shaped early colonial schools remained strong during the eighteenth century. The religious motivation of Reformation times was given further impetus by the evangelism and religious revivalism of the Great Awakening; the Humanistic motivation for the study of the classics held its place in the Latin grammar schools and in the new colleges; and the rationalistic motivation behind the linguistic, bookish, and mathematical studies remained strong. However, the new currents of political, economic, and scientific thought of the European Enlightenment were entering American education, not yet to challenge the superiority of the other aims, but gaining headway and finding such support that they were ready to challenge and even surpass them in the nineteenth century.

The political forces of democracy and nationalism began to affect educational theory to such an extent that some American leaders, as already noted, began to say that education in a democracy should be available to larger numbers of citizens. Despite the sentiments of democracy, however, the Latin grammar schools and most colleges maintained their essentially aristocratic character, and therefore it was left to the new private-venture schools and academies to meet the need for extending educational opportunity to wider groups in society. The economic influence of commercial capitalism took the form of a demand for more practical studies that would prepare for a life of useful occupations. When these demands met with little response from the Latin grammar schools and colleges, new institutions arose to serve these purposes.

The scientific outlooks likewise began to make themselves felt in education in various ways. Deism began to filter into some of the colleges as a reaction against the highly charged emotionalism of the Great Awakening. A good deal of religious skepticism appeared in some of the colleges in the 1790's along with such "radical" religious doctrines as Unitarianism. The scientific impact also began to be felt in the acceptance in some quarters of the empiricism and sense realism that stemmed from Comenius, Francke, and Locke. These expressed themselves most typically in a greater attention to the study of science in the private schools and some of the colleges.

Elementary Instruction

The elementary schools of the eighteenth century were essentially schools to teach young children the elements of English "letters" and religion; literacy was the prime goal, as achieved through reading religious materials. Little more was attempted, and little more was accomplished. Occasionally some writing and arithmetic were taught. More commonly, these subjects were taught in separate "writing" schools, which in general were considered to be somewhat more advanced than the reading schools. Reading was taught in the New England town schools, in the dame schools, by private tutors, in denominational schools, and in the charity schools of the Society for the Propagation of the Gospel in Foreign Parts.

The most influential of the reading books used was the *New England Primer*, which was based upon primers printed in England. First published in America just before the beginning of the eighteenth century, the *New England Primer* went through many editions by the end of the century. It illustrates above all how learning to read was thoroughly imbued with religious sentiments. It commonly began with the alphabet in capital and small letters, followed by lists of syllables and of words emphasizing moral concepts. Little children learned their letters by memorizing such words as abusing, bewitching, confounded, drunkenness, faculty, godliness, impudent, everlasting, fidelity, glorifying, and humility.

Then came the famous woodcuts illustrating the letters of the alphabet and accompanied by religious and moralistic rhymes, many of them reflecting the gloomy outlook of Puritanism. Reading material followed, usually under such headings as "The Dutiful Child's Promises" and "An Alphabet of Lessons for Youth," and including the Lord's Prayer, the Apostles' Creed, the Ten Commandments, the names of the books of the Old and New Testaments, religious verses and stories, and finally the Westminster catechism. The Roman and Arabic numerals were learned as a means "for the ready finding of any Chapter, Psalm, and Verse in the Bible." (For illustrations from the *Primer*, see pp. 258–259.)

Later in the century newer editions of the *New England Primer* began to reflect patriotic sentiments commensurate with the outlook of the new nation. For example, the early rhyme describing the letter K and expressing loyalty to the king of England had read, "Our King the Good, No man of blood." After the Revolution, patriotism became the motif: "Kings should be good, Not men of blood," "The British King, Lost states thirteen," or "Queens and Kings, Are gaudy things." Other changes reflected patriotic and nationalist sentiments; "Whales in the sea, God's voice obey" became "Great Washington brave, His country did save."

Not only did the patriotic motif begin to appear after the Revolution, but also a good deal of secular material was inserted. Stories about punishments for bad boys and girls no longer involved eternal suffering in hell but stressed the withholding of oranges, apples, cakes, and nuts. Furthermore, the practical values of learning to read began to replace its use in reading the Bible. For example, the *New England Primer* exhorted pupils in the following manner:

> He who ne'er learns his A.B.C.
> Forever will a blockhead be.
> But he who learns his letters fair
> Shall have a coach to take the air.

The *Primer* began to lose ground after the Revolution as more sprightly reading books appeared, one of the most famous of which was Noah Webster's "blue-backed speller" entitled *Elementary Spelling Book*. Emphasizing moralistic and patriotic sentences, the book was a popular favorite among primers for a hundred years after its publication in 1784. The secularizing of the elementary school curriculum, thus begun during the eighteenth century, was to make much more rapid strides in the nineteenth century.

Whereas relatively little attention was probably given to the improvement of teaching methods in the elementary schools, there is some evidence of a beginning of concern in this respect. As early as 1706 the Society for the Propagation of the Gospel in Foreign Parts issued rather elaborate instructions to its Anglican teachers. They were told what subjects to teach (reading, writing, arithmetic, catechism, prayers, and worship), and they were told to develop in their charges good manners and the virtues of honesty and truth. Especially interesting were the instructions to be kind and gentle to the children and to be sparing with corporal punishment.

Similarly, the Quaker teacher, Anthony Benezet, advocated patient understanding of innocent child nature, special attention to different aptitudes, and emphasis upon the pleasant and interesting rather than upon laborious drudgery. The most elaborate and perhaps the first entire book written in America on schoolteaching was that of Christopher Dock, a Mennonite schoolmaster in Pennsylvania. He described at length how he taught his children at different age and ability levels, appealed to their desire for praise and avoidance of blame rather than fear of the rod, and in general tried to instill a common understanding, sympathy, and mutual love between pupil and teacher. "Soft pedagogy" is at least 150 years old and deep in the American religious and educational tradition—but not as old nor as deep as the harsher puritanical strain of pedagogy.

New Types of Secondary Instruction

At the opening of the eighteenth century the dominant secondary school was the Latin grammar school taught by the public schoolmasters in the town schools of New England and by private tutors or religious teachers in other parts of the country. It was basically a college-preparatory institution, designed primarily to give its students a grounding in Latin grammar. It was thus essentially aristocratic, for only a relatively few boys could expect to go to college. Gradually, the secular aspects of life began to demand a newer type of secondary education. Two types of schools arose to meet these interests. The first was the private-venture school. The second type, known as the academy, came to dominate the field of secondary education by the end of the century.

Private-venture Schools. Responding to the interests of the rising commercial and trading classes early in the eighteenth century, many schoolmasters began to teach practical subjects that had greater and more direct vocational value than the classics. The basic language of their so-called "private schools" was English; thus, for the first time in America there was a conscious attempt to adapt educational institutions to a changing social situation. Inasmuch as their aim was not primarily preparation for college, the curriculum of these schools was not prescribed or circumscribed by college-entrance requirements. Rather, they were free to offer any courses for which there was a demand or for which a demand could be created.

The private schools were more flexible than the Latin grammar schools; they admitted anyone who wished to study and pay the fees, adults as well as youth, girls as well as boys. Students took whatever courses they felt would be valuable to them. Hence a kind of elective system was inaugurated, for there was no diploma or degree or prescribed curriculum. Classes were held at whatever hours students could come, early in the morning before working hours, at the noon hour, late in the afternoon, or in the evening after working hours. As a result, young people could go to school while they worked. A broadened clientele of middle-class youth made these schools more democratic than the Latin grammar

Fig. 21. Boston Latin School (1748–1810).

schools, which remained highly selective in character by reason of their more highly specialized college-entrance aim.

High on the list of studies taught by the private schools were the commercial subjects (bookkeeping, accounting, penmanship, and commercial arithmetic) designed to prepare clerks, accountants, bookkeepers, merchants, and bankers for jobs in business and trade. The mathematical subjects also were taught for their vocational usefulness in such increasingly important occupations as navigation and civil and military engineering. In many cases the mathematical teaching in the private schools was fully as good as that found in some of the colleges. The mathematical subjects included algebra, geometry, astronomy, trigonometry, calculus, navigation, surveying, optics, fortifications, and gunnery.

The modern languages, which found little acceptance in colleges or Latin grammar schools, were also quite common in the private schools—French as the polite language of high society, and Italian, Spanish, and Portuguese as the commercial languages of importance. Geography and history were widely advertised as of general value for everyone and of special value to traders and navigators. In addition, the private schools offered the classics for any who wished to prepare for college. The private schools thus did much to develop the "practical" and "modern" subjects that were disparaged for so long by classical Humanists.

The private schools were more democratic than the Latin grammar schools in another sense: they opened their doors for advanced education to girls. Some private schools allowed girls to attend with boys, some held special classes for girls, and others catered particularly to girls. The most common subjects for girls were reading, writing, arithmetic, geography, and French, but many other subjects were also offered in different schools —the general subjects of English grammar, history, and Latin; the vocational subjects of bookkeeping, accounting, and the modern languages; and the "polite" accomplishments of drawing, painting, singing, instrumental music, sewing, and penmanship. Hence, the groundwork of education for girls was being laid, upon which were later built the academies for girls, the "female seminaries," and eventually the colleges for women.

Franklin's Academy. As early as 1743 Benjamin Franklin had first proposed the establishment of an academy in Philadelphia, but he really pressed the matter in 1749 when he circulated his *Proposals Relating to the Education of Youth in Pennsylvania* and set out to collect funds for its foundation. The academy was finally given a charter by the state in 1753, and to it was added a charter for a college in 1755, from which developed the University of Pennsylvania. In his outline for an academy Franklin embodied the prevailing tendency of the private schools to offer utilitarian subjects for vocational preparation as well as classical languages for college preparation. He proposed that the new academy should have three departments, English, Latin, and mathematics; students should be allowed to choose their course according to the several occupations or professions for which they were preparing.

Benjamin Franklin's proposals included a wide range and variety of subjects that were in sharp contrast to the rather limited curriculum of the Latin grammar schools. Franklin proposed writing and drawing; arithmetic and accounts; geometry and astronomy; English grammar, composition, and literature; rhetoric and oratory; logic; history (universal and national history, ancient customs, moral, religious, and political); ancient and modern languages (Greek, Latin, German, French, Spanish); sciences (observation, experimentation, and natural history); history of invention, commerce, and manufacturing; and agriculture, gardening, and mechanics. Franklin further proposed that the academy be surrounded by gardens, meadows, and an orchard for use by the students in their studies and for physical exercise. Furthermore, the academy should be well equipped with a library, maps, mathematical instruments, and scientific apparatus.

It is apparent that Franklin represented the European influences of empiricism, sense realism, and the new science as well as his own experimental, commercial, and utilitarian interests. Significantly, also, he made no mention of religious or sectarian instruction, except for the history of religion, which was well within the deistic outlook. In practice, the academy did not work out as Franklin had planned, for some time later he was complaining that the English school had been subordinated to the Latin school. The classical tradition and college-entrance requirements proved to be too strong even for Franklin, and his academy became virtually another college-preparatory institution. Nevertheless, another step had been taken in the promotion of the practical, the modern, and the scientific studies. When other academies appeared, they had advanced considerably beyond the traditional Latin grammar school.

The Academy Movement. Although the private-venture schools had met a need, they apparently had gone too far in their departure from the classical and religious traditions of the Latin grammar schools. The theory behind Franklin's academy had been to combine the practical and modern with the classical, but he too had gone too far, for he had left out the religious element. The institutions that actually replaced the Latin grammar school were the academies, which absorbed into themselves the principal influences of the Enlightenment in America, not only the classical, the practical, and the scientific, but the religious as well.

The academies that were to have real influence were founded in the later part of the eighteenth century by the churches or by individuals with strong religious interests. The Dissenters' Academies in England had shown that religious schools could have a broad curriculum, and the Great Awakening gave the American impetus to establishing such schools for religious as well as practical purposes. The classics were also included, for the promoters of the academies wanted their children to be able to go on to college. In general, the academies combined the aims of college preparation with religious piety and vocational efficiency.

The academies differed in other respects from the Latin grammar schools and the private schools. They were usually boarding schools in which the students lived together away from home. Academies for girls also soon became common. The academies often came to be local substitutes for colleges. Indeed many of them were sooner or later transformed into colleges. Commonly, too, they were nonpublic institutions, supported by tuition from parents or by endowment from churches and from wealthy individuals. Support also came from several of the states, as the academies caught the public fancy and became centers of the deliberate efforts to train teachers.

Despite their private character, the academies were more liberal than the Latin grammar schools because of their wider appeal, their broader and more elastic curriculum, and their more inclusive aims. They helped to introduce into the secondary school curriculum English grammar, composition, and literature, English rhetoric, history, mathematics, the modern languages, some commercial subjects, and, especially for girls, the social arts of dancing, music, drawing, and needlework.

As the newer subjects became popular, there was greater demand for more textbooks in these fields. The first text in English grammar used in America was Thomas Dilworth's *New Guide to the English Tongue*. Soon American authors tried their hands at writing English grammars; the first of these authors were college teachers—Hugh Jones, professor at William and Mary, and Samuel Johnson, president of King's College. The most influential grammars, however, were written by Noah Webster and Lindley Murray late in the century.

The most noteworthy textbook in arithmetic was written by Isaac Greenwood, private schoolmaster and professor of mathematics at Harvard College, the title of whose book, published in 1729, revealed his practical outlook—*Arithmetic Vulgar and Decimal with the Application thereof to a Variety of Cases in Trade and Commerce*. History began to gain more attention, especially in the texts on reading and geography. Noah Webster inserted a good deal of historical material into his reader, and Jedidiah Morse included a good deal in his *Geography* published late in the century. Other texts began to appear in the commercial subjects, practical mathematics, and modern languages.

The Enlightenment and Great Awakening in Higher Education

During the eighteenth century, the Enlightenment concerns for science and practical utility gradually began to affect the religious outlook and curriculum of some of the colleges, but most of the colonial colleges held fairly strictly to the religious, Humanistic, and rationalistic aims of earlier days.

Liberalism at Harvard. Under the presidencies of John Leverett and Edward Holyoke from 1708 to 1769, Harvard's Congregationalism began to be affected by eighteenth-century Deism and Unitarianism. Holyoke's liberalism was enough to make the stricter Calvinists suspect Harvard and to provoke the overseers to try to extract oaths of orthodoxy from the tutors and to censor commencement theses. Despite such inspection and the return to fundamentalism demanded by the Great Awakening, Harvard maintained its liberal trend, while Yale, Princeton, and other colleges followed the popular evangelistic sectarianism of the Great Awakening.

By the beginning of the eighteenth century, the new Enlightenment science had begun to creep into the traditional studies of Harvard. The logic of Descartes, the geometry of Ramus, and the physics of Newton gradually gained a hearing. The astronomy of Copernicus, Galileo, Kepler, and Gassendi began to replace that of Aristotle, Ptolemy, and Dante. In 1728, Thomas Hollis established a professorship of mathematics and natural philosophy to which he contributed books and "philosophical apparatus." By 1769 these included skeletons, globes, microscopes, and mechanical instruments as well as the transactions of the English Royal Society and the French Academy of Sciences.

As the first Hollis professor of mathematics and natural philosophy, Isaac Greenwood wrote books on arithmetic, meteorology, mine damp, and the aurora borealis. He did much to bring the college into closer touch with the practical spirit of the age and to attract to Harvard practical-minded young men who might otherwise have gone to private-venture schools or into business. His successor, John Winthrop, who held the post from 1738 to 1779, proved to be the most accomplished scientific investigator in America next to Benjamin Franklin. By 1743, the Harvard curriculum included more of Enlightenment science and philosophy in the form of Isaac Watts's *Astronomy* and Locke's *Essay Concerning Human Understanding*.

In these ways Harvard had begun to show a definite interest in the new science and philosophy, though the paramount emphasis remained upon the classical languages and mathematics. By the end of the century the change had been made from the old Aristotelian science and philosophy to that of the Enlightenment.

The Great Awakening Reaffirms the Traditional Liberal Arts. When the College of William and Mary received its royal charter in 1693 under Anglican auspices, it was founded primarily for religious purposes, namely, to train ministers, to educate youth piously in good letters and manners, and to extend Christianity to the Indians. Its curriculum, similar to that of the Oxford colleges, did not change much during its first 85 years of existence. When Thomas Jefferson tried unsuccessfully to reform its course of study in 1779, there were only six instructors, two in divinity and Hebrew; one in logic, rhetoric, and ethics; one in physics, metaphysics, and mathematics; one in Latin and Greek; and one for teaching Indian boys the elements of religion. This curriculum was guided largely by the same interests as at Harvard, namely, to raise up an educated clergy for leadership in the church and state and to provide a liberal education for others who were destined to join the aristocracy.

Jefferson's proposals for the reform of William and Mary as submitted to the Virginia legislature in 1779 incorporated the basic ideals of the Enlightenment. He would have broadened and secularized the curriculum in the following ways: Theology and Bible study would have been replaced by study of the ancient languages and ecclesiastical history; modern foreign languages would have gained preeminence over the classics; great attention would have been given to the pure and applied sciences and to the social sciences in place of Aristotelian philosophy; and law and medicine would have had a large place. In general, the whole tone and purpose of the College would have been designed to prepare young men for leadership in public affairs, practical pursuits, and professional service, rather than for narrow scholarship, aristocratic intellectualism, or religious sectarianism. But Jefferson's proposals came 50 years too soon. Developments at Yale were more characteristic of the times.

The religious temper at Yale became even more marked under the spell of the Great Awakening. In 1735, the Connecticut General Court declared anew that the "one principal end proposed in erecting this college was to supply the churches in this Colony with a learned pious and orthodox Ministry." During most of the eighteenth century, its curricular development largely paralleled that of Harvard; the original course was changed gradually in the direction of the new science and philosophy of Newton and Locke.

The most significant difference, however, between Yale and Harvard up to the time of the American Revolution seems to have been that Yale gave greater emphasis to the religious nature of college education and the desirability of continuing the prescribed curriculum for religious ends. Whereas the religious position of Harvard had been considerably liberalized, the following statement of President Clap in 1754 illustrates the more traditional position of Yale:

> Colleges, are *Religious Societies*, of a Superior Nature to all others. For whereas *Parishes*, are Societies, for training up the *Common People;* Colleges, are *Societies of Ministers*, for training up Persons for the Work of the *Ministry.* . . . Some indeed, have supposed, that, the only Design of Colleges, was to teach the Arts, and Sciences. . . . But, it is probable, that there is not a College, to be found upon Earth, upon such a Constitution.[1]

This is the typical Reformation attitude, which reinforced the classical and Renaissance conception of a liberal education. These aristocratic and religious notions still purported to provide the liberal education suitable to a gentleman. All the colonial colleges were generally similar in their loyalty to this tradition and to an emphasis upon the study of divinity,

[1] Thomas Clap, *The Religious Constitution of Colleges, Especially of Yale-College in New Haven* (T. Green, New London, Conn., 1754), pp. 4 and 12.

the classics, mathematics, and philosophy. Their histories up to the Revolution showed little that was radically different except as noted in the following paragraphs.

A New Conception of Liberal Education. With the founding of King's College (Columbia) in New York City in 1754, there was a gradual shading off in the strictly religious aim. With the establishment of the College of Philadelphia in 1755 (University of Pennsylvania), there appeared a vastly wider conception of the aim and content of a liberal education, which implied that college studies should contribute to the commercial and civic usefulness of the many as well as to the religious and civic leadership of the few. The literary and aristocratic conception of a liberal education was challenged, however faintly, by a more practical and democratic conception of higher education.

King's College represented a new departure chiefly in the fact that the struggle over its founding led to a formal toleration of different religious beliefs. The charter provided that no persons should be denied entrance to the college or prevented from acquiring a degree or any of the benefits of the college because of his membership in any denomination or because of his religious beliefs. Although the college was founded nominally under Anglican auspices, the board of trustees included not only the rector of Trinity Church but also ministers from the Dutch Reformed, Lutheran, French, and Presbyterian churches. Toleration of different religious beliefs among the students was also authorized in the charters of Princeton, Brown, and other colleges, but the aim to provide ministers was uppermost in all but King's College and the College of Philadelphia.

With this freer religious atmosphere went a proposal to broaden the liberal arts at King's College to include many practical and scientific subjects useful for the more efficient pursuit of the commercial activities of the time. These proposals were formulated and published by Samuel Johnson, first president of King's College, whose desire to make college studies more useful for everyday life was perhaps intensified by his association with Franklin.

In spite of Johnson's public pronouncements, the literary and classical conception of a liberal education prevailed. The curriculum actually adopted at King's College in 1755 and again in 1762 was very similar to those of the traditional colleges with which King's College had to compete. The 4 years of study were heavily weighted with Latin and Greek grammar and literature, rhetoric, ethics, mathematics, and philosophy. Strict disciplinary control was enforced over the minutest details of student life. The actual practice at King's College did not fulfill the proposals.

The Reverend William Smith, the first provost of the college in Philadelphia, drew up its rather broad curriculum. Smith had attended the

University of Aberdeen, and it is possible that his curriculum for the Philadelphia college was framed substantially from the course that had shortly before (1753) been revised at King's College, Aberdeen. Although his Scottish training may have influenced him, Smith was also undoubtedly attracted by Franklin's theories, which clearly corresponded to those he had earlier formulated for himself. In his allegorical treatise entitled *A General Idea of the College of Mirania* (1753), Smith divided all "Miranians" into two classes, those intended for the learned professions and those intended for the trades, each class to have its own special school. He pointed out that there was little chance for the second class to receive useful instruction in the usual colleges, and he therefore proposed the establishment of a mechanics' school, which, he said, did not need much explanation because it was so much like Franklin's English school in Philadelphia.

Whatever the source of his ideas, Smith drew up "A Scheme of Liberal Education" that was accepted by the trustees of the Philadelphia college. It embraced the widest course of study and greatest variety of subjects of any college in America at the time. It seemed as if he were trying to crowd into the curriculum all the subjects that he had proposed for the Miranians. The college was planned to have three "Schools of Philosophy," in addition to the usual classical and rhetorical studies. These were to include "instrumental" philosophy (technology), moral philosophy (social sciences), and natural philosophy (physical sciences). A long list of miscellaneous readings to supplement the required lectures was appended to the curriculum. The effect of this plan was to extend considerably the conception of the liberal studies that a young man should be versed in, no matter what occupation he was to enter.

In summary, the Enlightenment of the eighteenth century wrought changes in the curriculum of the American colleges, especially in adding scientific and commercially useful subjects, to follow the trends of the times. Expansion in scientific knowledge, the refinement of skills needed in trade and commerce, and the prevalence of individualistic ideals of economic gain were responsible for what changes occurred. But the conception still held sway that a liberal education ought to be a complete round of prescribed studies heavily weighted on the linguistic and mathematical sides.

Although the new science and philosophy were added slowly to the prescribed curriculum of the denominational colleges, these still kept essentially to a liberal education embodying a study of Latin, Greek, mathematics, and philosophy as the best preparation for an aristocratic leadership in church and state. It was not until the forces of a highly industrial society were at work in the latter half of the nineteenth century that the traditional notion of a liberal education was really put upon the defensive.

Professional Education. Because the colonists followed the pattern of the English universities, they set up liberal arts colleges rather than universities on the medieval pattern. Therefore, the higher faculties of law, medicine, and theology were not present in the beginnings of American higher education. Education for these professions during most of the eighteenth century was gained by apprenticeship to a practicing lawyer, physician, or clergyman.

Study in the colleges no doubt contributed to the background appropriate for lawyers as the students read books on rhetoric, logic, and politics, but no specialized instruction in law was given until 1793, when a Kent professor of law was established at Columbia.

Likewise, in medicine, professional training was acquired when boys in their teens were apprenticed to physicians, to do the menial work and pick up what information they could. In general, American medicine lagged considerably behind European medicine in the eighteenth century and was shot through with quackery and old wives' tales. However, as the study of science began to gain ground and as more physicians came to America from England and France, special instruction in medicine began to appear in a few colleges, notably at those colleges where science had received particular emphasis, the college at Philadelphia, King's College, and Harvard.

Training in theology fared somewhat better because of the religious interests of most colleges. Students with a bent for theology could do special work with the professor of theology, who was often the president, or the young graduate might stay on after receiving his B.A. degree and receive theological instruction in the religious doctrines of the church that sponsored the college. He could then be apprenticed to a clergyman or teach school while waiting the call to a pastorate.

Chapter 12

SOCIAL FOUNDATIONS

OF MODERN EUROPEAN EDUCATION

THE STRUGGLE FOR THE MINDS OF MEN

Major Trends in Social Organization

Since the beginning of the nineteenth century four social trends have been particularly important for their impact upon education—nationalism, liberalism, industrialism, and capitalism. Interrelationships among these four trends and the political responses to them have produced much of the social conflict of the nineteenth and twentieth centuries.

Nationalism. The trend toward nationalism during Reformation and Enlightenment times moved rapidly to a culmination in the nineteenth century. The national state became the supreme unit of political authority of the modern world, as contrasted with the medieval and feudal world. Central to the ideal of nationalism was the conception of sovereignty. The sovereign state was assumed to be entirely independent of any legal or moral authority beyond its own borders. No matter whether the state was an absolute monarchy, a constitutional monarchy, or a republic, it was conceived to be the supreme political power possessing the right to determine its own boundaries, its own form of government, and its own internal arrangements.

In the process of building up political nationalism, most states appealed to the idea of cultural nationality. People began to think of themselves primarily as Frenchmen, Englishmen, Germans, Italians, Poles, Russians, and the like. Each nationality laid claim to a common historic background, a common language, common customs, and perhaps a common religious, artistic, and institutional life. More than ever before, it became important to the people of one nationality to be joined together in one national, political state. Great efforts were exerted to make the boundaries of the political state identical with the lines of cultural nationality. To this end it became important to foster in the people a strong feeling of loyalty to the state and pride in their nationality.

It was only natural, then, that education should be used as a prime means to develop the spirit of nationalism. During much of the nineteenth century, nationalism was often liberal in its aim to help nationality groups

338

achieve freedom from "foreign" oppressors and thus to achieve political self-determination. A great many of the revolutions and wars of the nineteenth century were undertaken by groups struggling to transform their cultural unity into political unity.

Liberalism and Democracy. Stemming from the great humanitarian movements of the Enlightenment period, liberalism won many victories. Nineteenth-century liberalism concentrated particularly upon achieving a greater measure of political democracy and fought for the extension of the voting rights to an ever larger proportion of the people. Coupled with the ideal of the consent of the governed in political life went the ideals of equality, individual worth, and the civil liberties as a fundamental necessity for a decent society. Many of the struggles of liberalism, centered in the effort to achieve and maintain freedom of speech, peaceful assembly, and petition; freedom of religion; and the rights of human reason to follow the truth wherever it might lead.

Within liberalism there was a continued struggle between two types. One elevated the ideal of individualism so high that it insisted upon a laissez-faire conception of the state in which progress was thought to be most possible if the state allowed individuals to seek their own interests. The second type of liberalism drew inspiration from the ideals of French humanitarianism and insisted that social progress was possible only if the state sought positively to reorganize institutions in the interest of the great majority of people and to raise the level of common life by serving the welfare of the greatest number.

Industrialism. Perhaps in the long perspective of history the most fundamental revolution of the nineteenth century was the Industrial Revolution. Nationalism had been several centuries in the making, and liberalism had appeared in other forms from Greek times on; but industrialism was something new under the sun. Never before had power-driven machinery appeared on the scene in any way to compare with the development of steam engines, water power, electricity, and, finally, atomic energy. The Enlightenment had developed the methods and ideas of modern science to a high degree, but a new era was ushered in during the latter part of the eighteenth century when science was finally applied to the production and distribution of goods. The essence of the Industrial Revolution was the development of technology, which affected all phases of the economy.

Technology meant that power-driven machines took the place of hand-operated machines and that the productivity of an individual was increased enormously. Mass production meant, further, that the making of goods could no longer take place in the homes or small shops of the workmen but now went on in a central place where the power was available, namely, in the factory.

Industrialism also meant that, as more goods were produced, more raw materials were necessary. Therefore, each country began to look about for the richest sources of raw materials and to cast covetous eyes upon the undeveloped regions of the world. It is highly important to remember that the industrial changes wrought in the nineteenth century came at a time when the dominant form of economic organization was capitalism.

Capitalism. As noted in preceding chapters, the first stage of capitalism, often called "mercantilism," had argued for strict government control and regulation of business. Then a second stage of capitalism became known as "laissez-faire capitalism" during the Enlightenment. Accordingly, it was felt that the economy rested upon the profit motive, free competition in an open market, and the private ownership of property. The basic urges and motives of men were thought to be the desire to acquire property, make money, and seek profit. Laissez-faire theory stated that, if the market were kept open for free competition without government interference, the money and price systems would automatically reach their "natural" levels through the operation of the laws of supply and demand. The aim was not so much to produce property as to *get* it, and it was assumed that the individual must be assured of the possibility of profit or the economic system would fail.

Now, with the emergence of power-driven machinery, a third stage of capitalism appeared, often called "industrial capitalism." The adherents of capitalism still maintained the ideas of laissez-faire economy despite the changed conditions in the production of goods. The whole relationship of the capitalist and the workers underwent a most significant change. Under earlier forms of capitalism the merchant had been a middleman, or entrepreneur, whose wealth enabled him to buy raw materials and hand them to the worker, who owned his own tools and produced the goods in his own home or in small shops. Under this arrangement the laborer was still a skilled workman somewhat independent of the entrepreneur.

With the development of the factory system, however, the entrepreneur became the owner of the machines and of the tools, as well as the buyer and seller of goods. The former skilled worker left his small shop and moved into the factory, where the tasks of working at machines tended to reduce him to the unskilled level. Whereas the worker had formerly done a complete job of many operations in the manufacture of whole articles, he now gradually began to concentrate upon one or a few specialized operations in the larger task of producing standardized goods. Owning no tools, the workers were now more than ever dependent upon the factory owner for their wages and their jobs. They soon turned to labor organizations as a means of protecting themselves against exploitation and of achieving better working conditions and wages. The modern labor movement arose as a protest and a reaction against the working conditions of industrial capitalism.

Major Social Programs of Action

In response to the four major trends of social organization just described, there were many proposals of plans to alleviate the conditions produced by the interaction of these patterns upon one another. The five most important types of programs, which appeared in different forms in different countries, may be identified as follows: conservatism, humanitarianism, socialism, communism, and fascism.

Conservatism. In general, conservatism was an attitude of mind that stressed the necessity of social stability and therefore expressed a great fear of change and novelty. Reacting against the French revolutionary ideals, the conservative ideal was perhaps stated most effectively by Edmund Burke in England. If possible, change should be reduced to a minimum. Whenever change was absolutely necessary, it should be undertaken with all possible regard for tradition, for the rights of property, and for the individual. All change was viewed as invalid if it did injustice to individuals; the greater freedom given to individuals, the better for society.

The conservative, however, was thinking of the individual as the man of property. He denied the revolutionary conception of equality, preferred to trust the elite, and feared the masses as brutal, ignorant, and emotional. All change must be orderly and gradual, for anything that threatened order threatened all of society. In general, conservatism stressed the values of capitalism, the religious tradition, and a nationalism that favored the interests of the aristocratic classes. It was consequently likely to discount and resist the demands of liberalism, for the people at large were deemed unable to discriminate and make wise decisions. The business of government should be left to the ruling classes—royalty, the aristocracy, the church, and the capitalists.

In general, conservatism was reflected in the Monarchist and Clerical parties in France; the Royalists, Conservatives, and Center party in Germany; and the Tories and Conservatives in England.

Humanitarianism. Stemming from the forces of liberalism and democracy in the Enlightenment, humanitarianism argued that the democratic state should seek reform of economic injustice by exerting regulation over the economy, guaranteeing a minimum basis of security for everyone, and planning affairs to enhance the welfare of all. The "welfare state" is its most modern form.

In some countries humanitarianism demanded a republican form of government, civil liberties, equality, and participation by the great majority of people in the government. In other countries it took the form of winning greater rights from the monarchy or ruling classes through more liberal constitutional arrangements. Humanitarianism won many victories in the nineteenth century and was reflected in the revolutions of the 1830's and 1840's on the Continent and in the reform movements in England. It relied on political and economic reforms as means of improving the social welfare of the great majority of the people.

Humanitarianism included the efforts of middle-class liberals, intellectuals, and many of the laboring classes, who joined together to attack the vested interests of the landed aristocracy, royalists, traditional churches, and wealthy industrialists. Humanitarianism felt that the ills of society could be removed by elevating the ideals of political liberalism, but it also often went hand in hand with nationalism in the interests of political self-determination for cultural nationalities. The belief was strongly held that the evils of industrialism and capitalism could be remedied by democratic political means. In general, the ideals of humanitarianism were reflected in the Republicans and Popular Republicans in France; the National Liberals and Christian Democrats in Germany; the Constitutional Democrats in Russia; and the Whigs and Liberals in England.

Socialism. After the middle of the nineteenth century, faith in piecemeal measures of political and economic reform began to weaken in some quarters. More radical proposals for thoroughgoing reform appeared, the most important of which was socialism. According to the socialist outlook of Karl Marx and Friedrich Engels, social change takes place by a historical process of struggle between opposites. Basic to the Marxist argument is the struggle between classes, between those who own property and those who have only their labor to rely upon. The history of mankind can be written in terms of the struggle between the owning classes (*bourgeoisie*) and the working classes (*proletariat*). This cleavage between owners and workers, Marx argued, is bound to increase because the workers do not receive a full or fair return for their labor under a capitalist system that favors private property. The political state under a capitalist system necessarily favors the capitalist class. The only real reform is thus for the state to own and manage the basic property, capital, and credit through which the production and distribution of goods are made possible in an industrial society.

Many socialist groups believed that the political forms of democracy and civil liberties of liberalism must be maintained while a socialist society was gradually created. Socialism should be voted into being by the people at the polls. Typical of these moderate and gradualist theories of socialism were the Socialists in France; the Social Democrats in Germany; the Christian Socialists, Utopian Socialists, Fabians, and Labor party in England; and the Social Democrats and the Menshevik (minority) Socialists in Russia. Socialists differed from the humanitarians in arguing that the democratic state must own and manage the basic means of production, not simply regulate them. Gradualist socialists also differed from revolutionary socialists in that they upheld the basic principles of political democracy and basic freedoms of liberalism.

Communism. The revolutionary socialists, or communists, made much more of the inherent and irreconcilable opposition between the interests of the capitalist, bourgeois class and those of the proletarian wage earners. As Marx was interpreted by Lenin and Stalin, the state has always been the instrument by which the ruling classes maintain themselves in power, protect their own interests, and exploit the workers. Since no ruling class will ever give up voluntarily its control over the coercive power of the state, the gradualist methods of moderate socialists are doomed to failure. The only realistic means of gaining control of the state is thus not by constitutional or democratic means but by force and violence. The working classes must seize power by revolution in order to use the state to improve the welfare of the masses of the people. In this revolutionary process the whole body of the proletariat will not be competent to take part. Therefore, a small, well-disciplined, conspiratorial party must engineer the revolution on behalf of the proletariat. This is the Communist party of Lenin and Stalin.

The first act of the Communist party after seizing power of the state is to destroy the capitalist system, liquidate the capitalist class and all other opposition, and institute a system of state ownership of the means of production and distribution of goods in the now classless society. This is supposed to be the transition period of state socialism. As soon as capitalism is destroyed and socialism is well established, the Communist party can then "enlighten" the whole proletariat in regard to its socialist responsibilities. When the proper attitude of mind of the proletariat is achieved, the state as historically known can then wither away and the dictatorship of the Communist party can be relaxed. In this final stage of pure communism there will no longer be any real conflict of interest between the party and the people in general; there will be no people for the proletariat to exploit.

The methods and assumptions of the Communist party are antidemocratic and antiliberal as well as anticapitalistic. The Communist party relies upon conspiracy, force, violence, and totalitarian methods of controlling the entire intellectual apparatus of a society as well as the political and economic system. Before it gains power, the Communist party claims adherence to the basic freedoms and uses them to achieve its conspiratorial purposes. But once it gains power, the Communist party refuses to permit freedom to others. Typical of the revolutionary socialist outlook were the early Bolshevik (majority) Socialists of Russia and now the Communist parties of all countries of the world which are part of a world-wide apparatus controlled by the Communist party of the Soviet Union.

Fascism. Before 1914 and immediately after the First World War, most people in western Europe felt that ultimately reason, liberalism, and democracy would prevail. Democratic gains were made in England and France, and in Germany under the Weimar Republic. Democratic governments were established or maintained in Switzerland, the Netherlands, Scandinavia, and Czechoslovakia. Most of the central European nations established republican forms of government.

Increasingly in the 1920's, however, the cause of reason and democracy began to suffer serious setbacks in many countries. Territorial disputes grew more heated; disarmament conferences failed; world-wide depression grew more acute; demands for the return of lost colonies became more insistent from Germany and Italy; jockeying for power in Europe became incessant; and most nations were not willing to give up enough sovereignty to the League of Nations to make it a genuine force for peace and international cooperation. In a deteriorating situation, new voices began to attack democracy and praise the social values of fascism as a release from the ills of war and depression that beset the peoples of the world.

Although fascism took many different forms, in all countries it had certain elements in common. It was opportunistic in character and tried to gain power by attacking anything that people disliked and by claiming to do everything that anybody wanted. It attacked in the same breath communism, socialism, capitalism, democracy, and liberalism. It professed to retain the ideal of private property but urged greatly centralized state control of the means of production and ownership. It appealed for the support of the working classes but destroyed free labor unions. It appealed especially for the support of the depressed lower middle classes and white-collar workers. It played upon fears and loyalties by preaching an extremely nationalistic patriotism. It exalted the ideas of war, expansion, and aggression as normal and natural for young vigorous nations in their attacks upon the decadent and weak democracies.

Fascism magnified the symbols of race as a means of fomenting and utilizing prejudices in order to unite a people against a real or fancied scapegoat, such as the Jews or the Poles, the communists or the capitalists. It proclaimed the essential inequality of peoples and rejected the liberal doctrines of freedom, equality, and democracy. It rejected as inefficient the ideal of political democracy and consent of the governed in the formulation of political decisions. It glorified the efficiency of a one-party system of the elite that by right could seize power and direct the destinies of the totalitarian state. All power resided in the leader, who somehow knew what was best for the rest of the people. Fascism, finally, relied upon terror, brute force, conspiratorial secrecy, ruthless suppression of all opposition, espionage, and propaganda to gain power and maintain the stability of the party. Once fascism was in power, all these methods plus complete control of all agencies of communication were used to justify, to spread, and to enforce acceptance of the party's policies.

Early forms of fascism appeared in Italy under Mussolini, but the most ruthless and powerful fascism existed in Germany under Hitler and the Nazis. Wherever the Germans were able to impose their will during World War II, fascist parties appeared, notably in the Vichy government of France during the German occupation. Native fascist groups arose in many countries of the world, some of them seeking to play their roles in cooperation with the Germans, while others simply sought power for their own purposes. Following World War II neofascist groups continued to plague reconstruction efforts in Germany, Italy, and elsewhere.

As these lines of economic interest were formed in the nineteenth and twentieth centuries, the greatest issue of modern times was posed: Could democracy and constitutional government solve the problems of an industrial society? The conservatives said that individualistic capitalism was essential to democracy; the liberals and humanitarians said that capitalism should be so reformed that economic and social democracy could go along with political democracy; the radicals said that true democracy could be achieved only when capitalism was rooted out of modern society; and the fascists resolutely set out to destroy democracy and all its works. The groundwork was laid for the continuing struggles of the twentieth century among fascism, communism, and democracy. In these struggles the role of education became ever more important.

Relations of Church and State

The power of the churches remained strong in the nineteenth century, gaining adherents as a reaction set in against the rationalism of the Enlightenment. The churches, however, had their troubles with nationalistic governments in the various countries, especially in France, Germany, and Italy. In general, the established churches were likely to be conservative and to side with the absolutist parties against the new liberalism.

In France the Roman Catholic Church regained some of its privileges and its status as the established church as a result of Napoleon's Concordat of 1801. It maintained this position, gaining strength under the Bourbon restoration, losing ground under the Second Republic, regaining strength under the Second Empire, and finally losing its favored position under the Third Republic. The Clericals (the political party favorable to the church) often paired off with the Royalists against the Republicans and Socialists of the Second and Third Republics. In 1901 the Third Republic became strong enough to pass the Association Act which provided that no religious order could exist without the approval of the government and no unauthorized order could teach in the schools. The next step was the Separation Act of 1905, which ended Napoleon's Concordat, abolished the state church, and required that within 10 years all teachers in state schools must be laymen.

In the twentieth century the Catholic Church continued largely to be the preferred church of those Frenchmen who adhered to any religious faith. Under the Vichy regime the church won back some of its privileges when a decree of 1942 canceled the Association Act of 1901, restoring to the religious orders full legal status as public utilities. Vichy France also enforced anti-Jewish regulations. The clerical point of view played a strong political role in France under the Fourth Republic as the Catholic outlook gained power through the Popular Republican party. The composition of the National Assembly was often so evenly divided that proposals to give state financial benefits to Catholic parents rocked the Republic as did the unpopular war in Indo-China or the high cost of living.

Despite the constitutional provisions for the separation of church and state, ways were found to aid Catholic schools by public funds. These provisions coincided with the stated policy of the Roman Catholic Church as contained in the papal encyclical of Pius XI, *The Christian Education of Youth*, issued in 1929. This affirmed the policy that the state has the obligation to aid Catholic parents to obtain a Catholic education for their children. It also affirmed the rights of the church and the family in the field of education, prior and superior to any right of the state to educate its citizens.

In Italy the Pope, long opposed to nationalism and liberalism because of their secularizing tendencies, looked with especial alarm upon the unification of Italy undertaken by Mazzini, Cavour, and Garibaldi. When the kingdom of Italy was established in 1861, the Papal States of Rome and Venetia were not included. Some of the reformers wished to capture Rome without the Pope's consent, but others felt that this step should not be taken against the wishes of the Pope and Louis Napoleon of France. Therefore, nothing further was done until the Franco-Prussian War, when Louis Napoleon withdrew his support of the Pope. Thereupon, with the approval of Bismarck, Victor Emmanuel conquered the Papal States, and an overwhelming majority of the people voted to become a part of the kingdom of Italy.

Despite this attitude of the people, the Pope refused to recognize the kingdom of Italy and retired to the Vatican, announcing himself to be a political prisoner. The Italian government gained Rome as its capital and recognized the Pope as representing a sovereign foreign state within the Vatican. The Pope maintained the theory that he was a prisoner until

1929, when a treaty and agreement were signed with Mussolini by which the Pope finally recognized the kingdom of Italy and in return the Roman Catholic Church was recognized as the state church of Italy.

In Italy the Roman Catholic Church continued to be by all odds the church of the people, surviving the Fascist dictatorship and even gaining political power as a result of the Concordat in 1929 with Mussolini's government. The articles of the Concordat became a part of the new constitution in 1947, thereby giving the Catholic Church a preferred place in the new Italian Republic. These provisions recognized Catholic instruction as an integral part of the public school system, gave public support to parish priests and Catholic teachers, much as civil servants were paid by the government, and made it possible for the Catholic Church to slow down, if not prohibit, the spread of Protestant doctrines in Italy. As a result, not only was the public school system oriented toward Catholicism, but also vigorous campaigns were waged to gain public moneys for aid to the Catholic private schools which rapidly increased following the close of the Second World War.

In the German states and in the Austrian Empire the state churches flourished throughout most of the nineteenth century. The Roman Catholic Church remained the established church in Austria and the southern German states, and the Lutheran Church in Prussia and other northern German states. Russia, Prussia, and Austria joined together following the Congress of Vienna in an attempt to establish the rule of religion on earth, but these allies were as much interested in maintaining the *status quo* of monarchy and aristocracy as in maintaining conservative religion. Austria signed a concordat with the Roman Catholic Church in 1850; and the Vatican Council in 1869 reaffirmed the supreme power and infallibility of the Pope.

With the beginning of the German Empire in 1871, Bismarck tried to woo the liberals of Prussia by suppressing the Roman Catholic Church, whose followers had organized the Center party in 1871. Preaching his *Kulturkampf* against any outside interference in the affairs of Germany and especially against the Roman Catholic Church, Bismarck severed diplomatic relations with the Pope, expelled the Jesuits in 1872, required state approval for the appointment of Roman Catholic priests, and insisted that only native Germans who had been educated in Germany could become Roman Catholic bishops. A large majority of Roman Catholic bishops were put into prison or driven into exile, but the Center party continued to gain strength. Bismarck therefore executed an about-face, accepted their support along with that of the conservatives, and turned his attention to suppressing the Socialists.

In Germany under the Nazis the churches received their most severe setbacks. Hitler took every means at his disposal to attack the clergy, destroy their power, and wean the younger generation away from religious teachings. The Nazis tried to set up a Nazi state church devoid of Christianity and persecuted Roman Catholic, Protestant, and especially Jewish leaders. By court order and otherwise, children were taken from parents who tried to teach Christianity or pacifism or resistance to Nazi ideas. Hitler tried to rewrite Christian history, claiming that divine guidance was on his side; in his anti-Jewish outbursts he even claimed that Christ was not a Jew but a good German Aryan. The churches, however, held out as best they could and throughout the Nazi regime constituted one of the few opposition forces to the Nazis. With the victory of the United Nations the German churches once more became free to undertake their activities and to reassert their influence in the schools.

In Russia before the Communist revolution the Greek Orthodox Church held a dominant position in the political life of the country, and the clergy ranked with the nobility among the privileged classes. When the Communists came into power, they immediately set about to liquidate the church as a bulwark of the old capitalistic and czarist regime. Karl Marx had written that religion is the "opium of the people"; Lenin had echoed this doctrine; and Stalin asserted that the party stood for science, whereas religion was diametrically opposed to science. Church properties were confiscated, and the clergy was forbidden to preach, teach, or undertake charitable activities. In educational and cultural activities, the youth were taught that Communism had no place for the old religion.

In the new Constitution of 1936, however, the principle of religious freedom was stated, but few gains were made by the church until the Second World War, when more official encouragement was given by the government. The church was no longer considered to be a threat to the security of the state, for it had supported the war against Germany. Although the church by no means recovered its lost ground, it was estimated in 1945 that there were more than 16,000 Greek Orthodox churches functioning in the Soviet Union, compared with 54,000 before the revolution. The church remained definitely in a subordinate position, but it was apparent that it could maintain itself as long as it did not oppose the Communist regime.

The role of the Protestant churches in society was marked by a renewed religious fervor and evangelism as a reaction against the intellectualism of the Enlightenment. This in turn led to a marked philanthropic effort to relieve the suffering of the underprivileged in the newly industrialized cities and to extend the opportunities of free or charity education to the children of the poor. The reaffirmation of religious faith led to a splitting and dividing process among Protestant churches that resulted in many new religious sects. Whereas there had been relatively few sects in the eighteenth century, several scores of identifiable groups had appeared by the end of the nineteenth century. Many missionary societies were formed to carry the gospel to all sections of the world. Throughout the nineteenth century the relations of the state and church in all European countries were crucial in respect to the support and control of education.

In England the Church of England retained its preferred and central place. During the nineteenth century it was generally allied with the Tories, the aristocracy, and the wealthy, but the growing liberalism in England permitted greater toleration for the nonconformist churches than elsewhere. Even the Roman Catholics gained headway following the Catholic Emancipation Act of 1829. This was in marked contrast to the lack of toleration that persisted in those countries, like Spain and Italy, where the Catholic Church continued to be the established church. In the twentieth century there were even signs that the Church of England was restless concerning its position of subservience to Parliament. In 1927 and 1928 Parliament refused to authorize changes in the Book of Common Prayer. By 1952 the Church of England was proposing that it keep its established status but be given greater freedom from parliamentary control. Representing about the same number of people as all the other Christian churches combined, the Church of England was finding that the established church in a religiously divided society had to pay a price in freedom for its privileges of legal support.

In their social points of view the churches everywhere were likely to be more conservative than not. The attacks of communism and socialism upon the churches reinforced the determination of many of them to resist radical or thoroughgoing social change. However, in various ways, some elements in the various churches began to preach more effectively the "social gospel" and to apply Christian ethics to economic and social affairs in order to achieve greater social justice. Pope Pius XI reiterated the pronouncement of Pope Leo XIII in favor of labor unionism, and the Malvern Conference in England outlined a forward-looking social program for non-Roman Catholic Christianity as viewed by reform elements in the Church of England.

Interdependence of the World

During the first half of the twentieth century the tempo of life—and of death—speeded up enormously. Prior to the First World War a rampant nationalism and imperialism characterized the foreign relations of the European countries though considerable progress toward social reform was taking place in domestic affairs. After the war, hope for peace and international cooperation through the League of Nations and for an extended liberalism and democracy in domestic affairs spread through several countries, only to be shattered by the world-wide depression of the 1920's and 1930's, accompanied by the rise of a militant fascism in Italy and Germany and communism in Russia.

As democracy, fascism, and communism came into rivalry in the 1930's, the world was once more plunged into an even greater and more destructive world war. Again the nations of the world hoped for peace and international cooperation by laying plans for the United Nations even before the end of the Second World War. The vast increase in industrial and technological development made it plain that the world was indeed one world in which the welfare of each nation was closely related with the welfare of all other nations.

The almost unbelievable advances of industrialism and science that produced the atomic bomb finally made it clear that the choice now was between one world and—no world. It was as simple as that, and yet the choice was hampered by the most complicated political, economic, and social conditions the world had ever seen. Could nationalism be so checked that genuine international cooperation could be achieved? Could the capitalistic countries work successfully with the communist countries? Could the democratic and communist countries continue the cooperation that won the war against fascism in order to safeguard an enduring peace? These were some of the underlying questions that faced the victorious nations as they began to survey the problems of the postwar world. Fundamental, too, was the question whether education, which had been so powerful in building nationalistic jealousies and hatreds in fascist and communist countries, could become as powerful in building attitudes and loyalties favorable to international and world cooperation.

The speed with which technological advances took place was breathtaking, and the most dramatic examples came to view in the greatly accelerated industrial strides that accompanied the Second World War.

In a few short years the first feeble flying machine of the Wright brothers had been developed into faster-than-sound airplanes that rendered no place on earth more than a few hours away from any other place on earth. The faint wireless messages of Marconi had become the globe-circling network of powerful radio stations and the wonders of radar that reached the moon. Above all, and almost beyond comprehension in its social implications, was the release of atomic energy that stunned the world with the atomic and hydrogen bombs. If, up to now, people around the world had been deaf and blind to the developing interdependence of nations arising from the development of industrialism, they could no longer disregard it—or did so at their peril. It was likely that the ramifications of the atomic age would outstrip the imagination. The world's hope was that it would not outrun social intelligence.

As technological industrialism made giant strides, more and more people throughout the world began to believe that the old conceptions of laissez-faire capitalism were becoming outmoded. The interdependence of the world required cooperative effort. Believers in capitalism itself realized this fact in their actual practice, despite the stated doctrines of free competition and individual effort.

Capitalism in the twentieth century changed from industrial capitalism to finance and corporate capitalism. The needs of large-scale financing and large-scale production led to corporate ownership, for which only large-scale banking and credit arrangements were suitable. This led in many countries to the growth of monopolies and international cartels to control production, distribution, and prices. World resources of raw materials were developed by these large-scale enterprises, and restraint of trade through high tariffs became a threat to the economic welfare of all nations.

This fact was dramatically brought home when the ordinary sources of raw materials, rubber, oil, food, and many other products were cut off by the successive events of the Second World War. This situation led to the scientific search for synthetic substitutes for these and other products. More important, however, was the realization that international efforts to control and stimulate world trade were imperative. Thus, the United Nations began to take steps toward cooperative commercial and financial arrangements. The economic welfare of one nation was found to be inextricably bound up with the welfare of all. This meant that the old conceptions of imperialistic domination of some peoples by others were also inappropriate in an interdependent world. No nation could live entirely by itself, nor could it, any longer, live by exploiting other nations.

The greatest fact of the postwar period was the emergence of Soviet Russia and the United States as the most powerful nations in the world. The hopes that the wartime alliance would be carried over into the postwar period were soon rudely shattered. The "cold war" between the East and the West, the "hot" wars in Korea, Indo-China, and China, and countless trouble spots around the world made it clear that uncertainty and tension were bound to afflict the world for many years to come. Debate after debate in the United Nations and conference after conference among the Big Four foundered on the rock of Russian intransigence. It became even more clear that here was no simple economic conflict between capitalism and communism, but rather a conflict of the largest proportions between whole ways of living and thinking. The basic Western tradition and ethos of liberalism, humanitarianism, and reason were challenged by the ethos of tyranny, terror, and coercion of mind as well as body. Counsels of desperation and hysterical calls for all-out war were easy to make. Counsels of patience and firmness were harder, but came from the realization of the holocaust that could be loosed upon the world by modern atomic war.

The West carried on its slow build-up of defensive power while it continued to talk with the Russians year after year. On the political and military front, the western nations joined in the mutual defense arrangements of the North Atlantic Treaty Organization in 1949. Six nations tried to create a unified European army, but this was long delayed by France's opposition to the rearming of Germany. Eight nations that saw communist expansionism as the chief threat to Asia formed the Southeast Asia Treaty Organization in 1954. In contrast, some 30 nations of Asia and Africa were invited in 1955 to a conference which symbolized the resurgence of nonwhite peoples against Western, white colonialism and imperialism and highlighted the critical role that the world's two largest nations, China and India, were likely to play in the future. On the economic front, the Marshall Plan for aid to 16 European nations by the United States began its work in 1948. Economic cooperation saved some countries from economic collapse, staved off communism, and speeded up the economic recovery of Europe following the war. Beginning in 1950, a slower but potentially still more powerful program of technological aid to underdeveloped countries was instituted by the United States under President Truman's Point Four program. In the realm of ideas, the struggle to shape men's minds throughout the world took the form of the "cold war." Because it could not or would not control all forms of communication as the Communist countries did, the West was at a disadvantage, but confidence grew that, if a "hot" war could be prevented, the power of freedom would win. But it would take determination, persistence, cooperation, and faith in the face of great odds. Education had had no greater task in all history.

ORGANIZED EDUCATION AND THE "ISMS"

Organized educational systems in Europe reflected the conflicting elements struggling for power in the various countries. In general, the forces of nationalism, capitalism, conservatism, and religion tended to reinforce the aristocratic character of educational institutions, while the forces of liberalism, humanitarianism, and socialism tended to make education more democratic. The struggle took different forms in different countries. During the nineteenth century the trends in France, Germany, and England had most influence upon American educational thought and practice. The educational systems of other states in Europe represented, in large part, variations of the patterns of these three countries. In general, European school systems in the twentieth century moved in the direction of greater centralized state and secular control. The changes in England

and France were more gradual; those in Nazi Germany and Communist Russia were more dramatic and thoroughgoing. The most impressive fact was the realization that education is an important agency of political control.

Nationalism and Liberalism in French Education

Napoleon and the First Republic. The most significant trend in France in the nineteenth century was the building of a strongly centralized state system of education. During the French Revolution, France had attempted to establish a state system of schools in order to achieve a democratic national unity. When Napoleon came to power, he immediately strove to reinforce the national character of schools, but the effect of his efforts was to reduce the democratic gains made by the Revolution. His Concordat of 1801 with the Roman Catholic Church was quickly followed by a law of 1802, which in general returned elementary schools to church control. Napoleon was favorably impressed with the work of the Institute of the Brothers of the Christian Schools; furthermore, he was really more interested in secondary education than in elementary education. It was through the secondary schools that he expected to train a loyal and efficient body of officials to help carry on his government.

The law of 1802 provided the framework for a state system of secondary schools under public control. Although private secondary schools were permitted to continue, the way was paved for the two most common types of public secondary schools, namely, the *lycée* for the larger towns and the *collège* for the smaller communes. The *lycée* became the standard secondary school of France, providing the preferred road to university study. It was typically a residential boarding school, received national funds for the construction of buildings and payment of teachers' salaries, catered to the aristocratic classes of society by charging fees, and maintained a highly classical and Humanistic course of study. The *collège* also gave preferment on the road to the higher faculties, but it received a greater share of support from the local community and therefore was often not so well endowed, physically or intellectually, as the *lycée*. Napoleon's law of 1802 also provided for the establishment of higher faculties of medicine, law, science, technology, theology, and other arts and sciences.

The First Empire. Napoleon's interest in a nationalistic system of education soon led to the law of 1806, issued after he became emperor and designed to bring all French education under his direct and personal control. The University of France was established as the supreme administrative organization to supervise all the public educational institutions of France. It was not a university in the usual American sense, but more nearly a centralized national department of education. A supreme master to be appointed by the emperor was the highest educational official. He received advice from a superior council of education made up of 26 or 30 members, also appointed by the emperor.

The whole country was divided into 27 administrative subdivisions for education, known as "academies"; each academy was to be headed by a rector, advised by a council, and aided by inspectors, all appointed by the master. The purpose of this hierarchy of public officials was to bring all public schools closely under national surveillance, provide inspection of the schools, supervise the teachers, and examine the students. A Superior Normal School to train teachers for the *lycées* was also established in 1810. Despite changes and modifications, the framework of French educational organization remained essentially as defined here for 150 years.

Monarchy. With the restoration of the Bourbon kings from 1814 to 1830 the generally reactionary measures of the kings were applied to education. The church was given much more of its former status in the schools, priests were appointed as principals and teachers in the public schools, and licensing of private teachers could be through bishops rather than through state authorities. In 1820 the title of superior master was changed to minister of public instruction.

The trend in favor of the church was somewhat reversed during the constitutional monarchy of Louis Philippe who ruled from the July revolution of 1830 until 1848. Under the leadership of Guizot as minister of public instruction, Victor Cousin was sent in 1831 to Prussia to report on the organization of German schools. The resulting law of 1833 provided the framework of French primary education.

This law required each commune to establish a public primary school, pay the teachers, and provide the school building (usually as a dwelling for the teacher as well). Fees were to be charged those parents who could afford to pay, but poor children could attend free of charge. If the commune could not afford to provide a school, the state was authorized to give help. Private schools (most of which were religious schools) were permitted to continue in operation, but the teachers of these schools had to be certified by the mayor of the commune as well as by the church. Likewise, the religious emphasis was somewhat lessened in the public primary schools by requiring that a child could not be forced to receive any religious instruction which his parents did not wish him to have.

In addition, a new type of advanced education was provided by the authorization of "higher primary schools" in the principal towns and cities of the departments, the 90-odd legal and political subdivisions of France. The higher primary schools were designed to offer to the graduates of the primary schools a vocational preparation in commercial, agricultural, or industrial subjects appropriate to the region. Furthermore, a primary normal school was to be established in each department for the training of teachers who were to teach in the primary schools.

Although primary education was not made free or compulsory, great progress had been made in providing a national and conservative type of education appropriate to a monarchy. In the late 1830's further progress was made in providing primary schools for girls, adult classes for boys beyond fourteen and for girls beyond twelve years of age, and infant schools for children of preschool age.

Second Republic. During the struggles to establish the Second Republic of 1848, it was apparent that an ardent democratic spirit motivated many of the primary teachers. They issued strongly democratic proposals to make primary education free, compulsory to age fourteen, and a liberalizing agency for greater opportunity among the common people. But as soon as the conservatives and monarchists gained the upper hand in the short-lived Second Republic, they set about to quash the liberal movement in education, especially through the law of 1850. The conservative and religious trend in this law was revealed when Louis Napoleon saw to it that bishops and church officials had a prominent place on the superior council and on the councils of the several academies.

Second Empire. It thus became easier for the clergy to teach in the public primary and secondary schools than had been the case under the July monarchy. The hierarchical system of state and local inspectors was reinforced and elaborated, so that the means were provided of hunting down the liberal teachers, who were charged with instigating the Revolution of 1848. As soon as Louis Napoleon became emperor in 1852, the process of "liberal-hunting" was intensified; teachers were discharged and even exiled; private and religious schools were urged to compete with the public schools; and the normal schools were put under close surveillance to ensure that they did not become soil for the growth of liberal social or educational ideas.

Third Republic. However, with the overthrow of the Second Empire and the establishment of the Third Republic in 1871, the pendulum began to swing back to a more liberal and democratic trend. Through a series of laws in the 1880's promoted by Jules Ferry, minister of public instruction, the modern form of French education was realized. In 1881 fees were abolished in the primary schools, and in 1882 compulsory attendance was required between ages six and thirteen. In 1886 the superior council lost its religious character, and professional educators made up the majority of its members. The Ministry of Public Instruction was given complete control over the details of curriculum, selection of textbooks, examination and appointment of teachers, and payment of all primary teachers' salaries.

Private, religious schools were more strictly supervised to ensure that the laws, spirit, and constitution of the Republic were not jeopardized. Furthermore, it was ruled that representatives of religious orders could not teach in the public schools and religious schools could not be authorized to act as public schools (as allowed in the law of 1850). Higher primary schools were encouraged and expanded to meet the needs for technical training as the industrialization of France proceeded rapidly. Secondary education for girls in their own *lycées* and *collèges* was fostered.

It is clear from this short survey that nationalism was a paramount factor in all French educational developments in the nineteenth century. Conservative, aristocratic, and religious influences predominated under the Bourbon restoration, the July monarchy, and the Second Empire. Liberal, constitutional, and democratic elements were stressed in the early days of the Second Republic and progressively under the Third Republic after 1880. France believed that a strongly centralized system of state education was the road to national unity, no matter whether the controlling power was monarchy, empire, or republic. Despite the democratic trends in the latter part of the century under the Third Republic, the aristocratic conception was strong enough to preserve a two-track system of education, one track for the lower classes and one track for the upper classes.

Under the Third Republic, France maintained its centralized system and its stand against religious instruction in the public schools. The association law in 1901 exerted state control over those religious orders which were still allowed to teach in public or private schools, and the Separation Act of 1905 ruled that within 10 years all teachers in elementary schools were to be laymen and all religious teaching orders suppressed. The agitation for religious instruction from ecclesiastical quarters did not cease, but the Socialist and Republican forces beat down all such attempts. Private schools, most of which were religious institutions, continued to exist and to enroll perhaps a third of French children, but they had to be approved by the Ministry of Education and could not be conducted by a religious order.

Meanwhile, the French educational system remained dualistic and class-conscious. Primary education remained almost the sole provision for the lower classes, secondary education being reserved for the upper classes. There were sporadic attempts to make the secondary schools available to lower-class children through scholarships, but not much progress was achieved. More attention was gradually given to a practical education in the higher primary schools and to technical and trade schools beyond the higher primary schools, but the secondary schools remained virtually aloof from the lower classes.

Following the First World War, considerable agitation was aroused by certain groups, particularly of war veterans, who urged a unitary school system for all, often referred to as the *école unique*. According to this system, free education would be available to all children, as far up the educational ladder as possible, including the university faculties. These agitations urged better trade and technical instruction, more continuation schools, and better opportunities for girls. However, the academic conservatism of the school system, dominated as it was by the aristocratic conception of secondary education, made the few gains negligible. In 1933, tuition fees began to be abolished for the *lycée*, beginning with the lowest class and then adding one class each year until all six grades were entirely free. This brought the process up to the opening of the Second World War.

Vichy France. Along with taking complete political control into his own hands after the fall of France in 1940, Marshal Pétain set about to reinstate the religious element in French schools. This attempt took two forms: an effort to reestablish religious instruction in state schools, and the revival of church teaching orders in their own religious schools, to which state money would be given. Under the Third Republic, no religious instruction in public schools had been permitted, but a half holiday a week had been allotted to allow students to receive religious instruction out of school if parents desired. Under a decree early in 1941, it was planned to give religious instruction on Thursday mornings in or near the school and to include 1½ hours of religious instruction in the regular course of study. This, of course, met great opposition from teachers who had been trained in the secular outlook, and sharp controversies arose between local teachers and local priests. Later in 1941 this decree was rescinded, but much damage had been done by reopening the issue.

In 1942 the ban on religious teaching orders dating back to 1901 and 1905 was lifted; they were given legal status and privileges by the state; and state funds were allocated to the religious schools. German authorities, seeing that dissension within France could be stimulated by such methods, encouraged the granting of state funds to the independent religious schools, which thereupon gained more power. In 1941 they had enrolled 1,200,000 students. In this way, religious controversies again became one of the most serious internal difficulties in France. Reinforcement of class lines was also a divisive technique. No transfer from primary to secondary education was allowed without a special examination, and tuition fees for secondary schools were restored to make the transfer still more difficult.

Fourth Republic. With the establishment of the provisional government in 1944, attention was again directed to the reform of the educational system. For a while it seemed likely that the public schools would revert to their secular policies, and public support of religious schools would be withdrawn. A committee for the reform of French education was appointed under the leadership of Paul Langevin, and in 1947 this committee published its plans.

As planned, compulsory education would be raised from thirteen to fifteen years of age, with compulsory part-time attendance to eighteen years for those with a job. The number of secondary schools was to be greatly increased, especially in the scientific, technical, and vocational fields. Also planned was a lessening of the power of the highly centralized system and more flexibility for local educational initiative. Thus the social-reform movements of France that gained such great headway during the Second World War pointed to greater democracy, more secular control, and less centralized authoritarianism in French education.

The reform looked toward greater equality of educational opportunity and more attention to individual aptitudes and the learning processes of children. To these ends it was proposed that education be organized on the unitary basis of a "ladder" system of schools. The sharp division between elementary and secondary education was to be eliminated. All education between the ages of seven and eighteen was to be a unified system known as the *"premier degré"* (first level), leading from a common education between ages seven and eleven to a period of education and vocational orientation between ages eleven and fifteen, and finally to a choice of practical, professional, or theoretical education between ages fifteen and eighteen. All higher education was to be looked upon as the *deuxième degré* (second level), consisting of advanced professional and technical preparation in the universities, institutes, and higher schools.

While the reform of French education has made some headway, the greatest difficulties have arisen from the unstable political character of the Fourth Republic, the severe economic problems, and the constant pressure of the Catholic Church upon the public schools. The financial situation has kept the public school system from expanding, whereas the Catholic schools have increased rapidly despite the legal restrictions against them. In 1951 the shaky coalition of conservative and center parties finally agreed to compromise with the church. In September, 1951, the National Assembly revised the secular policies of the Fourth Republic and passed two school-aid bills; one gave indirect aid to Catholic schools by granting scholarships at public expense to students in Catholic schools; the other gave direct aid to families of Catholic students by granting allotments to the Catholic parents' association. With such aid likely to increase as long as the Popular Republicans continued to be strong, the proportion of children in Catholic schools (about one-third in 1950) was likely to increase at the expense of the public schools.

Nationalism, Conservatism, and Fascism in German Education

France and Germany had much in common in their outlook and systems of education in the nineteenth century; indeed, they copied much from each other at various times. They both gave attention to nationalizing their schools, the principal difference being that at the end of the century the liberal tendencies were winning in France whereas the conservative forces were winning in Germany. Both nations established state school systems that were essentially aristocratic in their conception and practice.

During the reign of Frederick William III from 1797 to 1840 the struggles between conservatism and liberalism were prominent in German education. For 10 or 15 years after the defeat of Prussia by Napoleon in 1807, it looked as though liberalism might win. Prompted by such men as Stein, Fichte, Humboldt, and Süvern, the king allowed liberal ideas to be expressed as a means of regenerating Prussia and nationalizing Prussian education. These men felt that the best way to rejuvenate Prussia was to establish a democratic system of education of the "ladder" type in which every child would have an equal opportunity of climbing as far as his talents would enable him to go. In this way the class distinctions that divided Prussia socially might be lessened.

For a while it looked as though educational reform might proceed parallel with the social reforms of 1807 to 1811, when serfdom was abolished, towns were made independent of feudal control, and peasants gained a large share in the ownership of land. Fichte was made head of the University of Berlin, founded on liberal principles in 1809, and Humboldt was put in charge of Prussian education. Several teachers were sent to study Pestalozzian methods in Switzerland, and some of them came back to become heads of the public teacher-training schools and provincial departments of education. Elementary education in Prussia was on the way to becoming the most enlightened and advanced in the world, especially attracting the attention of French and American educators in the 1820's and 1830's.

The liberal trends were short-lived, however, and began to be nullified soon after the Congress of Vienna. His hand strengthened by the conservative reaction in Austria and Prussia, Frederick William III began to retreat from democratic principles and to reestablish religious and aristocratic control of education under his own supervision. The department of public instruction was shifted from the Department of Interior and made a branch of the Ministry of Religion, Education, and Public Health. The country was divided into provinces and subdivided into counties and local committees, each with a school board representing the various religious groups in the community. School inspection was largely in the hands of local ministers or priests.

Pestalozzian ideas of the regeneration of society through education began to give way to the ideals of religious, disciplinary, and military obedience. Frederick William III valued education, not as an agency for regenerating society, but as a means of making the common people satisfied with their lot, happy in their appointed place, and loyal to the king. By 1830 the two-track system of education was firmly established, the elementary schools for the common people (*Volksschulen*) serving over 90 per cent of the population and the secondary schools for the upper classes serving less than 10 per cent. Likewise, the repressive Carlsbad decrees of 1819 tried to stamp out liberalism among the faculties and student bodies of the universities.

The generally conservative reaction in Prussia was continued under Frederick William IV, who set out to surpass even the other Prussian kings in his absolute control of assertion of divine right. Far from looking upon education as a means of social improvement, he viewed the schools as a means of counteracting unauthorized religious and political ideas. He rebuked the elementary school teachers of Prussia for their part in the revolutions of 1848 and charged that they had been instrumental in stirring up the people to such outrageous acts as requesting a constitution. His regulations of 1854 were designed to reemphasize obedient habits and proper respect for religion and the king. He especially concentrated on the teacher-training institutions as a means of carrying out these aims. Once again the attempt to liberalize German education had failed; but the strength of education had been recognized by the upper classes, and they were determined more than ever that the schools should be used for *their* purposes.

German Empire. As soon as William I became emperor of the new "Second Reich" in 1871, he set out to use education as an instrument to unify the diverse elements in the new empire. Bismarck's *Kulturkampf* led to the school-inspection law of 1872, which was aimed to remove the control of school inspection from the clergy; but his abandonment of *Kulturkampf* soon left inspection still largely in church hands. The General School Regulations of 1872 recognized that the different religious groups in the German states that constituted the empire should not be driven out of the educational system but should be reconciled. Public schools should be constituted as Protestant, Roman Catholic, or Jewish, according to the dominant elements in the community. Where the community was divided, each kind of school should be maintained, or special instruction should be given by each of the different faiths. This conception of a public denominational school system in which the state maintained public schools for the benefit of the various religious groups produced many difficult problems.

Meanwhile, vocational and continuation schools became very popular in most German cities as a means of training skilled workers for the industrialization of Germany. More than any other nation, the Germans sponsored this type of education through local institutions. The regulations of 1872 further recognized the need for an education beyond the elementary level, and an intermediate, or middle, school was proposed for the children of artisans, small merchants, and tradesmen who could go beyond the minimum of education but were not expected to have the advantages of the secondary school.

Following his accession as emperor, William II issued a decree to the teachers of the schools, telling them that their prime purpose was to combat the dangerous doctrines of socialism and communism. The schools should teach that religion and a paternal monarchy would give labor all it needed if it would reject all socialistic doctrines. Thus, at the end of the century education was a highly centralized national agency, designed to inculcate nationalistic and conservative ideals that would produce patriotic Germans, knowing their place, promptly and efficiently obedient to orders, and habitually loyal to king and fatherland. Hitler had much in the German educational tradition to build upon.

Up to the First World War, German education remained strongly dualistic in structure and centralized in administration. The two-track system was maintained, and children at six years of age went to their respective schools, lower-class children to the *Volksschule* and upper-class children to the *Vorschule*, a preparation of 3 years before entering one of the secondary schools at nine years of age. Education continued to be compulsory from six to fourteen, and separate schools were maintained for boys and girls wherever possible. The religious control of education continued to be vexatious.

The Socialists and liberal groups opposed the sectarian public-school arrangements that had been devised, but they could not achieve complete separation of the churches from public education. Some gains were made, however. In addition to the sectarian public schools, some interdenominational schools were established in which the pupils went to separate religious teachers for instruction in their particular creed, and some secular schools were established in which there was no denominational religious instruction. The upper classes and conservative official groups repeatedly maintained that the schools should do all in their power to combat socialism. Industrial groups were active in extending scientific, technical, trade, and vocational education at all levels. The inculcation of national loyalties and the selective process to sort out the leaders from the followers remained the dominant aims and characteristics of German education.

Republic. After the First World War the Weimar Republic tried to reverse the aristocratic and centralized character of German schools. In the attempt to democratize the schools a unified 4-year fundamental course for all children from ages six to nine was established, called the *Grundschule*. The idea of this arrangement was to provide a common educational background for all children and to postpone the separation into elementary and secondary schools until the age of ten. It was also designed to give more chance for the children of the lower classes to pass over into the several secondary schools by means of scholarships and free tuition.

The second 4 years of the elementary school, known as the *Oberstufe*, was strengthened as a means of preparation for the trade, technical, and continuation schools; and more attention was given to the *Mittelschule*, which led to minor business, clerical, and official positions. New types of secondary schools appeared. Somewhat equivalent but separate secondary schools were established for girls.

In these ways the Weimar Republic attempted to make the opportunities more flexible for the masses of German children and to increase their opportunities for advancement. More authority for educational direction was given to the federal states of which the Republic was composed in order that the systems could be adopted to local needs. The churches in the various states also maintained a strong position in the public schools. The Roman Catholic Church, for example, supported the Republic because Prussia and the empire had favored Protestantism, whereas under the Republic the church could support denominational public education even in the Protestant strongholds.

As a result of the public denominational system there was little need for large numbers of private schools, and a very small proportion of German children went to private schools (some 3 or 4 per cent in the middle 1930's). There was some agitation for a unified school system (*Einheitschule*) along the lines of the proposed French *école unique*, but tradition was too strong and the life of the Republic was too short.

National Socialism. When the Nazis came to power in 1933, their first aim, of course, was to gain complete control of the educational system of Germany for their own purposes. This meant destroying the power of the federal states in education as well as in all other political matters and establishing a more completely centralized system of education than the empire had ever dreamed of. It meant, too, that the Nazis set about in all the ways they could think of to break the hold of the churches upon the schools. They would brook no opposition and no loyalties other than to the party.

On the surface, the Nazis also attacked the two-class, aristocratic system of education and turned their attention to building up the elementary schools at the expense of the secondary schools, with a corresponding drop in enrollment in the secondary schools. But in reality the aim was to use the mass schools to instill the Nazi ideology of followership in all children and then if necessary select a new aristocracy, or elite, based not upon economic class or intellectual achievement, but upon loyalty to the party.

Not only was the content of the school curriculum changed to suit Nazi purposes but all kinds of extraclass activities came to play an even larger part in the class instruction. These out-of-school activities attracted many youths, not only because of the privileges involved, but also because of their natural resistance to the highly formal, bookish, and overintellectualized character of most German schools. The Nazis perhaps went further in complete control of schools for political purposes than any other nation; they showed the world what a power education could be in achieving political and social ends, albeit for evil and destructive ends.

When the United Nations occupation authorities began their work in Germany in 1945, they immediately turned their attention to ways and means of creating a truly free and democratic education in Germany, a task of enormous proportions because the Nazis had done their work so well and because there was relatively so little in German tradition to build upon. The Potsdam agreement of 1945, which divided Germany into four occupied zones, stipulated that Nazi and militaristic doctrines should be eliminated from German schools in favor of democratic ideas. By 1947 the four occupying powers agreed upon 10 points of school reform that sounded very democratic. They included equal educational opportunity for all; free texts and school materials and scholarship grants; compulsory attendance from ages six to fifteen and part-time attendance to eighteen years; a ladder system, rather than a two-track system, of elementary and secondary schools; democratic citizenship education; international understanding; health and physical education; educational and vocational guidance; education of teachers in universities; and participation by the German people in the reform of their educational system. The United States and the Soviet Union would have abolished the denominational schools, but England and France would not agree.

By 1950–1951, however, it was clear that earlier agreement had resulted in little of common meaning between the Russian zone of the East and the zones of the West. The Russians proceeded to abolish the private and denominational schools and to infuse the entire system with Communist outlooks. Rule by fiat became the order of the day. Textbooks incorporated the dialectical materialism of Marxist-Leninist ideology; teachers were selected on the basis of their political reliability and loyalty to Communism; Russian language and literature were emphasized; and instructions issued to teachers ordered Russian pedagogical methods to be used, Russian heroes to be glorified, the ideals of freedom to be denied, and teachers to become active in the Communist party. Such great emphasis was put on scholarship grants that some 60 per cent of university students in the social-science fields were being subsidized by the state. Plans were made to increase the number of university students in the East zone from 35,000 to 50,000 by 1955. The entire objective was to create a younger generation molded by Communist philosophy in the shortest possible time.

In the Western zones much more attention was paid to the wishes of the German people. Reform was conducted by discussion rather than by fiat. As a result, much of the old two-track system was retained, with upper classes divided from lower classes. Furthermore, the denominational school system wherein religious instruction was supported by public funds was reestablished, especially upon the insistence of Catholic groups and aided by the power of the dominant Christian Democratic party. Religious influences grew steadily stronger.

The basic structure of German education was little changed. Children went to the *Grundschule* between ages six and ten. They then typically went in three different directions. Most of them finished up in the upper part of the *Volksschule;* a few of the lower-middle-class children went on to the 6-year *Mittelschule* as a preparation for lower jobs in trade, commerce, and the civil service. Upper-class children usually went on to the secondary schools, *Gymnasium* and *Oberschule,* to prepare for the universities.

Some progress was made in some of the states in expanding the elementary school from 4 to 6 years and thus delaying selection for the secondary schools until age twelve. New vitality in the German universities was marked, and great emphasis was put upon teacher education. Whether the relatively greater amounts of freedom in the Western zones could counterbalance the drive to conformity in the Eastern zone in a short period of time remained to be seen. The Western powers could see no alternative but to rely upon freedom.

Conservatism and Liberalism in English Education

Prior to the nineteenth century England's typical provision for elementary schools was through private, religious, and charitable associations, which raised funds by subscription and then established free charity schools for the poor who could not otherwise pay for the education of their children. It was long accepted that self-respecting parents would pay tuition for their children's education. The philanthropic measures begun in the eighteenth century were extended and redoubled in the early nineteenth century, largely as a result of the deplorable industrial conditions facing the working classes in the factory towns of England and Wales. Added to the sympathetic humanitarianism aroused by the Industrial Revolution were the religious sentiments stimulated by religious revivalism. There was also a desire to protect the vested interests of the upper classes against the unruly, ignorant, and undisciplined mob of workers now crowded into the unhealthy and congested cities.

Whereas the French Revolution had stimulated the liberals of France and Germany to propose national school systems for the benefit of the people, it stimulated the liberals of England to form charity organizations to help the underprivileged. Whereas the reaction against the French Revolution had led the conservatives of France and Germany to use their state school systems to keep the people in their place, it prompted the conservatives of England to form still more voluntary societies in order to provide a little education to make the people satisfied at small cost.

Any number of charitable agencies set out to furnish "ragged" schools for the poor and underprivileged, soup kitchens, orphan schools, reformatories, industrial schools, thrift brigades, and the like. Virtually all the religious denominations organized school societies to provide charity education. The most important agencies, however, concentrated on three types of schools: Sunday schools to give instruction to children who worked the rest of the week; monitorial schools to put education on a mass-production basis; and infant schools to provide a kind of nursery school education for three-, four-, and five-year-olds while their mothers worked in the factories.

In 1785 the Society for the Support and Encouragement of Sunday Schools in the Different Counties of England was founded. In 1808 the Royal Lancastrian Society for monitorial instruction was founded under nondenominational auspices, and in 1814 the name was changed to the British and Foreign School Society. In 1811 the National Society for Promoting the Education of the Poor in the Principles of the Established Church throughout England and Wales was organized to promote monitorial instruction under Anglican auspices. In 1836 the Home and Colonial Infant School Society was organized to promote the ideas propounded in 1799 by Robert Owen. By 1850 several thousand schools had been established by these and other school societies.

Despite all this voluntary activity, a number of investigations and reports found such large-scale inequalities and lack of opportunity for the vast majority of English children that agitation began for the government to take a hand. Under the leadership of such men as Lord Brougham, Blackstone, Bentham, James Kay-Shuttleworth, Dickens, Carlyle, and John Stuart Mill, efforts were made to extend free educational facilities for the working classes through state auspices with tax support. Parliament, however, moved slowly. Beginning in the early part of the century many bills were introduced and several motions were made in Parliament to grant financial aid to schools, but until the 1830's all such bills were defeated by the Tories, largely through fear that public education would make servants insubordinate to their masters.

As soon as the Whigs came to power in 1830, the first steps for government support were taken. In 1833 the first national aid to schools was granted by Parliament in the form of £20,000 to be given to the National Society and the British and Foreign Society for the construction of school buildings. Government support for the religious schools was to be the typical form of national interest in education for the next 35 or 40 years. Several times in the 1840's and 1850's the amounts of state aid were increased and extended to other school societies as well as the two just mentioned. In time, the national money could be used by the societies for maintenance and current expenditures as well as for the building of schoolhouses. In 1839 a committee of the Privy Council was appointed to administer the funds and provide inspectors to visit the schools to which money had been granted; in 1856 this committee was transformed into a Department of Education. Stimulated by the arguments that the industrialization of the country made it necessary for factory foremen and skilled workers to be able to read and write, the beginnings of state support were made.

Many liberals were not satisfied, however, with such halfhearted measures, and in 1850 a National Public School Association was formed to agitate for free, compulsory education supported entirely by the government through taxation. This, of course, met great opposition from the conservative and religious groups. The Anglicans wanted to maintain religious education; the dissenters wanted religious schools but did not want the Church of England to have a monopoly in the field; and both opposed the liberals, who proposed secular schools. In the midst of the agitation Parliament appointed in 1858 a committee known as the Newcastle Commission, whose investigations led it to recommend that free, compulsory education was undesirable, for the evils of a compulsion that invaded the individual's rights outweighed its advantages.

Finally, while Gladstone and the Liberal party were in power, an elementary-education act known as the Forster Act was passed in 1870. The country was divided into school districts under the jurisdiction of local school boards. The voluntary school societies were given a year to establish schools in any districts where they were needed. If this was not done, the school boards were authorized to establish public "board" schools to be supported partly by taxation and partly by fees from those parents who could afford to pay. They were to be free for those who could not pay tuition. The local boards were also authorized to make attendance compulsory from the ages of six to thirteen if they wished.

The religious question was solved by requiring the instruction in the board schools to be secular, while the voluntary schools could give religious instruction provided that children were not compelled to receive such instruction if their parents did not wish it. The modern "released-time" plan of religious instruction was foreshadowed when it was required that religious instruction should come at the beginning or at the end of the school day so that pupils could be withdrawn during those hours if the parents so desired.

As the century ended, a National Board of Education was created by joining the Department of Education and the Department of Science and Art in a single agency to deal with all kinds of elementary, secondary, and technical education. In contrast to the ministries of education in France and Germany, however, the English National Board of Education did not have the authority to appoint or discharge teachers, select text-books, prescribe the curriculum, or give examinations. Its primary duties were to enforce attendance, to pass on physical equipment, buildings, and qualifications of teachers, and to make suggestions and give aid concerning matters of curriculum and methods. This arrangement was based upon a distinction between the external setting of education, upon which the National Board of Education had compulsive power, and internal matters of curriculum and methods of teaching, which were left to local judgment and initiative.

Educational changes in England since 1900 were marked by a number of committee reports, debates, and tentative laws that were not fully carried out. In 50 years, however, definite progress was made toward establishing a more unified public system of schools. This development can be described in the light of the three major education acts of 1902, 1918, and 1944.

Balfour Act of 1902. This act was important because it set the basic character of public control until near the end of the Second World War. It abolished the old school boards and handed over public educational responsibility to the newly organized agencies of local government, namely, county councils, county boroughs, boroughs, and urban districts, which could levy taxes for the support of secondary as well as elementary schools. The old "board schools" came to be known as "council schools," that is, schools provided at public expense and under public control of the local councils. Privately and religiously sponsored schools continued to be known as "voluntary" schools. Conservative and ecclesiastical groups were able to insert provisions into the act that gave public tax funds to these voluntary schools. Liberals and reform church groups fought this aspect of the law—but to no avail—because it meant public support of religious instruction, especially favoring the Church of England.

In 1902 there were some 5,800 board schools and 14,000 voluntary schools. Inasmuch as the voluntary schools were older and in need of funds to bring them up to standard, it was decided that the easiest way to make educational facilities available to larger numbers of children was to subsidize the already existing voluntary schools. This dual system led to endless discussion and confusion concerning matters of control, finance, and religious instruction. When the Liberal and Labor parties come to power in 1905, they began to pass legislation to provide meals for poor children, nursery schools, medical care, recreation, and other facilities, but they could not remove the religious emphasis from the public schools.

Fisher Act of 1918. Out of the reform movement of the First World War came the Education Act of 1918, which made attendance compulsory to age fourteen, required part-time attendance at continuation schools to age sixteen, and removed all fees for public elementary schools. The local educational authorities were to impose taxes themselves and receive funds from the National Board of Education in order to carry out their plans for a thoroughgoing system of public elementary and secondary education, including continued support for the voluntary schools. Local educational authorities could provide nursery schools for children under five years, extend medical care, physical education, and recreation, and provide more scholarships to secondary schools.

In general, the theory of control was that the local educational authorities would have considerable freedom to provide education to meet their needs, along with stimulus, advice, and suggestions from the National Board of Education, which had the power to inspect both public and voluntary schools. These rather elaborate proposals, however, were never realized because the economy drives by conservative groups cut down educational budgets in the early 1920's. Further acts in 1921 and 1936 tried to realize some of these provisions, but they did not achieve a great deal.

Education Act of 1944. The movement for thorough reform, however, gained strength in the late 1930's and during the years of the Second World War. Finally a white paper on educational reconstruction was presented to Parliament in 1943 by R. A. Butler, president of the National Board of Education, the major proposals of which became the Education Act of 1944. These proposals were promoted by the Trades Union Congress, Cooperative Union, National Union of Teachers, and the Workers' Educational Association, along with the Labor party and liberals in the Conservative party. The provisions of the act would gradually extend the principle of free public education for all.

The National Board of Education was transformed into a Ministry of Education, which was to have greater centralized powers of leadership, control, and direction. The local educational authorities were now principally two, the county councils and the county-borough councils, which were to submit complete plans for the development of education in their jurisdictions for approval by the new minister of education. Each local educational authority was to make provision or secure appropriate facilities for three stages of education, somewhat analogous in principle to the ladder system, in which every child would have a chance to progress as far as his needs and abilities would carry him.

The three stages were as follows: *Primary education* included ages two through eleven; nursery schools or nursery classes were to be provided for children from two to five and separate primary schools from five through eleven. *Secondary* education was to include ages twelve through eighteen; attendance was to be compulsory through age fifteen and through age sixteen as soon as practicable. *Further education* was defined as being all education beyond the school-leaving age of fifteen or sixteen. It included compulsory attendance at county colleges for 1 day a week or 2 half days a week through age eighteen for those who were not in full-time attendance at some other educational institution. It included adult education as well as technical, commercial, and art education.

Provision was made for several kinds of control and support of primary and secondary schools. (1) *County schools* (formerly council schools) were entirely supported and controlled by the local educational authorities. (2) *Voluntary schools* were to be designated as (*a*) "aided schools," in which the private managers paid half of the expenses of repair and alteration to bring the school up to standard and the managers were to appoint and dismiss teachers and conduct denominational religious instruction; (*b*) "controlled schools," in which the local educational authority took on complete financial responsibility and appointed and dismissed teachers with approval of the private managers; and (*c*) "special-agreement schools," which had begun plans for joint public and private support under the Act of 1936. (3) *Assisted schools* were all private and religious schools that received some public funds but were not maintained by the local educational authority. (4) *Independent schools* (principally the old "public schools") included all other private schools. They had to be registered and inspected by the Ministry of Education. In these ways the power and control of public-education authorities were extended by utilizing and improving the private schools already in existence rather than by building a new public system of schools.

The provisions that caused the most concern and that were likely to be a source of difficulty had to do with religious education. The act provided that all county and voluntary schools should begin each day with collective worship of a nondenominational kind for all pupils and also that religious instruction should be given in all schools, the pupils to be excused if parents requested it. In county schools the religious instruction was to be nondenominational and in accordance with an agreed-upon syllabus drawn up by a conference of four committees representing the Church of England, other denominations in the local community, teachers' associations, and the local educational authority.

In controlled schools the agreed syllabus was to be taught, along with denominational instruction, for not more than two periods a week for those pupils whose parents desired it, such instruction to be given by "reserved teachers," who were to be appointed for the purpose. The reserved teachers were not to comprise more than one-fifth of the school's staff.

In aided schools, denominational religious instruction was to be under the control of the manager, but the agreed syllabus might be taught to those pupils whose parents preferred it. No teacher was to be disqualified because of his religious views in county, controlled, or special-agreement schools. This all meant that the religious element remained strong in English schools.

General provisions of the act included such liberal and humanitarian principles as the following: primary and secondary education to be conducted in separate schools; selection of pupils for secondary education to be based, not upon special-place examinations at the age of eleven as formerly, but upon the pupil's entire record and prospects; education to be provided according to the parents' wishes insofar as possible, including boarding-school provisions; special provisions made in separate schools or classes for any disability of mind or body; free medical inspection and treatment; free milk, meals, and clothing for those who needed them; enhanced facilities for recreation, social, and physical training in camps, playing fields, day centers, playgrounds, and swimming pools; and prohibition of child labor or any employment that the local educational authorities deemed harmful to the pupils' health or educational opportunities.

As the Second World War ended, it was clear that England had made major gains in achieving at last a more truly unified and democratic form of national education by the characteristic methods of gradualism and compromise. Whereas in 1944 only 1 out of 10 English children had the opportunity for secondary education and far fewer for higher education, the chances were that the way would increasingly be opened for greater opportunities for more children to go farther up the educational ladder.

An Education Act of 1945 for Scotland incorporated most of the principles just mentioned, and an Education Act in 1947 did the same for Northern Ireland. In 1872 Scotland had established the basis for a single-track system of schools almost 75 years before England and Wales had done so. Consequently, the vast majority of Scottish children had attended local public schools for a long time and had attended comprehensive secondary schools somewhat analogous to American high schools.

Whereas religious instruction was not controlled by the central authority, it was left to local authorities and generally followed Presbyterian principles. Freedom of conscience, however, permitted any parent to remove his child from the religious instruction if he wished.

It is, of course, dangerous to generalize too easily about whole nations and their educational systems as developed over a century, but certain facts concerning educational organization in France, Germany, and England seem to stand out. France and Germany were much more self-conscious than was England about generating a nationalistic spirit among their peoples. They arrived at roughly similar centralized systems of national education, whereas England was content to allow much more flexibility and scope to private and religious agencies. The military rivalry of France and Germany on the Continent perhaps accounts for some of their nationalistic emphasis. Germany had to stimulate a feeling of national unity within a few years, a process that had long been achieved in England. The French penchant for orderliness and logical patterns made a centralized system appropriate to France, whereas England was content with variety and lack of system because of a stronger, though more informal, sense of national unity despite political and economic diversity.

One thing common to all three countries, however, was their essentially aristocratic social organization, in which class distinctions were accepted as more rigid and more appropriate than in the United States. This meant that the educational systems of all three countries reflected the class distinctions in society. Despite centralized control in France and Germany as contrasted with decentralized control in England, all three countries agreed that elementary education was intended for the common people and that secondary education was to be reserved for the upper classes.

Elementary education was aimed not at producing democratic citizens but at fitting the ordinary people for the state in life to which they were thought to be destined, whereas secondary education was conceived as fitting the potential rulers of the nation to take their rightful places in the state, church, or business world. Whenever American education is compared with European education, this essential difference in social structure and purpose of education should be taken into account.

Communism in Russian Education

Czarist Russia. The Russian czars did relatively little for the education of the masses of the people. The upper classes, including the Greek Orthodox Church, felt that too much education, even mere literacy, might be dangerous for the regime. In line with traditional patterns, therefore, Russian education was based upon the highly aristocratic models of earlier centuries. It was designed to give educational advantages almost exclusively to the middle and upper classes, virtually as in feudal days. The Revolution of 1905, however, helped to spur the czar's government to action. In 10 years there were some seven or eight million students of all ages in all the schools and universities of Russia, though some 60 per cent of the population were still illiterate. When the Communist revolution took place in 1917, the revolutionists were confronted with the most neglected and impoverished educational system of any of the major nations of the world.

Soviet Russia. When the Communists came to power, they set out to secularize, socialize, and centralize Russian education. They confiscated church school property, abolished private schools, and began to set up a universal and free educational system completely under state control. In the course of time a unified system appeared, consisting of nurseries and nursery schools for children under three years of age (many located in the factories), all-day kindergartens for children from three to eight years, primary schools of 4 years (ages eight to twelve), secondary schools of 3 years (ages twelve to fifteen), and upper secondary schools of 3 years (ages fifteen to seventeen).

Above the secondary schools were the technical, scientific, agricultural, and university faculties. Parallel to the secondary schools were established special workers' faculties for the underprivileged city classes in the factories and for the peasants on the collective farms. In addition, there were a considerable number of institutions and extension classes for adult education in industrial, agricultural, commercial, and professional fields. Special attention was given at all levels to wiping out illiteracy and extending technical, cultural, and political education.

In the face of the need for propagating the Communist ideology the schools were completely converted to that task. The old aristocratic and selective methods were turned upside down as children of the privileged classes were denied opportunity to attend the higher schools and preference was given to the working classes. Coeducation became the rule in most schools, but since 1943 a definite tendency to segregate the sexes has been apparent. Despite the dominating centralized control, considerable freedom was allowed the autonomous republics in conducting schools in their own languages, though the central fact of Communist ideology was not, of course, a matter of choice. Whatever special privileges accrued to any groups took the form of privileges to the new "aristocracy" of the Communist party and the Red Army, training for which took place in special schools with rigorous methods.

As a result of all these changes, the numbers attending schools in Russia jumped to some 15,000,000 in 1929; 35,000,000 in 1936; and 47,000,000 in 1939. This vast expansion of educational facilities in little more than 20 years was not matched by any other country. In the twentieth century the Russians had farther to go than any other major country, and they went fast. The Communists showed, as the Nazis had shown, how effective education could be when turned wholeheartedly to the building of ideas and loyalties appropriate to a guiding policy in the hands of a well-organized and closely disciplined party that knew where it wanted to go and had the power to shape all educational agencies in that direction.

Improvement of the Teaching Profession

Teaching became a much more widely recognized profession in the nineteenth century than ever before. The building of national school systems on a mass basis in a relatively short period of time meant that whole new generations of teachers had to be prepared by direct methods in specific institutions for teacher training. An indication of the growing importance of the teaching profession is the way in which conservatives "viewed with alarm" the role of the teachers in the nineteenth-century revolutions in France and Germany. Reactionary leaders may have been looking for a scapegoat, and they naturally chose a fairly helpless group to blame, but the fact that they chose the teachers is indicative of the growing belief that it makes a difference what kind of schools and teachers a society has.

Although the provisions for teacher training in France, Germany, and England differed, they all held to the principle that elementary school teachers should receive a preparation different from that for secondary school teachers. This principle followed from the social and educational distinctions that were maintained in the two-track system of schools. Inasmuch as secondary schools were preparatory to and closely allied with universities, it was expected that universities should prepare teachers for the secondary schools. Inasmuch as elementary education did not lead to the universities, it was necessary to establish separate and "inferior" training institutions to prepare teachers for an inferior type of teaching. Social and educational inbreeding of teachers was accepted as normal and proper.

France. The training of secondary school teachers in France received a great impetus from public sources in 1810 when Napoleon established a Superior Normal School to prepare teachers for the *lycée* and *collège*. The Superior Normal School eventually came to be looked upon as a higher faculty of university standing, emphasizing university-grade instruction in the classics, mathematics, and other subjects appropriate to the secondary schools. By the middle of the century the most important degrees awarded at the Superior Normal School were in classical literature and grammar, philosophy, history, science, and mathematics. The acquisition of subject matter and of systematic knowledge was considered to be the chief instrument in the teacher's preparation for teaching. Graduation from a secondary school was requisite to entrance to the Superior Normal School. The class lines were rather rigidly drawn.

The law of 1833, which provided for primary normal schools to be established in each political department of France, gave a great stimulus to the training of teachers for elementary schools. A few years later, such normal schools were also provided for older girls who wished to become teachers in the primary schools for girls. Graduation from the primary schools was the normal requirement for entrance to the primary normal schools upon the passing of state examinations. Naturally enough, no one entitled to go to a secondary school and to the higher faculties would be interested in teaching in the "lower" schools. Courses in pedagogy and methods of teaching modeled somewhat on Pestalozzian lines were introduced into the normal schools in the 1830's and 1840's. Apparently these newfangled ideas were considered dangerous by the reactionary elements of the Second Republic and Second Empire, for the normal schools were the targets for particular reproach when teachers were being blamed for supporting the Republic.

The curriculum of the primary normal schools was thereupon narrowed, shorn of its "theory" and "methods," and reduced to the acquisition of the subject matter of the primary school subjects. Even the Superior Normal School received its share of rebuke. The degrees in philosophy were suspended, degrees were withheld from students who were suspected of liberal views, and instructors were forced to leave. After the establishment of the Third Republic the curriculum of the primary normal schools was expanded again, but all the details of entrance, subjects taught, textbooks used, and qualifications of the instructors in the normal schools were directed by the Ministry of Public Instruction. The system became a completely closed one, under state control and aimed at training efficient, competent, and loyal teachers.

Under the Third Republic the class distinctions in teacher training were even more rigid than in England. Elementary school teachers were trained in somewhat the following manner: After completing the primary school, the prospective teacher spent 2 years in a special preparatory course, then he went to the primary normal school, which offered a 3-year course; he was then ready to go back into the primary school as a teacher at about age eighteen or nineteen. One of these primary normal schools was located in each *département* of France. Here was almost complete inbreeding of elementary school teachers.

On the other hand, secondary school teachers were graduates of a *collège* or *lycée;* at the age of eighteen they went on for 2 or 3 years to teacher-training institutions connected with the various university faculties and then went back to teach in the secondary schools after passing a number of difficult and strict state examinations in the subject-matter fields. They thus had a strong humanistic, scholarly, and classical training, which served to maintain the traditional and conservative character of French secondary schools. The most influential of these higher normal schools was the Ecole Normale Supérieure of the University of Paris.

Under the Vichy government the reactionaries naturally turned to the teacher-training institutions in the effort to wipe out liberal and radical movements among elementary teachers. A decree in 1941 abolished the special primary normal schools and ordered prospective teachers to follow the regular higher primary school courses. This was undoubtedly a blow at the liberal and secular doctrines that had been taught in these training schools. Anti-Semitic decrees also made it difficult for many Jewish teachers to continue their work in the schools and universities, though some quietly returned when collaborationist enthusiasm began to decline. When the Vichy Ministry of Education became openly fascist, the teachers' organizations protested as vigorously as they could, and many teachers joined the underground resistance movements.

Under the reform plans of the Fourth Republic, efforts were made to reduce the traditional distinctions between the types of training offered to elementary and secondary school teachers. Distinctions remained, however, as in the United States, between those who prepared themselves in the common branches of the lower schools, with emphasis upon pedagogical methods, and those who prepared to teach the academic subjects on the higher levels, with emphasis upon the basic letters and sciences. France had not yet solved the problem of bringing together these principal competencies of teachers, subject matter and methods, theory and practice. The professional status of teachers continued to be protected by strict licensing and carefully planned salary scales, pensions, and social security.

Germany. As a result of the enthusiasm of the liberal movement of the early nineteenth century, the teacher-training institutions of Prussia soon became models for the world to follow. Before 1840, great improvements were made in preparation of elementary school teachers. Borrowing much from Pestalozzian ideas, new teachers' seminaries were set up under public control, the curriculum was broadened, and new courses were introduced in methods, theory, pedagogy, and "didactics." In 1848, the liberal teachers linked with their proposals for a more democratic school system a request that elementary teachers should be trained in the universities along with secondary teachers, but the reactionary movement killed their proposals.

The regulations of 1854 struck out the "dangerous" instruction in methods and theory, a move paralleling the effort to limit instruction in the teachers' seminaries to those subjects to be taught in the elementary schools. Some of the professional content, however, was restored by the regulations of 1872, which gave more freedom to such secular subjects as history of education, theory, psychology, and logic. But the German system did not allow university instruction for elementary teachers, and the principle of inbreeding remained paramount.

Meanwhile, the early liberal movement also affected the preparation of secondary school teachers. Some of the universities began to give special instruction in "pedagogical seminaries" in the subjects of the secondary schools. Prospective teachers in the secondary schools were required to pass state examinations before they could acquire certificates to teach. These examinations came to include the classics, mathematics, science, history, and geography. A year of practice teaching was also required for all new teachers. Such developments soon attracted the attention of many American educators who began to urge the improvement of American teacher training along Prussian lines. In fact, the dual system of training teachers in the United States for long followed European models of inbreeding. Only fairly recently has preparation for elementary teachers been raised to university levels of instruction in the United States.

At the beginning of the twentieth century German teacher training still reflected the familiar two-track system. Prospective elementary school teachers went to the 8-year elementary school, then to a 3-year special preparatory school, and then to a 3-year normal school in which the emphasis was upon routinized training in teaching the elementary school subjects. Inasmuch as the public elementary schools offered denominational religious instruction, the state normal schools were also denominational. Out of 201 state normal schools in Prussia in 1912, 126 were Protestant, 71 were Roman Catholic, and only 4 were nonsectarian in character.

Similarly, prospective secondary school teachers went through the 9-year secondary school (most often the *Gymnasium*) and then to a university, where they studied their subject-matter fields for some 4 years until they could pass comprehensive examinations in a major and minor subject. They generally had little training in educational methods or preparation for teaching as such. Scholarship and intellectual ability were considered to be sufficient qualifications for secondary school teachers. After a year or two of probationary teaching and the passing of a professional examination in education, the candidates were ready to be licensed as regular teachers.

During the Republic, efforts were made to break down the dual system and build more bridges between the elementary and secondary schools; the separate elementary normal schools were abolished in most of the federal states. Prospective elementary teachers were expected to go to the common 4-year *Grundschule*, then to the 9-year secondary school, and finally for 2 or 3 years to a university faculty or institute or to a separate teachers college of university rank where the emphasis was upon psychology and teaching methods. It was thereby hoped that the level of training of elementary teachers would be raised to that of the training of secondary teachers.

With the advent of the Nazis the teacher-training institutions went the way of all Nazi education. Students were put into brown shirts, and the principal qualifications for teaching thenceforth became party loyalty and membership in the Storm Troops. The prospective teacher had to be completely correct, in accordance with the party line, in belief and behavior. Tenure depended entirely on maintaining such a status. All teachers who survived from the Republic were, of course, scrutinized carefully for their political beliefs and the "dangerous" ones weeded out. All teachers' organizations were replaced by the National Socialist Teachers' Association, designed to reeducate teachers in Nazi doctrines or drive them from the schools. Newspaper readers in the United States in the late 1930's read of the book burnings at Salzburg and elsewhere conducted under the auspices of this organization.

As the United Nations occupation authorities looked forward to reconstructing education in Germany, the problem of finding appropriate democratically minded teachers was overwhelming. The chances were that a higher proportion of pre-Nazi teachers could be saved for postwar Germany from the elementary schools than from the secondary schools and universities. Coming as they did from the working and lower-middle classes, elementary teachers were more likely to have liberal, anti-Nazi, or Social Democratic outlooks upon which a democratic educational system could be built.

More than 70 per cent of the teachers under the Nazis had to be discharged, but efforts were made to discover and bring back into the schools those who had been teachers under the Republic. Some 40 teachers colleges were quickly established, and by 1947 some 8,000 teachers were being trained yearly. The students, averaging twenty-five to twenty-six years of age, were very earnest in their efforts to become teachers. Many were sent to the United States and other western countries to widen their horizons and take advantage of their enthusiasms. The greatest need was for professors to teach in the teachers colleges. Too many of them retained their old aristocratic conceptions of education. They were not Nazis, but neither were they democratic in training or outlook. Generations of formalistic and authoritarian attitudes in teacher training had to be overcome in a short time if the challenge from the East was to be met and countered.

England. As would be expected from the English voluntary system, the preparation of elementary school teachers in the nineteenth century was largely carried on by private and religious societies. Proposals for public training colleges for teachers met much the same fate as proposals for public schools. The result was that the government granted financial aid to the voluntary societies to help them support their training institutions, of which there were 32 in 1860. All but two of these were receiving government aid and were being inspected by the government, but the teaching staffs were regularly representative of the denominational faith that controlled the school.

In 1846, England set up an apprenticeship system of teacher training in which a student-teacher, assigned to a regular teacher in the school, received a government grant for support. The regular teacher to whom the apprentice was assigned also received payment; and the regulations for their working and teaching together were laid down by the government. Practice schools were very often maintained in connection with the teacher-training institutions. Much of the stimulus to teacher training came from the monitorial system of the day, for the large numbers of pupils required new techniques of teaching to replace individualized instruction. By 1890 training colleges were permitted in the university colleges, but in general the vast majority of secondary school teachers were considered to be properly prepared if they graduated from a secondary school and perhaps attended a university with an arts or science faculty.

The training of teachers in England thus traditionally followed the principles of the two-class system. Elementary school teachers went up through the elementary schools to the age of seventeen or so, were apprenticed to an experienced teacher for 2 to 5 years, and were then entitled to teach. Special teacher-training institutions, mostly under private and religious control, were established for preparing elementary school teachers in addition to the apprenticeship system.

Secondary school teachers were recruited from secondary school graduates. Some simply gained experience in teaching, and others went on to the universities for work in the academic subject-matter fields, sometimes topped off by a year of professional study of "education" in the university pedagogical department.

This system, as in France and Germany, established a rather high degree of inbreeding as between the elementary and secondary school systems. The National Board of Education controlled the public elementary teacher-training colleges up to the early 1920's and prescribed the courses of study. Since the early 1930's these prescriptions have been relaxed, and a good deal of local initiative has been allowed, the Board simply stating that teachers should be efficient.

In 1944 a national committee under the chairmanship of Sir Arnold

McNair recommended emergency as well as long-term measures to relieve the desperate shortage of teachers incurred by the war. Some 55 emergency training colleges were quickly established to give a 1-year intensive course to young men and women who had been engaged in national service. Within 4 years some 18,000 persons were prepared to teach by these emergency training colleges. In order to promote preparation of teachers on a long-term basis, Area Training Organizations were established with administrative centers in the several universities. These centers attempted to coordinate the efforts of training colleges, school systems, and universities in order to raise standards, improve courses of study, and promote the in-service as well as the preservice preparation of teachers. The establishment of single salary standards for elementary and secondary teachers was one further attempt to break down the old double-track system of teacher education.

Russia. When the Communists came to power in Russia, they had to use the main body of teachers already in the schools until they could train new teachers loyal to their revolutionary ideals. At the outset, therefore, they did not give too much power to teachers but aimed to capture directly the children and youth through party-controlled youth movements. Once the youth were won over, they in turn brought pressures and criticisms to bear upon those teachers who were reluctant to adopt the new ideology. Student control of discipline, administrative devices, and "reports" on the teachers were powerful weapons to bring the teachers into line.

Once teacher-training institutes were reorganized or created, a new generation of teachers began to man the schools. By 1930 or so, enough new teachers were ready and enough of the old teachers had been "re-educated" so that they could be given more power and authority in the schools. Elaborate decrees in the 1940's instructed children to obey without question the orders of teachers. Youth organizations were obliged to help teachers maintain discipline and to carry out their instructions. Children were no longer permitted to interfere with or criticize the work of the teachers. Political correctness was the supreme qualification of the Soviet teacher.

Considerable specialization became the rule in Soviet teacher education. Special pedagogical schools comparable to American 2-year normal schools were established to prepare teachers for the first four grades of the elementary schools. Separate teachers' institutes were designed for those who were preparing to teach in the intermediate grades 5, 6, and 7. Still other pedagogical institutes, comparable to American 4-year teachers colleges, prepared teachers for the upper grades 8, 9, and 10. The dominant motif in all teacher-training institutions was strict adherence to the ideology and goals of Soviet society as defined by the Communist party. To this end, special emphasis was put upon political studies as the very groundwork of pedagogical competence.

Out-of-school Agencies of Youth Education

In the twentieth century it became more than ever clear that agencies of education outside of the organized schools for children and youth could exert enormous influence. The radio, motion pictures, newspapers, periodicals, books, and rapid means of communication made easier the promotion of public discussion and the molding of public opinion.

In England, for example, adult education took enormous strides through such agencies as trade unions, political parties, church organizations, co-operatives, and university extension courses. Above all, the Workers' Educational Association, which had branches all over the country, furnished speakers and discussion-group leaders, and distributed large amounts of literature and films on public issues of all kinds. During the Second World War the Army Bureau of Current Affairs conducted an effective program for discussion of important problems among English soldiers and officers, and the civil-defense programs functioned similarly for the home front. The Youth Service also stimulated programs of health, recreation, and leisure-time activities in clubs and youth centers.

The Western democracies, however, lagged far behind Germany, Italy, and Russia in organizing out-of-school youth movements on a large scale. In pre-Nazi Germany at the beginning of the twentieth century a youth movement under the leadership of Karl Fischer found great popularity among German boys and girls of about ages fifteen to eighteen. It was a reaction against the increasing industrial, urban, and materialistic civilization of the times and represented the revival of a romantic spirit of freedom and rebellion against the restraints of intellectualized education. Trips into the country developed a back-to-nature feeling and an interest in the folklore and life of the rural and village regions.

The First World War changed the romantic spirit to an aggressive and disillusioned one; these youth proved to be fine tools for the Nazis, who quickly saw the value of organization as a means of capturing the loyalties of the younger generation and used them as a leverage against the anti-Nazi sentiments or indifference of older groups.

An organization known generically as the "Hitler Youth" was built up to embrace all children from ages ten to eighteen. A preparatory organization was for children from ten to fourteen years of age; in this, "character" development and physical training were emphasized. For youth from fourteen to eighteen the organization was to provide activities to interest the members and make good Nazis of them. Outings, hikes, camping, strenuous physical sports of all kinds, and evenings of singing, storytelling, marching, and radio entertainment made up the bulk of their out-of-school activities. At first the so-called "terrain sports" were claimed not to be military training, but by 1939 it was openly declared that pistol and rifle practice in attacking and defending imaginary battlegrounds was to be emphasized. Starting on a voluntary basis, the Hitler Youth was made compulsory in 1939 for all boys and girls from ten to eighteen.

Baldur von Schirach, Reich youth leader, held the post of a state secretary; his favorite phrase was "German youth belongs to the Fuehrer." Constant stress was put upon duty, obedience, German honor, character, spirit, courage, discipline, and leadership, all leading up to the desire to die for the fatherland and the Fuehrer. Special groups for training to become the elite in the Nazi party were organized and given a most rigorous and diabolical preparation for leadership. More than 7,000,000 belonged at one time to the Hitler Youth, by far the majority of German youth. For too long a time the democracies did not realize how seriously German youth were taking such "confessions of faith" as that delivered by Robert Ley, chief of the Labor Front, to 15,000 youth in Berlin in 1937.

> We believe on this earth solely in Adolf Hitler. We believe that National Socialism is the sole faith and salvation of our people. We believe there is a God in Heaven who has created us, led us, and publicly laid His blessing upon us. We believe that God has sent us Adolf Hitler so that Germany may receive a foundation for its existence through all eternity. Adolf Hitler, victory heil!

In addition to the military and ideological training of the Hitler Youth movement, which overshadowed the formal training in the schools, the Nazis reinforced the ideals of work and love for the soil, as well as promoting health and physical strength, by sending boys and girls of fourteen to fifteen years for a year of organized and directed work on the farms, a period known as the "land year." During the day they worked in the fields and had physical training; in the evenings they received nationalistic and political training in Nazi ideology. Likewise, the Labor Service was required for a half year for all boys at eighteen, prior to their 2 years of compulsory military service.

Thus, the party erected a complete structure of out-of-school education for all youth, designed to feed a strong and disciplined following into the Storm Troops, Elite Guard, and the party itself. Complete control of radio, newspapers, books, art, dramatic entertainment, and all the means of communication and propaganda gave the party enormous power. It was extremely clever in its appeal to the interests of youth by playing up the heroic ideals of self-sacrifice, obedience, and service to a cause. In these ways they produced the powerful and fanatical loyalties that the democracies so often underestimated.

The Soviet Russian techniques in developing youth organizations were somewhat similar to those of Germany. In Russia the Octobrists (ages eight to twelve), the Pioneers (ages ten to sixteen), and the Young Communists (ages fourteen to twenty-three) served analogous purposes to promote the Communist ideology and provide a pathway for entrance into the Communist party. The Soviet Union was extremely adept at developing cultural, dramatic, and art programs that solidified political awareness among youth and adult groups.

By 1950 the democracies could see what an enormously potent weapon the Communist party was forging in its youth organizations. The entire apparatus of Soviet mind control swung into action in the Communist countries of the postwar world. The organized group movements represented by the Stockholm "peace" campaign, the East Berlin Festival of Youth, and the "brain washing" of Korean prisoners of war served to remind that the Communists were relentless in their campaigns to capture the mind of youth. The entire picture of the Nazi youth groups described in the foregoing paragraphs could be repeated with the substitution of Communist for Nazi. Uniforms, marching, songs, hatred of scapegoats (Americans for Jews), and, above all, the unthinking enthusiasm for slogans were having the same effect all over again. Now, however, these attractions were reinforced by the feeling instilled in Communist youth that they were part of a world-wide movement to which the whole future belonged. The Western world could see it happening again. Could they learn the lesson from what they saw?

Chapter 13

INTELLECTUAL FOUNDATIONS
OF MODERN EUROPEAN EDUCATION

OLD AND NEW DIMENSIONS OF THOUGHT

Conflicts in Philosophy, Science, and Religion

Among the general intellectual trends of the nineteenth and twentieth centuries, two or three main currents may be mentioned as particularly relevant for understanding educational outlooks and methods. In the first half of the nineteenth century the dominant intellectual outlook came to be known as "absolute idealism." Stemming from the work of such German philosophers as Kant, Fichte, and Hegel, idealism represented a reaction against the scientific rationalism of the eighteenth-century Enlightenment. The effort of idealism was primarily to build a complete system of thought that would reintegrate man and nature and God into a great unity expressed by the term "Absolute." This outlook, related to romantic expressions in literature and the arts, generally tended to reinforce the religious temper against the scientific and positivistic temper.

Of all the tremendous scientific gains of the nineteenth century, the development of the theory of evolution was perhaps the most important and the most revolutionary in its whole impact upon the outlook of men. Stemming from the work of Linnaeus, Erasmus Darwin, Lamarck, and, above all, Charles Darwin, the evolutionary concept was elaborated not only as a specific biological explanation of the origin of life on this earth but also as a general interpretation of the development of man and his social institutions. Herbert Spencer and Thomas Huxley were preeminent in popularizing the broader applications of the doctrine of evolution. Consequently, they soon came into violent conflict with the established and traditional beliefs about the origin of the world and of man.

Backed by scientific investigations in many other fields of knowledge, evolution and science challenged the supremacy of religious and idealistic thought in the latter half of the nineteenth century. Despite a reassertion of idealism late in the century by Thomas Hill Green, Francis Herbert Bradley, and Bernard Bosanquet, the forces of science, evolution, and realism were emerging stronger than ever.

Sometimes the conflict of evolution and religion resulted in the attempt to reconcile the two, as in the case of the religious modernists, but it also

383

sometimes meant an out-and-out attack on orthodox religious beliefs. Leaders in the antireligious movement were Spencer and Huxley in England, Clemenceau in France, and Haeckel in Germany. They were not only active in speaking and writing, but they also formed societies to promulgate their ideas. The Rationalist Press Association was founded in England, and the International Freethinkers League was organized in 1880.

The religious forces, of course, were not without their resources, and they quickly rose to do battle. One defense was the movement in the nineteenth century known as "Christian Evidences," based on Butler's *Analogy of Natural and Revealed Religion* and Paley's *Natural Theology*. Their principal argument was that the existence of God is proved and demonstrated by the revelations of natural science. The wonderful adjustments of natural phenomena, they held, require the belief that nature has been designed by God and cannot be the result of accident or natural laws. In France the most effective defender of religion and Catholicism was Chateaubriand. In England notable defenses were made by the members of the Oxford movement, who denounced science and defended the faith. Of these John Henry Newman, who became a convert to Roman Catholicism and was made a cardinal of the church, was outstanding.

In the twentieth century the conflicts in religion, science, and philosophy continued in manifold ways. A few names are typical of several complex intellectual trends. Jacques Maritain in France was one of the leading Roman Catholic spokesmen for a return to the philosophy of St. Thomas Aquinas. Karl Barth in Germany and Switzerland represented a revival of orthodoxy in Protestant thought, stressing the power and righteousness of God, the sin of man, and the helplessness of man to be saved without the forgiveness of God. He argued for a return to Luther and Calvin and to Paul and Jeremiah.

In contrast, Jean-Paul Sartre in France was the outstanding spokesman for the atheistic version of existentialism. He insisted that, since God does not exist, man is on his own and must rely solely on his own efforts and will. Human values are not given to man from on high nor are they to be found in heaven; human destiny is found only in the realm of human action.

In philosophy, idealism found a forceful restatement by Benedetto Croce in Italy, whereas newer formulations of mathematical and scientific philosophy were made in their distinctive ways by Bertrand Russell, Alfred North Whitehead, and J. B. S. Haldane. The schools and the universities of the twentieth century rang with the cross fire of controversy in religion and philosophy as well as in politics and economics.

Religion versus Evolution. The fundamentalists in Protestantism held to the literal interpretation of the Bible that the world was specially created by God at a certain time in the past and that the species of living things have not changed since that time. For evidence they pointed to the description of creation in the Scriptures, which were divinely inspired and therefore could not be doubted.

Attacks upon the fundamentalist position during the nineteenth century took two principal forms. The first was based on a growing scientific and historical study of the origins of the Bible. It was pointed out that the Bible was written over a period of hundreds of years by a number of different human beings who recorded various stories and events much as any great literature is produced. Students of Biblical criticism and of comparative religions maintained that the doctrine of special creation was evolved by men in ancient times who did not have the advantage of the scientific knowledge now available. As this point of view gained headway, it was easier for the doctrine of evolution to gain adherents.

The second form of attack upon fundamentalist religion was based, of course, on the evolutionary conception of the nature of life. Evolution contended that during aeons of time the various species of life changed gradually from simple to more complex forms and that no species was fixed or changeless. In the natural process by which individual organisms interacted with their physical and social environments the various forms of life have appeared, of which the most complex is man. From the evidence of science and history, it was maintained that the earth and man are much older than had ever before been realized, that all species of life are branches of a common trunk of living things, and that species change from natural causes rather than as a result of a divine act of special creation.

Influenced by the sociological and population theories of Malthus, Darwin relied upon survival of the fittest and natural selection to explain the way in which living species changed. Evolution also drew upon the findings of geology and paleontology to show that the earth is 2 to 5 billion years old and that recent organisms have a much more complex structure than did the fossil remains of earlier times. Physiology, morphology, and chemistry showed that there is an essential likeness and continuity between the bodily structures and physiological processes of various types of animals and of man. Thus, the conception of change became enormously important not only in biology but in other fields of knowledge.

If change is an inherent part of the whole process of natural and human development, many began to argue, change is also an essential characteristic of social institutions. This meant that social institutions not only *can* be changed (as the Enlightenment humanitarians desired) but that social institutions *must* change because of the very nature of life and society. This application to society of the evolutionary conceptions of change stimulated optimism and hope in respect to human progress. It stimulated secularism because it focused attention upon life here and now rather than upon the next world. It stimulated the desire to study scientifically all aspects of social life with as much care, precision, and accuracy as had gone into the study of biology.

Idealism versus realism. The conflict between idealism and realism continued from the older controversies over the nature of the universe, but it took on new forms in the nineteenth century. It was the old battle between those who emphasized the preeminence of ideas and mental forms and those who emphasized the external world of nature and material things as the basic reality. Greek idealism had said that ideas are the supreme reality and that the objects of nature are simply passing fancies. Descartes had said that there are two realms equally real, one of mind and one of matter. Now, absolute idealism of the early nineteenth century tried to join mind and matter into a unity that made ideas and thought not only the supreme focus of individual attention but also the very structure of the universe itself. The idealists relied greatly upon faith, emotion, and mystical feeling. The towering philosophers of this outlook were Fichte, Schelling, and Hegel.

Whereas Kant had said that the individual mind must order its experience if it is to achieve knowledge, Fichte began to say that this is the process by which a universal mind, or Absolute, orders all the events of the world, nature, man, and social institutions. Hence, all experience takes place because the Absolute is experiencing and realizing itself. The objective world of nature is simply an expression of the Absolute mind, and all human beings act as they do because they are a part of this universal process. From all time the Absolute has been in the process of working out the relationships of man and nature, and in a sense this has been an evolutionary process.

God was viewed by idealism, not as a creator outside and beyond what He created, but rather as the creative intelligence or spirit within the whole process of physical and social development. Because the Absolute exists in everything, everything is shaped by a moral purpose. The highest manifestations of the Absolute are in man. Each man is an expression of the moral and spiritual qualities of the Absolute; therefore, as individual men work together in a common social and moral life, they express the unified moral purposes of the Absolute. Individual men can be good only as they cooperate actively in the processes of social institutions. Fichte's patriotic fervor after the defeat of Napoleon made his philosophy a groundwork element in the development of German nationalism. As individual Germans worked together to create a German nation, he urged, they were at the same time helping to express the Absolute's will on earth.

This philosophy of idealism was carried to its ultimate conclusions by Hegel, whose philosophy of history further helped to build up a theoretical justification for German nationalism. Beginning in the relatively subjective and disorganized mentality of individuals, the Absolute has been unfolding itself for centuries through the various stages of social institutions until it was finally being realized in its highest form in the Prussian state of Hegel's day. The basic social and moral process always goes through the three phases of thesis, antithesis, and synthesis. This view represents Hegel's dialectical method, some elements of which Marx relied upon in formulating his theory that every economic system generates its own opposite and thus contains the seeds of its own destruction.

In contrast to the metaphysical and mystical formulations of idealism, the philosophy of realism was reasserted with great strength in the nineteenth century. Turning its eyes away from the attempt to construct great systems of ideal perfection and absolute authority, realism oriented itself to the findings of natural science and the objectivity of the external world. It discounted the unity of all things and the reliance upon a supreme moral authority. Reality exists not in the ideas and will of a theoretical spiritual being but in the natural laws of the objective world. The facts and things and relationships of experience are real and exist independently of moral law and human minds.

This approach to science was formulated into a philosophy called "positivism" by Auguste Comte in the middle of the nineteenth century. Comte described three historical stages of philosophy, (1) the theological stage, in which the divine and supernatural were appealed to as explanations of natural phenomena; (2) the metaphysical stage, in which philosophers tried to build up complete systems of such abstract entities as substance, form, and Absolute in order to explain nature; and (3) the positive stage, in which science and scientific method were the agencies used to arrive at empirical explanations of nature.

In general, the effort of the realists was to build up a conception of a world of nature that was orderly, systematic, and knowable through the investigations of science and that did not need to rely upon spiritual or supernatural explanations of a religious or mystical kind. John Stuart Mill, Spencer, and Huxley made great efforts to spread this realistic view of the universe. The underlying assumption of Mill, for example, was a fixed reality in which physical things obey assured and uniform laws, acting in a predictable manner based upon the universal law of causation. He postulated a world of physical reality characterized by complete regularity of action. As idealism was likely to appeal to the religious and emotional temper, so did positivism and realism appeal to the secular temper of the times and attempt to incorporate science into philosophy.

The new scientific discoveries of the twentieth century led to a conception of the universe and of the nature of matter that overturned the nineteenth-century conception of science that had rested upon Newtonian physics. It also seemed to make necessary a revision of the traditional philosophic and religious conceptions of idealism. The rigidity of absolute natural laws that formed the basis of Newtonian physics was giving way to doctrines of relativity in the astronomical universe and of uncertainty in the subatomic universe.

The astronomers and physicists began to describe a new cosmos of unimaginable size in which our sun became an insignificant unit in our galaxy of astronomical bodies and our galaxy only one of perhaps a million galaxies of like proportions. Matter was no longer regarded as hard, rigid, indestructible, and obedient to certain fixed laws, as the laws of gravitation and the law of cause and effect in the Newtonian sense; it came to be looked upon as a way in which energy is organized. Somehow, the ultimate physical reality was conceived to be energy. The atom became, not a unitary and integral body, but a physical-energy system made up of electrons and neutrons operating in complex ways. The theories of relativity, quantum physics, electromechanics, and radioactivity produced a whole new conception of matter and energy.

The only way in which such relations could adequately be described was by means of a new mathematics to replace Newton's and Euclid's. Actual investigations with new instruments such as the atom-smashing cyclotron seemed to substantiate the calculations of such theoretical mathematicians as Henri Poincaré, Max Planck, and Albert Einstein. As the atom was broken up, analyzed, and studied, it became possible to produce hitherto unknown physical elements and to transmute matter from one form to another.

As discovery followed discovery in the physicists' laboratories, it became clear that the atomic age began, not with the dropping of the atomic bomb on Japan, but with the mathematicians and physicists who were beginning to lay the foundations in the opening years of the twentieth century. At all events, a reformulation of the traditional views of the universe was being forced by the new science of the twentieth century.

Conflicting Conceptions of Human Nature

The basic quarrel between idealism and realism expressed itself in conflicting conceptions, not only of the universe and nature, but of human nature as well. Religion emphasized the mental, moral, and intellectual aspects of human nature as expressions of the divine spirit on earth. Man was viewed as a distinct being separated by an impassable gulf from the rest of nature because of his moral and intellectual qualities. This idealization of human nature often branched out into a romantic and mystical glorification of the individual, especially exalting his emotions and feelings rather than his intellect as the guide to conduct.

The positivists, on the other hand, most often borrowed from science and evolution the description of man as continuous with nature but as the highest and most complicated form of natural life. Man developed his superior qualities of mind and conscience within the natural processes of evolution. Positivism led to the scientific study of human nature and the formulation of natural laws of human behavior to explain human conduct, on a par with scientific explanations of nature, the universe, and social institutions. The application of scientific methods of study to human nature was the principal effect of realism upon educational method in the nineteenth century.

Scientists began to study human physiology, the nervous system, the processes of sensation and perception, the physiology of the senses, and the laws of heredity and genetics and undertook experimental investigations of the mental processes. In this effort the work of Gall, Galton, Spencer, and Wundt was especially important. They began to operate on Mill's assumptions concerning the laws of the moral sciences. If we know all about a person, they felt, we can predict his conduct as certainly as we can predict physical events. We can build up a science of human nature in which there is no doubt that human thought, feelings, and actions work on the causal principle. The laws of the mind are general and universal laws that can be discovered by observation and experimentation much as the laws of nature may be discovered by scientific investigation.

From this kind of scientific psychology the laws of the formation of human character can be deduced. If we know how the mind works, then we have a ready-made structure upon which to hang our educational techniques. The naturalistic conception of man soon led to investigations that were to revolutionize the traditional conceptions of human learning and intelligence. This meant eventually a revolution in educational methods.

Although man seemed to be relegated to an incredibly insignificant place in comparison with the astrophysical universe that was being visualized by science, the twentieth century began to pay still more attention to the study of human nature. In general, the doctrines of evolution came to be more widely accepted than ever as anthropologists studied the origins of the race and psychologists studied the foundations of human behavior. Anthropology showed that man developed physically and culturally as he interacted with his environment over the long centuries of human development. Wherever science was free, anthropologists produced plenty of evidence to disprove the Nazi and fascist theories of racial purity and race superiority.

Anthropologists agreed that all men have a common ancestor. Whatever differences can be found among groups of people in skin or eye color, body size, shape of head or nose, or facial characteristics are relatively unimportant differences. Even if the major races are classified as Caucasoid, Mongoloid, and Negroid, the range of differences within one group is far greater than the differences among groups. Ethnic stocks have been so dispersed and mixed together for so long in all parts of the world that there is no such thing as a "pure" race. The differences among groups of people were agreed to be principally differences of culture, language, custom, and education.

Differences among individuals, however, were conceded to be great, no matter what the racial or ethnic background. Psychology turned to the matter of individual differences with enthusiasm. Much of this interest was devoted to a scientific investigation of sensory perceptions and motor reactions, following the lead of Wundt and other European psychophysiologists.

Another development in Europe that was to have great influence upon the conception of human nature was the development of psychoanalysis as worked out principally by Sigmund Freud, Alfred Adler, and Carl Gustav Jung. Their interest was primarily in explaining the reasons for mental abnormalities in adults. They all agreed in tracing back the difficulties in large part to the conflicts between individual and social desires that develop in the early years of childhood, principally between the ages of two to five.

The psychoanalysts held to a basically dualistic conception of mind and body as the ingredients of human nature, but they broke with the dominantly rationalistic conceptions that were current at the beginning of the twentieth century. They maintained that the mind is dualistic too, consisting of the conscious mind of rational choice and the subconscious motivations and drives that really give impetus to most human activities. As ideas, drives, and beliefs come into conflict within an individual, he must somehow meet the varying demands of social pressures. Some ideas and beliefs will therefore be suppressed, but rather than being sloughed off they are driven down to the subconscious level, where they continue to operate and often lead to abnormal behavior.

Freud explained the origin of most suppressed desires as due to interference with sex motives, defining sex broadly as the total driving force of the individual. Adler interpreted the basic human drive as the desire for power that comes when the child's sense of inferiority and helplessness in the face of social pressures lead him to try to achieve superiority. When blocked in these efforts, his drives to power are suppressed in childhood and then reassert themselves, usually in the form of abnormal or socially undesirable behavior, in adulthood. Jung defined the total driving force as the desire to express one's own individuality against the outside social pressures to conform.

Despite much opposition to the specific interpretations of the psychoanalysts, they have had enormous influence in turning the attention of educators to the importance of the early childhood years in shaping human behavior. They were forerunners of the mental-hygiene emphasis that began to be important later in the century. It meant that teachers and parents needed to be educated to be aware of the powerful impact of the early years upon the personality development of their children.

New Conceptions of Learning and Intelligence

The dominating theories of knowledge and the learning process were approached, as in the past, from two major points of view, the rational and the empirical. The rationalistic views were sympathetic to the idealistic and religious temper of thought, and the empirical views leaned upon scientific investigation for their evidence.

In general, rationalistic beliefs adhered to traditional outlooks stemming from Aristotle and St. Thomas Aquinas. The human mind is a mental and spiritual faculty that has the power to reach out and grasp the universal and necessary principles of ultimate truth. Cardinal Newman maintained this intellectualistic conception of knowledge and learning, definitely placing scientific knowledge in a lower position on the scale of intellectual virtues. This position has been described at length in previous chapters.

The empirical approach to knowledge and learning took several forms. John Stuart Mill argued that universal and necessary truths can be built up by experience through inductive methods. Mill was just as convinced as the rationalists were that permanent and necessary truths exist. He differed from them in insisting that such truths are revealed, not by an intellectual faculty of reason, but by the empirical processes of scientific and inductive methods. He provided the theoretical basis upon which much of the framework of a scientific philosophy and psychology was constructed in the nineteenth century.

Building upon a realistic conception of the external world and upon an empirical conception of the nature of knowledge, the most prominent psychology of learning of the mid-nineteenth century was associationism. It departed from the faculty psychology of idealism and rationalism and attempted to reduce all mental processes to that of association.

According to this view, whose famous exponents were Mill and Herbart, the mind and consciousness are formed by the process in which simple perceptions of external objects become associated with other perceptions. As these perceptions become associated in many complex combinations, an "apperceptive mass" of experience is built up in the individual. This constitutes the structure of his mind. When two ideas are linked in experience, a later stimulus from external causes will recall not only the original idea but also the one that has become associated with it.

The mind was thought to be a center in which ideas and perceptions constantly compete for recognition in the apperceptive mass. The mind develops as the perceptions become elaborated into ideas or conceptions or meanings. Perceptions do not remain in consciousness but are pushed back into the unconscious, where they are stored until called out by new perceptions or experiences. The more frequent, recent, or vivid the associations are, the more easily can an idea be called out of the unconscious into consciousness. The modern laws of learning related to frequency and recency as expressed by scientific psychology in the twentieth century are foreshadowed in these introspective theories of associationism.

Another form of an empirical approach to learning was the development of experimental psychology in the later nineteenth century. Psychology came to be looked upon as a scientific analysis of consciousness in which controlled experiment could produce quantitative results that would predict human behavior and learning. Many scientists began to insist that psychology and study of the mind must be based upon physiology. Therefore, psychologists turned to a study of the physiology of the senses. They investigated the sensory and motor nerves; they measured the speed of nerve impulses; they studied how the eye, ear, and speech organs work; and they tested the pressures necessary to cause sensations on the skin and in the tactile senses.

Above all, the experimental methods of scientific psychology were developed by Wilhelm Max Wundt in his laboratory at Leipzig. Wundt had much influence upon the development of scientific psychology in America. The tests of sensory discrimination conducted by Galton also gave an impetus to the study of individual differences and the development of intelligence testing.

Two trends were especially important in the early twentieth century: behaviorism and Gestalt psychology. Behaviorism applied rigorous scientific methods to human behavior. Its adherents concentrated on studying overt behavior, rejecting the introspective study of mental images, ideas, consciousness, will, and so on. They refused to speak of "mind" or mental activity and spoke only of behavior as it could be observed from the outside. They leaned heavily upon the work of Vladimir Bechterev and Ivan Petrovich Pavlov in Russia, who experimented with animals to arrive at the principles of the conditioned reflex.

By presenting food to a dog and ringing a bell at the same time under controlled conditions, Pavlov discovered that simply ringing the bell could call out the salivary flow which originally the food had produced. The principle was thus that, if two stimuli (food and bell), one of which is strong enough to evoke a reflex (salivary flow), occur often enough together, the second or formerly inadequate stimulus (bell) will be sufficient to evoke the response. The behaviorists began to build upon the fundamental principles of the conditioned reflex a whole theory of learning in which all the so-called "higher" processes of thought were considered to be built up by a like conditioning of responses to associated stimuli.

Gradually some psychologists in Europe and America became dissatisfied alike with the analytical methods of associationism and the purely objective methods of the conditioned reflex. This dissatisfaction took the form of a point of view having its origin in Germany and receiving the name Gestalt psychology. Under the leadership of Max Wertheimer, Wolfgang Köhler, and Kurt Koffka in the second decade of the twentieth century, the Gestaltists began to deny the principle that learning results from the connection between a specific stimulus and a specific response and the association of stimulus-response reflexes. They argued rather that the total situation affects the learning process and that the total activity of the body is involved in learning, not simply the sensory and motor nerves.

Gestalt psychology thus stressed the organic nature of the learning process. The learner responds as an organic whole, and he responds to a whole situation, not merely in an automatic, mechanistic, or piecemeal fashion. Insight and purposes become important elements in learning. Mere repetition was not considered sufficient for learning unless the individual by insight acquires the same goal for his activity that the teacher or experimenter has. Gestaltists also emphasized that growth and maturation are important means by which learners come to see the significance of the learning situation for them as they interact with their environment. The Gestalt psychology played an important part in influencing the development of a newer psychological outlook in America in the 1920's and 1930's.

Another very influential development in Europe had to do with procedures worked out by Alfred Binet and T. Simon in France. They were primarily interested in quickly identifying subnormal children, with capacities below those of normal children, in order to give them special help. Binet assumed that the mind is made up of different functions such as association, memory, motor skill, attention, reasoning, and will, all of which can be measured independently. He further assumed that these functions develop at about the same rate, so that a measurement of one or more functions at a given time will give a clue to the status of the others. He therefore worked out tests of association, memory, and attention, classified the items according to difficulty, and arrived at norms for different age levels. On this basis he devised the conception of "mental age," which gives a somewhat objective standard for the mental age of five-year-olds, six-year-olds, and so on. Binet's beginnings were rapidly picked up and expanded into a powerful intelligence-testing movement by an important group of psychologists in America during the early twentieth century.

Developments in the Arts and Sciences

The fields of scholarly and creative endeavor revealed somewhat the same contrast in outlooks that marked the fundamental views of the world and human nature. Somewhat akin to the idealist outlook in philosophy was the romanticism expressed in European literature, art, and music; and somewhat akin to the realistic outlook in philosophy were the major trends in the sciences and social sciences.

Harking back to the ideals of adventure and sentiment of the medieval romance for much of its inspiration, romanticism broke away from the classic emphasis upon simplicity, orderliness, clarity, and unity. Romanticism dealt in the strange, the subjective, the emotional, and the mysterious, glorifying the individual, freedom, and nature.

In contrast, the realist approach caused scholars to settle down to the serious task of examining, measuring, observing, checking, and generalizing the data derived from study of the physical, natural, and social world. Detailed and accurate description became the ultimate goal of the positivist in the sciences and social sciences and of the realist in literature and art.

In the nineteenth century the vernacular literature of the world definitely came of age. Even some of the classicists came to admit that the period was a creative one in literature that could stand next to the classical and Renaissance periods, even though not as a rival. The twentieth century witnessed notable achievements in the creative as well as the scholarly approach to the linguistic and literary arts. Scholars in the principal countries amassed enormous bodies of knowledge in philology and textual and literary criticism. Creative efforts in literature, drama, and poetry expressed the social trends of the new capitalistic industrialism, social reform, science, and Freudian psychology. In general, the romantic and sentimental tenor of nineteenth-century literature began to give way to a more realistic description of social forces and individual expressions of hope, despair, or anxiety.

Creative expression in the fine arts in the nineteenth century was perhaps overshadowed by the scientific, industrial, and technological advances. Except in France, the energies of men seemed to find expression in scientific investigation or in the building of a new industrial society rather than in the arts of painting and sculpture. France was easily the leader in painting. Following the romantic and dramatic themes, some painters turned to the realistic and accurate portrayal of the details of nature, and others painted landscapes with infinite regard for the exact tones of light and shade. The reaction of Cézanne against realism and impressionism laid the groundwork for the development of the various modernist schools of the twentieth century. In England Rossetti and William Morris urged that art and industrial design be more closely allied, to wipe out the ugliness of modern civilization and restore art to a social role in life and culture.

The developments in nineteenth-century music, however, reached the peak of creative expression, unmatched in any other comparable period of time. Its power and sweep were recognized so fully that it soon was known as "classical" music and became the standard by which all other music was to be judged. In architecture the emergence of industrial urban civilization pointed the way to architectural forms that not only expressed a functional design but would meet the needs of mass housing and better community planning.

The great steps taken in the field of the sciences during the Enlightenment were increased during the nineteenth century. Mention has already been made of the enormous advancement of the biological sciences, culminating in the theories of evolution. The study of the cellular structure of the animal and human organism, of heredity, pathology, embryology, and physiology kept pace, to say nothing of bacteriology, vaccines, anesthesia, the germ theory of disease, and antiseptic surgery in the field of medicine. Geology, paleontology, and geography gave new interpretations of the structure of the earth and its various manifestations that helped to support the evolutionary conceptions. The development of non-Euclidean geometry revealed significant trends in mathematics and astronomy. Practical work in astronomy was aided by the construction of improved telescopes and observatory equipment.

In physics the fundamental theories of heat, conservation of energy, the nature of electricity, and laws of thermodynamics were elaborated; and in chemistry the atomic theory and periodic law of the elements were probed. The formerly rigid lines between inorganic and organic existence began to be challenged by organic chemistry. The scientific investigations of human physiology and psychology have already been mentioned.

As a result of these great advances, science gained tremendous prestige and authority in the intellectual life of the world. The term "science" came to have at least three meanings. (1) It referred to the various bodies of organized knowledge, each with its own systematic and consistent statements of tested beliefs. (2) It came to mean a method for the discovery and refinement of experimental knowledge, relying upon careful observation, the formulation of hypotheses, the elaboration of consequences, and the testing and verifying of the hypotheses under controlled and measurable conditions. (3) It came to mean a whole philosophy, or world view, according to which events follow orderly procedures that can be discovered by the senses, measured accurately, and expressed in quantitative terms. In such a scientific philosophy the principle of continuity replaced the doctrine of dualism; and truth came to be looked upon as a relative rather than as an absolute means of guiding man to new and more valid conceptions of knowledge and action.

Stimulated by the great developments in science and by the efforts to achieve better social arrangements that grew out of the democratic movements of the nineteenth century, the study of human relationships took on a new importance. Positivism and realism led many scholars and writers to apply scientific methods to the study of society. For the first time, separate and distinct bodies of systematic knowledge in the social sciences were organized and differentiated from the traditional catch-all category of "philosophy" under which social institutions had been treated since ancient and medieval days. History, political science, economics, sociology, and anthropology appeared as distinct sciences.

Most of the history writing of the nineteenth century was strongly affected by the patriotic fervor that pervaded most countries, and many nationalistic histories of France, Germany, and England made their appearance. The effort was also made to write history with prime attention to accuracy and details that corresponded to the facts. A leader in this movement was Leopold von Ranke in Germany. In economics such classical economists as Malthus, Ricardo, and James Mill defended capitalism by formulating the "natural laws" of economics, but by the end of the century definite efforts were made to apply new statistical and historical methods to the realm of economic affairs.

Political science was largely devoted to defining terms and classifying forms of government according to their structure and type, but notable efforts were made to arrive at accurate descriptions and valid generalizations concerning political arangements in the works of Alexis de Tocqueville and James Bryce, both of whom took America as their object of study. Sociology was given form and status by the work of Saint-Simon, Comte, Spencer, and many others, most of whom attempted to describe society as an organism analogous to the individual person. Anthropology had not yet became a field of cultural study comparable in scope with the other social sciences but confined itself largely to measuring human skeletons and describing the development of tools and implements that had been produced in the various stages of man's evolution.

The practice and theory of law were greatly affected by the Napoleonic Code, which dominated the legal systems of the Continental nations. According to the prevailing view of the nineteenth century, the law was the system of regulations issued by the rulers or governing authorities of the state, and the study of law was simply the analysis of the body of laws in force in any state at any given time and place. Gradually, however, the notion spread that law should not be divorced from the ethics and customs of a people but should rather be considered as an outgrowth of the whole culture. Thus the common law of England gave greater place to the decisions of jurists on the basis of equity and common sense. As this outlook spread, it became more necessary for students of jurisprudence to study the broader history and institutions of a nation as a means of arriving at a more solidly grounded evaluation of the law.

The scientific and cultural investigations in the social sciences stimulated the secular trends in education. Less and less was society considered to be subject to divine or supernatural direction from above, but more and more the social good was thought to be derived from the effects of social arrangements upon the lives and welfare of people. In this process the utilitarianism of Jeremy Bentham and John Stuart Mill argued that the ethical good is to be determined by the greatest good of the greatest number of people. This, of course, meant that conceptions of morality and good might vary from time to time and from place to place. Evolution had a large place in this doctrine, and it soon was realized that a valid determination of social good would have to consider the whole complex of social institutions that bear on the welfare of a nation or society.

In the twentieth century, research and investigation concerning the nature of society and social forces were based upon an objective, scientific point of view as well as that of various social outlooks. Historical investigation and writing moved away from military and political annals to the tracing of the evolution of world civilization and of national cultures and the interpretation of the growth and decline of social institutions. Most social scientists were conscious of the imperative need to bring the social sciences to the level of effectiveness reached by the physical sciences and to control human institutions for the welfare of man instead of allowing chance to determine social progress.

TRADITION AND CHANGE IN EDUCATION

The forces of nationalism, conservatism, liberalism, and religion deeply affected the content and methods of education in the nineteenth and twentieth centuries. In general, conservatism was likely to stress a narrower curriculum, to resist new subjects, and exalt religious and nationalistic values in elementary education. It likewise expressed itself in favor of the aristocratic and Humanistic ideals of class distinctions in secondary education. Liberalism was likely to argue for a broader curriculum at all levels of education, the introduction of newer scientific and technical studies, and an emphasis upon humanitarian values that would enlarge social vision, reduce class distinctions, and develop the individual capacities of the common people as well as those of the upper classes.

Educators were not only torn by these conflicting social points of view, but they were pulled and hauled by the different intellectual demands discussed in the foregoing part of this chapter. Humanism, religion, and rationalism often combined to ignore or to try to withstand the criticisms of newer interpretations of educational method which came sometimes from science, sometimes from the naturalistic study of human nature, and sometimes from the philosophy of idealism itself.

Educational Theory

Pestalozzi. So much has been written about the ideas of Johann Heinrich Pestalozzi and his educational influence that it is difficult to do more than restate a few important generalizations. Much of Pestalozzi's fame was doubtless achieved because he not only wrote about educational theory but also conducted schools embodying his theories in practice for all to see. Many came to observe and carry back their enthusiasms about what they saw.

Furthermore, Pestalozzi was not a radical. He was profoundly religious and always put the religious and moral instruction of children at the top of his list of important aims of education. To be sure, he talked of social reform, and he had allied himself with liberal groups; but he looked upon the reform of society as a thing to be achieved by helping the individual to help himself. Apparently even this approach went too far for the conservatives of Prussia and France, but his sympathy for the downtrodden and underprivileged touched a responsive chord among the philanthropically minded middle classes. Likewise, Pestalozzi's emphasis upon the practical activities of children, starting with motor skills and leading to vocational competence in farming, trade, and industry, attracted those who were dissatisfied with the exclusively literary and linguistic emphasis of most schools of the day.

Above all, however, it was Pestalozzi's conceptions of learning that appealed to educators who were looking for new ways to teach the children of the common people. In this respect, too, Pestalozzi did not offend by his radicalism but attracted favorable attention by his application of Locke's empiricism and Rousseau's naturalism without giving up the doctrines of faculty psychology and religious sensitivity. His theory of individual development thus became his most effective contribution to educational theory and method. He looked upon the child as a unity made up of separate faculties of moral, physical, and intellectual powers, all of which were to be harmoniously developed by education.

His reliance upon naturalism is revealed by his insistence that the natural instincts of the child should provide the motives for learning, rather than prodding and compulsion from without. Cooperation and sympathy are the means by which to achieve discipline, rather than by physical punishment. In this way the natural powers of the child can develop and can be expressed freely and naturally. Since it is nature that gives the

Fig. 22. Johann Heinrich Pestalozzi.

drive to life, it is the job of the teacher to adapt instruction to the individual child according to his changing, unfolding nature and the various stages of his natural development.

Pestalozzi's reliance upon sense realism is also evident in his approach to educational method. Since sense perceptions are most important in the development of the mind of the young child, it is necessary to rely at the earliest stages upon observation of actual things and natural objects rather than upon books and reading. Pestalozzi devised a whole series of "object lessons" in order to give full play to the child's natural desire to develop his senses of sight, touch, and sound and as the means of acquainting him with the fundamentals of language, number, and form. Plants, animals, special models, tools, drawing, modeling, music, and geography were important items in Pestalozzi's program for developing the perceptive faculties.

Such methods made a great impression upon educators accustomed only to the reading of books, memorizing, and reciting. Pestalozzi's emphasis upon proceeding from the particular to the general, from the concrete to the abstract, was particularly impressive at a time when children were learning Latin with little understanding of its meaning.

Most important of all, Pestalozzi's methods were so well developed that it was soon recognized that a new kind of training was necessary for teachers if they were to be able to use such methods. Henceforth, teachers would need to study the nature of the child more closely in order to guide his development properly and to adjust instruction to his requirements and interests. Once this need had been recognized, an enormous step forward had been taken. At last schoolteaching could be looked upon as a profession that required special and professional preparation and not merely as a task for someone who could do little more than make quill pens or whittle strong birch rods—and use them. Pestalozzi made a lasting contribution to the rise of the teaching profession.

The poverty and the disintegration of family life that overtook the lower classes as a result of the French wars that devastated Switzerland at the end of the eighteenth century stirred Pestalozzi deeply. He strongly believed that society could be improved by helping individuals to develop their own powers, abilities, and feelings of self-respect and security. To this end, he established orphanages at Neuhof and Stanz for poor children whose fathers had been killed in the wars. Later he established boarding schools for boys at Burgdorf and finally at Yverdon, where he gained his greatest fame during the first quarter of the nineteenth century.

Conducting his schools with sympathy and gentleness, Pestalozzi tried to recapture the ideals of a sound family life with its emphasis upon mild discipline, loving care for children, and religious and moral inspiration. He broadened the conception of what the elementary curriculum should contain and, perhaps more than any other single person, helped to introduce into the elementary curriculum instruction in geography and nature study, drawing, and music, along with the more commonly accepted studies of reading, writing, and arithmetic.

In all these studies Pestalozzi emphasized the development of sense perceptions by associating models and actual objects with the symbols

Fig. 23. Pestalozzi's School at Stanz.

and meanings that described them. In his stress upon the importance of developing all the mental, physical, and moral powers of the individual by methods of sense realism and gentle discipline, Pestalozzi represented a much more liberal approach to elementary education than was common in the schools of his day.

Two other movements that reflected Pestalozzi's influence were later to affect American education. One was Philipp Emanuel von Fellenberg's institute at Hofwyl in which emphasis was put upon practical training in agricultural and industrial arts in order to spread technical knowledge and skills among the lower middle classes and peasants. In this way he hoped that the lower classes would be enabled to improve their social and economic status by increasing their ability to produce food, clothing, handicrafts, and all kinds of goods. The other influence was that of Friedrich Froebel, whose *kindergartens* for younger children became an important means of developing their mental, moral, and expressive powers before they entered the regular elementary schools.

Froebel. Friedrich Froebel taught with Pestalozzi and conducted his own schools in Switzerland and Germany. Froebel was impressed not only by the sense realism of Pestalozzi but also by the idealistic philosophy of his day. He formulated a whole philosophy of absolute idealism in which he assigned a place to education and the development of individuals. Froebel thought of the world and of the universe as a great unity in which there are no divisions between the realm of spirit and the realm of nature or between the individual and society. The Absolute appears in all nature as the guiding spirit and ultimate goal of existence; all things find their unity and their essence in God as his will is unfolded on earth.

Fitting education into this scheme of things, Froebel looked upon the child as an agency for the realization of God's will in human nature. Through education the child's spirit becomes linked with the spiritual unity of the Absolute. The purpose of education is to help the child unfold his powers so that he may enter into spiritual union with God. Since growth is an inherent aspect of the realization of the Absolute, the growth of children is a part of the expression of the divine essence. As the spiritual essence of the Absolute is active, creative, and morally good, so must the inherent powers of the child be allowed to develop freely in order that he may achieve unity with the Absolute. This freedom of activity gives the child a chance to develop his energies, his natural curiosity, and his spontaneous activity.

Froebel felt that the educative process should start with the small child of three or four years. He called the institution appropriate to young children the *kindergarten*, a garden where children grow. The characteristic methods of growth and learning for young children are play activities. Play is as natural and appropriate for small children as work is for adults.

Therefore, Froebel designed a variety of play activities to develop the whole nature of the child, his moral and emotional nature as well as his intellectual nature. To this end, drawing, clay modeling, painting and coloring, singing, dancing, dramatic stories, and the manipulation of blocks, patterns, paper and cardboard objects, balls, and cubes were all considered appropriate.

Fig. 24. Friedrich Froebel.

In tune with his idealistic philosophy a large measure of symbolism was assigned to these activities. The objects were thought to be "gifts of God" and the activities were felt to be divine "occupations," all leading to the closer identification of the child with the divine spirit and social unity. The handling of a ball or sphere was somehow supposed to give the child a sense of the perfect unity of all things, and sitting in a circle was supposed to make him feel his identification as an individual with his social group and eventually with the unity of all mankind in the Absolute.

Stripped of their symbolism and idealistic justification the ideals of Froebel were to become enormously influential in American education. A new respect for the child, for his individuality, and for the dynamic and active qualities of his nature meant a lessening of rigid discipline and the traditional formality of the school atmosphere. The emphasis upon manipulation of objects and freedom to explore and to express oneself produced a greater emphasis on activity and sense realism in place of the constant and regimented reading of books. The notion of group activity as a natural means of expression led to a realization of the importance of good social relationships as a desirable outcome of school and community life.

Viewing the child as inherently good led to the study of child nature and individual differences among children as proper guides to the educative process. Cooperation, creativeness, activity, growth, and freedom became bywords in educational theory and practice. In these various ways, the teaching of young children came to be recognized as an important function of the school, not merely as a preliminary to later instruction but also as a stage when the well-rounded development of the child's personality is important in its own right. An important foundation for the later conception of the "child-centered" school was laid by Froebel's *kindergarten*.

Herbart. A third important European influence upon American education in the nineteenth century was that of Johann Friedrich Herbart, famous German philosopher and psychologist. Whereas Pestalozzi had been particularly interested in the elementary school and Froebel in preschool education, Herbart found acceptance largely among secondary school and university teachers. Herbart's two principal contributions were his stress upon the social and moral character of education and his systematic formulation of "methods" of teaching.

Starting with the assumption that the most important aim of education is the development of sound character, Herbart insisted that education should be primarily moral in its outlook and intent. To Herbart this was not necessarily a religious conception of morality, but rather a matter of adjustment of the individual to society. To this end, he emphasized the study of history and literature as the best means of developing desirable social attitudes in children. He even went so far as to suggest that historical and literary studies should be the "core" of study upon which the child should concentrate his efforts and with which all other studies were to be correlated. These doctrines of concentration and correlation gave an impetus to the introduction of the social studies into American schools at a time when the classics and mathematics were struggling with the sciences for supremacy.

Despite his insistence upon the moral and social aims of education,

Herbart believed that these aims could be achieved primarily through an intellectual approach to the learning process. His whole psychology of associationism stressed the importance of developing clear ideas in students. He reduced emotion, will, and feeling to secondary qualities dependent upon the association of ideas in the mind. The teacher should

Fig. 25. Johann Friedrich Herbart.

therefore direct his attention primarily to the processes by which ideas are formed from perceptions and sensations.

Above all, the teacher must concentrate upon the problem of interest. Inasmuch as consciousness is made up of ideas associated in many ways, the teacher must see to it that new ideas are vitally associated with ideas already part of the experience of the learner. All school lessons should therefore be taught so that the connection is clear between the new ideas and the "apperceptive mass" of ideas already built up in the learner's mind.

Herbart's followers made of his insistence upon association and interest a rather rigid pattern that came to be known as the "five formal steps" of learning and teaching. These steps were "preparation," in which the teacher prepares the child's mind by recalling the appropriate ideas in the learner's experience to which the new material can be related; "presentation," in which the new facts or materials are given to the learner; "association," in which definite efforts are made to show connections, comparisons, and differences between new and old ideas; "generalization," or "abstraction," by which analysis of individual cases leads to general principles; and "application," in which the general principles are given meaning by reference to specific examples and practical situations.

At a time when reading, memory, and recitation were the principal methods of teaching, the Herbartian systematic and "scientific" methods became vastly popular. They spread rapidly through the institutions of teacher education in the United States and helped to stimulate the whole process of training teachers. In the hands of some, the new methods led to a vital professionalizing of education; in the hands of others, they were formalized into a stiff and unchanging pattern that saddled rigid "lesson plans" upon generations of teachers and their students.

Exerting less direct influence upon America but blazing the trail for modern educational outlooks and practices in Europe was Maria Montessori in Italy. Her popularity was greatest during the second decade of the twentieth century when her work was widely publicized and many visitors to Italy were struck with the vitality of Montessori herself and her schools. She stressed realistic methods of learning through sense experience reminiscent of those of Pestalozzi and Froebel, but she put more emphasis upon the freedom of the child. In her "houses for children" she infused a spirit of respect for the child and his personality and sought to free him to pursue learning through activities that interested and challenged him. The whole effort of teaching was looked upon as helping the child to learn rather than requiring him to acquire information through formal studies. Her work, though suppressed by Mussolini and the Fascist demands for national conformity, influenced schools in Switzerland, Holland, England, and, after the Second World War, India. Driven from Italy in 1933, Montessori sought to carry on her activities in other countries, often against great obstacles. She died in 1952, the same year that John Dewey died in America. For nearly 50 years she was the symbol of modern education for Europe, much as Dewey was in America. If she had been able to systematize her theories through an organized following or in the institutions that prepared teachers, they might have been translated more widely into practice in the schools of Europe.

Elementary Education

England. Generalizations about England in the early nineteenth century are difficult, for there were few laws regarding curriculum and no centralized curriculum making. In the main, however, the elementary curriculum of the voluntary schools was most commonly made up of the three R's and religion, whereas religious instruction in the government schools was prohibited by the Forster Act in 1870.

The Sunday school movement was initiated in 1780 by Robert Raikes, a newspaperman who sought to awaken public opinion to the need for education among the children who worked in factories from sunrise to sunset for 6 or even 7 days a week. Upon his initiative, voluntary schools were established in Gloucester to teach the three R's and the catechism to working children during their free time on Sundays. Sunday schools became a "movement" with the founding of the Society for the Support and Encouragement of Sunday Schools in the Different Counties of England. The idea spread to the United States, where such schools were popular in the first half of the nineteenth century.

Another specific educational response to the Industrial Revolution was the infant school, sponsored by Robert Owen, Scottish manufacturer, philanthropist, and socialist. In addition to agitating for reducing the hours of child labor, Owen was instrumental in establishing schools for small children whose parents worked all day in the factories. These schools likewise taught religion and some elements of the three R's, although much attention was directed at simply play, singing and dancing, and nursery care for three-, four-, and five-year-olds. As Pestalozzian ideas were introduced, the instruction put less emphasis upon books and more upon natural objects. The creation of societies for the spread of infant schools was another step in the recognition of the need for educational opportunities for young children.

Another means of making education available to larger numbers of children was the monitorial system developed almost simultaneously by Joseph Lancaster, a Quaker, and by Andrew Bell, an Anglican. Monitorial instruction meant that the older children were used as monitors, or helpers, for the teacher. The teacher taught the monitors a lesson, and then each monitor "taught" the lesson to 10 or 12 smaller children by repeating what he had learned. The small children recited aloud and in unison whatever was being taught. Wall placards and charts were used to aid in group instruction and to save money on books. The subject matter was still principally the catechism, reading, writing, spelling, and arithmetic. Corporal punishment was abolished, punishment being restricted to the dunce's cap and standing in the corner, and a system of merits and rewards was substituted to enlist the interest of the children. Children began to enjoy the marching, noisy activity, and rewards. The monitorial schools had a great vogue in the United States in the early nineteenth century.

One of the principal characteristics of English elementary schools has been the variety in curriculum arising out of local initiative and autonomy in curriculum building. The English also tended to believe that the family and home were the fundamental institutions and that the school was primarily a supplementary institution to give training that the home did not give. Even the education laws customarily laid the injunction upon parents to see that their children were educated, rather than laying the stress upon attending a school. This meant that character and moral training received a high place, whereas mastery of subject matter was relatively subordinate. Furthermore, subject matter itself was conceived rather narrowly, as revealed in the Education Act of 1921, which simply said that parents must cause their children from ages five to fourteen to receive elementary instruction in reading, writing, and arithmetic.

These were the only subjects found in virtually all elementary schools. Beyond that, each school could branch out as it saw fit to give instruction in such subjects as geography, history, nature study, drawing, music, physical training and hygiene, and manual and household arts. The amount of time given to these subjects varied; no textbooks were prescribed nationally, and no requirements were laid down concerning what they should contain. Religious instruction continued to play a large role in most elementary schools. The general practice was to give special-place examinations to determine which children at the age of eleven years should go to secondary schools and which should continue in the higher forms of the elementary school to receive additional training in the elementary branches of knowledge.

The broadening of the scope and conception of elementary education, however, was emphasized in the Education Act of 1944, which provided that education should be suited to the moral, mental, and physical needs of children and the community. In an attempt to destroy the traditional dual and class distinctions in education, the term "elementary" school is no longer supposed to be used, and the old special-place examinations have been abolished. The plan has been to expect all children to proceed from infant and nursery schools (below age six) to the primary school (ages five to eleven) to the secondary school (ages eleven to fifteen and eventually to sixteen). The official theory is now that the ladder system of schools has been established. The curriculum continues to vary from place to place. In many quarters more emphasis is being put upon project methods, community studies, and activity programs in addition to the regular systematic instruction. The goal is clear; the steps toward it will undoubtedly be very rapid in some places and much slower in others.

Diversity and tradition will continue to play their part in English primary education.

France. The conservative ideal of primary education in France was eloquently expressed by Napoleon in 1808, when he stated that the schools should teach the Roman Catholic religion, inculcate fidelity to the emperor, and produce citizens devoted to the church, the state, and their families. Following this ideal, the law of 1833 virtually fixed the primary school curriculum at the three R's and moral and religious instruction. This curriculum was somewhat broadened in 1850, when primary schools were allowed to include, if they wished, such studies as history, nature study, geography, drawing, and music.

The higher primary schools were designed to build upon these subjects and add such practical studies as geometry, surveying, agriculture, industrial arts, and commercial instruction. Because the higher primary school was shaped by the economic motive to improve competence on the farms and in the factories and cities, the higher primary schools had a difficult time achieving social acceptance because of the opposition of the secondary schools. The upper classes would not send their children to inferior schools, and the working classes often could not afford education beyond the rudiments because they needed the older children at home to contribute to the family income.

The principal changes in French primary education came with the Ferry law of 1882, which required the secular aspect of the curriculum to be expanded and its religious instruction to be narrowed. Although specific religious doctrines could not be taught, much was still made of moral instruction in the duties of children to God, family, and the Republic. The basic primary school curriculum thus came to include moral and civic instruction, the three R's, history, geography, nature study, science and mathematics, drawing, music, manual and household arts, and physical and military training.

The authoritarian role of the teacher, the strict discipline and obedience of pupils, and rigid adherence to state textbooks and curriculum marked the internal life of the schools. In French elementary schools the nationalistic element always was a direct and powerful part of teaching methods and curriculum. Along with nationalism the ideals of thoroughgoing mastery of subject matter played a large role. Therefore, much emphasis was put upon the acquisition of fundamental skills, facts, and organized knowledge. The kind and content of textbooks were rigidly prescribed by the national Ministry of Education, and state examinations, both oral and written, were given to all children at the age of eleven and again at the end of the higher primary school. The most common methods of teaching involved direct exposition by the teacher, questions and answers, copying dictation into an exercise book, and memorizing and reciting the material copied.

During the occupation by the Nazis great efforts were made to introduce texts friendly to Germany and weed out those which referred to German war guilt or atrocities in the First World War or which otherwise were anti-German. Under the Fourth Republic, plans were made to modernize elementary instruction along more progressive American lines, but the curriculum has been little changed; if anything, there has been greater emphasis than ever upon fundamental skills and knowledge in preparation for the secondary school. The state schools continue to rest upon secular rather than religious sanctions of morality, rationality, and culture.

Germany. Under the liberal impetus of the early nineteenth century, the German *Volksschule* for the common people was affected by Pestalozzian ideals. The basic curriculum was therefore broadened to include nature study, geography, drawing, and music, in addition to reading, writing, and arithmetic. The reliance upon religious and moral instruction and the development of loyalty to the nation, however, remained uppermost. History and literature extolling Germany soon came into the curriculum as a means of instilling nationalistic loyalities; physical education as a basis for military training also appeared.

These subjects constituted the basic elementary school curriculum throughout most of the nineteenth century, a curriculum shaped by religion and nationalism in order to produce obedient, loyal, and humble subjects of the monarchy and empire. The methods of instruction were likewise designed to emphasize discipline, obedience to the authority of the teacher, and reliance upon the authorized textbooks, rather than the development of initiative or resourcefulness among the students.

Under the Republic many elementary teachers in Germany became enthusiastic over "progressive" methods of teaching. They emphasized individual freedom from restraint and integrated subject matter as a reaction against the excessively controlled, authoritarian, and intellectualized subject matter of the imperial schools. Much stress was put upon the study of the local environment, trips, plays, music, and art as mediums of free expression. Printed courses of study were replaced by "suggestions."

Much attention was given to child psychology, the interests of pupils, and pleasanter relations between teachers and pupils to replace the formal discipline of bowing and heel clicking characteristic of the Prussian military tradition. Such freedom and individualism were, of course, resented by many Germans, and the excesses of such activity methods made inevitable an even more reactionary swing of the pendulum under the Nazis back to strict control, obedience, discipline, and authority of the teacher.

The content of the curriculum under the Nazis was entirely shaped around the nation's past, present, and future as visualized by the Nazis.

History was almost exclusively limited to the German aspects of history, glorifying ancient and mythical heroes and military achievements. The titles of textbooks were illuminating, for example, *In the Mists of Antiquity*, *Nordic Heroes*, *German Battles*, and *German Greatness in Sacrifice and Leadership*.

Glorification of the nation's present was reflected in a decreasing emphasis upon foreign languages. There was much emphasis upon German language, literature, culture, art, and music, "German" of course to be interpreted as "Aryan" and non-Jewish, which meant that the vast contributions of Jews to all these fields had to be eliminated. Geography was used to glorify Germany and to give children a further loyalty to all parts of the nation.

The nation's future was bound up in the study of biology, eugenics, and the "science of race purity." The interest here was in health, "correct" marriages among Aryans, and bearing and rearing children for the state. Economic and political study of the future role of Germany stressed the necessity of winning back the lost colonies, uniting those of German blood from all over the world into one great fatherland, and making Germany self-sufficient until such time as it could dominate the economic and political arrangements of the world.

The restoration of anything like objective knowledge or democratic teaching in German schools by the United Nations meant an enormous task of editing and writing new textbooks that would be democratic in outlook and yet as attractive, interesting, and vivid as the Nazi myths had been.

Russia. In their first attempts to reform the elementary schools in Russia the Communists adopted what they believed to be progressive methods, in which activities, project methods, student freedom, and political ideology were used to instill the new political ideals in the younger generation and "convert" the teachers. Individual marks and competition were abolished as a holdover from capitalistic ideology, and ability to perform in group cooperative work was extolled as the ideal.

However, after the first Five Year Plan, the Communists felt secure enough to return to the more traditional methods of giving organized and logical information to the people as a means of building a highly industrialized nation in a short time. An excellent description of the new attitude of Russian education is given by Professor George S. Counts.

The resources of the educational system were gradually directed to the "mastery of knowledge." Whereas in 1929 Soviet teachers commonly stated that their main task was to help achieve the goals of the first Five-Year Plan, by 1938 they agreed that their major responsibility was to assist the young in such a sober matter as mastering the Russian language, mathematics, science, technology, geography and history. The teaching of subjects was revived, "stable" or generally prescribed textbooks were carefully prepared, closely organized sequences of learning were established in every field, rigorous examinations and school marks were introduced, and in general a systematic curriculum resembling in its rigidity, severity and universality that of France was developed.[1]

The complete authority and discipline of the teacher were reestablished. The pupils' own responsibility for conscientious work, good grades, passing examinations, diligent study, strict obedience to the teacher, and personal appearance, manners, and conduct was stressed. National aims to build a Communist state and an industrial society took new forms in educational method and content, but these aims continued to pervade all that the schools did. Elementary education was definitely a political branch of the state, and in Russia the state was completely controlled by the Communist party.

The curriculum of the elementary school is dominated by the study of the Russian language and the native language of the region, more than half the time being devoted to these subjects. Arithmetic amounts to about one-quarter of the curriculum, and the rest of the time is devoted to history of the Soviet Union, geography, nature study, music, drawing, and physical training.

Secondary Education

In virtually all countries of Europe, secondary schools were designed for the upper classes as preparatory institutions for entrance to the universities and for leadership in the social class to which the youth's parents belonged. The logic of the system of secondary education maintained that a truly educated person should possess the traditional hallmarks of a liberal education, namely, the classics. Since only relatively few children in a nation were capable of mastering such subjects, they were the only ones thought to be entitled to a genuine education.

The strong hand of Humanism became even stronger in the nineteenth-century secondary schools. Conservatives tried their best to block the introduction of scientific and modern subjects into secondary education. Although they could not hold out entirely against the liberal demands for a more flexible and wider curriculum, they were able to protect the "best" schools from such inroads. Sometimes they were forced to allow new types of secondary schools to be established outside of the inner circle, but the general framework of secondary education as opposed to elementary education was successfully maintained. Most efforts to eliminate the rigid two-track arrangements for elementary and secondary education were defeated during the nineteenth century.

[1] George S. Counts, "Remaking the Russian Mind," *Asia and the Americas*, October, 1945, pp. 482–483.

England. The great "public" schools long set the standards and ideals for all other types of secondary school in England. The nine great "public" schools were usually considered to be Eton, Winchester, Charterhouse, Westminister, Rugby, Harrow, Shrewsbury, St. Paul's, and Merchant Taylor's. In these, classical Humanism continued to play the central role. The English set great store not only by the classics but by the corporate life of the boarding school as molders of the religious, moral, and intellectual life and of the manners and behavior appropriate to a gentleman's son. The community life of the English secondary schools was one principal way in which they differed from their counterparts in France and Germany.

Despite the hold of the "public" schools upon English life as exemplified by such famous schoolmasters as Thomas Arnold of Rugby, criticisms and attacks upon them increased during the nineteenth century. Demands for a more democratic and more practical type of education were made, but with relatively small results, even though such spokesmen as William Whewell, Thomas Huxley, and Herbert Spencer were doing their best to gain for science recognition as an essential ingredient in a liberal education. When new schools were established, they generally tried to follow the lead of the "public" schools and to appeal to a similar clientele among the upper classes. Many kinds of endowed schools, proprietary schools (in which the income was fed back into the corporation controlling the school), and private schools (conducted primarily for profit) were established.

After the middle of the century Parliament responded to the dissatisfaction being expressed and appointed several commissions to study the conduct of the secondary schools. The Clarendon Commission ended its study of the nine "public" schools by justifying the classical curriculum as the principal determinant in the molding of the English gentleman. It recommended more attention to the sciences, modern languages, and social studies, but in general the public schools were given a clean bill of health.

The Schools Inquiry Commission under Lord Taunton then studied all secondary schools and found a great diversity of quality and teaching standards, much of them bad. This commission made several far-reaching suggestions concerning reform of the curriculum, closer supervision by the state of the achievements of students and certification of teachers, and a more systematic organization. These suggestions apparently were too radical, however, for Parliament overlooked its report and passed the Endowed Schools Act of 1869, which simply appointed a commission to help the endowed schools to make more satisfactory plans for managing their endowments. Public control of "public" schools was too radical a step for England to take in the nineteenth century.

Although there was a steady growth of publicly supported secondary schools in England, the pace and tone of secondary education continued to be set by the great, privately supported "public" schools. Their classical, religious, and aristocratic patterns were largely imitated as far as possible by the endowed day schools and other private boarding schools. In the social estimation of England the public schools held high place as agencies for training leaders in government, business, and church, while at the same time they were increasingly criticized for their exclusive and selective character. Their hold was strong on the preferred civil, political, and managerial positions in England.

Despite the larger number of "free places" and scholarships that were being granted in the secondary schools, class distinctions and the economic level of parents played the largest roles in the selection of clientele. Pupils from the elementary schools were constantly outclassed in the examinations for scholarships because of the largely classical character of the examinations. Character training and "gentlemanliness" played a larger role in the public schools than severe intellectual training.

The Second World War brought new criticisms upon the public schools, and proposals were even made that they be taken over by the government. Their future role remained uncertain as genuine public secondary education expanded under the Education Act of 1944, but they will doubtless continue to play a large role, in influence if not in numbers, so long as much local autonomy and control over curriculum are left in the hands of headmasters and private school managers. The chances are, however, that they will never again play the exclusive and dominating role in a dualistic school system that was their privilege for so many generations.

During the postwar period four other types of secondary schools marked the educational scene in England: grammar schools, modern schools, technical schools, and comprehensive schools. The grammar schools sought to follow in large part the lead of the "public" schools in stressing a liberal arts education designed to prepare for the universities and the professions. The curriculum was nonvocational and highly academic in character. It emphasized foreign languages, especially Latin or Greek, along with standard subject-matter instruction in English language and literature, mathematics, science, history, and geography. Some attention was given to manual arts, domestic science, and physical training. These schools in 1948 enrolled something over a half million students.

The modern schools grew out of the upper levels of the old elementary schools. They stressed the general liberal arts in the lower grades and then offered a practical education appropriate to the vocational needs of students, the occupational demands of the community, and the social life of the locality. Community or regional studies were often developed along the lines of the American community-centered school or core program. The later years of the school often permitted the students to acquire direct vocational or prevocational studies in shop and laboratory. These schools, enrolling almost a million students in 1948, are likely to become the most popular secondary schools in England.

Technical schools have also gained somewhat since their first appearance in 1905. They claimed not to be vocational, industrial, or trade schools, but rather to stress those sciences and technologies upon which the dominant industries or businesses of the community rested. They enrolled some 70,000 students in the late 1940's.

Finally, in London a few comprehensive schools have been established, somewhat analogous to the American public high. These schools bring together under one roof courses representing the grammar, the modern, and the technical emphasis, giving students who specialize in one or the other type of study a chance to have a common social and community life.

France. In France the *lycée* was the highest type of secondary school, emphasizing Latin, Greek, and mathematics, with some provisions for philosophy and science in the last year. The *collège* was also a recognized secondary school but remained in a somewhat less respected position because it was generally found in the smaller towns and thus had less standing and fewer facilities. Both these schools became 7-year institutions, beginning at age eleven or twelve and ending at eighteen. They were designed as aristocratic schools for the upper classes and were dominated by classical Humanism.

Efforts were made in the latter half of the nineteenth century to give a larger place to science and the modern languages in the *lycée* and *collège*, but most of these efforts were defeated. At one point two different courses were instituted during the last 3 years of the school, when students were to have a choice between the classics and science, but the scheme did not work. Teachers were not as well trained in science as in the classics; the Humanists could therefore look down pityingly upon the scientific course as undisciplined and feeble.

Great controversies raged between the classicists and the modernists during the 1880's and 1890's, but the Third Republic did not depart from the Humanistic tradition as the recognized road to preferment in public affairs and university study. The modern subjects were largely kept out of the secondary schools and relegated to the higher primary schools. The Humanists were so convinced that real education meant classical education that they would brook no compromise until the twentieth century.

In 1902 Louis Liard was instrumental in introducing into the secondary schools a parallel course, which emphasized modern languages and science, alongside the classical course, which emphasized Greek and Latin. Both courses were to include a certain amount of history, geography, mathematics, and science, but the newer course was never fully recognized as equal in standards to the older classical subjects.

In reaction against the intrusion of modern subjects and after hot debates in the parliament of France, Léon Bérard decreed in 1923 that 4 years of Latin and 2 years of Greek were compulsory for all students in *lycées* and *collèges*. After 2 years, however, the choice between modern languages and Latin was restored, and in the highest grade of the *lycée* a choice was given between philosophy and mathematics. State examinations were held at the end of the secondary school, when the baccalaureate degree was awarded and admission to the university or technical facilities achieved.

To the horror of the Humanists, the Vichy government announced its intention to "deintellectualize" French secondary education along the lines of the German youth movement. Following the philosophy of "kitchen, church, and children," the proposal was to introduce manual training, domestic science, physical training, and other practical and vocational courses into the staid halls of the *lycée*. Fully as revolutionary was the proposal to abolish the philosophy course as the last year of the *lycée*. These proposals, of course, met determined resistance and were never fully carried out.

Under the Fourth Republic the dominant intellectual character of the secondary schools was maintained, but very significant new trends began to appear. Even before the Second World War, the closely knit character of the secondary schools began to loosen somewhat. An increasing number of scholarships went to able students irrespective of social class. Transfer from elementary to secondary "tracks" was made easier, gradual abolition of tuition fees was achieved in 1937, and the newer subjects gained respectability. Students could now major in the physical sciences in the final year as well as in mathematics or philosophy. The emphasis upon the classics in the lower grades was declining but continued strong.

In 1945 a remarkable experimental program was instituted for some 5,000 eleven-year-old pupils to emphasize an activity program roughly analogous to some of the methods of American progressive education. These "new classes" were to be added successively each year to the next higher grade. The content of the program in the mornings remained focused upon French language and literature, history, geography, modern language, natural science, and mathematics. In the afternoons attention was devoted to choices among the fine arts, music, and the applied arts. Recreational, health, and physical-education activities along with community studies were made compulsory. The underlying principles of attention to the growth and development of children, tests and measurements, guidance, and better teacher-student relationships all echoed modern trends in America. Attention to the creative talents of students and regard for their ideas and personality helped to break down the authoritarian methods of discipline by the teacher.

However, French education was not to be swept away by modern education. The hold of tradition was great, criticism of the newfangled "soft pedagogy" of these new classes was bitter, and loyalty to intellectualistic values was deep and strong. Neglect of the social sciences was common. Lectures by the teacher and note-taking by the students remained the basic methods of instruction. Library facilities in the schools were virtually nonexistent and other kinds of instructional and audio-visual materials were scarce. The bleakness of a regimented boarding-school life remained all too common.

The tremendous need for technical education as a basis for French industrial and military security was given little attention by secondary school educators. Vocational and technical education was offered in local or community preparatory vocational schools (2 or 3 years) and topped off by national vocational schools (3 to 4 years). Rapid increases in enrollments in these schools gave hope that this phase of French education would finally receive the attention it deserved. But it was likely to continue to be separated from the Humanistic and theoretical training available only in the secondary schools.

Germany. In the first half of the nineteenth century the classical *Gymnasium* emerged as the standard secondary school of Germany. It was a 9-year school for boys from the ages of nine to eighteen years and was the preferred road to the universities, public office, and the army. It emphasized, above all, the study of Latin and, to a lesser degree, Greek, mathematics, science, history, and geography. Religion continued to hold a high place. When the "leaving examination" taken at completion of the *Gymnasium* was recognized for admission to the universities, the status of the *Gymnasium* in German education was ensured.

All the attempts of liberals to increase the amount of science taught and introduce the modern foreign languages were defeated; even the efforts to make classical study a creative and liberalizing experience in the spirit of a new Humanism were defeated by the reactionary elements of the 1820's. The supremacy of a narrower study of Latin grammar and drill was maintained. This was a part of the repressive Carlsbad decrees, which reinforced strict supervision of the curriculum and weeded out any teachers or students who dared to deviate from the straight and narrow path of obedience and loyalty to the king.

The achievements in science and the gains of the Industrial Revolution, however, were not to be completely denied, and after the middle of the century newer types of schools were recognized, if not on a par with the *Gymnasium*, at least as better than elementary schools. One of these was the *Realgymnasium*, which represented a compromise according to which

Latin was retained but Greek was omitted in order to give more time to science and modern languages. Although these schools were attacked by conservatives on the basis that they failed to give real mental discipline, they were finally accorded the right to give leaving examinations in science, mathematics, and modern languages that entitled the graduate to enter the universities.

A third type of school also gained some recognition on the fringes of secondary education against the objections of the conservatives. This was the *Oberrealschule*, which was so radical that it omitted Latin as well as Greek and shaped its curriculum entirely around the sciences, mathematics, modern languages, and social studies. It was, of course, attacked as utterly lacking in "culture" and discipline because it omitted the classics.

All these schools were 9-year institutions, but each had its 6-year counterparts from which students could go on to the 9-year schools; the 6-year schools were, respectively, the *Progymnasium*, the *Realprogymnasium*, and the *Realschule*.

The multiplication of secondary schools went much further in Germany than it did in France or England, especially under the impetus of the democratic educational reforms of the Weimar Republic. Whereas France really had only two versions of the same type of secondary school (*lycée* and *collège*) as roads to the universities, Germany provided at least six types of schools that led to higher education in technical or academic subjects. Until the Nazi regime, however, the *Gymnasium* continued to be the preferred route, much like the *lycée* in France and the public school in England.

The Nazis set out to reduce the hold of the traditional secondary schools upon university preparation. They took away the sixth day of each week from classes and gave the time to the Hitler Youth activities; they reduced the importance of the classics; and they restricted the attendance of Jewish students. As a result, the program of the German *Gymnasium* was cut by 2 to 3 years in the time devoted to class instruction, and the attendance declined by 25 to 30 per cent. The German secondary school system was greatly reduced in intellectual and scholarly standing in comparison with the school systems of most other nations of the Western world. Whether this standing could be recovered along democratic lines in a reconstructed Germany remained to be seen.

The secondary schools in Western Germany after the Second World War maintained their specialized character, but the number of different kinds of institutions was cut down considerably. The main secondary schools continued to be the *Gymnasium* and the *Oberschule*. The *Gymnasium* emphasized English, Latin, and Greek as foreign languages, along with German, history, geography, mathematics, science, and religion. The *Oberschule* made it possible for a student to major in the sciences or in foreign languages (in which case he had large amounts of English, Latin, and French). A third type of secondary school, the *Aufbauschule* (created during the Weimar Republic), made it possible for some of the lower-middle-class children from the *Mittelschule* to prepare for the universities, but they remained on the fringes of the secondary school scene.

Russia. In the 1940's the Soviet government revitalized its secondary school curriculum in a way that reflected a new approach to intellectual and cultural matters. New emphasis was given to Russian history, literature, and the arts as well as to science and technology. Great interest in the United States, England, and Canada was aroused among Russian students as a result of the cooperation in the Second World War, and despite the opposing economic outlooks there was evidence of great eagerness to know about American and English life. The study of English grammar and literature also became of widespread interest.

By 1948 the complete 10-year secondary school curriculum in Russia gave greatest attention to the subjects of mathematics and the physical and natural sciences. Next came Russian language and literature. The rest of the time was divided among history of the U.S.S.R., modern languages, physical and military training, and writing, drafting, and singing. Segregation of the sexes became widespread in most of the secondary schools, especially in the urban centers. As the "cold war" heightened in the 1950's, it seemed unlikely that the old isolationism surrounding the building of socialism in one nation could give way to a larger international concern.

Higher Education

England. The English universities began to recover a measure of their old vitality with the beginning of the nineteenth century. During the first half of the century, Oxford commenced to reform its examination system from within so that a student needed more adequate preparation for passing his examinations. Honors courses were designed to permit greater specialization than the regular "pass courses" and to provide added inducements for the student to attain a high degree of scholarship. The first honors courses were in the classics and mathematics. Then, with Parliamentary acts to reform the universities, other honors courses were added. At Cambridge, mathematics continued to gain in importance during the early nineteenth century; it had been the first subject in which a tripos (honors-course examination) was held (1747). Then triposes were added in civil law (1815), classics (1824), moral sciences (1851), and natural sciences (1850).

Although this marked an advance over the lethargy of the eighteenth century, the English universities were still far behind the German universities in scientific research and freedom of teaching and learning. Courses were still prescribed, and all religions but Anglicanism were proscribed. Not until 1871 were the English universities freed from doctrinal tests for all degrees, fellowships, and university and college offices. Prospective clergymen still were required to give evidence of Anglican orthodoxy.

Controversy over the functions of universities took two forms: debates concerning the relative value of science versus literature as the main subjects of study, and wholesale criticisms of the established university systems as developed in England. In his famous essay *What Knowledge Is of Most Worth?* Spencer insisted that the physical sciences provide the knowledge that is most valuable for the guidance and conduct of life as well as for mental discipline. He advocated that science should be given a greater place in education, because it is so much more efficacious than the classical literature in preparing for the main functions of human living. These include self-preservation and bodily health, the gaining of a livelihood, the activities of parenthood and citizenship, and the relaxations and pleasures of leisure and art.

By means of speeches and writings, Huxley carried the banner of scientific studies through the British Isles and the United States. He eulogized the value of science for promoting mental discipline as well as for the practical information that it conveyed. In *Science and Culture*, Huxley pointed out how the introduction of the scientific studies had met the continued opposition of the classicists and even of businessmen at first, but he argued that neither the subject matter of nor the mental discipline afforded by the classics justified the expenditure of time given to them. For real culture, an exclusively scientific education is as good as an exclusively classical one, but both literary and scientific studies are needed to prevent undesirable mental twists in the educated man.

Matthew Arnold was the most vigorous opponent of Huxley and Spencer. He attacked the utilitarian aims of scientific and practical subjects on the ground that they might drive out true "culture." He defended the classical languages and literature as the best means of developing the spiritual and moral qualities of man and of arriving at his famous ideal of culture—"to know the best which has been thought and said in the world." The counterpart of this controversy in England over the place and functions of science versus the classics was carried on vigorously in the United States.

Another means by which the ideal of university education received more explicit formulation both in Europe and in America was the great amount of general criticism that was being leveled at the universities.

Cardinal Newman's idea of a university, for example, was that it is a place for teaching universal knowledge and aiming at "intellectual culture." In a liberal education, knowledge should be acquired for its own sake, with no ulterior motive, whereas, in a professional or useful education, knowledge is to be acquired as a basis for social service. The university should disseminate knowledge of the liberal sort only. Thus its highest aim is to cultivate the intellect.

Huxley formulated a quite different idea of a university in his inaugural address as rector of the University of Aberdeen. "In an ideal University, as I conceive it, a man should be able to obtain instruction in all forms of knowledge, and discipline in the use of all the methods by which knowledge is obtained." He then outlined the various fields of knowledge that he would include; among them there should be no question of relative importance or superiority. It is very evident, however, that he proposed much more of the scientific subjects than was customary in the English universities of the day.

Spencer, Huxley, Arnold, and Newman were merely examples of the wide discussion concerning university education that took place during the latter half of the nineteenth century in both Europe and the United States. Gradually, the notion gained currency that a true university is one in which all branches of knowledge are taught and investigated. The teacher should have the freedom to follow the truth wherever it leads him, and the student should have the freedom to study whatever pleases him or best suits his needs and capacities. The German universities most nearly approached this conception of a university and therefore became the source of inspiration for many of the changes in American higher education in the nineteenth century.

Higher education in England has been dominated by the two universities, Oxford and Cambridge. Traditionally, their emphasis has been not so much upon research as upon instruction that would lead to the type of social, moral, and political character appropriate to the ruling classes of England. Despite the constantly growing number of scholarships and free places, the principal opportunity for attendance has doubtless belonged to the more privileged families. The close relationship between an Oxford or Cambridge degree and a high government position has long been apparent.

Over the years, opportunities for higher education somewhat in the manner of American state universities have been steadily expanding. Notable are such provincial universities as Birmingham, Bristol, Durham, Leeds, Liverpool, Manchester, Reading, and Sheffield, and the Scottish universities at Aberdeen, Edinburgh, and Glasgow.

The University of London consists of about 30 loosely coordinated and semiautonomous institutions, including undergraduate colleges (King's

College and University College); several schools of special interest, such as the London School of Economics; the Imperial College of Science and Technology; the Institute of Education; and several research institutes, hospitals, teacher-training schools, and the like. The University of London also acts as an administrative body for giving examinations and granting degrees for these constituent institutions and for other institutions in the United Kingdom and abroad.

Enrollment in British universities has more than doubled since the Second World War and may continue to increase as educational opportunity is made more available through the new secondary schools and as government aid is used to expand scholarships for able and deserving students. In English universities the honors course with its specialization and higher scholarly standards is usually preferred to the pass courses, whereas in the Scottish universities the more general course with its concern for breadth and comprehensiveness is likely to be more favored. Controversy over the place of the sciences and technology in relation to the humanities continues to be lively. It is especially related to the almost inevitable tendency of government grants to be made in a way that favors technological research, although so far the University Grants Committee has maintained the principle that government funds should be given with no strings attached and with the traditional autonomy of the universities preserved.

France. The University of Paris, along with other French universities, virtually ceased to exist during the French Revolution, and it was not reestablished until 1896, when the separate faculties set up by Napoleon were again combined to constitute the University of Paris. Throughout most of the nineteenth century, university instruction was carried on in separate faculties of letters, science, medicine, and law, which operated under strict regulations laid down by the Ministry of Education. Attendance at lectures and exercises was compulsory; the courses of instruction were prescribed for each year; and state examinations had to be passed before the student could be promoted from one year to the next. In contrast to the situation in Germany, much of the active scientific research went on outside the faculties, often in connection with the Academy of Sciences.

Several kinds of state institutions made up the opportunities for higher education in France. Before the Second World War there were 17 universities, one in each of the *academies* (national administrative divisions for education). The universities had two principal aspects: the *faculties*, which normally included letters, science, law, medicine, and pharmacy, for general instruction and research; and the *institutes* for specialized research or study within a faculty or for research that cut across the traditional subject-matter fields, such, for example, as industrial chemistry, radium, optics, psychology, statistics, ethnology, linguistics, art and archeology, physical education, and the like.

There were also several kinds of *higher schools* for specialized instruction in fields outside of the regular university faculties and institutes. Some were technical and scientific, such as the schools of polytechnics, military and naval science, aeronautics, mines, forestry and agriculture, and engineering and industry. Others, administered by the Ministry of Education, included the Superior Normal Schools for secondary and elementary school teaching, schools of arts, crafts, and music, and technical schools.

The faculties, institutes, and higher schools regularly required some sort of secondary school diploma or baccalaureate degree for entrance, in addition to qualifying examinations. They granted various licenses after 2 or 3 years of study; the doctorates, which usually entailed an additional 2 or 3 years of study; and the *agrégation*, which was issued on the basis of competitive examinations to instructors in the secondary schools and professors in the higher faculties.

In addition to the degree-granting institutions, there were several publicly supported institutions for advanced study whose courses of lectures were public and free but did not lead to examinations or degrees. Notable among these were the Collège de France, the National Museum of Natural History, and the National Academy of Arts and Crafts. Finally, there were the private and religious institutions of higher education, which offered a wide range of study in many fields but which in general were overshadowed by the public institutions in respect to recognition and support.

Despite this diversity of higher educational institutions, the opportunity for gaining degrees and passing state examinations has generally been limited to the relatively exclusive clientele coming up from the secondary schools. If the Fourth Republic follows through its early intention to widen the scope of secondary education and make it more fully available to a larger cross section of the population, it may be that university reform will follow in the same direction.

In general, French higher education has not kept pace with advances in other countries. It has been wedded to traditional subject matters and to traditional methods of teaching and research. Its facilities and laboratories have been outmoded. The reform movement, as represented by the Langevin commission, has urged a revitalizing to overcome the strict separation of the technical from the theoretical that has long marked French higher education. An example of this was the establishment of the National School of Administrators to give better preparation for public administration. If this and similar movements could be expanded to bring together the basic cultural and intellectual foundations and practical training experience, a new day might dawn in French professional education. Another suggestion has been to bring the higher schools for technical training into closer association with the university faculties and research institutes.

Germany. During the nineteenth century German universities made substantial strides toward freedom for the individual professor and for the individual student. Despite reactionary attempts in the early decades to stamp out liberalism in the universities, Humboldt made of Berlin a university of independence and freedom. Instruction was carried on, not in the form of a prescribed curriculum, but in a situation in which the professor had freedom to teach what he thought best and the student freedom to study what he desired. In the early part of the century the most important studies were philosophy, the classical humanities, philology, and history. By the end of the second decade, however, mathematics and science were flourishing, and during the second half of the century they became the dominating studies.

As the interest in speculative philosophy was overshadowed by the rise of research in the physical sciences, an ever-increasing specialization in the fields of investigation took place. Consequently, the number of departments increased; the number of professors in each department multiplied many times; and the greater need of specializing in order to reach a competent degree of scholarship led to the free use of the elective principle. According to this principle, the student was not required to follow a round of prescribed studies but was free to select the field of study in which he wished to specialize and to attend what lectures he needed in order to obtain his degree. The faculties of the German universities were nearly equivalent to what Americans know as graduate and professional schools. The English and American conception of an undergraduate "college" was not a part of German higher education. The highest ideal of the German university was the training of the research specialist.

Up to the 1930's many educators in the United States looked upon the German universities as furnishing the highest levels of teaching and research and therefore as the best universities in the world. The renown of Berlin, Munich, Heidelberg, Göttingen, Halle, Jena, Freiburg, Hamburg, Bonn, Cologne, Frankfort, Breslau, and Königsberg, along with a dozen others, was very impressive. The freedom of teaching and learning for professors and students; the autonomy of the faculties of philosophy (arts and sciences), medicine, law, and theology; the quality of research; and the objectivity of science and knowledge were highly regarded. In addition, a number of scientific and technical institutions outside of the universities were often considered of equal standing for advanced research and teaching.

When the Nazis came to power, however, they instituted a program to turn the universities to their own uses, to make party loyalty the principal requirement for students and professors, and to wipe out the "decadent" liberal notions that science and knowledge should be objective. Knowledge and science could no longer be nonnational or international in outlook but had to be subordinated to Nazi ideology. In 1936 Bernhard Rust, minister of education, proclaimed:

> Science is not a free and independent construction, fitting into neither space nor time, but is a specific accomplishment of the national spirit. For the first time the political duty of the young scientist and his scientific duty have been unified. The Fuehrer summons them. They shall lay hand to the undertaking that has been presented to German science.

Professors who did not suit the Nazi ideas of race, religion, or politics were vigorously attacked. Many who could not adjust their positions were weeded out or "liquidated." New courses were announced on such subjects as folk and race, Nazi philosophy and race theory, foundations of National Socialist philosophy, and the nature of ancient German religions. Student enrollment between 1932 and 1935 dropped virtually 50 per cent. In 1936 the Nazis conducted a celebration to mark the five hundred and fiftieth anniversary of the founding of Heidelberg, and all major universities in the world were invited to send representatives. Many accepted and sent delegates, others accepted with reservations, and others refused, led by Birmingham, Cambridge, and Oxford.

In 1937 the two hundredth anniversary of Göttingen was celebrated with the full panoply of Nazi uniforms, marching, cheering, speeches, and spectacular show. Delegates came from 30 foreign universities. The *New York Times* correspondent closed his report of the scene with the words, "Most of the foreign delegates stood rigidly at attention giving the Hitler salute along with their German colleagues."

It was clear that many educators were confused by the spectacle of Nazi control of German universities. Some laid full blame upon the Nazis for destroying the ideals of free and objective research and teaching. Others, blaming the Nazis fully as much, also held the German universities themselves to be not entirely blameless. They recalled the traditional aristocratic and undemocratic character of the German universities, which had led them to retire to their ivory towers in unconcern for the political and social trends of their times. Today, no one can miss the tragic point: universities cannot reject their social responsibility in a crisis and cannot maintain their traditional liberalism without taking active leadership in sustaining a free and democratic society.

Russia. During the nineteenth century the nobility spurned the Russian universities, and the peasant and working classes were shut out. Therefore, the largest element in the student body usually came from liberal, constitution-minded middle classes. The students were often considered to be dangerous revolutionaries by the aristocratic ruling classes. They justified the aristocracy's fears by constant agitation for liberal reforms and by supporting the Revolution of 1905.

During the First World War, plans were made to restore some of the autonomy earlier gained by the universities and to emphasize research and higher investigation rather than specific preparation for public service. The universities, representing middle-class outlooks as they did, opposed the revolution of October, 1917, and therefore received the full force of Communist attacks.

When the Soviet regime came to power, the first steps were to abolish entrance requirements, state examinations, and degrees, and to open the universities to all persons, both men and women, sixteen years of age and over. Since the young peasants and workers had no educational background fitting them for university study, new institutions known as *Rabfacs*, or workers' faculties, were established to give a concentrated 3 years of study to prepare the lower-class students for entrance. By 1932 a half million students were enrolled in the *Rabfacs* and, despite great opposition, rapidly invaded the halls of the universities.

In 1922 a thoroughgoing reorganization of higher education was announced. The universities were made a part of the state system of education, and numerous other higher schools were established, intended both to prepare specialists and scientific workers in the various vocations and to spread knowledge among the masses. Entrance examinations were restored, and this time preference was given to students of proletarian origin and background, who received maintenance at state expense.

Now that the higher schools had become a political arm of the Communist party, the curriculum of the higher schools and universities played up social and political studies in order to spread the Marxist gospel. Physical education and military training were also made compulsory. As was the case in the lower schools in the 1920's, students and youth organizations were given much responsibility in running the institutions as a means of breaking the hold of faculties who were not in sympathy with the Soviet ideology. Student groups, newspapers, meetings, excursions, entertainment, and discussions played a large role in the activities of the institutions. Competition for grades was abolished in favor of the principle of equal rewards and group responsibility. Students set out to reduce illiteracy among the adult population, work on the farms and factories during vacations and in emergencies, and help in establishing collective farms and conducting elections.

After 1929 the character of Soviet higher institutions changed once more, much as lower schools had changed with the beginning of the first

Five Year Plan. The stress was now upon the mastery of knowledge as a means of preparing professional and specialized scientific personnel. Neutral or antagonistic professors were liquidated, and a great campaign was conducted to fill the student body with proletarian Communists. The doctrine that science must serve Communism became the over-all aim, much as the Nazis stated that science must serve National Socialism. Higher institutions were set up in connection with many factories; thus, centers of production also became centers of education.

As the second Five Year Plan got under way in 1933, methods of instruction became more standardized. Individual marks, examinations, and degrees were restored, along with an emphasis upon greater discipline for students and greater authority for the professors. More general education in the social studies and sciences was offered, in addition to the professional and practical training for productive work, physical education, and military training.

By 1946 the number of higher institutions had been expanded enormously and had been brought under all-union control, except the pedagogical institutes which were left to the ministries of education in the several republics. In 1949 there were some 31 universities, 19 polytechnical institutes, and several hundred specialized institutes devoted to metallurgy, medicine, transportation, aviation, pedagogy, and the like. Soviet higher education put emphasis upon establishing a large number of separate and specialized institutions rather than bringing many fields of interest together into large universities. Very rapid increases in enrollments brought additional thousands of students into Soviet higher institutions in the postwar years. By 1955 the Soviet Union produced more scientists in one year than the United States did.

World Cooperation in Education

As the Second World War drew to a close, voices were raised in many countries urging that the cooperation of the United Nations in war should be extended to education in the peace. More and more people began to realize how much the war had been promoted by educational systems that devoted themselves entirely to the nationalistic aims of aggressor nations. In 1944, preparatory commissions met in London and elsewhere to draw up plans for an international agency of education. In November, 1945, delegates from 43 of the United Nations met in London and approved the charter for the United Nations Educational, Scientific, and Cultural Organization (UNESCO). Soviet Russia, refusing to participate in the proceedings, has never joined and has kept its major satellites out of the organization.

The principal objectives of UNESCO were to promote international peace, to improve international cooperation and understanding through the educational systems of the various nations, to reduce illiteracy by means of vast programs of fundamental education, to aim at equality of educational opportunity for all people in the various nations, and to combat doctrines of racial superiority and inferiority and national misunderstandings. Only if men and women everywhere are educated to want world peace can peace be achieved. As UNESCO's preamble stated, "Since wars begin in the minds of men, it is in the minds of men that the defenses of the peace must be constructed."

Fig. 26. The Work of UNESCO. (*Courtesy of* UNESCO.)

The principal methods to achieve these ends were to be extensive interchange of scholars, students, and educational materials, help for the ruined educational facilities of the devastated countries, cooperative methods to extend scientific and cultural research, revision of textbooks and instructional materials, and international seminars on educational and scientific problems. It was clearly recognized that unless the various mediums of mass communication (press, radio, movies, and the like) fully supported the objectives of UNESCO the efforts of schools alone would achieve relatively little.

Although some persons desired greater authority for UNESCO to control or supervise educational systems that might become a danger to the peace, the charter specifically safeguarded the integrity and independence of each nation's schools against interference by the international agency. The success of UNESCO clearly depended upon the genuine will and desire of the member nations to promote world peace. If such a will remained strong, UNESCO could doubtless promote international cooperation.

If it succeeded in promoting and strengthening the desire for peace among the peoples of the world, it could become one of the most important agencies ever devised. As the atomic bomb and the touch-and-go relations of Russia and the United States became the number-one political problem of the postwar period, more and more people began to feel that efforts to achieve international understanding must be redoubled.

Another indication of the growing sense of need for world cooperation in education was the establishment of the World Organization of the Teaching Profession at a meeting of delegates from 30 nations at Endicott, N.Y., in August, 1946. President William F. Russell of Teachers College, Columbia University, was chosen the first president. The principal purpose was to secure greater unity among the professional teachers' organizations of the world, to extend full and free education to all without discrimination, to improve the status of teachers, to advise agencies of the United Nations, and to promote the physical, social, and intellectual conditions of cooperation upon which world peace and security must rest. In August, 1952, W.O.T.P. and two other teachers' organizations agreed to form the World Confederation of Organizations of the Teaching Profession.

No greater task faced the men of good will and the educators of the world than to create an atmosphere in which mutual understanding and agreement could be reached by discussion and the free uses of intelligence rather than by resort to fear, force, and violence.

Chapter 14

NINETEENTH-CENTURY AMERICA:

SOCIAL FOUNDATIONS OF EDUCATION

GROWING PAINS OF THE NEW NATION

During the nineteenth century, institutions and ideas continued to be transplanted in America from many countries of Europe. Millions of people came to the United States, bringing their diversified cultures with them, but America was no longer merely a hothouse in which these institutions and ideas flourished as replicas of the Old World. A new environment, new soil, and new atmosphere, nurturing the mixtures of peoples and nationalities, helped to produce a culture that began to make its own distinctive contributions to Western civilization. Not the least important of these was the public school idea.

In nineteenth-century United States the political and economic patterns of life began to overshadow the religious as claimants upon the energies and loyalties of men. The United States was becoming an increasingly secular society in which religious institutions still played a strong part but no longer the leading role. This shift in emphasis did not take place without bitter struggles and much searching of the hearts and minds of men. These struggles found their counterpart in the conflicts between political and religious authorities for control of schools, colleges, and the means of education. The growth of political democracy, the expanding role of government, and the growth of nationalism contributed to the conception of public education that took root and flourished despite strong opposition from many quarters.

The Struggle for Democracy

General Political Developments. From the election of Jefferson as president in 1800, the Jeffersonian Republicans and their successor, the Democratic party, won every national election until 1860, with the exception of the Whig victories in 1840 and 1848. In general, during the early part of the century, the Republican-Democrats received their support from the independent farming groups of the South and West and the laboring classes of the cities of the East. This coalition elected Jefferson, Madison, Monroe, John Quincy Adams, Jackson, and Van Buren. By stressing states' rights, low tariffs, popular suffrage, and opposition

430

to special privileges, the Democrats appealed to the agrarian interests of the "common man" until the 1830's, when the question of slavery and industrial benefits to business brought a change in the alignment of forces.

The Federalists and their successors, the Whigs, were able to elect Harrison and Tyler in 1840 and Taylor and Fillmore in 1848. The Whigs generally proposed high tariffs for the protection of business and industrial interests. With the heightening of the slavery issue, Lincoln was elected in 1860 by the new Republican party (successor to the Whigs) on a platform of free land, high tariff, and opposition to slavery, designed to appeal to the farmers of the West as well as to the industrial groups of the East.

In the latter part of the nineteenth century the party control of the federal government was exactly reversed. The Republicans elected all the presidents up to 1900 with the exception of the two separate terms of Grover Cleveland. After Lincoln and Johnson, all the Republican presidents were military men of greater or lesser importance, Grant, Hayes, Garfield, Arthur, Benjamin Harrison, and McKinley. The Republicans generally drew up platforms in favor of high tariffs, free land, civil-service reform, and "sound money," which appealed to the business, industrial, and propertied classes of the East and West. Increasingly, however, discontent arose among the agrarian and debtor groups, whose dissatisfaction with the major parties was embodied in many new parties. These had only minor effects as far as elections were concerned but they often forced the major parties to adopt many of their proposals.

Labor groups formed a series of labor parties as early as 1872. The Free Soil party, which had as its object to keep slavery out of the territories, and the Know-Nothing party, which attempted to render Roman Catholics and the foreign-born population politically powerless, attracted discontented persons for widely varying reasons. Agrarian and labor groups made greater headway with their Independent party (1876), known as "Greenbackers," and especially with the People's party, known as "Populists," which polled a million votes in 1892. The Democratic party in 1896, with strong Populist support, gave the Republicans a close race in which Bryan polled 6,500,000 votes against 7,100,000 for McKinley.

Growth of Political Democracy. Enormously important for the future of American political life was the extension of the ballot to wider and wider elements in the population. At the beginning of the nineteenth century the privilege of voting was limited by property and religious qualifications, but by the middle of the century white manhood suffrage was virtually won. In the 1820's and 1830's, especially, the new states of the West came into the Union with constitutions guaranteeing universal manhood suffrage (at least for white men), and many of the eastern states liberalized their voting requirements under the impact of the Republican-

Democrats. The election of Andrew Jackson in 1828 is usually taken as the signal that the process of extending the vote to small farmers and laborers was well on its way.

Then with the Emancipation Proclamation and the Thirteenth, Fourteenth, and Fifteenth Amendments to the Constitution in the 1860's the principle of universal manhood suffrage, including Negroes as well as whites, was established, although methods of circumventing the principle were devised by literacy tests, poll taxes, and "grandfather clauses" in the South. Vast efforts to extend the voting privilege to women were made in the nineteenth century, with success on a state basis in the 1890's in Wyoming, Utah, Colorado, and Idaho, but without success on a national basis until the Nineteenth Amendment in 1920.

Meanwhile, other gains were made for democratic political control, especially through the efforts of the labor and agrarian parties. Property qualifications for holding office were gradually abolished. Secret ballots replaced party ballots, a step toward eliminating intimidation of voters by politicians and employers. Presidential electors and senators were elected directly by the people instead of by state legislatures or party machines. Presidential candidates were nominated by national conventions rather than by party caucuses. These gains all helped to make the electoral process more democratic.

Expanding Role of Government. Despite the arguments for and against increasing the power of the federal government, the trend was unmistakably in the direction of expanding the role of the government in the affairs of the new nation. Though the Jeffersonian Democrats adhered to a narrow conception of the functions of the federal government in comparison with that of state governments, their presidents often actually helped to enlarge the federal government's powers. As president, Jefferson conducted the Louisiana Purchase in 1803 which added vast areas of the West to the nation, and he imposed the embargo of 1807 upon English goods, which vitally affected all American industry and agriculture.

Monroe raised tariffs, annexed Florida, and formulated the Monroe Doctrine, warning European nations away from the shores of the Americas. Jackson would not go along with the doctrine of states' rights when he helped to prevent secession of South Carolina over higher tariffs. Under Polk, Texas, California, New Mexico, and Arizona were added to the western territories, until the boundaries of the nation spanned a continent. Under Pierce, the power of the nation was exerted when Commodore Perry opened up Japan to Western trade. In all these ways Democratic administrations laid the groundwork for a vast nation in which the power of the federal government was bound to expand. A decentralized political authority could no longer be sufficient.

As the Civil War approached, however, the Democratic party began to stress the rights of states to govern themselves. The Republican party took up the cudgels for a strong federal government. Inheriting the arguments for a permanent union as set forth by Webster and other Whigs, the Republicans gave to Lincoln the task of preventing the federal government from falling apart in civil war. The power of the federal government emerged from the Civil War enhanced and strengthened.

In the later years of the century, several steps were taken by the federal government to control the rampant individualism and monopolistic methods of big business. The measures to increase income taxes, control railroad rates by the Interstate Commerce Commission, and regulate monopoly by the Sherman Antitrust Act, although not applied rigorously at first, foreshadowed the trend toward even greater federal authority. Interestingly enough, roots of the "welfare state" were being nourished by the Republicans more than by the Democrats in the later nineteenth century.

Nationalism and Imperialism. Born in an international war of revolution, the new nation tried to keep out of "foreign wars" and entangling alliances during its early days. Despite demands to help our "former French ally," Adams and Jefferson stayed out of the actual fighting of the Napoleonic wars, but Madison finally plunged in. As a result of the War of 1812, a new spirit of nationalism swept the country. We were "on our way" and set out to win a continent by treaty, purchase, and war with Mexico and with the various Indian tribes.

Each new success, despite opposition from some quarters, enhanced the spirit of nationalism. For a time, it looked as though the Civil War would bring the edifice toppling down, but after the wounds of reconstruction were bound up the sense of nationhood emerged stronger than ever. The expansion westward and the growth of industrial power completed the process. By the end of the century, the nation was ready to undertake deliberate imperialistic ventures that elevated even higher the nationalistic spirit.

About 1890 such men as Alfred Thayer Mahan, Josiah Strong, Henry Cabot Lodge, Theodore Roosevelt, and Albert Jeremiah Beveridge began to preach the doctrine that the United States was now an adult among nations and must play an adult role in power politics. The continent had been won, and therefore new markets were necessary. The argument followed that a large navy, world-wide naval bases, and an aggressive foreign policy would lead to new outlets for agricultural products and more raw materials for industry, which would be helpful to farmers, industry, and labor alike. Also, it would be a spiritual good to bring American civilization and Christianity to the heathen of the world.

The road to imperialism was paved with high-sounding intentions. The Spanish-American War, the acquisition of Puerto Rico, the Philippines,

Guam, and Hawaii, and the suppression of the Boxer Rebellion in China were the result. It was clear that the world was shrinking in size and that a "natural" isolation was steadily being broken down over a century of rapid change and expansion. By the end of the nineteenth century the several American states had been welded into one nation, but the trends that were creating "one world" were yet to be recognized.

Individualism versus Humanitarianism. Cutting across much of the political development just described were two underlying outlooks concerning the role of government in American society. One outlook may be called "individualism." It stemmed from the laissez-faire and conservative conception of the state (see pages 338 to 341). According to individualism, the government should refrain from regulatory control and should allow the maximum of freedom to individual initiative and business enterprise. Only through such individual effort will the wheels of society turn at maximum efficiency and each individual receive compensation in wages or profits commensurate with his effort and initiative.

If in this process any individual does not receive much return but is poor or unemployed, he has only his own improvidence, laziness, or carelessness to blame. He cannot expect government to intervene in his behalf but can only rely upon the charitable instincts of the more fortunate to help him out. Private charity and philanthropy are the proper means of relieving distress, for government aid not only will make the poor even less self-reliant but also will stifle the initiative of the more able and make the rich poorer so that they cannot help the more unfortunate. The individualistic outlook was not only congenial to the interests of the capitalistic well to do as a justification for their own business practices, but conditions of life in the early half of the nineteenth century seemed to justify its acceptance by great numbers of independent farmers and small owners.

However, in the latter part of the century, increasingly severe depressions, the concentration of wealth in fewer hands, and the spread of poverty and bad working conditions led to a stronger assertion of the humanitarian doctrines. According to social humanitarianism (see pages 341 to 342), the government is the only agency that can cope adequately with big business. It was argued that government should become more active in promoting the public welfare and in regulating the conditions under which great masses of people had to earn their living. Reformers of many shades of opinion, ranging from humanitarianism to socialism, began to urge greater participation by the government in public affairs. Minor political parties, labor organizations, agrarian organizations, scholars, and intellectuals preached of reform somewhat akin to the liberal, social democratic, and humanitarian doctrines of Europe.

The feeling that "there ought to be a law" was deep in the American tradition, and demands were made for many types of legislation to be enacted by state and federal governments: factory laws to improve safety and sanitation in industry, maximum-hour and minimum-wage laws, responsibility of employers for compensation for injury to workers, unemployment insurance, old-age pensions, government control of public utilities, public-health measures, city planning and improvement of housing conditions, conservation of natural resources, prison reform, and more humane punishment for crimes.

Along with these demands for social legislation went agitation for public education, sponsored especially by labor organizations, humanitarians, and middle-class liberals. Other groups were organized to agitate for abolition of slavery, for temperance, and for woman's rights. By the end of the century the abolition of slavery had been accomplished, and the achievement in public education had outdistanced most of the other reforms.

The Struggle for Equality of Opportunity

Perhaps the most significant long-term trend in American economic life during the nineteenth century was the shift from an agrarian to an industrial society. At the opening of the century most people made their living from the land; by the end of the century the impact of industrialism and manufacturing was making itself felt in all parts of the country. The conflict between agricultural interests and industrial interests came to play a large part in the political, economic, and social life of the people. Accompanying industrial changes were the growth of city life, the easier and more rapid means of communication and transportation, the dominance of capitalistic enterprise, and the growth of organized labor. Cutting across these trends was the great increase in population, added to by the influx of immigrants. All these developments had profound effects upon American education.

As great numbers of people moved rapidly westward, vast land areas were relatively soon in private hands, individual or corporative. It was possible for the government to announce in 1893 that there was no more frontier (defined as an area in which there are more than two but less than six persons per square mile). For a century the frontier had been a great attraction to all kinds of persons from the East and from foreign lands. It had stimulated the ideals of individualism and equality to a greater degree than in any other country in the world, and it helped to fix these ideals as a part of the American dream of opportunity for all. But, even before the end of the century, new conditions were arising to make this dream of opportunity less possible of achievement.

The Industrial Revolution that had begun in England in the last third of the eighteenth century swept the United States in the first half of the nineteenth century. Whereas the typical artisan and mechanic of 1800 had done his work at home or in his small shop, the trend to the factory type of manufacturing was well on its way by the 1820's, and the Northeast turned rapidly to industrial production with power-driven machinery. By the middle of the century the capital value of city and manufacturing property was greater than the capital value of agricultural property, and by 1890 the value of all manufactured products had surpassed the value of all agricultural products. It is significant that the closing of the frontier came at about the same time as this fundamental shift from agrarian to industrial interests.

Closely associated with industrial development were rapid advances in science and technology, for new inventions made this degree of industrialization possible. As these technological advances resulted in mass production of goods, they also speeded up their transportation and distribution. The means of communication paralleled the means of transportation. The reliance of one part of the nation upon the others was producing a degree of interdependence that only a few realized at the time.

Another vastly important aspect of industrialization was the growth of city life. As the factory system replaced household and domestic methods of production, people began to flock to the manufacturing centers, first in New England and the middle states and then in the Middle West. As workers crowded into the cities, amid desperate conditions of filth, squalor, and overcrowding, the slum areas became a startling threat to health, morals, and sanitation, the effects of which are still seen in the tenement areas of all our large cities today.

In 30 years, from 1840 to 1870, the population of the United States doubled; in 30 years, from 1870 to 1900, it doubled again. Contributory to this amazing expansion, of course, was the immigration from Europe. Of the 76,000,000 people in America in 1900 about 10,000,000 were foreign-born, not counting the generations of children born to earlier immigrants from many lands. Of equal importance was the changing character of the immigrant population.

Between 1820 and 1860 most came from the northern European countries, especially from Ireland and Germany. After the middle of the century the great sources of immigration shifted from northern to southern and eastern Europe. Whereas people from the latter areas had been less than 1 per cent of the immigration in the 1820's, the proportion jumped to two-thirds at the end of the century. In many of the larger cities the foreign-born population came to represent 30, 40, and even more than 50 per cent of the total population.

Despite the difficulties confronting these newcomers, they never faced such extensive legal restrictions as did the American Negro. At the end of the Civil War several southern states adopted "black codes" designed to preserve white supremacy by law. The federal government countered with a civil rights act and the Thirteenth, Fourteenth, and Fifteenth Amendments. The Fourteenth Amendment, adopted in 1868, eventually came to be the most controversial of these amendments. It prohibited the states from infringing the life, liberty, or property of any American citizen without due process of law and forbade the states to deny any citizen equal protection of the laws. The southern states, however, proceeded to adopt "Jim Crow" laws and constitutional provisions enforcing legal segregation upon Negroes in public places, conveyances, theaters, hotels, and schools. Dual school systems, one for whites and one for Negroes, were established in 17 southern states and Washington, D.C.

Efforts to break down legal segregation were met by the decisions of state and federal courts upholding the principle that segregation was legal so long as equal facilities for both races were maintained. This doctrine went back at least as far as the Roberts case in Boston in 1849 when the supreme court of Massachusetts decided that Boston could maintain segregated school systems. The "separate but equal" doctrine was firmly incorporated in the famous case of *Plessy v. Ferguson* in 1896 when the United States Supreme Court upheld the right of railroads to segregate passengers according to race. The Plessy case became the most important legal bulwark supporting segregated public schools until the middle of the twentieth century.

Meanwhile, American Negroes were having difficulties in making social, economic, and political adjustments. At the time of the Civil War about one-third of the population of the South was made up of Negroes, the great majority of whom were slaves. After their emancipation, great numbers of Negroes found that their freedom had been achieved without appreciable improvement in their economic security. Indeed, many found themselves in even worse condition, for their chance of becoming independent landowners was very small. Some went back to work as wage earners for plantation owners, some were able to become tenant farmers, and others drifted to the cities of the North, where they found it difficult to compete in the skilled trades because of their lack of technical training.

Beset by social, political, and economic discrimination from all sides, the Negro often found his lot desperate and at best only tolerable. As the century drew to a close, the ideal of equality of opportunity and freedom, which had been a part of the American dream, was becoming ever more difficult of achievement for large sections of the American population who found that they were not accepted as "real" Americans because of their race or national background. This denial of the American dream put public education to the test in a way that no other cultural development had done.

The nineteenth century was the high point in the pervasive influence of capitalism. It saw the shift from a commercial type of capitalism to industrial capitalism, or, as some writers put it, from merchant capitalism to employer capitalism. As in Europe, the capitalist changed his economic role from that of a middleman between the worker and the buyer to that of the employer of labor, owner of the factory, machines, and tools of production, manager of the enterprise, and seller of the finished goods. This shift in the role of the capitalist began to take place with the inauguration of the factory system in the early part of the century and proceeded with greater and greater rapidity after the Civil War. In this process, the corporation as a business device, and a highly successful one, entered the scene. Corporations expanded in size so enormously that they gained control of raw materials and natural resources as well as factories, railroads, and other means of production and distribution.

Whereas industrial capitalism professed equality of opportunity for all, the realization of the ideal of equality to any such degree as claimed was prevented by the closing of the frontier, the spread of monopoly, the factory system, the growing concentration of wealth, and the control of government by the wealthy interests.

Meanwhile, as the capitalists used the individualistic and laissez-faire ideals of historic liberalism to justify their role in society, labor was beginning to use the social humanitarian ideals of liberalism to defend itself. The labor movement in America arose, as elsewhere, as a protest and reaction against the excesses of capitalism. At the beginning of the nineteenth century independent workmen and mechanics began to lose their status as the merchant capitalists set the workers to competing with one another for hire in a process that forced wages down. Thus, the skilled workers began to organize into trade unions or craft unions in order to improve their bargaining power and keep wages up.

In 1827 in Philadelphia 15 trade unions joined together and formed the Mechanics' Union of Trade Associations. Meeting with preliminary success, the movement soon expanded, and a political party was organized in 1828 called the Workingmen's party, designed to agitate for legislation that would extend the rights of labor. Drawing upon the humanitarian and democratic ideals of liberalism, the labor groups argued for free public education as one of the means of improving the condition of working people. Organized labor was a potent factor in extending the political suffrage in the Jacksonian era and in contributing to the "public school revival."

The opposition of the capitalists, the depression of 1837, the adoption of many of their proposed reforms by the major political parties, and the disintegration of the Workingmen's party led to a decline of the labor movement in the 1840's, but after the Civil War the trend was upward again. In 1866 the National Labor Union was formed in order to unite local and city unions into a national association. It soon began to extend its efforts from simply bargaining for higher wages to the actual production of goods through producers' cooperatives. This was too radical for the times; the bitter opposition of manufacturers resulted in its decline in 6 years.

The next and much more important effort at national organization was the Knights of Labor, which appeared in the 1870's in the effort to unite all workers into one union, regardless of race, color, sex, or creed. The Knights of Labor gained considerable strength, claimed as many as 700,000 members, and won several notable strikes, especially against the railroads. Agitation for an 8-hour day became one of their activities; but the opposition became extremely bitter, and the charge was made that the Knights of Labor were really anarchistic and extremely radical.

Meanwhile, a different type of labor organization, known as the American Federation of Labor, began to gain strength from 1886 on. Basing its organization upon the principle of uniting all craft unions into a national federation rather than into one big union for all American workers, the American Federation of Labor appealed principally to skilled workers and concentrated on collective bargaining for higher wages, shorter hours, and better working conditions. It opposed the more radical efforts of Marxist, socialist, or anarchist groups and refrained from direct political action or affiliation with one political party. Under the leadership of Samuel Gompers, who was president from 1886 to 1924 with the exception of one year, the American Federation of Labor worked for labor bureaus in the state and national governments, state factory laws to increase the safety of workers, compensation for injury, equal pay for men and women, abolition of child labor, and the extension of public schools.

In general, membership in labor unions of various kinds, including the powerful railroad brotherhoods, which began to increase in the last years of the nineteenth century, was soon well over the million mark. Organized labor not only worked to better its own conditions but also supported social legislation that would achieve public education, extend the suffrage, control monopolies, and abolish prison for debt. It was one of the most effective agencies for promoting the welfare of the common people against the injustices, poverty, and inequalities facing the underprivileged groups handicapped and thwarted by industrial conditions beyond their individual control.

Stemming from the social humanitarianism of France, the transcendentalism of Germany, and the romantic ideals of England, a new American humanitarianism struck out to improve social conditions in many ways. It took the form of almost innumerable societies to prevent poverty, abolish slavery, soften criminal codes, improve prison conditions, extend woman's rights, prevent intemperance, and help the insane, the blind, the deaf, and the handicapped.

Approaching reform in a variety of ways, groups were formed to achieve a more humane community life for selected persons. Religious communities went into seclusion to seek the perfect life apart from the destructive influences of an industrial and capitalistic society. For example, the Perfectionist religion of John Humphrey Noyes produced the Oneida Community, based on the radical and primitive communism of Christianity.

Many secular communal groups also appeared in the early nineteenth century. The socialistic ventures of Robert Owen and Robert Dale Owen at New Harmony, Ind., and elsewhere attracted scores of people. Even more extensive were the several communities established according to the socialistic doctrines of Charles Fourier, who had preached the common ownership of land and common labor as means of achieving a self-sufficient community life. Brook Farm at West Roxbury, Mass., was probably the most famous of these.

In all, there were dozens of different experiments along these and other lines in the nineteenth century, reflecting the ferment of reform ideas that emerged in reaction to the sordidness and stifling quality of industrial conditions. But the industrial and capitalistic trends made wider achievement of social reform impossible without a greater organized effort than could be put forth by small and isolated community efforts. The social-welfare movement thus began to appear, signalized by the establishing of such settlement houses as Stanton Coit's Neighborhood Guild in New York and Jane Addams's Hull House in Chicago and by the publications of Jacob Riis attacking tenement conditions. By 1900 a hundred settlement houses were operating in various cities. On a national scale the American Red Cross began to provide help for those suddenly afflicted by disasters beyond their control.

Sectarianism and Secularism

America remained predominantly a Protestant society during the nineteenth century, but the influence of Protestantism was less all-embracing than it had been at the beginning of the century. The important principle of liberty of religious conscience and separation of church and state was achieved by the liberal and democratic efforts of the late eighteenth and early nineteenth centuries. Yet conservative religious outlooks often went hand in hand with conservative political and economic ideals. In the early part of the century the orthodox churches were closely allied with Federalism, whereas liberal and radical religious aims often found expression in the reform movements of this period. Unitarianism in New England provided an outlet for social reform in the Utopian and Perfectionist societies already mentioned.

Religious revivalism and emotionalism were marked in the first decades of the nineteenth century, almost paralleling the Great Awakening of the eighteenth century. The revivalistic movement found especially fertile ground in the new West as the settlers took their own churches with them and responded to the greater flexibility, informality, and individualism of frontier life. Churches in the East became greatly concerned about spreading the gospel in the West. The American Bible Society in 1816 and the American Home Missionary Society in 1826 set out to convert the West as well as to send missionaries to foreign lands. The circuit riders and itinerant ministers and preachers became a common feature of western life, just as the local church became one of the most important centers of frontier community life. Thousands of new members were swept into the churches by these methods. Between 1800 and 1850 church membership increased 10 times while the total population was increasing only five times.

Meanwhile, the great new influx of immigrants in the 1830's and 1840's and again after the 1880's brought in thousands who had Roman Catholic and Jewish backgrounds. Most of the Irish immigrants and many German immigrants of the early period were loyal Roman Catholics; and a great majority of the immigrants from Austria-Hungary, Poland, Italy, Russia, and southeastern Europe of the later period were Roman Catholic or Jewish.

As Protestants felt their way of life challenged by Roman Catholicism, they often turned upon Roman Catholics as undemocratic and un-American. The Know-Nothing party of the 1850's and the American Protective Association of the 1880's and 1890's focused this resentment in organized form. These movements were largely expressions of rural, middle-western antagonism against the industrial cities, where most of the Roman Catholics had settled. The American Protective Association was a secret society in which the members were pledged to vote against Roman Catholics and discriminate against them in employment. The ideal of fair play and religious toleration was having a hard test.

Perhaps more than any other country, the United States has seen the segmentation of religious groups and the establishment of dozens of new cults appealing to the dissatisfied and restless. By the end of the century Americans were confronted by some 150 sects that claimed their religious loyalties. If the Protestant churches were grouped together, they represented some 18,000,000 members, of which the Methodists, Baptists, Presbyterians, Lutherans, and Congregationalists were the largest groups. The Roman Catholic Church, larger by far than any one Protestant church, represented some 10,000,000 members. Jews accounted for perhaps

1,000,000. Throughout the century the number of church members increased more rapidly, in proportion, than did the total population; James Bryce judged that no country in Europe could match America in respect to the influence of churches upon the people.

The strength and vitality of the churches in America were in no small measure the result of the principles of religious freedom and the separation of church and state as embodied in the First Amendment and in the bills of rights of the several state constitutions. Virtually every state as it came into the Union in the nineteenth century adopted the principles that the state guaranteed freedom of religious conscience and that the state would not use public funds to aid or support one or any number of churches. The new states either followed the formula adopted in such early constitutional provisions as those of Pennsylvania, New Jersey, and North Carolina or in Jefferson's statute for religious freedom in Virginia or in the wording of the First Amendment itself.

Up to 1876 new states followed voluntarily the historic principles of separation of church and state. After 1876 the Congress stipulated that new states must adopt irrevocable ordinances to the same effect. By the end of the nineteenth century the American people came closer to agreeing to these principles than at any time in their history. As applied to education, it was widely accepted that no public funds would be given to religious schools and no religious instruction would be given in the public schools. In the course of the twentieth century, however, these principles were to be severely challenged, and many of the battles had to be fought all over again.

As the century moved into its later decades, the growing secularism of life, especially represented by industrialism, urbanization, and newer intellectual trends growing out of the theory of evolution, affected organized religions in different ways. The increase of wealth in the cities gave enormous financial support to the established churches. Great churches were built, money flowed to improve church services and music, and city congregations often became aristocratic and exclusive. It soon became clear that the laboring classes could not easily attend without embarrassment the services of certain churches that catered to the wealthy classes. It was also clear from sermons delivered in some of the exclusive city churches that little attention was being given to the conditions of the laboring classes.

Liberalism and the spirit of reform did appear among many church leaders, however. Some liberal churches directly aided labor, under the leadership of such men as Horace Bushnell, Washington Gladden, and Josiah Strong and of the Christian Socialist Society of the 1880's. Liberal Episcopalians formed a society for the advancement of the interests of labor, and the Pope's encyclical in 1891 recognized the rights of labor.

The observance of Sunday in the Puritan tradition began to be weakened as the European immigrants brought with them their less rigid ideas concerning the proper activities for the Sabbath. This caused concern among many groups, who organized Sabbath societies to reinforce a more ascetic observance of Sunday. Other churches turned to secular methods to hold and attract membership, instituting weekday activities such as the sewing circle, gymnastic activities, child-care agencies, and reading and discussion groups.

Interdenominational cooperation existed in many different forms, as in the Young Men's Christian Association, the Young Women's Christian Association, the Christian Endeavor Society, and the World's Student Christian Federation. Religiously minded persons found outlets for their reform interest in the cooperative efforts of the Prohibition party, the Women's Christian Temperance Union, and many other organizations. Interdenominational revival movements aided many of the Protestant churches, under the leadership of such men as Dwight L. Moody, in the latter decades of the century.

The greatest intellectual and secular challenge to the churches of the later nineteenth century was undoubtedly the spread of the doctrines of biological evolution. Some of the churches combated these with a reassertion of extreme fundamentalism and the literal interpretation of the Bible, simply denying their validity. Others began to try to reconcile the scientific implications of evolution with religious beliefs, under the leadership of such men as Henry Ward Beecher, Washington Gladden, John Fiske, and Lyman Abbott. This battle over evolution symbolized the onrush of secular forces that were weakening the intellectual hold of the churches upon the minds of the people and were making the problems for public education ever more acute.

A DISTINCTIVE SYSTEM OF PUBLIC EDUCATION

In the process of becoming a nation, the United States, though possessing a high spirit of confidence and optimism, was torn by all kinds of difficulties. American education in the nineteenth century shared these difficulties and these optimisms. When Americans decided that government should expand its role for the benefit of all the people, they naturally turned to public education as one of the most important of governmental functions. When Americans decided that they must become and remain a united nation, they turned to the public schools to help achieve their goals.

Education was caught up in the conflicts and controversies that marked these decisions. Shall we give everyone an equal opportunity for life, liberty, and the pursuit of happiness? Let the schools help. Shall we give everyone a chance to make a better living? Let the schools train for jobs. Shall we provide a haven for the oppressed peoples of the world? Let the schools help to make them Americans. But it was not as easy as all this.

Many Americans felt that only a relatively few were able to profit from education, and therefore they fought against the establishment of public schools. Many Americans felt that working people should not be allowed to rise too rapidly from their inherited places in society, and therefore they fought against expanding public education. The trend, however, was unmistakable. The forces of democracy, industrialism, and humanitarianism all pointed to the establishment of something new under the sun, a free public school system dedicated to the proposition that equality of educational opportunity is essential for the achievement of a truly democratic society.

The Public School Idea Wins

The idea of a public school system supported at public expense to achieve democratic purposes was not a completely new idea, as we have seen, but it had not yet been fulfilled in any country in the world at the beginning of the nineteenth century. The United States took up the idea and pushed further toward its achievement, despite notable shortcomings, than any other country had done by the end of the century. This was not accomplished without bitter struggles and controversies.

In general, the public school idea was promoted by middle-class liberals, reformers, and humanitarians, by the labor movement and working classes of the cities, and by the organized agrarian and Populist movements during the latter part of the century. In general, the public school idea was opposed by social, political, and economic conservatives of all classes, by industrial and business interests that included large taxpayers, by the southern aristocrats, and by certain religious and non-English-speaking groups who saw a threat to their private control of religious and foreign-language schools.

Transition from Private to Public Control. The real battle began with the upsurge of democratic ideals in the Jacksonian era of the 1820's and 1830's and was waged hotly for three or four decades until the legal principles of public control were won. The battle continued in the last decades of the century as the movement to put the principles into action gained momentum. The main argument in favor of public schools was that the fortunes of a democratic society depend upon a free and equal opportunity for all the children of all the people to develop themselves to their fullest capacity. Not only do the state and society depend for their welfare upon such a school system, but also does the individual's chance to make something of himself and rise out of whatever unfortunate circumstances he may have inherited. Only by providing free schools at public expense can these social and individual aims be achieved, the argument went; and only by providing secular schools free from sectarian religious doctrines can the principle of separation of church and state be maintained so as to avoid the difficulties that most European countries experienced with established state churches.

The main arguments against public control of schools were that private interests and initiative are undermined by public schools. The wealth of the privileged and able classes of society should not be taxed to provide an education for the poor and ignorant classes of society, who cannot profit from such education. Education should properly be reserved for those intellectually able to profit from it and financially able to pay for it. It was assumed that there is a natural and high correlation between intelligence and income. Furthermore, many religious groups argued that secular and therefore "godless" schools would destroy the moral and religious foundations of society and would, in fact, prejudice the financial endowments of established private and religious school systems. Within this framework of argument, the political, economic, and legal struggles were carried on at a high pitch of intensity throughout most of the century.

The transition from the private school idea to the public school idea was a difficult one and took different forms in different parts of the country but there were usually three crucial arenas in which the battle had to be fought. First and foremost was the struggle to achieve the principle that truly public schools must be free to all children and therefore must be supported by general taxation. Second, the fight to broaden the scope of control and support from the local district to a state-wide basis had to be won in order to provide decent schooling for all children of a state. Third, public schools had to be freed of sectarian religious control if they were to strengthen the common bonds of democracy among all people rather than divide them on ideological grounds. Any one of these battles would have been hard enough to win separately. When they were combined, the task assumed gigantic proportions.

Growth of Public Support. The principal achievement of the nineteenth century was to destroy the traditional notion that free education should be provided only for the poor and underprivileged and to establish the conception that free education should be designed for everyone, irrespective of financial status.

At the beginning of the century the most common plan, outside of New England, was to provide education under private auspices, charging fees and tuition for those who could afford to pay, and offering free education on a charity basis for those who could not pay. Very often parents of underprivileged children had to declare themselves paupers in order to take advantage of free educational opportunities for their children. Thus, "free" education meant education connected with charity and the stigma of pauperism. In several of the middle-eastern and southern states this pauper conception for free public schools was written into the state laws or constitutions.

The reformers and humanitarians therefore had two major tasks to perform. First, they had to combat the ideas that free education and public education were only for the poor. They took the only position they believed consistent with a democratic conception of society and insisted that free and public education could be achieved only if common schools were supported at public expense and were open equally to all economic and social levels of the population. Secondly, they went to work to change the laws and to get communities and state legislatures to provide the funds for free public schools. The Jeffersonian Republicans, the Jacksonian Democrats, the New England liberals and humanitarians, and the labor and Populist movements all worked in their various ways for these ends.

As noted in an earlier connection (see pages 317 to 318), schools had been supported in a large number of ways, including tuition, rate bills, endowments, bequests, gifts, lotteries, licenses, and taxes. The task of the public school enthusiasts was to replace these specialized and limited forms of support with direct taxation sufficient to meet the full needs of public schools for everyone. This was, of course, the most difficult task, for it meant spreading the burden of support for public schools among all the taxpayers, even those who had no children in the public schools. To win this battle required all the talents and energies of public-spirited persons throughout the whole range of public and private life.

Two types of indirect public support paved the way for direct support, namely, federal grants for education and permanent common school funds in the various states. Considerable indirect public support for public schools came from the federal government through grants of land and money to the states. It is estimated that nearly 150,000,000 acres of public land were given by the federal government to the states, the income from which was used for educational purposes. More than half of this amount came from grants of the sixteenth section of each township under the provision of the Ordinances of 1785 and 1787 (see pages 315 to 317). When Ohio was admitted to the Union in 1803 as the first state carved out of the old Northwest Territory, each township in Ohio was granted the sixteenth section to be used for common schools. Later on, several states in the West where land values were low received two and even more sections in each township for common schools.

During the course of the century several other types of federal aid were devoted by the states to public schools. For example, the so-called "5 per cent fund" was the result of an agreement whereby the federal government gave to a state 5 per cent of the proceeds from the sale of public lands within that state, if the state did not tax the federal land within its boundaries. Other grants included salt lands and swamplands that were given to the states for improvement and sale, the income from these often going to education. Likewise, the Surplus Revenue Deposit Act of 1837 distributed among the state treasuries a surplus of $28,000,000 then in the federal treasury. This was apportioned on the basis of the number of Congressional representatives each state had in Congress. The Internal Improvement Act of 1841 also benefited many states, for they interpreted "internal improvement" to include the building of school-houses, along with roads and bridges.

Higher education also profited from federal aid in the form of the seminary grants of an entire township for each state to be used for higher education. All states received these grants except the original 13 states, Vermont, Maine, Kentucky, and Texas. Much more important for higher education in the long run was the Morrill Act of 1862 and later sup-plementary grants, which gave large amounts of public land to the vari-ous states for the establishment of agricultural and mechanical colleges. These were the so-called "land-grant colleges" (see pages 466 to 467). Also, the Hatch Act of 1887 provided additional federal funds to the land-grant agricultural colleges to promote scientific research in affili-ated agricultural experiment stations.

The second form of indirect public support for education was perma-nent school funds, the income from which was to be used by the states for the operation and maintenance of common schools. The principal of these state funds was usually made up of the money derived from the various federal grants just mentioned (except the seminary and Morrill grants), fines, property forfeitures and escheat, and sometimes a mill tax on property. Great hopes were held for these funds by their advocates in the early days. They even evoked the objection from opponents that they would produce far more than the states would ever need for their schools and that therefore the states were squandering their money.

However, the funds generally produced a pitifully small proportion of the money needed for public schools as the school systems expanded to meet growing needs. Mismanagement of the funds, embezzlement, poor investments, and, above all, the growing need for larger and larger outlays of money meant that the funds fell far below the original expectations. They did help, however, to establish the idea that public funds should be used for public schools.

During the 1830's and 1840's the principal struggle for public support of schools shifted to the problem of direct taxation. There were two stumbling blocks. One was the prevailing belief that free education was proper only for poor, or "pauper" children. The other obstacle was the use of rate bills, by which the public schools levied a special tax upon those parents who had children in school. The more children of a family in school, the more the parents paid to supplement the meager funds derived from taxation. This, of course, imposed a greater burden upon the underprivileged groups with large families, who could not afford to pay and who therefore could not send their children to public schools. The battle raged during the middle 50 years of the nineteenth century but was virtually won by 1875 in nearly all states.

In general, the laws concerning pauper education and rate bills had to be altered or wiped off the statute books and new laws passed. Although the process varied in many states, three stages of development were fairly well marked. In the early stage, the best that many states could do was to pass laws permitting local districts to tax themselves for schools if the people voted for it. This local option in some cases took the form of levying taxes only upon those who desired to be taxed and in other cases of taxing everyone if the vote so determined. A second stage appeared when the states passed laws offering state aid as an inducement to local districts to tax themselves and giving state aid only to those districts which did so. Finally, most of the states passed laws compelling local districts to tax themselves up to a certain amount for the support of public schools.

When this final stage was reached, the vast resources of the local real-property tax were at the disposal of public education. In time it came to carry the greatest burden of public school support, amounting to approximately three-fourths of all public school funds in the United States. The rest was made up of state taxes (on inheritance, corporations, sales, and income), federal aid, and permanent school funds, in that order. In the nineteenth century the great task was to establish the principle and practice that direct taxes should be used for public schools. In the twentieth century the great task was to broaden school support from a state-wide to a nationwide basis, in order to give more equal educational opportunity for all children of the nation, no matter in what state they might happen to live.

Growth of Centralized Control. In order to achieve greater equality of educational opportunity for all children by means of genuine public support, it seemed clear to educational reformers that the inherited district system of local control needed to be supplemented by a more highly unified and centralized state control. In an earlier connection it has been noted that the eighteenth century produced a rather large measure of local and decentralized control. Now the nineteenth century witnessed a reversal of that trend as the reformers struggled for greater state control. In other words, there have been in America two authentic traditions of educational control, one leading to decentralized and local administration, the other leading to more centralized control as represented in county, city, and state administrative units.

As the great westward migrations took place in the nineteenth century, the people from New England took with them to the West their tradition of district control and the people from the South took with them their tradition of private, religious, or county control. Under the frontier and agrarian conditions of the West, these traditions seemed adequate for a time when there were no strong state governments.

However, it soon became apparent that the district system was extremely limited in its ability to provide adequate schools for all. Despite the great loyalties to the district school engendered among the American people and their belief that it was more democratic than a more centralized form of control, the trend of the times was toward widening the size of the community that should be organized for educational purposes. That the community should be the state rather than local units seemed clear to those who recognized the needs for a genuine democratic education in the new industrial society of the nineteenth century.

The effort was therefore made to induce the various state legislatures to reassert their authority concerning public schools by organizing county, city, or district units for administrative purposes. Thus, by public agitation, by laws passed in the legislatures, and by legal decisions in the state and federal courts, it was generally established by the last quarter of the nineteenth century that the states constituted the final legal power in public education. Smaller units operated therefore under the enabling laws of the states and at the direction of the states.

The states then began to set up organized school systems to carry out the laws of the legislature and to allocate and supervise the distribution of state funds to the local units. In some states, beginning with New York in 1812, a state superintendent of public instruction was established as the chief school official for the state. After a good deal of pulling and hauling and false starts in which the office was created, abolished, and created again, it became fairly common and fairly well established in most states by the end of the century. Then, too, it became necessary to establish state departments of education to take over the added tasks of enforcing school laws, publishing reports, supervising schools, and establishing minimum requirements for taxation, qualifications of teachers, building codes, and courses of study.

In the middle decades of the century, it became clear that the states needed larger units of administration and organization than could be achieved under the local autonomy of the district system. So the county system of administration was often adopted in which a county superintendent of schools operated under the authority of a county school committee or board of education. Functioning as the chief executive officer of the county, which was a legal subdivision of the state, the county superintendent carried out the state laws in his county, gathered data for the state, supervised local school officials, distributed the state funds, and aided in the collection of school taxes.

A similar process took place in the cities as they grew in size and as the growth of great numbers of autonomous school districts, each with tax-levying functions, seemed inappropriate to the demands of modern city life. The states began to require the cities to establish boards of education to conduct the affairs of the city systems under the leadership of a city superintendent of schools. Beginning in the 1830's in such cities as Buffalo, Louisville, Providence, St. Louis, and Springfield, Mass., the movement spread until most cities of reasonable size had established unitary systems by the end of the century. Thus, in another respect, the old face-to-face handling of school problems by the people in their town or district school meetings or by elected school committeemen was no longer feasible under the conditions of city life where thousands were to be served by the public schools.

Consequently, the modern patterns of city school administration began to appear. At first the boards of education tried to keep in their own hands direct control over the various activities of the school system. The members of the board, elected by the people or appointed by the mayor, tried to handle directly the many details of administration through standing committees on instruction, curriculum, attendance, finance, buildings, and the like. As the school systems expanded in the later nineteenth century, it became increasingly evident that such procedures were extremely inadequate and inefficient.

The demand for efficiency and expertness led to a greater reliance upon the superintendent and his staff of administrative officers. It was natural to turn for a model to the contemporary industrial and business type of organization, which was being praised for its efficient management of large-scale industrial operations. Recognizing and fearing the inexpertness and even incompetence of many teachers, administrators felt it logical to keep a high degree of authority and supervision in their own hands rather than trusting too much to the relatively poorly trained teachers.

It was therefore generally agreed that the board of education should confine itself to matters of broad educational policy representing the public and the community and should leave to the superintendent and his staff the day-to-day execution and administration of the board's policies. The superintendent was usually elected by the people or was appointed by the board of education. He in turn chose his staff and the teachers with the approval of the board, drew up the budget for approval of the board, and supervised directly through his staff the operation of the system. With the improvement in the qualifications and training of teachers, however, it has more recently been asserted that teachers should begin to play a larger role in the professional policies and conduct of their school systems as a means of achieving greater democratic participation of all persons directly concerned with the educational enterprise.

Although the American people were willing to take great strides in the greater centralization of public education into county, city, and state units, they were not willing to extend the principle to the federal, or national, basis. It seemed clear that the federal government had the right to provide educational facilities for military purposes. Therefore, the military academy at West Point was established in 1802 for the training of army officers, and a similar institution for the training of naval officers was established at Annapolis in 1845. Likewise, the federal government assumed the responsibility of education for Indians on their reservations, under the Office of Indian Affairs in the Department of Interior, and for a while gave special assistance in the education of former Negro slaves, under the Freedmen's Bureau established in 1865.

In general, however, the functions of the federal government were limited to the extensive federal grants already mentioned. This meant that the states were willing, even eager, to receive financial support and aid from the federal government, but they were not willing to have the federal government extend its control over the state systems of education. Several bills were introduced into Congress in the 1870's and 1880's proposing direct federal support for general education, but they were never enacted into law.

The most extreme of these bills was introduced by Representative George F. Hoar, Republican from Massachusetts, in 1870. The Hoar bill was designed to compel states to establish efficient systems of education and, in effect, to establish a national system of education. Any state that proved to be delinquent in this respect would be subject to control by a federally appointed state superintendent of schools and by federal inspectors, and to a federal tax for support of its schools. Great opposition was marshalled among citizens and educators, and the bill did not even come to a vote. In the 1870's other bills were introduced to provide proceeds from the sale of public lands for education. The Perce bill passed in the House and the Burnside bill passed in the Senate, but neither passed in both houses.

In the 1880's Senator Henry W. Blair, Republican of New Hampshire, introduced a bill five different times providing for money grants to the states to aid them in creating effective systems of public schools. The bill passed in the Senate three times but no action was taken in the House. The Blair bills created a great deal of public discussion. In general, they were favored by organized labor, by important segments of organized business, by public school educators (especially the National Education Association), by some Protestant groups, and by most of the Republican party. Opposition was expressed principally by leaders of private schools and higher institutions, by parochial school educators (especially the Roman Catholic Church), by some Protestant groups, and by the majority of Democrats. This was the last great effort to achieve federal support for general education until the period following the Second World War.

It was recognized, however, that the federal government should share in the field of national education in some measure. Consequently, a federal Department of Education was established in 1867. Fearing that such a department might get out of hand, several states raised objections, and the separate department was transformed into an Office of Education within the Department of Interior. In 1870 it became the Bureau of Education. Despite its change in name, its function remained primarily that of collecting information and statistical data, conducting research, and disseminating information concerning the status and progress of American education. Henry Barnard was the first United States commissioner of education, followed during the nineteenth century by John Eaton, N. H. R. Dawson, and William T. Harris. During a century when France and Germany were building strong national systems of education, the United States was unwilling to take any steps that would seem to put very much control in the hands of the national government. Financial aid for special purposes, especially for vocational education, was considered appropriate, but not general federal support or control. The forces of decentralization were too strong for that.

No Public Funds for Religious Schools. America was able to build a strong public school system not only because the people came to believe in public education but also because public funds were not for long diverted to the support of private or religious schools. The nineteenth century was marked by bitter struggles, but by the end of the century the principle was widely established that public funds should not be granted to religious schools. This practice followed the principle of separation of church and state as expressed in the First Amendment of the United States Constitution and in the constitutional provisions and legal enactments of the several states. This was a critical factor in the establishment of a vital system of public education. If America had followed the patterns of England, or some of the provinces of Canada, or of other countries, it is likely that the distinctive values of a widespread system of common schools could not have been achieved.

Critical struggles over this issue ensued in several states prior to the Civil War; most noteworthy were those in New York and Massachusetts. In the early decades of the century the New York legislature granted public funds to the Free School Society of New York City and to three other religious and philanthropic societies to aid them in support of their charity schools. Thereafter, in the 1830's when the Roman Catholic population increased rapidly, the Catholic Church sought public funds for the support of its parochial schools. In the early 1840's Bishop John Hughes led the campaign to gain support from tax funds for Catholic schools, but these demands were refused by the New York city council. Despite the effort to carry on the fight in the state elections, the New York legislature settled the issue in an act of 1842, declaring

> No school above mentioned, or which shall be organized under this act, in which any religious sectarian doctrine or tenet shall be taught, inculcated, or practised, shall receive any portion of the school moneys to be distributed by this act. . . .

In Massachusetts a similar struggle was carried on before the Civil War, but the victory again went to the public school forces as defined in a constitutional amendment of 1855 which declared:

> All moneys raised by taxation in the towns and cities for the support of public schools, and all moneys which may be appropriated by the state for the support of common schools, shall be applied to, and expended in, no other schools than those which are conducted according to law, under the order and superintendence of the authorities of the town or city in which the money is to be expended; and such moneys shall never be appropriated to any religious sect for the maintenance, exclusively, of its own school.

Following the Civil War the same trend to prohibit the use of tax funds for sectarian schools was maintained. The dominant attitude of the states is typified in the new constitution of Illinois in 1870:

> Neither the general assembly nor any county, city, town, township, school district, or other public corporation shall ever make any appropriation or pay from any public fund whatever, anything in aid of any church or sectarian purpose, or to help support or sustain any school, academy, seminary, college, university or other literary or scientific institution, controlled by any church or sectarian denomination whatever; nor shall any grant or donation of land, money or other personal property ever be made by the State or any such public corporation to any church or for any sectarian purpose.

By 1900 the principle of separation of church and state had been nearly universally applied to this issue of public funds for religious schools. The battle to reserve public funds exclusively for public schools was more nearly won by the end of the nineteenth century than at any time before or since. The whole issue, however, was to be reopened again in the middle of the twentieth century on the national as well as on the state and local levels.

How the Battle in the States Was Won

The problem of breaking away from the inherited English tradition that schools should be controlled and supported by private or religious agencies was, at bottom, one to be solved by arousing public opinion to demand public schools. In 1800 most people believed that education was a matter of private initiative or church responsibility and that only the financially able were entitled to education. Then the humanitarian and philanthropic idea gained currency that poor children should have a better chance for a rudimentary education. Some people believed that free education for the poor should be expanded by the churches, by secular charitable agencies, or at public expense. The churches therefore began to provide charitable education for the poor, free school societies were formed to extend free education for those poor children not served by the church schools, and the states began to pass laws for free schools for poor children.

Various types of school societies engaged the efforts and received the contributions of many philanthropically minded persons. They sought individual contributions, formed associations, and established schools. Some of these societies had special interests in mind and were direct outgrowths of similar societies in England. In the 1820's, infant school societies were formed in Boston, Philadelphia, New York, and other cities to provide free instruction for poor children below the ages of seven or eight years. Sunday school societies were organized in similar cities to give the rudiments of secular instruction to poor children on Sundays, but the churches soon took over the Sunday school idea and made religious instruction the principal aim. Monitorial school societies on the model of the Lancasterian schools in England gained widespread popularity because of the relatively low cost of instruction for many pupils. These societies helped to show that education was a possibility for the ordinary people.

Meanwhile, a number of "free school societies" grew up in Baltimore, Washington, Philadelphia, Providence, Albany, N.Y., and elsewhere to consolidate the efforts within the cities to provide free schools for poor children. The most famous was the Free School Society of New York City organized in 1805 by Mayor DeWitt Clinton and other prominent citizens. The society solicited funds, built schoolhouses, trained and paid teachers, and in 50 years had given instruction to more than a half a million children. Thereupon, it turned over its assets to the New York City public schools, which had begun to appear in the 1840's.

As democratically minded persons began to observe the activities of these free school societies in the first two decades of the nineteenth century, it began to occur to some that the distinction between private education for the well to do and charity education for the poor produced an unfortunate and invidious distinction inappropriate for a democratic society. Therefore, from the 1820's on, many groups began to agitate and work for free public schools open equally to all. The enlightened middle classes and the labor groups provided the backbone of this movement, which gained headway against stiff opposition in the 1830's and 1840's.

Organizations were formed to this end, notably the American Institute of Instruction in Boston, the Pennsylvania Society for the Promotion of Public Schools, and the Western Academic Institute in Cincinnati. Such agencies for general diffusion of popular knowledge as the American Lyceum and the many mechanics' and workingmen's institutes took up the cause. In the early decades of the century, labor organizations and labor conventions in New York, Philadelphia, and elsewhere added their voices to the clamor for public schools free from the stigma of pauperism and supported by public funds. The American Federation of Labor from its organization in 1881 onward has had a consistently effective record of energetic advocacy of public education.

Leaders in the public education movement came from the middle social classes, who had already had the advantages of educational opportunities, but they could not have achieved their aims without the political support of the working and laboring classes, who made their strength tell at the polls. Many labor organizations in city and state elections favored those candidates who stood for public education. The important role of labor in this struggle has often been overlooked by writers on the subject, who have consciously or unconsciously played down the efforts of the unnamed and unknown supporters in the ranks of labor. The contribution of middle-class leaders was great indeed, but there is enough credit and to spare for all.

New England. As might be expected from its long interest in public education, extending back to the laws of 1642 and 1647, Massachusetts soon became the scene of active agitation for state control and support of public schools. James G. Carter and Horace Mann took the leadership in this movement. They persuaded the legislature to establish a state board of education in 1837 and a school fund to aid local units in the support of schools. Carter argued long and hard for the establishment of public high schools and normal schools.

Through his position as secretary of the state board of education from 1837 to 1848, Horace Mann was able to put into effect a program of state support for public high schools, state normal schools, and increased support for common schools. He strengthened the ideal of state organization and supervision of schools as against the decentralized district system, raised teachers' salaries and improved their training and qualifications, lengthened the school year, and improved the standards of school buildings. Above all, he acted as a publicist and awakener of public interest in state schools through his extensive lecturing and writing, his 12 annual reports, and his editing of the *Common School Journal*. His influence extended far beyond the confines of Massachusetts as a result of his travels and conferences and the public attention that his activities received.

Somewhat the same process took place in Connecticut and Rhode Island. Thomas H. Gallaudet and Henry Barnard were active in Con-

Fig. 27. Horace Mann.

necticut in establishing a state board of education, for which Barnard acted as secretary from 1838 until it was abolished in 1842. Barnard went to Rhode Island for 4 years to organize the work of its new state board of education and then returned to Connecticut. For many years thereafter, as editor of the *American Journal of Education* from 1855 to 1882 and as the first United States commissioner of education from 1867 to 1870, he was a great influence in raising the standards of professional education.

Middle States. Stimulated by the democratic forces of the early decades of the century, New York State passed a school law of 1812 that undertook to establish a state system of common schools under a state superintendent of schools, the first in the United States. This represented a dual system, for the University of the State of New York under the Board of Regents had been established in 1784 to take responsibility for secondary and higher education. The law of 1812 provided for school commissioners to be elected in each town and school trustees to be elected in each district. Teachers' salaries were to be paid by town taxes, which were to be matched by aid from the state school fund, such moneys to be allocated to local districts upon the basis of the number of children aged five to fifteen years. Local districts were to raise money by taxes to build schools and operate them. In addition, rate bills were to be levied upon parents according to the number of children they had in school.

This system was abolished in 1821 through the efforts of conservative forces, but the struggle continued. For example, a convention of workingmen in New York City in 1829 agitated for greater state support of schools "to insure the opportunity to every individual of obtaining a competent education before he shall have arrived at the age of maturity." The state system was restored in effect in 1851, and by 1867 the rate bills were abolished. From then on, the common school system rested entirely upon taxation and state aid.

In Pennsylvania a school law of 1802 established a system by which those children whose parents declared themselves to be paupers were allowed to attend private schools free of charge, the expenses to be paid by the county. Various public school societies protested against this pauper-school act, and again the laboring groups began to bring their weight to bear. The Workingmen's Association of Philadelphia passed resolutions in 1829 and 1830 similar to that of New York City and publicized the attitudes toward public schools expressed by candidates for the legislature. In 1834 the legislature passed a school law establishing public school districts throughout the state, but so many counties, especially in German Lutheran strongholds, opposed the idea of public schools taught in English that the whole system was in danger of collapse. Finally, under the leadership of Thaddeus Stevens, the opposition was broken down, and the law was saved. By 1838 a great majority of counties had accepted the law, and a state school system was under way. In New Jersey a similar pauper-school law was rejected, and after 1838 a genuine public school system was made possible.

The South. The movement for public education took hold more slowly in the southern states than elsewhere in the country. Before the Civil War, several states in the South initiated arrangements that had the outward form of state school systems, but the strong aristocratic traditions of private and religious schools stood in the way. "Free" education in the South continued to mean charity or pauper education much longer than elsewhere. The rigid caste distinction between white and Negro and the class distinction between the planter, or owning, group and the tenants and poor whites remained firm by reason of the desire of the upper classes to retain political, economic, and social power. Some of the southern states established common school funds early in the century, and many established state superintendents of schools with subordinate county systems.

Before the Civil War, attention to education for Negroes was pitifully lacking. Some states even had laws prohibiting the education of Negroes in school subjects. Most of what could pass for education involved the teaching of skills to Negroes to enable them to do agricultural and semiskilled work on plantations. During the early reconstruction period, under President Lincoln's plans, some of the southern states enacted laws providing for the education of Negroes, and this process went much further during the Congressional reconstruction period from 1868 to 1876.

Such efforts, of course, evoked enormous resistance from the majority of the white classes, for to them the idea of giving education to Negroes was the height of absurdity and folly. Their conception of the Negroes as an inherently inferior race incapable of intelligence or education made them fearful of the consequences. And, of course, the taxes that would be necessary for genuine public education for all touched them where it hurt most. They looked with suspicion upon the efforts made by Northerners to stimulate education for Negroes in the South.

Nevertheless, many northern religious and philanthropic societies sent men and money into southern schools and colleges. The United States government established the Freedmen's Bureau in 1865 to give an over-all supervision to these efforts. Several Negro colleges were established, notably Fisk University in 1865, Hampton Institute in 1868, Atlanta University in 1867, and Tuskegee Institute in 1881. The George Peabody Fund and the Slater Fund poured money and workers into the South to help pay teachers' salaries, improve teacher training, and build schools.

Despite these efforts, progress was slow in providing public education for both Negroes and whites. After 1876, when the upper-class whites came back into power in the South, many of the laws for public education were either revoked or disregarded. The easiest way was simply not to vote adequate funds for Negro schools. It is true that the economic resources of the South were extremely limited in comparison with those of other parts of the country, but it is also true that the dominant classes made matters even worse by insisting upon a dual system for whites and Negroes, which was much more expensive. Without money to go around, the Negro schools obviously suffered most. Despite the efforts of some forward-looking Southerners and humanitarian Northerners, the Negro schools continued to be a disgrace in a democratic nation. White teachers received little enough; Negro teachers received a mere pittance.

What gains were made came under the leadership of such men as Henry Ruffner, Charles F. Mercer, and General S. C. Armstrong in Virginia, Calvin H. Wiley and S. S. Ashley in North Carolina, J. K. Jillson in South Carolina, John Eaton in Tennessee, Robert J. Breckenridge in Kentucky, A. G. Brown and Henry R. Pease in Mississippi, and William F. Perry in Alabama. Even so, a measure of their effectiveness was the fact that by 1900 compulsory-attendance laws were not to be found in any southern state. Less than half the children in the South actually attended school, and only 1 out of every 70 who started the first grade ever reached the eighth grade. Other parts of the country were not perfect by any means, but nowhere else did the ideal of equality of educational opportunity fall so short in practice.

The West. In general, the western states developed their systems of public education rapidly and in some respects even outstripped the East. There was no entrenched tradition of private education, and many of the constitutions of the western states carried strong statements or provisions for public schools when the states were first admitted. In the old Northwest Territory of Ohio, Indiana, Michigan, Illinois, and Wisconsin the Ordinances of 1785 and 1787 laid down the principle of public common schools as a framework for later developments. The settlers from New England and the East carried with them the tradition of public schools, and they relatively soon were able to adopt strong state organizations of education against the opposition of Southerners who had settled in the southern regions of Ohio, Indiana, and Illinois.

Thus by the 1850's and 1860's these states of the Middle West had made great strides in wiping out the system of rate bills, levying taxes for common schools, and organizing state departments of education. These developments were accomplished through the efforts of such men as Samuel Lewis, Calvin E. Stowe, and Samuel Galloway in Ohio, Caleb Mills in Indiana, Ninian Edwards in Illinois, and John D. Pierce and Isaac Crary in Michigan.

A similar process took place in the new states of the plains, mountains, and Pacific areas of the trans-Mississippi West. Superintendents were appointed or elected, school funds established, taxes levied, and compulsory-attendance laws passed. Private and religious schools were, of course, predominant in the early days, but these traditions were more easily changed in the freer and more flexible atmosphere of the frontier West. The ideal of equality of opportunity that was so much a part of the development of the West found rapid realization in the public school ideal of free education for all at public expense.

An American System of Schools Takes Shape

Despite variations among states, the nineteenth century was the formative period in which an American conception of education began to appear in fairly clear outline. Whereas most European countries maintained a dual system of schools frankly designed to separate the upper classes from the lower classes, the United States launched a democratic system designed to provide equality of opportunity for everyone to go as far upward as his talents and abilities would take him. Furthermore, this opportunity should be available at public expense under state auspices and should begin at the lowest levels and extend through the university.

The so-called "ladder system" meant that secondary education would be a continuation of elementary education and higher education would follow secondary education. The conception of a universal, free, coeducational, and compulsory school system contrasted sharply with the European two-track system of separate schools for upper and lower classes, free education for lower classes in elementary schools, tuition schools for the upper classes in secondary schools, and often separate schools for boys and girls.

Likewise, the American ideal of secular schools free from sectarian control contrasted sharply with the common European practice according to which state churches or authorized religions kept a large measure of influence in the state schools. The principle of secular public schools was not established without a bitter struggle. Many of the states in the early decades of the century authorized public funds to be allocated to religious schools, but some men, notably Horace Mann in Massachusetts, saw great danger in this practice and lashed the use of tax moneys to subsidize sectarian religious teaching. Against the charge that public schools were becoming "godless schools," Mann and others declared that sectarian instruction would wreck the public schools. Mann even had to fight attempts by the religious groups to abolish the state board of education.

In other states, some religious groups tried to block the spread of public schools or to divide public funds among public and parochial schools. In the 1830's, 1840's, and 1850's this was a vital issue all over the country. The public school idea became involved in the anti-Roman Catholic issues brought to a head by the Native-American party in the 1840's and the Know-Nothing party in the 1850's. Although the victory of secular public schools had apparently been won in principle by 1900, the problem has continued to plague American education down to the present time.

Linked to the problem of secular education was the growing idea that the development of a truly democratic nation required compulsory attendance. The great influx of immigrants from nearly every country of Europe in the nineteenth century made the problem of assimilation more acute than ever as the various groups with their different languages, customs, and traditions tended to congregate in isolated groups in the large cities. Hence, the public schools were called upon to provide a means to accelerate the process of assimilation.

When voluntary measures did not seem to work rapidly enough, compulsory-attendance legislation began to appear in the state legislatures. The first such law was passed in Massachusetts in 1852, and most other states had taken up the idea by 1900, except in the South. The states, of course, varied in the age limits they set for compulsory attendance, the length of school term during which they required attendance, and the strictness with which they enforced the laws. It had become clear to many, however, that with the great variety of religious backgrounds present in the United States the public schools could not hold to a specific kind of religious instruction. Therefore, the compulsory-attendance idea ran head on into the problem of sectarian and private schools.

The United States ensured freedom for private and religious schools for those who preferred them but proceeded to provide public secular schools at public expense. This was done on the theory that church and state should remain separate in educational as well as in political functions and that a democratic society requires a universal system of public education. By the middle of the century more students were enrolled in public elementary and secondary schools than in private and religious schools. Once the principle had been established, the public schools expanded enormously and rapidly.

Elementary Schools. With the great influx of children into the common schools, it soon became clear that the little one-room district school with its individual teaching methods for a wide range of ages could no longer be satisfactory. The two principal changes in elementary school organization were, therefore, the development of the class method of teaching and the graded system of grouping children by age levels. The unitary district school was gradually divided into primary schools, for younger children from ages five or six to nine or ten, and intermediate, or grammar, schools, for children of ages ten to fourteen.

This process, which varied considerably in different cities and states, soon produced a primary school for grades 1 through 4 and a grammar school for grades 5 through 8. In general, the graded schools in which one grade was aimed at one age level became fairly widespread by the end of the Civil War. In the next 20 or 25 years the primary and grammar grades were gradually brought together again to produce a single elementary school for grades 1 through 8. By 1900 the 8-year graded school was the most common type of American elementary school.

The development of the graded and class system was doubtless influenced not only by the increased number of children but also by the expansion in the subjects of the elementary school curriculum. It was also influenced by the example of the European systems, especially German, as reported by such Americans as Horace Mann, Henry Barnard, Calvin E. Stowe, John Griscom, and others. A teacher now could specialize somewhat by teaching only one grade and age level by the class method, rather than the whole range of children individually. The graded system, first receiving attention in Boston in the middle of the century through Superintendent John D. Philbrick, soon spread rapidly throughout the country.

Secondary Schools. At the beginning of the nineteenth century the most common secondary schools were the academies supported by private or religious sponsors. There were also a considerable number of Latin grammar schools, principally supported by the towns in New England. The entering age for these schools was usually around ten to twelve years, and the courses were 4 to 6 years in length. As the academies began to emphasize subjects requiring a command of English, they also began to institute preparatory departments to give the younger children a grounding in the fundamentals before they entered the academy proper. If this process had continued uninterruptedly, the United States might have produced a dual system of schools similar to that of the European countries.

However, in the 1820's and thereafter, the democratic forces in the United States began to demand a type of secondary school that would give at public expense a more useful education for children who had completed the primary and grammar grades of the elementary schools. The public high school was designed to meet this demand and to overcome the growing undemocratic and "class" character of the academies. The laboring groups had no opportunity for higher education of a more practical and non-college-preparatory sort so long as the Latin grammar schools and the academies remained as the only secondary school institutions.

Therefore, in Boston in 1821 an English classical school was established (later it became the English high school) designed for boys of twelve years of age or older who were not planning to go to college. It was originally a 3-year high school emphasizing English, mathematics, and social studies of a more practical nature. In 1827 Massachusetts passed a law requiring such high schools to be established in every town of 500 or more families.

By 1860 there were over 300 such high schools in the country, most of them located in Massachusetts, New York, and Ohio. In the last years of the century the expansion was enormous. By 1900 there were some 6,000 public high schools enrolling more than 80 per cent of all secondary school students. The public high school, in the process of outstripping the academies, became normally a 4-year institution, coeducational, and designed to prepare for college as well as directly for life.

The expansion in the establishment of public high schools before 1870 was slowed by the opposition of taxpayers' groups and by religious organizations that had large investments in private academies, which they saw jeopardized by public high schools. As has been the case in other great depressions, the industrialists, following the panic of 1873, attacked the idea of public education because of the expense involved. They demanded retrenchment in educational budgets and especially opposed the extension of public high schools, which, they said, made the workers dissatisfied with the prevailing wage scale.

Moreover, school boards were uncertain as to whether they had the legal right to levy taxes for the support of high schools. In the 1870's, however, a series of judicial decisions in Michigan, Illinois, and elsewhere laid a sound legal basis for the development of public high schools.

The most famous of these decisions was the Kalamazoo case, decided in the supreme court of Michigan in 1874. The complainants had sought to restrain School District No. 1 of Kalamazoo from levying taxes to support a high school and to determine the right in general of school authorities to support free high schools and to offer foreign-language instruction. The complainants admitted the right of the state to establish common schools but argued that secondary education was generally agreed to mean instruction in the classics and modern languages and was therefore intended to be an accomplishment of the few to be paid for by them. Secondary education did not include practical education for all to be supported at public expense.

The court decided against the complainants, however, stating that the legislation and policy of the state had always been intended to furnish not only the rudiments of education to everyone but advanced education as well, to poor and rich alike, as a practical advantage and not as a matter of culture for a few wealthy persons. Justice Cooley cited as precedents the Massachusetts laws of 1642, 1647, and 1787, the Ordinance of 1787, the territorial legislation of Michigan in 1817, Michigan school laws of 1821, 1827, and 1833, and the Michigan constitutions of 1835 and 1850.

Inasmuch as the intent in these legal precedents was to establish a complete system of education, the court found it unthinkable that the state could legally provide elementary and university instruction but that parents would be obliged to send their children abroad or pay tuition in private schools in order to obtain preparation for the state university. The clear legal right of the school board to levy taxes for public high schools was affirmed.

With the legal basis clear, local school boards felt free to establish high schools as the demand arose. State legislatures were also encouraged to pass legislation permitting local boards to proceed, to offer state aid to those districts which did establish high schools, and finally to compel high schools to be established in certain districts throughout the state. By the end of the century the high school had taken its place as the normal continuation of the elementary school.

Higher Education. The nineteenth century witnessed the beginning of democratic experiment in higher education, no less than in elementary and secondary education. No other country tried to establish so many institutions of higher education. Almost every religious denomination was active in founding colleges as a means of spreading their religious doctrines as well as of providing a general education for the youth of the land. The most active denominations were the Presbyterians, Methodists, Baptists, Congregationalists, Roman Catholics, and Episcopalians. They worked individually, and they worked jointly in such organizations as the Society for the Promotion of Collegiate and Theological Education at the West. According to Donald G. Tewksbury, 182 permanent colleges were established before the Civil War, along with dozens more that died after a shorter or longer time.

Despite the prevalence of the theory that higher education should be under religious control, the movement for state universities that had begun in the late eighteenth century gained increasing momentum in the nineteenth century. Borrowing from French Enlightenment ideas, many humanitarians believed with Thomas Jefferson that the doctrine of democracy required public higher education as well as public lower education.

The most decisive legal move was precipitated when democratic forces tried to gain control of Dartmouth College. When John Wheelock became president in 1799, he tried to cast off the more conservative political and religious doctrines of his father as predecessor. His Jeffersonian Republican ideas brought him into conflict with the Federalist board of trustees. The board of trustees ousted Wheelock in 1815, whereupon the Republican state legislature passed a law in 1816 converting Dartmouth into a state university, adding 11 new members to the board of trustees, and appointing Wheelock as president of the new Dartmouth University. The old college refused to accede to this innovation, and the two institutions tried to exist alongside each other for a year or two. The old board of trustees brought suit in the New Hampshire supreme court to recover control of the college, but their plea was denied. They therefore retained Daniel Webster to appeal the case to the United States Supreme Court in 1818.

In the famous Dartmouth College case of 1819, Chief Justice John Marshall wrote the decision reversing the New Hampshire supreme court

Fig. 28. Free Academy, New York City (Now College of the City of New York).

465

and declaring the legislature's Act of 1816 to be unconstitutional. The Republicans had argued that, whereas the state had contributed to the support of Dartmouth, its self-perpetuating board of trustees gave it an undemocratic organization and control, not in accord with the spirit of free government and free education. The Federalists argued, however, that Dartmouth College was a corporation whose charter from the king of England had the force of a contract which the state could not impair. The decision had far-reaching economic and political ramifications, but it meant specifically for colleges that the philanthropic endowments of private colleges would be safe from encroachment by the states. This encouraged private donors to give money to the private colleges and stimulated the states to establish their own universities under state control.

The state-university movement was the principal response to democratic demands for public higher education. Twenty state universities were founded before the Civil War, but they met vigorous opposition from the private and religious colleges in many ways. The religious groups often tried to prevent the passage of enabling laws in the legislatures and they tried to transfer state moneys and land grants to religious institutions. Even after the establishment of many state universities, the religious groups often continued their efforts to insert religious interests in the new universities or reduce their funds to insignificance. The score in the contest between state and church for control of higher education was more than even. For the few cases in which states tried to take over private institutions, there were many cases where the religious groups tried to control the state universities.

Up to the Civil War the state universities were far behind the private colleges in their influence upon American higher education. However, with the passage of the Morrill act by Congress in 1862, the great impetus to the state-university movement began. The Morrill act granted to each state 30,000 acres of public land for each of its members in Congress. The money was to be used for the establishment of agricultural and mechanical colleges that would teach the liberal arts as well as the sciences appropriate to agriculture, engineering, mining, and forestry. Some of the states set up separate "A and M" colleges; others gave the money to their state universities. With this impulse the state universities became a great force in American higher education by the end of the century.

Higher education, in general, made huge strides as great private fortunes were poured into such established institutions as Harvard, Yale, Columbia, and Princeton and into the founding of such new institutions as Johns Hopkins, Chicago, Leland Stanford, and Cornell. Professional education in medicine, law, and theology was stimulated, and technical institutions like Rensselaer, Massachusetts Institute of Technology, Purdue, and others responded to the growing technological demands of American society. In the last quarter of the century the number of students in undergraduate colleges more than doubled, reaching more than 100,000 in 1900, while the enrollment in all kinds of postsecondary institutions reached nearly 250,000.

Beginnings of a Teaching Profession

Preservice Training of Teachers. With the tremendous expansion in publicly supported education throughout the nineteenth century, increased provision for the preparation of teachers was clearly necessary. In the early years of the century most of the training of teachers was done in the liberal arts colleges and the academies. There was little in the way of specific attention to the task of teaching; rather, it was felt that knowledge of the subject-matter field was enough. For elementary school teaching, the qualifications beyond religious orthodoxy and good moral character were vague and informal.

As early as the 1820's, however, a definite movement to provide specific preparation for teaching gained headway as normal schools began to be established. Taking their characteristics somewhat from European examples, normal schools were designed to prepare teachers for work in the elementary schools. The word "normal" came from the French word meaning a model or a rule, connoting that the object of the institution was to give teachers rules for teaching.

The first normal schools in America were private schools such as those promoted by Samuel R. Hall at Concord, Vt., in 1823 and by James G. Carter at Lancaster, Mass., in 1827. The first state normal school was established in 1839 at Lexington, Mass., at the instigation of Horace Mann and Charles Brooks and with Cyrus Peirce as principal. By 1860 there were 11 state normal schools in eight states, and by 1898 there were 167 public normal schools in the United States, or slightly less than the number of private normal schools (including those conducted by religious denominations). In the latter nineteenth century, county normal schools and municipal normal schools, such as those in Boston, Philadelphia, Baltimore, Trenton, St. Louis, and San Francisco, made their appearance.

Most normal schools admitted students directly from the elementary schools, and even as late as 1900 the most common requirement for admission was only 2 years of high school work. The courses of study varied in length, 2 years being the most common. In general, most of the curriculum was devoted to study and mastery of the elementary school subjects, with additional work in philosophy, psychology, history of education, and observation and practice teaching. Although there was great variety in the courses taught, nearly all normal schools eventually included some sort of observation and practice teaching performed either

in a "model" school conducted by the normal school or in the public
. schools.

The influence of Prussian and French state systems of education and
teacher training helped to spur the American states to develop their
normal schools. The report of Victor Cousin on the Prussian system was
given wide currency in America, along with the reports of such Americans as Horace Mann, Henry Barnard, Calvin Stowe, Charles Brooks, John
Griscom, William C. Woodbridge, and Edward Sheldon. In Oswego,
N.Y., Edward Sheldon became enthusiastic about the educational methods
of Pestalozzi and brought some Pestalozzian-trained teachers to Oswego
in the 1860's to help his staff improve their teaching. When Oswego became a state normal school, these ideas were taken up by other normal
schools, and the influence began to spread rapidly in the United States.
Other influential normal schools were the Illinois State Normal University at Normal, Ill., and the New York State Normal College at
Albany.

Some liberal arts colleges began to give lectures on the "art of teaching" and pedagogy, notably New York University in 1832, Brown in
1850, and Michigan in 1860. In the 1870's and 1880's regular professorships and departments of education began to be established at such institutions as Iowa, Michigan, Wisconsin, North Carolina, and Johns Hopkins.

Toward the end of the century, teaching as a profession began to be
recognized sufficiently to warrant the establishment of graduate instruction in education. New York University established graduate courses in
1888. Similarly, the New York College for the Training of Teachers was
launched in 1888 under the presidency of Nicholas Murray Butler; its
name was changed to Teachers College in 1892. When Teachers College
first petitioned the Columbia University council to become affiliated with
the university, it met with the reply " . . . there is no such subject as
education and, moreover, it would bring into the university women who
are not wanted." In 1898, however, Teachers College became affiliated
with Columbia University and developed graduate work of a high level
under the leadership of James E. Russell, dean from 1897 to 1927.

Despite the jaundiced eye with which "education" was viewed by the
established academic institutions and subject-matter fields, graduate study
in education made its way rapidly in colleges and universities and began
making great contributions to the improvement of elementary and secondary school teaching.

Upgrading of Experienced Teachers. In addition to the notable extension of preservice training for teachers in educational institutions, many
steps were taken to improve the quality of teaching through in-service
training for experienced teachers. Much of the development of supervisory functions undertaken by state, city, and county superintendents,

principals, and supervisors was designed to improve the quality of instruction among teachers already on the job.

Teachers' institutes of a day or two to 5 or 6 weeks' duration were started by Henry Barnard in Connecticut in 1839, and the idea spread rapidly to most states. Study during the summer months was originated in 1873 under Louis Agassiz of Harvard in his summer courses at Nantucket for teachers of natural history. Eventually, summer schools became one of the most popular agencies for in-service education of teachers.

Fig. 29. Kindergarten Training School, New York State Normal College, 1878.

Several universities began to give extension courses on and off the campus, home-study courses, and library lectures.

Periodicals for teachers appeared as far back as the *Academician* (1818). William Russell's *American Journal of Education* (1826 to 1831) and, above all, Henry Barnard's *American Journal of Education* (1855 to 1881) were of great interest. Textbooks for teachers began with Samuel R. Hall's *Lectures on Schoolkeeping* (1829), but their influence was rather slight until the professors of education at the end of the century began to publish books on a wide variety of topics.

Teachers' Associations. Another important means of improving the status and quality of the teaching profession was the relatively large number of teachers' organizations that sprang up in the nineteenth century.

Among the more important were the American Institute of Instruction (1830), consisting mostly of New England scholars and college educators, and the National Teachers Association (1857) which became the National Education Association in 1870. Despite the fact that the National Education Association had only 2,300 members by 1900, it was the most influential of the national organizations. Much wider in their contact with classroom teachers were the numerous city, county, and state teachers' associations that spread throughout the country.

By publishing magazines, holding meetings and institutes, passing resolutions on all kinds of school policies, and petitioning legislatures and city councils, such teachers' organizations were able to improve the economic status of teachers by obtaining better salaries, better working conditions, and better schools. Although they were not socially radical in any sense, they soon came to realize the importance of group action for school reform.

Meanwhile, salaries began slowly to improve, so that by the end of the century schoolteachers ranked in income somewhat above the level of common laborers and somewhat below that of skilled laborers. A wide differential existed between salaries for men teachers and women teachers and between those for city teachers and rural teachers. Despite the improvement in teachers' salaries, they were still far below that of professional workers in other fields. The influx of women into the profession and the low estimation of the teacher's role held by the public in general helped to prevent further increase.

Qualifications for teachers continued to improve, as longer periods of college study were required and as states began to centralize the issuing of licenses and certificates for teaching, thus prompting local communities to raise their standards. Gradually, too, the voluntary and mutual societies for death benefits, illness, and old-age pensions began to give way to public and state retirement and pension systems.

Teachers were drawn largely from the lower middle classes of American life. Their personal lives were subjected to heavy social pressures by the community in which they worked. Then as now many women looked upon teaching as an interim employment while waiting for marriage. These facts, coupled with low salaries, meant that few teachers stayed very long in the profession. Great gains were made in the nineteenth century, but a long distance remained to be traveled before teaching could become a genuine profession worthy of its role in society.

Out-of-school Agencies of Education

Organized education of youth and adults outside of the regularly constituted school and university systems took tremendous strides in the nineteenth-century United States. The spread of knowledge was promoted by philanthropic and humanitarian agencies as well as by some commercial ventures. These organized movements spread through all social classes in the population, including the laboring classes of the cities as well as the white-collar and professional classes.

Mechanics' institutes, workingmen's and merchants' libraries, and lectures for industrial and commercial workers became very popular as ordinary people were imbued with the idea that knowledge gave power. The Boston Apprentices' Library was formed in 1820 and the Boston Mechanics' Institute in 1826. By 1829 the New York Apprentices' Library had 10,000 volumes and by the middle of the century was serving three-quarters of a million people, principally working-class people. "Mercantile libraries" for young workers in business offices also became very popular after the 1820's.

Many of these organizations sponsored lectures, discussions, debates, and public events of various kinds. Employers and philanthropically minded members of the wealthier classes also promoted adult education in such forms as the Lowell Institute in Boston (1836), Cooper Union in New York City (1859), and Peabody Institute in Baltimore.

On a larger scale and serving the rural regions as well as the urban communities, the lyceum movement became an important agency for adult education in the first half of the nineteenth century. First organized by Josiah Holbrook in Millbury, Mass., in 1826, the lyceum sponsored lectures, forums, public discussion, and reading material on all kinds of scientific and social subjects, including support for the public school movement. Beginning as local discussion groups, the lyceums began to command the services of some of the best speakers and orators of the day, who often went about the circuit giving popular lectures. By 1834 some 3,000 communities boasted lyceums.

In the latter part of the century the religiously motivated Chautauqua movement served large adult audiences throughout the country. Originated by Lewis Miller and Bishop John H. Vincent of the Methodist Episcopal Church, the Chautauqua Assembly was organized in 1874 at Chautauqua Lake, N.Y., as a summer training course for religious workers. Local Chautauquas eventually appeared in hundreds of communities. In 1878 the Chautauqua Literary and Scientific Circle provided a 4-year reading course in literary, social, scientific, and religious studies. Stemming from the religious motivation for youth and adult education were the Young Men's Christian Association, the Young Men's Hebrew Association, and the Young Women's Christian Association. Reaching the younger age levels, the Boy Scouts of America soon became a nationally effective agency for out-of-school education.

The public thirst for knowledge expressed itself in many other ways. Paralleling in many respects the public school movement was the growth of public libraries. Free public libraries appeared early in the century in Boston and other New England towns. New Hampshire passed the first state law allowing public funds to be used for the establishment of public libraries on a state-wide basis. With the stimulus given by Enoch Pratt and Andrew Carnegie later in the century and the founding of the American Library Association in 1876, the public-library movement gained great momentum.

The improvement in printing methods and the public demand for reading matter made possible all kinds of easily available published materials. Penny newspapers and cheaply priced books and magazines were put out in increasingly large numbers. The urge for self-improvement among women was revealed in the establishment of hundreds of women's clubs and literary circles, eventually resulting in the organization of the General Federation of Women's Clubs in 1889.

The eagerness for improvement reached all social levels of the population: upper- and middle-class women's clubs as well as the settlement houses for the underprivileged classes; scholarly and professional societies as well as mechanics' institutes; the lyceum and Chautauqua as well as the Metropolitan Museum of Art (1870) and the American Museum of Natural History (1869); the county fairs as well as the New York stage. In these and many other ways the education of the American people, outside of regular educational institutions, gained momentum along with the education of their children and youth in schools and colleges.

Chapter 15

NINETEENTH-CENTURY AMERICA:
INTELLECTUAL FOUNDATIONS OF EDUCATION

COMPETING CLAIMS UPON THE AMERICAN MIND

American intellectual life in the nineteenth century continued to borrow heavily from European sources, but it also began to assert itself not only by adapting European importations to American conditions but also by making distinctive contributions that often in turn influenced Europe. In the first half of the century the influence of French humanitarianism remained strong, its ideals of liberty, equality, and social progress continuing to feed American conceptions of democracy. From England came scientific and technological invention, economic individualism, and romantic literature that appealed especially to American middle classes. From Germany came idealistic and transcendental philosophy along with romanticism. Gradually, interest in other countries increased as immigrants from other parts of Europe flooded into America.

Meanwhile, American nationalism began to assert itself. The decades before the Civil War saw the growth of a feeling that American intellectual life should break the bond with Europe and create modes of expression and methods of thinking more appropriate to the freer conditions of the new American nation. After the Civil War the ideal of nationality was greatly enhanced, but the influence of European thought continued to be strong, especially as found in the scholarly and scientific ideals of the German universities. As the century drew to a close, American philosophy, literature, and art made distinctive contributions that could only be described as American. The contributions of nearly all the nations of Europe were represented in the work and ideas of immigrants who became Americans.

Religion and Philosophy

Traditional Religious Outlooks. Throughout the nineteenth century the traditional beliefs in supernatural religion continued to be influential among the masses of people as well as among religious leaders. Christian theism remained the most common conception of the world and of the relation of man to nature. The world of spirit was sharply defined in contrast to the world of matter. God created the world, as described in the

473

Bible. Man consists of a soul and a body, the two elements in him being in constant opposition. Human nature is set off by an impassable gulf from the rest of nature by virtue of the spiritual qualities given to man by God.

The Calvinistic tradition was reasserted in the manner of Jonathan Edwards by such men as Nathaniel Walker, who aided in the foundation of Yale's Divinity School in the early part of the century. Andover Theological Seminary was founded by Calvinists in 1808 to combat the liberal religious trends of Unitarianism, which had appeared at Harvard. In the latter part of the century, fundamentalism was reasserted by such conservative theologians as Laurens Perseus Hickok, president of Union College, Charles Hodge of Princeton, and William G. T. Shedd of Union Theological Seminary. Outside of the orthodox churches, the popularity of supernaturalism in various forms was reflected in such movements as spiritualism, theosophy, and Christian Science.

Liberal Religious Outlooks. Meanwhile, several efforts to liberalize traditional supernaturalism were being made. One of the most important of these was Unitarianism, which denied the conception of an angry God and of original sin. Unitarians rejected the doctrine of the Trinity and emphasized the beneficence and loving-kindness of God, the human qualities of Jesus, and the inherent goodness and perfectibility of man's nature. As expressed by William Ellery Channing, religion became a matter not so much of dogma and theology as of cultivating the ethical spirit of God in the heart of man. Largely humanistic in tone, it urged the individual to seek truth according to the Scriptures and to express his religious convictions in improving society. Unitarianism fed the social reform movements of New England in the early nineteenth century and represented a return to the essentially liberal emphasis that early Protestantism had placed upon freedom of conscience.

Later in the century when science and evolution began to challenge the authority of traditional supernatural religions, several notable efforts were made to reconcile religion with evolution. Some American scholars followed the lead of the European higher criticism in Biblical scholarship and the study of comparative religions. Outstanding were Philip Schaff of Union Theological Seminary, Orello Cone of St. Lawrence University, and James Freeman Clarke. The modernist effort to liberalize the traditional religious outlooks by incorporating the findings of evolutionary science was led by Henry Ward Beecher, Phillips Brooks, Washington Gladden, Lyman Abbott, and, above all, John Fiske. Despite the efforts of fundamentalists to stem the tide of modernism by heresy trials and bitter attacks, the hold of uncompromising supernaturalism was not as strong at the end of the century as it was at the beginning.

Idealism and Transcendentalism. Stemming from Unitarianism but adding to it an adaptation of German idealism, an American transcendental philosophy found considerable expression in the early nineteenth-century writings of such men as Ralph Waldo Emerson, Theodore Parker, and Henry David Thoreau. They were deeply affected by the mystical idealism of Kant, Fichte, and Schleiermacher, but they rejected much of the absolutistic and nationalistic qualities of German idealism in favor of an exaltation of individualism that seemed more appropriate to the American temper. Stressing the goodness of God, the transcendentalists emphasized above all the inalienable worth of the individual, who represents in his nature the divine presence of God. Man should be trusted implicitly because the spirit of God exists in the individual soul. This conception of divine immanence in man led the transcendentalists to rely upon human will and conscience as the guide to morality and to attack as evil all political or economic institutions that restrict the activities of man in his efforts to achieve a better society.

In the latter part of the century Hegelian idealism attracted such American philosophers as George Herbert Palmer, Josiah Royce, George Sylvester Morris, George H. Harrison, and C. C. Everett. Idealism became the most influential outlook of American professional philosophers in the last decades of the century, much stimulated by the *Journal of Speculative Philosophy* founded by William T. Harris, superintendent of schools in St. Louis. His influence touched in quite different ways the points of view of Nicholas Murray Butler and John Dewey. Impressed by the idealists' emphasis upon the organic relationship between society and the individual, Dewey was also greatly influenced by the doctrines of evolution and pragmatism.

Evolution and Pragmatism. Perhaps the most distinctively American contribution to the intellectual life of the nineteenth century was the development of pragmatism, a philosophical orientation largely based upon the broad principles of evolutionary theory. The theory of evolution challenged the religious doctrine that the world and man were specially created by divine intervention and that the human being is a form of living being absolutely different from the rest of nature. In direct opposition to the religious outlook, the startling theories of evolution stated that the earth was not created at a moment in time but was millions of years old, that by natural processes the simpler forms of life became more complex, and that man and all living things were branches of a common stock of life. Thomas Huxley and Robert Ingersoll carried the war into the theological camps, and Herbert Spencer applied the evolutionary concepts and the doctrines of the survival of the fittest to the fields of ethics, politics, history, economics, and social development in general.

Not only was religious authority challenged by evolutionary science, but the whole philosophical position of idealism and the "genteel tradition" was attacked by the new philosophy of pragmatism. The original tradition of Calvinism in America and the early nineteenth-century influence of German idealism had led most American philosophers to envisage a monistic universe in which everything had a fixed place in relation to the whole and in which truth was looked upon as uniform, fixed, and eternal.

The prevailing conditions of American frontier life, however, with its wilderness to be conquered and its dangers, uncertainties, and constant struggle for existence, had shaped an "American mood" that was out of sympathy with the finalities of philosophic idealism. Established order, routine, and finality became less vital to Americans than initiative, enterprise, and innovation. From the temper of American life and from the example of Darwinism and the sciences, Charles Peirce and William James formulated a pragmatic philosophy that they felt was more appropriate to the changed conditions of life.

Pragmatism looked upon the universe as essentially incomplete and changing. The varieties of existence and of experience were set over against the organic unity and homogeneity of idealism. The appearance of novelty was considered to be a genuine fact of experience. Belief in the immediate experience of human beings rather than appeal to remote authority of religion or philosophy was considered the court of last resort in validating ideas. In other words, truth is not a single and closed body of knowledge that holds good despite all the experience of men; truth depends upon the consequences that occur when men act in certain ways. Truth is subject to change whenever better methods of acting and thinking are devised to meet the exigencies of life.

Inasmuch as law, religion, government, art, and science were thus looked upon as receiving meaning and value from what they accomplish, it was but a step to look upon education as valuable only insofar as it accomplishes what is desired. After the turn of the century, the experimentalism of John Dewey and his followers made it even more difficult for advocates of a completely closed metaphysical system and static body of truth to hold their own.

Trends in Psychology

Somewhat parallel to the trends noted above, the dominant beliefs about how people learn underwent a marked change in the nineteenth century. During the first half of the century the traditional rationalism of Europe had been used by American writers to support a faculty psychology and mental discipline as the basis of the learning process. The mind was looked upon as a special spiritual creation quite different in essence from the physical body. The mind, common to all men as distinguished from animals, consists of distinct and identifiable faculties, each governing and directing certain mental powers. In the latter part of the century the faculty psychology was challenged by psychological outlooks modeled upon the scientific methods that were becoming so useful in the study of nature. As a result, the learning process came to emphasize specific learnings rather than a general mental discipline.

Faculty Psychology versus Experimental Psychology. According to faculty psychology, the mind was conceived as consisting of separate, independent, and ready-made capacities, or faculties, such as memory, judgment, reason, will, imagination, and taste. These faculties were considered to be merely potential until brought into actuality by training or practice. The exercise and strengthening of one faculty was thought to transfer beneficially to other faculties.

Development of the powers of the mind had been set up, especially by a Yale faculty report of 1828, as the supreme aim of education. The classics and mathematics had been looked upon as the best means of bringing about this development of the intellectual powers. For the exercise of the faculties, the form of studies was considered more important than their content. Thus, for example, when the older studies of the school or college curriculum were attacked for the reason that they were not practical or useful enough, their supporters defended them with the doctrines of faculty psychology. They said that the classics and mathematics should retain their position in the curriculum because their form was more valuable for mental discipline than that of such so-called "practical" studies as the physical sciences and modern languages.

So long as faculty psychology remained the dominating theory of the learning process, the defenders of mental discipline and of the traditional prescribed studies held their position securely. Advocates of the newer subjects, however, attacked the classics, mathematics, and traditional philosophy because they were not sufficiently adapted to the varying interests, capacities, and prospective pursuits of the students. This latter view was increasingly supported by the findings of a newer empirical psychology. As the nineteenth century drew to its close, faculty psychology lost its dominance in educational philosophy and psychology.

The "associational school" of psychology in Europe had, for example, declared that faculty psychology distinguished too minutely among different mental powers that actually were not mutually exclusive or independent of one another. Associationism tried to reduce all mental processes to the single process of association. The mind was looked upon as made up of groups of ideas that had become associated in different ways and with varying emphases. Memory, reason, emotion, and invention were conceived not as independent faculties of the mind but merely as different ways in which simple perceptions had become associated with more complicated perceptions and ideas. Thus, it was believed that *specific* ideas rather than independent mental faculties determined an individual's memory and reason.

Experimental psychology, as it developed in the United States, gave close attention to the scientific study of psychology and recognized that sensory, motor, and physiological processes greatly affect mental development. Influenced by the laboratory methods of Wundt and the theory of evolution, actual experiments by G. Stanley Hall, Joseph Jastrow, and Edward Lee Thorndike were based on a functional theory of mind. Far from being a separate entity or faculty, the mind is really the functioning of the organism in adjusting its behavior more adequately to its environment. In the field of learning, "behavior" became more important than "consciousness." William James said at Harvard that mind is in "what it does."

Furthermore, experimental psychology was supported by studies in heredity and original nature conducted by such men as Francis Galton, James McKeen Cattell, and Edward Lee Thorndike. The startling findings as to "individual differences" as early as the 1880's led progressive educators gradually to emphasize the differing capacities of individuals and to recognize the need for taking account of these varying abilities and interests in the learning process. As the theories of mental discipline and transfer of training became suspect in view of the new experimental psychology, each individual began to be looked upon as worth developing in his own way for his own sake. Since the nature of each individual had been found to differ from that of every other, the notion gained strength that each individual should receive special attention through special studies if he is to attain maximum growth and development.

Development of American Educational Theory

At the close of the century two other voices were being heard that eventually were to help modify American education in important ways. During his teaching at Johns Hopkins and his presidency of Clark University, G. Stanley Hall carried on many investigations and produced dozens of writings dealing with the psychological development of children and adolescents. His great contribution was to turn the attention of educators to the need for the careful study of child development. In his application of evolutionary doctrines to child study he often offered fanciful analogies that later brought him much criticism. His recapitulation theories, for example, that the child in his growth processes follows the evolutionary development of the race gained him not only great popularity but also much opposition. He found certain distinct stages in the development of the individual that parallel the changes in human society from the primitive stage to hunting, to cave dwelling, to early civilization, and to later civilization. His extensive writings on almost all phases of education, and particularly on the psychology of adolescence, made his name widely known until well into the twentieth century.

Much more influential in the long run was the work of John Dewey, who began to write on educational topics in the last decade of the century. His best-known educational works before 1900 were *Interest as*

Fig. 30. John Dewey.

Related to Will (1896), *My Pedagogic Creed* (1897), and *The School and Society* (1899). These works, which stated the general theory underlying Dewey's interest in the experimental elementary school at the University of Chicago (1896), heralded a revolt against the dominance of the religiously motivated moral aim, the disciplinary aim, and the informational aim, which ruled elementary education throughout most of the nineteenth century. He argued that schools should strive to elevate moral aims based upon civic and social experience, vocational and practical usefulness, and individual development. The outline of thought contained in these works formed the groundwork of Dewey's philosophy of education, which was elaborated in form and extended in practice throughout the first half of the twentieth century.

Dewey's philosophy of education took the form of a restatement of the aims of education in the light of the rapid social changes that had taken place in American society in the nineteenth century. According to Dewey, education has two sides, the psychological and the social, neither of which may be subordinated or neglected. On the one hand, the basis for education is the psychological nature of the individual child. The teacher must utilize the activity springing from a child's nature and make it coincide with his efforts. On the other hand, teachers must be familiar with the social situation in order to interpret properly the child's activities and transfer them into social channels. Education proceeds by the participation of the individual in social relationships with his fellow human beings.

When the psychological approach is isolated from the social, education produces either a barren and formal development of the mental powers, with no idea of the use to which they are to be put, or a forced and external education, resulting in subordinating the freedom of the individual to a preconceived notion of society. Dewey attacked both the older attitude of formal indoctrination and the newer type of education, which attempted to train the individual slavishly for a specific adult life. He proposed instead that the child be put in complete possession of all his powers, capacities, skills, and judgment. This can be achieved only if teachers begin with an insight into the psychological interests and habits of the child, using them as springboards to social development. Education is thus an active process whereby immediate experience is continuously redirected toward more significant social behavior.

Schools must be set up to include both social and individual goals. Dewey considered the school as primarily a social institution; the processes in the school are not basically different from the social processes outside of the school. The school is simply that form of social life in which are concentrated all the factors that will most effectively and rapidly bring the child to share in the accumulated knowledge and skills of the race. The school must take account of the home and play life, which are the sources of the child's principal experiences. The best moral training is received, not in the form of dictates or discipline from the teacher, but as the child is obliged to develop proper social relationships with others in the school. Hence, the teacher should not impose fiats or try to form rigid habits in the child but should select appropriate learning situations for the child and assist him in responding to them.

The mere linking of the words "school" and "society" in the title of Dewey's book had a great effect on the minds of laymen and teachers— that of emphasizing the close relationships existing between the two.

Dewey pointed out that modifications of method and curriculum should consist in efforts to meet the needs of a new society. This changed social situation was marked by the application of science to the means of production and distribution, by great manufacturing centers, and by rapid means of communication. Habits of discipline and responsibility that were earlier formed in an agrarian and family system of economy can no longer be so given, and it is the duty of the school to help with this function of education.

Dewey believed the school to be a fundamental method of social progress and reform. Education should be one of the important agencies by which society can formulate its own purposes, organize its means of attainment, and shape itself in the direction it wishes to move. This is the essence of a democratic social order. The handing down of ready-made concepts is the mark of an autocratic social order. With the advance of social as well as political democracy, which requires change and progress to prevent itself from reverting to autocracy, a new "social education" is needed. This social education, in Dewey's sense, should endeavor to make vocational interests or special interests of many kinds a means for promoting the common life.

Dewey was also insistent upon constant experimentation, to learn more about child nature in order to adapt school practices to its effective development. Inasmuch as child nature is inherently active and bubbling over with the impulse to do, it is the function of education to release and direct the impulses evident in the school. According to Dewey, these impulses are of four kinds: the social impulse of communication or conversation; the constructive impulse to make things; the impulse to investigate things; and the impulse of artistic or creative expression.

Thus the school should not rely upon mere listening but should be arranged so that the child can learn by active experience and learn to think by managing experience. Since the proper solution of a problem demands intelligent thinking, thinking becomes the main element in the ability to cope with new situations. Dewey defined thinking as bringing the meanings of past experience to bear on the interpretation of new situations.

Accordingly, the subject matter and method of the school should be adapted to child needs. Dewey found that a general mistake was made of introducing the child too abruptly to special studies that have little relation to his own social life. Rather, the social life of the child should be the basis of correlation or concentration in his growth and development. Thus, the so-called "expressive," or "constructive," activities, such as manual arts, household arts, drawing, music, and nature study, should be used as means of introducing the child to more formal subjects. For example, language is primarily a means of social communication; yet much of its value is lost because it is taught as a separate study with the social element lacking.

In emphasizing the importance of the interests of the child, Dewey made another contribution to the enrichment of education. Interests, said Dewey, are signs of growing powers and as such require careful and constant observation. They should be neither excessively humored nor excessively repressed. Repression results in weak intellectual curiosity and lack of initiative, whereas unguided humoring results in transiency, caprice, and whim. Misconceptions of interest come from ignoring its moving, developmental nature. To protect pedagogical theory from a merely internal conception of mind and from a strictly external conception of subject matter, Dewey believed that interest should be viewed as a unified activity that links the child with subject matter.

The genuine principle of interest is involved when the individual identifies himself with the fact to be learned or the action proposed. Interest provides the moving, or driving, force, whereas effort comes into play in the degree to which the achievement of the activity is postponed or made remote by obstacles. The effort to overcome obstacles or perform tasks stimulates thinking and reflection, which are the only really educative activities. Interest cannot be genuinely added or attached to a formal subject; it must be inherently contained in the activity in which the child engages. These activities are physical, constructive, intellectual, and social activities. To charge Dewey with anti-intellectualism is to misunderstand or misinterpret him.

Such, then, were some of Dewey's conceptions of education in the late nineteenth century. In his theory of the desirable interaction of the individual and the social, Dewey stressed the fact that the psychological nature of the child must not be divorced from the social situation but must be used as the basis for directing his energies into socially useful channels. Rousseau's naturalism had emphasized the importance of child nature and minimized environment. The child's nature was conceived as inherently good and if freed from all constraint of environment would naturally tend to unfold into the right kind of adulthood. On the other hand, the religious tradition had emphasized the importance of the discipline of environment in curbing the individual's nature, which was supposed to be inherently bad. While paying his respects to naturalism and discipline alike, Dewey believed that neither the psychological nature of the individual nor the social environment of the culture could be slighted but that a democratic society could be attained only by the proper interaction of the two.

The Value of Knowledge

One of the most impressive facts concerning the nineteenth-century United States is the enormous and rapid expansion that took place in nearly all fields of organized knowledge. Few developments had so great or so direct an effect upon the character of American education. The influence of science, scientific methods, and the evolutionary theory played a large part in this process. Bitter controversies developed concerning the role that knowledge should play in society and in education.

Expansion and Specialization of Knowledge. As investigation and research added great masses of material to the traditional bodies of knowledge, many new and relatively independent "subjects" were organized. The older bodies of knowledge were divided and subdivided into ever more specialized elements. A college professor of "natural history" at the beginning of the century took for his field the whole range of organic life. At the end of the century, natural history had been broken down into the various biological and natural sciences, including botany, zoology, physiology, psychology, paleontology, ornithology, entomology, and anthropology. What had simply been called "natural philosophy" became subdivided into such specialized physical sciences as astronomy, physics, chemistry, mineralogy, geology, meteorology, and physical geography. In the same manner "moral philosophy" was transformed and differentiated into the social sciences of history, economics, political science, and sociology. Indeed, by the end of the century a scholar could no longer take even the whole of one of these newer fields for his special interest but had to specialize in ever more narrow aspects of zoology, or physics, or history.

This process of expansion and specialization of knowledge was hastened by the attempt to apply scientific methods to nearly all fields of knowledge and by the organization of professional associations of scholars and specialists in the various fields. The success of the scientific method was soon apparent as scientists were impelled by colleges and universities, by business and industry, and by the government to investigate the whole range of natural and physical phenomena. Practical and profit motives were strong, as well as the theoretical impetus. The desire to create better machines for the production of goods, to improve agricultural products, to find better sea lanes, and to develop ocean and overland transportation all played their parts.

The formation of professional associations of scholars and scientists was highly accelerated. Before the Civil War most of the societies were local in scope, with the exception of such outstanding organizations as the American Academy of Arts and Sciences, the American Medical Association, and the American Association for the Advancement of Science. After the Civil War the national type of association became more popular, and a great acceleration in their establishment took place in the 1870's, 1880's, and 1890's. Among the many, only a few can be mentioned, for example, the American Philological Association, American Library Association, American Bar Association, Modern Language

Association, American Chemical Society, American Mathematics Society, American Historical Association, American Economics Association, American Psychological Association, and American Philosophical Association. In the process of forming associations the principle of specialization was at work, as shown, for example, by the fact that the mining engineers, mechanical engineers, and electrical engineers all formed separate societies within 10 or 15 years.

This wide range of activity was stimulated not only by practical considerations but by the effort to apply the scientific method to fields other than the physical and natural sciences. Scholars in the social sciences, language and literature, and the arts were trying to make their work "scientific," to gather detailed information and accurate facts, to classify and describe their phenomena as carefully as the physical scientists were doing in their laboratories.

For this ideal many American scholars looked to the German universities for their inspiration. In the hundred years after 1812 nearly 10,000 American scholars went to Germany, and many thousands more were affected by the scholarly ideal of specialized research. The older ideal of broad scholarship ranging over as many fields of knowledge as possible was replaced by the ideal that a scholar should exhaustively explore a narrow segment.

The "Genteel Tradition" versus Social Responsibility. With the growing importance of knowledge of many kinds, it was only natural that there should be differences of opinion concerning the use to which knowledge should be put—indeed, concerning its whole purpose. One outlook held to the ideal that knowledge is valuable simply for its own sake. Literature, language, science, history, art, and music are the hallmarks of culture and scholarship and should express the most refined and purest sentiments of human nature.

According to this "genteel tradition," the quiet, reserved, and undisturbed pursuit of truth or expression of beauty should not be jarred by the harsh realities of the outside world. Romanticism, "escape" literature, the remote, the sentimental, and the adventurous were marks of the genteel tradition, exemplified by such writers as Longfellow, Lowell, and Holmes.

While the belles-lettres of the genteel tradition were likely to be steeped in romanticism or refinement, the sciences could not very well be romantic, but they could and did elevate the ideal of objectivity and social neutrality. Following the lead of the German universities, American scientists and social scientists began to say that "pure" truth and "pure" knowledge are the aim of all research and all study. Truth for its own sake, undefiled by practical applications in nature or in society, came to be the watchword. The corollary was often an idealization of an intellectual elite as the guardian of truth and beauty, the masses of people being considered inherently incapable of entrance into the portals of true scholarship.

In reaction against the exaltation of "culture" was the belief that knowledge has a social function to perform and should not merely hide away in its ivory tower. This reaction took many and varied forms. One form was the nationalistic emphasis of the early nineteenth century, which began to glorify the new republic, its ideals, its people, and its setting in a new continent. Much literature, history, and science were stimulated by this nationalistic zeal to turn knowledge and forms of expression to the uses of the new nation.

Another form drew its inspiration from business enterprise and industrialism, which joined together to idealize the practicality of life and to insist that knowledge should promote the practical business of living. This stimulus included not only the desire to use technology to improve methods of production but also the individualistic optimism that knowledge is the open-sesame by which the individual may raise himself in the social scale. "Practicality" could mean a generous insistence that the welfare of an industrial society depends upon the application of science to nature, or it could mean a narrow demand that historians and economists defend the profit motive in the interests of the enterprise system.

A third form of the doctrine of social responsibility was the belief that knowledge should improve the welfare of the great majority of the people in a democracy. From the reform movements of the early nineteenth century to the social-welfare movements of the late nineteenth century, the demand continued to grow that the test of literature, science, social science, and art should be their functioning in the public interest. Knowledge must not be locked up in its intellectual hideaways; it must not be neutral to injustice and corruption; it must not be confined to an aristocratic elite; it must not defend the privilege and entrenched interests of the *status quo*. Rather, investigation should be undertaken with a view to the improvement of democracy, and its fruits should be spread as widely among the population as possible.

Stimulated by these different views of the social role of the arts and sciences, a great galaxy of scholars and writers produced a prodigious amount of material in the various fields of knowledge, from which American education drew sustenance and had to select elements for emphasis. Differences of opinion as to what should be selected and for what purposes led to many educational controversies.

Language Arts and Literature. Several developments in the linguistic and literary arts had significance for education in the nineteenth century, only a few of which can be mentioned. First of all, the traditional hold of Humanism gave a continued strength to the classics, but there was no doubt that the ramparts were about to be stormed. In the early part of the century many bitter battles were fought by the classicists in the effort to maintain the superiority of the classical languages and literature over modern languages and literature. The classicists used the arguments of the genteel tradition against the modernists; proponents of modern languages, interestingly enough, used the arguments of practicality to justify their claims to equality with the classics.

Then, as modern languages gained headway through the century, the classicists and the modernists often joined together to defend the literary tradition against the practicality of their common enemy, the physical and natural sciences, The battle between literature and science, embodied by Huxley, Spencer, and Arnold in England, was repeated in America. But, despite their antagonism to science as such, students of both classical and modern languages stressed the specialized research and "scientific" investigation that had become popular in the German universities. New editions and better translations of much of the world's great literature were produced, and extensive studies made in philology and literary criticism.

Much more than in the scholarly study of literature were the current trends of thought reflected in the creative literature being written by American authors. Even though reliance upon England remained very strong, the early nineteenth century saw the rise of a distinctively American type of literature, reflecting the development of cultural nationality. Some idealized the romantic retreat from reality; others stressed social reform. Some expressed great faith in the common people; others were definitely antidemocratic. Some glorified the "effete" East; others revealed the vitality and rough-and-ready venturesomeness of the West.

In the latter part of the century, realistic descriptions of the dreadful impact of industrialism and business capitalism upon the underprivileged groups were accompanied by a direct appeal for social reform. In one way or another, reform writers depicted the greed, corruption, and monopolistic methods of big business and took the part of the common people as represented by the farmer and laborer in difficult straits through no fault of their own.

In these and other ways American literature was responding to the call for greater social responsibility. In general, however, it was the "safer" and more refined literature of the genteel tradition that found its way into the schools and colleges of the nation. Educators were dominated by the ideals of scholarly research and purely intellectual virtues, as well as by the conservative political and economic outlooks of the times.

Science and Mathematics. The rise of the various fields of physical and natural science to a place of great importance and popularity was one of the principal intellectual events of the nineteenth century. It may be that the greatest creative discoveries in science were made by Europeans, but the range and quality of American achievement were rapidly increasing. The establishment of the *American Journal of Science* in 1818 by Benjamin Silliman signalized the appearance of a genuinely American science.

Scientists reflected the varying outlooks concerning the social role of knowledge. In the early days of the century many scientists either resisted the idea of evolution or tried to show that there was no essential contradiction between evolution and religion. In the latter part of the century those scientists who were impressed by the scholarly ideals of the genteel tradition ignored the question and went about their work, while those who felt strongly about the matter joined in defending evolution and arguing for the practicality of science against the intellectual isolationism of academic literature. Gradually, by virtue of the weight of scientific research, the academic war between science and literature was being decided in favor of the former. Scientific studies were accepted in the curriculum by college and school faculties, at first in a subordinate position, then on a basis of equality, and finally in a dominant position.

The scientific movement was one of the most important factors in breaking down barriers between intellectuals and the common people. Especially in the early part of the century, the interest in scientific facts amounted to a popular rage. Societies for the dissemination of scientific knowledge sprang up in all parts of the country, and thousands of people were brought into closer touch with the marvels of science through mechanics' institutes, libraries, popular books, and lyceum lectures. Scientists themselves, however, were divided concerning this movement. Some preferred to think of science as the peculiar function of an intellectual elite working in their laboratories at the universities.

Social Sciences. Borrowing much from scientific influence but making much headway in their own right, social scientists expanded their work enormously during the nineteenth century. They followed the general pattern of specialization and subdivided their materials into such separate disciplines as history, economics, political science, sociology, and anthropology. The American Revolution was the object of much interest among historians of the early decades of the century. Histories of the various colonies and states continued to be written, while the new spirit of nationalism led other historians to turn their attention to the United States in general. In the middle decades of the century historians expanded their efforts and began to write on a wide variety of topics.

Meanwhile economics, political economy, and political science began to receive their share of special attention. The Revolution and the Civil War stimulated a great deal of writing on the political nature of the new nation. In the later decades of the century the political economists were divided on the conflict between individualism and social reform as stimulated by Darwinism and by the new industrial conditions of life.

Sociology and anthropology became distinct "sciences" during the nineteenth century. Many studies of ancient societies, primitive cultures, and the American Indians laid the groundwork for modern anthropology. Sociology exerted still greater influence in the later decades of the century. Some sociologists looked upon social evolution in Darwinian terms of virtually automatic and uncontrolled change; others emphasized the possibility of controlling and directing the process of social change as a means of promoting the general welfare through social reform. Schools and the means of education were often thought of as great agencies of social improvement.

EXPANSION AND REFORM IN THE EDUCATIONAL PROGRAM

Most of the educational problems inherited from the nineteenth century can be traced in some measure to the vast expansion of the school system. The nineteenth-century United States was marked by an enormous expansion in population. There was a vast increase in building the things that were needed to exploit the resources of a new continent. The curriculum at all levels of education expanded rapidly, and scores of new subjects were added to meet all kinds of demands. As indicated in the preceding pages, American culture revealed the interplay of several major factors, democracy, nationalism, capitalism, science, industrialism, the religious tradition, Humanism, and a new psychology. Out of this welter of forces appeared several distinctive and dominating aims for education.

Educational Aims

The principal aims of education in the nineteenth century can be identified and defined in many ways, but at least six outstanding conceptions were at work at the different levels of the educational system. Although they overlap to a considerable degree, they are given here to indicate some guidelines for the discussion that follows.

Character and Moral Development. Stemming from the great influence that organized religion exerted in American education, the ideal of character development through religion remained a dominant aim in the nineteenth century. Bulwarked by the religious and Humanistic traditions, "moral training" was closely identified through much of the century with the ideals of Christian character and was often considered to be impossible apart from specific religious training. As secular values in morality gained headway, character development continued to be emphasized as a function of the public schools despite the absence of sectarian religious instruction. This aim was influential at all levels from elementary school through the liberal arts college.

Mental Discipline. Rooted in the European traditions of idealistic and rationalistic philosophy, the ideal of mental discipline was current in the early part of the century and then gained great popularity in the middle and later decades. This aim put little stress upon the acquisition of knowledge and information as such but rather emphasized the training of the mental faculties and the cultivation of the intellectual powers apart from any specific application to practical affairs. The disciplinary theory, strongly supported by the religious and Humanistic traditions, was most often used to justify the extensive teaching of the classics and mathematics. It was especially popular in the liberal arts colleges and was often used to support the college-preparatory functions of the academies and high schools.

Literacy and Information. The ideal of universal literacy and of the acquisition of specific factual knowledge challenged the disciplinary ideal. Literacy achieved through the fundamental processes of the three R's had been a goal of elementary education and received support from the religious tradition ever since the Protestant Reformation. During the nineteenth century the democratic doctrines of universal suffrage gave added impetus to literacy as a prime function of the common school. The acquisition of information as such was also stimulated by the popularity of scientific knowledge at all social levels of the population.

Backed by the scientific tradition, the ideal of scholarly research, and the new stimulus-response psychology of Thorndike, the informational aim gained great headway over mental discipline. It was used to justify the introduction of the sciences and specialized knowledge of all kinds into the high school and college. It helped to fix upon schools the idea that education was virtually equivalent to the mastery of systematic bodies of knowledge organized into subject-matter fields. It was used to justify lectures, memorizing, drill, recitation methods based upon learning of textbook materials, and the ability to pass examinations as a test of mastery.

Vocational and Practical Aims. With the great advances in science, technology, industrialism, capitalism, and democracy, the vocational and practical aim gained an increasing place in American education in the nineteenth century. Joining with the informational aim, the ideal of practical usefulness challenged the hold of mental discipline and justified the introduction of specific courses to help prepare high school and college students for getting jobs in a wider and wider variety of occupations. The sciences and their applications to industry, business, and agriculture were strengthened by the capitalistic doctrine that everyone should be trained to make a living in order to get ahead in the world and by the democratic ideal that everyone should have the opportunity to fit himself for some lifework.

Great battles were fought between the proponents of disciplinary, or cultural, studies and the proponents of vocational, or practical, studies. New studies that had gained recognition on the basis of their practicality were often justified as disciplinary in the face of demands that still newer subjects be recognized. Entrance into traditional institutions was sought for the newer subjects on the grounds that they were just as strongly disciplinary as the older studies. Once they were admitted, it was claimed that they possessed superiority over the older studies in that they were practical as well. The history of the various sciences and modern languages furnishes examples of both these tactics. The practical and vocational aim, of course, was especially strong among the non-college-preparatory studies of the high schools and the technical courses in the colleges.

Civic or Social Aim. Whereas the social aim in secondary and higher education had earlier been couched in aristocratic terms and glorified training for leadership, the democratic and nationalistic forces of the nineteenth century began to stress the importance of citizenship education for all. With the growing complexities of social life, it became apparent to many that the schools and colleges needed to make more direct efforts to train the citizenry of the nation for their duties and responsibilities. This aim gave great support to the introduction of the social studies at all levels of education and helped to stimulate interest in history, government, and economics. Although Americanization programs often reached extremes of patriotic fervor and nationalism, nevertheless this aim was extremely important in helping the schools to play their role in welding a nation out of many divergent parts and to instill basic democratic attitudes among the people.

Individual Development. The individualistic conception of man that was promoted jointly by capitalism, by a frontier democracy, and by the newer psychology of individual differences gained some headway in educational circles in the nineteenth century. The philosophy of naturalism that stemmed from Rousseau and Pestalozzi gave American educators an interest in developing the capacities of each individual to the full. This conception first entered the educational system most prominently at the lower levels and gradually worked its way upward. It was supported by a capitalistic individualism that looked upon the individual as of prime importance and upon society as simply an aggregate of well-developed individuals. When this ideal was further supported by a psychology of individual differences, it seemed clear to many that the principal aim of education was to enable the child to develop according to his own needs, interests, and capacities.

In general, this individualistic aim was not as influential in the nineteenth century as other aims, but it did gain currency in some quarters and helped to justify the elective system as a means by which students might freely choose the studies of most value to them. It therefore supported the practical and vocational aims and was most often found among non-college-preparatory subjects in opposition to the ideal of mental discipline. In the twentieth century it became one of the dominating conceptions in educational theory.

Elementary Education

The desire to develop good moral character and literacy outran all others in the elementary schools of the nineteenth century, although the practical, social, and individual aims were gathering momentum. Of course, sheer physical discipline, as a means of keeping order in school and punishment for misconduct, could be relied upon by teachers when all other aims seemed fruitless.

European Influences. Throughout the century a series of specific influences from Europe were at work in American education. From England came the Sunday schools, the infant schools, and the monitorial schools (see pages 407 to 408), all of which helped to provide a transition from private to public school systems. The infant school spread the notion that schools had a responsibility to children as young as ages four, five, and six. The monitorial schools helped to prove that class instruction might be better than individual instruction or at least could be effective for moral, literacy, and informational purposes. Likewise, they showed that discipline through rewards and social punishment was more effective than corporal punishment.

From Germany came the ideas of Pestalozzi, Froebel, and Herbart. Pestalozzian ideas (see pages 398 to 402) were adapted to American practices. Newer methods of teaching the three R's were developed; more attention was given to the study of nature and concrete objects; the practical usefulness of geography, drawing, music, home economics, and industrial arts was recognized; and a psychological rather than a strictly logical organization of subject matter was designed to meet the learning needs of individuals. In the hands of enthusiastic and well-trained teachers, these newer methods promoted better learning; but as the methods became stiffly formalized, the ideal of simply passing on information more efficiently came to dominate.

Froebel's *kindergarten* (see pages 402 to 404) stressed the moral-religious, the social, and the individual aims. Two of Froebel's students, Johannes Kraus, who was in America in the 1850's, and Mrs. Carl Schurz, who established the first kindergarten in America at Watertown, Wis., in 1856 (taught in German), helped to spread the kindergarten idea. Elizabeth Peabody, Horace Mann's sister-in-law, established a kindergarten taught in English in Boston in the 1860's, and William T. Harris added kindergartens to the public school system of St. Louis. By 1880 they had appeared in some 30 states, and by 1900 there were some 4,500 kinder-gartens in the United States, more than two-thirds of which were pri-vately sponsored.

The kindergarten's emphasis upon development of the individual child's capacities through play activities, greater freedom of movement, and social attitudes of cooperation gradually helped to relieve the rigid discipline and formal atmosphere of the elementary schools. Francis W. Parker, as superintendent of schools in Quincy, Mass., and as principal of the Cook County Normal School in Chicago, is given the credit for much of the success of this movement during the 1880's and 1890's.

The ideas of Herbart (see pages 404 to 406) had great vogue in Amer-ica in the last two decades of the century, much as Pestalozzian ideas were popular earlier. The initial Herbartian stimulus tended to stress the social aim of education through the social studies and literature. When, however, his science of teaching through the five formal steps was systematized into lesson plans, the informational aim came strongly to the fore. Herbartian methods eventually were used largely as a means to attain more effective mastery of subject matter. Herbartianism be-came prominent in normal schools and teachers colleges through the in-fluence of such men as Charles De Garmo, Charles A. McMurray, and Frank McMurry and through the National Herbart Society (1895), which later became the National Society for the Study of Education.

Although all the foreign influences upon American elementary educa-tion cannot be mentioned here, the increasing attention to education for handicapped children should be noted. The democratic ideal that all children should have an opportunity to develop themselves drew atten-tion to the unfortunate deaf, blind, crippled, and feeble-minded. After a visit to France in 1816, Thomas H. Gallaudet helped to establish a school for the deaf in Hartford, Conn., in 1817. He advocated the use of finger or sign language as the principal means of instruction. State schools for the deaf appeared as early as the 1820's and 1830's.

Also from France came a stimulus to education for the blind, through the efforts of Dr. Samuel Gridley Howe, who helped to establish the Perkins Institute for the Blind in Boston in 1832. As the idea spread to New York, Philadelphia, and elsewhere, state schools began to appear. Great impetus was given to the work by the adoption of the Braille method of reading and by the action of Congress in allowing the post-office department to send materials for the blind free through the mails.

The study of feeble-minded children was a part of Edouard Séguin's work in France and Gallaudet's work in the United States. The first state institution was the Massachusetts School for Idiotic and Feeble-minded Youth in 1851. As interest in the work spread, classes for subnormal children appeared in the public schools in Providence in 1893 and rapidly thereafter in other school systems.

Private schools for crippled children were established in New York in the 1860's. Later in the century special attention to the crippled was given in public schools and in special state institutions in various parts of the country. The crowded and unhealthy character of city life also drew attention to the need for the rehabilitation of delinquent children. Although the early conceptions were largely disciplinary and emphasized punishment in "reform schools" or "industrial schools" run by the states, the public school systems gradually began to institute more appropriate reeducative methods.

Expansion of the Elementary School Curriculum. The many details of the expansion of the curriculum of the elementary school in the nineteenth century cannot be described here, but the fact of expansion is of the utmost importance. The differences in the way the curriculum developed were enormous, for no one pattern was common in various schools, cities, or states. In the course of the century the rather narrow studies of the three R's in the dame schools, district schools, reading schools, and writing schools were expanded to include many of the studies that had been taught in the academies and early high schools.

First and foremost in the elementary curriculum was the study of the English language, in accordance with the aim to increase literacy among the general population. Whatever the names given in various schools to this study, it most commonly included reading, writing, spelling, and eventually the rules of grammar, rhetoric, and composition.

Among the hundreds of authors who wrote books on these subjects the most influential were doubtless Noah Webster, Lindley Murray, and William Holmes McGuffey. Webster's "blue-backed speller," grammar, and reader were enormously popular. The speller was doubtless the most widely used schoolbook during most of the century. Expressing the ideals of patriotic nationalism, it represented the new civic and social aim for education as well as the literacy aim. Murray's *English Grammar*, representing the disciplinary and literacy aims, was patterned on the long-recognized divisions of grammar as defined in Latin grammars, namely, orthography, inflection, syntax, and prosody. McGuffey's graded series of readers reflected the dominant middle-class virtues of religious morality, patriotism, and prudent practical morality as a means of getting ahead in life.

The next most influential subject in the elementary school was undoubtedly arithmetic, which received impetus principally from the disciplinary and practical aims. In the earliest decades the most common procedure in teaching arithmetic was for the teacher to write out or dictate the problems to the pupils, who then tried to solve them by applying the appropriate rules, the teacher then correcting the answers.

An important advance in the method of teaching arithmetic was made when Warren Colburn published his mental arithmetic in 1821, which followed Pestalozzi's ideas of psychological and inductive organization of subject matter. In the early part of the century, arithmetic gained in popularity because of its practical usefulness, but in the latter part of the cen-

20. Billy saw that he looked very sad, and asked him what was the matter.

21. The poor old man said he was very hungry. He had had nothing to eat for a long time, and he could not work, as he was old and blind.

22. Then Billy, without saying a word, brought the rest of the cake. He said, "Here, old man, is some cake for you," and put it into the old man's hat.

23. The fiddler thanked him, and Billy was happier than if he had eaten ten cakes.

EXERCISES.—Will you tell us all about Harry's cake? Peter's? Billy's? Which of the boys do you like best?

Fig. 31. A Page from the McGuffey Readers Showing the Emphasis on Moral Education. (From Harvey C. Minnich (ed.), *Old Favorites from the McGuffey Readers,* American Book, New York, 1936. Courtesy of American Book Company.)

tury it was further justified because of its disciplinary values. Nature study also appeared in various forms on a much smaller scale as a result of the "object methods" of Pestalozzi.

Next in importance were the various social studies, principally geography and American history. The Massachusetts school laws of 1824 and 1827 required geography in addition to the study of English and arithmetic. American history was required by state law as early as 1827 in Vermont and 1857 in Massachusetts. American history textbooks appeared in large numbers during the first half of the nineteenth century in response to the rise of nationalism and the civic and social aims for education. Texts by Charles A. Goodrich and Peter Parley (Samuel G. Goodrich) led the field. The social-civic interest also led to the study of government, civics, and political economy as early as the 1830's and 1840's. This interest expanded in the later nineteenth century.

One of the best examples of the influence of the dominant political and economic ideals of the early nineteenth century upon the school curriculum is furnished by an elementary textbook entitled *First Lessons in Political Economy*, written in 1835 by the Reverend John McVickar, professor at Columbia College. Here can be seen at work most clearly the religious-moral aims, the civic-social aims of patriotism and economic individualism, and the practical efforts to get ahead. McVickar's glorifying of the traditional laissez-faire economic system, his opposition to governmental interference in business, and his defense of natural laws in economics are seen throughout his book. In a last chapter on How to Make Money, McVickar idealized the individualistic conception of the American dream as follows:

If he has good health and is industrious, even the poorest boy in our country has something to trade upon; and if he be besides well-educated and have skill in any kind of work, and add to this, moral habits and religious principles, so that his employers may trust him and place confidence in him, he may then be said to set out in life with a handsome capital, and certainly has as good a chance of becoming independent and respectable, and perhaps *rich*, as any man in the country. "Every man is the maker of his own fortune." All depends upon setting out on the right principles, and they are these:

1. Be Industrious—time and skill are your capital.
2. Be Saving—whatever it be, live within your income.
3. Be Prudent—buy not what you can do without.
4. Be Resolute—let your economy be always of to-day, not tomorrow.
5. Be Contented and Thankful—a cheerful spirit makes labor light, and sleep sweet, and all around *happy*, all which is much better than being *only* *rich*.[1]

[1] John McVickar, *First Lessons in Political Economy; for the Use of Primary and Common Schools* (Hilliard, Gray, and Co., Boston, 1835), pp. 86–88.

In addition to the various English studies, arithmetic, and the social studies, the elementary school curriculum also came to give some attention to drawing, music, and physical education, although they always remained in a subordinate position in respect to time and emphasis. Drawing entered some monitorial schools early in the century, and by the 1860's the schools in Boston, New York, Philadelphia, and some cities of the West were beginning to include it. Generally, at first, drawing was a matter of copying such standardized objects as vases and pitchers by using geometric circles and ellipses, but gradually freehand drawing became more popular. The teaching of drawing was influenced in one direction by the practical interest in mechanical drawing for industrial purposes and in another direction by the psychological interest in the development of manual and physical skills along Pestalozzian lines as a means of developing individual capacities.

Music, primarily as expressed in singing and choral work, became popular in the early decades of the century. It was especially promoted by Lowell Mason who wrote instruction manuals for music teachers and persuaded the Boston public schools to introduce the subject into the system in the 1830's and 1840's. The idea spread to other cities, and later in the century the teacher-training institutions began to give special attention to it.

By the middle of the century some educators became interested in health and physical education, but acceptance was rather slow. The study of hygiene and physiology was promoted by the antialcohol and antitobacco interests. Physical education in the form of calisthenics, exercises, and playground activities began to appear in the 1850's and 1860's. In the last decade of the century medical examinations were instituted in the schools of Chicago, New York, and Philadelphia.

Secondary Education

The nineteenth century saw substantial shifts in the character and aims of secondary education. At the beginning of the century the academy was the dominating secondary institution, regularly offering classical departments for college preparation and "English departments" for non-college-preparatory purposes. As the century progressed, the academies began to put much greater stress upon the college-preparatory subjects of the classical departments, with a consequent emphasis upon religious-moral and disciplinary aims.

Meanwhile, the original intention of the public high school had been to provide practical and non-college-preparatory studies. In the latter decades of the century it began to expand its offerings to include the college-preparatory as well as the non-college-preparatory functions. The public high school therefore often developed classical courses, English and historical courses, scientific courses, commercial and business courses, technical and industrial-arts courses, and home-economics courses. By the end of the century the religious-moral aim was being challenged by more secular aims. Disciplinary and Humanistic ideals died hard because of the needs of college preparation, but they were often overshadowed by the informational, social-civic, vocational and practical, and individual-development aims.

These changes reflected the cultural patterns of a society in which religious and Humanistic traditions were being confronted by the secular trends of democracy, nationalism, science and technology, industrialism, and capitalism. The inherited European conceptions of an aristocratic, religious, and Humanistic secondary education were losing ground to the democratic and secular forces that looked toward a secondary education for all American youth.

Not only were more boys going on to secondary school, but opportunities for girls expanded as a part of the new experiment in democratic secondary education. In the early nineteenth century this took the form of the "female academies" and "female seminaries" under the leadership of such reformers as Emma Willard, Catherine Beecher, and Mary Lyon. They had to fight the traditional social attitudes, which insisted that woman's place was in the home to rear children and care for a family and that women were inherently inferior intellectually to men. Despite these obstacles, girls' schools were established by Emma Willard at Troy, N.Y., in 1821, by Catherine Beecher at Hartford, Conn., in 1828, and by Mary Lyon at Mount Holyoke, Mass., in 1838.

With this much gained, the advancing political and social democracy of the time began to make it possible for the sphere of women's activities to be expanded to include business, industry, and the professions, especially teaching. When this happened, and as a corollary to it, girls were admitted to high schools on a coeducational basis. By the end of the century they showed their interest and abilities by going to high school in large numbers and soon excelling the boys in their studies. With such an enormously expanded clientele it is no wonder that the secondary schools had to expand their courses of study accordingly.

Expansion of the Secondary School Curriculum. Just as in the case of the elementary school, the basic fact in secondary education was the rapid increase in the number of studies and the length of time devoted to them in secondary schools. Although figures do not mean much because of the variation in the names of subjects, nevertheless it is probably true that at the beginning of the century 10 to 12 titles would have covered most of the subjects taught in the academies. By the end of the century a hundred titles would not have done the same for the high schools. Whatever the number, however, it is clear that by the end of the century no one student could expect to study even a small proportion of the subjects offered in a reasonably large high school. The development of the elective system was therefore a physical necessity. The closed and prescribed course of study that all students followed in common was no longer possible to maintain.

The addition to the curriculum of the new subjects pressing for admission, however, was not gained without great opposition from those who favored the traditional college-preparatory subjects. If the century is taken as a whole, including academies as well as high schools, it is certainly true that the college-preparatory subjects dominated the scene, as against the non-college-preparatory subjects. Within the college-preparatory subjects the preferred positions were given for the longest period of time to the foreign languages, mathematics, English, science, and social studies.

College-preparatory Studies. Foreign languages long held their preferred status, bulwarked as they were by the religious and Humanistic traditions which dominated the colleges and which insisted that language study provided the best preparation for college. For most of the century, foreign languages meant Latin, of course, and, to a lesser degree, Greek, which never made as much headway in the public high schools as it did in the academies. Despite great variety, the commonest Latin course included grammar in the first year and then Caesar's *Commentaries*, Cicero's *Orations*, and Vergil's *Aeneid* in the following years. From the 1880's onward, French and German struggled to gain a place of equality alongside Latin. Although this place was never fully admitted by the confirmed classicists, the modern languages had gained a firm foothold by the end of the century.

Mathematics stood with the foreign languages in importance, for it had the sanction not only of the religious and disciplinary traditions but also of the practical aim. Arithmetic was popular in the academies and high schools, but it eventually came to be an elementary school subject. Algebra and geometry became the most widely taught mathematical studies in the secondary schools. Both the college-preparatory and the non-college-preparatory emphasis laid claim to the importance of algebra and geometry. For disciplinary purposes, it was argued that the memorizing of definitions, axioms, rules, and equations was unparalleled in respect to logical organization and difficulty as a means of training the mental faculties. For practical purposes, it was easy to argue that the knowledge of algebra and geometry was essential for the study of navigation, surveying, and the whole range of technical and scientific studies that supported the developing industrial society of the later nineteenth century. Trigonometry, mensuration, and astronomy also were taught in some secondary schools.

The various scientific studies showed a steady gain throughout most of the century. "Natural philosophy" rode to popularity on the wave of enthusiasm for scientific and useful knowledge that arose in the early decades of the century, and it was supported by the informational and practical aims. In the latter part of the century the great advances in physical science gave further impetus to the teaching of physics and chemistry, which were made into logically organized bodies of subject matter in order to prove that their disciplinary values were equal or even superior to those of the classics. To a lesser extent, physical geography, geology, and mineralogy also received some attention.

What had been known simply as "natural history" in the academies and early high schools gradually became known as biology; or it was divided into botany, for the study and classification of plants, and zoology, for the study of the structure of animal life. Early teaching of natural history proclaimed that it revealed the divine plan on earth and was thus supported by the religious aim as well as the informational and practical; but as the implications of evolution aroused bitter conflicts between religion and science, the teaching of biology became more secular in emphasis. The attempt was made to organize it as logically as the other disciplinary subjects in order to claim for it disciplinary values, but it never could quite compete with physics in this respect. After the middle of the century physiology gained some headway as a result of Darwinism and the reformers' attacks upon the use of alcohol and tobacco.

The increased study of the English language arts was also one of the most important developments in the secondary school curriculum. At the beginning of the century the study of English was definitely in an inferior position. The Latin grammar schools had paid little attention to it. Although the academies had begun to give it much greater attention, the classical departments in many academies so dominated the scene that "English courses" were definitely considered to be inferior and principally designed for those unable to follow the classical course. However, the democratic and nationalistic trend in American life greatly helped to promote the study of English. Claims for larger attention rested upon its social and civic, practical, and individual (leisure) values. These were the common arguments for non-college-preparatory studies in the early part of the century, but the disciplinary argument was soon adopted in favor of English to justify its recognition as a college-preparatory subject.

Grammar was the commonest form of English to be taught, but soon more and more attention was given to English composition, rhetoric, declamation and forensics, logic, and English literature. Proponents of English literature tried to maintain that it was as valuable for discipline as classical literature, a point that the classicists would never admit. When American literature gained some standing, the argument between the values of English and American authors ensued. To the end of the century, English authors far outweighed American in the time and attention given to them in the high schools.

The social studies likewise started the century in an inferior position but improved in their status throughout the country. History was promoted first by the religious-moral, informational, social-civic, and practical aims and was thus largely a non-college-preparatory subject. It was also justified in the latter part of the century on disciplinary grounds, but its claims could never be fully established. Ancient history received a high proportion of time in comparison with modern European history, a fact that reflected the classical and Humanistic tradition.

European history often outweighed American history, although the growing nationalism of the nineteenth century stimulated the study of American history for patriotic and Americanization purposes. As more texts on American history were written and as the states began to require its teaching, American history began to be accepted for college entrance in the last decades of the century. Most of the content of history textbooks was political and military in nature, relatively little attention being given to social or cultural history.

Geography was also popular, especially in the first year of high school, and was increasingly accepted for college entrance. It was largely informational and descriptive in content, stressing the location of rivers, mountains, cities, and states. Some attention, too, was given to "moral and political philosophy," governmental and constitutional forms, civics, and political economy. These studies were stimulated especially by the informational and social-civic aims, which received their impetus from the democratic and nationalistic elements in American society and which saw a need for citizenship training among the youth of the nation.

Non-college-preparatory Studies. The other studies that entered the secondary school curriculum did so as non-college-preparatory subjects. They remained virtually in that inferior position throughout the century. Industrial arts, home economics, commercial studies, and agriculture received their prime impetus from vocational and practical aims. Others, such as the arts and physical education, were stimulated principally by the values of individual development. In general, the so-called "vocational studies" received attention, in the middle of the century, in private institutions outside of the public high schools and then were gradually admitted to the expanded high schools or to special vocational high schools.

In the early part of the century the manual-labor movement, stemming from Pestalozzi and Fellenberg in Europe, gained wide popularity in the United States. The idea was sponsored by such men as William McClure and Joseph Neef, who organized the Manual Labor Society for Promoting Manual Labor in Literary Institutions in 1831. Many academies took up the idea and tried to combine farming or industrial work with regular study. The character-forming aim, as well as the social and practical aims, was set forth by the manual-labor enthusiasts. They saw in the idea a chance for students to engage in useful work that would help them to pay the cost of schooling while developing habits of democratic cooperation, independence, health, and industry. The strength of the academic tradition was too great, however, and the movement declined rapidly in the 1850's. It was important principally as indicating a temper among the people that was gradually to force secondary education to take account of it.

More influential in American secondary education was the manual-training movement, which became popular in the latter part of the century. It had two principal phases. It started out along Pestalozzian lines to give exercise to the motor skills, along with intellectual and moral training. It gave high place to the individual aims of self-development through sensory activities and was even justified because of its disciplinary values. In the last two decades of the century the motive changed, however, to absorb more fully the practical and vocational aim, as businessmen and manufacturers saw the values in such work for training boys and girls to become better prepared for jobs in industry.

President John D. Runkle of the Massachusetts Institute of Technology was impressed by the manual-training exhibit of Finnish, Russian, and Swedish students on display at the Philadelphia Centennial Exposition. He urged that similar work be done in the high schools of the United States. High schools for manual training were established at the Massachusetts Institute of Technology, Washington University in St. Louis, and elsewhere in connection with universities and public school systems. In 1895 Massachusetts required manual training to be taught in the high schools of all cities of 30,000 or more in population. Typical subjects in manual-training courses and manual-training high schools were woodworking, clay modeling, iron forging, foundry and sheet-metal work, machine-shop work, and mechanical drawing. Drawing was stimulated both by the individual-development ideal as a means of expression and also by the practical desires of industry and business to make it useful for occupational training.

Home economics, or domestic science, has had a longer history in the United States than manual training, tracing back to the time of Emma Willard, Catherine Beecher, Harriet Beecher Stowe, and Ellen H. Richards. It also was the victim of conflicting desires among its proponents. Some wanted to make it scientific and disciplinary, accompanied by a thorough study of physics and chemistry and biology. Others wanted to make it a useful and practical training for the family duties of girls. Home economics was cited by some of the progressive educators of the day as a helpful and practical activity to supplement intellectual studies as, for example, in John Dewey's school at the University of Chicago and in the Horace Mann School at Teachers College in New York. It also was looked upon as a vocational course for girls somewhat parallel to manual training for boys. It entered the manual-training high schools in the form of sewing, dressmaking, millinery, and home management.

Commercial studies became increasingly important from the vocational and practical standpoint as American business and industry expanded in the nineteenth century. Some academies and early high schools taught bookkeeping, penmanship, and commercial arithmetic, but shortly after the Civil War a great boom was given to commercial subjects by the private business colleges that sprang up in virtually all cities of any size by the end of the century. Commercial studies began to be offered on a large scale in the high schools during the last two decades of the century, and by the end of the century several commercial high schools had been established in New York, Philadelphia, Pittsburgh, Washington, D.C., and elsewhere.

Interest finally turned to agriculture, which somehow seemed to many to be the farthest removed from the college-preparatory ideal and therefore the lowest in the scale of intellectual pursuits. Through the efforts principally of the land-grant colleges, about a dozen agricultural high schools had been established by the end of the century.

Music, art, and physical education fared scarcely better than the most "practical" of the vocational studies, for they had only the aim of individual development to justify them. They were not even vocationally useful. Music and art could not qualify under the religious-moral, disciplinary, informational, or civic ideals. Indeed, many thought of them as dilettante studies perhaps suitable for girls but generally wasteful of the taxpayers' money. They remained on the fringe of an American culture that glorified success in the economic and business world.

Physical education prospered somewhat more because it had the backing of interest in health and physical activity, which could more easily be understood and accepted. New ideas of physical training, exercise, and calisthenics came in from Germany, Sweden, and France to stimulate the interest in gymnastics. By the 1880's and 1890's many city school systems were developing programs in physical training along the rather formal lines of German and Swedish exercises. Although an increasing number of high schools offered music, art, and physical training, the general estimate of their academic standing is shown by the fact that they seldom carried credit for high school graduation and therefore almost never carried credit for entrance to college.

Standardization of the High School Curriculum. It soon became clear that the persons who were most concerned about the expansion of the high school curriculum were the college educators. They saw utter confusion developing in the high schools, which apparently were bound to teach anything to anyone. When these high school graduates began knocking at the doors of the colleges for admission, what were they to do? It was one thing when the colleges could count upon most secondary school graduates having studied the classics and mathematics; it was disturbing when they began to study science, English, and the social studies; but when they began to offer manual training or home economics, the colleges felt that the line had to be drawn.

The high schools became more interested in offering a wide and flexible course of study to their students as they admitted an ever higher proportion of youth of high school age. The colleges, on the other hand, were interested in having students come to them with a more uniform background of subject matter. The best way to remedy the situation from the point of view of the colleges was to bring order into the high schools by standardizing the high school curriculum for those who wished to go to college. This they set out to do in the way they knew best, by working through college-entrance requirements.

Some steps were taken before the problem became too acute when separate colleges began the process of accrediting certain high schools. Under the leadership of President James Burrill Angell, the University of Michigan in 1871 established a commission to inspect the high schools of the state and evaluate the quality of teaching, character of the curriculum, and standards achieved by the students. If the high school met the approval of the commission, its graduates were to be admitted to the university without further examination. By the end of the century some 200 colleges and universities were using some form of this accrediting device.

It soon became apparent, however, that students were going to cross state lines to go to college. The accrediting system was therefore not broad enough. Consequently, regional standardizing agencies were developed in order to arrive at understandings among groups of colleges and secondary schools concerning the standards of achievement to be met by the secondary schools if they wanted their graduates to be admitted easily to college.

By the end of the century most of the country was covered by the following agencies: the New England Association of Colleges and Preparatory Schools (1885), the Association of Colleges and Preparatory Schools of the Middle States and Maryland (1892), the North Central Association of Colleges and Preparatory Schools (1894), the Association of Colleges and Preparatory Schools of the Southern States (1895), and the College Entrance Examination Board (1899). These associations did much to improve the standards of secondary schools in the direction that the colleges wanted to see them go. They served to bulwark the college-preparatory idea in high schools, but the standardizing process was still not on a national scale. To this problem the National Education Association turned its attention in the 1890's in two very influential reports.

The Committee of Ten on Secondary School Subjects was appointed under the chairmanship of President Charles William Eliot of Harvard in 1892, and its report was published in 1893. The Committee of Ten consisted of seven college presidents or professors and three secondary school educators. It appointed nine subcommittees to consider the following subject-matter fields in detail: (1) Latin; (2) Greek; (3) English; (4) other modern languages (French and German); (5) mathematics; (6) physics, chemistry, and astronomy; (7) natural history (botany, zoology, and physiology); (8) history, civil government, and political economy; (9) geography (physical geography, geology, and meteorology). Most of the members of the subcommittees were likewise college presidents or professors, with a sprinkling of secondary school administrators and a very few teachers. The subjects to be treated by the subcommittees revealed what the Committee of Ten believed were appropriate secondary school subjects, namely, college-preparatory studies.

The recommendations of the Committee of Ten are interesting as revealing principally a disciplinary, informational, and subject-matter outlook on education, with an occasional acknowledgment of the moral and social aims. It was recommended that all subjects should be started earlier and studied longer than was presently the case. Only the Latin and Greek committees were apparently satisfied with the amount of time given to their subjects. It was also recommended that all subjects should be considered as equivalent in value. No matter what subjects a student took he would have had 4 years of strong and effective mental training. Further, there should be no distinction made between those students intending to go to college and those not so intending.

Despite these protestations concerning equivalence of studies, the committee showed its bias in favor of language study when it recommended four types of model courses, all of which required foreign languages. The classical course was to include three foreign languages (two ancient and one modern); the English-classical course, two foreign languages (one ancient and one modern); the modern language course, two modern languages; and the scientific course, one foreign language.

In a similar vein the Committee on College Entrance Requirements in its report of 1899 gave its stamp of approval to the following college-preparatory subjects: Latin, Greek, French, German, English, history, civics and economics, geography, mathematics, biology, and chemistry. The length of time a subject was studied in high school became as important as what was studied. If a student went to class for 4 hours a week for a year, this work was to be counted as a unit, acceptable to the colleges for admission and equal to any other college-entrance subject. Although the committee approved the elective system, realizing that students could not take all the courses offered in high school, prejudice was shown again in favor of the foreign languages when it recommended that certain constants should be in every college entrant's program, namely, 4 years, or units, of foreign language, 2 years of mathematics, 2 years of English, 1 year of history, and 1 year of science.

Apparently, in the view of the colleges, foreign languages were twice as important as English and mathematics and four times as important as history and science. Likewise, English and mathematics were twice as important as history and science. Although the committee stated that it hoped that the secondary school curriculum would be flexible and practical as well as disciplinary, its real reliance upon the disciplinary and Humanistic tradition was all too clear in its recommended units. It protested that all subjects were equal in value if studied an equal amount of time, but it obviously believed that some studies were more valuable than others.

Despite the standardizing movement and the quantitative arrangements that had been devised for judging college entrance, the underlying problems of a common general education for all American youth had not genuinely been faced.

Higher Education

Some of the cultural forces that helped to bring about fundamental changes in the character of American higher education were as follows: the gradual substitution of secular for religious authority in the political, social, and intellectual activities of life; the growth of commerce and industry and of a corresponding acquisitive spirit; the enormous expansion of systematized knowledge, particularly in the physical and social sciences; the advance of democracy and of the idea of individual freedom; and the growth of the concept of naturalism and of the innate worth of individuals. One of the most important changes wrought by these factors was the decline of the prescribed curriculum and the acceptance of the elective system of studies. In this process a new conception of a liberal education emerged. As a result, the long-standing religious-moral and disciplinary aims were challenged by the newer informational, social-civic, practical, and individual aims of education.

Reform in the Early Nineteenth Century. Secular ideas were strongly injected into American higher education through the efforts of Thomas Jefferson, who was instrumental in the founding of the University of Virginia. In his plans for the University of Virginia in 1818, Jefferson desired that all subjects useful to modern times should be taught. The sciences, history, politics, and the modern languages should be put on an equality with the classics, mathematics, and philosophy. He also wished the university to train for political leadership as well as for practical, scientific, and scholarly pursuits. Jefferson's plans for college reform were important for the development of American higher education, for he enunciated the doctrines that the university should be conceived on a large scale, should be supported by the state and free from sectarian control, and should allow the student freedom to prepare himself for whatever future position he desired.

Also influential was the work of George Ticknor, who brought to Harvard in 1819 German ideals of advanced scholarship and of freedom for teacher and learner. Ticknor set out to break up the prescribed curriculum and substitute election of studies and methods of thorough scholarship. His justification for these reforms was that Harvard must meet the demands of the community for a useful education in scientific, technical, and mechanical studies and must meet the competition of rising technical schools. He further supported his plans by showing that the prescribed studies had been so extended by the addition of new fields of knowledge that a student could not study all of them without sacrificing scholarship; for proper learning the studies should be more adapted to the capacities, interests, and future pursuits of the students.

These goals for higher education, however, did not by any means go unchallenged in the 1820's and 1830's. Perhaps the most influential and comprehensive statement of the opposing position was made by the faculty of Yale in its famous report of 1828 (see page 477). Yale defended the ideal of religious and mental discipline through a narrow prescribed curriculum of classical studies as the best means of liberal education. Yale became a sort of champion for the conservative ideal of college education as Harvard was for the progressive ideal.

The currents of unrest, however, were strong, and many colleges took steps toward various kinds of reform. Some of the plans were abortive and, in the face of determined opposition, amounted to little more than a statement drawn up by a board of trustees or a report written by a few progressive faculty members. Other plans were tried halfheartedly for a few years and then given up. Still others served as springboards for further development when the time was ripe after the Civil War. Three responses to the demands for curriculum change took place in the first half of the century.

1. Parallel courses. The most common kind of effort to reform the college curriculum was to set up entirely separate courses, parallel to the prescribed classical course. Thus, the integrity of the classical course could be retained, and the B.A. degree would remain unimpaired, but there would still be a chance for students to get an education in the

"scientific" or "literary" course. In these new parallel courses, the classical studies were either diminished, or they entirely disappeared to make way for the physical and biological sciences, English and modern languages, and social sciences.

In this way, there were attempts in some colleges to make concessions to the "practical" needs of the times; but, in most educational and religious circles, the traditional classical course was still looked upon as the only true route to a genuine liberal education. The new courses did not usually set such high standards for admission as did the classical course; that is, they did not require as much Latin or Greek. They were allowed to grant, not the bachelor-of-arts degree, which was jealously reserved for the classical course, but only a diploma or, later, such new degrees as the bachelor of science, bachelor of philosophy, and bachelor of letters. This multiplication of courses and degrees became one of the most characteristic features of American colleges.

2. Independent technical schools. One very compelling reason why the colleges became interested in scientific and practical courses was the beginning of technological education on a high level as represented in the founding of Rensselaer Polytechnic Institute, Worcester Polytechnic Institute, and Massachusetts Institute of Technology.

Stephen Van Rensselaer, for example, established his school in 1824 with the purpose of " . . . affording an opportunity to the farmer, the mechanic, the clergyman, the lawyer, the physician, the merchant, and in short, to the man of business or of leisure, of any calling whatever, to become practically scientific." It was emphasized that students would not only receive literary exercises but also would be given proper development of manual abilities by appropriate muscular exercises. In this way, the student was to become familiar with the most important scientific manipulations and "particularly with those which will be most useful in the common concerns of life." Here was a direct menace to and a source of keen competition for the literary colleges.

3. Affiliated scientific schools. A few of the older colleges attempted to meet the competition and to silence the cries of the reformers by establishing "schools of science" separate from the regular college. In this way, the college could retain its classical emphasis and give the traditional training to those students who wished to become clergymen, teachers, scholars, or merely "cultured" persons, whereas the scientific school could give a training to those who were intended for leadership in business or industry. Such were Sheffield Scientific School at Yale, Lawrence Scientific School at Harvard, Chandler School of Science at Dartmouth, and others at Princeton, Pennsylvania, Columbia, and elsewhere.

University Reform in the Later Nineteenth Century. The most effective theory of higher education in the middle of the nineteenth century was formulated by President Francis Wayland of Brown University. He advocated making Brown into a real university by offering courses in all the major branches of knowledge and by devising new courses to meet the mechanical, agricultural, and industrial needs of the people. He saw that the curriculum was too crowded to justify requiring students to cover the whole round of studies and that the college must adapt itself to meet the needs of all classes of society or lose essential patronage to the technical schools.

Another outstanding proponent of the idea of creating a genuine university and allowing election of studies was Henry Tappan at the University of Michigan. Taking inspiration from the German universities, Tappan argued that a university must be secular and supported by the state in order to be able to offer courses in all the subjects of human knowledge, to ensure freedom of research and of study, and to adapt itself properly to the needs of the state. Furthermore, it should be the crown of a complete state system of schools.

Above all, the most influential spokesman for adapting the American college to the modern forces of a scientific age was President Charles William Eliot at Harvard. By virtue of his public utterances, of actually changing Harvard's curriculum, and of his ability to secure funds to carry out his ideas, Eliot for 40 years was preeminent in the leadership of higher education and the development of the elective system in the United States. He strove to make of Harvard a university in which all the branches of modern knowledge could be taught and investigated. He expanded the notion of a liberal education as represented by the B.A. degree to include, on a level with the older studies, the modern subjects of English, French, German, history, economics, politics, and the physical sciences.

Eliot advocated a greater freedom for students in all phases of university life—freedom through the elective system and freedom to govern themselves in order to develop a sense of responsibility and self-reliance. He urged a greater recognition of the individual nature of students in order that they might develop adequately according to their particular needs, interests, and abilities. The better students should be allowed to progress at their own rate and to finish the college course in 3 years, if they desired, by using the elective system. The idea of accelerated programs of study was born with the elective system. Eliot opened the doors of Harvard to the demand for greater specialized, technical, and professional training.

Other prominent advocates of university reform were Andrew Dickson White at Cornell, Frederick A. P. Barnard at Columbia, Daniel Coit Gilman at Johns Hopkins, David Starr Jordan at Leland Stanford, and William Rainey Harper at Chicago. Influenced by Prussian examples and by the University of Michigan, President White's theories for Cornell embodied the close union of liberal and practical studies in a nonsectarian institution in close relationship with the state school system. Consequently, a greater emphasis was put upon modern languages and historical and scientific studies, with a corresponding freedom of election for the student. Combined with White's leadership was the desire of Ezra Cornell and the intention of the Morrill Act to promote agricultural and mechanical subjects that would appeal particularly to the farming and industrial classes of society.

Impressed by the phenomenal success of Harvard, Michigan, and Cornell in attracting students, President Barnard at Columbia reversed his earlier opposition to the elective system and advocated it as the best means of placing Columbia alongside these more progressive higher institutions. He was frank to admit that popular judgment of college studies must be the criterion of their value, regardless of what educators thought of that judgment.

At Johns Hopkins, President Gilman provided seven different undergraduate courses all leading to the B.A. degree and thus fully admitted the new subjects to a level of equality with classical studies in the acquisition of a liberal education. At Leland Stanford, President Jordan set out to give students any specialized courses they desired, but he also required students to concentrate on a "major" subject in the last 2 years of college besides taking a number of electives. At Chicago, President Harper set up a junior college, for those who desired or could afford to study for only 2 years, and a senior college in which a large amount of election was allowed.

Opposed to such reforms was a large group of conservative college educators, represented especially by Noah Porter of Yale and James McCosh and Andrew West of Princeton, who defended the traditional college. They advocated retaining the prescribed curriculum with its limited number of studies, its mental discipline, its emphasis upon classical and mathematical studies, its opposition to specialized, technical, and professional subjects, its idea of close supervision of student life and morals, and its dominating religious tone. They argued that a liberal education was best promoted by continuing these conditions of college life.

General Trends in Higher Education. In spite of the efforts of the conservative groups, the character of colleges and universities began to change during the nineteenth century in the following identifiable ways:

1. The narrowly prescribed curriculum of a few subjects gave way to an elective curriculum of many subjects.

2. The conception of a liberal education (as represented by the B.A. degree) was widened to include on an equality with the traditional sub-

jects such new studies as English, the modern languages, the physical sciences, and the social sciences.

3. The ideal of the small undergraduate college began to lose ground in favor of the German ideal of a large university where research as well as instruction in the major branches of knowledge could be carried on. The lecture and laboratory began to encroach upon classroom recitation as methods of instruction.

4. The so-called "cultural" studies (classics, mathematics, and philosophy), which had long monopolized the prescribed curriculum, now had to make way for scientific and technical subjects (the so-called "practical" studies), which were useful as a preparation for specialized careers in the professions or in business, industry, or the academic world. Specialization in the graduate courses required more and more specialization in undergraduate courses.

5. The notion of mental discipline, or development of "intellectual power," through the study of the ancient classics and mathematics gave way to the notion that knowledge of subjects especially appropriate to each individual was a proper aim of college education. The practice of treating all students alike in the learning process gave way to the increasing attempt to provide for differing interests, abilities, and future occupations of different individuals.

6. The religious tone of college education began to yield to an increasing secularism as a result of a curriculum in which the secular aim to prepare for citizenship and an occupation was paramount.

7. The close and strict supervision of all phases of student life by the college administration began to weaken in favor of a greater freedom for the student to develop his own sense of responsibility and self-reliance.

8. The aristocratic nature of higher education as represented in the scarcity value of a college degree began to give way to the democratic notion that college education should be open to all classes of society and should try to develop civic responsiblity and social understanding as well as occupational efficiency among the majority of young men and women.

The democratic movement in higher education offered greater educational opportunities for women at the college level. In the East this took the form principally of separate colleges for women, such as Vassar, Wellesley, Smith, Mount Holyoke, and Bryn Mawr. Other women's colleges were established as semi-independent institutions affiliated with large universities, notably Barnard at Columbia, Radcliffe at Harvard, and Sophie Newcomb at Tulane. In the West the more common provision for women was in the form of coeducation. Oberlin was established in the 1830's on the basis of sex equality for women and race equality for Negroes. In the 1850's and later, coeducation appeared at Antioch and at other private colleges, but principally at such state universities as Utah, Michigan, Ohio, and Wisconsin.

Technical and professional education in the universities not only gave greater attention to the long-established professions of law, medicine, and theology, but also began to give some recognition to the newer occupational fields that were struggling to become full-fledged professions. Among these were agriculture, business, journalism, architecture, library science, and the various professional aspects of teaching and education.

Chapter 16

AMERICA IN THE TWENTIETH CENTURY:
SCHOOL AND SOCIETY

THE SEARCH FOR SECURITY

American education in the twentieth century was affected by a wide range of social outlooks as well as by the institutional forces to be described in this chapter. Many of these ideas paralleled the points of view discussed earlier (see pages 338 to 345). They provoked fundamental controversies that were in turn reflected in education. Although a detailed analysis of such points of view cannot be undertaken here, something of the range of outlook can be suggested.

Social Ideas

Four or five general social outlooks were proposed to the American people at various times during the twentieth century as programs for political and economic action. They might be identified as traditional conservatism, humanitarianism, socialism, communism, and fascism.

The conservative position held rather closely to the historic ideals of individualistic and laissez-faire liberalism as developed in the eighteenth and nineteenth centuries. In general, this position affirmed that the principles of traditional capitalism and free enterprise were basically sound and that public welfare would best be served by releasing business and industry from government control and regulation. Conservative spokesmen laid the blame for the depression of the middle 1930's upon the restrictive policies of the New Deal that caused business to lose confidence and profits because of the interference of government. Their principal program was to keep the government out of business but to use it as an umpire to ensure free competition and to restrain monopoly in the interests of freedom for individual enterprise. Democracy to them meant the reaffirmation of capitalism and the profit system with a minimum of government planning, which could only lead, if unchecked, to regimentation and the destruction of freedom. In their view the basic character of American society was sound. The principal support for this position seemed to come from the Republican party, the wealthy and upper middle classes, and a large number of small businessmen and farmers.

512

A more aggressive outlook toward liberal reform was taken by an increasing number of persons, whose ideas stemmed from the humanitarian and social trends of eighteenth- and nineteenth-century liberalism. The outlook was represented principally by the New Deal of President Roosevelt and the Fair Deal of President Truman in the Democratic party. In general, according to this position, capitalism needed drastic reforms in order to make it appropriate to the changed conditions of industrial society. The proponents of this view set out to expand the powers of government to regulate business and monopoly practices, increase the buying power of the people, and ensure the social security and welfare of larger numbers of people. Cooperation of government, business, labor, and consumer in planning economic affairs became a fundamental principle of action and was considered to be an authentic embracing of the democratic ideal. In general, the liberal reformers felt that historic capitalism must be reconstructed if it were to weather the political and economic storms of the twentieth century. This position drew its support principally from lower-middle-class groups, labor, small business, farmers, and liberal intellectuals. It was agreed that collective action was necessary, but that it could and must be carried on within the framework of political democracy.

The socialist and communist orientations stemmed from a Marxist view, which held that capitalism is basically a sick economy in which the profit motive prevents a fair distribution of the goods of the world. Therefore, capitalism must be done away with, and state control must substitute for private enterprise a nonprofit, planned economy. The present state is simply an instrument of control by which the capitalist groups maintain themselves in power. Advocates of this orientation split on fundamental methods of procedure. The Socialist party under men like Norman Thomas insisted that the forms of political democracy should be used in both short- and long-range efforts. Power should be won by constitutional methods of voting, and owners should be compensated fairly when the basic industries were taken over by the government. The Communist party under Earl Browder and later William Z. Foster believed rather that power should be seized by force in a crisis. The government should be in the hands of a dictatorship of the Communist party in the short range until such time as genuine democracy could be achieved in the classless society of the longer-range future.

The Socialists and Communists split sharply over the war policies of the United States. Many Socialists maintained a pacifist and isolationist policy on the ground that any war was a bad war. The Communists opposed the Second World War as an imperialist war until Soviet Russia was attacked and then supported America's participation as a world war against fascism. The American Communist party in general followed the policy that a world communist order must be built around support for the Soviet Union.

Fascism, of course, held that the whole notion of a democratic and liberal society was false. Power should rest in the hands of an elite, who should attack with all means of violence and intrigue those who stood in the way, capitalists, labor unions, liberals, and communists. To gain strength from the underprivileged groups and to build a strong, disciplined, single party, attacks should be made upon Jews, Negroes, and other minority groups of various "foreign" nationalities. The fascist doctrines of violence, force, and authoritarianism were openly expressed by only a few American intellectuals, notably Lawrence Dennis; but, under the cover of other phraseology, fascist tendencies appeared in hate groups appealing to all classes of people from the wealthiest to the poorest. Wherever the principles and practices of democratic due process, freedom, and equality were undermined, there was fascism.

Political Trends

After 1900 impressive gains were made, despite opposition from conservative forces, in the direction of political reform and social legislation designed to promote the general welfare of the people. Although the gains may have seemed inadequate to some extremists, the character of political life in the 1950's showed enormous changes from that of 1900. What had been shouted down as radical or nonsensical in 1900 had become accepted principles of governmental responsibility by mid-century.

The trend toward more widespread social legislation was unmistakable, taking place more slowly under the Republicans and more rapidly under the Democrats. In general, the majority view in the Republican party was likely to represent conservatism and the majority view of the Democratic party humanitarianism (see pages 341 to 342). Protest votes recorded by various minor political parties reached their peak during Republican control early in the century and declined somewhat as the New Deal seemed to respond to the public desire for greater government participation in achieving a measure of economic and social welfare.

As business and industry grew in power and size, so did the power and regulatory controls of government. The trend toward greater authority for the federal government was the central political fact of the twentieth century. Controversies were waged hotly as to whether or not this was a desirable trend. Some, alarmed by totalitarian trends in Europe, declared that increased governmental authority was the inevitable "road to serfdom." Others believed that American ingenuity in social invention could make government, even big and powerful government, still more democratic than it was.

Reform Movements. When McKinley was reelected president in 1900, the Republicans had stood on their record of sound business achievement during the prior few years. When Theodore Roosevelt became president upon the assassination of McKinley in 1901, he aroused some enthusiasm among reformers for his "Square Deal" attacks upon trusts, his efforts to conserve the resources of the country under federal control, and his upholding of the rights of labor in the anthracite-coal strike of 1902. After William Howard Taft had won the election of 1908, he also attacked the trusts and supported the income-tax amendment to the Constitution. Despite such policies as these, however, the high tariff of 1909 and other measures led certain progressives under the leadership of the elder Senator Robert M. La Follette of Wisconsin to organize a revolt from the Republican party in the election of 1912.

In that year the Republicans renominated Taft, the Progressives nominated Roosevelt, and the Democrats put forward Woodrow Wilson. With the split among the Republicans, Wilson was elected; but the large vote for Roosevelt and votes of nearly a million for Eugene V. Debs on the Socialist ticket revealed a growing dissatisfaction with both major parties. Wilson immediately set out to expand social legislation in line with his doctrines of the "New Freedom." Further efforts were made to break up large trusts charged with restraint of trade, and the Federal Trade Commission was established in 1914, a recognition that the government should not allow unlimited competition and should regulate business and industry in the interests of the public welfare.

Meanwhile, the ferment of social reform during the first two decades of the twentieth century was being reflected on a broad front of social legislation in the various states. Many state legislatures passed laws regulating the hours of labor, safety and sanitary measures, compulsory accident-insurance and public-health measures, housing, public utilities, natural resources, income and inheritance taxes, old-age pensions, and benefits for widows and dependent children. In all these ways the conception was growing that democratic government had the right and obligation to prevent business practices that endangered the health and security of the people and to promote the general welfare by public regulation and control.

In addition to the expansion of the role of government, great gains were made in improving the political processes of democracy, by which control was put more directly into the hands of the people. This took the form of attack upon rule by party bosses and political caucuses. The Seventeenth Amendment to the Constitution was approved in 1913, providing for the direct election of senators by the people of the several states. By 1910 many states of the South and West required direct primary elections as the means by which candidates were chosen by the people of the respective parties.

The methods of balloting were reformed, and precautions were taken to ensure secrecy by the use of the Australian ballot and by voting machines. Voting rights for women met success in state after state, until finally the Nineteenth Amendment in 1920 gave equal suffrage to women throughout the country. These reforms did not, of course, entirely prevent party abuses; political bosses in the large cities learned new ways to "get out the votes," and the primaries of the Democratic party in the South (tantamount to election) excluded Negroes by various means. Despite many such imperfections, however, the elections of the 1950's were generally much more honest and representative of the genuine will of the people than elections had been in the nineteenth century.

Republican Normalcy. On a wave of dissatisfaction and unrest following the First World War the Democrats were swept out of national office, and the Republican candidates, Warren G. Harding and Calvin Coolidge, were elected. From 1920 to 1932, the Republicans remained in power, arguing that "normalcy" had returned under their leadership and that the greatest prosperity known to man was of their making. In general, big business and industry felt much freer to conduct their affairs without government control and regulation.

The general feeling of prosperity during the 1920's militated against continued proposals for social legislation, but some gains were made, sometimes with the support of and sometimes against the will or indifference of Coolidge and Hoover. Coolidge favored an amendment abolishing child labor, but he opposed extension of the income and inheritance taxes, government ownership of Muscle Shoals, and aid to farmers.

Hoover favored an agricultural marketing bill to give relief to farmers, and labor was reinforced in its struggle for collective bargaining by the anti-injunction law of 1932 under the leadership of Senator George W. Norris and Representative Fiorello H. La Guardia, both Republicans. When the crash of 1929 occurred, Hoover foresaw "prosperity just around the corner" but gradually took steps to meet the depression by proposing a public works program, loans to large business and industrial concerns, and loans to property owners. The depression became so acute, however, that the voters were dissatisfied with Republican attempts to stem the tide and elected Franklin D. Roosevelt and the Democratic party by an overwhelming majority in 1932.

The New Deal and the Fair Deal. For over 12 years President Roosevelt remained in office, smashing all traditions against a third term and achieving the unparalleled distinction of being elected for a fourth term. Taking office in the dark days of March, 1933, with most of the major banks in the country closed, President Roosevelt set out to restore confidence, relieve suffering, prime the pump of business, and move toward social reform on a broad front. Many of the steps the New Deal took were not new, but they were taken so rapidly and vigorously that enormous changes occurred between 1933 and the beginning of the Second World War. Only some of the high lights can be mentioned here.

Extensive measures for control and regulation of the banking, credit, and currency structure of the nation were instituted to prevent bank failures and fluctuations in the values of money and to protect the funds of bank depositors. Vast sums were loaned to all sorts of institutions and individuals. Many and varied efforts were made to stimulate employment and regulate prices and production of goods, stocks and bonds, and public utilities.

The attack on unemployment took the form not only of pump priming by loans to business but also of direct aid to less privileged Americans in an effort to restore the buying power of the people and thus stimulate production. The Federal Emergency Relief Administration helped states to meet their ever-mounting relief rolls; the Civilian Conservation Corps and the National Youth Administration provided jobs and training for youths; the Civilian Works Administration subsidized many kinds of temporary service jobs; the Public Works Administration stimulated public building programs; and the Works Progress Administration gave a variety of jobs to millions of unemployed. New conceptions of public planning on a broad scale were carried out by the Tennessee Valley Authority, the Soil Conservation Service, the Rural Electrification Administration, the Resettlement Administration, and the National Housing Agency. Direct aid to the unfortunate and the principle of a minimum of security below which the government would not allow persons to go were involved in the Social Security Act, which provided a wide range of benefits for the unemployed, the dependent, the handicapped, and the aged.

Encouragement to organized labor was given by the National Labor Relations Act which created the National Labor Relations Board to enforce the principles and practices of collective bargaining. For unorganized labor the Wages and Hours Act set minimum wages of 40 cents an hour and a maximum of 40 hours a week in many enterprises. Despite much opposition, the major elements of the New Deal program seem to have been the kind of solution to the problem of the critical depression years that enlisted the support of the majority of Americans.

In 1943 the National Resources Planning Board, appointed by President Roosevelt, presented its postwar program for extending social security, social service, and full employment. Although it met the hostility of conservative members of Congress and although the board itself ceased to exist because the House of Representatives refused to appropriate funds for its continuance, the "new bill of rights" that it constituted met a ready response among socially minded persons who felt government and private enterpise should cooperate to achieve a fuller life for all the people. The board's program included the following points:

(1) *The right to work*, usefully and creatively through the productive years;

(2) *The right to fair pay*, adequate to command the necessities and amenities of life in exchange for work, ideas, thrift, and other socially valuable service;

(3) *The right to adequate food, clothing, shelter, and medical care;*

(4) *The right to security*, with freedom from fear of old age, want, dependency, sickness, unemployment, and accident;

(5) *The right to live in a system of free enterprise*, free from compulsory labor, irresponsible private power, arbitrary public authority, and unregulated monopolies;

(6) *The right to come and go, to speak or to be silent*, free from the spying of secret political police;

(7) *The right to equality before the law*, with equal access to justice in fact;

(8) *The right to education*, for work, for citizenship, and for personal growth and happiness;

(9) *The right to rest, recreation, and adventure*, the opportunity to enjoy life and take part in an advancing civilization.

Upon the sudden death of President Roosevelt in April, 1945, and the end of the war against Germany and Japan, President Harry S. Truman promptly outlined his plans for removing wartime controls and at the same time speeding reconversion and extending social legislation, largely in the framework of the New Deal. During the remainder of his first term and after his reelection in 1948, President Truman's proposals for his Fair Deal program quite consistently included the following points: a federally supported program of unemployment compensation; an increase in minimum wage standards; "full employment" regulations, according to which government public works would be developed if private enterprise did not provide jobs for all; creation of a permanent Fair Employment Practices Commission to prevent racial and religious discrimination by employers and labor unions; support for farm prices and a crop-insurance program; compulsory military service; a federal slum-clearance program and federal aid in building millions of new homes; liberal provisions for the medical care, education, and rehabilitation of veterans; a large program for conservation of natural resources; and extensive federal programs for health insurance, social security, and federal aid to education. Despite the difficulties that this broad program ran into, it pointed to the need for the federal government to be squarely in the middle of the process of creating a better life for Americans.

The New Republican Conservatism. With the election of General Dwight D. Eisenhower as president in 1952 many signs pointed to the intention of the new Republican administration to reduce the role of the federal government in American political and economic life and to elevate the role of business and industry. Prominent businessmen with little political experience were brought into top government posts, career civil servants and diplomats were retired, and thousands of employees were dropped from the federal payrolls. The federal budget was cut, taxes were cut, and labor felt that it had few friends in the government. Vast offshore oil lands were given over to state control. Educators had hoped that Senator Lister Hill's amendment would be passed to authorize the federal government to retain control of the coastal oil lands and use the revenues from them for federal aid to education, but this proposal was killed in the early days of the new Republican Congress in 1953.

During the first half of President Eisenhower's administration his legislative program was overshadowed by internal struggles for the control of the Republican party. The Republican campaign of 1952 had hammered away on the theme that the Democrats were no longer entitled to govern because they were responsible for war in Korea, corruption in Washington, and communism in government. An early truce in Korea gave the Republicans a chance to claim credit for this part of their campaign promises, but the other two issues continued to plague and divide the Republican party. The quarrels between Senator Joseph R. McCarthy of Wisconsin and the administration boiled over into open conflict between the Department of the Army and the McCarthy forces.

For many months the president's legislative program was bogged down over the issue of McCarthyism, as legislative investigations tried to find communists in the State Department, the overseas information service, the armed forces, defense industries, schools, colleges, the press, the clergy, and philanthropic foundations. The year 1953 was called the "Year of Accusation." In 1954 the country was treated to the spectacle of an investigation into the charges and countercharges over the role of Senator McCarthy's investigative staff and then into the activities of Senator McCarthy himself. Educators were especially disturbed by the prevailing climate of fear, suspicion, and attacks upon freedom of thought and teaching that marked the first half of the first Republican administration in 20 years.

Contradictions in the American Economy

In the first 50 years of the twentieth century it became increasingly clear that certain great contradictions were appearing between the promises of nineteenth-century capitalism and actual practices in American economic life. Perhaps the most striking discrepancies had to do with production of goods and the distribution of incomes. Scientific studies made in the 1930's showed that even in 1929 the total productive powers of the country were operating at 20 to 30 per cent below capacity of the then existing production plant. In the depression year of 1932 production fell to 50 to 60 per cent of capacity.

Even more striking was the inequality in the distribution of incomes. Figures of the National Resources Committee for the year 1935–1936 showed that 27 per cent of American families received less than $750 a year; 42 per cent, less than $1,000 a year; 64 per cent, less than $1,500 a year; 83 per cent, less than $2,000 a year; and 91 per cent, less than $3,000 a year. Not only was "one-third of a nation ill-housed, ill-clothed, and ill-fed," but the concentration of income in the higher brackets was astonishing. Three per cent of the families at the top of the scale received an aggregate income about equal to that of the lowest 50 per cent. One per cent at the top received almost as much as 40 per cent at the bottom. It seemed clear that there was "widespread poverty in the midst of potential plenty."

Incomes and production, however, jumped tremendously between the two World Wars. The proportion of total national income that went to the few at the top was declining. Between 1920 and 1944 the number of employed workers increased from 42,000,000 to 63,000,000, and the total national income more than doubled as it rose from 48 billion dollars to 121 billion dollars. Much of this was made possible by the enormous improvement of industrial techniques and mass production. While the average of weekly hours of work dropped from nearly 60 hours in 1920 to 46 hours in 1944, the net output per man-hour almost doubled. These achievements proved that high production and high employment were possible for the American economy. The basic question was how to maintain this high level under "normal" conditions.

It had become clear that the problem of constantly expanding employment had not been met, for investigators found that the number of unemployed became greater in each depression, the most severe of which were in 1907 to 1909, 1921 to 1922, and 1930 to 1933. Advocates of free enterprise argued that depressions were simply a part of the natural business cycle and were to be expected. But as unemployed rolls mounted to the extremes of the early 1930's, many began to wonder what was natural about it and turned to the government for aid. The historic doctrines of laissez-faire capitalism had been designed to keep government out of business; but when the depths of the depression hit business and industry so hard, businessmen and industrialists turned to the government for help just as enthusiastically as did the unemployed. Whereas the historic capitalist doctrines had put faith in the profit motive as the essential economic ingredient of human nature, it became clear that, for the nine-tenths who owned no property and who relied upon salaries or wages for income, profit had given way to security as the principal economic motive for work and effort.

The historic theory of free competition in an open market operating according to automatic laws of supply and demand had also given way to the actual practices of price fixing and regulation of production by great corporations and monopolies. More and more people began to feel that if these practices were to continue they would prefer that prices, production, and wages were regulated by the joint efforts of government, labor, and management, rather than leaving such matters entirely in the hands of private owners and management. Whereas advocates of free enterprise had proclaimed that planning was alien to the American way of life, many began to see that a great amount of economic planning went into the management of huge corporations; and they began to insist that government and labor should have a larger share in planning in order to ensure that the benefits of planning would accrue to the general welfare.

Whereas individualistic capitalism had insisted that freedom of opportunity and enterprise could exist only under private auspices, many Americans began to suggest that an unmodified capitalism was a threat to the continued freedom and welfare of the majority of people, who had less and less opportunity to rise unaided as individuals in the economic scale. All these doubts and questions about historic capitalism led to the increasing support for social legislation by the government that culminated in the New Deal and the Fair Deal. The industrial and technological trends that had begun in the nineteenth century had now progressed so far that technical efficiency could produce a higher standard of living for all if only the economic system could be kept working efficiently. This became the principal political and economic problem for democracy to solve as the twentieth century wore on.

Social Trends

One of the most significant social developments in the twentieth century was the growth of organized labor. As economic power became ever more concentrated in the hands of bankers, financiers, huge corporations, employers, and owners, the only recourse of the unpropertied workers was to organize more solidly in order to gain somewhat equivalent economic power. This trend, which seemed so hopeful to millions of workers, seemed most ominous to employers. Although radical elements in the labor movement were represented by the Industrial Workers of the World (organized in 1905 by Eugene V. Debs and others) and by the Communists after 1920, the main stream of organized labor was content to work within the established economic system.

In general, labor set out to achieve its aims of a great share in the economic goods of the nation through strikes and collective bargaining as means to achieve higher wages, shorter working hours, better conditions of work, and greater security for workers and their families. Entering the twentieth century with something less than 1,000,000 members in organized labor, the movement grew, despite setbacks during the great depressions, until it had enrolled approximately 15,000,000 by the middle of the century.

Another social trend of vast importance was the decline in the rate of population growth. Population continued to increase in the twentieth century but, with immigration reduced to a trickle, the rate of increase declined in 25 years to such an extent that it was estimated that, somewhere around 1970 or 1980, the United States would have a stationary population. However, the steady decline in the birth rate that had been apparent for decades was halted by an increase beginning in 1941. This grew to such proportions that schools were greatly overcrowded as the population "bulge" caused rapid increases in enrollments in the late 1940's and 1950's. Perhaps even more important was the fact that the reproduction index was lower in the cities than in the rural sections and that the highest birth rates were in the rural South, which had the poorest economic and educational conditions in the nation. The large cities no longer maintained their populations by their own births.

Likewise of vast importance for the status of the family was the great influx of women into business and industry, a trend enormously accelerated by the Second World War. Juvenile delinquency increased rapidly, and the effects upon moral and mental welfare were hard to calculate. The tremendous migrations of warworkers to and from all parts of the country uprooted families and created disturbing social problems of adaptation for countless communities. The normal complexities of life, to be expected from improvements in inventions, technology, and communication, were further complicated and expanded by the unsettled conditions of the Second World War. Severe adjustments faced families and education in the postwar period.

Intergroup Relations

An important realm in which the American ideal of democratic opportunity for all was not fully realized in practice was in the relationships among religious, nationality, and racial groups. The United States preached equality of opportunity, but prejudices, hatreds, and active discriminations against large numbers of Americans continued to be a source of conflict and unrest. Many such prejudices arose from economic insecurity and fear of unemployment or economic competition. It is noteworthy that the hate campaigns rose in intensity in war periods and in economic depressions. Intergroup relations posed enormously important and difficult problems for American education.

Religious Groups. Organized religious groups continued to play a large role in twentieth-century American life. Membership continued to increase until in 1952 more than 92,000,000 people representing 250 denominations were counted as church members. According to the *Yearbook of American Churches*, edited by the National Council of Churches of Christ in America, these figures represent rapid gains and are the highest ever reported.

The largest single denomination was the Roman Catholic Church, with some 30,200,000 members; the various Baptist Conventions accounted for nearly 17,500,000; Methodists, 11,000,000; the principal Lutheran churches, 6,000,000; Episcopalians, over 2,400,000; Presbyterians, 3,500,-000; Disciples of Christ, 1,800,000; Congregationalists, 1,200,000; and Jewish congregations, 5,000,000. In round numbers, the principal Protestant denominations totaled some 54,200,000; the Roman Catholic Church, 30,200,000; Jewish congregations, 5,000,000; and Eastern Orthodox, 2,300,000.

The official stand of the major religious bodies was, of course, against religious intolerance and bigotry, but religious antagonisms were fostered by many groups that drew from one or more of the recognized denominations. Following the First World War, the Ku Klux Klan was revived among Protestant followers and expanded its objects of hate to include principally Roman Catholics and Jews as well as Negroes. In the early 1920's it spread to most of the states in the Union and is estimated to have embraced some 2,500,000 people in 1923. Organized anti-Semitic campaigns became popular in the early 1920's through many organizations and publishing ventures as well as by whispering campaigns and discrimination in employment, business, educational institutions, clubs, hotels, and resorts. Following the depression of the early 1930's and the rise of Nazism in Europe, anti-Semitism was also sponsored in the United States by the German-American Bund and by all kinds of Brown Shirts, Silver Shirts, and White Shirts.

Men and women of good will of all religious faiths began to organize to combat the hate campaigns that reappeared following the Second World War. Notable among many were the National Council of Churches of Christ in America, the National Conference of Christians and Jews, the American Jewish Congress, and the National Catholic Welfare Council. On the legal and political front, several steps were taken to promote amity and prevent discrimination against ethnic and racial as well as religious groups. Outstanding were the Fair Employment Practices Committee appointed at the national level by President Roosevelt and supported by President Truman, state action such as the New York State

Commission against Discrimination and governors' commissions in many states, and hundreds of local mayors' committees on interracial and inter-religious cooperation. The FEPC, however, succumbed on June 30, 1946, to the postwar reaction. Its final report showed a rise of discriminatory practices.

Nationality Groups. In the early part of the twentieth century the flood of immigration from Europe reached its peak, especially from central, eastern, and southern Europe. Despite the cutting off of large-scale immigration in the 1920's, the proportion of first- or second-generation citizens of foreign birth was very high. In 1930, some 12 per cent of the total population was foreign-born, and another 20 per cent had foreign-born or mixed parents. In addition, some 10 per cent of Americans were Negroes. Therefore, substantially less than 60 per cent of Americans were native white persons with native-born parents. The United States was truly a mixture of nearly all the nationalities of the world; but, despite the ideal of welcome to all peoples, Americans still consciously or unconsciously fostered group prejudices against the more recent immigrant groups. The McCarran-Walter Act and federal legislation prompted by fear of communism made it very difficult for displaced persons and refugees from the fascist and communist tyrannies to gain admittance to the United States.

Organized hate groups fostered prejudice against "foreigners" and "aliens," but even more pervasive were the stereotypes used by authors of books, newspapers, radio, motion pictures, and plays. In 1944 the Writers' War Board asked the Bureau of Applied Social Research at Columbia University to investigate the stereotypes in common use. It was found that writers generally fostered the false impression that the United States was a Protestant, white, Anglo-Saxon nation with a sprinkling of largely "undesirable" persons of different religious, racial, and national stocks. Short stories seemed to be the worst offenders, with more than 90 per cent of the heroes pictured as Anglo-Saxons and the villains or unscrupulous characters nearly always "foreigners." Advertisers were admittedly snobbish in their popular appeal, and the press and radio were generally not as liberal or conscientious as the comic cartoon books, the stage, and the novel. As the Second World War progressed, however, many notable contributions to better understanding of group relations were made by an increasing number of authors.

Race Relations. The largest minority racial group in the United States, the Negroes, comprised about 10 per cent of the population, and the problems of Negro-white relationships constituted one of the most critical points at which the American ideal of equality of opportunity had not been fully realized.

The Second World War brought the problem of race and color to the forefront again as the United Nations fought against the racial doctrines of the Nazis and Japanese as much as against their political doctrines. At home, the problem became acute as mass movements of Negroes to war-industry centers took place and as violence broke out in many industrial centers. The housing situation was critical, and discrimination in employment was still high in many industries, but great gains were made through the efforts of the Fair Employment Practices Committee and of progressive employers and unions.

Despite the defense of white supremacy by influential persons in the South and in the United States Senate, political gains were made against the poll tax and for the freedom of Negroes to vote in Democratic primaries of the South, as a result of the Supreme Court decision in the Texas primary case. Despite segregation in many branches of the armed forces, conditions improved as the war ended and as criticism was leveled at the army and navy. The press, stage, and screen supported equality of opportunity for Negroes, and many community groups as well as national organizations marshaled their forces to the same end. All the principal churches began similar campaigns.

Notable among other groups that began to redouble their efforts were the Common Council for American Unity, the Council against Intolerance in America, the Julius Rosenwald Fund, the National Association for the Advancement of Colored People, the National Urban League, and the Southern Regional Council. A flood of literature and programs of action was formulated as people of good will sensed the difficulties of the postwar period and realized that the victory might be lost at home if intergroup relations deteriorated sufficiently to deny to millions of Americans the values for which they had worked and fought.

Sensing the importance of civil rights for all as a part of the American democratic ideal, President Truman appointed a Committee on Civil Rights which issued its report in 1947, entitled *To Secure These Rights*. This was a sweeping indictment of segregation and discrimination based upon race, color, creed, or national origin. The report proposed a broad legislative and educational program to eliminate segregation and discrimination from American life. Included were proposals to make lynching a federal offense, to outlaw poll taxes, to end segregation in the armed forces, and to assure equality of opportunity in employment, in health and public services, in housing, and in education. Of great significance was the proposal that state legislatures should enact "fair educational practice laws for public and private educational institutions, prohibiting discrimination in the admission and treatment of students based on race, color, creed, or national origin." As a result of the arousal of public interest and organized effort, considerable gains were made in the fields of housing, equal travel facilities, the armed services, and in education.

EDUCATIONAL OPPORTUNITY AND EDUCATIONAL CONTROL

Equalizing Educational Opportunity

One of the most important issues facing educational administration in the last 50 years has been the problems of providing more equal educational opportunity for all American children and youth. The rapid growth of attendance did not blind careful students to the fact that enormous inequalities continued to exist in the quality and amount of education available to various groups in the population. The more industrialized and therefore richer states could spend more on education and thus provide better opportunities. In 1940, for example, the average expenditure per pupil in the whole country was something over $80; but nine southern states spent less than $50 per pupil, and eight other states spent more than $100 per pupil. Mississippi spent only $25 per pupil, less than one-third of the nation's average and less than one-fifth spent by New York State. By 1950 several states were spending only one-fourth as much per pupil as other states were spending. The poorer states had to exert greater effort than the richer states even to maintain this relationship.

It was clear, too, that, within the states, the urban and industrial areas were more advantageously situated than the rural and farming regions. So long as local units provided the bulk of school support, those units with greater population and greater wealth could spend more money on schools and thus provide better schools. Likewise, great inequalities were apparent in the provision of educational opportunities for Negro children as compared with white children; in the southern states the average expenditure per Negro child was about one-fourth to one-half what it was for each white child. Thus, in general, the inequality was enormous, either because some communities simply did not have enough money to provide decent education or because they did not wish to spend equal amounts for all groups in the population, or both.

Attempts to equalize these discrepancies took several forms. Within the states, equalization funds were set up to distribute state aid to the local communities on a basis that would help the poorer districts. Forward-looking states adopted the general principle that the entire wealth of the state should be tapped to serve the entire population of the state. Various kinds of formulas were developed to give state aid to communities on the basis of their need and ability to raise funds for schools, the number of children to be educated, and their willingness to tax themselves as fully as possible for the support of schools. Many states raised funds by state income taxes and by other taxes in order to give aid to those communities which could not meet their needs unaided.

Likewise, many states set out to consolidate local rural school districts into larger units in order to provide more efficient schools at less cost.

By pooling their resources on a county basis, local districts could provide fewer but better schools, served by school buses and manned by better-paid and better-trained teachers. The consolidation movement met vigorous opposition from many enthusiasts for local and decentralized control, who feared that the county or state would usurp their rights, but the trend toward consolidation continued despite opposition.

Inequalities for Negroes were attacked more or less vigorously at the state level. Much of the effort to improve Negro schools came from private foundations such as the General Education Board, Peabody Fund, John B. Slater Fund, the Jeannes Fund, and the Julius Rosenwald Fund. Even those southern states which developed a desire to improve Negro education found themselves handicapped by lack of funds to match their desires. Some states did set out to equalize facilities and teachers' salaries for Negroes and whites in their separate school systems. Some states responded more or less willingly to the demand for equalization; others did just enough to try to prevent more drastic changes.

Rapid steps were taken, however, to force equalization by court action. In 1938 the United States Supreme Court ruled in the Gaines case that the University of Missouri must provide equal facilities of legal education for Negro students. In June, 1950, the Supreme Court again ruled that the University of Texas must admit a Negro student to its law school (Sweatt case) and that the University of Oklahoma must provide free and equal access to its facilities for a Negro graduate student in education (McLaurin case). By 1954 *The New York Times* estimated that some 2,000 Negro students had been admitted to white colleges and universities in the South, most of them in graduate and professional schools. All the evidence seemed to show that this had been done with a minimum of difficulty and maximum of satisfaction to all concerned.

These gains were followed by concerted legal action to wipe out segregation itself in the public schools of the 17 states and the District of Columbia where segregated school systems were still required by law. In December, 1952, five cases went to the United States Supreme Court to test the constitutionality of segregation. The Supreme Court was asked to declare segregation itself to be unconstitutional and to overthrow the "separate but equal" doctrine of *Plessy v. Ferguson* (see page 437). These decisions, delayed for more than a year, promised to be among the most momentous facing the Supreme Court in all its history. At least two southern states, Georgia and South Carolina, took steps to abolish their public school systems and turn the schools over to private agencies if the Supreme Court should declare segregation to be unconstitutional. The American belief in equality of educational opportunity was to receive its most severe test.

In May, 1954, the Supreme Court issued its unanimous decision in which the Plessy doctrine was reversed and the segregated school systems were declared unconstitutional under the Fourteenth Amendment because they denied equal educational opportunity to Negro children. The court held that segregation in and of itself produced inequality and that separate facilities are inherently unequal even though the physical facilities may be equal. The basic argument of the decision was as follows:[1]

> Today, education is perhaps the most important function of state and local governments. Compulsory school attendance laws and the great expenditures for education both demonstrate our recognition of the importance of education to our democratic society. It is required in the performance of our most basic public responsibilities, even service in the armed forces. It is the very foundation of good citizenship. Today it is the principal instrument in awakening the child to cultural values, in preparing him for later professional training, and in helping him to adjust normally to his environment. In these days, it is doubtful that any child may reasonably be expected to succeed in life if he is denied the opportunity of an education. Such an opportunity, where the state has undertaken to provide it, is a right which must be made available to all on equal terms.
>
> We come then to the question presented: Does segregation of children in public schools solely on the basis of race, even though the physical facilities and other "tangible" factors may be equal, deprive the children of the minority group of equal educational opportunities? We believe that it does.
>
> . . . To separate them from others of similar age and qualifications solely because of their race generates a feeling of inferiority as to their status in the community that may affect their hearts and minds in a way unlikely ever to be undone. . . . "A sense of inferiority affects the motivation of a child to learn. Segregation with the sanction of law, therefore, has a tendency to retard the educational and mental development of Negro children and to deprive them of some of the benefits they would receive in a racially integrated school system". . . .
>
> We conclude that in the field of public education the doctrine of "separate but equal" has no place. Separate educational facilities are inherently unequal. Therefore, we hold that the plaintiffs and others similarly situated for whom the actions have been brought are, by reason of the segregation complained of, deprived of the equal protection of the laws guaranteed by the Fourteenth Amendment.

The Supreme Court then asked for assistance of all interested parties to present rearguments having to do with the issuance of decrees to enforce the decision and promote desegregation of schools. Great difficulties remained. The attitudes inculcated for 200 years would not be easily changed, and some groups and some states were sure to drag their heels and perhaps even defy the Supreme Court. But up to the middle of 1955

[1] *Brown v. Board of Education*, May 17, 1954.

remarkable success had been achieved in orderly desegregation in some of the border states and in Washington, D.C. The problem was by no means fully settled, but the Court's decision was a great and historic policy statement, reaffirming the best of the American tradition of devotion to equality of educational opportunity.

Federal Participation in Education

Despite the gains made in equalizing educational opportunity by county, state, and private agencies, it rapidly became clearer, especially during the depression of the early 1930's, that genuine equality could not be achieved for all American children unless the federal government entered the field of school support in a substantial way. The pressure for federal aid to education increased from many quarters, and a series of federal-aid bills were introduced into Congress. However, up to 1954 no federal-aid bill had been passed for the support of general education in America, and none seemed likely to pass in the foreseeable future. It looked for a while as though federal aid was possible when the Taft-Thomas bill passed the Senate in 1948 and again in 1949, but each time it was blocked in the House of Representatives over the religious issue. The real stumbling block was clearly and evidently the reluctance of some groups to provide public funds for parochial schools and the determination of the Roman Catholic Church to oppose federal aid unless it included their parochial schools.

The question of federal aid to education seemed settled, at least for the duration of Republican control of Congress, when the Hill amendment to the offshore oil lands bill was defeated in 1953. President Eisenhower in February, 1955, proposed federal legislation to provide funds for school buildings to meet the shortage of classrooms, but his proposals were opposed by most schoolmen as too complicated, too slow, and too little. Curiously enough, the role of the two major parties had reversed since the nineteenth century. Whereas the Republicans had sponsored federal-aid bills in the 1870's and 1880's, it was the Democratic party that favored aid to education in its party platforms in 1944, 1948, 1952, and President Truman had included actual sums in several of his proposed budgets.

More and more educators were coming to realize the need for federal funds, but many continued to be afraid of federal control. The centralizing forces that were evident in political and economic realms were especially feared in educational matters. Many opposed federal support because they felt that control should remain in the hands of the states and were convinced that federal control would inevitably follow federal support. Southern states and southern congressmen opposed any bill that would provide for equal distribution of funds to Negro schools. Most

Protestants and Jews opposed any bill that would give federal aid to parochial schools as well as to public schools. Roman Catholic groups favored such bills but opposed any federal-aid bill that ruled out support for private and parochial schools. Taxpayers' alliances and economy groups opposed all federal aid of any kind. With these groups pulling and hauling in different directions, the issue was unsolved, but the problem remained.

Perhaps the most definitive policy statement on the problem by educators was made in 1945 in a pamphlet entitled *Federal-State Relations in Education*, prepared jointly by the Educational Policies Commission of the National Education Association and the Problems and Policies Committee of the American Council on Education. These groups deplored the centralizing trends of the federal government and its tendency to control education, but they insisted that the federal government must participate in the support of education. They disapproved of the Civilian Conservation Corps (CCC), National Youth Administration (NYA), and Servicemen's Readjustment Act (commonly called the "G.I. Bill of Rights") as permanent agencies of the federal government, but they noted that the Congress had responded to emergency situations when the states did not.

The principles proposed were that the predominant control of education should remain at state and local levels but that the federal government should continue to exercise, within properly defined limitations, certain educational functions. The federal government should provide financial assistance to the states on the basis of school populations and wealth of the states. It should deal with established state agencies to which it should give the money and should expect in return simply an audit and report on how the money was used. The federal government should also exercise leadership of a stimulating but noncoercive character in the form of investigations, research, conferences, and publications. Federal control of education should be limited to certain special undertakings like the Military and Naval Academies. These views probably represented the majority opinion of American educators.

Despite the fact that no bill for federal aid to general education had been passed by mid-century, the federal government was spending some 3.5 billion dollars a year by 1950. The trend toward federal support of education that began in the nineteenth century was accelerated in the twentieth century, but it was on a piecemeal basis rather than as a carefully planned and integrated service. Congress saw a special need or responded to special demands and thereupon made provisions for special educational aids. Only a few of the outstanding developments can be mentioned here. In 1914 the Smith-Lever Act provided for agricultural extension services to disseminate useful knowledge relating to farm methods and home economics throughout the rural areas of the nation. County agricultural agents were authorized to work with farmers and housewives to improve their practices and raise the level of farm life. Lectures, meetings, conferences, classes, publications, and demonstrations

School Board Journal

This Journal was founded 1890 by WILLIAM GEORGE BRUCE.

VOL. XXXI, No. 6.   MILWAUKEE—NEW YORK, DECEMBER, 1905.   SUBSCRIPTION PRICE $1 PER YEAR.

Fig. 32. A Cartoon Demanding Improvement in School Building Facilities 1905). (*Courtesy of The Bruce Publishing Company, Milwaukee.*)

were provided by federal funds, to be matched dollar for dollar by those states which accepted the provisions of the act.

In 1917 the Smith-Hughes Act provided vocational instruction in secondary schools for agricultural, home-economics, trade, and industrial subjects. A Federal Board of Vocational Education and state boards were set up to administer the federal funds, which were to be matched dollar for dollar by the states. The money was to be used to pay the salaries of agricultural, home-economics, and trades and industrial teachers, to help states prepare teachers in these subjects, and to conduct research in the various fields. In 1929 the appropriations for vocational education were increased by the George-Reed Act, and in 1936 the George-Deen Act extended federal aid to instruction in the distributive or selling occupations in secondary schools. Vocational rehabilitation of handicapped persons also received federal aid through the Vocational Rehabilitation Act of 1920 and the Social Security Act of 1935.

An enormous impetus was given to federal support of specialized educational needs during the depression years by the New Deal. The Civilian Conservation Corps was established in 1933 to give relief, employment, and vocational training for unemployed youths. An educational and work program was devised for the various camps in which the young men helped to conserve and develop the national parks, forests, and other resources. The National Youth Administration was established in 1935 to provide work for unemployed youth, lend aid in finding jobs, give vocational training, and provide financial aid to attend school or college. Despite their great utility in preparing warworkers, the CCC and the NYA drew increasing criticism in 1942 and 1943 until they were finally closed entirely.

The Works Project Administration (WPA) provided money for work-relief payments for unemployed teachers and for an extensive educational program of nursery schools, vocational training and rehabilitation, workers' education, adult education, and national citizenship education for foreign-born residents of the United States. The Public Works Administration (PWA) provided extensive grants and loans to communities and states for the construction of school buildings. In these and many other ways, education shared in the federal government's attempts to meet the economic emergency.

With the deterioration of the international situation in the late 1930's, the federal government began to sponsor educational measures of national defense. In 1938 the Civil Aeronautics Authority (CAA) sponsored programs for the training of pilots, and in 1940 large federal funds began to be distributed through the United States Office of Education (this name was restored in 1929) for the training of defense workers in schools and colleges. In 5 years, the war-training program gave vocational preparation to some 12,000,000 persons at a cost of $500,000,000. The most popular courses were on aviation and automotive services, radio and electricity, machine shops, shipbuilding, and welding.

With the tapering off of the civilian war-training program in 1945, the government's program for educational benefits to veterans swung into high gear. The Servicemen's Readjustment Act of 1944 (G.I. Bill of Rights) provided returning servicemen and servicewomen with tuition, subsistence, and supplies for study in school or college. Between 1945 and 1954 more than 8,000,000 veterans had received benefits totaling 14 billion dollars in college, school, and on-the-job training. A special act for similar benefits to veterans of the Korean War passed in 1952. Disabled veterans were entitled to other benefits and somewhat larger subsistence amounts.

Following the Second World War, the federal government continued large grants to colleges and universities for fundamental research and training of personnel in fields of importance to national security. Emphasis was put upon science, technology, agriculture, industry, medicine, and public health. By 1952 the federal government was spending $300,-000,000 for these purposes.

In 1939 the United States Office of Education was transferred from the Department of Interior to the newly organized Federal Security Agency, along with the Public Health Service, Social Security Board, and other agencies. From the 1920's on, there was a movement to establish a federal department of education with a member of the president's cabinet as head, but this was not realized for some 30 years. In 1953 the Federal Security Agency was transformed into the Department of Health, Education, and Welfare, with a secretary in the president's cabinet.

Problems of Administration and Control

Public versus Private Control. The right of the state to support public educational institutions from preschool to adult education was no longer questioned. Compulsory-school-attendance laws of some kind had been passed in all states by 1918, even though they varied in the length of time and the age limits within which attendance was required. All states had organized state departments or state boards of education, and the legal authority of state legislatures was fully established. However, the question of the rights of the state with regard to private and parochial schools was unsettled until an important judicial decision in the early 1920's.

The Oregon legislature passed a law in 1922 requiring every child in Oregon to attend a public school between the ages of eight and sixteen years. This struck at the heart of the parochial and private school systems, but in 1925 the United States Supreme Court ruled the law unconstitutional. The court declared that the child was a creature of the parents rather than of the state and that therefore the parents had the inherent right to educate their child by sending him to any school they deemed best for his welfare. Furthermore, the court ruled that the state had no right to destroy the value of the property of the private schools without due process of law.

The court reaffirmed the right of the state to require all children to be educated, but not to specify that they must attend a public school in order to acquire that education. It also reaffirmed the right of the state to supervise and inspect all schools, private, parochial, and public, in order to see that they meet the minimum requirements for education in a democracy. Thus, the right of private and religious schools to exist alongside the public schools was guaranteed, but the issue persisted. Most people continued to believe that the public schools should be the principal agency whereby the youth of America was to be educated. But a persistent and growing minority believed that private education should receive greater attention and even aid from public sources.

Public school educators noted with great concern that the proportion of children attending nonpublic schools was rapidly increasing. In 1937–1938 approximately 9.5 per cent of elementary and secondary children were in nonpublic schools; by 1949–1950 it was 11.8 per cent, and the prediction was that it would be nearly 14 per cent by 1960 if the present trend continues. Approximately 90 per cent of these private school enrollments were in Roman Catholic schools. A steady and very strong campaign was undertaken by Catholic leaders to get all Catholic children into Catholic schools. Some Protestants, too, were redoubling their efforts to expand the number of their denominational schools. These were potential threats to the idea of a common school system established with such cost and effort in the nineteenth century.

In answer to the question "Should public funds be used for religious schools" there were three types of answers.

1. In the main, the Roman Catholic Church answered "Yes." Spokesmen for the Church argued that the parochial schools provided a public service by helping children to meet the compulsory attendance laws. It was therefore only just that parochial schools be aided in this task in order to relieve Catholic parents from the burden of "double taxation," that is, of paying public school taxes and also supporting their own schools. Beneath this argument was the basic presupposition that the Church and the family had a right to conduct education that was prior and superior to that of the state. It was argued that church and state should "cooperate" in this matter. No harm would come to the principle of separation of church and state so long as the state aided all churches equally and fairly and did not show preference for one church above others.

2. The second answer given by many Catholics and many Protestants was a qualified "Yes." Here it was argued that the state could not give *direct* support to religious schools because that would violate the separation of church and state. But, on the other hand, it was perfectly proper

for the state to use public funds for such indirect support as paying for transportation of children to parochial schools and providing them with free textbooks, free lunches, and free health and medical services. This argument was based upon the premise that such "auxiliary services" were welfare benefits to the child and not aids to the school. Such benefits should be given to all children, no matter what school they attended. The majority decision of the United States Supreme Court in the Everson case in 1948 seemed to support this practical adjustment, although the constitutional principle was there clearly stated that "No tax in any amount, large or small, can be levied to support any religious activities or institutions, whatever they may be called, or whatever form they may adopt to teach or practice religion."

3. The third answer to the question about public funds for religious schools was "No." This answer was given by many Protestants, most Jews, and most public school educators, including the National Education Association. This position argued that indirect aid, as well as direct aid, to religious schools must be prohibited if the values of the long struggle for separation of church and state were to be maintained. The Everson decision was used here also to show that either kind of aid would violate the First Amendment of the Constitution and in effect reintroduce "an establishment of religion" in the United States. In the Everson case, the Supreme Court had said that an establishment of religion means that neither the federal government nor the state governments can "pass laws which aid one religion, aid all religions, or prefer one religion over another." This was taken to mean not only that preferential aid to one church was prohibited, but also that nonpreferential aid to many or all churches was likewise prohibited. Not only was genuine separation required on principle but there seemed to be no place logically to stop once aid was begun even on a small scale.

These problems continued to plague public education in the middle of the century and no clear-cut decision was in sight. The battles were bound to be fought out in hundreds of localities and dozens of states for years to come.

The response to a second question, "Should religious instruction be given in the public schools?" also elicited three types of response.

1. One response to this question, given principally by Protestants and Roman Catholics, was "Yes, religious instruction should be given in the public schools." Some adherents of this position might like to see their own sectarian religion become the basis of public school instruction but they knew that this was a practical impossibility so long as many strong churches continued to prosper in the United States. The most promising way to insert sectarian religious instruction into the public school has therefore come to be the weekday released-time plan. This gave parents

the opportunity to have their children receive instruction in their preferred faith by approved instructors for certain hours set aside each week to allow children to leave their regular classes and attend religious classes.

The United States Supreme Court stirred up great controversy when it decided in the McCollum case in 1948 that such religious classes could not be conducted within the public school buildings of Champaign, Ill. "This is beyond all question a utilization of the tax-established and tax-supported public school system to aid religious groups to spread their faith. And it falls squarely under the ban of the First Amendment . . . " as the court interpreted it in the Everson case. Religious groups were mollified somewhat, however, when the Supreme Court decided, in the Zorach and Gluck case in 1952, that the New York City plan of released-time instruction was permissible because the religious classes were held off school property. This decision was viewed as a reversal by the court's minority who argued that the principles laid down in the McCollum case had been ignored.

2. A second answer to the question was "Yes, there should be more religious instruction in the public schools, but it should be *nonsectarian* instruction." This position was taken almost entirely by Protestants who argued that the common basis of so much of American culture was Christian in its origin that these common religious teachings could form the basis of nonsectarian instruction. Most often this took the form of reading the Bible in the schools each day. Under Protestant stimulus, some 12 states passed laws requiring Bible reading and some 25 other states permitted the practice in one way or another.

The practice has been objected to by Catholics and Jews on the grounds that the Bible used is most often the King James Version and therefore sectarian in their eyes. At least six state courts have ruled that the Bible is a sectarian document and therefore cannot be read in the public schools. A definitive decision might have been reached in 1952 when the Doremus case was decided by the United States Supreme Court, but the majority ruled that the appellants had not shown enough injury before the law because their children were no longer in the public schools, and therefore the constitutional question was not decided. Meanwhile, the effect was to permit the practice of Bible reading in those states where it was already required or permitted.

3. The third response to the question was "Religious instruction—no; factual study of religion—yes." More and more public school educators who could not go along with the first two responses were still concerned that some attention should be paid to religion in the public schools. They were opposed to the inculcation of religious doctrines either by sectarian or nonsectarian instruction. They felt, however, that religion is so im-

portant as a phase of American culture that it should be studied wherever appropriate in connection with such regular school subjects as history and social studies, literature, music, and the fine arts. In this way, American youth could become religiously literate and gain an appreciation of the importance of religious values without violating the separation of church and state. Careful, objective, factual study of religion would achieve these goals. This point of view was promoted by the Committee on Religion and Education of the American Council on Education and by the Educational Policies Commission.

It should be noted that there were divisions of opinion within all religious groups as to the advisability of these various responses. The controversies aroused rocked many communities when the proposals were made. Many public school educators and many citizens believed that all these plans had elements of threat to the separation of church and state. They maintained that the best way to serve American democracy and to prevent the ill effects of European experience with religious instruction in public schools was to keep the two as separate as possible.

Local Administration of Schools. From the 1920's onward, it became increasingly clear to some educators that the theory of public control of education through a lay board of education was not working out in practice to the best interests of all the people. Studies showed that school boards appointed by mayors and even school boards elected by the people were not representative of a cross section of the population. School boards were composed in greatest numbers of professional men (physicians, lawyers, and clergymen) and businessmen, representing the upper-middle and wealthier classes in the communities. As representatives of organized labor and minority groups began to become members of school boards, their composition became more representative of the total population.

Another trend toward more democratic administration of education began to appear when teachers in some school systems began to gain some voice in the making of school policies, a development that took place largely after 1930. The inherited administrative arrangements of the nineteenth century were highly centralized and authoritarian as schools adopted the business and industrial methods of "efficiency" in running the school system. Gradually, many educators began to argue that educational institutions were not analogous to industrial or military establishments. If teachers were to develop democratically minded students, the teachers themselves must develop democratic habits by taking part in decisions that concerned them. Most school administrators met the idea with cool indifference or active hostility, but some began to put it to the test.

In Shaker Heights, Ohio, for example, a staff council was formed to take full responsibility for the formulation of those school policies which the school board normally handed over to the superintendent of schools. The superintendent agreed to be bound by the decisions of the staff council, composed of 48 members. Fifteen members were administrative officers, including the superintendent, and 33 were teachers. Superintendent Arthur K. Loomis reported that the participation of the teaching staff in the formulation of policies had improved the morale of the staff and had resulted in better and wiser decisions than would have otherwise been possible. The mistake was not made of confusing policy making with executive authority. The province of the staff council was to make decisions of policy and then delegate to the proper administrative officers full authority to act and carry out the decisions.

The movement for democratic administration gained slowly, but it seemed to be in line with the best outlook that began to permeate curriculum building, supervisory practices, and instructional methods. As administrators and teachers alike learned to work cooperatively in the educational enterprise, the best interests of all concerned were increasingly being served. Some schools even began to give a voice to students, parents and members of the community in matters of concern to them. The idea of a "community school" closely related to the needs and welfare of the surrounding community gained wide attention in the middle decades of the century.

Pressures upon the Schools. The value of a cooperative and unified professional staff including both administrators and teachers was borne in upon an increasing number of educators as they faced the growing pressures upon the schools from various sources. Wise administrators soon learned that their position was much stronger when authority flowed in two directions than when all decisions rested in their hands or with the board of education alone. Strong economy drives were instituted during the depression to force retrenchment of school budgets. Taxpayers' alliances and groups of all kinds brought pressures to bear to cut school budgets. Administrators found that a cooperative effort of the whole staff in making budget decisions, in publicizing the educational and social values of the school program, and taking leadership in the community brought greater returns than when administrators faced the demands alone.

Patriotic and veterans' organizations demanded flag salutes, loyalty oaths for teachers, and an emphasis on patriotism. Religious organizations demanded religious instruction in public schools or the exclusion of instruction on sex, evolution, or other matters. Legislatures passed laws requiring the teaching of American history or the prohibition of the teaching of the German language. In these and many other ways, special-interest groups besieged the schools to serve their interests. A wishy-washy stand by the schools simply meant that the group with the most power could sway the legislature, the board of education, or the superintendent. A well-thought-out program of public education effectively presented to the public could do much to help educators stand out against ill-advised pressures.

Wise educators marshaled organizations favoring good education in the community and their own professional staff to formulate good educational policies and defend them before the public. It seemed clear that the profession could not and should not isolate itself from the community but rather should take into account a larger proportion of the community when it made its decisions. It was desirable to meet the community needs, but it was dangerous to define the community simply in terms of the most vociferous or well-organized minorities. That school system was strongest which had developed a continuous and cooperative program of communication and conference with forward-looking and democratically minded groups in the community.

Changes in Organization

The structure or, rather, structures of the American school system went through many modifications in the first half of the twentieth century in response to increased enrollments, community demands upon the schools, and the constantly changing plans of educators to meet new needs. The organization of educational institutions varied from state to state and with different localities in many states. This variation imparted flexibility and the ability to adapt to different conditions, but it also meant that unequal quality and quantity of education were often provided in different parts of the country. The general trend, however, was to extend the amount of education under public auspices to the lower and higher age levels. At the opening of the twentieth century the most common form of organization was an 8-year elementary school, a 4-year high school, and a 4-year college, with some kindergartens provided below the elementary school and professional, technical, and graduate schools beyond the college. During the first half of the twentieth century, certain significant changes took place that extended and expanded this organization.

Preelementary Education. By the middle of the century it had become clear that public responsibility for education was being extended to include nursery schools for two- and three-year-old children and kindergartens for four- and five-year-olds. The nursery school movement was rather slow in developing until the depression years of the 1930's, when federally supported nursery schools were inaugurated by the WPA of the New Deal. By 1938, some 300,000 children had been enrolled in 1,500 emergency nursery schools, most of which were housed in public school buildings. Forward-looking educators urged that the emergency pattern of nursery schools, maternity care, and parent education, stimulated by the depression and war program, should become a permanent part of public education. By 1948, however, only about 10 per cent of all cities were maintaining nursery schools and the trend seemed to be toward curtailment rather than expansion.

The kindergarten had been developed in the nineteenth century to provide educational facilities for children younger than the normal school-beginning age of six. By 1950, some 750,000 children were enrolled in public kindergartens and another 145,000 in private kindergartens. As might be expected, most of these were in urban centers. About 60 per cent of all city school systems maintained public kindergartens.

Both the nursery school and the kindergarten were in large part a response to the urban and industrial character of twentieth-century life, in which a higher percentage of mothers began to transfer some of their energies from child care to business and industry. These institutions were justified even more urgently, however, on the grounds that young children need the social activity of group life and the guidance in mental, moral, and emotional development that could be provided by trained teachers to supplement the training provided by the home. Indeed, such teachers could help to improve the quality of home life itself by working with parents to improve their knowledge and insight into child development and child care. Early childhood education and parent education had become an important frontier for educational workers.

Elementary Education. As already noted, the dominant type of elementary school in 1900 was an 8-year school in which children normally started at the age of six and graduated at the age of fourteen. Even this pattern varied, however, for many southern states had 7-year elementary schools, and many New England states had 9-year elementary schools. Criticism of this arrangement was heard increasingly from 1910 on, and the idea of a junior high school began to spread after its beginnings in California and Ohio. It was argued that the growth patterns of adolescent children of thirteen, fourteen, and fifteen years of age required special attention as a means of transition from elementary to secondary education.

Thus the junior high school, designed as a separate institution to include the seventh, eighth, and ninth grades, began to gain in popularity. This development meant a 6-year elementary school, a 3-year junior high school, and a 3-year senior high school, often known as the "6-3-3 plan." By 1950 the 6-3-3 plan had far outstripped the 8-4 plan. Throughout the wide variety of plans that were devised, the 6-year elementary school was definitely the most popular by mid-century. The junior high school never became very popular in rural sections, where the shortage of teachers and fewer children meant that the dominant pattern remained an 8- or 7-year elementary school. Where consolidated rural schools became common, the junior high school was more popular.

The 1920's and 1930's saw such a rapid development of the junior high school that it was difficult to say whether elementary schools included six grades or eight grades. But many educators were less concerned about the grades to be included than in seeing that children received an education appropriate to their stage of development in a unitary and integrated plan. One item of major concern was the enormous increase in elementary school enrollment. It had increased from 16,000,000 to nearly 24,000,000 between 1900 and 1930, then began to decline steadily during the 1930's until it went below 20,000,000 in 1938. The decline in the birth rate and restriction of immigration were largely responsible. Contrary to earlier expectations, elementary school enrollments did not stabilize but increased sharply after 1947 when the rising birth rate of the Second World War began to have its effect. By 1954 the number enrolled jumped to an all-time high of well over 26,000,000 and was expected to reach 29,000,000 by 1957.

Secondary Education. The organizational definition of secondary education was even more difficult to determine. In 1900 it was more simple, for secondary education generally referred to the 4 years of high school that stood between the 8-year elementary school and the 4-year college. With the growth of the junior high school, however, many educators began to include the junior high school in secondary education, which added 2 years to secondary education. Then another new institution known as the "junior college" appeared with some prominence immediately after the beginning of the century and was often thought of as adding 2 years to the upper end of secondary education.

The junior college movement expanded rapidly after 1920, especially in the West. In 1915 there were some 74 junior colleges enrolling 2,300 students. By 1952 there were some 586 junior colleges enrolling 575,000 students. The prospects were that enrollments would continue to rise. The movement had become firmly embedded in the American educational system and was expanding in conception to include technical institutes and "community colleges." Thus, vocational, technical, and semiprofessional preparation could go along simultaneously with general education for personal and civic purposes.

It is clear that there were a good many different conceptions of the organizational pattern for secondary education. Some localities held to the 8-4 plan. Some established a 6-3-3 arrangement and considered the junior college as higher education. Others began to experiment with a 6-6 arrangement, considering grades 7 through 12 as a unitary 6-year high school. Some with an 8-year elementary school were thinking of secondary education as a unitary 6-year institution including the junior college years (8-6 plan). Still others were thinking of a 6-4-4 plan in which grades 7 through 10 were considered a lower secondary school and grades 11 through 14 an upper secondary school.

Whatever the plan, the trend was definitely in the direction that the majority of American youth would find educational facilities easily available to them up to the age of twenty. Whether education would go beyond that age no one could say, but it was clear that the expectation had steadily risen in the course of a hundred years. It took a battle in the nineteenth century to provide public education for all children up to ages thirteen or fourteen; it was even harder to establish the terminal age at seventeen or eighteen (the end of high school).

The road seemed easier in the twentieth century, for the public began to recognize the values of extended schooling. That this realization was actually not long in coming was shown by the phenomenal rise in public high school enrollments from about 500,000 in 1900 to 1,000,000 in 1910, 2,000,000 in 1920, over 4,000,000 in 1930, and approximately 7,000,000 in 1940. After a decline to around 6,000,000 in the early 1950's, secondary school enrollments were well over 7,000,000 in 1954 and expected to continue to rise sharply.

Higher Education. The task of defining American higher education became fully as baffling. First of all was the question whether the first 2 years of college should be considered as secondary education. Some educators believed that it would be so considered. President Robert M. Hutchins went so far as to recommend giving the B.A. degree at the end of the second year to signify the end of general education. Arrayed firmly against such suggestions, however, were the advocates of the 4-year liberal arts college, who maintained that its integrity should be preserved.

At the beginning of the twentieth century the 4-year college was the predominant institution of higher education. However, it began to lose its unique position as the junior college nibbled away at the first 2 years and as professional and technical education started to bite into the second 2 years. The growth of large universities with their professional, technical, and graduate faculties began to dominate the offerings of the undergraduate colleges so that preparation for advanced specialized work became a prominent goal of college instruction, especially during the last 2 years of the 4-year college.

Enrollment advanced by leaps and bounds, increasing from nearly 250,000 in 1900 to nearly 1,500,000 just before the Second World War. After drastic declines during the war years, enrollment in higher institutions boomed to the all-time high of 2,500,000 in 1949. As the flood of veterans receded, enrollments dropped for a few years, but started up again in 1952, reaching 2,500,000 by 1954.

One of the outstanding trends in higher education was the increasing proportion of public funds that went into the support of colleges and universities in the twentieth century. State universities, land-grant colleges, and municipal colleges came to overshadow the private institutions in numbers of students. From the depression years of the early 1930's onward, the resources of private fortune that had fed college endowments began to dry up, and many colleges found themselves in financial difficulties. The onset of the Second World War made the problem still more acute. High taxes on income and the great decrease in enrollment of men students brought many privately endowed institutions to the brink of disaster. Many colleges were able to tide themselves over the war years only with the help of an increased enrollment of women and with government funds derived from war activities. Public support from state and federal funds was apparently another permanent feature of higher education in America. In the post-war years new sources of revenue from business and industry were also being tapped in the form of grants for research, scholarships, faculty salaries, and other projects.

The Teaching Profession

Social Status of Teachers. In the twentieth century the status of teachers improved considerably; but, in comparison with other occupations, teaching was fairly low in the scale of financial returns. Average salaries of all public school teachers increased from about $325 a year in 1900 to approximately $1,350 in 1940. They more than doubled in 10 years after 1940 and reached the all-time high in 1951–1952 of $3,300 on the average for the whole country. This was below the average of all wage and salary earners in the country, while physicians earned four times as much as teachers, lawyers three times as much, and dentists well over twice as much.

The average of $3,300 did not tell the whole story by any means. The director of research for the National Education Association found that in the early 1950's the average salary for teachers in Mississippi was $1,475 while it was more than $4,500 in New York. Sixteen states paid some of their teachers as little as $25 a week or less. Rural teachers were paid less than city teachers, and Negro teachers less than white. It was no wonder that teachers left the schools by the thousands in the early 1940's to engage in war work of a more remunerative kind. Estimates indicated that there was a shortage of some 75,000 to 100,000 teachers before the war ended. Added to this was the estimate that from one-sixth to one-half of all elementary school teachers were below minimum standards of preparation.

The low financial return for teachers became an urgent concern of many educators, who urged that teachers' salaries should be based upon cost-of-living requirements to ensure a decent standard of living for teachers in comparison with occupations requiring similar preparation and competence. They also urged that salaries be based upon training and experience rather than the grade level or subject taught, for the tradition had been to pay secondary school teachers more than elementary school teachers. Furthermore, extra allowances should be paid to married men with families, and annual increments should be given over a fairly long period of time to keep initiative and interest high. Certification requirements, tenure provisions, and sick-leave and retirement allowances have been improved in recent years. These all helped to compensate somewhat in greater security for the lack of financial reward. Much remained to be done in these respects, however.

Doubtless, part of the reason for the low financial status of the teaching profession was the fact that most teachers were women, who were somehow expected to be able to live on less than men. If they were single or had husbands at work, the assumption was probably true. In addition, women teachers have often not felt that it was "dignified or respectable" to agitate for higher salaries or press their claims upon legislatures or boards of education as almost all other organized groups have done. In 1900, about 70 per cent of public school teachers were women; this increased to about 85 per cent in 1920, following the First World War, when many men had gone into the service. The percentage of women dropped to about 80 per cent in 1934, rose again during the Second World War, and then leveled off at about 80 per cent after the Second World War.

Social pressures upon teachers have been great. The public has been very eager to make its teachers toe the mark of respectability and conform to the dominant mores of the community. Studies have shown that the private and public lives of teachers have been more subject to public approval or disapproval than those of almost any other group in the community, aside from the clergy. Smoking, drinking, cardplaying, "dating," and dancing have rivaled radicalism for public disapproval. Discrimination against Negroes, Roman Catholics, Jews, pacifists, militarists, and divorced or married women has had free rein in various communities, depending upon the times and upon the character of the population.

Teachers as a rule have been recruited from the agricultural and lower middle classes in American society. This social composition of the teaching profession has been modified somewhat in recent years but remains substantially true. Ordinarily, teachers have not brought to teaching a background of organized labor that would prompt them to work actively for higher salaries, nor have they had a wealthy background that would enable them to overcome the relatively meager salary scales. Raising the social estimation of teaching seems to be a matter of raising salaries in order to attract more competent persons to the profession and raising the standards of preparation and qualifications for teaching in order to command a higher return for services rendered.

Academic Freedom. The whole problem of academic freedom has been a thorny one in the twentieth century, for teachers have been put under a wide variety of pressures to support certain causes and to avoid others. The nature of "hot" controversial issues has changed with the times and has varied with localities. In one community at one time a pacifist teacher might get into trouble; in another community a militaristic teacher would be in trouble. In the 1920's the battles between fundamentalist religion and evolutionary science were bitter. In the 1930's the "Red scares" were numerous, and many teachers with liberal or even New Deal proclivities were subject to being labeled as communists. Until late in the 1920's teachers who joined labor unions or were outspoken in favor of labor were subject to "yellow-dog" contracts, in which it was stipulated that they would be discharged if they joined a union. This attitude still prevails in many parts of the country, but gains have been made.

In the 1940's and 1950's the hottest issues centered upon "subversive" ideas and actions of teachers. International tensions arising out of the "cold war" with Russia and the "hot" war in Korea and elsewhere were combined with political maneuvering at home to make the loyalty of teachers a prime target for patriotic and superpatriotic groups. Several kinds of steps were taken to ensure the orthodoxy of teachers and to weed out those thought to be dangerous or disloyal.

By 1952 some 30 states had passed laws requiring teachers to swear special oaths of loyalty to the state and federal governments. Most professional organizations opposed loyalty oaths on two grounds: They discriminated against teachers and infringed their rights of freedom of belief and association; and they were ineffective because no real subversive would have scruples about taking such an oath. In 1952 the United States Supreme Court declared an Oklahoma oath law for teachers to be unconstitutional under the First and Fourteenth Amendments (*Wieman v. Updegraff*).

A second type of approach has been the passage of laws to make it possible to discover and dismiss teachers who belong to the Communist party or other identified subversive organizations. Perhaps the most celebrated of these was the Feinberg law of New York State passed in 1949 and tested through the courts until finally declared constitutional by the United States Supreme Court by a six-to-three decision in 1952. The Feinberg law authorized the state Board of Regents to draw up a list of subversive organizations. Thereupon, any teacher who was found, after hearing and trial, to belong to one of the listed subversive organizations was to be considered disqualified for holding a teaching position in the public schools of the state. Those who favored the Feinberg law argued that a teacher's associations must be reckoned in determining fitness to teach. Those who opposed it argued that political beliefs and associations are not subject to scrutiny or approval by the state and that the law accepts the repugnant principle of guilt by association.

The major professional organizations were agreed that disloyal and incompetent teachers should not be retained as teachers. They disagreed as to the criteria of determining disloyalty and incompetence. The National Education Association and the American Federation of Teachers held that membership in the Communist party automatically disqualified a teacher. The American Association of University Professors and the American Civil Liberties Union held that competence in scholarship and teaching should be the only test of fitness to teach. All were agreed that no teacher should be ousted on the basis of rumor or unsubstantiated charges and that no teacher should be discharged except after all the safeguards of a fair hearing by competent colleagues had been ensured.

More serious than all other aspects of these campaigns for orthodoxy was the atmosphere of fear, suspicion, timidity, and anxiety that developed in schools and colleges throughout the land. Self-appointed censors and accusers kept after teachers so energetically that few dared to discuss even the basic issues of public policy that filled the press, radio, and television. A wave of legislative investigations at the state and federal levels highlighted the years following the Second World War and reached their peak in the early 1950's. In May, 1951, *The New York Times* found "a subtle, creeping paralysis of freedom of thought" pervading college campuses. Faculty members avoided the discussion of controversial issues in classrooms or in public, and students refused to join humanitarian causes for fear of being labeled subversive and thus being penalized when it came to finding jobs. In June, 1953, the National Education Association reported that school teachers were afraid to discuss the most common controversial issues with their students and that the academic freedom of teachers was in greater jeopardy than at any time in the past 100 years.

As a result of the interplay of these social forces, some educators proposed that controversial issues should not be treated at all by teachers but rather that they should teach only what is commonly accepted by the community. Other educators proposed that teachers should deal with controversial issues but should treat all sides fairly and remain completely neutral, leaving it to the students to decide what positions they would take. This view has often been summarized in the phrase "Teach students *how* to think but not *what* to think."

Still other educators urged that teachers must face controversial issues openly and fairly, indicating what positions the various community groups take on the issues and what the teacher himself believes. They insisted that the teacher must make a selection from the whole range of possible materials to be taught and that such selection inevitably reveals the underlying assumptions and point of view of the teacher. Therefore, they argued, it is more conducive to good teaching for the teacher to state his point of view rather than attempt to conceal it and insist that he has no ideas on the subject himself.

If teachers think through such problems carefully and make their decision on the basis of solid study and scholarship, then they should be free to teach the values of democracy as they see it. In the last analysis, academic freedom will be won when the community is convinced of the integrity and honesty of its teachers. Academic freedom can be promoted by improving the preparation of teachers, by extending tenure laws, and by building strong professional organizations of teachers that will support honest teaching and defend it from attacks by pressure groups desirous only of serving their own special interests. On the other hand, some basis that is regularized should still be available for removing incompetent and genuinely subversive teachers after a fair hearing and the consideration of accurate evidence openly arrived at.

Preservice Education of Teachers. The preservice education of prospective teachers has expanded its purposes and raised its standards in many ways. The older conception of "training" as embodied in the earlier normal schools has been replaced by a much broader conception of "teacher education." Since 1920 the trend has been away from the normal school idea and toward the teachers-college idea. In 1920, there were 137 state normal schools; by 1952, only a handful. Whereas a normal school usually offered a year or two of training beyond high school, a teachers college usually requires high school graduation for admission, offers 4 years of college-grade work, and grants a bachelor's degree at the end of the course.

Many new teachers colleges were founded, and many normal schools became teachers colleges. In 1920, there were 46 teachers colleges; by 1952, there were more than 200 accredited teachers colleges, most of which were state institutions. Among the most important of the private institutions are Teachers College of Columbia University and George Peabody College for Teachers in Nashville, Tenn. Many of the teachers colleges award a master's degree and a few the doctor's degree in addition to the bachelor's degree. Some states are requiring new teachers to acquire a master's degree before they begin to teach in a high school.

The preservice education of teachers is coming to be recognized as including the following four elements: general education, subject-matter specialization, foundations of education, and induction to teaching.

General education is intended to give the prospective teacher a broad acquaintance with the major fields of organized knowledge and of human activities. Nowadays these are usually thought of as the social sciences, the physical and natural sciences, the humanities, and the arts.

Subject-matter specialization in the field in which the prospective teacher will teach is usually required as a special competence in addition to a general education. This usually consists of courses in the subject matter and related fields, and in methods of teaching in those fields, and general study of curriculum development and the work of the teacher.

The foundations of education are usually intended to give the prospective teacher a wide acquaintance with the purposes and function of education in its various social relationships and with educational problems that are common to all teachers, no matter what subject they may teach. The foundations' function is usually fulfilled through courses in philosophy or principles of education, history of education, educational sociology, the social foundations of education, educational psychology, and human growth and development. Some institutions are attempting to weave the elements of these separate foundational approaches into an integrated orientation to the whole field of education.

The induction to teaching is intended to give prospective teachers the opportunity to apply in actual teaching situations the principles and knowledge that they have acquired in their other work. Induction thus is coming to be looked upon as a continuing process that includes observation of instruction, participation in teaching procedures, and laboratory experiences, and culminates in actual student teaching or practice teaching.

In-service Education of Teachers. In addition to the improvement in preservice education, there has been a vast increase in the opportunities for the in-service education of teachers in the last 50 years. One of the most important agencies of regular in-service education of teachers has been supervision of instruction. Formerly, supervision was conceived as inspection by administrators of classroom management by teachers. Elaborate check lists were developed by which administrators and supervisors would rate teachers in many detailed respects. Standardized tests were given to pupils as a means of determining how well the teacher was doing his work. As a result of such means, the supervisory officer would tell the teacher how to improve.

In recent years, the trend has been toward a more democratic and cooperative conception of supervision in which supervisors and teachers worked together on the individual learning and personality problems of pupils and on developing appropriate curricular materials and methods. The growth of this conception of supervision was heralded when the Department of Supervisors and Directors of Instruction of the National Education Association became the Association for Supervision and Curriculum Development.

Summer study at higher institutions has become another of the most popular and important direct methods of professional growth for in-service teachers. Most institutions of teacher education have also made special provisions by which teachers can engage in part-time study by attendance at late afternoon or evening classes in off-campus centers or at a nearby institution or by home-study work.

Another most important development in in-service education in recent years has been the workshop movement, which has tried to increase the participation of the teacher in his professional growth. Above all, the workshop principle has centered special attention upon the individual problems that a teacher faces in his own situation. A great amount of individual conference work, small-group work, reading and study, and provision for recreational and artistic outlets characterizes most workshops.

In addition to these methods, the various professional organizations have provided direct means of in-service growth for teachers. The National Education Association, the largest educational organization in America, includes numerous affiliated associations of a specialized kind. The American Federation of Teachers (affiliated with the American Federation of Labor), the National Society of College Teachers of Education, the John Dewey Society, the American Educational Research Association, and the National Society for the Study of Education are smaller but influential national organizations of educators, who find considerable professional stimulus from their work in these groups. There are also numerous national organizations of teachers devoted to one or more of the recognized subject-matter fields, such as the National Council for the Social Studies, the National Council of Teachers of English, and many others. Finally, hundreds of local teachers' associations enroll many teachers and carry on active professional programs.

Outstanding in the improvement of the education of teachers has been the great amount of research and investigation on a wide range of professional problems that has occurred in the past 50 years. In the forefront of this process has been the work of professional educators at teachers colleges and schools of education throughout the country.

Extensive surveys have also had much influence. One of the earliest of these was the study made by W. S. Learned and W. C. Bagley for the Carnegie Foundation for the Advancement of Teaching, published in 1920. A second study, the Commonwealth Teacher Training Study, used the methods of job analysis to discover specific lists of activities and traits desirable for teachers. It was conducted by W. W. Charters and D. Waples from 1925 to 1928 and was financed by the Commonwealth Fund of New York. A third and more extensive study was the National Survey of Teacher Education, authorized by Congress and conducted from 1928 to 1931 under the leadership of Professor E. S. Evenden of Teachers College, Columbia University. It was published in six volumes in 1933 by the United States Office of Education.

One of the most important recent agencies for the improvement of teacher education has been the Commission on Teacher Education of the American Council on Education. The commission, headed by Professor Karl W. Bigelow of Teachers College, was established for the 5-year period from 1938 to 1943 to make an over-all study of the problems of teacher education on a national scale. Perhaps the most important aspect of the commission's work has been the field study project, in which some 35 or 36 institutions were invited to work cooperatively on the improvement of teacher education. The staff of the commission set up consultative services, workshops, institutes, and agencies for the sharing of experiences among the cooperating institutions. The purpose of the commission was not to lay down specific patterns for all institutions to follow but to help a variety of institutions to improve and evaluate their own programs.

Out-of-school Agencies of Education

Nonschool agencies of education in the twentieth century expanded so greatly in range and variety that only a few outstanding examples can be mentioned here. The family, of course, has continued to be the first and most important educative agency in the lives of most children, but the character of family life has been so greatly affected by industrialization, urbanization, depression, and wars that special agencies have grown up to improve the quality of family care and upbringing of children.

Increased attention to child study, mental hygiene, and parent education has taken many forms. Child-guidance clinics supported by community-welfare agencies, hospitals, and schools have made available psychiatrists, psychologists, pediatricians, and social psychiatric workers to help with the care of children. The Child Study Association of America has been prominent in this process. The parent-education movement has also grown rapidly, resulting in the organization of the National Congress of Parents and Teachers, a federation of parent-teachers associations with branches in all states and a membership of 2,500,000. Recognizing that the social and emotional difficulties of parents often account for emotional disturbances in children, this movement has tried to educate parents by conferences, publications, discussion, and instruction.

Churches have also continued to be important nonschool agencies of education. In addition to regular church services and spiritual guidance, many church organizations have provided activities largely educational in nature. Especially among Protestant denominations these have included Sunday schools enrolling some 20,000,000 children, young people's societies enrolling some 3,500,000 youth, summer-vacation church schools, and summer camps and conferences. The Young Men's Christian Association, Young Women's Christian Association, and Jewish and Roman Catholic groups have continued to carry out extensive educational programs.

A large number of organized groups for boys and girls have focused around such agencies as the Boy Scouts, Girl Scouts, Girl Reserves, Camp Fire Girls, Hi-Y, Junior Red Cross, youth hostels, neighborhood centers, and settlement houses. The informal and autonomous voluntary groups like the "gangs," clubs, and "dens" of New York City have attracted the interests and enlisted the loyalties of many boys and girls who resisted parental and adult supervision.

From the time of the depression, the youth who were not in school became one of the most acute problems of American life. The American Youth Commission was established in 1935 by the American Council on Education to study the whole problem of youth in America. A notable series of publications, research studies, and investigations was produced under the direction first of Homer P. Rainey and later of Floyd W. Reeves. In 1937 it was estimated that there were approximately 20,000,000 youth between the ages of sixteen and twenty-four in the United States; of these about 20 per cent were in school, 40 per cent employed, 15 per cent married women, and 25 per cent unemployed. The percentage of unemployed and of those who felt that they were in "dead-end" jobs was much higher in depression years. It was to relieve this desperate situation of frustration, cynicism, and idleness that the Civilian Conservation Corps and the National Youth Administration were organized by the New Deal.

The CCC was established in 1933 and ended in 1942, when the war industries, military service, and political opposition had reached their crescendo. Unemployed youth from families on relief provided the largest proportion of enrollees, most of whom were in their teens. Enrolling as many as 520,000 youth in 2,600 camps in 1935, the CCC set youth to work primarily on soil and forest conservation and public works. Operated under the supervision of the War Department, the camps also developed educational programs in reading and writing for illiterate youth as well as regular academic and vocational courses at elementary and secondary school levels. In 18 months from May, 1940, to November, 1941, some 665,000 CCC youth received vocational training in some 4,000 courses useful for national defense. These courses included motor mechanics, metal- and woodwork, electrical work, welding, and airplane construction, as well as a large number of other activities.

The NYA was established in 1935 as a part of the WPA and transferred in 1939 to the Federal Security Agency until it was abolished in 1943. The principal aims of the NYA were (1) to give financial aid to students in secondary or higher institutions so that they could work part time and thus stay in school and (2) to give work experience and training to unemployed youth in order to prepare them for regular jobs. The student-aid program had benefited more than 2,000,000 students by the end of 1941–1942, after which this phase of the program was abolished. The work program gave all kinds of vocational training to young men and women between sixteen and twenty-four, as well as sewing, music, art, and recreational activities. In 1940–1941 virtually all the efforts of the NYA were devoted to training youth for defense industries, and by April, 1942, some 30,000 youth were trained each month for war production.

Adult Education. In addition to the organized educational activities already mentioned, there was a great development of a wide variety of adult-education activities, especially since 1920. It became increasingly clear that the personal, occupational, political, economic, and cultural needs of millions of adults were not being met by organized educational agencies. The Department of Adult Education of the National Education Association was organized in 1924 and the American Association of Adult Education in 1926. The two were combined in 1951 to form the Adult Education Association with the intention to coordinate training for leadership in the adult-education movement.

The oldest interests of adult education have been the removal of illiteracy and the Americanization of the foreign-born. When it was apparent in 1930 that more than 4 per cent of the adult population was still illiterate, the WPA conducted a wide program to teach adults to read and write. In 1940, when 5,000,000 resident aliens were required to register with the government, a National Citizenship Education Program was sponsored by the Department of Justice, with the cooperation of WPA, under the direction of Dean William F. Russell of Teachers College, to reach the more than 4,000,000 aliens who might become desirable American citizens. New methods and new techniques were developed by outstanding educators to make this more than simply literacy education and to promote social, political, and cultural understanding of the American way of life.

Regular night and day classes for adults have expanded under local and state as well as federal auspices. Institutions like the New School for Social Research, Town Hall, Cooper Union, and Brooklyn Institute in New York City have broadened their activities. Public-forum movements like those of Des Moines, Chicago, Cleveland, New York, San Francisco, and Springfield, Mass., have attracted large numbers of people. Leaders in the field urge the establishment of community councils to coordinate the broad front of adult-education activities by the cooperation of all interested agencies, public and private.

Special organizations of many kinds aimed their activities at particular elements in the community. Settlement houses, public-health nurses, private nursing and social-work agencies, like the Henry Street Settlement and the Henry Street Visiting Nurse Service in New York, helped families who were ill and who needed care for children and the aged. The Cooperative Extension Service of the United States Department of Agriculture was probably the largest and most effective adult-education agency in the world.

In the cities, labor unions and other groups expanded workers' education. The International Ladies Garment Workers established an educational director as early as 1916, and later, under the leadership of Mark Starr, it conducted one of the most extensive and effective educational programs for workers. The Workers' Education Bureau of America was established in 1921, and many other labor unions developed educational programs. The Summer School for Workers, begun at the University of Wisconsin in 1925, conducted a series of institutes for laboring men and women in a broad range of subjects, including not only special union problems but also political, economic, educational, consumer, international, journalistic, and public-speaking topics.

Libraries and museums began to think of their function as broadly educational and took steps to bring more people within the range of their activities and to extend their influence beyond their own walls. As early as 1910, the American National Red Cross began its educational programs, which reached hundreds of thousands in the war years and included instruction in first aid, home nursing, nutrition, work for nurses' aids, swimming, diving, lifesaving, and accident prevention, besides its various volunteer special services and disaster preparedness. Women's organizations sometimes sponsored definite educational programs, such as those provided by the League of Women Voters and the American Association of University Women. Radio networks gave thought to serious educational programs, and a vast new vista of possibilities was opened up by commercial and educational television. In many other ways and through countless organizations of a business, labor, civic, and fraternal nature, the education of the American public was promoted, sometimes for special interests, and sometimes in the interests of the general welfare.

Chapter 17

AMERICA IN THE TWENTIETH CENTURY:
IDEAS AND EDUCATION

CONFLICTING AUTHORITIES IN EDUCATION

In the first half of the twentieth century American educators were increasingly required to reassess their educational traditions. Just as the tempo of social affairs created problems for education, so did the range and scope of intellectual controversy impinge upon education. Confusion and conflict were persistent earmarks of the educational arena. When educators tried to ignore the conflict or simply remained unaware of the intellectual confusion, they lost leadership to forces outside education. When they tried to please all sides or to select indiscriminately from the several points of view in an eclectic fashion, they found themselves beset by social pressures that regarded the schools as an inviting battleground for the achievement of their special interests. The most thoughtful approach among professional leaders was to try to understand clearly the basic intellectual forces at work in our society and to make informed choices that could be defended judiciously yet fearlessly.

Three general types of orientation were discernible in their influence upon education. Some educators and philosophers relied on the authority of tradition for their principal assumptions concerning educational content and method. Others looked to modern science for their authority in describing the world, human behavior, and the educative process. Still others appealed to the cultural conceptions of man and society as providing the basic ingredients of a defensible philosophy of human nature, knowledge, and education.

Appeal to the Traditional Foundations of Education

The most vigorous spokesmen for a return to traditional values of the past as the basic guideposts for modern education came from religious leaders of the Protestant and Roman Catholic persuasions and from writers who affirmed philosophical positions resting upon idealism, Humanism, and intellectualism.

Protestantism. Three rather distinct outlooks were present within Protestantism during the first half of the twentieth century, namely, fundamentalism, liberalism or modernism, and neo-orthodoxy or neo-

554

protestantism. Fundamentalism gained new vigor in the first three decades of the twentieth century, partly as a reaction against the evolutionary and scientific movement of the late nineteenth century and partly as a result of the upsetting of social and moral values attendant upon the First World War. It maintained its loyalty to the authority of the Bible as the literal word of God and as the absolute divine guide to conduct in this world and to salvation in the next world. One phase of the resurgence of Protestant fundamentalism consisted of attacks upon the public schools for their secular and godless character. Two principal means were sought for the reinsertion of religious teaching in the public schools. Several states required daily Bible reading in the public schools, and the released-time plan for religious instruction also gained support. Efforts were made to ban instruction in science and evolution which seemed to contradict the Biblical stories of creation of the world and of man. Some fundamentalist sects objected to teaching in geography that the world was round when the Bible seemed to assert that it was flat.

The clash of fundamentalism and science was highlighted in Tennessee in 1925, when John Thomas Scopes, a high school teacher, was brought to trial because of teaching the doctrines of evolution in violation of state law. Scopes was defended by Clarence S. Darrow and prosecuted by William Jennings Bryan. The right of teachers to rely upon findings of biological science rather than upon the literal interpretation of the Bible in describing the origin of man was argued with great skill and attracted much public attention. The trial showed that religion and science had not been reconciled in the public mind and that fundamentalism was still a powerful force, especially in rural areas.

Between the two World Wars liberalism and modernism gained considerable headway among Protestant leaders who could no longer reject completely the findings of modern science in the physical and human world. Some modernists relaxed the insistence that the Bible was the literal, divinely inspired word of God, and regarded the Bible as simply the best resource and guide the world knows for ethical and moral behavior. Similarly, stress was put upon Jesus as an ethical and human teacher rather than as Christ, the divine Son of God. Others stressed social improvement and the "social gospel" as the prime ways in which good Christians could realize God's will on earth. Some modernists joined in the demand for released time and Bible reading, but others felt that religious instruction was the province of the home and church and should be kept out of the public schools.

After the Second World War a resurgence of neo-orthodoxy appeared with considerable force in the Protestant churches and theological schools. This involved an effort to accept the valid findings of science but at the same time to reassert the values of the Bible as the basic rule of faith and the divinity of Christ as the only means of salvation for man. Neo-orthodoxy stressed God's power in contrast to the evil inherent in human nature. Salvation could be achieved only by a recognition of God's sovereignty over human affairs and of man's weakness and inability to solve his own problems without divine grace and assistance. Neo-orthodoxy added its voice to the demands for increased attention to religion in the public schools.

Catholicism. Underlying all statements of the Roman Catholic position was the encyclical of Pope Pius XI in 1929, entitled *The Christian Education of Youth.* Catholicism elaborated the dualism between the supernatural order of eternity and permanence, embracing God and all things sacred and spiritual, as against the natural order of change and flux, embracing the physical world of material values and practices. Man too has a dual nature in which his immortal soul is the means of salvation and his physical body the seat of original sin and of human desires and appetites. Man is set off from the rest of nature by an impassable gulf because of the supernatural gift of his soul and faculty of reason.

The rational faculties are the prime instruments of education and learning and are the means by which truth is discovered, insofar as man's finite powers can ascertain the truth. The mind's principal role is cognitive, that is, the acquisition, discovery, and verification of preestablished truth. Since all truth and knowledge originate in the supernatural order, man does not share in creating knowledge but simply in acquiring the principles of truth, which are permanent and eternal.

The highest knowledge is supernatural revelation, to be ascertained as far as possible by reason, but beyond that by faith. Values for human conduct and destiny come from the supernatural world as interpreted by the church. Therefore, no education is complete or can, indeed, be true education unless it is permeated at every stage with religious values and religious discipline. Much reliance was put upon the classics and Scholastic philosophy as educational instruments, in addition to religious instruction.

Since Catholic philosophy insisted that the only true education must be permeated with the Catholic religion in every aspect of curriculum and instruction, education must be preeminently in the hands of the church and the family. The rights of the state were viewed as definitely subordinate to those of the church. Therefore the principal obligation of the state toward education is to help support the church and the family in their educational efforts. Protestants could agree that moral instruction must rest upon religious sanctions, but they objected to state support for Catholic schools.

Humanism. In addition to the sectarian religious outlooks of Protestantism and Catholicism, there were other powerful philosophic points of view that did not profess sectarian religion but did have close affinity to traditional religious values. For example, the philosophy of idealism which had been so powerful in the late nineteenth century continued to play a prominent role, despite a decline in relative importance. Idealists stressed the central significance of spiritual values in human personality and the spiritual self as the most vital source of human values, freedom, and knowledge. They were likely to emphasize the role of the great intellectual, literary, and religious heritage of the West as the prime essential of educational content and method. Science and technology were viewed as definitely inferior to language, literature, and religion in the educational program. Idealism was often close to Humanism in its conceptions of mental discipline and absolute truth as presuppositions upon which to build education.

Stemming from the historic philosophic outlooks of idealism, rationalism, and dualism, a philosophy of human nature and education that looked to the Great Tradition for sustenance, and therefore properly called "conservative," continued to be stated forcibly and effectively in the twentieth-century United States. Among the most extreme conservative outlooks was one that took the name "New Humanism." Although there were, of course, differences in the position of those who called themselves Humanists, nevertheless there were certain fundamental assumptions that they all accepted sufficiently to warrant thinking of them primarily as "literary" Humanists.

In general, the New Humanism involved a defensive reaction against the upsetting implications of modern social and scientific theories. In social theory, it reasserted the claims of an aristocratic and social conservatism against the humanitarian demands of social reform. Irving Babbitt stated explicitly that Humanism was interested in the discipline of the few rather than in a benevolence toward all men and in the perfection of the individual rather than in the elevation of mankind as a whole. Humanism demanded a renewed emphasis upon the ascetic qualities of "intellectual discipline" to control moral conduct more severely in order to keep a firm rein upon spontaneity and naturalism. Intellectually, the New Humanism repudiated the leadership of the natural and social sciences in the affairs of life and reverted in essence to traditional philosophy as represented by Plato, Aristotle, and medieval Scholasticism.

Among the most extreme of the Humanists (but implicitly represented in all), the most fundamental postulate was the reaffirmation of the essential dualism between man and nature. They believed in an *absolute* distinction between man and the world of nature. Man has certain unique, universal, and eternal qualities that set him off from the lower forms of nature. In other words, the extremists denied the essential implications of the evolutionary doctrine that the natural and social sciences had been at such pains to establish. Here the Humanist approach closely paralleled the traditional faculty psychology, for the Humanists spoke of human nature as if it were a separate substance or entity.

The faculties that distinguish man from lower animals were often described as conscience, reason, sense of beauty, and religion. The Humanists insisted that moral conscience is a part of man's original endowment. Conscience does not admit of degrees, for it is absolute. Reason is a universal ability to draw distinctions and form judgments. Man's sense of beauty is curiously independent of time and sets him immeasurably above the rest of the animal world. Finally, some Humanists stated, the religious instinct is universal in man. These qualities of human nature cannot be described by the scientific method; rather, this conception of human nature has come down to us from ancient classical thought, supported by the Christian religion and medieval thought.

These assumptions of Humanism have specific implications for distinctive conceptions of knowledge, truth, and human values. The Humanist believed in absolute standards of value by which the knowledge or truth of a situation may be tested. Values for the Humanist were somehow related to a sphere of existence that is above and beyond nature and that gives to knowledge and truth an unchanging and authoritative character. Knowledge, then, took on the character of a fixed body of true principles, which are to be handed down as the heritage of the race.

Stemming from this desire to introduce order into the chaotic world of society by appealing to a higher and fixed realm of values that lies behind the flux and flow of experience, the Humanist's conception of learning and of education took form. Learning has to do especially with that faculty of human nature which is termed reason, or intellect, and the main aim of learning is thus the discipline and development of the intellectual powers of discrimination and judgment. The Humanist argument followed that the studies that best present the enduring principles of absolute truth and that most effectively develop the intellect are contained in the great literature of the past, namely, the Humanistic studies.

Intellectualism. Gaining wide public notice in the 1930's and 1940's, an offshoot of literary Humanism, sometimes known as "intellectualism" or "rational Humanism," also called upon traditional conceptions of human nature and intelligence in support of its claims. Intellectualists agreed in many respects with the Humanists but had a less exclusive interest in the literary and linguistic emphasis. Drawing upon many of the historic mainsprings of Catholic philosophy but believing that religious doctrine could not be the synthesizing agency for American education, the intellectualists turned to traditional philosophy and the liberal arts for their standards of educational value.

Just as the conservative followers of the Great Tradition adhered to an underlying philosophy of rationalism, so did the intellectualists adhere to a theory of knowledge and psychology that, if not identical with the traditional faculty psychology of discipline, at least tended to emphasize the intellectual function as distinct from the other activities of human beings. Of the two realms of life that dualism posits, the intellectualists definitely preferred the realm of mind as opposed to that of the body, or matter. They identified education with development of the mind and tended to disparage the other aspects of human activity. Their psychology prompted them to extol the benefits of "intellectual training," "cultivation of the intellect," "intellectual power," and "mental discipline." In their writings, there was much emphasis upon a return to "first principles" and "fundamental concerns."

There seemed to be three crucial points in the intellectualist theory of knowledge. (1) There is a separate faculty of intellect, or reason, which is somehow capable of reaching out and grasping truth. (2) Truth in its ultimate form is absolute and fixed and serves to give order to such lower forms of knowledge as scientific knowledge of the physical world and empirical knowledge of practical affairs. (3) The curriculum in the school and college should be predominantly intellectual in content and method and should remain free of defilement by worldly matters.

These fundamental assumptions led the intellectualists to decry the great attention being given by American education to scientific and technical studies, to practical experience, and to the freedom and interests of students as means to effective learning. They outlined what they believed to be the permanent studies appropriate to all youth at all times and in all places inasmuch as all men have a common and permanent human nature. They relied upon the traditional liberal arts of the Middle Ages, the rationalistic idealism of the Great Tradition, and a faculty psychology of formal discipline. Primary place in general education was given to the reading of the great books of the past and the study of formal grammar, rhetoric, logic, and mathematics as means of training the mind. When the intellectual virtues have been properly cultivated, they argued, the educated person would be fully equipped to solve problems of practical conduct and experience. The distinctive function of school and college is, however, intellectual in nature and not practical or moral.

Appeal to the Scientific Foundations of Education

Reacting against the conceptions of the traditionalists just outlined, many educators in the twentieth-century United States turned to modern science for their standards of authority and methods of work. Borrowing from the Newtonian conceptions of science and the Positivism of Auguste Comte and Herbert Spencer in the nineteenth century, modern realists began to describe the world as a machine that obeyed fixed and immutable natural laws in which supernatural and rationalistic interpretations had little or no place.

Believing fully in the scientific method, they assumed that human nature could be investigated and analyzed by scientific methods with as much precision as the physical universe and physical phenomena. Discarding dualistic conceptions of human nature, they described man as a complicated machine whose behavior could be predicted and even controlled with a high degree of accuracy and certainty. Man was therefore looked upon as an inherent part of nature, although somewhat more complex in his structure and behavior than the animals. Even so, it was assumed that much could be learned about man from the scientific study of animals. Most American psychologists in the first half of the twentieth century were brought up in the atmosphere of a scientific realism.

Connectionism. In the field of psychology, the development was so tremendous that only one or two generalizations can be made here. The experimental and scientific methods that had been envisioned in the latter nineteenth century developed with enormous rapidity in the many different fields of learning, instincts, individual differences, and emotions. E. L. Thorndike attacked the introspective and "faculty" psychology of an earlier day. At Teachers College, Columbia University, he virtually created "educational psychology" as he attempted to apply the methods of the exact sciences to certain educational problems. With the publication of his three monumental volumes, entitled *Educational Psychology*, in 1913, attention in the United States began to turn more and more to an "objective" psychology for the answers to problems of original nature, learning, and individual differences.

By his insistence that learning is highly specific, Thorndike made a frontal attack upon the doctrines of mental discipline, which had long held that certain studies are uniquely valuable for "training the mind" and enabling it to transfer its operations to any field whatever. Thorndike asserted that the reflex arc in the nervous system is the hereditary unit of behavior, rather than a group of substantive "faculties." Learning consists, not in a general training of unformed and spiritual faculties, but in the establishment of specific bonds of connection between a situation S and a response R. These S-R bonds are established in two major ways, according to Thorndike's famous laws of learning—by exercise and by satisfying effect. According to the law of exercise, modifiable connections between a stimulus and a response are strengthened as they are used and are weakened when not used. Other things being equal, the more frequently and the more recently the bonds are strengthened by practice, the stronger the connections and hence the more effective the learning. According to the law of effect, modifiable connections tend to be stamped in when the learning is satisfying and pleasant for the learner, and bonds tend to be weakened when the result is unsatisfying or annoying. Other things being equal, connections are established more easily when the action system is ready to act and less easily when it is not ready to act (law of readiness).

Under the impact of Thorndike's connectionist psychology, mental discipline received a major setback, especially in the elementary and secondary school practices of the United States. Thorndike pointed out that transfer of training occurs only when the content or the method of a school subject is similar to the use to which it is to be put. In other words, if students are to be educated for specific ends, they should study those subjects which contribute directly to those ends. This theory gave great support to the new scientific and social studies for which there was a growing demand throughout the country. Hence, specialized studies entered more easily into the elementary and secondary schools, but they were not accepted as readily in the traditional liberal-arts courses of colleges, which held more stubbornly to the doctrines of discipline.

Another characteristic development was the creation of applied psychology to deal with industrial and educational problems of guidance, personnel selection and training, advertising appeal, and other phases of human relations. Clinical and abnormal psychology grew in proportion, to deal with variants from the average types of mental and emotional adjustment. Psychiatry was developed to deal more directly with the physiological bases of psychological phenomena.

More extreme in their interpretations of man as a completely measurable mechanism were the behaviorists who gained widespread attention after the First World War. Aspiring to be able to predict human behavior with as much certainty as the physicist predicts physical phenomena, the behaviorists set out to formulate definite laws of human behavior on the basis of observable, external relationships. They discarded all concepts of consciousness, will, and sensation and simply described the measurable and outward aspects of behavior, building up most of their laws of learning upon the conditioning process developed by Pavlov. Children are born, they stated, only with simple, inherited, and unlearned reflexes of fear, love, and rage as expressed in outward signs of attraction, rejection, crying, and other physiological responses. The whole complex of learned responses is built up by the acquisition of habits and verbal manipulations that become associated with the simple unlearned responses.

Another way in which the scientific method was applied to the study of human nature was in the development of objective and standardized tests. The testing and measurement movement had a great rage in the 1920's and 1930's as a means of making education scientific. This faith in science was simply stated: Whatever exists at all exists in some amount; anything that exists in amount can be measured; and measurement in education is, in general, the same as measurement in the physical sciences.

Testing was applied to nearly all school subjects in the form of achievement tests and was perhaps the most characteristic feature of scientific educational procedure in the 1920's.

Much reliance was also put upon intelligence testing and the measurement of the intelligence quotient (I.Q.). Lewis Terman developed and refined the Binet tests and made them suitable for American use in the Stanford Revision; Thorndike and others helped to develop group tests of intelligence and aptitude for the army in the First World War; and vast use was made of group tests of all kinds in the Second World War. There was much discussion concerning the permanence of the I.Q., most psychologists maintaining that native intelligence as measured by I.Q. tests is not affected significantly by differences of environment or education. It was assumed that intelligence tests measure inherited capacity and not achievement, but most tests relied upon some kind of acquired knowledge as evidence of original ability. Other psychologists in the 1930's began to question these assumptions, and the battles between the advocates of heredity and of environment, between nature and nurture, became more severe.

The battle was not over, but significant gains had been made by the environmentalists. All this debate seemed to the advocates of experimentalism to have stated the problem mistakenly, for they had long said that human behavior is a matter of interaction between the individual and his environment, neither of which can be neglected in the educative process.

Appeal to the Cultural Foundations of Education

Reacting against the traditional religious and philosophical outlooks as well as the "positivistic" science of educational psychologists, a point of view often known as "experimentalism" or "cultural naturalism" began to gain more and more adherents during the twentieth century. Experimentalism attempted to adjust philosophy more closely to the requirements of an age committed to human freedom, democracy, and modern science. Under the intellectual leadership of John Dewey, a new and progressive outlook for American education was formulated. Drawing upon the philosophical traditions of naturalism, empiricism, and pragmatism, and upon new evidence from the social sciences, anthropology, Gestalt psychology, and social psychology, experimentalism set out to design a philosophy appropriate for twentieth-century American education.

The significant thing about the experimentalist position was that it attempted to devise a theory of education that would adequately assimilate the new social-science disciplines. It was apparent to the experimentalists that an adequate theory of education must take account of the best evidence that had been developed by modern natural science, social science, and psychology.

Of prime significance here was the conception of culture and the role of culture in the development of individuals (see Chapter 1). It was apparent to the experimentalists that the foundations of education were to be found in the culture which gives meaning and significance to education. To understand individual behavior and to formulate desirable goals for education, one must study the culture in which they function. The essence of the American culture was found to reside in the social ideals of democracy and the intellectual ideals of free and disciplined intelligence. These were the authorities for the cultural foundations of American education.

The other side of the experimentalist picture was a movement at all levels of education to give much more attention to the individual student and to his personal development than had been possible in the standardized school situation. The converse of the demand of democratic education was that the individual should not be lost in the masses of new students who filled the schools and colleges. Here it was that the new conceptions of science and psychology contributed to a changed conception of human nature and of individuality.

Human Nature. In general, experimentalism denied the traditional distinctions or dualisms that divided man from nature, mind from body, individual from society, and knowledge from action. On the contrary, it interpreted the findings of science to mean that man is essentially a part of nature and, in common with other organisms, lives in constant interaction with his physical and cultural environment. On this basis, the individual is not something discrete and separate from society but develops his own unique individuality and personality as a result of his participation in and through the social situation. In other words, human nature was viewed, not as something fixed and eternal from all time, but as a mode of reaction developed in and through the surrounding culture. Differences in the culture of individuals elicit such differences in the way they act and believe that it is misleading to say that human nature is the same everywhere in spite of its surrounding social environment.

Thus, life was viewed as a continual interactive adjustment between an active cultural environment and an active individual. Behavior arises when a condition of equilibrium between the individual and the environment has been upset, causing tension or disturbance in the individual, who seeks to restore the equilibrium by acting upon the environment. In this process, the individual is changed by his behavior, and the environment is also changed by his behavior.

Learning. Some of the implications for educational practice that arose out of this position may be stated briefly. First, from the point of view of the culture, it was apparent that education must stress much more the *vital connection between the school and the culture* of the surrounding community and larger society. The student must gain a much more genuine understanding of the problems of society, and therefore he must give much more time to study of the culture. Studying must put a far greater reliance upon a wide variety of materials and activities in order that the student may see the relationship of one problem to other problems and to make preliminary efforts at solving the problems. Such solving must rely more and more upon the cooperation of students in carrying on social activities together and at arriving at group decisions, based not so much upon authority or majority voting as on a genuine consensus which is reached through discussion and working together with the teacher.

Secondly, from the point of view of the individual, the implications of the experimentalist position were fully as far-reaching. The conception of *growth* in education resulted in a much greater respect for the individual student and for his development as a unique personality. Furthermore, the conception of the *active* character of experience proved to be exceedingly fruitful for educational theory and practice. Since experience is the interaction of the individual and his environment, then knowing and meaning arise only when there is an active response on the part of the learner. That learning is viewed as best which encourages the learners under the guidance of the teacher to take the initiative in planning, carrying out, and judging their own activities. Learning is best when students themselves have freedom to carry out those activities which seem to be in line with their own genuine purposes and interests. The test of learning thus becomes, not the ability to recite in class or write an examination, as much as the ability to act intelligently in subsequent experiences.

A third implication of the experimentalist approach was the conception of *wholeness*. The whole organism contributes to the responses that the individual makes. Thus, learning becomes a matter of all that the student takes away from a situation in physical, mental, and emotional attitudes as well as intellectual meanings. From the point of view of the individual, wholeness, or integration, of response is achieved when the individual makes effective adjustments within as he faces the situation without. If the learner faces effectually a sufficient variety of situations, he integrates himself as a personality; but when a number of such interactions are sufficiently inadequate to upset the normal balance of the individual, incipient maladjustments follow.

Because the individual interacts with his social environment, made up of other people, institutions, customs, laws, and systems of thought and belief, education must more and more take account of all these factors in order to promote most effectively the whole personal and social development of the individual.

Intelligence. In reaction against the traditional rationalism of earlier philosophies as well as the positivist outlooks of scientific psychology, the experimentalists laid stress upon a different conception of thinking and intelligence. Thinking was viewed not simply as a function of a separate faculty of "reason" or of conditioned behavior but essentially as a matter of problem solving.

In his widely influential book *Democracy and Education,* published in 1916, Dewey emphasized the importance of science and of scientific method as central in the governing of human affairs of all kinds. In the scientific method, he found principles of procedure that gave him a clue to a conception of experience, knowledge, and thinking widely at variance with the notion of a separate faculty of intellect held by the rationalists and intellectualists. His theory closely associated knowledge and thinking with action and with the consequences of action.

Dewey thus arrived at a description of thinking that rested upon the scientific method of problem solving. In other words, problem solving becomes *the* method of human *intelligence* in the conduct and control of human affairs. Mind is not a separate faculty for dealing with "ideas" but is the name given to all human activities that approach experience intelligently with the intent to remake human experience and to accomplish real changes in events with the purpose of improving and enriching human life and enjoyment. Thinking as problem solving involves four steps: a sense of a disturbance, or *problem,* to be solved; *observation* of the conditions surrounding the problem; formulation of suggested *hypotheses,* or *plans* of *action,* with their possible consequences if acted upon; actual and active experimental *testing* to see if the hypotheses when acted upon give the desired consequences.

Then, basing educational method upon this process of thinking, Dewey reached the following implications for education: The student must be in the center of genuine situations of experience and continuously engaged in activities in which he is interested when the *problem* confronts him as a genuine stimulus to thought. He must possess or obtain the proper information to make *observations* that are necessary for dealing with the problem. Suggested solutions, or *hypotheses,* must occur to him, and he must be responsible for developing them in an orderly way. Finally, he must have the opportunity and the occasion to *test* his ideas by applying them in practice in order to make their meaning clear and to discover for himself their validity. Thus, educational method really consists in the method of thinking made conscious and realized in action.

Some experimentalists were not satisfied with this formulation of the thinking process and did not believe that the essentially fact-finding nature of the scientific method was appropriate to decisions that involve the guidance of conduct. In the Twenty-eighth Yearbook of the National Society of College Teachers of Education (1942), entitled *The Discipline of Practical Judgment in a Democratic Society*, Professor R. Bruce Raup and his associates outlined their suggestions for developing good decisions concerning what people *should* do in various kinds of situations. They argued that intelligence is not simply the scientific method of fact finding or simply what is measured by an intelligence test. Intelligence is a form of deliberative action that embraces wise decisions arrived at cooperatively and democratically in the light of facts and values to be served.

Practical judgments, therefore, include simple decisions as to what to do, the formulation and carrying out of general policies with respect to action, and the reconstruction of underlying assumptions and normative principles concerning how people in general should act. Practical intelligence must include three phases: (1) the projection of a desired state of affairs or an ideal situation, (2) the survey of the existing relevant facts in the present situation, and (3) designing and carrying out a program of action that will proceed from the present situation to the desired state of affairs. Direct attention to the development of practical intelligence in the schools and colleges is one of the most important ways in which educational methods proposed by certain of the experimentalists differed from the "mind training" of the intellectualists and the "scientific method" of the realists.

Social Role of the Arts and Sciences

Science and Mathematics. Enriched by the coming to America of such notable scientists as Albert Einstein and other refugee scholars from Nazism and Fascism, American science made rapid strides, absorbed the developments from Europe, and began further to branch out.

Even more impressive to the average person than "pure" research were the new inventions and technological applications of science, for these they could see. The development of the airplane from the Wright brothers' model early in the century to Lindbergh's solo flight across the Atlantic in 1927, and finally to jet-propelled and rocket planes took less than 50 years; many had seen the whole process in their lifetimes. Air conditioning, television, prefabricated houses, plastics, and synthetic goods of all kinds were close to the experience of millions and were soon to be demanded by millions more. On top of it all came the realization of harnessing atomic energy in the hydrogen bomb, in radioactive isotopes, in atomic submarines, and in other atomic power plants.

Most scientists in the early twentieth century had held to the doctrines of social neutrality and objectivity. They denied that scientists had any responsibility for the uses to which their "pure" research was put and defended the investigation of science apart from social implications as the only true approach to research. Abraham Flexner became a symbol of this outlook. The First World War left more people in doubt as to this retreat from social responsibility. After the atomic bomb was dropped in the Second World War and the hydrogen bomb tests proved to be so devastating, the storm broke.

Many of the atomic scientists themselves took the lead in demanding social control of scientific investigation through the United Nations or a world government in order to prevent scientific competition that might lead to terrible destruction among nations. Some scientists even began to insist that science was not purely "objective"; that the scientist did not and could not approach his work with a mind entirely empty of assumptions and values; and that scientific knowledge must be sought, within the context of cultural forces and conditions, with awareness of its relationship to practice and conduct.

Engineers had seen this more clearly than "pure" scientists in their studies of technological applications of science to society. Witness the Society of Industrial Engineers in their report on technocracy, and Harold Loeb and the Brookings Institution in their reports on the potential capacity of production in America. The National Planning Board and the National Resources Planning Board saw the need to utilize science for public welfare. It was later clear to all what strides could be made when scientists worked cooperatively on a project of urgent national concern, as on the government's atomic program known as the "Manhattan Project." A cooperative and coordinated program in research could achieve in 3 or 4 years what might take individual scientists in universities and private foundations many times longer to do. Some began to wonder what might be achieved in peacetime pursuits under similar conditions. The trend was away from the separation of knowledge and action as preached by traditional philosophies; the trend was toward a close relation between knowledge and action as urged by the experimentalists.

Social Sciences. One of the most significant developments in American scholarship in the twentieth century was the increased attention given to the social sciences by a large number of scholars and writers. The trend was toward an increasingly realistic description of American institutions and how they worked, toward the relating of political, economic, and social forces to American culture and the welfare of the people. Despite the assumptions of many that social science must be just as scientific as the physical and natural sciences and not take sides in social affairs, an increasing number of social scientists began to assert that social interpretation was a legitimate and even primary part of their task. Whatever interpretations they made were based ultimately upon the social values they held and upon the kind of social relationships they felt to be desirable in American life.

Joint enterprises and cooperative efforts of social scientists resulted in the monumental and extremely important volumes of the *Encyclopaedia of the Social Sciences,* edited by E. R. A. Seligman and Alvin Johnson, and the *Dictionary of American Biography.* The Social Science Research Council formed after the First World War took the lead in the effort to coordinate research in the field. The American Historical Association promoted several cooperative studies; the most important for education was the analysis and interpretation of its Commission on the Social Studies in the Schools. The New Deal did much to enlist economists, sociologists, and government experts from colleges and universities as consultants and planners. This brought forth the jeers of opponents concerning the "Brain Trust" and "egg heads," but the conservatives moved to enlist like support on their side. The National Association of Manufacturers, the Chamber of Commerce, and the Republican party soon had scholars studying, writing, and speaking on their behalf.

Before the First World War and the great depression, most social scientists were confident that the basic structure of American society was sound, but in the early 1930's there was a growing chorus of criticism as social scientists tried to find reasons for the economic collapse. More and more they began to believe that the United States must move toward social reform more or less rapidly and that social knowledge is useful as a guide in social planning and social action.

The Arts. American literature came into its own in the twentieth century, breaking away at last from its too complete reliance upon Europe. Romance, history, or sex furnished the material for much writing, but realistic descriptions of social conditions surrounding all classes began to play a larger role and ranged from cynical factualism to vigorous and earnest social reformism. Novels, short stories, and newspaper columnists had millions of readers.

Perhaps more widely read than any other form of publication were the "comic" books, the "pulp" magazines, and the sports writers in the large dailies. Americans were probably more likely to be magazine readers than any other people, and millions of copies were sold each week or each month.

Scholars became interested in the role of language in communication. "Semantics" was a byword for those who emphasized that the meanings of words are not fixed and stable but take on different meanings in relation to the situation or context in which they are used. All in all, the American language and American letters began to drop their exclusive allegiance to the Great Tradition and to reflect the trends toward social reform and experimentalism.

American art and music in the twentieth century also began to break away from traditional forms and traditional themes and give expression to a new spirit reflecting the social trends of the times. "Form should follow function" became the slogan for those who tried to give a more realistic and more liberal expression in art forms to the new life of the times. In general, the effort was made to make the fine arts more functional and to ensure better design in the practical arts.

Modern architecture continued to gain adherents. Despite the controversies over the architectural designs of Radio City, the Chicago World's Fair of 1933, the New York World's Fair of 1939–1940, and the United Nations buildings, it was clear that modern design was gaining headway against tradition in office buildings, private homes, and public housing.

One of the most important ways in which American art was brought closer to the people grew out of the emergency measures of the New Deal during the depression. Designed originally to give relief to unemployed writers, artists, actors, and musicians, the project was so carefully planned and carried out that it showed what widespread benefits could be gained for popular taste and enjoyment. The Federal Arts Project was organzied in 1933 under the Works Progress Administration. Its divisions included the Federal Art Project, the Federal Music Project, the Federal Theater Project, and the Federal Writers' Project.

Not only were hundreds of persons given employment but thousands more all over the country attended classes in all the arts and listened to concerts and saw plays at low prices. American folk art was catalogued in the *Index of American Design*, indigenous American music was stimulated in all parts of the country, American folklore was collected, and extremely valuable guides to American states, rivers, and national resources were written. To be sure, all the creative work was not of the highest caliber, but Americans for the first time gained a sense of what federal patronage of the arts could mean in bringing the arts close to the people. It was a great experiment in the education of the American public. It led many to wonder whether private patronage of the arts had not gone too far in widening the gap between the public and the artist. Some began to wonder if the social role of the arts and sciences would not be greatly improved if sponsorship of the arts were patterned somewhat along the lines of education, in which public and private sponsorship existed side by side.

CROSSCURRENTS IN THE EDUCATIONAL PROGRAM

Reinterpretation of Aims

The preceding section outlined some of the contradictory intellectual authorities to which American educators and the public appealed during the first half of the twentieth century. As curriculum makers went about the task of reassessing the educational program at all levels, they were beset by these conflicting claims. They may be restated briefly as follows:

1. Religious and moral values. Some people criticized the schools for not paying enough attention to religion as the basis for sound moral principles. Others argued that moral values should be grounded in the common life of the democratic community and culture and that religion in a free society should be the province of home and church.

2. Intellectual discipline and intelligence. Some people stressed intellectual discipline as the chief goal of education, such discipline to be achieved through the traditional bodies of academic subject matter. Others argued that the main goal of discipline should be attained by free intelligence developed in and through a wide range of problem-solving activities calling for the exercise of sound practical judgments.

3. Acquisition of knowledge. Some persons felt that systematic knowledge of the type produced by academic scholarship should be the starting point for curriculum content. Others believed that functional knowledge could best be achieved by starting with the experience of students and moving toward the organized knowledge of adults as the end point.

4. Individual and social needs. Some educators came to the conclusion that the principal goal of the educative process was to enable the student to fulfill his individual needs and interests. Others insisted that education for citizenship should be the prime goal of education in the modern world.

5. Vocational and general education. Practical-minded persons argued that education was derelict in its duty if it did not give students a practical training for some job in life and for earning a living. Others were equally convinced that the distinctive task of schools and colleges was to give students a well-rounded liberal education that would fit them to lead a full and worthwhile life, leaving specialized technical training to other agencies.

The interplay of these various outlooks led to a variety of new claims upon the educational program. In the first two decades of the century the traditional religious and philosophical outlooks continued to stress moral development and mental discipline as the paramount aims of education. However, the rise of a scientific psychology and realistic philosophy began to stress the informational and practical aspects of education, and a few voices here and there began to urge the claims of individual development and social needs for education.

In the 1920's interest in individual development was accelerated by the growing power of the psychology of individual differences and the dominant individualism of American life. Greater attention was therefore given in education to individualizing instruction. In the 1930's, 1940's, and 1950's the events of depression and the World Wars drew the attention of educators to the claims of industrialism and technology and evoked efforts to think of democracy in social as well as individualistic terms. Consequently, greater attention was devoted to preparing students to play their parts in a democratic society.

The change from a stress upon individual development to a stress upon the social needs of youth was well illustrated in the change of outlook among "progressive" educators. With the organization of the Progressive Education Association in 1918, the dominant interest for 15 or 20 years was to release the individual capacities of children in the "child-centered" school. All kinds of new methods and activities were devised to aid the development of individuals. In the middle 1930's the critical social situation in the United States and in the world made it clear to the "frontier" group of progressive educators that the aims and curriculum of schools and colleges should consider more fully the needs of society and should be based upon a rounded conception of the desirable social system that should be achieved in the United States. Prominent spokesmen among progressive educators urged that the traditional aims of education should be reinterpreted in the light of the newer conceptions of a cultural view of human nature and an experimentalist view of democratic society.

According to this view, character and moral development are prime requisites for education. Character was conceived as arising from the interaction of the individual with his cultural environment. Moral instruction in the public schools was to be achieved not by religious injunctions but by increasingly intelligent participation in democratic processes. Discipline remained an important aspect of educational aims but was to be developed not so much by authority stemming from the teacher as by the social requirements involved as the individual takes part in group activities.

Information and knowledge were still considered to be important, not as ends in themselves, but as means to a more intelligent solving of problems recognized as important to the learner. Vocational and practical aims took a paramount position, not in a category separate and distinct from other aims, but closely allied to the general development of character, discipline, and knowledge—knowledge and action always to be closely related. Individual development is a most important quality of democratic education, but it was increasingly seen that individual capacities are developed most effectively as an integral part of the social process.

The interactive process means that individuals realize their potentialities in and through a genuinely democratic social participation. The well-developed individual cannot be considered apart from the consideration of a desirable social order. All good education rests upon a good society.

As this kind of reinterpretation of educational aims gained headway in American education, many changes took place in the curriculum and methods at all levels of the schools and colleges, but not without vigorous opposition from educationally and socially conservative groups. The trend was unmistakably in favor of the newer outlooks until a reaction set in following the Second World War. Progressive education was put on the defensive by traditionalist forces in the 1940's and 1950's. Many of the gains of 50 years' experience were threatened, and the outcome was by no means assured. Much depended upon the strength and vitality of the organized profession and the institutions that prepared teachers.

Elementary Education

As the century opened, the traditional subject-matter curriculum was in the saddle in elementary schools. Paramount stress was laid upon the acquisition of knowledge and skill in the fundamental operations of reading, writing, spelling, and arithmetic. Lesser stress was given to elementary science, history, geography, music, art, and physical education. The earliest efforts to reform the elementary curriculum were various attempts to individualize instruction. One of these reforms centered in the "project method," which borrowed its ideals from the practical fields of manual training, home economics, and agriculture. Gradually the project idea was transferred to almost all other subjects as a means of giving the pupil a chance to work on actual practical problems as nearly lifelike in quality as possible.

Often the project became a "unit" of work designed to give a comprehensible and definite amount of knowledge through activities to be undertaken by the student. Projects and units became the rage in the first three decades of the century. They even became the basis for a thoroughgoing reorganization of the elementary school curriculum in the Dalton plan and the Winnetka plan. At Dalton, Mass., in the early 1920's, Helen Parkhurst devised a series of projects, units, or large problems known as "contracts." A contract set forth a definite amount of reading, exercises, and written work to be done in a specified amount of time, usually 3 or 4 weeks. At Winnetka, Ill., Superintendent Carleton Washburne instituted an arrangement by which a certain number of projects or units were assigned to each grade level and students were allowed to proceed at their own individual rate in mastering the subject matter of the projects.

Individualized instruction was thus a matter of adjusting the speed of achievement to the abilities of the children, but the subject matter to be mastered was constant for all. In this way, the brighter students could advance more rapidly, and the slower students were given necessary help in acquiring the minimum standards.

Another and even more popular device to individualize instruction was the effort to classify students into different groups according to their academic ability. Known as "ability groups," "homogeneous groups," and

"XYZ groups," these arrangements swept the country in the 1920's, largely as a result of the new findings of the psychology of individual differences and the intelligence-testing movement. Most commonly, students were divided according to scholastic aptitude as measured by intelligence tests. Thus, the brightest pupils could be given extra work in an "enriched" program and not be held back by the slower pupils; the average students did somewhat less than the brightest; and the slowest, or

Fig. 33. Children Studying Arithmetic in a Modern Elementary School. (*Courtesy of Associated Public School Systems.*)

"dull," students could be helped to achieve the minimum essentials. Individualized instruction in this way could be achieved by keeping the promotion rate constant for all, but the curriculum could be adjusted to varying abilities.

In the 1930's, many elementary educators felt that a still more thorough-going attack upon the elementary school curriculum should be made. They argued that projects, units, contracts, ability grouping, and the like, were simply devices for improving the acquisition of subject matter. They urged that the real basis for organization should be the experiences of the learners. Therefore, the curriculum should be conceived, not as a course of study consisting of subject matter to be learned, but as the total range of experiences involved in the school activities. The idea of the "experience" curriculum revolved around the "activities movement." The leading exponent of this view was William H. Kilpatrick at Teachers College, Columbia University.

The activity program meant many things to many people, but it most often meant that the learner should be viewed as a "whole" and that learning is best when activities are purposeful and interesting to the learner. The learner was viewed as active and creative; he should have a part in initiating, planning, carrying out, and evaluating his activities. "Learning by doing" became the watchword, and great emphasis was put upon freedom for the learner to engage in activities deemed important by him and to criticize intelligently his own learning process.

Since learning is not a specific thing but involves the acquisition of attitudes and habits as well as knowledge, the integration of the whole personality of the learner is the ultimate aim of the educative process. The test of learning is not the ability to pass factual examinations but the way the individual behaves in subsequent experiences. The individual learns only what he "accepts to act on" and what he brings away from the situation in knowing, thinking, and feeling. Much attention was given in the activity program to discussion, trips, making things, dramatic and pictorial representation, and sharing experiences through displays and assembly programs, as well as reading books and writing reports.

The early progressive schools in the 1920's and 1930's began to bring down upon their heads the accusation of conservatives that they were simply coddling pupils and catering to their passing interests. Criticism was leveled at the lack of discipline and bad manners among progressive students, as well as their failure to grasp the fundamental information and skills deemed necessary by traditional and "essentialist" educators. The individualistic methods of the early progressives also were increasingly criticized by those who began to stress the social needs of modern American youth.

In the 1930's and 1940's an ever larger company of educators insisted that the whole educational process must be considered a social process. Group activities in learning through cooperative efforts, the dealing with vital social problems rather than casual interests of children, and a vital connection between the school and community were paramount in their proposals. Above all, these newer progressive critics insisted that education must rely upon a fundamental democratic philosophy of society in which the curriculum is built and carried out through democratic methods of study, discussion, and cooperation. Some progressives said that the democratic philosophy is served simply in the *process* by which teachers and students cooperatively work out their activities; others said that democratic education must be geared to a *program* of social reform, as well as relying upon democratic school arrangements.

As a result of these criticisms, the curriculum began to be shaped by the needs of society as well as by the interests of pupils. It was believed by many that the needs of children cannot be separated from a conception of a desirable kind of society in which they are to live. It seemed clear that the school experiences should be planned not only with references to good learning activities of individual children but with reference to the social significance of the problems that children face and solve.

"Areas of living," "persistent life situations," and "common learnings" in a democratic society became key concepts for the cooperative building of the school program. Children should not be allowed to neglect the development of abilities in such areas as home and family life, personal relationships, social and civic responsibilities, economic and occupational life, and health, recreation and leisure activities. Educators continued to be divided in their outlooks concerning whether or not such a curriculum should be based upon a fairly well defined kind of society toward which educators should move.

Regardless of the outcome of these controversies, most progressive educators were urging the expansion of the services of the elementary school to include more attention to such activities as child study and mental hygiene; educational and vocational guidance, counseling, and personnel services; medical and health education, recreation, and physical education; and special treatment of exceptional children ranging from the farthest above normal to the farthest below normal in physical, mental, and emotional characteristics.

Growing attention to the emotional needs of children as well as to their intellectual and physical needs was one of the most significant developments in the middle decades of the century. Wide-ranging studies in child development and mental hygiene called attention to the irrational or nonrational wellsprings of human behavior and motivation. Borrowing from the research and theories of psychoanalysis, mental hygiene began to highlight the behavior problems that arise in the wake of maladjustments in family and group life. Educators became more than ever aware that the earliest years of the child's life can have momentous influence upon his later development. The psychology of personality and adjustment was an increasingly popular and important concern of educators as they realized that teaching could be seriously handicapped if the teacher ignored the emotional development of the child and tried to deal solely with intellectual training and academic knowledge.

Secondary Education

Several factors in the twentieth century led many educators to believe that a thoroughgoing revision of the secondary school curriculum was as essential as reform in the elementary curriculum. One of these factors was the change in the character of the high school population. In 1900, only about 10 per cent of youth of secondary school age were actually in school; by 1930 the percentage had jumped to about 50 per cent; and by 1954 it was up to 85 per cent. This was a phenomenal increase and represented an educational experiment of vast proportions. It virtually was something new under the sun. No other nation had tried to educate the vast majority of its population to such an advanced age.

This meant that a much wider range of social and economic background as well as of scholastic aptitude was represented in the secondary schools than ever before. It meant also that the aim of college preparation was no longer the dominant purpose of the high school. Whereas about 75 per cent of high school graduates had gone on to college in 1900, only about 25 per cent of high school graduates went to college in 1950. With these changes, it became clear to many that the traditional aristocratic and relatively exclusive character of secondary education must give way to a kind of secondary education that would meet the needs of the students it dealt with.

Another change in secondary education was the continued multiplication of subjects and courses in the high school. All subjects expanded enormously as a result of the new industrial, scientific, and scholarly activities. The high schools were flooded with courses in English; social studies; science; mathematics; commercial, home-economics, and vocational studies; art; music; foreign languages; and physical education. This multiplication of subjects meant that the elective system was standard practice, and the subject curriculum of separate, isolated, and discrete subjects carried the day. Students were likely to specialize excessively or scatter their efforts over a large number of subjects having little relation to each other. In view of this "suicidal specialization" and "excessive smattering," many educators began to urge a reorganization of the curriculum in order to give more continuity and unity to the students' programs.

One step in this direction was taken by the Commission on Reorganization of Secondary Education, which issued its famous *Cardinal Principles of Secondary Education* in 1918. The commission urged that secondary education should provide for specialization through selection of elective courses and also for uniformity through common activities that all students would pursue. These specializing and unifying functions were to be related to the seven principal objectives of secondary education: health, command of the fundamental processes, worthy home membership, a vocation, civic education, worthy use of leisure time, and ethical character. From that time on, many efforts were made to achieve a greater "correlation" and "fusion" of subject matter in order to overcome the specialized subject matters.

Some schools grouped the various subjects into "broad fields" of knowledge in the effort to show the relationships between groups of studies. The most common "broad fields" were language arts, social studies, science and mathematics, and the arts and music. Students were often required to take a certain amount of work in each of the broad fields in order to acquire a general acquaintance with the several basic fields of organized knowledge. "Survey courses" were developed to give a general understanding of the broad fields and were designed for all students, in place of the more highly specialized courses suitable to the interests of the specialist in a narrow field.

"Problems courses" were devised to give the opportunity for students to become acquainted with basic social problems or broad themes of human development, the understanding of which required drawing upon a wide range of subject matter that cut across the traditional subject fields. The study of a whole culture, for example, would draw upon literature, language, history, politics, economics, science, art, and music as they were needed. Sometimes the "problems" were defined in terms of "unemployment," "problems of American democracy," "transportation and communication," "industrial society," and the like. Other programs tried to go beyond these reorganizations and use the techniques of the activities program and experience curriculum as they were being developed in the elementary school. The social studies often took the lead in these efforts to correlate or integrate the learning activities of students.

The trend was definitely toward providing a common background of outlook, knowledge, and experience for all students. This often took the form of a "core curriculum," or "core course," required of all students for a large share of their school time. The whole trend was sometimes designated as the "general-education movement." It was claimed that thereby the evils of the elective system and separate subjects could be remedied and students would achieve a more integrated understanding of social development and of their own role in a democratic society.

This process was aided by the support given to the social aims of education by influential publications of the Educational Policies Commission of the National Education Association, the American Historical Association's Commission on the Social Studies, the American Council on Education, and the Progressive Education Association. In contrast, traditionalists were reacting to the confusions in American education by urging a return to the study of the great heritage of the past as a means of unifying educational experiences.

One of the most significant developments in secondary education ·in the twentieth century was the cooperative program undertaken by the Commission on the Relation of School and College of the Progressive Education Association, popularly known as the "Experiment of the

Thirty Schools" or the "Eight Year Study." Beginning in 1933 under the direction of Wilford Aikin, the commission enlisted some 30 public and private high schools to reorganize their programs and arranged with some 200 colleges to accept the graduates of these schools with no college-entrance requirements other than the recommendation of the principals of the schools.

Here was a broad attack upon the problem to see if high school graduates of "progressive" schools could do as well in college as did graduates

Fig. 34. Four Leaders in Progressive Education.
From left to right: John Dewey, William H. Kilpatrick, George S. Counts, and Boyd H. Bode.
(Philosophy of Education Conference, Teachers College, Columbia University, 1948).

of traditional schools who met the usual college-entrance requirements. Each school was left to its own devices within a framework of general principles: greater mastery and continuity of learning, a clearer understanding of the problems of our civilization, the development of a sense of social responsibility, release of creative energies, greater freedom for students and teachers, and an emphasis upon guidance and counseling of students. The schools offered programs ranging from the "broad-fields" and "problems" type of approach to an "experience" curriculum centered in some enduring interest, need, or vocational objective of individual students.

The first graduates of the progressive schools went to college in 1936, and a follow-up study was undertaken to see how well the whole group did in academic subjects, college life, and personal development. The evaluation staff under the direction of Ralph Tyler compared 1,475 graduates of the progressive schools with an equal number of students from traditional schools. Each progressive student was paired with one from a traditional high school of equivalent age, sex, race, intelligence, scholastic achievement in high school, and general economic and social background.

By careful analysis, study, and observation the evaluation staff discovered that the progressive students earned a slightly higher total average of grades in college and more academic and nonacademic honors than the traditional students. The progressive students were more often judged to possess a high degree of intellectual curiosity and drive, to be precise, systematic, and objective in their thinking, to demonstrate a high degree of resourcefulness in meeting new situations, to participate more frequently in appreciative and art experiences as well as in most student activities, and to have developed a better orientation toward the choice of a vocation and a more active concern for what was going on in the world.

An interesting point was that the graduates of the six most progressive schools (which changed their programs most radically from the traditional program) did better in college than the graduates of the six least progressive schools (which changed their programs least from the traditional program). The range of social and economic background in the progressive schools was as great as in the average public high school, but the proportion of low-income groups was not as large as in the country as a whole. However, of comparable students with equal scholastic aptitude, it was found that the student from the lower socioeconomic group did better in college.

These careful and extensive studies seemed to show without doubt that changes in high school programs made for non-college-preparatory reasons did not handicap those students who did go to college and undoubtedly gave to all students a more useful kind of education in meeting their individual and social problems.

Higher Education

As the twentieth century opened, the elective system seemed to be the answer to the college curriculum problems raised, on the one hand, by the tremendous additions to knowledge achieved by the physical and social sciences and, on the other, by the growing demands of a young democracy that more and more youth should be given the advantages of higher education. As the colleges and universities expanded to meet these practical needs, however, many critics arose to attack the universities for what they were doing. In general, the critics seemed to range themselves into two opposing groups, which for the lack of better terms have been called the "conservatives" and the "progressives."

The conservatives, who formed an unbroken link with the scholarly traditions of the past, wished to preserve as far as possible the traditional conception of a liberal education. They claimed that the universities had degenerated into mere "service stations" for all sorts of industrial, commercial, and agricultural enterprises. They insisted that the university must return to its proper function of improving the "intellectual" quality of university training. On the other hand, the progressives said that modern society was so complex and changing so rapidly that the college must give the student an integrating and unifying experience in order to prepare him more directly for living in an interdependent society.

Although the elective system may have met definite needs in American life of the nineteenth century by adding technical and practical subjects to the curriculum, it now appeared that it had become encumbered with a vast variety of requirements as to hours, credits, prerequisites, and degrees. Since the highly specialized and unrelated subjects of the elective system did not give the needed integration to students, the progressive educators felt that new courses and new colleges should be devised which would attempt to do so. It thus seemed that the rule of the elective system was not to go unchallenged.

Both the conservatives and the progressives agreed that the free elective system as it had developed with highly specialized courses of narrow subject matter was educationally bad, but they differed in their proposals for reform. Both conservatives and progressives were suggesting more prescription, but they differed radically concerning the kinds of studies that they would prescribe. They both agreed that the common elements in education and life should receive greater emphasis in the prescribed studies, but they differed as to what those common qualities were. They both favored greater integration and correlation of knowledge, but they differed as to how these could be achieved and what studies best showed the interrelationships of knowledge.

For example, the general-education movement, which proposed to provide greater integration through stressing common bodies of knowledge, ranged all the way from the conservative proposals of President Hutchins to the experimentalist proposals of progressive educators who took their cue from John Dewey's philosophy. Between these two extremes, the majority of college educators seemed to be trying to patch up the college curriculum with compromises between the principles of election and prescription, taking inspiration now from the conservatives and now from the progressives.

The principal efforts to reform the college curriculum have been of three general types: (1) attempts to revise course requirements; (2)

efforts to give greater attention to individual students; (3) efforts to break down narrow subject-matter fields and to prescribe the study of larger and more interrelated fields of knowledge.

Revision of Course Requirements. The earliest and ultimately the commonest methods of reforming the curriculum have been various arrangements in which certain studies are prescribed and others are left to student choice. Most commonly this effort has accepted as valuable the customary type of subject-matter course dealing with a relatively narrow segment of knowledge, and it has retained the traditional reliance upon lectures, assignments, and recitation, or "quiz," sections.

Stemming from the efforts of A. Lawrence Lowell when he became president of Harvard in 1909, the principle of concentration and distribution struck a compromise between prescription and election. In this way, students were required to concentrate some courses in one field of knowledge and at the same time to distribute their other selections so that they would be somewhat acquainted with other important fields of knowledge. A variant was the method that required the student to take enough credits within one department to count as a "major" and then to take fewer credits in one or more other departments to make up a "minor" or "minors" in those fields.

Individualized Instruction. A second kind of general approach intended to break the academic lockstep of credits and units involved special provisions by which each student would receive more individual attention to his interests and learning needs. Among the efforts to individualize college instruction were tutorial and preceptorial plans. At such colleges as Princeton, Harvard, and Vassar, students were assigned to tutors, or preceptors, whose function was to advise and help them with their classwork or in preparation for their final or comprehensive examinations. In this way, the individual abilities or disabilities of students might more easily be discovered and appropriate measures taken to give them special work better adapted to their own peculiar needs than would be possible in large lecture or recitation classes.

Another form of individualized instruction was embodied in the honors plan (customarily identified with Swarthmore) and the independent-study plan (Leland Stanford). In both cases, the main intention was to give the more able students a chance to branch out for themselves and to proceed more rapidly than the speed of the average classes would allow. Under the close guidance of a faculty member, the student was directed to an individual plan of study, which he followed independently, without being held to the usual requirements and class obligations.

Taking a cue from the honors plan of reading, some colleges have so arranged their programs that students may be relieved from class attendance during some parts of the year in order to concentrate for a period on reading and study uninterrupted by the necessities of class attendance. Other colleges have applied the technique of individual conferences or small discussion groups for use among all students rather than for just a few. Informality became the keynote, and spirited discussions and group activities have had a better chance of flourishing than was possible in the traditional stiff and formal atmosphere of the recitation room. The formal atmosphere of large classes has also been dissipated by some colleges through their emphasis upon such field activities as excursions into the surrounding community, a year of study abroad and other traveling plans, and periods of work or study with community agencies.

The most thoroughgoing efforts to individualize instruction were probably found in the few progressive colleges that consciously tried to begin with the student's own interests and to develop for him an appropriate course of study that grew out of his own experience and purposes. Thus, at Bennington, Sarah Lawrence, and Bard, students have had a great deal of freedom to work out their own programs of study along with their instructors and to criticize their own efforts and activities in an effort to judge the value of their work for others and for themselves. Despite the great emphasis upon individual interests by the progressive colleges, there was evident a growing tendency to see that the student's interests not only served as a starting point for the experience curriculum but also that they revealed to him the ever-widening implications of his activity for social welfare.

Greater Prescription. The third method of reforming the college curriculum was the formation of several kinds of new prescribed courses, designed to break down the customary narrow compartmentalization of subject matter, to provide a more integrated approach to knowledge and society, and to afford students the common funds of knowledge necessary to intelligent participation in modern society.

Some colleges abolished the many specialized departments and created in their place a relatively few divisions that offered fewer and broader courses of study. Typical broad fields were the social sciences, natural sciences, languages and literature, philosophy and religion, and fine arts. Students were then required to become reasonably proficient in each of these major areas. In this way, the former sharp lines between departments were eradicated, and the divisions sometimes tried to meet the needs not only of students who planned to be specialists in that field but also of those who were just exploring or who had decided to specialize in other fields. The Harvard report of 1945 signalized the effort of Harvard to move in this direction.

One of the most popular methods for achieving a greater degree of integration in the college curriculum has been the survey course. Survey courses have been framed with many different purposes in view and with many different names attached to them. The second quarter of the century saw a great mushroom growth of "orientation courses," "correlated courses," "coordinated courses," "integrated courses," and "cooperating courses." Some have aimed at giving freshmen an orientation into college study or into the various fields of knowledge. Some have aimed at giving a bird's-eye view for all beginners in a particular field. Some have been devised particularly as an introduction to a field for students who will never take more work in that field. And some have been required as a first course for all who intend to specialize further in that field. Frequently, all these aims have been combined, and a single course has borne the burden of achieving these different aims for different students.

A less popular but perhaps more effective technique for reforming the college curriculum has been the centering of study in a whole culture epoch, or civilization. As a whole people was viewed in its efforts to solve its major problems of political and social control, industry, science, wealth, war, unemployment, leisure, and fundamental world view, the student had a good chance to integrate his knowledge and to focus it upon social action. Perhaps the most thoroughgoing example of this approach was the Experimental College headed by Alexander Meiklejohn at the University of Wisconsin from 1927 to 1932. Other techniques have involved the study of pressing personal needs that face the individual, such as physical health, sex, marriage and home relationships, vocation, leisure, social and civic relationships, and religious attitudes. A final approach to the problem of prescription has been made, notably at St. John's College, by centering the curriculum in the required reading of specified "great" books.

Whatever the name given to such revisions or reforms and whatever the specific aims and details with which they were worked out, at least two aims commonly stood out in the more progressive of these experimental colleges and courses. One was to give more attention to the needs of the individual student and greater meaning to his college study than was possible in large impersonal courses and lectures. The second was to relate college study more closely to the needs of present-day society and to give students a more integrated approach to their study of and participation in modern life. Prescribed courses came back into favor as the colleges tried to make certain that all students would gain a common understanding of the problems of man, society, and the world at large.

As the colleges and universities of the United States turned from their war experiences to plan their programs for the coming years, they took stock of what the Second World War had meant to them. If they were wise, they realized that the emergency demands for vocational, technical, and scientific training reflected not only the needs of a nation at war but the needs of an industrial nation in peace. They realized that they could not maintain the old snobbery concerning "practical education" and that both "cultural" and "practical" aims must be synthesized into a new outlook appropriate to modern life. They realized also that no amount of intellectual or cultural or vocational training would be worthwhile if their program was not oriented around the goal of social responsibility for achieving and maintaining a democratic society in the United States and in the world.

The college experience should be such that after college days the young people of the United States would know how to live democratically in an interdependent world and would strive earnestly for a truly democratic society in that world. There will be little profit to the United States or to the world if we train vast numbers of professional workers, engineers, technical experts, and teachers who have not a deep-seated desire and ability to make their skills contribute to the creation and maintenance of a free and democratic society. To enable them to become liberally educated persons with high professional and vocational competence and an urgent sense of social responsibility for democracy should be the goal of higher education in the United States.

SELECTED REFERENCES

The following materials have been selected to provide a working bibliography for further reading or investigation.

The first part, entitled *General Books*, is a list of references that cover a wide range of time and place and that can be used as companion reading for the whole of this volume.

The second part, entitled *Books for Further Reading by Chapters*, is a list of references that deal with topics specifically related to the chronological periods referred to in the respective chapters in this volume.

In both parts the references have been grouped under two or three headings. The first consists of original writings by authors who represent important social, intellectual, or educational points of view of the period involved. The second consists principally of interpretive and historical writings about the cultural trends of the period. The third consists of general and specialized studies in the history of education of the respective chapters and chronological periods.

In this way the reader may quickly select readings that will give him a cross section of the social, intellectual, and educational outlooks and practices of the time. Appropriate use of the original writings as well as of the interpretive and secondary sources can substantially aid an understanding of the history of culture and education.

GENERAL BOOKS

COLLECTIONS OF ORIGINAL WRITINGS IN WESTERN CULTURE AND EDUCATION

Baumer, Franklin L. van: *Main Currents of Western Thought; Readings in Western European Intellectual History from the Middle Ages to the Present*, Knopf, New York, 1952.

Bettenson, H. S. (ed.): *Documents of the Christian Church*, Oxford, New York, 1947.

Brubacher, John S. (ed.): *Eclectic Philosophy of Education*, Prentice-Hall, New York, 1951.

Coker, F. W. (ed.): *Readings in Political Philosophy*, 2d ed., Macmillan, New York, 1938.

Columbia College, Columbia University: *Introduction to Contemporary Civilization in the West, A Source Book*, 2 vols., Columbia University Press, New York, 1946.

Cubberley, E. P.: *Readings in the History of Education*, Houghton Mifflin, Boston, 1920.

Dennis, Wayne (ed.): *Readings in the History of Psychology*. Appleton-Century-Crofts, New York, 1948.

Fitzpatrick, Edward A. (ed.): *Readings in the Philosophy of Education*, Appleton-Century-Crofts, New York, 1936.

Guerlac, H.: *Selected Readings in the History of Science*, Cornell University Press, Ithaca, N.Y., 1950.

Hart, J. K.: *Creative Moments in Education*, Holt, New York, 1931.

Hutchins, Robert M., and Mortimer J. Adler: *Great Books of the Western World*, 54 vols., Encyclopaedia Brittanica, Chicago, 1952.

Kilpatrick, W. H. (ed.): *Source Book in the Philosophy of Education*, rev. ed., Macmillan, New York, 1934.

Leach, Arthur F.: *Educational Charters and Documents, 598 to 1909*, Cambridge, New York, 1911.

Painter, F. V. N.: *Great Pedagogical Essays: Plato to Spencer*, American Book, New York, 1905.
Robinson, J. H.: *Readings in European History*, 2 vols., Ginn, Boston, 1904–1906.
Ulich, Robert (ed.): *Three Thousand Years of Educational Wisdom*, Harvard University Press, Cambridge, Mass., 1954.

INTERPRETIVE WRITINGS ON WESTERN CULTURE

Baker, Herschel: *The Dignity of Man*, Harvard University Press, Cambridge, Mass., 1947.
Barnes, Harry Elmer: *An Intellectual and Cultural History of the Western World*, Random House, New York, 1937.
Brinton, Crane: *Ideas and Men; The Story of Western Thought*, Prentice-Hall, New York, 1950.
Butterfield, Herbert: *The Origins of Modern Science*, Macmillan, New York, 1951.
Collingwood, R. G.: *Idea of Nature*, Oxford, New York, 1945.
Dampier, W. C.: *History of Science*, rev. ed., Cambridge, New York, 1949.
Durant, Will: *The Story of Philosophy*, Simon and Schuster, New York, 1933.
Fromm, Erich: *Escape from Freedom*, Rinehart, New York, 1941.
Kline, Morris: *Mathematics in Western Culture*, Oxford, New York, 1953.
Kohn, Hans: *Idea of Nationalism*, Macmillan, New York, 1944.
Murphy, Gardner: *Historical Introduction to Modern Psychology*, Harcourt, Brace, New York, 1929.
Randall, J. H.: *The Making of the Modern Mind*, rev. ed., Houghton Mifflin, Boston, 1940.
Robinson, J. H.: *Mind in the Making*, Harper, New York, 1921.
Russell, Bertrand: *History of Western Philosophy*, Simon and Schuster, New York, 1945.
Sabine, G.: *A History of Political Theory*, Holt, New York, 1937.
Sandys, J. E.: *A History of Classical Scholarship*, 3 vols., Cambridge, New York, 1903–1908.
Sarton, George: *Introduction to the History of Science*, 3 vols., Williams & Wilkins, Baltimore, 1927–1947.
Seligman, E. R. A., and Alvin Johnson (eds.): *Encyclopaedia of the Social Sciences*, 15 vols., Macmillan, New York, 1930–1935.
Thorndike, Lynn: *A Short History of Civilization*, rev. ed., Appleton-Century-Crofts, New York, 1948.
Toynbee, Arnold: *The Study of History*, Oxford, New York, 1947.
Whitehead, A. N.: *Science and the Modern World*, Macmillan, New York, 1925.
Wightman, W. P. D.: *The Growth of Scientific Ideas*, Yale University Press, New Haven, Conn., 1953.

THE HISTORY OF EUROPEAN EDUCATION

Bolgar, R. R.: *The Classical Heritage and Its Beneficiaries*, Cambridge University Press, New York, 1954.
Boyd, William: *The History of Western Education*, 6th ed., Macmillan, New York, 1952.
Brickman, W. W.: *A Guide to Research in Educational History*, New York University Bookstore, New York, 1949.
Brubacher, John S.: *A History of the Problems of Education*, McGraw-Hill, New York, 1947.

Butts, R. Freeman: *The College Charts Its Course*, McGraw-Hill, New York, 1939.

Cole, Percival R.: *A History of Educational Thought*, Oxford, New York, 1931.

Cubberley, E. P.: *The History of Education*, Houghton Mifflin, Boston, 1920.

Eby, F., and C. F. Arrowood: *The Development of Modern Education*, Prentice-Hall, New York, 1934 (2d ed., 1952).

———— and ————: *The History and Philosophy of Education; Ancient and Medieval*, Prentice-Hall, New York, 1940.

Good, H. G.: *A History of Western Education*, Macmillan, New York, 1947.

Graves, F. P.: *A History of Education before the Middle Ages*, Macmillan, New York, 1909.

————: *A History of Education during the Middle Ages*, Macmillan, New York, 1910.

————: *A History of Education in Modern Times*, Macmillan, New York, 1913.

Kane, W.: *An Essay toward a History of Education*, Loyola Press, Chicago, 1935.

Kandel, I. L.: *History of Secondary Education*, Houghton Mifflin, Boston, 1930.

Knight, E. W.: *Twenty Centuries of Education*, Ginn, Boston, 1940.

Marique, P.: *History of Christian Education*, 3 vols., Fordham University Press, New York, 1924–1932.

McCormick, P. J.: *History of Education*, 3d ed., Catholic Education Press, Washington, D.C., 1953.

Monroe, Paul: *Cyclopedia of Education*, 5 vols., Macmillan, New York, 1911–1919.

————: *Textbook in the History of Education*, new ed., Macmillan, New York, 1920.

Moore, E. C.: *The Story of Instruction: The Beginnings*, Macmillan, New York, 1936.

————: *The Story of Instruction: The Church, the Renaissance and the Reformations*, Macmillan, New York, 1938.

Mulhern, James: *A History of Education*, Ronald, New York, 1946.

Quick, R. H.: *Essays on Educational Reformers*, Appleton-Century-Crofts, New York, 1907.

Reisner, E. H.: *The Evolution of the Common School*, Macmillan, New York, 1930.

————: *Historical Foundations of Modern Education*, Macmillan, New York, 1927.

————: *Nationalism and Education since* 1789, Macmillan, New York, 1922.

Ulich, Robert: *History of Educational Thought*, American Book, New York, 1945.

Woody, Thomas: *Liberal Education for Free Men*, University of Pennsylvania Press, Philadelphia, 1951.

COLLECTIONS OF ORIGINAL WRITINGS IN AMERICAN CULTURE AND EDUCATION

Barnard, Henry (ed.): *American Journal of Education*, 32 vols., 1855–1882.

Blau, Joseph L. (ed.): *American Philosophic Addresses*, 1700–1900, Columbia University Press, New York, 1946.

Brubacher, John S. (ed.): *Eclectic Philosophy of Education*, Prentice-Hall, New York, 1951.

Commager, Henry S.: *Living Ideas in America*, Harper, New York, 1951.

Cubberley, E. P.: *Readings in Public Education in the United States*, Houghton Mifflin, Boston, 1934.

Elliott, E. C., and M. M. Chambers (eds.): *Charters and Basic Laws of Selected American Universities and Colleges*, Carnegie Foundation, New York, 1934.

Hinsdale, B. A.: *Documents Illustrative of American Educational History*, U.S. Commissioner of Education Report, 1892–1893, Vol. II, 1895.

Hacker, Louis: *The Shaping of the American Tradition,* Columbia University Press, New York, 1946.

Klain, Zora (ed.): *Educational Activities of New England Quakers: A Source Book,* Westbrook, Philadelphia, 1928.

Knight, Edgar W.: *A Documentary History of Education in the South before* 1860, 5 vols., University of North Carolina Press, Chapel Hill, N.C., 1949–1953.

————: *Reading in Educational Administration,* Holt, New York, 1953.

————, and C. L. Hall: *Readings in American Educational History,* Appleton-Century-Crofts, New York, 1951.

Monroe, Paul: *Readings in the Founding of the American Public School System,* University Microfilms, Ann Arbor, Mich., 1940.

Smith, Bernard: *The Democratic Spirit,* 2d ed., Knopf, New York, 1945.

Thorp, Willard, Merle Curti, and Carlos Baker: *American Issues,* 2 vols., Lippincott, Philadelphia, 1954.

INTERPRETIVE WRITINGS ON AMERICAN CULTURE

Beard, Charles A., and Mary R. Beard: *The Rise of American Civilization,* new ed. rev. and enl., 2 vols. in 1, Macmillan, New York, 1933.

Blau, Joseph L.: *Men and Movements in American Philosophy,* Prentice-Hall, New York, 1952.

Brogan, D. M.: *The American Character,* Knopf, New York, 1944.

Cohen, Morris: *American Thought,* Free Press, Glencoe, Ill., 1954.

Commons, John R., and associates: *History of Labour in the United States,* 4 vols., Macmillan, New York, 1918–1935.

Curti, Merle: *The Growth of American Thought,* Harper, New York, 1943.

Gabriel, Ralph H.: *The Course of American Democratic Thought,* Ronald, New York, 1940.

Green, Evarts B.: *Religion and the State,* New York University Press, New York, 1941.

Hansen, Marcus L.: *The Immigrant in American History,* Harvard University Press, Cambridge, Mass., 1940.

Morison, S. E., and H. S. Commager: *The Growth of the American Republic,* 2 vols., 4th ed., Oxford, New York, 1950.

Parrington, V. L.: *Main Currents in American Thought,* 3 vols., Harcourt, Brace, New York, 1927–1930.

Pfeffer, Leo: *Church, State, and Freedom,* Beacon Press, Boston, 1953.

Roback, A. A.: *A History of American Psychology,* Library Publishers, New York, 1952.

Schlesinger, A. M., and D. R. Fox (eds.): *History of American Life,* 13 vols., Macmillan, New York, 1927–1948.

Schneider, Herbert W.: *A History of American Philosophy,* Columbia University Press, New York, 1946.

Stokes, Anson Phelps: *Church and State in the United States,* 2 vols., Harper, New York, 1950.

Werkmeister, W. H.: *The History of Philosophical Ideas in America,* Ronald, New York, 1949.

White, Morton G.: *Social Thought in America,* Viking, New York, 1949.

HISTORY OF AMERICAN EDUCATION

Beale, Howard K.: *A History of Freedom of Teaching in American Schools,* Scribner, New York, 1941.

Brickman, William W.: *A Guide to Research in Educational History*, New York University Bookstore, New York, 1949.

Brown, E. F.: *The Making of Our Middle Schools*, Longmans, New York, 1903.

Brubacher, John S.: *A History of the Problems of Education*, McGraw-Hill, New York, 1947.

Burns, James A.: *The Growth and Development of the Catholic School System in the United States*, Benziger, New York, 1912.

Butts, R. Freeman: *The American Tradition in Religion and Education*, Beacon Press, Boston, 1950.

————: *The College Charts Its Course*, McGraw-Hill, New York, 1939.

————, and Lawrence A. Cremin: *A History of Education in American Culture*, Holt, New York, 1953.

Cubberley, E. P.: *Public Education in the United States*, Houghton Mifflin, Boston, 1934.

Curti, Merle: *The Social Ideas of American Educators*, Scribner, New York, 1935.

Edwards, Newton, and Herman G. Richey: *The School in the American Social Order*, Houghton Mifflin, Boston, 1947.

Elsbree, Willard S.: *The American Teacher*, American Book, New York, 1939.

Gabriel, Ralph (ed.): *The Pageant of America*, Vol. X, Yale University Press, New Haven, Conn., 1928.

Hofstadter, Richard, and Walter P. Metzger: *The Development of Academic Freedom in the United States*, Columbia University Press, New York, 1955.

Kandel, I. L.: *History of Secondary Education*, Houghton Mifflin, Boston, 1930.

Knight, E. W.: *Education in the United States*, 3d rev. ed., Ginn, Boston, 1951 (c1922).

McGucken, William J.: *The Jesuits and Education; The Society's Principles and Practice, Especially in the United States*, Bruce, Milwaukee, 1932.

Monroe, Paul: *Founding of the American Public School System*, Macmillan, New York, 1940.

Noble, S. G.: *A History of American Education*, Rinehart, New York, 1954.

Reisner, E. H.: *The Evolution of the Common School*, Macmillan, New York, 1930.

————: *Nationalism and Education since 1789*, Macmillan, New York, 1922.

Tewksbury, Donald G.: *The Founding of American Colleges and Universities before the Civil War*, Teachers College, Columbia University, New York, 1932.

Ulich, Robert: *History of Educational Thought*, American Book, New York, 1945.

Woody, Thomas: *A History of Women's Education in the United States*, 2 vols., Science Press, New York, 1929.

COMPILATIONS AND BIBLIOGRAPHIES

The student should also be on the alert to make use of such compilations of historical materials as are contained in:

Barnard, Henry: *American Journal of Education*, 32 vols., 1855–1882.

Dictionary of American Biography, Scribner, New York, 1928–1936.

Monroe, Paul (ed.): *Cyclopedia of Education*, 5 vols., Macmillan, New York. 1911–1919.

Rivlin, Harry N. (ed.): *Encyclopedia of Modern Education*, Philosophical Library, New York, 1943.

U.S. Bureau of Education: *Circulars of Information*, 1887–1903 (especially for education in the several states).

For especially good bibliographies, see:

American Educational Research Association: "Historical and Philosophical Foundations of Education," Chap. 1, in "The Social Framework of Education," *Review of Educational Research*, Vol. 22, February, 1952.

————: "History of Education and Comparative Education," *Review of Educational Research*, Vol. 6, October, 1936.

————: "History of Education and Comparative Education," *Review of Educational Research*, Vol. 9, October, 1939.

Brickman, William W.: "Educational Literature Reviews" in *School and Society*, Oct. 26, 1946; Dec. 28, 1946; April 26, 1947; Nov. 29, 1947; March 27, 1948; March 5, 1949; May 28, 1949; March 4, 1950; May 6, 1950; Oct. 28, 1950; and Dec. 30, 1950.

————: *A Guide to Research in Educational History*, New York University Bookstore, New York, 1949.

Brubacher, John S.: *A History of the Problems of Education*, McGraw-Hill, New York, 1947.

BOOKS FOR FURTHER READING BY CHAPTERS

Chap. 1. The Beginnings of Culture and Education in the Eastern Mediterranean World

ANTHROPOLOGICAL WRITINGS

Benedict, Ruth: *Patterns of Culture*, Houghton Mifflin, Boston, 1934.

Boas, Franz (ed.): *General Anthropology*, Heath, New York, 1938.

————: *The Mind of Primitive Man*, Macmillan, New York, 1938.

Childe, V. Gordon: *Man Makes Himself*, Watts, London, 1939.

Counts, George S.: "Primitive Education," in *Encyclopaedia of Social Sciences*, Macmillan, New York, 1930–1935.

Goldenweiser, Alexander A.: *History, Psychology, and Culture*, Knopf, New York, 1933.

Herskovits, Melville J.: *Man and His Works; The Science of Cultural Anthropology*, Knopf, New York, 1948.

Hooton, Ernest Albert: *Up from the Ape*, 2d ed., Macmillan, New York, 1949.

Howells, William White: *Mankind So Far*, Doubleday, New York, 1944.

Kluckhohn, Clyde: *Mirror for Man*, McGraw-Hill, New York, 1949.

Kroeber, A. L.: *Anthropology*, Harcourt, Brace, New York, 1923, 2d ed., 1933; 3d ed., 1948.

Linton, Ralph: *The Cultural Background of Personality*, Appleton-Century-Crofts, New York, 1945.

————: *The Study of Man*, Appleton-Century-Crofts, New York, 1936.

Malinowski, B.: "Culture," in *Encyclopaedia of the Social Sciences*, 4:621–646, Macmillan, New York, 1930–1935.

————: *The Dynamics of Culture Change*, Yale University Press, New Haven, Conn., 1945.

Mead, Margaret: *Coming of Age in Samoa*, Blue Ribbon, New York, 1936.

————: *Growing Up in New Guinea*, Blue Ribbon, New York, 1933.

————: *Sex and Temperament in Three Primitive Societies*, Morrow, New York, 1935.

Miller, Nathan: *The Child in Primitive Society*, Brentano's, New York, 1928.

Weidenreich, Franz: *Apes, Giants and Man*, University of Chicago Press, Chicago, 1946.

Wissler, Clark: *Man and Culture; An Introduction to Social Anthropology*, Crowell, New York, 1923.

HISTORY OF EARLY CIVILIZATIONS AND EDUCATION

Bates, E. S.: *The Bible Designed to Be Read as Living Literature*, Simon and Schuster, New York, 1936.

Bevan, Edwin R., and Charles Singer (eds.): *The Legacy of Israel*, Oxford, New York, 1927.

Boas, Franz: *Race, Language and Culture*, Macmillan, New York, 1940.

Boyle, Mary E.: *Man Before History*, Little, Brown, Boston, 1926.

Breasted, James Henry: *Ancient Times; A History of the Early World*, Ginn, Boston, 1935.

Cambridge Ancient History, 12 vols., Cambridge University Press, New York, 1923–1939.

Childe, V. Gordon: *The Dawn of European Civilization*, Knopf, New York, 1925.

Goldenweiser, Alexander A.: *Early Civilization*, Knopf, New York, 1922.

Moore, G. F.: *History of Religions*, 2 vols., Scribner, New York, 1913–1920.

Peake, Harold J.: *Early Steps in Human Progress*, Lippincott, Philadelphia, 1933.

Pfeifer, Robert H.: *Introduction to Judaism and the Old Testament*, new ed., Harper, New York, 1948.

Swift, Fletcher Harper: *Education in Ancient Israel*, Open Court, La Salle, Ill., 1919.

Woody, Thomas: *Life and Education in Early Societies*, Macmillan, New York, 1949.

Chaps. 2 and 3. Greek Culture

ORIGINAL WRITINGS

Aristotle: *Basic Works* (ed. by R. McKeon), Random House, New York, 1941.

Bakewell, C. M.: *Sourcebook in Ancient Philosophy*, rev. ed., Scribner, New York 1939.

Burnet, John: *Aristotle on Education*, Harvard University Press, Cambridge, Mass., 1928.

Homer: *The Complete Works of Homer*, Modern Library, New York, n.d.

Isocrates: *Orations* (tr. by J. H. Freese), London, 1894.

Livingstone, R. W. (ed.): *The Legacy of Greece*, Oxford, New York, 1928.

Monroe, Paul: *Sourcebook of the History of Education for the Greek and Roman Period*, Macmillan, New York, 1913.

Oates, W. J., and C. T. Murphy: *Greek Literature in Translation*, Longmans, New York, 1946.

Plato: *The Dialogues of Plato* (trans. by B. Jowett), 2 vols., Random House, New York, 1937.

———: *The Republic of Plato* (trans. by F. M. Cornford), Oxford, New York, 1954.

———: *The Works of Plato* (ed. by Irwin Edman), Modern Library, New York, 1930.

Thucydides: *History of the Peloponnesian War* (tr. by Richard Crawley), Everyman's Library, Dent, London, 1910.

Xenophon: *Memorabilia* and *Cyropaedia* in *Works* (tr. by H. G. Dakyns), London, 1890.

INTERPRETIVE WRITINGS

Allan, D. J.: *The Philosophy of Aristotle*, Oxford, New York, 1952.

Barker, Ernest: *The Political Thought of Plato and Aristotle*, Putnam, New York, 1906.

Burnet, J.: *Early Greek Philosophy*, 4th ed., A. & C. Black, London, 1930.

Cambridge Ancient History, 12 vols., Cambridge, New York, 1923–1939.

Crossman, R. H. S.: *Plato Today*, Oxford, New York, 1939.

Dickinson, G. Lowes: *The Greek View of Life*, Beacon Press, Boston, 1951.

Durant, Will: *The Life of Greece*, Simon and Schuster, New York, 1939.

Gomperz, T.: *Greek Thinkers*, 4 vols., J. Murray, London, 1905–1920.

Greene, W. C.: *The Achievement of Greece*, Harvard University Press, Cambridge, Mass., 1923.

Hamilton, Edith: *The Greek Way*, New American Library (Mentor), New York, 1948.

Jaeger, Werner: *Paideia, the Ideals of Greek Culture*, 2 vols., 2d ed., Oxford, New York, 1943–1945.

Jaeger, W. W.: *The Theology of the Early Greek Philosophers*, Oxford, New York, 1952.

Kitto, H. D. F.: *The Greeks*, Penguin, Harmondsworth, Middlesex, England, 1951.

Lavell, C. F.: *The Biography of the Greek People*, Houghton Mifflin, Boston, 1934.

Lovejoy, A. O.: *The Great Chain of Being*, Harvard University Press, Cambridge, Mass., 1936.

Nettleship, R. L.: *Lectures on the Republic of Plato*, St. Martin's, New York, 1936.

Nilsson, M. P.: *A History of Greek Religion*, 2d ed., Oxford, New York, 1949.

Robin, Leon: *Greek Thought and the Origins of the Scientific Spirit*, Knopf, New York, 1928.

Rostovtzeff, Mikhail I.: *A History of the Ancient World; The Orient and Greece*, Oxford, New York, 1926.

————: *Social and Economic History of the Hellenistic World*, 3 vols., Oxford, New York, 1941.

Sandys, J. E.: *A History of Classical Scholarship*, Vol. I, Cambridge, New York, 1903.

Sarton, George: *A History of Science; Ancient Science through the Golden Age of Greece*, Harvard University Press, Cambridge, Mass., 1952.

Shorey, Paul: *What Plato Said*, University of Chicago Press, Chicago, 1933.

Tarn, W. W.: *Hellenistic Civilization*, E. Arnold, London, 1927.

Taylor, A. E.: *Plato, the Man and His Work*, 3d ed., MacVeagh, New York, 1929.

Taylor, A. E.: *Socrates, the Man and His Thought*, Doubleday, New York, 1953.

Van Hook, Larue: *Greek Life and Thought*, Columbia University Press, New York, 1937.

HISTORY OF GREEK EDUCATION

Adamson, J. E.: *The Theory of Education in Plato's Republic*, S. Sonnenschein, London, 1903.

Burnet, John: *Aristotle on Education*, Harvard University Press, Cambridge, Mass., 1928.

Capes, W. W.: *University Life in Ancient Athens*, Stechert, New York, 1922.

Davidson, Thomas: *Aristotle and Ancient Educational Ideals*, Scribner, New York, 1892.

————: *Education of the Greek People*, Appleton, New York, 1894.

Dobson, J. F.: *Ancient Education and Its Meaning to Us*, Longmans, New York, 1932.

Forbes, Clarence A.: *Greek Physical Education*, Appleton-Century-Crofts, New York, 1929.

Freeman, K. J.: *Schools of Hellas*, 3d ed., St. Martin's, New York, 1932.

Laurie, S. S.: *Historical Survey of Pre-Christian Education*, Longmans, London, 1895.
Lodge, Rupert C.: *Plato's Theory of Education*, Harcourt, Brace, New York, 1948.
Nettleship, R. L.: *The Theory of Education in the Republic of Plato*, University of Chicago Press, Chicago, 1906.
Walden, J. W. H.: *The Universities of Ancient Greece*, Scribner, New York, 1909.
Wilkins, A. S.: *National Education in Greece in the Fourth Century B.C.*, Stechert, New York, 1911.
Woody, Thomas: *Life and Education in Early Societies*, Macmillan, New York, 1949.

Chap. 4. The Roman World

ORIGINAL WRITINGS

Augustine: *Concerning the Teacher and On the Immortality of the Soul*, Appleton-Century-Crofts, New York, 1938.
Augustine: *Confessions*, Everyman's Library, Dutton, New York, 1950.
Bailey, Cyril (ed.): *The Mind of Rome*, Oxford, New York, 1926.
Bettenson, H. S. (ed.): *Documents of the Christian Church*, Oxford, New York, 1947.
Cicero: *De Oratore*, G. Bell, London, 1903.
Chase, W. J.: *The Ars Minor of Donatus*, University of Wisconsin Press, Madison, Wis., 1926.
———: *The Distichs of Cato*, University of Wisconsin Press, Madison, Wis., 1922.
Guinagh, Kevin, and A. P. Dorjahn: *Latin Literature in Translation*, Longmans, New York, 1942.
Lewy, H. (ed.): *Philo, Philosophical Writings, Selections*, East and West Library, Oxford, 1946.
Lucretius: *On the Nature of Things* (tr. by W. E. Leonard), Dutton, New York, 1916.
Marcus Aurelius: *Meditations* (ed. by A. S. L. Farquharson), Oxford, New York, 1944.
Monroe, Paul: *Sourcebook of the History of Education for the Greek and Roman Period*, Macmillan, New York, 1913.
Oates, W. J. (ed.): *Basic Writings of St. Augustine*, 2 vols., Random House, New York, 1948.
Plutarch: "On the Nature of Children" in *Moralia* (tr. by F. C. Babbitt), Heinemann, London, 1927.
Quintilian: *Institutes of Oratory* (selections by H. H. Horne), New York University Bookstore, New York, 1936.
Turnbull, Grace H.: *Essence of Plotinus*, Oxford, New York, 1934.
Vitruvius: *De Architectura*, Putnam, New York, 1931.

INTERPRETIVE WRITINGS

Altheim, F.: *A History of Roman Religion*, Dutton, New York, 1938.
Artz, Frederick B.: *The Mind of the Middle Ages, A.D. 200–1500: An Historical Survey*, Knopf, New York, 1953.
Bailey, Cyril (ed.): *The Legacy of Rome*, Oxford, New York, 1924.
Bevan, E. R., and C. Singer: *Legacy of Israel*, 2d ed., Oxford, New York, 1928.
Boak, A. E. R., and Richard Hudson: *A History of Rome to 565 A.D.*, 3d ed., Macmillan, New York, 1945.
Cambridge Ancient History, 12 vols., Cambridge, New York, 1923–1939.
Cambridge Mediaeval History, Vol. I., 2d ed., Cambridge, New York, 1924.

Cochrane, C. N.: *Christianity and Classical Culture*, Oxford, New York, 1940.

Durant, Will: *Caesar and Christ; A History of Roman Civilization and Christianity from Their Beginnings to A.D. 325*, Simon and Schuster, New York, 1944.

Greene, W. C.: *The Achievements of Rome*, Harvard University Press, Cambridge, Mass., 1934.

Goodenough, E. R.: *An Introduction to Philo Judaeus*, Yale University Press, New Haven, Conn, 1940.

Hamilton, Edith: *The Roman Way*, Norton, New York, 1932.

McGiffert, A. C.: *A History of Christian Thought*, 2 vols., Scribner, New York, 1932–1933.

Moore, Frank G.: *The Roman's World*, Columbia University Press, New York, 1936.

Munro, D. C., and G. C. Sellery: *Mediaeval Civilization*, Appleton-Century-Crofts, New York, 1904.

Rand, E. K.: *Founders of the Middle Ages*, 2d ed., Harvard University Press, Cambridge, Mass., 1929.

Schweitzer, Albert: *Quest of the Historical Jesus*, new ed., Macmillan, New York, 1948.

Showerman, Grant: *Rome and the Romans*, Macmillan, New York, 1933.

Starr, Chester G.: *The Emergence of Rome as Ruler of the Western World*, Cornell University Press, Ithaca, N.Y., 1950.

Taylor, H. O.: *Classical Heritage of the Middle Ages*, Macmillan, New York, 1911.

———: *The Mediaeval Mind*, 2 vols., Macmillan, New York, 1925.

Wolfson, H. A.: *Philo; Foundations of Religious Philosophy in Judaism, Christianity, and Islam*, 2 vols., Harvard University Press, Cambridge, Mass., 1948.

HISTORY OF ROMAN EDUCATION

Abelson, Paul: *The Seven Liberal Arts*, Teachers College, Columbia University, New York, 1906.

Cole, P. R.: *Later Roman Education*, Teachers College, Columbia University, New York, 1909.

Dobson, J. F.: *Ancient Education and Its Meaning to Us*, Longmans, New York, 1932.

Gwynn, Aubrey: *Roman Education from Cicero to Quintilian*, Oxford, New York, 1926.

Haarhoff, T.: *Schools of Ancient Gaul*, Oxford, New York, 1920.

Hodgson, Geraldine: *Primitive Christian Education*, T. Clark, Edinburgh, 1906.

Laurie, S. S.: *Historical Survey of Pre-Christian Education*, Longmans, New York, 1924.

Marique, Pierre J.: *History of Christian Education*, Fordham University Press, New York, 1924.

Smail, W. M.: *Quintilian on Education*, Oxford, New York, 1938.

Wilkins, A. S.: *Roman Education*, Macmillan, New York, 1905.

Woody, Thomas: *Life and Education in Early Societies*, Macmillan, New York, 1949.

Chaps. 5 and 6. The Middle Ages

ORIGINAL WRITINGS

Chase, W. J.: *The Ars Minor of Donatus*, University of Wisconsin Press, Madison, Wis., 1926.

———: *The Distichs of Cato*, University of Wisconsin Press, Madison, Wis., 1922.

Coulton, G. G. (ed.): *Life in the Middle Ages*, 4 vols., Macmillan, New York, 1930.

Jones, C. W.: *Mediaeval Literature in Translation*, Longmans, New York, 1950.

Leach, A. E.: *Educational Charters and Documents, 598–1909*, Cambridge, New York, 1911.

Mayer, Mary H.: *The Philosophy of Teaching of St. Thomas Aquinas*, Bruce, Milwaukee, 1929.

McKeon, R. (ed.): *Selections from Medieval Philosophers*, 2 vols., Modern Library, New York, 1929–1930.

Norton, A. O.: *Readings in the History of Education: Medieval Universities*, Harvard University Press, Cambridge, Mass., 1909.

Paetow, L. J. (ed.): *Battle of the Seven Arts*, University of California Press, Berkeley, Calif., 1914.

Pegis, A. (ed.): *The Basic Writings of Aquinas*, 2 vols., Random House, New York, 1945.

Poole, R. L.: *Illustrations of the History of Mediaeval Thought and Learning*, 2d rev. ed., Macmillan, New York, 1940.

Rose, J. B., and M. M. McLaughlin, (eds.): *The Portable Medieval Reader*, Viking, New York, 1949.

Seybolt, Robert F. (tr.): *The Manuale Scholarium*, Harvard University Press, Cambridge, Mass., 1921.

Symonds, John A.: *Wine, Women and Song*, Mosher, Portland, Maine, 1918.

Thorndike, Lynn: *University Records and Life in the Middle Ages*, Columbia University Press, New York, 1944.

Waddell, Helen: *The Wandering Scholars*, Constable, London, 1927.

INTERPRETIVE WRITINGS

Adams, Henry: *Mont St. Michel and Chartres*, Houghton Mifflin, Boston, 1936.

Arnold, T., and A. Guillaume (eds.): *The Legacy of Islam*, Oxford, New York, 1931.

Artz, Frederick B.: *The Mind of the Middle Ages, A.D. 200–1500: An Historical Survey*, Knopf, New York, 1953.

Baynes, N. H., and H. Moss (eds.): *Byzantium*, Oxford, New York, 1948.

Cambridge Mediaeval History, 2d ed., 8 vols., Cambridge, New York, 1924–1936.

Cornish, F. W.: *Chivalry*, Macmillan, New York, 1911.

Crump, C. G., and E. F. Jacob: *The Legacy of the Middle Ages*, Oxford, New York, 1926.

Davis, W. S.: *Life on a Mediaeval Barony*, Harper, New York, 1923.

Durant, Will: *The Age of Faith*, Simon and Schuster, New York, 1950.

Easton, S. E.: *Roger Bacon and His Search for a Universal Science*, Oxford, New York, 1952.

Gilson, E.: *History of Christian Philosophy in the Middle Ages*, Random House, New York, 1955.

————: *Reason and Revelation*, Scribner, New York, 1938.

————: *Spirit of Mediaeval Philosophy*, Scribner, New York, 1936.

Haskins, C. H.: *The Renaissance of the Twelfth Century*, Harvard University Press, Cambridge, Mass., 1927.

————: *Studies in the History of Medieval Science*, Harvard University Press, Cambridge, Mass., 1929.

Luchaire, Achille: *Social France at the Time of Philip Augustus*, Peter Smith, New York, 1929.

McGiffert, A. C.: *A History of Christian Thought*, 2 vols., Scribner, New York, 1932–1933.

Munroe, D. C., and G. C. Sellery: *Mediaeval Civilization*, Appleton-Century-Crofts, New York, 1904.

Paetow, L. J.: *Guide to the Study of Mediaeval History*, 2d ed., Appleton-Century-Crofts, New York, 1931.

Painter, Sidney: *Mediaeval Society*, Cornell University Press, Ithaca, N.Y., 1951.

Pirenne, Henri: *Medieval Cities; Their Origin and the Revival of Trade*, Princeton University Press, Princeton, N.J., 1925.

Powicke, F. M.: *The Christian Life in the Middle Ages*, Oxford, New York, 1935.

————: *Ways of Mediaeval Life and Thought*, Beacon Press, Boston, 1951.

Rand, E. K.: *Founders of the Middle Ages*, Harvard University Press, Cambridge, Mass., 1929.

Taylor, H. O.: *The Classical Heritage of the Middle Ages*, 3d ed., Macmillan, New York, 1911.

————: *The Mediaeval Mind*, 4th ed., 2 vols., Harvard University Press, Cambridge, Mass., 1949.

Thompson, J. W.: *The Middle Ages*, 2 vols., Knopf, New York, 1931.

Waddell, Helen: *Peter Abelard*, Holt, New York, 1933.

Walsh, J. J.: *The Thirteenth, Greatest of Centuries*, 5th ed., Catholic Summer School Press, New York, 1924.

HISTORY OF EDUCATION IN THE MIDDLE AGES

Abelson, Paul: *The Seven Liberal Arts*, Teachers College, Columbia University, New York, 1906.

Compayre, G.: *Abelard and the Origin of the Universities*, Scribner, New York, 1893.

Duckett, Eleanor S.: *Alcuin, Friend of Charlemagne; His World and His Work*, Macmillan, New York, 1951.

Graham, Hugh: *Early Irish Monastic Schools*, Talbot, Dublin, 1923.

Haskins, C. H.: *The Rise of Universities*, Holt, New York, 1923.

Kibre, Pearl: *The Nations in the Mediaeval Universities*, Medieval Academy of America, Boston, 1948.

Laurie, S. S.: *Rise and Early Constitution of Universities*, Appleton-Century-Crofts, New York, 1903.

Leach, A. F.: *Schools of Medieval England*, Methuen, London, 1915.

Loomis, Louis: *Mediaeval Hellenism*, Ph.D. dissertation, Columbia University, New York, 1906.

Mullinger, J. Bass: *The Schools of Charles the Great*, Stechart, New York, 1911.

Paetow, A. J.: *The Arts Course at Medieval Universities*, University of Illinois Press, Urbana, Ill., 1910.

Parry, A. W.: *Education in England in the Middle Ages*, University of London Press, London, 1920.

Rait, R. S.: *Life in the Medieval University*, Cambridge, New York, 1912.

Rashdall, Hastings: *Universities of Europe in the Middle Ages*, new ed., Oxford, New York, 1936.

Schlachner, Nathan: *The Medieval Universities*, G. Allen, London, 1938.

Watson, Foster: *The English Grammar Schools to 1660*, Cambridge, New York, 1908.

West, A. F.: *Alcuin and the Rise of Christian Schools*, Scribner, New York, 1892.

Chap. 7. The Renaissance

ORIGINAL WRITINGS

Ascham, Roger: *The Scholemaster* (ed. by D. C. Whimster), Methuen, London, 1934.

Born, Lester K. (ed.): *The Education of a Christian Prince, by Desiderius Erasmus*, Columbia University Press, New York, 1936.

Cassirer, Ernst, P. O. Kristeller, and J. H. Randall: *The Renaissance Philosophy of Man*, University of Chicago Press, Chicago, 1948.

Castiglione, Baldassare: *The Book of the Courtier* (tr. by L. E. Opdycke), Scribner, New York, 1903 (also Everyman's Library, 1951).

Elyot, Thomas: *The Boke Named the Governour*, 2 vols., Kegan Paul, Trench, London, 1883.

Hudson, H. H. (tr.): *Erasmus' Praise of Folly*, Princeton University Press, Princeton, N.J., 1944.

Montaigne, Michel de: *Education of Children*, Appleton, New York, 1899.

More, Thomas: *Utopia* (tr. by Ralph Robinson), Murry & Son, London, 1869.

Watson, Foster: *Vives: On Education*, Cambridge, New York, 1913.

Woodward, W. H.: *Desiderius Erasmus Concerning the Aim and Method of Education*, Cambridge, New York, 1904.

————: *Vittorino da Feltre and Other Humanist Educators*, Cambridge, New York, 1905.

INTERPRETIVE WRITINGS

Artz, Frederick: *The Mind of the Middle Ages, A.D. 200–1500; An Historical Survey*, Knopf, New York, 1953.

Burckhardt, Jacob: *The Civilization of the Renaissance in Italy*, Macmillan, London, 1890.

————: *Renaissance in Italy*, Phaidon, London, 1937.

Durant, Will: *The Renaissance*, Simon and Schuster, New York, 1953.

Ferguson, W. K.: *The Renaissance*, Holt, New York, 1940.

————: *The Renaissance in Historical Thought; Five Centuries of Interpretation*, Houghton Mifflin, Boston, 1948.

Hulme, E. M.: *The Renaissance, the Protestant Revolution and the Catholic Reformation in Continental Europe*, Appleton-Century-Crofts, New York, 1914.

Hyma, Albert: *Renaissance to Reformation*, Eerdmans, Grand Rapids, Mich., 1951.

Robinson, J. H., and H. W. Rolfe: *Petrarch: The First Modern Scholar and Man of Letters*, Putnam, New York, 1909.

Roeder, Ralph: *The Man of the Renaissance*, Viking, New York, 1933.

Sandys, J. E.: *A History of Classical Scholarship*, Vol. II, Cambridge, New York, 1903.

Smith, P.: *Erasmus*, Harper, New York, 1923.

Symonds, J. A.: *Renaissance in Italy*, Modern Library, New York, 1935.

————: *A Short History of the Renaissance in Italy*, Holt, New York, 1894.

Taylor, H. O.: *Thought and Expression in the Sixteenth Century*, 2d ed., Macmillan, New York, 1930.

Thompson, J. W., and others: *Civilization of the Renaissance*, University of Chicago Press, Chicago, 1929.

Zweig, Stefan: *Erasmus of Rotterdam*, Viking, New York, 1934.

HISTORY OF EDUCATION IN THE RENAISSANCE

Baldwin, T. W.: *William Shakespeare's Small Latine and Less Greeke*, 2 vols., University of Illinois Press, Urbana, Ill., 1944.

Clark, Donald L.: *John Milton at St. Paul's School; A Study of Ancient Rhetoric in English Renaissance Education*, Columbia University Press, New York, 1948.

Hyma, Albert: *Erasmus and the Humanists*, Appleton-Century-Crofts, New York, 1930.

Leach, A. F.: *Schools of Medieval England*, Methuen, London, 1915.

McMahon, Clara P.: *Education in Fifteenth-century England*, Johns Hopkins Press, Baltimore, 1947.

Rashdall, Hastings: *Universities of Europe in the Middle Ages*, new ed., Oxford, New York, 1936.

Chap. 8. Religious Reformation and Scientific Revolution

ORIGINAL WRITINGS

Bacon, Francis: *Advancement of Learning and Novum Organum*, rev. ed., Willey, New York, 1944.

Calvin, John: *Institutes of the Christian Religion*, 7th American ed., Presbyterian Board of Christian Education, Philadelphia, 1936.

Champagnac, E. T. (ed.): *Ludus Literarius, or the Grammar Schools, by John Brinsley*, Constable, London, 1917.

————: *Mulcaster's Elementarie*, Oxford, New York, 1925.

————: *A New Discovery of the Old Art of Teaching Schoole, by Charles Hoole*, Liverpool University Press, Liverpool, 1913.

Comenius, John Amos: *The Great Didactic*, 2 vols., A. & C. Black, London, 1910.

————: *The Orbis Pictus*, Bardeen, Syracuse, N.Y., 1887.

Eby, Frederick (ed.): *Early Protestant Educators*, McGraw-Hill, New York, 1931.

Fitzpatrick, E. A.: *St. Ignatius and the Ratio Studiorum*, McGraw-Hill, New York, 1933.

Keatinge, M. W.: *Comenius*, McGraw-Hill, New York, 1931.

Leach, A. F.: *English Schools at the Reformation*, Archibald Constable, Westminster, England, 1896.

Luther, Martin: "Selections," in Dr. Eliot's Five-foot Shelf, *Harvard Classics*, Collier, New York, 1910.

Milton, John: *Milton on Education*, Yale University Press, New Haven, Conn., 1928.

Painter, F. V. N.: *Great Pedagogical Essays*, American Book, New York, 1905.

————: *Luther on Education*, Lutheran Publication Society, Philadelphia, 1889.

Turnbull, G. H.: *Hartlib, Dury and Comenius*, Liverpool University Press, Liverpool, 1947.

Young, Robert F. (ed.): *Comenius in England*, Oxford, New York, 1932.

INTERPRETIVE WRITINGS

Allen, J. W.: *History of Political Thought in the Sixteenth Century*, Methuen, London, 1928.

Anderson, F. H.: *The Philosophy of Francis Bacon*, Chicago University Press, Chicago, 1948.

Bainton, Roland: *Here I Stand*, Abingdon, Nashville, Tenn., 1950.

Burtt, E. A.: *Metaphysical Foundations of Modern Physical Science*, Harcourt, Brace, New York, 1927.

Butterfield, Herbert: *The Origins of Modern Science, 1300–1800*, Macmillan, New York, 1951.

Clark, G. N.: *The Seventeenth Century*, Oxford, New York, 1929.

Crombie, A. C.: *Augustine to Galileo; The History of Science*, Harvard University Press, Cambridge, Mass., 1953.

Hulme, E. M.: *The Renaissance, the Protestant Revolution and the Catholic Reformation in Continental Europe*, Appleton-Century-Crofts, New York, 1914.

Hyma, A.: *The Brethren of the Common Life*, Eerdmans, Grand Rapids, Mich., 1950.

Janelle, P.: *Catholic Reformation*, Bruce, Milwaukee, 1949.

Jones, R. F.: *Ancients and Moderns*, Washington University Press, St. Louis, 1936.

Laski, Harold: *The Rise of Liberalism; the Philosophy of a Business Civilization*, Harper, New York, 1936.

McGiffert, A. C.: *Protestant Thought before Kant*, Scribner, New York, 1911.

Ornstein, M.: *Role of Scientific Societies in the Seventeenth Century*, Chicago University Press, Chicago, 1928.

Reichenbach, Hans: *The Rise of Scientific Philosophy*, University of California Press, Berkeley, Calif., 1951.

Smith, Preserved: *The Age of the Reformation*, Holt, New York, 1923.

————: *A History of Modern Culture*, Vol. I, Holt, New York, 1930.

Stebbing, George: *The Story of the Catholic Church*, Sands, London, 1915.

Tawney, R. H.: *Religion and the Rise of Capitalism, A Historical Study*, Harcourt, Brace, New York, 1926.

Taylor, H. O.: *Thought and Expression in the 16th Century*, Macmillan, New York, 1920.

Weber, Max: *The Protestant Ethic and the Spirit of Capitalism*, Scribner, New York, 1930.

Willey, Basil: *Seventeenth Century Background*, Chatto & Windus, London, 1934.

Wolf, Abraham: *A History of Science, Technology, and Philosophy in the Sixteenth and Seventeenth Centuries*, Macmillan, New York, 1935.

Woodhouse, A. S. P.: *Puritanism and Liberty*, Dent, London, 1938.

HISTORY OF EDUCATION

Adamson, J. W.: *Pioneers of Modern Education*, Cambridge, New York, 1905.

Barnard, H. C.: *The French Tradition in Education*, Cambridge, New York, 1922.

Battersby, W. J.: *De La Salle: A Pioneer of Modern Education*, Longmans, New York, 1949.

De Montmorency, J. E. G.: *The Intervention of the State in English Education*, Cambridge, New York, 1902.

Farrell, Allan P.: *The Jesuit Code of Liberal Education; Development and Scope of the Ratio Studiorum*, Bruce, Milwaukee, 1938.

Fitzpatrick, Edward A.: *La Salle, Patron of All Teachers*, Bruce, Milwaukee, 1951.

Monroe, Will S.: *Comenius and the Beginnings of Educational Reform*, Scribner, New York, 1900.

Paulsen, Friedrich: *German Education, Past and Present*, Scribner, New York, 1912.

————: *German Universities and University Study*, Scribner, New York, 1906.

Robbins, C. L.: *Teachers in Germany in the Sixteenth Century*, Teachers College, Columbia University, New York, 1912.

Schwickerath, Robert: *Jesuit Education; Its History and Principles*, Herder, St. Louis, 1904.

Watson, Foster: *English Grammar Schools to 1660*, Cambridge, New York, 1908.

Wood, Norman: *The Reformation and English Education*, Routledge, London, 1931.

Chap. 9. The Reformation in America

ORIGINAL WRITINGS

Littlefield, George E.: *Early Schools and School-books of New England*, Club of Odd Volumes, Boston, 1904.

Meriwether, Colyer: *Our Colonial Curriculum, 1607–1776*, Capital Publishing Company, Washington, D.C., 1907.

Miller, Perry, and Thomas H. Johnson: *The Puritans*, American Book, New York, 1938.

Parsons, Elsie Clews: *Educational Legislation and Administration of Colonial Governments*, Macmillan, New York, 1899.

Seybolt, Robert F.: *Apprenticeship and Apprenticeship Education in Colonial New England and New York*, Teachers College, Columbia University, New York, 1916.

————: *The Public Schools of Colonial Boston 1635–1775*, Harvard University Press, Cambridge, Mass., 1935.

Wigglesworth, Michael: *The Day of Doom*, Spiral, New York, 1929.

INTERPRETIVE WRITINGS

Adams, J. T.: *The Founding of New England*, Atlantic Monthly, Boston, 1921.

Dorfman, Joseph: *The Economic Mind in American Civilization*, 1606–1865, Vol. I, Viking, New York, 1946.

Jernegan, Marcus W.: *Laboring and Dependent Classes in Colonial America*, 1607–1783, University of Chicago Press, Chicago, 1931.

Miller, Perry: *The New England Mind, the Seventeenth Century*, Macmillan, New York, 1939.

Morris, Richard B.: *Government and Labor in Early America*, Columbia University Press, New York, 1946.

Nettels, Curtis P.: *The Roots of American Civilization*, Appleton-Century-Crofts, New York, 1938.

Parrington, V. L.: *Main Currents in American Thought*, Vol. I, *The Colonial Mind*, 1620–1800, Harcourt, Brace, New York, 1927.

Priestly, Herbert I.: *The Coming of the White Man*, 1492–1848, Macmillan, New York, 1929.

Schneider, Herbert W.: *The Puritan Mind*, Holt, New York, 1930.

Sweet, William W.: *Religion in Colonial America*, Scribner, New York, 1942.

Wertenbaker, T. J.: *The First Americans*, 1607–1690, Macmillan, New York, 1927.

————: *The Founding of American Civilization; The Middle Colonies*, Scribner, New York, 1938.

————: *The Old South; The Founding of American Civilization*, Scribner, New York, 1942.

Wish, Harvey: *Society and Thought in Early America*, Longmans, New York, 1950.

HISTORY OF EDUCATION

Burns, J. A.: *The Catholic School System in the United States*, Benziger, New York, 1908.

Fleming, Sandford: *Children and Puritanism*, Yale University Press, New Haven, Conn., 1933.

Gould, Elizabeth: *Ezekiel Cheever, Schoolmaster*, Palmer, Boston, 1904.

Holmes, Pauline: *A Tercentenary History of the Boston Public Latin School, 1635–1935*, Harvard University Press, Cambridge, Mass., 1935.

Kilpatrick, W. H.: *The Dutch Schools of New Netherland and Colonial New York*, U.S. Bureau of Education, Bulletin 12, 1912.

Knight, E. W.: *Public Education in the South*, Ginn, Boston, 1922.

Monroe, Paul: *Founding of the American Public School System*, Macmillan, New York, 1940.

Morison, S. E.: *The Founding of Harvard College*, Harvard University Press, Cambridge, Mass., 1935.

————: *Harvard College in the Seventeenth Century,* 2 vols., Harvard University Press, Cambridge, Mass., 1936.

Small, Walter H.: *Early New England Schools,* Ginn, Boston, 1914.

Suzzalo, Henry: *The Rise of Local School Supervision in Massachusetts,* Teachers College, Columbia University, New York, 1906.

Tewksbury, D. G.: *The Founding of American Colleges and Universities before the Civil War,* Teachers College, Columbia University, New York, 1932.

Tuer, Andrew: *History of the Horn-book,* Scribner, New York, 1897.

Wells, Guy F.: *Parish Education in Colonial Virginia,* Teachers College, Columbia University, New York, 1923.

Chap. 10. The Age of Reason and Enlightenment

ORIGINAL WRITINGS

Adamson, J. W.: *The Educational Writings of John Locke,* E. Arnold, London, 1912.

————: *Pioneers of Modern Education,* Cambridge, New York, 1905.

Bacon, Francis: *Advancement of Learning and Novum Organum,* rev. ed., Willey, New York, 1944.

Barker, Ernest: *Social Contract; Essays by Locke, Hume, and Rousseau,* Oxford, New York, 1947.

Boyd, William (ed.): *The Minor Educational Writings of Jean Jacques Rousseau,* Blackie, Glasgow, 1910.

De La Fontainerie, François: *The Conduct of the Schools of Jean Baptiste de La Salle,* McGraw-Hill, New York, 1935.

————: *French Liberalism and Education in the Eighteenth Century,* McGraw-Hill, New York, 1932.

Descartes, René: *Discourse on Method,* Everyman's Library, Dent, London, 1949.

Greene, T. M. (ed.): *Kant, Selections,* Scribner, New York, 1929.

Hobbes, Thomas: *Leviathan,* Everyman's Library, Dutton, New York, 1950.

Hume, David: *Enquiry Concerning Human Understanding,* Open Court, La Salle, Ill., 1926.

Locke, John: *Essay Concerning Human Understanding,* Open Court, La Salle, Ill., 1933.

————: *Some Thoughts Concerning Education,* Cambridge, New York, 1902.

Machiavelli: *The Prince,* Farrar, Strauss, & Young, New York, 1946.

Montaigne, *Essays,* Heritage, New York, 1947.

Montesquieu: *Spirit of the Laws,* Hafner, New York, 1949.

Paine, Thomas: *Age of Reason,* Liberal Arts Press, New York, 1948.

————: *Rights of Man,* Everyman's Library, Dutton, New York, 1951.

Redman, B. R.: *Portable Voltaire,* Viking, New York, 1949.

Rousseau, Jean Jacques: *Emile,* Everyman's Library, Dutton, New York, 1950.

Rand, B. (ed.): *Modern Classical Philosophers,* Houghton Mifflin, Boston, 1908.

INTERPRETIVE WRITINGS

Becker, Carl: *The Heavenly City of the Eighteenth Century Philosophers,* Yale University Press, New Haven, Conn., 1932.

Boyd, William: *From Locke to Montessori,* Harrap, London, 1914.

Bruford, W. H.: *Germany in the Eighteenth Century,* Cambridge, New York, 1935.

Bury, J. B.: *The Idea of Progress,* Macmillan, New York, 1920.

Laski, Harold J.: *The Rise of Liberalism,* Harper, New York, 1936.

Lecky, W. E. H.: *History of the Rise and Influence of the Spirit of Rationalism in Europe*, rev. ed., Appleton, New York, 1876.

Maritain, Jacques: *Three Reformers: Luther, Descartes, and Rousseau*, Scribner, New York, 1929.

Martin, Kingsley: *French Liberal Thought in the Eighteenth Century*, Little, Brown, Boston, 1929.

Mowat, R. B.: *The Age of Reason; the Continent of Europe in the 18th Century*, Houghton Mifflin, Boston, 1934.

Palmer, R. R.: *Catholics and Unbelievers in Eighteenth Century France*, Princeton University Press, Princeton, N.J., 1939.

Shorr, Philip: *Science and Superstition in the Eighteenth Century*, Columbia University Press, New York, 1940.

Smith, Preserved: *A History of Modern Culture*, Vol. II, Holt, New York, 1934.

Stephen, Leslie: *English Thought in the Eighteenth Century*, Putnam, New York, 1876.

Wolf, Abraham: *A History of Science, Technology, and Philosophy in the Eighteenth Century*, Macmillan, New York, 1939.

HISTORY OF EDUCATION

Birchenough, Charles: *History of Elementary Education in England and Wales*, W. B. Clive, London, 1925.

Boyd, William: *The Educational Theory of Jean Jacques Rousseau*, Longmans, New York, 1911.

Davidson, Thomas: *Rousseau and Education According to Nature*, Scribner, New York, 1898.

De Montmorency, J. E. G.: *State Intervention in English Education*, Cambridge, New York, 1902.

Dobbs, A. E.: *Education and Social Movements*, 1700–1850, Longmans, New York, 1919.

Farrington, F. E.: *French Secondary Schools*, Longmans, New York, 1910.

————: *The Public Primary School System of France*, Teachers College, Columbia University, New York, 1906.

Hans, Nicholas: *History of Russian Educational Policy*, King, London, 1931.

Paulsen, F.: *German Universities and University Study*, Scribner, New York, 1906.

Smith, Frank: *A History of English Elementary Education*, 1760–1902, University of London Press, London, 1931.

Chap. 11. Enlightenment and Revolution in America

ORIGINAL WRITINGS

Arrowood, Charles F.: *Thomas Jefferson and Education in a Republic*, McGraw-Hill, New York, 1930.

Boyd, J. P.: *Papers of Thomas Jefferson*, Vols. I–VIII, Princeton University Press, Princeton, N.J., 1950–1953.

Butler, Vera M.: *Education as Revealed by New England Newspapers Prior to 1850*, Majestic Press, Philadelphia, 1935.

Brumbaugh, Martin G.: *The Life and Works of Christopher Dock*, Lippincott, Philadelphia, 1908.

Cubberley, E. P., and E. C. Elliott: *State and County School Administration*, Vol. II, Source Book, Macmillan, New York, 1915.

Edwards, Jonathan: *Representative Selections*, American Book, New York, 1935.

Evans, Henry R., and Edith A. Wright (eds.): *Expressions on Education by Builders of American Democracy, U.S. Office of Education, Bulletin* 1940, No. 10, 1941.

Ford, Paul L. (ed.): *The New England Primer*, Dodd, Mead, New York, 1899.

Hansen, A. O.: *Liberalism and American Education in the Eighteenth Century*, Macmillan, New York, 1926.

Heartman, Charles F.: *The New England Primer, Issued Prior to* 1835, Bowker, New York, 1934.

Honeywell, Roy J.: *The Educational Work of Thomas Jefferson*, Harvard University Press, Cambridge, Mass., 1931.

Johnson, Clifton: *Old-time Schools and Schoolbooks*, Macmillan, New York, 1904.

Meriwether, Colyer: *Our Colonial Curriculum*, 1607–1776, Capital Publishing Company, Washington, D.C., 1907.

Miller, Perry, and Thomas H. Johnson: *The Puritans*, American Book, New York, 1938.

Padover, Saul K. (ed.): *The Complete Jefferson*, Duell, Sloan, & Pearce, New York, 1943.

Parsons, Elsie Clews: *Educational Legislation and Administration of Colonial Governments*, Macmillan, New York, 1899.

Seybolt, Robert F.: *Apprenticeship and Apprenticeship Education in Colonial New England and New York*, Teachers College, Columbia University, New York, 1916.

Seybolt, R. F.: *The Evening School in Colonial America*, University of Illinois Press, Urbana, Ill., 1925.

————: *The Private Schools of Colonial Boston*, Harvard University Press, Cambridge, Mass., 1935.

————: *The Public Schools of Colonial Boston*, 1635–1775, Harvard University Press, Cambridge, Mass., 1935.

————: *Source Studies in American Colonial Education: The Private School*, University of Illinois Press, Urbana, Ill., 1925.

Woody, Thomas: *Educational Views of Benjamin Franklin*, McGraw-Hill, New York, 1931.

————: *Quaker Education in the Colony and State of New Jersey*, University of Pennsylvania Press, Philadelphia, 1923.

INTERPRETIVE WRITINGS

Adams, J. T.: *Provincial America*, 1690–1763, Macmillan, New York, 1928.

Cobb, Sanford H.: *The Rise of Religious Liberty in America*, Macmillan, New York, 1902.

Dorfman, Joseph: *The Economic Mind in American Civilization*, 1606–1865, 2 vols., Viking, New York, 1946.

Fleming, Sandford: *Children and Puritanism*, Yale University Press, New Haven, Conn., 1933.

Greene, Evarts B.: *The Revolutionary Generation*, 1763–1790, Macmillan, New York, 1943.

Herskovits, Melville J.: *The Myth of the Negro Past*, Harper, New York, 1941.

Jernegan, Marcus W.: *Laboring and Dependent Classes in Colonial America*, 1607–1783, University of Chicago Press, Chicago, 1931.

Kiefer, Monica: *American Children through Their Books*, 1700–1835, University of Pennsylvania Press, Philadelphia, 1948.

Miller, Perry: *The New England Mind*, Macmillan, New York, 1939.

Morais, Herbert W.: *Deism in Eighteenth Century America*, Columbia University Press, New York, 1934.

Morris, Richard B.: *Government and Labor in Early America*, Columbia University Press, New York, 1946.

Mott, Frank L.: *A History of American Magazines*, 1741–1850, Appleton-Century-Crofts, New York, 1930.

Nettels, Curtis P.: *The Roots of American Civilization*, Appleton-Century-Crofts, New York, 1938.

Parrington, V. L.: *Main Currents in American Thought*, Vol. I, *The Colonial Mind*, 1680–1800, Harcourt, Brace, New York, 1927.

Perry, Ralph Barton: *Puritanism and Democracy*, Vanguard, New York, 1944.

Schneider, Herbert: *The Puritan Mind*, Holt, New York, 1930.

Sweet, William W.: *Religion in Colonial America*, Scribner, New York, 1942.

Van Doren, Carl: *Benjamin Franklin*, Viking, New York, 1938.

Wertenbaker, T. J.: *The Founding of American Civilization; the Middle Colonies*, Scribner, New York, 1938.

———: *The Old South; the Founding of American Civilization*, Scribner, New York, 1942.

Wish, Harvey: *Society and Thought in Early America*, Longmans, New York, 1950.

HISTORY OF EDUCATION

Bell, Sadie: *The Church, the State, and Education in Virginia*, Science Press, New York, 1930.

Cassidy, F. P.: *Catholic College Foundations and Development in the United States* (1677–1850), Catholic University of America Press, Washington, D.C., 1924.

Gambrell, Mary L.: *Ministerial Training in 18th Century New England*, Columbia University Press, New York, 1937.

Holmes, Pauline: *A Tercentenary History of the Boston Public Latin School*, 1635–1935, Harvard University Press, Cambridge, Mass., 1935.

Jackson, George L.: *The Development of School Support in Colonial Massachusetts*, Teachers College, Columbia University, New York, 1909.

Kemp, W. W.: *The Support of Schools in Colonial New York by the Society for the Propagation of the Gospel in Foreign Parts*, Teachers College, Columbia University, New York, 1913.

Kilpatrick, W. H.: *The Dutch Schools of New Netherland and Colonial New York*, U.S. Bureau of Education, Bulletin 12, 1912.

Kirkpatrick, J. E.: *Academic Organization and Control*, Antioch Press, Yellow Springs, Ohio, 1931.

McGucken, W. J.: *The Jesuits and Education*, Bruce, Milwaukee, 1932.

Monroe, Paul: *Founding of the American Public School System*, Macmillan, New York, 1940.

Small, Walter H.: *Early New England Schools*, Ginn, Boston, 1914.

Suzzallo, Henry: *The Rise of Local School Supervision in Massachusetts*, Teachers College, Columbia University, New York, 1906.

Taylor, Howard C.: *The Educational Significance of the Early Federal Land Ordinances*, Teachers College, Columbia University, New York, 1922.

Tewksbury, Donald G.: *The Founding of American Colleges and Universities before the Civil War*, Teachers College, Columbia University, New York, 1932.

Updegraff, Harlan: *The Origin of the Moving School in Massachusetts*, Teachers College, Columbia University, New York, 1908.

Walsh, James J.: *Education of the Founding Fathers; Scholasticism in the Colonial Colleges*, Fordham University Press, New York, 1935.

Warfel, Harry: *Noah Webster, Schoolmaster to America*, Macmillan, New York, 1936.

Wells, Guy F.: *Parish Education in Colonial Virginia*, Teachers College, Columbia University, 1923.

Woody, Thomas: *Early Quaker Education in Pennsylvania*, Teachers College, Columbia University, New York, 1920.

Chaps. 12 and 13. Modern European Education

ORIGINAL WRITINGS

Anderson, L. F.: *Pestalozzi*, McGraw-Hill, New York, 1931.

Arnold, Matthew: *Culture and Anarchy*, Cambridge, New York, 1932.

———: *Reports on Elementary Schools*, 1852–1882, Macmillan, London, 1899.

Burns, Emile (ed.): *A Handbook of Marxism*, Random House, New York, 1935.

Cavenagh, F. A. (ed.): *James and John Stuart Mill on Education*, Cambridge University Press, New York, 1931.

Comte, Auguste: *A General View of Positivism*, Routledge, London, 1908.

Counts, George S., and Nucia P. Lodge: *I Want to Be Like Stalin*, John Day, New York, 1947.

Darwin, Charles: *The Origin of Species*, Modern Library, New York, 1936.

Fletcher, S. S., and J. Welton: *Froebel's Chief Writings on Education*, Longmans, New York, 1912.

Freud, Sigmund: *An Outline of Psychoanalysis*, Norton, New York, 1949.

Froebel, Friedrich: *The Education of Man*, Appleton, New York, 1887.

Green, J. A.: *Pestalozzi's Educational Writings*, Longmans, New York, 1912.

Green, T. M. (ed.): *Kant, Selections*, Scribner, New York, 1929.

Gentile, Giovanni: *The Reform of Education*, Harcourt, Brace, New York, 1922.

Herbart, J. F.: *Outlines of Educational Doctrine*, Macmillan, New York, 1901.

———: *The Science of Education*, Heath, Boston, 1895.

Kandel, I. L.: *French Elementary Schools: Official Courses of Study*, Teachers College, Columbia University, New York, 1927.

———: *The Reform of Secondary Education in France*, Teachers College, Columbia University, New York, 1924.

——— and Thomas Alexander: *Reorganization of Education in Prussia*, Teachers College, Columbia University, New York, 1927.

Kant, Immanuel: *Educational Theory* (tr. by E. F. Buchner), Lippincott, Philadelphia, 1904.

———: *On Education* (tr. by Annette Churton), Heath, Boston, 1900.

Knight, E. W.: *Reports on European Education*, McGraw-Hill, New York, 1930.

Newman, John Henry Cardinal: *The Idea of a University*, Longmans, New York, 1927.

Pestalozzi, J. H.: *How Gertrude Teaches Her Children*, Allyn & Unwin, London, 1915.

———: *Leonard and Gertrude*, Heath, Boston, 1885.

Spahr, Margaret: *Readings in Recent Political Philosophy*, Macmillan, New York, 1935.

Spencer, Herbert: *Education: Intellectual, Moral, and Physical*, Appleton, New York, 1883.

Turnbull, G. T.: *The Educational Theory of J. G. Fichte*, Liverpool University Press, Liverpool, 1926.

Ziemer, Gregor A.: *Education for Death; the Making of the Nazi*, Oxford, New York, 1941.

INTERPRETIVE WRITINGS

Arendt, Hannah, *The Origins of Totalitarianism*, Harcourt, New York, 1951.

Babbitt, Irving: *Rousseau and Romanticism*, Houghton Mifflin, Boston, 1919.

Baron, Salo W.: *Modern Nationalism and Religion*, Harper, New York, 1947.

Barzun, Jacques: *Berlioz and the Romantic Century*, Little, Brown, Boston, 1950.

———: *Darwin, Marx, Wagner*, Little, Brown, Boston, 1941.

Benn, A. W.: *History of English Rationalism in the Nineteenth Century*, 2 vols., Longmans, New York, 1906.

Bernal, John D.: *The Social Function of Science*, Routledge, London, 1939.

Boas, George: *Our New Ways of Thinking*, Harper, New York, 1930.

Bowen, H. C.: *Froebel and Education through Self-activity*, Scribner, New York, 1899.

Brinton, Crane: *English Political Thought in the Nineteenth Century*, Harvard University Press, Cambridge, Mass., 1949.

Buckner, E. F.: *The Educational Theory of Immanuel Kant*, Lippincott, Philadelphia, 1904.

Connell, W. F.: *The Educational Thought and Influence of Matthew Arnold*, Routledge, London, 1950.

Crossman, R.: *The God That Failed*, Harper, New York, 1949.

DeGarmo, Charles: *Herbart and the Herbartians*, Scribner, New York, 1896.

Goodfriend, Arthur: *If You Were Born in Russia*, Farrar, Straus & Young, New York, 1950.

Hayes, C. J. H.: *Essays on Nationalism*, Macmillan, New York, 1926.

———: *The Historical Evolution of Modern Nationalism*, Richard R. Smith, New York, 1931.

Hayward, F. H.: *Three Historical Educators: Pestalozzi, Froebel, Herbart*, Ralph, Holland & Company, London, 1905.

Heimann, Eduard: *Communism, Fascism, or Democracy?*, Norton, New York, 1938.

Hobson, J. A.: *The Evolution of Modern Capitalism*, rev. ed., G. Allen, London, 1926.

Hook, Sidney: *From Hegel to Marx*, Reynal & Hitchcock, New York, 1936.

Joad, C. E. M.: *Decadence*, Faber, London, 1948.

Johnson, F. Ernest (ed.): *Religion and the World Order*, Harper, New York, 1944.

Kohn, Hans: *The Idea of Nationalism*, Macmillan, New York, 1948.

———: *The Twentieth Century: A Mid-way Account of the Western World*, Macmillan, New York, 1949.

Laski, Harold J.: *The Rise of Liberalism*, Harper, New York, 1936.

Leighton, J. A.: *Social Philosophies in Conflict; Fascism and Nazism, Communism, Liberal Democracy*, Appleton-Century-Crofts, New York, 1937.

Mackenzie, Millicent: *Hegel's Educational Theory and Practice*, S. Sonnenschein, London, 1909.

Makintosh, H. R.: *Types of Modern Theology*, Scribner, New York, 1937.

Mangone, Gerard J.: *A Short History of International Organization*, McGraw-Hill, New York, 1954.

Masters, Dexter: *One World or None*, McGraw-Hill, New York, 1946.

McKeon, R. (ed.): *Democracy in a World of Tensions*, University of Chicago Press, Chicago, 1951.

Mead, G. H.: *Movements of Thought in the Nineteenth Century*, Univeristy of Chicago Press, Chicago, 1936.

Merriam, C. E.: *The New Democracy and the New Despotism*, McGraw-Hill, New York, 1939.

Merz, J. T.: *History of European Thought in the Nineteenth Century*, 4 vols., Blackwood, Edinburgh, 1907–1914.

Northrop, F. S. C.: *The Meeting of East and West; An Inquiry Concerning World Understanding*, Macmillan, New York, 1946.

Ogg, F. A.: *European Governments and Politics*, Macmillan, New York, 1929.

Ruggiero, Guido de: *History of European Liberalism*, Oxford, New York, 1927.

Schilpp, P. A. (ed.): *The Philosophy of John Dewey*, Northwestern University Press, Evanston, Ill., 1939.

Schweitzer, Albert: *Quest for the Historical Jesus*, Macmillan, New York, 1938.

Somervell, D. C.: *English Thought in the Nineteenth Century*, Longmans, New York, 1938.

Whitehead, A. N.: *Science and the Modern World*, Macmillan, New York, 1925.

HISTORY OF EDUCATION

Adamson, J. W.: *English Education*, 1789–1902, Cambridge, New York, 1930.

Alexander, Thomas: *Prussian Elementary Schools*, Macmillan, New York, 1918.

————: *Training of Elementary Teachers in Germany*, Teachers College, Columbia University, New York, 1929.

———— and Beryl Parker: *The New Education in the German Republic*, John Day, New York, 1929.

Archer, R. L.: *Secondary Education in the 19th Century* [England], Cambridge, New York, 1921.

Barker, Ernest: *British Universities*, Longmans, New York, 1946.

Becker, Carl H.: *Secondary Education and Teacher Training in Germany*, Teachers College, Columbia University, New York, 1931.

Birchenough, Charles: *History of Elementary Education in England and Wales from 1800 to the Present Day*, University Tutorial Press, London, 1938.

Brinkmann, Carl: *Recent Theories of Citizenship in Its Relation to Government*, Yale University Press, New Haven, Conn., 1927.

Chambers, M. M. (ed.): *Universities of the World outside U.S.A.*, American Council on Education, Washington, D.C., 1950.

Counts, George S., and Nucia P. Lodge: *The Country of the Blind; The Soviet System of Mind Control*, Houghton Mifflin, Boston, 1949.

De Montmorency, J. E. G.: *State Intervention in English Education*, Cambridge, New York, 1902.

Education in Britain: An Outline of the Educational System, rev. ed., British Information Services, Reference Division, London, 1948.

Engelmann, Susanne E.: *German Education and Re-education*, International Universities Press, New York, 1945.

Farrington, F. E.: *French Secondary Schools*, Longmans, New York, 1910.

————: *The Public Primary School System of France*, Teachers College, Columbia University, New York, 1906.

Gaus, John M.: *Great Britain: A Study of Civic Loyalty*, University of Chicago Press, Chicago, 1929.

Hans, Nicholas: *History of Russian Educational Policy*, 1701–1917, King, London, 1931.

Hays, C. J. H.: *France, A Nation of Patriots*, Columbia University Press, New York, 1930.

Harper, S. N.: *Civic Training in Soviet Russia*, University of Chicago Press, Chicago, 1929.

Holland, Kenneth: *Youth in European Labor Camps*, American Council on Education, Washington, D.C., 1939.

Johnson, William H. E.: *Russia's Educational Heritage*, Rutgers University Press, New Brunswick, N.J., 1950.

Kandel, I. L.: *Comparative Education*, Houghton Mifflin, Boston, 1933.

———: *The Making of Nazis*, Teachers College, Columbia University, New York, 1935.

——— (ed.): *Educational Yearbooks of the International Institute*, Teachers College, Columbia University, New York, 1924–1944.

King, Beatrice: *Russia Goes to School*, Heinemann, London, 1948.

Kneller, George F.: *The Educational Philosophy of National Socialism*, Yale University Press, New Haven, Conn., 1941.

Lawrence, Evelyn (ed.): *Friedrich Froebel and English Education*, Philosophical Library, New York, 1953.

Learned, W. S.: *The Quality of the Educational Process in the United States and Europe*, Carnegie Foundation, Bulletin 20, New York, 1927.

Leese, John: *Personalities and Power in English Education*, Arnold, Leeds, England, 1950.

Lilge, Frederic: *The Abuse of Learning; The Failure of the German University*, Macmillan, New York, 1948.

Mack, E. C.: *Public Schools and British Opinion*, 2 vols., Columbia University Press, New York, 1941.

Mallet, Charles E.: *A History of the University of Oxford*, 3 vols., Methuen, London, 1924–1927.

Marrara, H. R.: *The New Education in Italy*, S. F. Vanni, New York, 1936.

Merriam, C. E.: *The Making of Citizens; A Comparative Study of Methods of Civic Training*, University of Chicago Press, Chicago, 1931.

Meyer, Adolph E.: *The Development of Education in the 20th Century*, 2d ed., Prentice-Hall, New York, 1949.

Miles, Donald W.: *Recent Reforms in French Secondary Education*, Teachers College, Columbia University, New York, 1953.

Moehlman, A. H., and J. S. Roucek (eds.): *Comparative Education*, Dryden, New York, 1952.

Mullinger, J. Bass: *The University of Cambridge*, 3 vols., Cambridge, New York, 1873–1911.

Paulsen, Friedrich: *German Education* (tr. by T. Lorenz), T. Fisher Unwin, London, 1908.

———: *German Universities and University Study*, Scribner, New York, 1906.

Pinkevitch, A. P.: *The New Education in the Soviet Republic*, John Day, New York, 1929.

Reisner, E. H.: *Nationalism and Education since 1789*, Macmillan, New York, 1922.

Russell, James E.: *German Higher Schools*, Longmans, New York, 1913.

Smith, Frank: *A History of English Elementary Education, 1760–1902*, University of London Press, London, 1931.

Wenke, Hans: *Education in Western Germany*, Library of Congress, Washington, D.C., 1953.

Wilhelm, Theodor, and Gerhard Grafe: *German Education Today*, Terramare Office, Berlin, 1936.

Woody, Thomas: *New Minds, New Men*, Macmillan, New York, 1932.

World Handbook of Educational Organization and Statistics, UNESCO, Education Clearing House, Paris, 1951.

Wymer, Norman: *Dr. Arnold of Rugby*, Robert Hale, London, 1953.

The Yearbook of Education, Evans Brothers, London, 1932 to present.

Chaps. 14 and 15. Nineteenth-century America

ORIGINAL WRITINGS

Arrowood, C. F.: *Thomas Jefferson and Education in a Republic*, McGraw-Hill, New York, 1930.

Barnard, Henry: *American Journal of Education*, 32 vols., 1855–1882.

Brubacher, John S.: *Henry Barnard on Education*, McGraw-Hill, New York, 1931.

Butler, Vera M.: *Education as Revealed by New England Newspapers Previous to 1850*, Majestic Press, Philadelphia, 1935.

Burton, Warren: *The District School As It Was* (ed. by Clifton Johnson), Crowell, New York, 1928.

Caldwell, Otis W., and Stuart A. Courtis: *Then & Now in Education*, World, Yonkers, N.Y., 1924.

Common School Assistant (New York), Albany, N.Y., 1836–1840.

Common School Journal (Massachusetts), Marsh, Capen, Lyon & Webb, etc., Boston, 1839–1852.

Connecticut Common School Journal, Case, Tiffany & Burnham, etc., Hartford, Conn., 1838–1866.

Curoe, Philip R. V.: *Educational Attitudes and Policies of Organized Labor in the United States*, Teachers College, Columbia University, New York, 1926.

Dewey, John: *The Child and the Curriculum*, University of Chicago Press, Chicago, 1902.

———: *The Educational Situation*, University of Chicago Press, Chicago, 1904.

———: *My Pedagogic Creed*, E. L. Kellogg, New York, 1897.

———: *The School and Society*, University of Chicago Press, Chicago, 1899.

Eliot, Charles W.: *Educational Reform*, Century, New York, 1898.

Gilman, Daniel C.: *University Problems in the United States*, Appleton-Century, New York, 1898.

Goodsell, Willystine: *Pioneers of Women's Education*, McGraw-Hill, New York, 1931.

Honeywell, Roy J.: *The Educational Work of Thomas Jefferson*, Harvard University Press, Cambridge, Mass., 1931.

James, William: *Pragmatism, A New Name for Old Ways of Thinking*, Longmans, New York, 1907.

———: *Talks to Teachers on Psychology*, new ed., Holt, New York, 1939.

Johnson, Clifton: *Old-time Schools and Schoolbooks*, Macmillan, New York, 1917.

Knight, E. W.: *Reports on European Education*, McGraw-Hill, New York, 1930.

Life and Works of Horace Mann, 5 vols., Lee and Shepard, Boston, 1891.

Parker, Francis W.: *Talks on Pedagogics*, E. L. Kellogg, New York, 1894.

Peterson, Houston (ed.): *Great Teachers*, Rutgers University Press, New Brunswick, N.J., 1946.

Porter, Noah: *The American Colleges and the American Public*, Charles C. Chatfield, New Haven, Conn., 1870.

Tappan, Henry Philip: *University Education*, Putnam, New York, 1851.
Washington, Booker T.: *Up from Slavery*, Doubleday, New York, 1927.

INTERPRETIVE WRITINGS

Adams, Henry: *The Education of Henry Adams*, Houghton Mifflin, Boston, 1922.
Bowers, David F.: *Foreign Influences in American Life*, Princeton University Press, Princeton, N.J., 1944.
Brooks, Van Wyck: *The Flowering of New England* (1815–1865), Dutton, New York, 1938.
————: *New England: Indian Summer*, Dutton, New York, 1940.
Bryce, James: *The American Commonwealth*, 2 vols., Macmillan, New York, 1907.
Cargill, Oscar: *Intellectual America: The March of Ideas*, Macmillan, New York, 1941.
Cole, Arthur C.: *The Irrepressible Conflict*, 1850–1865, Macmillan, New York, 1934.
Commager, Henry S.: *The American Mind*, Yale University Press, New Haven, Conn., 1950.
Coulter, E. Merton: *The South During Reconstruction*, 1865–1877, Louisiana State University Press, Baton Rouge, La., 1947.
Counts, George S.: *The Prospects of American Democracy*, John Day, New York, 1938.
————: *The Social Foundations of Education*, Scribner, New York, 1934.
Ditzion, Sidney: *Arsenals of a Democratic Culture*, American Library Association, Chicago, 1947.
Dorfman, Joseph: *The Economic Mind in American Civilization*, 1606–1865, Vol. II, Viking, New York, 1946.
Fish, Carl R.: *The Rise of the Common Man*, 1830–1850, Macmillan, New York, 1927.
Gabriel, R. H.: *The Course of American Democratic Thought*, Ronald, New York, 1940.
Hansen, Marcus L.: *The Immigrant in American History*, Harvard University Press, Cambridge, Mass., 1940.
Harris, Herbert: *American Labor*, Yale University Press, New Haven, Conn., 1938.
Hayes, Cecil B.: *The American Lyceum: Its History and Contribution to Education*, U.S. Office of Education, Bulletin 12, 1932.
Hicks, John D.: *The Populist Revolt*, University of Minnesota Press, Minneapolis, 1931.
Hofstadter, Richard: *Social Darwinism in American Thought*, University of Pennsylvania Press, Philadelphia, 1945.
James, Henry: *Charles W. Eliot*, 2 vols., Houghton Mifflin, Boston, 1930.
Kiefer, Mary Monica: *American Children Through Their Books:* 1700–1835, University of Pennsylvania Press, Philadelphia, 1948.
Krout, John A., and Dixon Ryan Fox: *The Completion of Independence*, 1790–1830, Macmillan, New York, 1944.
Leidecker, Kurt F.: *Yankee Teacher: The Life of William Torrey Harris*, Philosophical Library, New York, 1946.
Mathews, Basil: *Booker T. Washington, Educator and Interracial Interpreter*, Harvard University Press, Cambridge, Mass., 1948.
Mead, George H.: *Movements of Thought in the Nineteenth Century*, University of Chicago Press, Chicago, 1936.
Miller, Perry: *The Transcendentalists*, Harvard University Press, Cambridge, Mass., 1950.

Mumford, Lewis: *The Brown Decades; A Study of the Arts in America*, 1865–1895, Harcourt, Brace, New York, 1931.

Nevins, Allan: *The Emergence of Modern America*, 1865–1878, Macmillan, New York, 1927.

Parrington, V. L.: *Main Currents in American Thought*, Vol. II, *The Romantic Revolution in America*, 1800–1860; Vol. III, *The Beginnings of Critical Realism in America*, 1860–1900, Harcourt, Brace. New York, 1927–1930.

Perry, Ralph Barton: *Puritanism and Democracy*, Vanguard, New York, 1944.

Schlesinger, Arthur M.: *The Rise of the City*, 1878–1898, Macmillan, New York, 1933.

Schlesinger, Arthur M., Jr.: *The Age of Jackson*, Little, Brown, Boston, 1945.

Spitz, David: *Patterns of Anti-democratic Thought*, Macmillan, New York, 1949.

Tarbell, Ida M.: *The Nationalizing of Business*, 1878–1898, Macmillan, New York, 1936.

Tocqueville, Alexis De: *Democracy in America*, 2 vols., Knopf, New York, 1945.

Turner, F. J.: *The Frontier in American History*, Holt, New York, 1920.

Tyler, Alice Felt: *Freedom's Ferment*, University of Minnesota Press, Minneapolis, 1944.

Wiener, Philip P.: *Evolution and the Founders of Pragmatism*, Harvard University Press, Cambridge, Mass., 1949.

Wish, Harvey: *Society and Thought in Early America*, Longmans, New York, 1950.

————: *Society and Thought in Modern America: A Social and Intellectual History of the American People from* 1865, Longmans, New York, 1952.

Wittke, Carl: *We Who Built America*, Prentice-Hall, New York, 1939.

Woodward, Comer Vann: *Origins of the New South*, Louisiana State University Press, Baton Rouge, La., 1951.

HISTORY OF EDUCATION

Anderson, L. F.: *History of Manual and Industrial School Education*, Appleton-Century-Crofts, New York, 1926.

Bittner, W. S.: *The University Extension Movement*, U.S. Bureau of Education, *Bulletin* 84, 1919.

Boas, Louise: *Women's Education Begins; the Rise of the Women's Colleges*, Wheaton College Press, Newton, Mass., 1935.

Bond, Horace Mann: *The Education of the Negro in the American Social Order*, Prentice-Hall, New York, 1934.

Borrowman, Merle L.: *The Liberal and Technical in Teacher Education; A Historical Survey of American Thought*, Teachers College, Columbia University, New York, 1955.

Brown, S. W.: *The Secularization of American Education*, Teachers College. Columbia University, New York, 1912.

Butts, R. F.: *The College Charts Its Course*, McGraw-Hill, New York, 1939.

Carlton, Frank T.: *Economic Influences upon Educational Progress in the United States*, University of Wisconsin Press, Madison, Wis., 1908.

Cremin, Lawrence A.: *The American Common School*, Teachers College, Columbia University, New York, 1951.

Culver, Raymond B.: *Horace Mann and Religion in the Massachusetts Public Schools*, Yale University Press, New Haven, Conn., 1929.

Dearborn, Ned H.: *The Oswego Movement in American Education*, Teachers College, Columbia University, New York, 1925.

DeGarmo, Charles: *Herbart and the Herbartians*, Scribner, New York, 1895.

Douglas, Paul: *American Apprenticeship and Industrial Education*, Columbia University Press, New York, 1921.

Eckleberry, R. H.: *The History of the Municipal University in the United States*, *U.S. Office of Education, Bulletin* 2, 1932.

Grizzell, Emit Duncan: *Origin and Development of the High School in New England before* 1865, Macmillan, New York, 1923.

Harper, C. A.: *A Century of Public Teacher Education*, American Association of Teachers Colleges, New York, 1939.

Hayes, Cecil B.: *The American Lyceum*, *U.S. Office of Education, Bulletin* 12, 1932.

Hinsdale, B. A.: *Horace Mann and the Public School Revival in the United States*, Scribner, New York, 1937.

Holmes, D. O. W.: *The Evolution of the Negro College*, Teachers College, Columbia University, New York, 1934.

Jackson, Sidney L.: *America's Struggle for Free Schools*, American Council on Public Affairs, Washington, D.C., 1942.

Kirkpatrick, J. E.: *Academic Organization and Control*, Antioch Press, Yellow Springs, Ohio, 1931.

Klein, Arthur J.: *Survey of Land-grant Colleges and Universities*, *U.S. Office of Education, Bulletin* 9, 1930.

Lee, Gordon C.: *The Struggle for Federal Aid: First Phase*, Teachers College, Columbia University, New York, 1949.

Monroe, Paul: *Founding of the American Public School System*, Macmillan, New York, 1940.

Monroe, W. S.: *History of the Pestalozzian Movement in the United States*, Bardeen, Syracuse, N.Y., 1907.

————: *Teaching-Learning Theory and Teacher Education*, 1890–1950, University of Illinois Press, Urbana, Ill., 1952.

Morison, S. E.: *The Development of Harvard University since the Inauguration of President Eliot* (1869–1929), Harvard University Press, Cambridge, Mass., 1930.

Mosier, Richard D.: *Making the American Mind*, King's Crown, New York, 1947.

Pangburn, Jessie M.: *The Evolution of the American Teachers College*, Teachers College, Columbia University, New York, 1932.

Pierce, Bessie L.: *Public Opinion and the Teaching of History*, Appleton-Century-Crofts, New York, 1926.

Rugg, Harold: *American Life and the School Curriculum*, Ginn, Boston, 1936.

Stout, John E.: *The Development of High-school Curricula in the North Central States from 1860 to 1918*, University of Chicago Press, Chicago, 1921.

Swift, F. H.: *A History of Public Permanent Common School Funds in the United States*, 1795–1905, Holt, New York, 1911.

Taylor, Howard Cromwell: *The Educational Significance of the Early Federal Land Ordinances*, Teachers College, Columbia University, New York, 1922.

Tewksbury, D. G.: *The Founding of American Colleges and Universities before the Civil War*, Teachers College, Columbia University, New York, 1932.

Tharp, Louise Hall: *Until Victory; Horace Mann and Mary Peabody*, Little, Brown, Boston, 1953.

Thursfield, Richard: *Henry Barnard's Journal of Education*, Johns Hopkins Press, Baltimore, 1946.

Thwing, C. F.: *A History of Higher Education in America*, Appleton-Century-Crofts, New York, 1906.

Williams, E. I. F.: *Horace Mann, Educational Statesman*, Macmillan, New York, 1937.

Chaps. 16 and 17. Twentieth-century America

ORIGINAL WRITINGS

APPEAL TO THE TRADITIONAL FOUNDATIONS OF EDUCATION

American Council on Education, Committee on Religion and Education: *The Relation of Religion to Public Education,* Washington, D.C., 1947.

Babbitt, Irving: *Literature and the American College,* Houghton Mifflin, Boston, 1908.

Barzun, Jacques: *Teacher in America,* Little, Brown, Boston, 1945.

Bell, Bernard I.: *The Crisis in Education,* McGraw-Hill, New York, 1949.

Bestor, Arthur E.: *Educational Wastelands,* University of Illinois Press, Urbana, Ill., 1953.

Butler, J. Donald: *Four Philosophies and Their Practice in Education and Religion,* Harper, New York, 1951.

Butler, Nicholas Murray: *The Meaning of Education,* Scribner, New York, 1915.

Cunningham, W. F.: *The Pivotal Problems of Education,* Macmillan, New York, 1940.

Deferrari, R. J.: *Vital Problems of Catholic Education in the United States,* The Catholic University of America Press, Washington, D.C., 1939.

Demiashkevich, Michael: *An Introduction to the Philosophy of Education,* American Book, New York, 1935.

Flexner, Abraham: *The American College: A Criticism,* Appleton-Century-Crofts, New York, 1908.

———: *Universities, English, German, American,* Oxford, New York, 1930.

Foerster, Norman: *The American State University,* University of North Carolina Press, Chapel Hill, N.C., 1937.

Grattan, C. Hartley (ed.): *The Critique of Humanism; A Symposium,* Brent, Warren & Putnam, New York, 1930.

Highet, Gilbert: *The Art of Teaching,* Knopf, New York, 1950.

Horne, Herman H.: *A Democratic Philosophy of Education,* Macmillan, New York, 1932.

Hutchins, Robert M.: *The Higher Learning in America,* Yale University Press, New Haven, Conn., 1936.

———: *The Conflict in Education,* Harper, New York, 1953.

Johnson, F. Ernest (ed.): *American Education and Religion,* Harper, New York, 1952.

Kandel, I. L.: *Conflicting Theories of Education,* Macmillan, New York, 1939.

Livingstone, Richard: *On Education,* Macmillan, New York, 1944.

Lodge, Rupert C.: *Philosophy of Education,* Harper, New York, 1947.

Maritain, Jacques: *Education at the Crossroads,* Yale University Press, New Haven, Conn., 1943.

———: *True Humanism,* Scribner, New York, 1938.

Meiklejohn, Alexander: *Education Between Two Worlds,* Harper, New York, 1942.

Nash, Arnold S. (ed.): *Protestant Thought in the Twentieth Century,* Macmillan, New York, 1951.

Niebuhr, Reinhold: *Moral Man and Immoral Society,* Scribner, New York, 1932.

———: *The Nature and Destiny of Man,* 2 vols., Scribner, New York, 1941–1943.

Nock, Albert Jay: *The Theory of Education in the United States,* Harcourt, Brace, New York, 1932.

Redden, John, and Francis Ryan: *A Catholic Philosophy of Education,* Bruce, Milwaukee, 1942.

Ulich, Robert: *Fundamentals of Democratic Education*, American Book, New York, 1940.

Van Doren, Mark: *Liberal Education*, Holt, New York, 1943.

Van Dusen, Henry P.: *God in Education*, Scribner, New York, 1951.

West, Andrew F.: *The Value of the Classics*, Princeton University Press, Princeton, N.J., 1917.

Williams, Daniel Day: *What Present-day Theologians Are Thinking*, Harper, New York, 1952.

APPEAL TO THE SCIENTIFIC FOUNDATIONS OF EDUCATION

Bagley, W. C.: *Determinism in Education*, Warwick and York, Baltimore, 1928.

———: *Education and Emergent Man*, Ronald, New York, 1934.

Bobbitt, Franklin: *How to Make a Curriculum*, Houghton Mifflin, Boston, 1924.

Breed, F. S.: *Education and the New Realism*, Macmillan, New York, 1939.

Charters, W. W.: *Curriculum Construction*, Macmillan, New York, 1925.

Finney, Ross L.: *A Sociological Philosophy of Education*, Macmillan, New York, 1928.

Gates, Arthur I., and others: *Educational Psychology*, 3d ed., Macmillan, New York, 1948.

Howerth, I. W.: *Theory of Education*, Appleton-Century-Crofts, New York, 1929.

Judd, Charles H.: *Education and Social Progress*, Harcourt, Brace, New York, 1934.

Monroe, Walter S., and Max Engelhart: *The Scientific Study of Educational Problems*, Macmillan, New York, 1937.

Morrison, H. C.: *Basic Principles of Education*, University of Chicago Press, Chicago, 1934.

National Society for the Study of Education: *Learning and Instruction*, Forty-ninth Yearbook, Part I, University of Chicago Press, Chicago, 1950.

———: *Psychology of Learning*, Forty-first Yearbook, Part II, University of Chicago Press, Chicago, 1942.

Thorndike, Edward L.: *Educational Psychology*, 3 vols., Teachers College, Columbia University, New York, 1913–14.

———: *Human Nature and the Social Order*, Macmillan, New York, 1940.

———: *Selected Writings from a Connectionist's Psychology*, Appleton-Century-Crofts, New York, 1949.

Watson, John B.: *Behaviorism*, Norton, New York, 1930.

APPEAL TO THE CULTURAL FOUNDATIONS OF EDUCATION

American Historical Association, Commission on the Social Studies in the Schools: *Conclusions and Recommendations*, Scribner, New York, 1934.

Baker, Melvin: *Foundations of John Dewey's Educational Theory*, Columbia University Press, New York, 1955.

Benne, Kenneth D.: *A Conception of Authority; an Introductory Study*, Teachers College, Columbia University, New York, 1943.

Berkson, I. B.: *Education Faces the Future*, Harper, New York, 1943.

———: *Preface to an Educational Philosophy*, Columbia University Press, New York, 1940.

Bode, Boyd H.: *Progressive Education at the Crossroads*, Newson, New York, 1938.

Brameld, Theodore: *Patterns of Educational Philosophy*, World, Yonkers, N.Y., 1950.

Brubacher, John S.: *The Public Schools and Spiritual Values*, Seventh Yearbook of the John Dewey Society, Harper, New York, 1944.

Childs, John L.: *Education and Morals*, Appleton-Century-Crofts, New York, 1950.

————: *Education and the Philosophy of Experimentalism*, Appleton-Century-Crofts, New York, 1931.

Conant, James B.: *Education and Liberty*, Harvard University Press, Cambridge, Mass., 1953.

Counts, George S.: *Dare the School Build a New Social Order?* John Day, New York, 1932.

————: *Education and American Civilization*, Teachers College, Columbia University, New York, 1952.

————: *Education and the Promise of America*, Macmillan, New York, 1945.

Cowley, Malcolm (ed.): *After the Genteel Tradition*, Norton, New York, 1936.

Dewey, John: *A Common Faith*, Yale University Press, New Haven, Conn., 1934.

————: *Democracy and Education*, Macmillan, New York, 1916.

————: *Experience and Education*, Macmillan, New York, 1938.

————: *How We Think*, Heath, Boston, 1933.

————: *Human Nature and Conduct*, Holt, New York, 1922.

Hook, Sidney: *Education for Modern Man*, Dial, New York, 1946.

Kallen, Horace W.: *The Education of Free Men*, Farrar, Strauss & Young, New York, 1949.

Kilpatrick, W. H.: *Education for a Changing Civilization*, Macmillan, New York, 1926.

————: *The Educational Frontier*, Appleton-Century-Crofts, New York, 1933.

————: *Foundations of Method*, Macmillan, New York, 1925.

————: *Philosophy of Education*, Macmillan, New York, 1951.

————: *Selfhood and Civilization*, Macmillan, New York, 1941.

————: *The Teacher and Society*, First Yearbook of the John Dewey Society, Appleton-Century-Crofts, New York, 1937.

Linton, Ralph: *The Cultural Background of Personality*, Appleton-Century-Crofts, New York, 1945.

———— (ed.): *The Science of Man in the World Crisis*, Columbia University Press, New York, 1945.

Lynd, Robert S.: *Knowledge for What? The Place of Social Science in American Culture*, Princeton University Press, Princeton, N.J., 1939.

Mead, George H.: *Mind, Self, and Society*, University of Chicago Press, Chicago, 1936.

National Society of College Teachers of Education: *The Discipline of Practical Judgment in a Democratic Society*, University of Chicago Press, Chicago, 1943.

Newcomb, Theodore: *Social Psychology*, Dryden, New York, 1950.

Newlon, Jesse H.: *Education for Democracy in Our Time*, McGraw-Hill, New York, 1939.

Otto, Max: *The Human Enterprise*, Appleton-Century-Crofts, New York, 1940.

Raup, R. Bruce, and others: *The Improvement of Practical Intelligence*, Harper, New York, 1950.

Readings in the Foundations of Education, 2 vols., Teachers College, Columbia University, New York, 1941.

Robinson, James Harvey: *The Humanizing of Knowledge*, rev. and enl., Doubleday, New York, 1926.

Rugg, Harold O.: *Democracy and the Curriculum*, Third Yearbook of the John Dewey Society, Appleton-Century-Crofts, New York, 1939.

————: *Foundations for American Education*, World, Yonkers, N.Y., 1947.

Smith, B. Othanel, and others: *Readings in the Social Aspects of Education,* Interstate, Danville, Ill., 1951.
Thayer, Vivian T.: *The Attack upon the American Secular School,* Beacon Press, Boston, 1951.

INTERPRETIVE WRITINGS

Boas, George: *Our New Ways of Thinking,* Harper, New York, 1930.
Bode, Boyd H.: *Conflicting Psychologies of Learning,* Heath, Boston, 1929.
Brown, W. A.: *Church and State in Contemporary America,* Scribner, New York, 1936.
Burtt, Edwin A.: *Types of Religious Philosophy,* Harper, New York, 1939.
Cargill, Oscar: *Intellectual America; The March of Ideas,* Macmillan, New York, 1941.
Commager, Henry S.: *The American Mind,* Yale University Press, New Haven, Conn., 1950.
Conant, James B.: *On Understanding Science,* Yale University Press, New Haven, Conn., 1947.
Counts, George S.: *The Social Foundations of Education,* Scribner, New York, 1934.
Faulkner, Harold U.: *From Versailles to the New Deal,* Yale University Press, New Haven, Conn., 1950.
————: *The Quest for Social Justice,* 1898–1914, Macmillan, New York, 1931.
Harris, Herbert: *American Labor,* Yale University Press, New Haven, Conn., 1939.
Heidbreder, Edna: *Seven Psychologies,* Appleton-Century-Crofts, New York, 1933.
Hofstadter, Richard: *Social Darwinism in American Thought,* University of Pennsylvania Press, Philadelphia, 1945.
Hook, Sidney: *Reason, Social Myth, and Democracy,* John Day, New York, 1940.
Hulfish, H. Gorden (ed.): *Educational Freedom in an Age of Anxiety,* Twelfth Yearbook of the John Dewey Society, Harper, New York, 1953.
Johnson, F. Ernest: *The Social Gospel Re-examined,* Harper, New York, 1940.
Krikorian, Yervant H. (ed.): *Naturalism and the Human Spirit,* Columbia University Press, New York, 1944.
Lerner, Max: *Ideas Are Weapons; the History and Uses of Ideas,* Viking, New York, 1939.
Lynd, Robert S., and Helen M. Lynd: *Middletown, A Study in Contemporary American Culture,* Harcourt, Brace, New York, 1929.
———— and ————: *Middletown in Transition; A Study in Cultural Conflicts,* Harcourt, Brace, New York, 1937.
MacIver, R. M.: *Academic Freedom in Our Time,* Columbia University Press, New York, 1955.
Morris, Charles W.: *Paths of Life,* Harper, New York, 1942.
Myrdal, Gunnar: *An American Dilemma,* Harper, New York, 1944.
Pfeffer, Leo: *Church, State, and Freedom,* Beacon Press, Boston, 1953.
Recent Social Trends in the United States, Report of the President's Research Committee on Recent Social Trends, McGraw-Hill, New York, 1933.
Robinson, James Harvey: *The New History,* Macmillan, New York, 1912.
Schlesinger, Arthur M., Jr.: *The Vital Center,* Houghton Mifflin, Boston, 1949.
Slosson, Preston W.: *The Great Crusade and After,* 1914–1928, Macmillan, New York, 1931.
Spitz, David: *Patterns of Anti-democratic Thought,* Macmillan, New York, 1949.
Sutherland, R. L.: *Color, Class and Personality,* American Council on Education, Washington, D.C., 1942.

Warner, W. L., and others: *Color and Human Nature, Negro Personality Development in a Northern City,* American Council on Education, Washington, D.C., 1941.
————, M. Meeker, and K. Eells: *Social Class in America,* Science Research, Chicago, 1949.
Wecter, Dixon: *The Age of the Great Depression,* Macmillan, New York, 1948.
Wish, Harvey: *Society and Thought in Modern America: A Social and Intellectual History of the American People from 1865,* Longmans, New York, 1952.

HISTORY OF EDUCATION

Aikin, W. M.: *The Story of the Eight-year Study,* Harper, New York, 1942.
American Council on Education, Commission on Teacher Education: *The Improvement of Teacher Education,* Washington, D.C., 1946.
Armstrong, W. Earl, E. V. Hollis, and Helen Davis: *The College and Teacher Education,* American Council on Education, Washington, D.C., 1944.
Ashmore, Harry: *The Negro and the Schools,* University of North Carolina Press, Chapel Hill, N.C., 1954.
Beale, Howard K.: *Are American Teachers Free?* Scribner, New York, 1936.
Bell, Howard M.: *Youth Tell Their Story,* American Council on Education, Washington, D.C., 1938.
Bogue, Jesse P.: *The Community College,* McGraw-Hill, New York, 1950.
Brameld, Theodore: *Workers' Education in the United States,* Fifth Yearbook of the John Dewey Society, Appleton-Century-Crofts, New York, 1941.
Brubacher, John S.: *Modern Philosophies of Education,* rev. ed., McGraw-Hill, New York, 1950.
Bunker, F. F.: *The Junior High School Movement—Its Beginnings,* W. F. Roberts, Washington, D.C., 1935.
Caswell, Hollis L. (ed.): *The American High School,* Harper, New York, 1946.
———— and D. S. Campbell: *Curriculum Development,* American Book, New York, 1935.
———— and A. Wellesley Foshay: *Education in the Elementary School,* 2d ed., American Book, New York, 1950.
Commission on Financing Higher Education: *Nature and Needs of Higher Education,* Columbia University Press, New York, 1952.
Counts, George S.: *Social Composition of Boards of Education,* University of Chicago Press, Chicago, 1927.
Duffus, R. L.: *Democracy Enters College,* Scribner, New York, 1936.
Fine, Benjamin: *Democratic Education,* Crowell, New York, 1946.
————: *Our Children Are Cheated,* Holt, New York, 1947.
Gallagher, Buell G.: *American Caste and the Negro College,* Columbia University Press, New York, 1938.
Harvard University, Report of the Harvard Committee: *General Education in a Free Society,* Harvard University Press, Cambridge, Mass., 1945.
Hofstadter, Richard, and C. DeWitt Hardy: *The Development and Scope of Higher Education in the United States,* Columbia University Press, New York, 1952.
Hollingshead, August: *Elmtown's Youth,* Wiley, New York, 1949.
Hollinshead, Byron S.: *Who Should Go to College,* Columbia University Press, New York, 1952.
Hollis, E. V.: *Philanthropic Foundations and Higher Education,* Columbia University Press, New York, 1938.
Kandel, Isaac L.: *The Impact of War upon American Education,* University of North Carolina Press, Chapel Hill, N.C., 1948.

Kandel, Isaac L.: *Twenty-five Years of American Education*, Macmillan, New York, 1924.

Knight, Edgar W.: *Fifty Years of American Education*, Ronald, New York, 1952.

Koos, Leonard V.: *The Junior College*, University of Minnesota Press, Minneapolis, 1924.

————: *The Junior College Movement*, Ginn, Boston, 1925.

McMurry, Charles A., and Frank M. McMurry: *The Method of the Recitation*, Macmillan, New York, 1911.

Meiklejohn, Alexander: *Education between Two Worlds*, Harper, New York, 1942.

Millett, John D.: *Financing Higher Education in the United States*, Columbia University Press, New York, 1952.

Monroe, Walter S.: *Teaching-Learning Theory and Teacher Education, 1890–1950*, University of Illinois Press, Urbana, Ill., 1952.

National Education Association, Educational Policies Commission: *Education and Economic Well-being in American Democracy*, Washington, D.C., 1940.

————: *Education for All American Children*, National Education Association, Washington, D.C., 1944.

————: *Education for All American Youth*, National Education Association, Washington, D.C., 1944.

————: *Federal-State Relations in Education*, American Council on Education, Washington, D.C., 1945.

————: *Moral and Spiritual Values in the Public Schools*, National Education Association, Washington, D.C., 1951.

————: *Public Education and the Future of America*, National Education Association, Washington, D.C., 1955.

————: *The Purposes of Education in American Democracy*, National Education Association, Washington, D.C., 1938.

————: *The Structure and Administration of Education in American Democracy*, National Education Association, Washington, D.C., 1938.

————: *The Unique Function of Education in American Democracy*, National Education Association, Washington, D.C., 1937.

National Society for the Study of Education: *General Education*, Fifty-first Yearbook, Part I, University of Chicago Press, Chicago, 1952.

————: *Modern Philosophies and Education*, Fifty-fourth Yearbook, Part I, University of Chicago Press, Chicago, 1955.

Pierce, Bessie L.: *Civic Attitudes in American School Textbooks*, University of Chicago Press, Chicago, 1930.

Prall, Charles E.: *State Programs for the Improvement of Teacher Education*, American Council on Education, Washington, D.C., 1946.

————: and Leslie C. Cushman: *Teacher Education in Service*, American Council on Education, Washington, D.C., 1944.

President's Commission on Higher Education: *Higher Education for American Democracy*, Harper, New York, 1948.

Rank, Otto: *Modern Education* (tr. by Moxon), Knopf, New York, 1932.

Raup, R. Bruce: *Education and Organized Interests in America*, Putnam, New York, 1936.

Reutter, E. Edmund, Jr.: *The School Administrator and Subversive Activities*, Teachers College, Columbia University, New York, 1951.

Russell, James E.: *Federal Activities in Higher Education after the Second World War*, King's Crown, New York, 1951.

Sayers, Vern L.: *A First Course in Philosophy of Education*, Holt, New York, 1952.

Smith, B. Othanel, and others: *Fundamentals of Curriculum Development*, World, Yonkers, N.Y., 1950.

Stout, John Elbert: *The Development of High-school Curricula in the North Central States from 1860 to 1918*, University of Chicago Press, Chicago, 1921.

Stratemeyer, Florence B., and others: *Developing a Curriculum for Modern Living*, Teachers College, Columbia University, New York, 1947.

Taba, Hilda, and William Van Til (eds.): *Democratic Human Relations; Promising Practices in Intergroup and Intercultural Education in the Social Studies*, National Council for the Social Studies, Washington, D.C., 1945.

Thayer, V. T., and others: *Reorganizing Secondary Education*, Appleton-Century-Crofts, New York, 1939.

Todd, Lewis Paul: *Wartime Relations of the Federal Government and the Public Schools*, 1917–1918, Teachers College, Columbia University, New York, 1945.

U.S. Office of Education (E. S. Evenden, director): *National Survey of the Education of Teachers*, 6 vols., *Bulletin* 10, 1933.

Warner, W. L., R. Havighurst, and M. B. Loeb: *Who Shall be Educated?*, Harper, New York, 1944.

Woelfel, Norman: *Molders of the American Mind; A Critical Review of the Social Attitudes of Seventeen Leaders in American Education*, Columbia University Press. New York, 1933.

INDEX